Accounting II

AC 116

Warren | Reeve | Duchac

Australia • Brazil • Japan • Korea • Mexico • Singapore • Spain • United Kingdom • United States

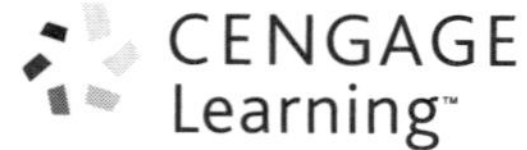

Accounting II: AC 116

Warren | Reeve | Duchac

Executive Editors:
Maureen Staudt
Michael Stranz

Senior Project Development Manager:
Linda DeStefano

Marketing Specialist:
Sara Mercurio
Lindsay Shapiro

Senior Production / Manufacturing Manager:
Donna M. Brown

PreMedia Supervisor:
Joel Brennecke

Rights & Permissions Specialist:
Kalina Hintz
Todd Osborne

Cover Image:
Getty Images*

* Unless otherwise noted, all cover images used by Custom Solutions, a part of Cengage Learning, have been supplied courtesy of Getty Images with the exception of the Earthview cover image, which has been supplied by the National Aeronautics and Space Administration (NASA).

For product information and technology assistance, contact us at
Cengage Learning Customer & Sales Support, 1-800-354-9706
For permission to use material from this text or product,
submit all requests online at **cengage.com/permissions**
Further permissions questions can be emailed to
permissionrequest@cengage.com

ISBN-13: 978-1-111-07278-0

ISBN-10: 1-111-07278-7

Cengage Learning
5191 Natorp Boulevard
Mason, Ohio 45040
USA

Cengage Learning is a leading provider of customized learning solutions with office locations around the globe, including Singapore, the United Kingdom, Australia, Mexico, Brazil, and Japan. Locate your local office at: **international.cengage.com/region**

Cengage Learning products are represented in Canada by Nelson Education, Ltd.

For your lifelong learning solutions, visit **www.cengage.com/custom**

Visit our corporate website at **www.cengage.com**

Printed in the United States of America

Custom Contents: Accounting II- AC 116

CHAPTER 8

Sarbanes-Oxley, Internal Control, and Cash

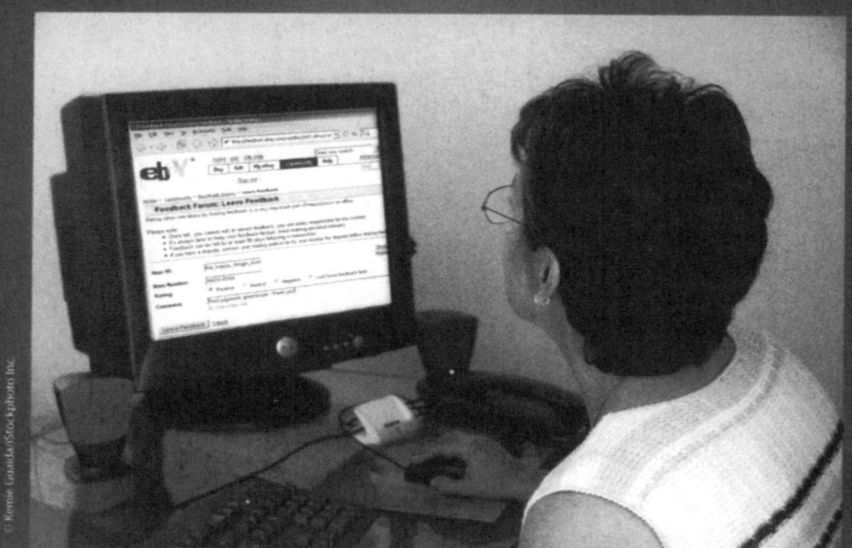
© Kemie Gould/iStockphoto Inc.

eBAY INC.

Controls are a part of your everyday life. At one extreme, laws are used to limit your behavior. For example, the speed limit is a control on your driving, designed for traffic safety. In addition, you are also affected by many nonlegal controls. For example, you can keep credit card receipts in order to compare your transactions to the monthly credit card statement. Comparing receipts to the monthly statement is a control designed to catch mistakes made by the credit card company. Likewise, recording checks in your checkbook is a control that you can use at the end of the month to verify the accuracy of your bank statement. In addition, banks give you a personal identification number (PIN) as a control against unauthorized access to your cash if you lose your automated teller machine (ATM) card. Dairies use freshness dating on their milk containers as a control to prevent the purchase or sale of soured milk. As you can see, you use and encounter controls every day.

Just as there are many examples of controls throughout society, businesses must also implement controls to help guide the behavior of their managers, employees, and customers. For example, eBay Inc. maintains an Internet-based marketplace for the sale of goods and services. Using eBay's online platform, buyers and sellers can browse, buy, and sell a wide variety of items including antiques and used cars. However, in order to maintain the integrity and trust of its buyers and sellers, eBay must have controls to ensure that buyers pay for their items and sellers don't misrepresent their items or fail to deliver sales. One such control eBay uses is a feedback forum that estabilishes buyer and seller reputations. A prospective buyer or seller can view the member's reputation and feedback comments before completing a transaction. Dishonest or unfair trading can lead to a negative reputation and even suspension or cancellation of the member's ability to trade on eBay.

In this chapter, we will discuss controls that can be included in accounting systems to provide reasonable assurance that the financial statements are reliable. We also discuss controls over cash that you can use to determine whether your bank has made any errors in your account. We begin this chapter by discussing the Sarbanes-Oxley Act of 2002 and its impact on controls and financial reporting.

After studying this chapter, you should be able to:

1. Describe the Sarbanes-Oxley Act of 2002 and its impact on internal controls and financial reporting.
   - Sarbanes-Oxley Act of 2002
2. Describe and illustrate the objectives and elements of internal control.
   - Internal Control
   - Objectives of Internal Control
   - Elements of Internal Control
     - Control Environment
     - Risk Assessment
     - Control Procedures
     - Monitoring
     - Information and Communication
   - EE 8-1 (page 360)
   - Limitations of Internal Control
3. Describe and illustrate the application of internal controls to cash.
   - Cash Controls Over Receipts and Payments
   - Control of Cash Receipts
   - Control of Cash Payments
4. Describe the nature of a bank account and its use in controlling cash.
   - Bank Accounts
   - Bank Statement
   - EE 8-2 (page 366)
   - Using the Bank Statement as a Control Over Cash
5. Describe and illustrate the use of a bank reconciliation in controlling cash.
   - Bank Reconciliation
   - EE 8-3 (page 370)
6. Describe the accounting for special-purpose cash funds.
   - Special-Purpose Cash Funds
   - EE 8-4 (page 372)
7. Describe and illustrate the reporting of cash and cash equivalents in the financial statements.
   - Financial Statement Reporting of Cash

At a Glance | Menu | Turn to pg 374

South-Western

Describe the Sarbanes-Oxley Act of 2002 and its impact on internal controls and financial reporting.

Sarbanes-Oxley Act of 2002

During the financial scandals of the early 2000s, stockholders, creditors, and other investors lost billions of dollars.[1] As a result, the United States Congress passed the **Sarbanes-Oxley Act of 2002**. This act, often referred to as *Sarbanes-Oxley*, is one of the most important laws affecting U.S. companies in recent history. The purpose of Sarbanes-Oxley is to restore public confidence and trust in the financial reporting of companies.

Sarbanes-Oxley applies only to companies whose stock is traded on public exchanges, referred to as *publicly held companies*. However, Sarbanes-Oxley highlighted the importance of assessing the financial controls and reporting of all companies. As a result, companies of all sizes have been influenced by Sarbanes-Oxley.

The ex-CEO of WorldCom, Bernard Ebbers, was sentenced to 25 years in prison.

Sarbanes-Oxley emphasizes the importance of effective internal control.[2] **Internal control** is defined as the procedures and processes used by a company to:

1 Exhibit 2 in Chapter 1 briefly summarizes these scandals.

2 Sarbanes-Oxley also has important implications for corporate governance and the regulation of the public accounting profession. This chapter, however, focuses on the internal control implications of Sarbanes-Oxley.

1. Safeguard its assets.
2. Process information accurately.
3. Ensure compliance with laws and regulations.

Sarbanes-Oxley requires companies to maintain effective internal controls over the recording of transactions and the preparing of financial statements. Such controls are important because they deter fraud and prevent misleading financial statements as shown below.

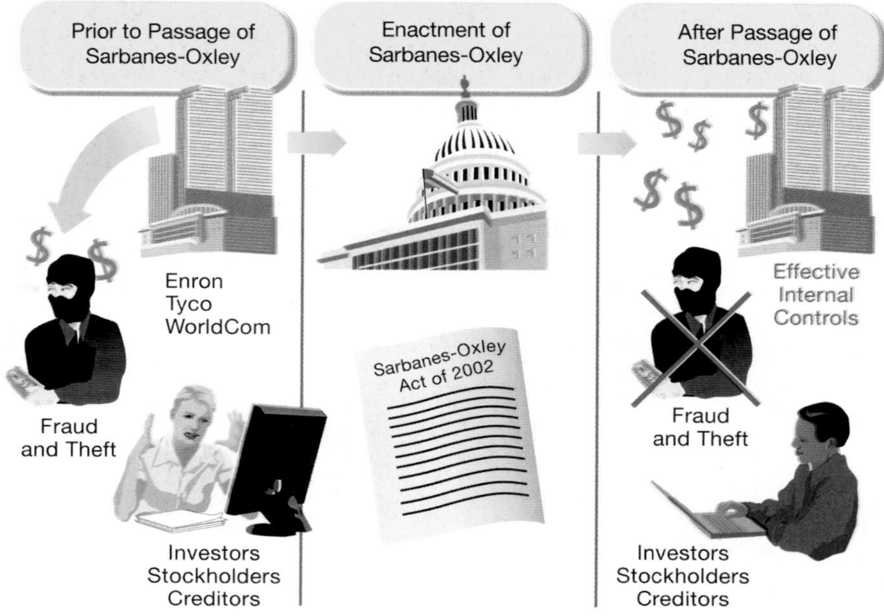

It is estimated that companies spend millions each year to comply with the requirements of Sarbanes-Oxley.

Sarbanes-Oxley also requires companies and their independent accountants to report on the effectiveness of the company's internal controls.[3] These reports are required to be filed with the company's annual 10-K report with the Securities and Exchange Commission. Companies are also encouraged to include these reports in their annual reports to stockholders. An example of such a report by the management of Nike is shown in Exhibit 1.

Exhibit 1

Sarbanes-Oxley Report of Nike

Management's Annual Report on Internal Control Over Financial Reporting

Management is responsible for establishing and maintaining adequate internal control over financial reporting . . . , Under the supervision and with the participation of our Chief Executive Officer and Chief Financial Officer, our management conducted an evaluation of the effectiveness of our internal control over financial reporting based upon the framework in *Internal Control—Integrated Framework* issued by the Committee of Sponsoring Organizations of the Treadway Commission. Based on that evaluation, our management concluded that our internal control over financial reporting is effective as of May 31, 2007. . . .

PricewaterhouseCoopers LLP, an independent registered public accounting firm, has audited . . . management's assessment of the effectiveness of our internal control over financial reporting . . . and . . . the effectiveness of our internal control over financial reporting . . . as stated in their report . . . .

MARK G. PARKER
Chief Executive Officer and President

DONALD W. BLAIR
Chief Financial Officer

3 These reporting requirements are required under Section 404 of the act. As a result, these requirements and reports are often referred to as 404 requirements and 404 reports.

Exhibit 1 indicates that Nike based its evaluation of internal controls on *Internal Control—Integrated Framework*, which was issued by the Committee of Sponsoring Organizations (COSO) of the Treadway Commission. This framework is the standard by which companies design, analyze, and evaluate internal controls. For this reason, this framework is used as the basis for discussing internal controls.

2 Describe and illustrate the objectives and elements of internal control.

Internal Control

Internal Control—Integrated Framework is the standard by which companies design, analyze, and evaluate internal control.[4] In this section, the objectives of internal control are described followed by a discussion of how these objectives can be achieved through the *Integrated Framework's* five elements of internal control.

Information on *Internal Control—Integrated Framework* can be found on COSO's Web site at **http://www.coso.org/.**

Objectives of Internal Control

The objectives of internal control are to provide reasonable assurance that:

1. Assets are safeguarded and used for business purposes.
2. Business information is accurate.
3. Employees and managers comply with laws and regulations.

These objectives are illustrated below.

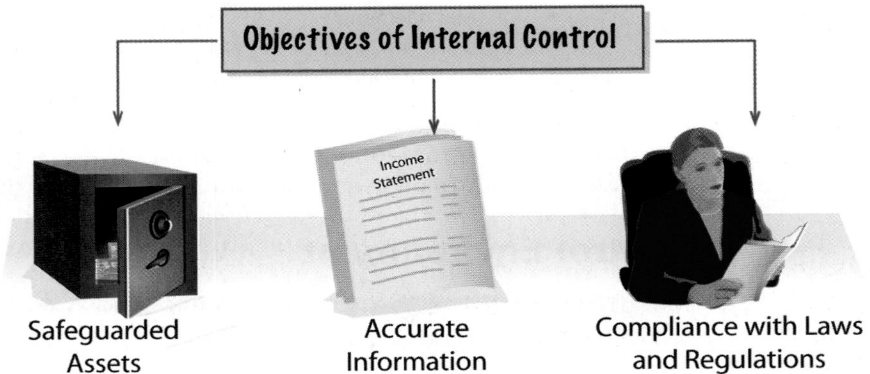

The Association of Certified Fraud Examiners has estimated that businesses will lose over $650 billion, or around 5% of revenue, to employee fraud.

Source: *2006 Report to the Nation: Occupational Fraud and Abuse*, Association of Certified Fraud Examiners.

Internal control can safeguard assets by preventing theft, fraud, misuse, or misplacement. A serious concern of internal control is preventing employee fraud. **Employee fraud** is the intentional act of deceiving an employer for personal gain. Such fraud may range from minor overstating of a travel expense report to stealing millions of dollars. Employees stealing from a business often adjust the accounting records in order to hide their fraud. Thus, employee fraud usually affects the accuracy of business information.

Accurate information is necessary to successfully operate a business. Businesses must also comply with laws, regulations, and financial reporting standards. Examples of such standards include environmental regulations, safety regulations, and generally accepted accounting principles (GAAP).

Elements of Internal Control

The three internal control objectives can be achieved by applying the five **elements of internal control** set forth by the *Integrated Framework*.[5] These elements are as follows:

1. Control environment
2. Risk assessment

4 *Internal Control—Integrated Framework* by the Committee of Sponsoring Organizations of the Treadway Commission, 1992.

5 Ibid., 12–14.

3. Control procedures
4. Monitoring
5. Information and communication

The elements of internal control are illustrated in Exhibit 2.

Exhibit 2

Elements of Internal Control

In Exhibit 2, the elements of internal control form an umbrella over the business to protect it from control threats. The control environment is the size of the umbrella. Risk assessment, control procedures, and monitoring are the fabric of the umbrella, which keep it from leaking. Information and communication connect the umbrella to management.

Control Environment

The **control environment** is the overall attitude of management and employees about the importance of controls. Three factors influencing a company's control environment are as follows:

1. Management's philosophy and operating style
2. The company's organizational structure
3. The company's personnel policies

Management's philosophy and operating style relates to whether management emphasizes the importance of internal controls. An emphasis on controls and adherence to control policies creates an effective control environment. In contrast, over-emphasizing operating goals and tolerating deviations from control policies creates an ineffective control environment.

The business's organizational structure is the framework for planning and controlling operations. For example, a retail store chain might organize each of its stores as separate business units. Each store manager has full authority over pricing and other operating activities. In such a structure, each store manager has the responsibility for establishing an effective control environment.

The business's personnel policies involve the hiring, training, evaluation, compensation, and promotion of employees. In addition, job descriptions, employee codes of ethics, and conflict-of-interest policies are part of the personnel policies. Such policies can enhance the internal control environment if they provide reasonable assurance that only competent, honest employees are hired and retained.

Risk Assessment

All businesses face risks such as changes in customer requirements, competitive threats, regulatory changes, and changes in economic factors. Management should identify such risks, analyze their significance, assess their likelihood of occurring, and take any necessary actions to minimize them.

Control Procedures

A bank officer who was not required to take vacations stole almost $5 million by printing fake certificates of deposit. The theft was discovered when the bank began requiring all employees to take vacations.

Control procedures provide reasonable assurance that business goals will be achieved, including the prevention of fraud. Control procedures, which constitute one of the most important elements of internal control, include the following as shown in Exhibit 3.

1. Competent personnel, rotating duties, and mandatory vacations
2. Separating responsibilities for related operations
3. Separating operations, custody of assets, and accounting
4. Proofs and security measures

Exhibit 3

Internal Control Procedures

Competent Personnel, Rotating Duties, and Mandatory Vacations A successful company needs competent employees who are able to perform the duties that they are assigned. Procedures should be established for properly training and supervising employees. It is also advisable to rotate duties of accounting personnel and mandate vacations for all employees. In this way, employees are encouraged to adhere to procedures. Cases of employee fraud are often discovered when a long-term employee, who never took vacations, missed work because of an illness or another unavoidable reason.

An accounting clerk for the Grant County (Washington) Alcoholism Program was in charge of collecting money, making deposits, and keeping the records. While the clerk was away on maternity leave, the replacement clerk discovered a fraud: $17,800 in fees had been collected but had been hidden for personal gain.

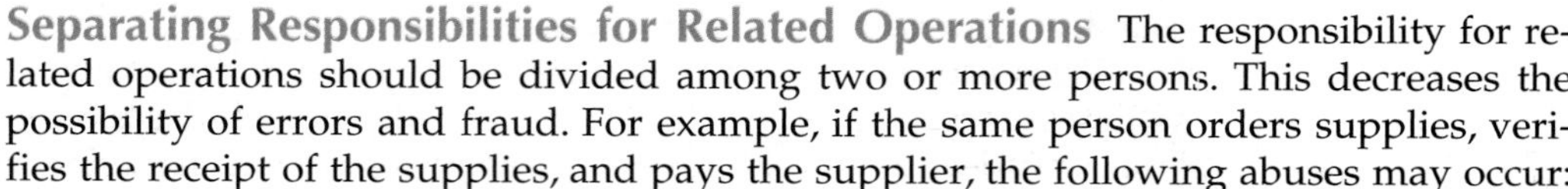

Separating Responsibilities for Related Operations The responsibility for related operations should be divided among two or more persons. This decreases the possibility of errors and fraud. For example, if the same person orders supplies, verifies the receipt of the supplies, and pays the supplier, the following abuses may occur:

1. Orders may be placed on the basis of friendship with a supplier, rather than on price, quality, and other objective factors.
2. The quantity and quality of supplies received may not be verified; thus, the company may pay for supplies not received or that are of poor quality.
3. Supplies may be stolen by the employee.
4. The validity and accuracy of invoices may not be verified; hence, the company may pay false or inaccurate invoices.

For the preceding reasons, the responsibilities for purchasing, receiving, and paying for supplies should be divided among three persons or departments.

An accounts payable clerk created false invoices and submitted them for payment. The clerk obtained the checks, cashed them, and stole thousands of dollars.

Separating Operations, Custody of Assets, and Accounting The responsibilities for operations, custody of assets, and accounting should be separated. In this way, the accounting records serve as an independent check on the operating managers and the employees who have custody of assets.

To illustrate, employees who handle cash receipts should not record cash receipts in the accounting records. To do so would allow employees to borrow or steal cash and hide the theft in the accounting records. Likewise, operating managers should not also record the results of operations. To do so would allow the managers to distort the accounting reports to show favorable results, which might allow them to receive larger bonuses.

Proofs and Security Measures Proofs and security measures are used to safeguard assets and ensure reliable accounting data. Proofs involve procedures such as authorization, approval, and reconciliation. For example, an employee planning to travel on company business may be required to complete a "travel request" form for a manager's authorization and approval.

Integrity, Objectivity, and Ethics in Business

TIPS ON PREVENTING EMPLOYEE FRAUD IN SMALL COMPANIES

- Do not have the same employee write company checks and keep the books. Look for payments to vendors you don't know or payments to vendors whose names appear to be misspelled.
- If your business has a computer system, restrict access to accounting files as much as possible. Also, keep a backup copy of your accounting files and store it at an off-site location.
- Be wary of anybody working in finance that declines to take vacations. They may be afraid that a replacement will uncover fraud.
- Require and monitor supporting documentation (such as vendor invoices) before signing checks.
- Track the number of credit card bills you sign monthly.
- Limit and monitor access to important documents and supplies, such as blank checks and signature stamps.
- Check W-2 forms against your payroll annually to make sure you're not carrying any fictitious employees.
- Rely on yourself, not on your accountant, to spot fraud.

Source: Steve Kaufman, "Embezzlement Common at Small Companies," Knight-Ridder Newspapers, reported in *Athens Daily News/Athens Banner-Herald,* March 10, 1996, p. 4D.

Documents used for authorization and approval should be prenumbered, accounted for, and safeguarded. Prenumbering of documents helps prevent transactions from being recorded more than once or not at all. In addition, accounting for and safeguarding prenumbered documents helps prevent fraudulent transactions from being recorded. For example, blank checks are prenumbered and safeguarded. Once a payment has been properly authorized and approved, the checks are filled out and issued.

Reconciliations are also an important control. Later in this chapter, the use of bank reconciliations as an aid in controlling cash is described and illustrated.

A 24-hour convenience store could use a security guard, video cameras, and an alarm system to deter robberies.

Security measures involve measures to safeguard assets. For example, cash on hand should be kept in a cash register or safe. Inventory not on display should be stored in a locked storeroom or warehouse. Accounting records such as the accounts receivable subsidiary ledger should also be safeguarded to prevent their loss. For example, electronically maintained accounting records should be safeguarded with access codes and backed up so that any lost or damaged files could be recovered if necessary.

Monitoring

Monitoring the internal control system is used to locate weaknesses and improve controls. Monitoring often includes observing employee behavior and the accounting system for indicators of control problems. Some such indicators are shown in Exhibit 4.[6]

Evaluations of controls are often performed when there are major changes in strategy, senior management, business structure, or operations. Internal auditors, who are independent of operations, usually perform such evaluations. Internal auditors are also responsible for day-to-day monitoring of controls. External auditors also evaluate and report on internal control as part of their annual financial statement audit.

Exhibit 4

Warning Signs of Internal Control Problems

Warning signs with regard to people

1. Abrupt change in lifestyle (without winning the lottery).
2. Close social relationships with suppliers.
3. Refusing to take a vacation.
4. Frequent borrowing from other employees.
5. Excessive use of alcohol or drugs.

Warning signs from the accounting system

1. Missing documents or gaps in transaction numbers (could mean documents are being used for fraudulent transactions).
2. An unusual increase in customer refunds (refunds may be phony).
3. Differences between daily cash receipts and bank deposits (could mean receipts are being pocketed before being deposited).
4. Sudden increase in slow payments (employee may be pocketing the payments).
5. Backlog in recording transactions (possibly an attempt to delay detection of fraud).

6 Edwin C. Bliss, "Employee Theft," *Boardroom Reports*, July 15, 1994, pp. 5–6.

Information and Communication

Information and communication is an essential element of internal control. Information about the control environment, risk assessment, control procedures, and monitoring is used by management for guiding operations and ensuring compliance with reporting, legal, and regulatory requirements. Management also uses external information to assess events and conditions that impact decision making and external reporting. For example, management uses pronouncements of the Financial Accounting Standards Board (FASB) to assess the impact of changes in reporting standards on the financial statements.

Example Exercise 8-1 Internal Control Elements 2

Identify each of the following as relating to (a) the control environment, (b) risk assessment, or (c) control procedures.

1. Mandatory vacations
2. Personnel policies
3. Report of outside consultants on future market changes

Follow My Example 8-1

1. (c) control procedures
2. (a) the control environment
3. (b) risk assessment

For Practice: PE 8-1A, PE 8-1B

Limitations of Internal Control

Internal control systems can provide only reasonable assurance for safeguarding assets, processing accurate information, and compliance with laws and regulations. In other words, internal controls are not a guarantee. This is due to the following factors:

1. The human element of controls
2. Cost-benefit considerations

The *human element* recognizes that controls are applied and used by humans. As a result, human errors can occur because of fatigue, carelessness, confusion, or misjudgment. For example, an employee may unintentionally shortchange a customer or miscount the amount of inventory received from a supplier. In addition, two or more employees may collude together to defeat or circumvent internal controls. This latter case often involves fraud and the theft of assets. For example, the cashier and the accounts receivable clerk might collude to steal customer payments on account.

Cost-benefit considerations recognize that cost of internal controls should not exceed their benefits. For example, retail stores could eliminate shoplifting by searching all customers before they leave the store. However, such a control procedure would upset customers and result in lost sales. Instead, retailers use cameras or signs saying *We prosecute all shoplifters.*

3 Describe and illustrate the application of internal controls to cash.

Cash Controls Over Receipts and Payments

Cash includes coins, currency (paper money), checks, and money orders. Money on deposit with a bank or other financial institution that is available for withdrawal is also considered cash. Normally, you can think of cash as anything that a bank would accept for deposit in your account. For example, a check made payable to you could normally be deposited in a bank and, thus, is considered cash.

The Internet has given rise to a form of cash called "cybercash," which is used for Internet transactions, such as being used in conjunction with PayPal.

Businesses usually have several bank accounts. For example, a business might have one bank account for general cash payments and another for payroll. A separate ledger account is normally used for each bank account. For example, a bank account at City Bank could be identified in the ledger as *Cash in Bank—City Bank*. To simplify, we will assume in this chapter that a company has only *one* bank account, which is identified in the ledger as *Cash*.

Cash is the asset most likely to be stolen or used improperly in a business. For this reason, businesses must carefully control cash and cash transactions.

Control of Cash Receipts

To protect cash from theft and misuse, a business must control cash from the time it is received until it is deposited in a bank. Businesses normally receive cash from two main sources.

1. Customers purchasing products or services
2. Customers making payments on account

Fast-food restaurants, such as McDonald's, receive cash primarily from over-the-counter sales. Internet retailers, such Amazon.com, receive cash primarily through electronic funds transfers from credit card companies.

Cash Received from Cash Sales An important control to protect cash received in over-the-counter sales is a cash register. The use of a cash register to control cash is shown below.

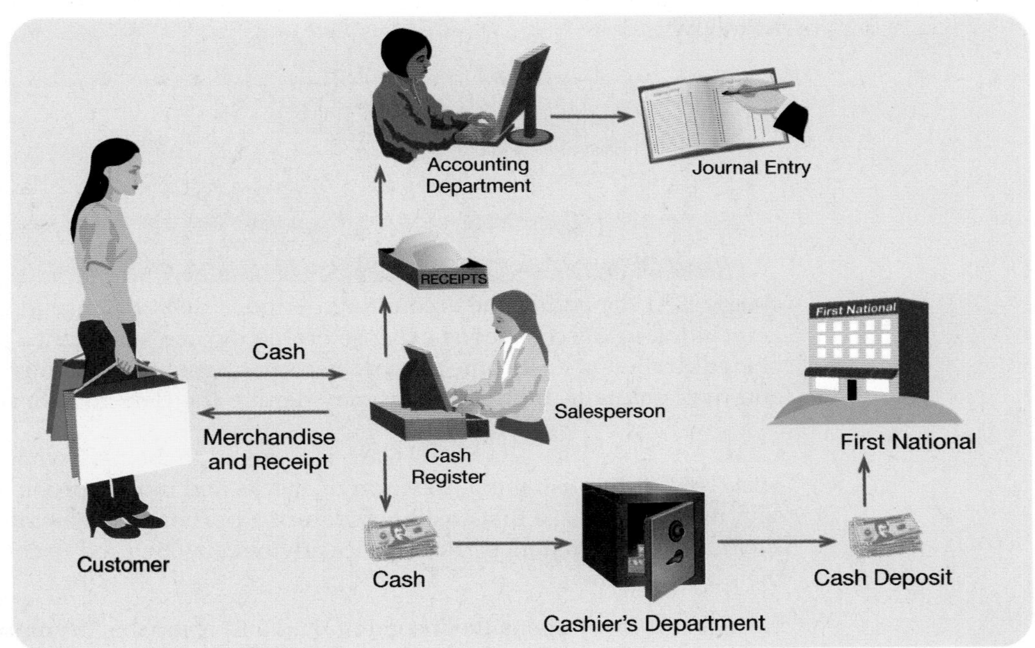

A cash register controls cash as follows:

1. At the beginning of every work shift, each cash register clerk is given a cash drawer containing a predetermined amount of cash. This amount is used for making change for customers and is sometimes called a *change fund*.
2. When a salesperson enters the amount of a sale, the cash register displays the amount to the customer. This allows the customer to verify that the clerk has charged the correct amount. The customer also receives a cash receipt.

3. At the end of the shift, the clerk and the supervisor count the cash in the clerk's cash drawer. The amount of cash in each drawer should equal the beginning amount of cash plus the cash sales for the day.
4. The supervisor takes the cash to the Cashier's Department where it is placed in a safe.
5. The supervisor forwards the clerk's cash register receipts to the Accounting Department.
6. The cashier prepares a bank deposit ticket.
7. The cashier deposits the cash in the bank, or the cash is picked up by an armored car service, such as Wells Fargo.
8. The Accounting Department summarizes the cash receipts and records the day's cash sales.
9. When cash is deposited in the bank, the bank normally stamps a duplicate copy of the deposit ticket with the amount received. This bank receipt is returned to the Accounting Department, where it is compared to the total amount that should have been deposited. This control helps ensure that all the cash is deposited and that no cash is lost or stolen on the way to the bank. Any shortages are thus promptly detected.

Salespersons may make errors in making change for customers or in ringing up cash sales. As a result, the amount of cash on hand may differ from the amount of cash sales. Such differences are recorded in a **cash short and over account**.

To illustrate, assume the following cash register data for May 3:

Cash register total for cash sales	$35,690
Cash receipts from cash sales	35,668

The cash sales, receipts, and shortage of $22 ($35,690 – $35,668) would be recorded as follows:

May	3	Cash		35,668	
		Cash Short and Over		22	
		Sales			35,690

If there had been cash over, Cash Short and Over would have been credited for the overage. At the end of the accounting period, a debit balance in Cash Short and Over is included in Miscellaneous expense on the income statement. A credit balance is included in the Other income section. If a salesperson consistently has large cash short and over amounts, the supervisor may require the clerk to take additional training.

Cash Received in the Mail Cash is received in the mail when customers pay their bills. This cash is usually in the form of checks and money orders. Most companies design their invoices so that customers return a portion of the invoice, called a *remittance advice*, with their payment. Remittance advices may be used to control cash received in the mail as follows:

1. An employee opens the incoming mail and compares the amount of cash received with the amount shown on the remittance advice. If a customer does not return a remittance advice, the employee prepares one. The remittance advice serves as a record of the cash initially received. It also helps ensure that the posting to the customer's account is for the amount of cash received.
2. The employee opening the mail stamps checks and money orders "For Deposit Only" in the bank account of the business.
3. The remittance advices and their summary totals are delivered to the Accounting Department.
4. All cash and money orders are delivered to the Cashier's Department.
5. The cashier prepares a bank deposit ticket.

6. The cashier deposits the cash in the bank, or the cash is picked up by an armored car service, such as Wells Fargo.
7. An accounting clerk records the cash received and posts the amounts to the customer accounts.
8. When cash is deposited in the bank, the bank normally stamps a duplicate copy of the deposit ticket with the amount received. This bank receipt is returned to the Accounting Department, where it is compared to the total amount that should have been deposited. This control helps ensure that all cash is deposited and that no cash is lost or stolen on the way to the bank. Any shortages are thus promptly detected.

Separating the duties of the Cashier's Department, which handles cash, and the Accounting Department, which records cash, is a control. If Accounting Department employees both handle and record cash, an employee could steal cash and change the accounting records to hide the theft.

Cash Received by EFT Cash may also be received from customers through **electronic funds transfer (EFT)**. For example, customers may authorize automatic electronic transfers from their checking accounts to pay monthly bills for such items as cell phone, Internet, and electric services. In such cases, the company sends the customer's bank a signed form from the customer authorizing the monthly electronic transfers. Each month, the company notifies the customer's bank of the amount of the transfer and the date the transfer should take place. On the due date, the company records the electronic transfer as a receipt of cash to its bank account and posts the amount paid to the customer's account.

Companies encourage customers to use EFT for the following reasons:

1. EFTs cost less than receiving cash payments through the mail.
2. EFTs enhance internal controls over cash since the cash is received directly by the bank without any employees handling cash.
3. EFTs reduce late payments from customers and speed up the processing of cash receipts.

Howard Schultz & Associates (HS&A) specializes in reviewing cash payments for its clients. HS&A searches for errors, such as duplicate payments, failures to take discounts, and inaccurate computations. Amounts recovered for clients range from thousands to millions of dollars.

Control of Cash Payments

The control of cash payments should provide reasonable assurance that:

1. Payments are made for only authorized transactions.
2. Cash is used effectively and efficiently. For example, controls should ensure that all available purchase discounts are taken.

In a small business, an owner/manager may authorize payments based on personal knowledge. In a large business, however, purchasing goods, inspecting the goods received, and verifying the invoices are usually performed by different employees. These duties must be coordinated to ensure that proper payments are made to creditors. One system used for this purpose is the voucher system.

Voucher System A **voucher system** is a set of procedures for authorizing and recording liabilities and cash payments. A **voucher** is any document that serves as proof of authority to pay cash or issue an electronic funds transfer. An invoice that has been approved for payment could be considered a voucher. In many businesses, however, a voucher is a special form used to record data about a liability and the details of its payment.

In a manual system, a voucher is normally prepared after all necessary supporting documents have been received. For the purchase of goods, a voucher is supported by the supplier's invoice, a purchase order, and a receiving report. After a voucher is prepared, it is submitted for approval. Once approved, the voucher is recorded in the accounts and filed by due date. Upon payment, the voucher is recorded in the same manner as the payment of an account payable.

Many businesses and individuals are now using Internet banking services, which provide for the payment of funds electronically.

In a computerized system, data from the supporting documents (such as purchase orders, receiving reports, and suppliers' invoices) are entered directly into computer files. At the due date, the checks are automatically generated and mailed to creditors. At that time, the voucher is electronically transferred to a paid voucher file.

Cash Paid by EFT Cash can also be paid by electronic funds transfer systems. For example, many companies pay their employees by EFT. Under such a system, employees authorize the deposit of their payroll checks directly into their checking accounts. Each pay period, the company transfers the employees' net pay to their checking accounts through the use of EFT. Many companies also use EFT systems to pay their suppliers and other vendors.

4 Describe the nature of a bank account and its use in controlling cash.

Bank Accounts

A major reason that companies use bank accounts is for internal control. Some of the control advantages of using bank accounts are as follows:

1. Bank accounts reduce the amount of cash on hand.
2. Bank accounts provide an independent recording of cash transactions. Reconciling the balance of the cash account in the company's records with the cash balance according to the bank is an important control.
3. Use of bank accounts facilitates the transfer of funds using EFT systems.

Bank Statement

Banks usually maintain a record of all checking account transactions. A summary of all transactions, called a **bank statement**, is mailed to the company (depositor) or made available online, usually each month. The bank statement shows the beginning balance, additions, deductions, and the ending balance. A typical bank statement is shown in Exhibit 5.

Checks or copies of the checks listed in the order that they were paid by the bank may accompany the bank statement. If paid checks are returned, they are stamped "Paid," together with the date of payment. Many banks no longer return checks or check copies. Instead, the check payment information is available online.

The company's checking account balance *in the bank records* is a liability. Thus, in the bank's records, the company's account has a credit balance. Since the bank statement is prepared from the bank's point of view, a credit memo entry on the bank statement indicates an increase (a credit) to the company's account. Likewise, a debit memo entry on the bank statement indicates a decrease (a debit) in the company's account. This relationship is shown below.

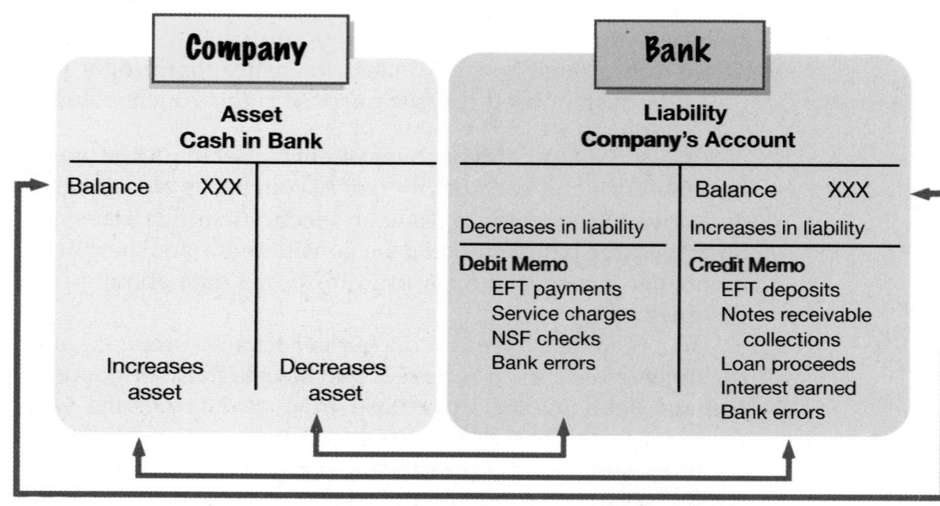

Exhibit 5

Bank Statement

MEMBER FDIC

PAGE 1

VALLEY NATIONAL BANK OF LOS ANGELES

LOS ANGELES, CA 90020-4253 (310)555-5151

POWER NETWORKING
1000 Belkin Street
Los Angeles, CA 90014 -1000

	ACCOUNT NUMBER	1627042
	FROM 6/30/09	TO 7/31/09
	BALANCE	4,218.60
22	DEPOSITS	13,749.75
52	WITHDRAWALS	14,698.57
3	OTHER DEBITS AND CREDITS	90.00CR
	NEW BALANCE	3,359.78

CHECKS AND OTHER DEBITS						DEPOSITS	DATE	BALANCE
No. 850	819.40	No. 852	122.54			585.75	07/01	3,862.41
No. 854	369.50	No. 853	20.15			421.53	07/02	3,894.29
No. 851	600.00	No. 856	190.70	No. 857	52.50	781.30	07/03	3,832.39
No. 855	25.93	No. 858	160.00			662.50	07/05	4,308.96
No. 860	921.20	NSF	300.00			503.18	07/07	3,590.94
No. 880	32.26	No. 877	535.09			ACH 932.00	07/29	4,136.66
No. 881	21.10	No. 879	732.26	No. 882	126.20	705.21	07/30	3,962.31
		SC	18.00			MS 408.00	07/30	4,352.31
No. 874	26.12	ACH	1,615.13			648.72	07/31	3,359.78

EC — ERROR CORRECTION ACH — AUTOMATED CLEARING HOUSE
MS — MISCELLANEOUS
NSF — NOT SUFFICIENT FUNDS SC — SERVICE CHARGE

* * * * * * * * *

THE RECONCILEMENT OF THIS STATEMENT WITH YOUR RECORDS IS ESSENTIAL.
ANY ERROR OR EXCEPTION SHOULD BE REPORTED IMMEDIATELY.

A bank makes credit entries (issues credit memos) for the following:

1. Deposits made by electronic funds transfer (EFT)
2. Collections of note receivable for the company
3. Proceeds for a loan made to the company by the bank
4. Interest earned on the company's account
5. Correction (if any) of bank errors

A bank makes debit entries (issues debit memos) for the following:

1. Payments made by electronic funds transfer (EFT)
2. Service charges
3. Customer checks returned for not sufficient funds
4. Correction (if any) of bank errors

Customers' checks returned for not sufficient funds, called *NSF checks*, are customer checks that were initially deposited, but were not paid by the customer's bank. Since the company's bank credited the customer's check to the company's account when it was deposited, the bank debits the company's account (issues a debit memo) when the check is returned without payment.

The reason for a credit or debit memo entry is indicated on the bank statement. Exhibit 5 identifies the following types of credit and debit memo entries:

EC: Error correction to correct bank error
NSF: Not sufficient funds check
SC: Service charge
ACH: Automated clearing house entry for electronic funds transfer
MS: Miscellaneous item such as collection of a note receivable on behalf of the company or receipt of a loan by the company from the bank

The above list includes the notation "ACH" for electronic funds transfers. ACH is a network for clearing electronic funds transfers among individuals, companies, and banks.[7] Because electronic funds transfers may be either deposits or payments, ACH entries may indicate either a debit or credit entry to the company's account. Likewise, entries to correct bank errors and miscellaneous items may indicate a debit or credit entry to the company's account.

Example Exercise 8-2 Items on Company's Bank Statement 4

The following items may appear on a bank statement:

1. NSF check
2. EFT deposit
3. Service charge
4. Bank correction of an error from recording a $400 check as $40

Using the format shown below, indicate whether the item would appear as a debit or credit memo on the bank statement and whether the item would increase or decrease the balance of the company's account.

Item No.	Appears on the Bank Statement as a Debit or Credit Memo	Increases or Decreases the Balance of the Company's Bank Account

Follow My Example 8-2

Item No.	Appears on the Bank Statement as a Debit or Credit Memo	Increases or Decreases the Balance of the Company's Bank Account
1	debit memo	decreases
2	credit memo	increases
3	debit memo	decreases
4	debit memo	decreases

For Practice: PE 8-2A, PE 8-2B

Using the Bank Statement as a Control Over Cash

The bank statement is a primary control that a company uses over cash. A company uses the bank's statement as a control by comparing the company's recording of cash transactions to those recorded by the bank.

The cash balance shown by a bank statement is usually different from the company's cash balance, as shown in Exhibit 6.

7 For further information on ACH, go to **http://www.nacha.org/**. Click on "About Us," and then click on "What is ACH?"

Exhibit 6

Power Networking's Records and Bank Statement

Bank Statement

Beginning balance		$ 4,218.60
Additions:		
Deposits	$13,749.75	
Miscellaneous	408.00	14,157.75
Deductions:		
Checks	$14,698.57	
NSF check	300.00	
Service charge	18.00	(15,016.57)
Ending balance		$ 3,359.78

Power Networking Records

Beginning balance	$ 4,227.60
Deposits	14,565.95
Checks	(16,243.56)
Ending balance	$ 2,549.99

Power Networking should determine the reason for the difference in these two amounts.

Differences between the company and bank balance may arise because of a delay by either the company or bank in recording transactions. For example, there is normally a time lag of one or more days between the date a check is written and the date that it is paid by the bank. Likewise, there is normally a time lag between when the company mails a deposit to the bank (or uses the night depository) and when the bank receives and records the deposit.

Differences may also arise because the bank has debited or credited the company's account for transactions that the company will not know about until the bank statement is received. Finally, differences may arise from errors made by either the company or the bank. For example, the company may incorrectly post to Cash a check written for $4,500 as $450. Likewise, a bank may incorrectly record the amount of a check.

Integrity, Objectivity, and Ethics in Business

CHECK FRAUD

Check fraud involves counterfeiting, altering, or otherwise manipulating the information on checks in order to fraudulently cash a check. According to the National Check Fraud Center, check fraud and counterfeiting are among the fastest growing problems affecting the financial system, generating over $10 billion in losses annually. Criminals perpetrate the fraud by taking blank checks from your checkbook, finding a canceled check in the garbage, or removing a check you have mailed to pay bills. Consumers can prevent check fraud by carefully storing blank checks, placing outgoing mail in postal mailboxes, and shredding canceled checks.

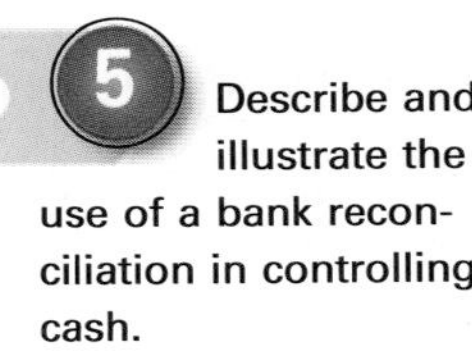

5 Describe and illustrate the use of a bank reconciliation in controlling cash.

Bank Reconciliation

A **bank reconciliation** is an analysis of the items and amounts that result in the cash balance reported in the bank statement to differ from the balance of the cash account in the ledger. The adjusted cash balance determined in the bank reconciliation is reported on the balance sheet.

A bank reconciliation is usually divided into two sections as follows:

1. The *bank section* begins with the cash balance according to the bank statement and ends with the *adjusted balance.*
2. The *company section* begins with the cash balance according to the company's records and ends with the *adjusted balance.*

The *adjusted balance* from bank and company sections must be equal. The format of the bank reconciliation is shown below.

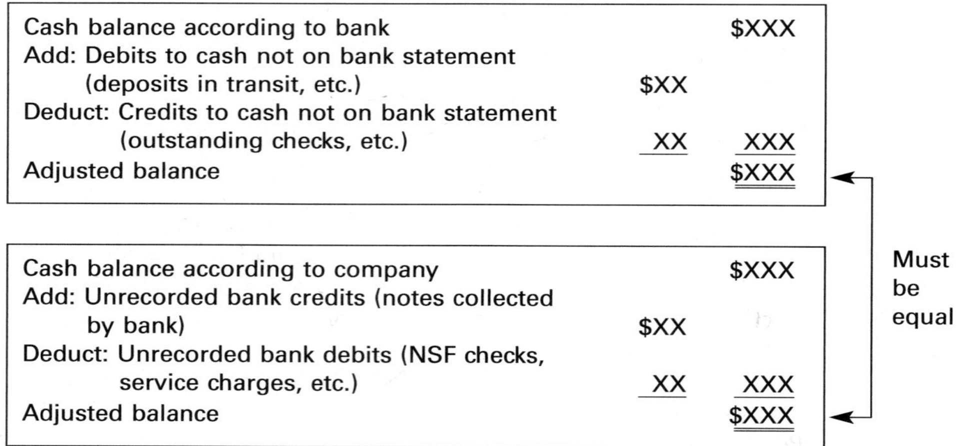

Cash balance according to bank		$XXX
Add: Debits to cash not on bank statement (deposits in transit, etc.)	$XX	
Deduct: Credits to cash not on bank statement (outstanding checks, etc.)	XX	XXX
Adjusted balance		$XXX

Cash balance according to company		$XXX
Add: Unrecorded bank credits (notes collected by bank)	$XX	
Deduct: Unrecorded bank debits (NSF checks, service charges, etc.)	XX	XXX
Adjusted balance		$XXX

A bank reconciliation is prepared using the following steps:

Bank Section of Reconciliation

Step 1. Enter the *Cash balance according to bank* from the ending cash balance according to the bank statement.

Step 2. *Add deposits not recorded by the bank.*
Identify deposits not recorded by the bank by comparing each deposit listed on the bank statement with unrecorded deposits appearing in the preceding period's reconciliation and with the current period's deposits.

Examples: Deposits in transit at the end of the period.

Step 3. *Deduct outstanding checks that have not been paid by the bank.*
Identify outstanding checks by comparing paid checks with outstanding checks appearing on the preceding period's reconciliation and with recorded checks.

Examples: Outstanding checks at the end of the period.

Step 4. Determine the *Adjusted balance* by adding Step 2 and deducting Step 3.

Company Section of Reconciliation

Step 5. Enter the *Cash balance according to company* from the ending cash balance in the ledger.

Step 6. *Add credit memos that have not been recorded.*
Identify the bank credit memos that have not been recorded by comparing the bank statement credit memos to entries in the journal.

Examples: A note receivable and interest that the bank has collected for the company.

Step 7. *Deduct debit memos that have not been recorded.*
Identify the bank debit memos that have not been recorded by comparing the bank statement debit memos to entries in the journal.

Examples: Customers' not sufficient funds (NSF) checks; bank service charges.

Step 8. Determine the *Adjusted balance* by adding Step 6 and deducting Step 7.

Step 9. Verify that the Adjusted balances determined in Steps 4 and 8 are equal.

The adjusted balances in the bank and company sections of the reconciliation must be equal. If the balances are not equal, an item has been overlooked and must be found.

Sometimes, the adjusted balances are not equal because either the company or the bank has made an error. In such cases, the error is often discovered by comparing the amount of each item (deposit and check) on the bank statement with that in the company's records.

Any bank or company errors discovered should be added or deducted from the bank or company section of the reconciliation depending on the nature of the error. For example, assume that the bank incorrectly recorded a company check for $50 as $500. This bank error of $450 ($500 − $50) would be added to the bank balance in the bank section of the reconciliation. In addition, the bank would be notified of the error so that it could be corrected. On the other hand, assume that the company recorded a deposit of $1,200 as $2,100. This company error of $900 ($2,100 − $1,200) would be deducted from the cash balance in the company section of the bank reconciliation. The company would later correct the error using a journal entry.

To illustrate, we will use the bank statement for Power Networking in Exhibit 5. This bank statement shows a balance of $3,359.78 as of July 31. The cash balance in Power Networking's ledger on the same date is $2,549.99. Using the preceding steps, the following reconciling items were identified:

Step 2. Deposit of July 31, not recorded on bank statement: $816.20
Step 3. Outstanding checks:

Check No. 812	$1,061.00
Check No. 878	435.39
Check No. 883	48.60
Total	$1,544.99

Step 6. Note receivable of $400 plus interest of $8 collected by bank not recorded in the journal as indicated by a credit memo of $408.
Step 7. Check from customer (Thomas Ivey) for $300 returned by bank because of insufficient funds (NSF) as indicated by a debit memo of $300.00.
Bank service charges of $18, not recorded in the journal as indicated by a debit memo of $18.00.

In addition, an error of $9 was discovered. This error occurred when Check No. 879 for $732.26 to Taylor Co., on account, was recorded in the company's journal as $723.26.

The bank reconciliation, based on the Exhibit 5 bank statement and the preceding reconciling items, is shown in Exhibit 7.

The company's records do not need to be updated for any items in the *bank section* of the reconciliation. This section begins with the cash balance according to the bank statement. However, the bank should be notified of any errors that need to be corrected.

The company's records do need to be updated for any items in the *company section* of the bank reconciliation. The company's records are updated using journal entries. For example, journal entries should be made for any unrecorded bank memos and any company errors.

The journal entries for Power Networking, based on the bank reconciliation shown in Exhibit 7, are as follows:

July	31	Cash		408	
		Notes Receivable			400
		Interest Revenue			8
	31	Accounts Receivable—Thomas Ivey		300	
		Miscellaneous Expense		18	
		Accounts Payable—Taylor Co.		9	
		Cash			327

Exhibit 7

Bank Reconciliation for Power Networking

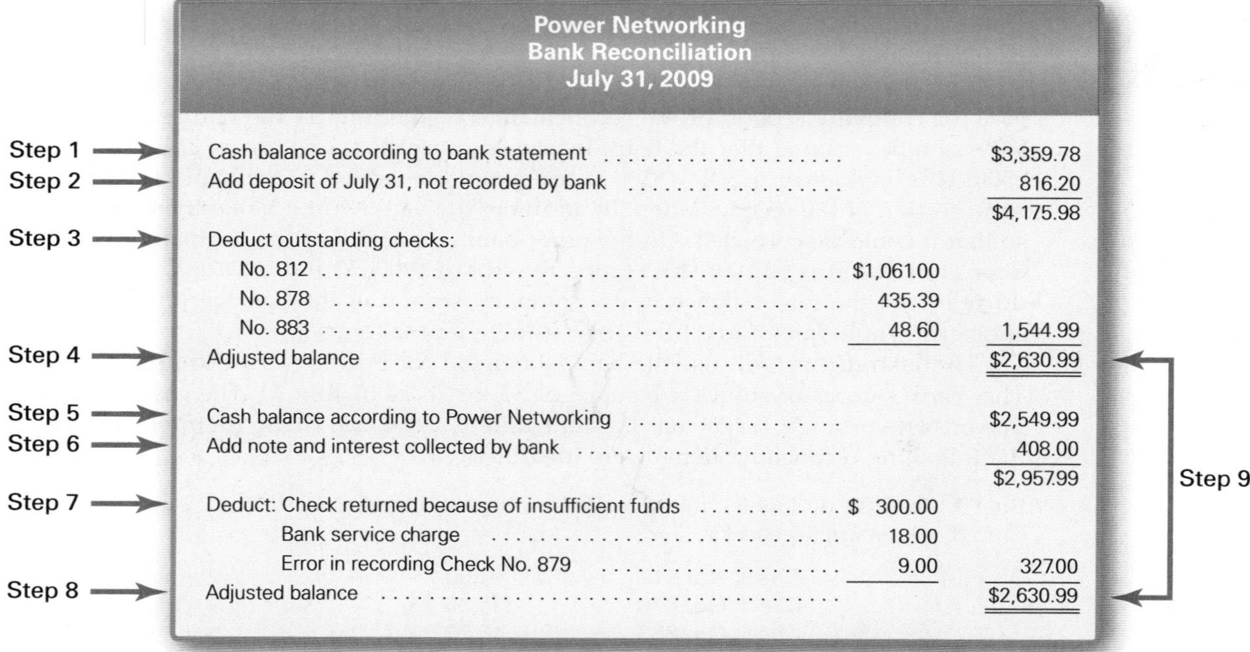

Power Networking
Bank Reconciliation
July 31, 2009

Step			
Step 1	Cash balance according to bank statement		$3,359.78
Step 2	Add deposit of July 31, not recorded by bank		816.20
			$4,175.98
Step 3	Deduct outstanding checks:		
	No. 812	$1,061.00	
	No. 878	435.39	
	No. 883	48.60	1,544.99
Step 4	Adjusted balance		$2,630.99
Step 5	Cash balance according to Power Networking		$2,549.99
Step 6	Add note and interest collected by bank		408.00
			$2,957.99
Step 7	Deduct: Check returned because of insufficient funds	$ 300.00	
	Bank service charge	18.00	
	Error in recording Check No. 879	9.00	327.00
Step 8	Adjusted balance		$2,630.99

Step 9

After the preceding journal entries are recorded and posted, the cash account will have a debit balance of $2,630.99. This cash balance agrees with the adjusted balance shown on the bank reconciliation. This is the amount of cash on July 31 and is the amount that is reported on Power Networking's July 31 balance sheet.

Businesses may reconcile their bank accounts in a slightly different format from that shown in Exhibit 7. Regardless, the objective is to control cash by reconciling the company's records with the bank statement. In doing so, any errors or misuse of cash may be detected.

To enhance internal control, the bank reconciliation should be prepared by an employee who does not take part in or record cash transactions. Otherwise, mistakes may occur, and it is more likely that cash will be stolen or misapplied. For example, an employee who handles cash and also reconciles the bank statement could steal a cash deposit, omit the deposit from the accounts, and omit it from the reconciliation.

Bank reconciliations are also important computerized systems where deposits and checks are stored in electronic files and records. Some systems use computer software to determine the difference between the bank statement and company cash balances. The software then adjusts for deposits in transit and outstanding checks. Any remaining differences are reported for further analysis.

Example Exercise 8-3 Bank Reconciliation 5

The following data were gathered to use in reconciling the bank account of Photo Op:

Balance per bank	$14,500
Balance per company records	13,875
Bank service charges	75
Deposit in transit	3,750
NSF check	800
Outstanding checks	5,250

a. What is the adjusted balance on the bank reconciliation?

b. Journalize any necessary entries for Photo Op based on the bank reconciliation.

(continued)

Follow My Example 8-3

a. $13,000, as shown below.
Bank section of reconciliation: $14,500 + $3,750 − $5,250 = $13,000
Company section of reconciliation: $13,875 − $75 − $800 = $13,000

b.

Accounts Receivable	800	
Miscellaneous Expense	75	
Cash		875

For Practice: PE 8-3A, PE 8-3B

Integrity, Objectivity, and Ethics in Business

BANK ERROR IN YOUR FAVOR

You may sometime have a bank error in your favor, such as a misposted deposit. Such errors are not a case of "found money," as in the Monopoly® game. Bank control systems quickly discover most errors and make automatic adjustments. Even so, you have a legal responsibility to report the error and return the money to the bank.

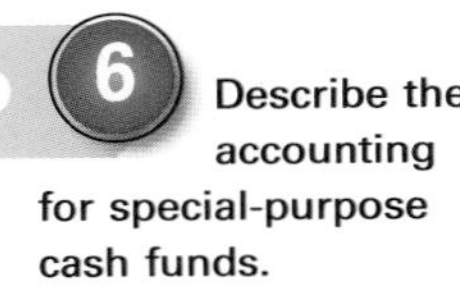

6 Describe the accounting for special-purpose cash funds.

Special-Purpose Cash Funds

A company often has to pay small amounts for such items as postage, office supplies, or minor repairs. Although small, such payments may occur often enough to total a significant amount. Thus, it is desirable to control such payments. However, writing a check for each small payment is not practical. Instead, a special cash fund, called a **petty cash fund**, is used.

A petty cash fund is established by estimating the amount of payments needed from the fund during a period, such as a week or a month. A check is then written and cashed for this amount. The money obtained from cashing the check is then given to an employee, called the *petty cash custodian*. The petty cash custodian disburses monies from the fund as needed. For control purposes, the company may place restrictions on the maximum amount and the types of payments that can be made from the fund. Each time money is paid from petty cash, the custodian records the details on a petty cash receipts form.

The petty cash fund is normally replenished at periodic intervals, when it is depleted, or reaches a minimum amount. When a petty cash fund is replenished, the accounts debited are determined by summarizing the petty cash receipts. A check is then written for this amount, payable to Petty Cash.

To illustrate, assume that a petty cash fund of $500 is established on August 1. The entry to record this transaction is as follows:

Aug.	1	Petty Cash		500	
		Cash			500

The only time Petty Cash is debited is when the fund is initially established, as shown in the preceding entry, or when the fund is being increased. The only time Petty Cash is credited is when the fund is being decreased.

At the end of August, the petty cash receipts indicate expenditures for the following items:

Office supplies	$380
Postage (debit Office Supplies)	22
Store supplies	35
Miscellaneous administrative expense	30
Total	$467

The entry to replenish the petty cash fund on August 31 is as follows:

Aug.	31	Office Supplies		402	
		Store Supplies		35	
		Miscellaneous Administrative Expense		30	
		Cash			467

Petty Cash is not debited when the fund is replenished. Instead, the accounts affected by the petty cash disbursements are debited, as shown in the preceding entry. Replenishing the petty cash fund restores the fund to its original amount of $500.

Companies often use other cash funds for special needs, such as payroll or travel expenses. Such funds are called **special-purpose funds**. For example, each salesperson might be given $1,000 for travel-related expenses. Periodically, each salesperson submits an expense report, and the fund is replenished. Special-purpose funds are established and controlled in a manner similar to that of the petty cash fund.

Example Exercise 8-4 Petty Cash Fund

6

Prepare journal entries for each of the following:

a. Issued a check to establish a petty cash fund of $500.

b. The amount of cash in the petty cash fund is $120. Issued a check to replenish the fund, based on the following summary of petty cash receipts: office supplies, $300 and miscellaneous administrative expense, $75. Record any missing funds in the cash short and over account.

Follow My Example 8-4

a.	Petty Cash	500	
	Cash		500
b.	Office Supplies	300	
	Miscellaneous Administrative Expense	75	
	Cash Short and Over	5	
	Cash		380

For Practice: PE 8-4A, PE 8-4B

Describe and illustrate the reporting of cash and cash equivalents in the financial statements.

Financial Statement Reporting of Cash

Cash is normally listed as the first asset in the Current Assets section of the balance sheet. Most companies present only a single cash amount on the balance sheet by combining all their bank and cash fund accounts.

A company may temporarily have excess cash. In such cases, the company normally invests in highly liquid investments in order to earn interest. These investments are called **cash equivalents**.[8] Examples of cash equivalents include U.S. Treasury bills, notes issued by major corporations (referred to as commercial paper), and money market funds. In such cases, companies usually report *Cash and cash equivalents* as one amount on the balance sheet.

The balance sheet presentation for cash for Mornin' Joe is shown below.

Mornin' Joe
Balance Sheet
December 31, 2010

Assets	
Current assets:	
Cash and cash equivalents	$235,000

Banks may require that companies maintain minimum cash balances in their bank accounts. Such a balance is called a **compensating balance**. This is often required by the bank as part of a loan agreement or line of credit. A *line of credit* is a preapproved amount the bank is willing to lend to a customer upon request. Compensating balance requirements are normally disclosed in notes to the financial statements.

Financial Analysis and Interpretation

For companies that are either starting up or in financial distress, cash is critical for their survival. In their first few years of operations, startup companies often report losses and negative net cash flows. In these cases, the ratio of cash to monthly cash expenses (negative cash flow for operating activities) is useful for assessing how long a company can continue to operate without additional financing or without generating positive cash flows from operations. Likewise, this ratio can be used to assess how long a business may continue to operate when experiencing financial distress. In computing cash to monthly cash expenses, the amount of cash on hand can be taken from the balance sheet, while the monthly cash expenses can be estimated from the operating activities section of the statement of cash flows.

The ratio of cash to monthly cash expenses is computed by first determining the monthly cash expenses. The monthly cash expenses are determined as follows:

$$\text{Monthly Cash Expenses} = \frac{\text{Negative Cash Flows from Operations}}{12}$$

The ratio of cash to monthly cash expenses can then be computed as follows:

$$\text{Ratio of Cash to Monthly Cash Expenses} = \frac{\text{Cash and Cash Equivalents as of Year-End}}{\text{Monthly Cash Expenses}}$$

To illustrate these ratios, we use Northwest Airlines Corporation, a major carrier of passengers and cargo with service to approximately 900 cities in 160 countries. For the year ending December 31, 2005, Northwest Airlines reported the following data (in millions):

Negative cash flows from operations	$ (436)
Cash and cash equivalents as of December 31, 2005	1,284

Based on the preceding data, the monthly cash expenses, sometimes referred to as cash burn, were $36.3 million per month ($436/12). Thus, as of December 31, 2005, the cash to monthly cash expenses ratio was 35.4 ($1,284/$36.3). That is, as of December 31, 2005, Northwest would run out of cash in less than three years unless it changes its operations, sells investments, or raises additional financing. Northwest Airlines was able to reorganize and for the year ending December 31, 2006, generated $1,245 million in positive cash flows from operations.

8 To be classified a cash equivalent, according to FASB Statement No. 95, the investment is expected to be converted to cash within 90 days.

Business Connection

MICROSOFT CORPORATION

Microsoft Corporation develops, manufactures, licenses, and supports software products for computing devices. Microsoft software products include computer operating systems, such as Windows, and application software, such as Microsoft Word™ and Excel.™ Microsoft is actively involved in the video game market through its Xbox and is also involved in online products and services.

Microsoft is known for its strong cash position. Microsoft's June 30, 2007, balance sheet reported over $23 billion of cash and short-term investments, as shown below.

Balance Sheet
June 30, 2007
(In millions)
Assets

Current assets:	
Cash and equivalents	$ 6,111
Short-term investments	17,300
Total cash and short-term investments	$23,411

The cash and cash equivalents of $6,111 million are further described in the notes to the financial statements, as shown below.

Cash and equivalents:	
Cash	$3,040
Mutual funds	132
Commercial paper	179
U.S. government and agency securities	1
Corporate notes and bonds	2,425
Municipal securities	334
Total cash and equivalents	$6,111

At a Glance 8

1 Describe the Sarbanes-Oxley Act of 2002 and its impact on internal controls and financial reporting.

Key Points	Key Learning Outcomes	Example Exercises	Practice Exercises
The purpose of the Sarbanes-Oxley Act of 2002 is to restore public confidence and trust in the financial statements of companies. Sarbanes-Oxley requires companies to maintain strong and effective internal controls and to report on the effectiveness of the internal controls.	• Describe why Congress passed Sarbanes-Oxley. • Describe the purpose of Sarbanes-Oxley. • Define *internal control.*		

2 Describe and illustrate the objectives and elements of internal control.

Key Points	Key Learning Outcomes	Example Exercises	Practice Exercises
The objectives of internal control are to provide reasonable assurance that (1) assets are safeguarded and used for business purposes, (2) business information is accurate, and (3) laws and regulations are complied with. The elements of internal control are the control environment, risk assessment, control procedures, monitoring, and information and communication.	• List the objectives of internal control.		
	• List the elements of internal control.		
	• Describe each element of internal control and factors influencing each element.	8-1	8-1A, 8-1B

3 Describe and illustrate the application of internal controls to cash.

Key Points	Key Learning Outcomes	Example Exercises	Practice Exercises
A cash register is one of the most important controls to protect cash received in over-the-counter sales. A remittance advice is a control for cash received through the mail. Separating the duties of handling cash and recording cash is also a control. A voucher system is a control system for cash payments that uses a set of procedures for authorizing and recording liabilities and cash payments. Many companies use electronic funds transfers to enhance their control over cash receipts and cash payments.	• Describe and give examples of controls for cash received from cash sales, cash received in the mail, and cash received by EFT.		
	• Describe and give examples of controls for cash payments made using a voucher system and cash payments made by EFT.		

4 Describe the nature of a bank account and its use in controlling cash.

Key Points	Key Learning Outcomes	Example Exercises	Practice Exercises
Bank accounts help control cash by reducing the amount of cash on hand and facilitating the transfer of cash between businesses and locations. In addition, the bank statement allows a business to reconcile the cash transactions recorded in the accounting records to those recorded by the bank.	• Describe how the use of bank accounts helps control cash.		
	• Describe a bank statement and provide examples of items that appear on a bank statement as debit and credit memos.	8-2	8-2A, 8-2B

5 Describe and illustrate the use of a bank reconciliation in controlling cash.

Key Points	Key Learning Outcomes	Example Exercises	Practice Exercises
The bank reconciliation begins with the cash balance according to the bank statement. This balance is adjusted for the company's changes in cash that do not appear on the bank statement and for any bank errors. The second section begins with the cash balance according to the company's records. This balance is adjusted for the bank's changes in cash that do not appear on the company's records and for any company errors. The adjusted balances for the two sections must be equal. The items in the company section must be journalized on the company's records.	• Describe a bank reconciliation.		
	• Prepare a bank reconciliation.	8-3	8-3A, 8-3B
	• Journalize any necessary entries on the company's records based on the bank reconciliation.	8-3	8-3A, 8-3B

6 Describe the accounting for special-purpose cash funds.

Key Points	Key Learning Outcomes	Example Exercises	Practice Exercises
Special-purpose cash funds, such as a petty cash fund or travel funds, are used by businesses to meet specific needs. Each fund is established by cashing a check for the amount of cash needed. At periodic intervals, the fund is replenished and the disbursements recorded.	• Describe the use of special-purpose cash funds.		
	• Journalize the entry to establish a petty cash fund.	**8-4**	8-4A, 8-4B
	• Journalize the entry to replenish a petty cash fund.	**8-4**	8-4A, 8-4B

7 Describe and illustrate the reporting of cash and cash equivalents in the financial statements.

Key Points	Key Learning Outcomes	Example Exercises	Practice Exercises
Cash is listed as the first asset in the Current Assets section of the balance sheet. Companies that have invested excess cash in highly liquid investments usually report *Cash and cash equivalents* on the balance sheet.	• Describe the reporting of cash and cash equivalents in the financial statements.		
	• Illustrate the reporting of cash and cash equivalents in the financial statements.		

Key Terms

bank reconciliation (367)
bank statement (364)
cash (360)
cash equivalents (373)
cash short and over account (362)
compensating balance (373)
control environment (356)
electronic funds transfer (EFT) (363)
elements of internal control (355)
employee fraud (355)
internal control (353)
petty cash fund (371)
Sarbanes-Oxley Act of 2002 (353)
special-purpose funds (372)
voucher (363)
voucher system (363)

Illustrative Problem

The bank statement for Urethane Company for June 30, 2009, indicates a balance of $9,143.11. All cash receipts are deposited each evening in a night depository, after banking hours. The accounting records indicate the following summary data for cash receipts and payments for June:

Cash balance as of June 1	$ 3,943.50
Total cash receipts for June	28,971.60
Total amount of checks issued in June	28,388.85

Comparing the bank statement and the accompanying canceled checks and memos with the records reveals the following reconciling items:

a. The bank had collected for Urethane Company $1,030 on a note left for collection. The face amount of the note was $1,000.
b. A deposit of $1,852.21, representing receipts of June 30, had been made too late to appear on the bank statement.
c. Checks outstanding totaled $5,265.27.
d. A check drawn for $139 had been incorrectly charged by the bank as $157.
e. A check for $30 returned with the statement had been recorded in the company's records as $240. The check was for the payment of an obligation to Avery Equipment Company for the purchase of office supplies on account.
f. Bank service charges for June amounted to $18.20.

Instructions

1. Prepare a bank reconciliation for June.
2. Journalize the entries that should be made by Urethane Company.

Solution

1.

Urethane Company
Bank Reconciliation
June 30, 2009

Cash balance according to bank statement		$ 9,143.11
Add: Deposit of June 30 not recorded by bank	$1,852.21	
Bank error in charging check as $157 instead of $139	18.00	1,870.21
		$11,013.32
Deduct: Outstanding checks		5,265.27
Adjusted balance		$ 5,748.05
Cash balance according to company's records		$ 4,526.25*
Add: Proceeds of note collected by bank, including $30 interest	$1,030.00	
Error in recording check	210.00	1,240.00
		$ 5,766.25
Deduct: Bank service charges		18.20
Adjusted balance		$ 5,748.05

*$3,943.50 + $28,971.60 – $28,388.85

2.

June	30	Cash		1,240.00	
		Notes Receivable			1,000.00
		Interest Revenue			30.00
		Accounts Payable—Avery Equipment Company			210.00
	30	Miscellaneous Administrative Expense		18.20	
		Cash			18.20

Self-Examination Questions (Answers at End of Chapter)

1. Which of the following is *not* an element of internal control?
   A. Control environment
   B. Monitoring
   C. Compliance with laws and regulations
   D. Control procedures
2. The bank erroneously charged Tropical Services' account for $450.50 for a check that was correctly written and recorded by Tropical Services as $540.50. To reconcile the bank account of Tropical Services at the end of the month, you would:
   A. add $90 to the cash balance according to the bank statement.
   B. add $90 to the cash balance according to Tropical Services' records.
   C. deduct $90 from the cash balance according to the bank statement.
   D. deduct $90 from the cash balance according to Tropical Services' records.
3. In preparing a bank reconciliation, the amount of checks outstanding would be:
   A. added to the cash balance according to the bank statement.
   B. deducted from the cash balance according to the bank statement.
   C. added to the cash balance according to the company's records.
   D. deducted from the cash balance according to the company's records.
4. Journal entries based on the bank reconciliation are required for:
   A. additions to the cash balance according to the company's records.
   B. deductions from the cash balance according to the company's records.
   C. both A and B.
   D. neither A nor B.
5. A petty cash fund is:
   A. used to pay relatively small amounts.
   B. established by estimating the amount of cash needed for disbursements of relatively small amounts during a specified period.
   C. reimbursed when the amount of money in the fund is reduced to a predetermined minimum amount.
   D. all of the above.

Eye Openers

1. (a) Why did Congress pass the Sarbanes-Oxley Act of 2002? (b) What is the purpose of the Sarbanes-Oxley Act of 2002?
2. Define *internal control.*
3. (a) Name and describe the five elements of internal control. (b) Is any one element of internal control more important than another?
4. How does a policy of rotating clerical employees from job to job aid in strengthening the control procedures within the control environment? Explain.
5. Why should the responsibility for a sequence of related operations be divided among different persons? Explain.
6. Why should the employee who handles cash receipts not have the responsibility for maintaining the accounts receivable records? Explain.
7. In an attempt to improve operating efficiency, one employee was made responsible for all purchasing, receiving, and storing of supplies. Is this organizational change wise from an internal control standpoint? Explain.
8. The ticket seller at a movie theater doubles as a ticket taker for a few minutes each day while the ticket taker is on a break. Which control procedure of a business's system of internal control is violated in this situation?
9. Why should the responsibility for maintaining the accounting records be separated from the responsibility for operations? Explain.
10. Assume that Yvonne Dauphin, accounts payable clerk for Bedell Inc., stole $73,250 by paying fictitious invoices for goods that were never received. The clerk set up accounts in the names of the fictitious companies and cashed the checks at a local bank. Describe a control procedure that would have prevented or detected the fraud.
11. Before a voucher for the purchase of merchandise is approved for payment, supporting documents should be compared to verify the accuracy of the liability. Give an example of supporting documents for the purchase of merchandise.

12. The accounting clerk pays all obligations by prenumbered checks. What are the strengths and weaknesses in the internal control over cash payments in this situation?
13. The balance of Cash is likely to differ from the bank statement balance. What two factors are likely to be responsible for the difference?
14. What is the purpose of preparing a bank reconciliation?
15. Do items reported as credits on the bank statement represent (a) additions made by the bank to the company's balance or (b) deductions made by the bank from the company's balance? Explain.
16. Oak Grove Inc. has a petty cash fund of $1,500. (a) Since the petty cash fund is only $1,500, should Oak Grove Inc. implement controls over petty cash? (b) What controls, if any, could be used for the petty cash fund?
17. (a) How are cash equivalents reported in the financial statements? (b) What are some examples of cash equivalents?

Practice Exercises

PE 8-1A
Internal control elements
obj. 2
EE 8-1 p. 360

Identify each of the following as relating to (a) the control environment, (b) control procedures, or (c) monitoring.

1. Hiring of external auditors to review the adequacy of controls
2. Personnel policies
3. Safeguarding inventory in a locked warehouse

PE 8-1B
Internal control elements
obj. 2
EE 8-1 p. 360

Identify each of the following as relating to (a) the control environment, (b) control procedures, or (c) information and communication.

1. Management's philosophy and operating style
2. Report of internal auditors
3. Separating related operations

PE 8-2A
Items on company's bank statement
obj. 4
EE 8-2 p. 366

The following items may appear on a bank statement:

1. Bank correction of an error from posting another customer's check to the company's account
2. EFT deposit
3. Loan proceeds
4. NSF check

Using the format shown below, indicate whether each item would appear as a debit or credit memo on the bank statement and whether the item would increase or decrease the balance of the company's account.

Item No.	Appears on the Bank Statement as a Debit or Credit Memo	Increases or Decreases the Balance of the Company's Bank Account

PE 8-2B
Items on company's bank statement
obj. 4
EE 8-2 p. 366

The following items may appear on a bank statement:

1. Bank correction of an error from recording a $3,200 deposit as $2,300
2. EFT payment
3. Note collected for company
4. Service charge

Using the format shown below, indicate whether each item would appear as a debit or credit memo on the bank statement and whether the item would increase or decrease the balance of the company's account.

Item No.	Appears on the Bank Statement as a Debit or Credit Memo	Increases or Decreases the Balance of the Company's Bank Account

PE 8-3A
Bank reconciliation

obj. 5

EE 8-3 p. 370

The following data were gathered to use in reconciling the bank account of East Meets West Company:

Balance per bank	$19,340
Balance per company records	6,480
Bank service charges	50
Deposit in transit	2,500
Note collected by bank with $250 interest	8,250
Outstanding checks	7,160

a. What is the adjusted balance on the bank reconciliation?
b. Journalize any necessary entries for East Meets West Company based on the bank reconciliation.

PE 8-3B
Bank reconciliation

obj. 5

EE 8-3 p. 370

The following data were gathered to use in reconciling the bank account of Crescent Moon Company:

Balance per bank	$11,200
Balance per company records	9,295
Bank service charges	25
Deposit in transit	1,650
NSF check	600
Outstanding checks	4,180

a. What is the adjusted balance on the bank reconciliation?
b. Journalize any necessary entries for Crescent Moon Company based on the bank reconciliation.

PE 8-4A
Petty cash fund

obj. 6

EE 8-4 p. 372

Prepare journal entries for each of the following:
a. Issued a check to establish a petty cash fund of $300.
b. The amount of cash in the petty cash fund is $95. Issued a check to replenish the fund, based on the following summary of petty cash receipts: store supplies, $120 and miscellaneous selling expense, $75. Record any missing funds in the cash short and over account.

PE 8-4B
Petty cash fund

obj. 6

EE 8-4 p. 372

Prepare journal entries for each of the following:
a. Issued a check to establish a petty cash fund of $500.
b. The amount of cash in the petty cash fund is $140. Issued a check to replenish the fund, based on the following summary of petty cash receipts: repair expense, $260 and miscellaneous selling expense, $84. Record any missing funds in the cash short and over account.

Exercises

EX 8-1
Sarbanes-Oxley internal control report

obj. 1

Using Wikpedia **(www.wikpedia.com)**, look up the entry for Sarbanes-Oxley Act. Look over the table of contents and find the section that describes Section 404.
What does Section 404 require of management's internal control report?

EX 8-2
Internal controls
objs. 2, 3

Blake Gable has recently been hired as the manager of Jittery Jim's Canyon Coffee. Jittery Jim's Canyon Coffee is a national chain of franchised coffee shops. During his first month as store manager, Blake encountered the following internal control situations:

a. Blake caught an employee putting a case of 100 single-serving tea bags in her car. Not wanting to create a scene, Blake smiled and said, "I don't think you're putting those tea bags on the right shelf. Don't they belong inside the coffee shop?" The employee returned the tea bags to the stockroom.
b. Jittery Jim's Canyon Coffee has one cash register. Prior to Blake's joining the coffee shop, each employee working on a shift would take a customer order, accept payment, and then prepare the order. Blake made one employee on each shift responsible for taking orders and accepting the customer's payment. Other employees prepare the orders.
c. Since only one employee uses the cash register, that employee is responsible for counting the cash at the end of the shift and verifying that the cash in the drawer matches the amount of cash sales recorded by the cash register. Blake expects each cashier to balance the drawer to the penny *every* time—no exceptions.

State whether you agree or disagree with Blake's method of handling each situation and explain your answer.

EX 8-3
Internal controls
objs. 2, 3

Anasazi Earth Clothing is a retail store specializing in women's clothing. The store has established a liberal return policy for the holiday season in order to encourage gift purchases. Any item purchased during November and December may be returned through January 31, with a receipt, for cash or exchange. If the customer does not have a receipt, cash will still be refunded for any item under $100. If the item is more than $100, a check is mailed to the customer.

Whenever an item is returned, a store clerk completes a return slip, which the customer signs. The return slip is placed in a special box. The store manager visits the return counter approximately once every two hours to authorize the return slips. Clerks are instructed to place the returned merchandise on the proper rack on the selling floor as soon as possible.

This year, returns at Anasazi Earth Clothing have reached an all-time high. There are a large number of returns under $100 without receipts.

a. How can sales clerks employed at Anasazi Earth Clothing use the store's return policy to steal money from the cash register?
b. What internal control weaknesses do you see in the return policy that make cash thefts easier?
c. Would issuing a store credit in place of a cash refund for all merchandise returned without a receipt reduce the possibility of theft? List some advantages and disadvantages of issuing a store credit in place of a cash refund.
d. Assume that Anasazi Earth Clothing is committed to the current policy of issuing cash refunds without a receipt. What changes could be made in the store's procedures regarding customer refunds in order to improve internal control?

EX 8-4
Internal controls for bank lending
objs. 2, 3

First Kenmore Bank provides loans to businesses in the community through its Commercial Lending Department. Small loans (less than $100,000) may be approved by an individual loan officer, while larger loans (greater than $100,000) must be approved by a board of loan officers. Once a loan is approved, the funds are made available to the loan applicant under agreed-upon terms. The president of First Kenmore Bank has instituted a policy whereby he has the individual authority to approve loans up to $5,000,000. The president believes that this policy will allow flexibility to approve loans to valued clients much quicker than under the previous policy.

As an internal auditor of First Kenmore Bank, how would you respond to this change in policy?

EX 8-5
Internal controls
objs. 2, 3

One of the largest losses in history from unauthorized securities trading involved a securities trader for the French bank, Societe Generale. The trader was able to circumvent internal controls and create over $7 billion in trading losses in six months. The trader apparently escaped detection by using knowledge of the bank's internal control systems learned from a previous back-office monitoring job. Much of this monitoring involved the use of software to monitor trades. In addition, traders are usually kept to tight spending limits. Apparently, these controls failed in this case.

What general weaknesses in Societe Generale's internal controls contributed to the occurrence and size of the losses?

EX 8-6
Internal controls
objs. 2, 3

An employee of JHT Holdings, Inc., a trucking company, was responsible for resolving roadway accident claims under $25,000. The employee created fake accident claims and wrote settlement checks of between $5,000 and $25,000 to friends or acquaintances acting as phony "victims." One friend recruited subordinates at his place of work to cash some of the checks. Beyond this, the JHT employee also recruited lawyers, who he paid to represent both the trucking company and the fake victims in the bogus accident settlements. When the lawyers cashed the checks, they allegedly split the money with the corrupt JHT employee. This fraud went undetected for two years.

Why would it take so long to discover such a fraud?

EX 8-7
Internal controls
objs. 2, 3

Bizarro Sound Co. discovered a fraud whereby one of its front office administrative employees used company funds to purchase goods, such as computers, digital cameras, compact disk players, and other electronic items for her own use. The fraud was discovered when employees noticed an increase in delivery frequency from vendors and the use of unusual vendors. After some investigation, it was discovered that the employee would alter the description or change the quantity on an invoice in order to explain the cost on the bill.

What general internal control weaknesses contributed to this fraud?

EX 8-8
Financial statement fraud
objs. 2, 3

A former chairman, CFO, and controller of Donnkenny, Inc., an apparel company that makes sportswear for Pierre Cardin and Victoria Jones, pleaded guilty to financial statement fraud. These managers used false journal entries to record fictitious sales, hid inventory in public warehouses so that it could be recorded as "sold," and required sales orders to be backdated so that the sale could be moved back to an earlier period. The combined effect of these actions caused $25 million out of $40 million in quarterly sales to be phony.

a. Why might control procedures listed in this chapter be insufficient in stopping this type of fraud?
b. How could this type of fraud be stopped?

EX 8-9
Internal control of cash receipts
objs. 2, 3

The procedures used for over-the-counter receipts are as follows. At the close of each day's business, the sales clerks count the cash in their respective cash drawers, after which they determine the amount recorded by the cash register and prepare the memo cash form, noting any discrepancies. An employee from the cashier's office counts the cash, compares the total with the memo, and takes the cash to the cashier's office.

a. Indicate the weak link in internal control.
b. How can the weakness be corrected?

EX 8-10
Internal control of cash receipts
objs. 2, 3

Victor Blackmon works at the drive-through window of Buffalo Bob's Burgers. Occasionally, when a drive-through customer orders, Victor fills the order and pockets the customer's money. He does not ring up the order on the cash register.

Identify the internal control weaknesses that exist at Buffalo Bob's Burgers, and discuss what can be done to prevent this theft.

EX 8-11
Internal control of cash receipts
objs. 2, 3

The mailroom employees send all remittances and remittance advices to the cashier. The cashier deposits the cash in the bank and forwards the remittance advices and duplicate deposit slips to the Accounting Department.

a. Indicate the weak link in internal control in the handling of cash receipts.
b. How can the weakness be corrected?

EX 8-12
Entry for cash sales; cash short
objs. 2, 3

The actual cash received from cash sales was $36,183, and the amount indicated by the cash register total was $36,197. Journalize the entry to record the cash receipts and cash sales.

EX 8-13
Entry for cash sales; cash over
objs. 2, 3

The actual cash received from cash sales was $11,279, and the amount indicated by the cash register total was $11,256. Journalize the entry to record the cash receipts and cash sales.

EX 8-14
Internal control of cash payments
objs. 2, 3

El Cordova Co. is a small merchandising company with a manual accounting system. An investigation revealed that in spite of a sufficient bank balance, a significant amount of available cash discounts had been lost because of failure to make timely payments. In addition, it was discovered that the invoices for several purchases had been paid twice. Outline procedures for the payment of vendors' invoices, so that the possibilities of losing available cash discounts and of paying an invoice a second time will be minimized.

EX 8-15
Internal control of cash payments
objs. 2, 3

Digital Com Company, a communications equipment manufacturer, recently fell victim to a fraud scheme developed by one of its employees. To understand the scheme, it is necessary to review Digital Com's procedures for the purchase of services.

The purchasing agent is responsible for ordering services (such as repairs to a photocopy machine or office cleaning) after receiving a service requisition from an authorized manager. However, since no tangible goods are delivered, a receiving report is not prepared. When the Accounting Department receives an invoice billing Digital Com for a service call, the accounts payable clerk calls the manager who requested the service in order to verify that it was performed.

The fraud scheme involves Matt DuBois, the manager of plant and facilities. Matt arranged for his uncle's company, Urban Industrial Supply and Service, to be placed on Digital Com's approved vendor list. Matt did not disclose the family relationship.

On several occasions, Matt would submit a requisition for services to be provided by Urban Industrial Supply and Service. However, the service requested was really not needed, and it was never performed. Urban would bill Digital Com for the service and then split the cash payment with Matt.

Explain what changes should be made to Digital Com's procedures for ordering and paying for services in order to prevent such occurrences in the future.

EX 8-16
Bank reconciliation
obj. 5

Identify each of the following reconciling items as: (a) an addition to the cash balance according to the bank statement, (b) a deduction from the cash balance according to the bank statement, (c) an addition to the cash balance according to the company's records, or (d) a deduction from the cash balance according to the company's records. (None of the transactions reported by bank debit and credit memos have been recorded by the company.)

1. Bank service charges, $15.
2. Check drawn by company for $160 but incorrectly recorded as $610.

3. Check for $500 incorrectly charged by bank as $5,000.
4. Check of a customer returned by bank to company because of insufficient funds, $3,000.
5. Deposit in transit, $15,500.
6. Outstanding checks, $9,600.
7. Note collected by bank, $10,000.

EX 8-17
Entries based on bank reconciliation
obj. 5

Which of the reconciling items listed in Exercise 8-16 require an entry in the company's accounts?

EX 8-18
Bank reconciliation
obj. 5
✔ Adjusted balance: $13,680

The following data were accumulated for use in reconciling the bank account of Commander Co. for March:

a. Cash balance according to the company's records at March 31, $13,065.
b. Cash balance according to the bank statement at March 31, $12,750.
c. Checks outstanding, $4,170.
d. Deposit in transit, not recorded by bank, $5,100.
e. A check for $180 in payment of an account was erroneously recorded in the check register as $810.
f. Bank debit memo for service charges, $15.

Prepare a bank reconciliation, using the format shown in Exhibit 7.

EX 8-19
Entries for bank reconciliation
obj. 5

Using the data presented in Exercise 8-18, journalize the entry or entries that should be made by the company.

EX 8-20
Entries for note collected by bank
obj. 5

Accompanying a bank statement for Euthenics Company is a credit memo for $18,270, representing the principal ($18,000) and interest ($270) on a note that had been collected by the bank. The company had been notified by the bank at the time of the collection, but had made no entries. Journalize the entry that should be made by the company to bring the accounting records up to date.

EX 8-21
Bank reconciliation
obj. 5
✔ Adjusted balance: $11,740

An accounting clerk for Grebe Co. prepared the following bank reconciliation:

Grebe Co.
Bank Reconciliation
August 31, 2010

Cash balance according to company's records		$ 4,690
Add: Outstanding checks	$3,110	
Error by Grebe Co. in recording Check No. 1115 as $940 instead of $490	450	
Note for $6,500 collected by bank, including interest.	6,630	10,190
		$14,880
Deduct: Deposit in transit on August 31	$4,725	
Bank service charges	30	4,755
Cash balance according to bank statement		$10,125

a. From the data in the above bank reconciliation, prepare a new bank reconciliation for Grebe Co., using the format shown in the illustrative problem.
b. If a balance sheet were prepared for Grebe Co. on August 31, 2010, what amount should be reported for cash?

EX 8-22
Bank reconciliation

obj. 5

✔ Corrected adjusted balance: $11,960

Identify the errors in the following bank reconciliation:

Rakestraw Co.
Bank Reconciliation
For the Month Ended April 30, 2010

Cash balance according to bank statement			$11,320
Add outstanding checks:			
No. 315		$450	
360		615	
364		850	
365		775	2,690
			$14,010
Deduct deposit of April 30, not recorded by bank			3,330
Adjusted balance			$10,680
Cash balance according to company's records			$ 7,003
Add: Proceeds of note collected by bank:			
Principal	$4,000		
Interest	120	$4,120	
Service charges		18	4,138
			$11,141
Deduct: Check returned because of insufficient funds		$ 945	
Error in recording April 20 deposit of $5,300 as $3,500		1,800	2,745
Adjusted balance			$ 8,396

EX 8-23
Using bank reconciliation to determine cash receipts stolen

objs. 2, 3, 5

First Impressions Co. records all cash receipts on the basis of its cash register tapes. First Impressions Co. discovered during June 2010 that one of its sales clerks had stolen an undetermined amount of cash receipts when she took the daily deposits to the bank. The following data have been gathered for June:

Cash in bank according to the general ledger	$ 7,865
Cash according to the June 30, 2010, bank statement	18,175
Outstanding checks as of June 30, 2010	5,190
Bank service charge for June	25
Note receivable, including interest collected by bank in June	8,400

No deposits were in transit on June 30.

a. Determine the amount of cash receipts stolen by the sales clerk.
b. What accounting controls would have prevented or detected this theft?

EX 8-24
Petty cash fund entries

obj. 6

Journalize the entries to record the following:

a. Check No. 8193 is issued to establish a petty cash fund of $800.
b. The amount of cash in the petty cash fund is now $294. Check No. 8336 is issued to replenish the fund, based on the following summary of petty cash receipts: office supplies, $295; miscellaneous selling expense, $120; miscellaneous administrative expense, $75. (Since the amount of the check to replenish the fund plus the balance in the fund do not equal $800, record the discrepancy in the cash short and over account.)

EX 8-25
Variation in cash flows

obj. 7

Mattel, Inc., designs, manufactures, and markets toy products worldwide. Mattel's toys include Barbie™ fashion dolls and accessories, Hot Wheels™, and Fisher-Price brands. For a recent year, Mattel reported the following net cash flows from operating activities (in thousands):

First quarter ending March 31	$ (326,536)
Second quarter ending June 30	(165,047)
Third quarter ending September 30	(9,738)
Fourth quarter December 31	1,243,603

Explain why Mattel reports negative net cash flows from operating activities during the first three quarters yet reports positive cash flows for the fourth quarter and net positive cash flows for the year.

EX 8-26
Cash to monthly cash expenses ratio

During 2010, Bezel Inc. has monthly cash expenses of $250,000. On December 31, 2010, the cash balance is $1,750,000.

a. Compute the ratio of cash to monthly cash expenses.
b. Based on (a), what are the implications for Bezel Inc.?

EX 8-27
Cash to monthly cash expenses ratio

Delta Air Lines is one of the major airlines in the United States and the world. It provides passenger and cargo services for over 200 domestic U.S. cities as well as 70 international cities. It operates a fleet of over 800 aircraft and is headquartered in Atlanta, Georgia. Delta reported the following financial data (in millions) for the year ended December 31, 2004:

Net cash flows from operating activities	$(1,123)
Cash, December 31, 2004	1,811

a. Determine the monthly cash expenses. Round to one decimal place.
b. Determine the ratio of cash to monthly expenses. Round to one decimal place.
c. Based on your analysis, do you believe that Delta will remain in business?

EX 8-28
Cash to monthly cash expenses ratio

Acusphere, Inc., is a specialty pharmaceutical company that develops new drugs and improved formulations of existing drugs using its proprietary microparticle technology. Currently, the company has three products in development in the areas of cardiology, oncology, and asthma. Acusphere reported the following data (in thousands) for the years ending December 31, 2006, 2005, 2004, and 2003:

	2006	2005	2004	2003
Cash as of December 31*	$ 59,750	$ 51,112	$ 45,180	$ 54,562
Net cash flows from operating activities	(48,089)	(30,683)	(19,319)	(15,507)

*Includes cash equivalents and short-term investments.

1. Determine the monthly cash expenses for 2006, 2005, 2004, and 2003. Round to one decimal place.
2. Determine the ratio of cash to monthly expenses as of December 31, 2006, 2005, 2004, and 2003. Round to one decimal place.
3. Based on (1) and (2), comment on Acusphere's ratio of cash to monthly operating expenses for 2006, 2005, 2004, and 2003.

Problems Series A

PR 8-1A
Evaluate internal control of cash
objs. 2, 3

The following procedures were recently installed by The Louver Shop:

a. Each cashier is assigned a separate cash register drawer to which no other cashier has access.
b. At the end of a shift, each cashier counts the cash in his or her cash register, unlocks the cash register record, and compares the amount of cash with the amount on the record to determine cash shortages and overages.
c. Vouchers and all supporting documents are perforated with a PAID designation after being paid by the treasurer.
d. Disbursements are made from the petty cash fund only after a petty cash receipt has been completed and signed by the payee.
e. All sales are rung up on the cash register, and a receipt is given to the customer. All sales are recorded on a record locked inside the cash register.
f. Checks received through the mail are given daily to the accounts receivable clerk for recording collections on account and for depositing in the bank.
g. The bank reconciliation is prepared by the accountant.

Instructions

Indicate whether each of the procedures of internal control over cash represents (1) a strength or (2) a weakness. For each weakness, indicate why it exists.

PR 8-2A
Transactions for petty cash, cash short and over
objs. 3, 6

Hallihan Company completed the following selected transactions during June 2010:

June 1. Established a petty cash fund of $500.

12. The cash sales for the day, according to the cash register records, totaled $13,115. The actual cash received from cash sales was $13,129.

30. Petty cash on hand was $38. Replenished the petty cash fund for the following disbursements, each evidenced by a petty cash receipt:

    June 2. Store supplies, $55.

    10. Express charges on merchandise purchased, $80 (Merchandise Inventory).
    14. Office supplies, $35.
    15. Office supplies, $40.
    18. Postage stamps, $42 (Office Supplies).
    20. Repair to fax, $100 (Miscellaneous Administrative Expense).
    21. Repair to office door lock, $35 (Miscellaneous Administrative Expense).
    22. Postage due on special delivery letter, $27 (Miscellaneous Administrative Expense).
    28. Express charges on merchandise purchased, $40 (Merchandise Inventory).

30. The cash sales for the day, according to the cash register records, totaled $16,850. The actual cash received from cash sales was $16,833.

30. Increased the petty cash fund by $125.

Instructions

Journalize the transactions.

PR 8-3A
Bank reconciliation and entries
obj. 5

✔ 1. Adjusted balance: $13,445

The cash account for Interactive Systems at February 28, 2010, indicated a balance of $7,635. The bank statement indicated a balance of $13,333 on February 28, 2010. Comparing the bank statement and the accompanying canceled checks and memos with the records reveals the following reconciling items:

a. Checks outstanding totaled $4,118.
b. A deposit of $4,500, representing receipts of February 28, had been made too late to appear on the bank statement.
c. The bank had collected $5,200 on a note left for collection. The face of the note was $5,000.
d. A check for $290 returned with the statement had been incorrectly recorded by Interactive Systems as $920. The check was for the payment of an obligation to Busser Co. for the purchase of office supplies on account.
e. A check drawn for $415 had been incorrectly charged by the bank as $145.
f. Bank service charges for February amounted to $20.

Instructions

1. Prepare a bank reconciliation.
2. Journalize the necessary entries. The accounts have not been closed.

PR 8-4A
Bank reconciliation and entries
obj. 5

✔ 1. Adjusted balance: $15,430

The cash account for Fred's Sports Co. on June 1, 2010, indicated a balance of $16,515. During June, the total cash deposited was $40,150, and checks written totaled $43,600. The bank statement indicated a balance of $18,175 on June 30, 2010. Comparing the bank statement, the canceled checks, and the accompanying memos with the records revealed the following reconciling items:

a. Checks outstanding totaled $6,840.
b. A deposit of $4,275, representing receipts of June 30, had been made too late to appear on the bank statement.

c. A check for $640 had been incorrectly charged by the bank as $460.
d. A check for $80 returned with the statement had been recorded by Fred's Sports Co. as $800. The check was for the payment of an obligation to Miliski Co. on account.
e. The bank had collected for Fred's Sports Co. $3,240 on a note left for collection. The face of the note was $3,000.
f. Bank service charges for June amounted to $35.
g. A check for $1,560 from ChimTech Co. was returned by the bank because of insufficient funds.

Instructions

1. Prepare a bank reconciliation as of June 30.
2. Journalize the necessary entries. The accounts have not been closed.

PR 8-5A
Bank reconciliation and entries
obj. 5

✔ 1. Adjusted balance: $11,178.59

Rocky Mountain Interiors deposits all cash receipts each Wednesday and Friday in a night depository, after banking hours. The data required to reconcile the bank statement as of July 31 have been taken from various documents and records and are reproduced as follows. The sources of the data are printed in capital letters. All checks were written for payments on account.

BANK RECONCILIATION FOR PRECEDING MONTH (DATED JUNE 30):

Cash balance according to bank statement		$ 9,422.80
Add deposit of June 30, not recorded by bank		780.80
		$10,203.60
Deduct outstanding checks:		
No. 580	$310.10	
No. 602	85.50	
No. 612	92.50	
No. 613	137.50	625.60
Adjusted balance		$ 9,578.00
Cash balance according to company's records		$ 9,605.70
Deduct service charges		27.70
Adjusted balance		$ 9,578.00

CASH ACCOUNT:
Balance as of July 1 $9,578.00

CHECKS WRITTEN:
Number and amount of each check issued in July:

Check No.	Amount	Check No.	Amount	Check No.	Amount
614	$243.50	621	$309.50	628	$ 837.70
615	350.10	622	Void	629	329.90
616	279.90	623	Void	630	882.80
617	395.50	624	707.01	631	1,081.56
618	435.40	625	158.63	632	62.40
619	320.10	626	550.03	633	310.08
620	328.87	627	318.73	634	503.30

Total amount of checks issued in July $8,405.01

MEMBER FDIC

AMERICAN NATIONAL BANK
OF DETROIT

DETROIT, MI 48201-2500 (313)933-8547

ROCKY MOUNTAIN INTERIORS

PAGE 1

ACCOUNT NUMBER

FROM 7/01/20– TO 7/31/20–

	BALANCE	9,422.80
9	DEPOSITS	6,086.35
20	WITHDRAWALS	8,237.41
4	OTHER DEBITS AND CREDITS	3,685.00CR
	NEW BALANCE	10,956.74

CHECKS AND OTHER DEBITS						DEPOSITS	DATE	BALANCE
No.580	310.10	No.612	92.50			780.80	07/01	9,801.00
No.602	85.50	No.614	243.50			569.50	07/03	10,041.50
No.615	350.10	No.616	279.90			701.80	07/06	10,113.30
No.617	395.50	No.618	435.40			819.24	07/11	10,101.64
No.619	320.10	No.620	238.87			580.70	07/13	10,123.37
No.621	309.50	No.624	707.01			MS 4,000.00	07/14	13,106.86
No.625	158.63	No.626	550.03			MS 160.00	07/14	12,558.20
No.627	318.73	No.629	329.90			600.10	07/17	12,509.67
No.630	882.80	No.631	1,081.56	NSF	450.00		07/20	10,095.31
No.628	837.70	No.633	310.08			701.26	07/21	9,648.79
						731.45	07/24	10,380.24
						601.50	07/28	10,981.74
		SC	25.00				07/31	10,956.74

EC — ERROR CORRECTION
MS — MISCELLANEOUS
NSF — NOT SUFFICIENT FUNDS
OD — OVERDRAFT
PS — PAYMENT STOPPED
SC — SERVICE CHARGE

* * * * * * * * *

THE RECONCILEMENT OF THIS STATEMENT WITH YOUR RECORDS IS ESSENTIAL.
ANY ERROR OR EXCEPTION SHOULD BE REPORTED IMMEDIATELY.

CASH RECEIPTS FOR MONTH OF JULY 6,158.60

DUPLICATE DEPOSIT TICKETS:
Date and amount of each deposit in July:

Date	Amount	Date	Amount	Date	Amount
July 2	$569.50	July 12	$508.70	July 23	$731.45
5	701.80	16	600.10	26	601.50
9	819.24	19	701.26	31	925.05

Instructions

1. Prepare a bank reconciliation as of July 31. If errors in recording deposits or checks are discovered, assume that the errors were made by the company. Assume that all deposits are from cash sales. All checks are written to satisfy accounts payable.
2. Journalize the necessary entries. The accounts have not been closed.
3. What is the amount of Cash that should appear on the balance sheet as of July 31?
4. Assume that a canceled check for $125 has been incorrectly recorded by the bank as $1,250. Briefly explain how the error would be included in a bank reconciliation and how it should be corrected.

Problems Series B

PR 8-1B
Evaluating internal control of cash
objs. 2, 3

The following procedures were recently installed by C&G Hydraulics Company:

a. The bank reconciliation is prepared by the cashier, who works under the supervision of the treasurer.
b. All mail is opened by the mail clerk, who forwards all cash remittances to the cashier. The cashier prepares a listing of the cash receipts and forwards a copy of the list to the accounts receivable clerk for recording in the accounts.
c. At the end of the day, cash register clerks are required to use their own funds to make up any cash shortages in their registers.
d. At the end of each day, all cash receipts are placed in the bank's night depository.
e. At the end of each day, an accounting clerk compares the duplicate copy of the daily cash deposit slip with the deposit receipt obtained from the bank.
f. The accounts payable clerk prepares a voucher for each disbursement. The voucher along with the supporting documentation is forwarded to the treasurer's office for approval.
g. After necessary approvals have been obtained for the payment of a voucher, the treasurer signs and mails the check. The treasurer then stamps the voucher and supporting documentation as paid and returns the voucher and supporting documentation to the accounts payable clerk for filing.
h. Along with petty cash expense receipts for postage, office supplies, etc., several postdated employee checks are in the petty cash fund.

Instructions

Indicate whether each of the procedures of internal control over cash represents (1) a strength or (2) a weakness. For each weakness, indicate why it exists.

PR 8-2B
Transactions for petty cash, cash short and over
objs. 3, 6

Padilla's Restoration Company completed the following selected transactions during March 2010:

Mar. 1. Established a petty cash fund of $800.
10. The cash sales for the day, according to the cash register records, totaled $11,368. The actual cash received from cash sales was $11,375.
31. Petty cash on hand was $193. Replenished the petty cash fund for the following disbursements, each evidenced by a petty cash receipt:
Mar. 3. Store supplies, $275.
7. Express charges on merchandise sold, $120 (Delivery Expense).
9. Office supplies, $18.
13. Office supplies, $13.
19. Postage stamps, $9 (Office Supplies).
21. Repair to office file cabinet lock, $40 (Miscellaneous Administrative Expense).
22. Postage due on special delivery letter, $18 (Miscellaneous Administrative Expense).
24. Express charges on merchandise sold, $90 (Delivery Expense).
30. Office supplies, $16.
31. The cash sales for the day, according to the cash register records, totaled $14,690. The actual cash received from cash sales was $14,675.
31. Decreased the petty cash fund by $50.

Instructions

Journalize the transactions.

PR 8-3B
Bank reconciliation and entries
obj. 5

✔ 1. Adjusted balance: $8,613

The cash account for Discount Medical Co. at April 30, 2010, indicated a balance of $4,604. The bank statement indicated a balance of $9,158 on April 30, 2010. Comparing the bank statement and the accompanying canceled checks and memos with the records revealed the following reconciling items:

a. Checks outstanding totaled $5,225.
b. A deposit of $3,150, representing receipts of April 30, had been made too late to appear on the bank statement.
c. The bank had collected $4,120 on a note left for collection. The face of the note was $4,000.
d. A check for $2,490 returned with the statement had been incorrectly recorded by Discount Medical Co. as $2,409. The check was for the payment of an obligation to Goldstein Co. for the purchase of office equipment on account.
e. A check drawn for $170 had been erroneously charged by the bank as $1,700.
f. Bank service charges for April amounted to $30.

Instructions

1. Prepare a bank reconciliation.
2. Journalize the necessary entries. The accounts have not been closed.

PR 8-4B
Bank reconciliation and entries
obj. 5

✔ 1. Adjusted balance: $9,360

The cash account for Inky's Bike Co. at July 1, 2010, indicated a balance of $12,470. During July, the total cash deposited was $26,680, and checks written totaled $31,500. The bank statement indicated a balance of $16,750 on July 31. Comparing the bank statement, the canceled checks, and the accompanying memos with the records revealed the following reconciling items:

a. Checks outstanding totaled $12,850.
b. A deposit of $5,100, representing receipts of July 31, had been made too late to appear on the bank statement.
c. The bank had collected for Inky's Bike Co. $2,675 on a note left for collection. The face of the note was $2,500.
d. A check for $370 returned with the statement had been incorrectly charged by the bank as $730.
e. A check for $320 returned with the statement had been recorded by Inky's Bike Co. as $230. The check was for the payment of an obligation to Ranchwood Co. on account.
f. Bank service charges for July amounted to $25.
g. A check for $850 from Hallock Co. was returned by the bank because of insufficient funds.

Instructions

1. Prepare a bank reconciliation as of July 31.
2. Journalize the necessary entries. The accounts have not been closed.

PR 8-5B
Bank reconciliation and entries
obj. 5

✔ 1. Adjusted balance: $13,893.32

Reydell Furniture Company deposits all cash receipts each Wednesday and Friday in a night depository, after banking hours. The data required to reconcile the bank statement as of June 30 have been taken from various documents and records and are reproduced as follows. The sources of the data are printed in capital letters. All checks were written for payments on account.

JUNE BANK STATEMENT:

MEMBER FDIC

AMERICAN NATIONAL BANK OF DETROIT

DETROIT, MI 48201-2500 (313)933-8547

PAGE 1

ACCOUNT NUMBER

FROM 6/01/20– TO 6/30/20–

	BALANCE	9,447.20
9	DEPOSITS	8,691.77
20	WITHDRAWALS	8,014.37
4	OTHER DEBITS AND CREDITS	3,370.00CR
	NEW BALANCE	13,494.60

REYDELL FURNITURE COMPANY

CHECKS AND OTHER DEBITS				DEPOSITS	DATE	BALANCE
No.731	162.15	No.736	345.95	690.25	6/01	9,629.35
No.739	60.55	No.740	237.50	1,080.50	6/02	10,411.80
No.741	495.15	No.742	501.90	854.17	6/04	10,268.92
No.743	671.30	No.744	506.88	840.50	6/09	9,931.24
No.745	117.25	No.746	298.66	MS 3,500.00	6/09	13,015.33
No.748	450.90	No.749	640.13	MS 210.00	6/09	12,134.30
No.750	276.77	No.751	299.37	896.61	6/11	12,454.77
No.752	537.01	No.753	380.95	882.95	6/16	12,419.76
No.754	449.75	No.755	272.75	1,606.74	6/18	13,304.00
No.757	407.95	No.759	901.50	897.34	6/23	12,891.89
				942.71	6/25	13,834.60
		NSF	300.00		6/28	13,534.60
		SC	40.00		6/30	13,494.60

EC — ERROR CORRECTION
MS — MISCELLANEOUS
NSF — NOT SUFFICIENT FUNDS
OD — OVERDRAFT
PS — PAYMENT STOPPED
SC — SERVICE CHARGE

* * * * * * * * *

THE RECONCILEMENT OF THIS STATEMENT WITH YOUR RECORDS IS ESSENTIAL.
ANY ERROR OR EXCEPTION SHOULD BE REPORTED IMMEDIATELY.

CASH ACCOUNT:
Balance as of June 1 $9,317.40

CASH RECEIPTS FOR MONTH OF JUNE $9,601.58

DUPLICATE DEPOSIT TICKETS:
Date and amount of each deposit in June:

Date	Amount	Date	Amount	Date	Amount
June 1	$1,080.50	June 10	$ 896.61	June 22	$ 987.34
3	854.17	15	882.95	24	942.71
8	840.50	17	1,606.74	30	1,510.06

CHECKS WRITTEN:
Number and amount of each check issued in June:

Check No.	Amount	Check No.	Amount	Check No.	Amount
740	$237.50	747	Void	754	$ 449.75
741	495.15	748	$ 450.90	755	272.75
742	501.90	749	640.13	756	113.95
743	671.30	750	276.77	757	407.95
744	506.88	751	299.37	758	259.60
745	117.25	752	537.01	759	901.50
746	298.66	753	830.95	760	486.39

Total amount of checks issued in June $8,755.66

BANK RECONCILIATION FOR PRECEDING MONTH:

Reydell Furniture Company
Bank Reconciliation
May 31, 20—

Cash balance according to bank statement		$ 9,447.20
Add deposit for May 31, not recorded by bank		690.25
		$10,137.45
Deduct outstanding checks:		
No. 731	$162.15	
736	345.95	
738	251.40	
739	60.55	820.05
Adjusted balance		$ 9,317.40
Cash balance according to company's records		$ 9,352.50
Deduct service charges		35.10
Adjusted balance		$ 9,317.40

Instructions

1. Prepare a bank reconciliation as of June 30. If errors in recording deposits or checks are discovered, assume that the errors were made by the company. Assume that all deposits are from cash sales. All checks are written to satisfy accounts payable.
2. Journalize the necessary entries. The accounts have not been closed.
3. What is the amount of Cash that should appear on the balance sheet as of June 30?
4. Assume that a canceled check for $260 has been incorrectly recorded by the bank as $620. Briefly explain how the error would be included in a bank reconciliation and how it should be corrected.

Special Activities

SA 8-1
Ethics and professional conduct in business

During the preparation of the bank reconciliation for New Concepts Co., Peter Fikes, the assistant controller, discovered that City National Bank incorrectly recorded a $710 check written by New Concepts Co. as $170. Peter has decided not to notify the bank but wait for the bank to detect the error. Peter plans to record the $540 error as Other Income if the bank fails to detect the error within the next three months.

Discuss whether Peter is behaving in a professional manner.

SA 8-2
Internal controls

The following is an excerpt from a conversation between two sales clerks, Ross Maas and Shu Lyons. Both Ross and Shu are employed by Hawkins Electronics, a locally owned and operated electronics retail store.

Ross: Did you hear the news?

Shu: What news?

Ross: Jane and Rachel were both arrested this morning.

Shu: What? Arrested? You're putting me on!

Ross: No, really! The police arrested them first thing this morning. Put them in handcuffs, read them their rights—the whole works. It was unreal!

Shu: What did they do?

Ross: Well, apparently they were filling out merchandise refund forms for fictitious customers and then taking the cash.

Shu: I guess I never thought of that. How did they catch them?

Ross: The store manager noticed that returns were twice that of last year and seemed to be increasing. When he confronted Jane, she became flustered and admitted to taking the cash, apparently over $7,000 in just three months. They're going over the last six months' transactions to try to determine how much Rachel stole. She apparently started stealing first.

Suggest appropriate control procedures that would have prevented or detected the theft of cash.

SA 8-3
Internal controls

The following is an excerpt from a conversation between the store manager of Yoder Brothers Grocery Stores, Lori Colburn, and Terry Whipple, president of Yoder Brothers Grocery Stores.

Terry: Lori, I'm concerned about this new scanning system.

Lori: What's the problem?

Terry: Well, how do we know the clerks are ringing up all the merchandise?

Lori: That's one of the strong points about the system. The scanner automatically rings up each item, based on its bar code. We update the prices daily, so we're sure that the sale is rung up for the right price.

Terry: That's not my concern. What keeps a clerk from pretending to scan items and then simply not charging his friends? If his friends were buying 10-15 items, it would be easy for the clerk to pass through several items with his finger over the bar code or just pass the merchandise through the scanner with the wrong side showing. It would look normal for anyone observing. In the old days, we at least could hear the cash register ringing up each sale.

Lori: I see your point.

Suggest ways that Yoder Brothers Grocery Stores could prevent or detect the theft of merchandise as described.

SA 8-4
Ethics and professional conduct in business

Ryan Egan and Jack Moody are both cash register clerks for Organic Markets. Lee Sorrell is the store manager for Organic Markets. The following is an excerpt of a conversation between Ryan and Jack:

Ryan: Jack, how long have you been working for Organic Markets?

Jack: Almost five years this November. You just started two weeks ago . . . right?

Ryan: Yes. Do you mind if I ask you a question?

Jack: No, go ahead.

Ryan: What I want to know is, have they always had this rule that if your cash register is short at the end of the day, you have to make up the shortage out of your own pocket?

Jack: Yes, as long as I've been working here.

Ryan: Well, it's the pits. Last week I had to pay in almost $40.

Jack: It's not that big a deal. I just make sure that I'm not short at the end of the day.

Ryan: How do you do that?

Jack: I just shortchange a few customers early in the day. There are a few jerks that deserve it anyway. Most of the time, their attention is elsewhere and they don't think to check their change.

Ryan: What happens if you're over at the end of the day?

Jack: Lee lets me keep it as long as it doesn't get to be too large. I've not been short in over a year. I usually clear about $20 to $30 extra per day.

Discuss this case from the viewpoint of proper controls and professional behavior.

SA 8-5
Bank reconciliation and internal control

The records of Anacker Company indicate a July 31 cash balance of $9,400, which includes undeposited receipts for July 30 and 31. The cash balance on the bank statement as of July 31 is $6,575. This balance includes a note of $4,000 plus $160 interest collected by the bank but not recorded in the journal. Checks outstanding on July 31 were as follows: No. 370, $580; No. 379, $615; No. 390, $900; No. 1148, $225; No. 1149, $300; and No. 1151, $750.

On July 3, the cashier resigned, effective at the end of the month. Before leaving on July 31, the cashier prepared the following bank reconciliation:

Cash balance per books, July 31		$ 9,400
Add outstanding checks:		
No. 1148	$225	
1149	300	
1151	750	1,175
		$10,575
Less undeposited receipts		4,000
Cash balance per bank, July 31		$ 6,575
Deduct unrecorded note with interest		4,160
True cash, July 31		$ 2,415

Calculator Tape of Outstanding Checks:
0 *
225 +
300 +
750 +
1,175 *

Subsequently, the owner of Anacker Company discovered that the cashier had stolen an unknown amount of undeposited receipts, leaving only $1,000 to be deposited on July 31. The owner, a close family friend, has asked your help in determining the amount that the former cashier has stolen.

1. Determine the amount the cashier stole from Anacker Company. Show your computations in good form.
2. How did the cashier attempt to conceal the theft?
3. a. Identify two major weaknesses in internal controls, which allowed the cashier to steal the undeposited cash receipts.
   b. Recommend improvements in internal controls, so that similar types of thefts of undeposited cash receipts can be prevented.

SA 8-6
Observe internal controls over cash

Group Project

Select a business in your community and observe its internal controls over cash receipts and cash payments. The business could be a bank or a bookstore, restaurant, department store, or other retailer. In groups of three or four, identify and discuss the similarities and differences in each business's cash internal controls.

SA 8-7
Cash to monthly cash expenses ratio

OccuLogix, Inc., provides treatments for eye diseases, including age-related macular degeneration (AMD). The company's treatment system, called the RHEO system, consists of an Octonova pump and disposable treatment sets that improve microcirculation in the eye by filtering high molecular weight proteins and other macromolecules from the patient's plasma. OccuLogix reported the following data (in thousands) for the years ending December 31, 2006, 2005, 2004, and 2003:

	2006	2005	2004	2003
Cash as of December 31*	$15,536	$41,268	$60,040	$1,239
Net cash flows from operating activities	(14,548)	(18,710)	(5,382)	(2,375)

*Includes cash equivalents and short-term investments.

1. Determine the monthly cash expenses for 2006, 2005, 2004, and 2003. Round to one decimal place.
2. Determine the ratio of cash to monthly expenses as of December 31, 2006, 2005, 2004, and 2003. Round to one decimal place.
3. Based on (1) and (2), comment on OccuLogix's ratio of cash to monthly operating expenses for 2006, 2005, 2004, and 2003.

Answers to Self-Examination Questions

1. **C** Compliance with laws and regulations (answer C) is an objective, not an element, of internal control. The control environment (answer A), monitoring (answer B), control procedures (answer D), risk assessment, and information and communication are the five elements of internal control.
2. **C** The error was made by the bank, so the cash balance according to the bank statement needs to be adjusted. Since the bank deducted $90 ($540.50 — $450.50) too little, the error of $90 should be deducted from the cash balance according to the bank statement (answer C).
3. **B** On any specific date, the cash account in a company's ledger may not agree with the account in the bank's ledger because of delays and/or errors by either party in recording transactions. The purpose of a bank reconciliation, therefore, is to determine the reasons for any differences between the two account balances. All errors should then be corrected by the company or the bank, as appropriate. In arriving at the adjusted cash balance according to the bank statement, outstanding checks must be deducted (answer B) to adjust for checks that have been written by the company but that have not yet been presented to the bank for payment.
4. **C** All reconciling items that are added to and deducted from the cash balance according to the company's records on the bank reconciliation (answer C) require that journal entries be made by the company to correct errors made in recording transactions or to bring the cash account up to date for delays in recording transactions.
5. **D** To avoid the delay, annoyance, and expense that is associated with paying all obligations by check, relatively small amounts (answer A) are paid from a petty cash fund. The fund is established by estimating the amount of cash needed to pay these small amounts during a specified period (answer B), and it is then reimbursed when the amount of money in the fund is reduced to a predetermined minimum amount (answer C).

CHAPTER 9

Receivables

©Tetra Images/Jupiter Images

OAKLEY, INC.

The sale and purchase of merchandise involves the exchange of goods for cash. However, the point at which cash actually changes hands varies with the transaction. Consider transactions by Oakley, Inc., a worldwide leader in the design, development, manufacture, and distribution of premium sunglasses, goggles, prescription eyewear, apparel, footwear, and accessories. Not only does the company sell its products through three different company-owned retail chains, but it also has approximately 10,000 independent distributors.

If you were to buy a pair of sunglasses at an Oakley Vault, which is one of the company's retail outlet stores, you would have to pay cash or use a credit card to pay for the glasses before you left the store. However, Oakley allows its distributors to purchase sunglasses "on account." These sales on account are recorded as receivables due from the distributors.

As an individual, you also might build up a trusted financial history with a local company or department store that would allow you to purchase merchandise on account. Like Oakley's distributors, your purchase on account would be recorded as an account receivable. Such credit transactions facilitate sales and are a significant current asset for many businesses. In this chapter, we will describe common classifications of receivables, illustrate how to account for uncollectible receivables, and demonstrate the reporting of receivables on the balance sheet.

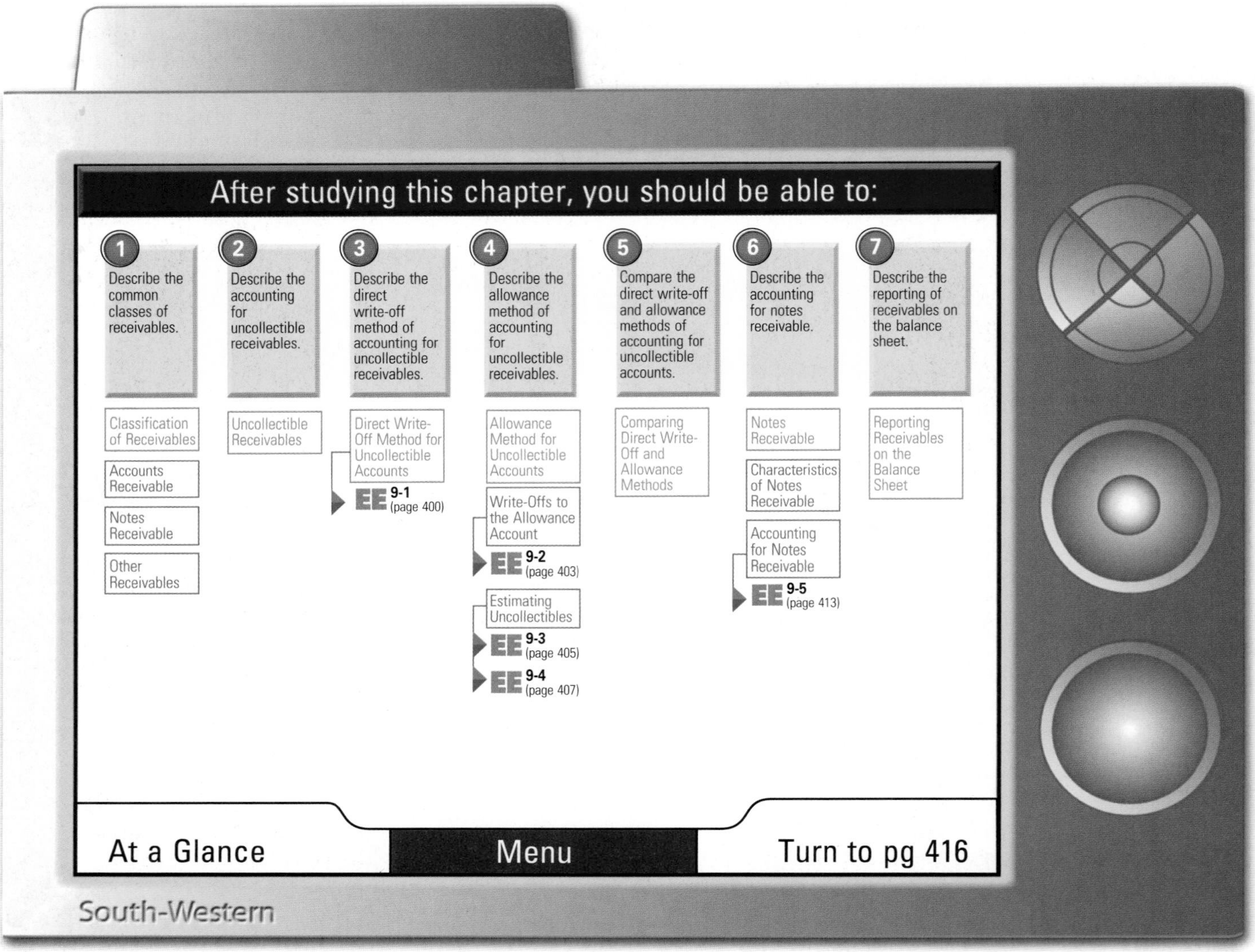

After studying this chapter, you should be able to:

1. Describe the common classes of receivables.
   - Classification of Receivables
   - Accounts Receivable
   - Notes Receivable
   - Other Receivables
2. Describe the accounting for uncollectible receivables.
   - Uncollectible Receivables
3. Describe the direct write-off method of accounting for uncollectible receivables.
   - Direct Write-Off Method for Uncollectible Accounts
     - EE 9-1 (page 400)
4. Describe the allowance method of accounting for uncollectible receivables.
   - Allowance Method for Uncollectible Accounts
   - Write-Offs to the Allowance Account
     - EE 9-2 (page 403)
   - Estimating Uncollectibles
     - EE 9-3 (page 405)
     - EE 9-4 (page 407)
5. Compare the direct write-off and allowance methods of accounting for uncollectible accounts.
   - Comparing Direct Write-Off and Allowance Methods
6. Describe the accounting for notes receivable.
   - Notes Receivable
   - Characteristics of Notes Receivable
   - Accounting for Notes Receivable
     - EE 9-5 (page 413)
7. Describe the reporting of receivables on the balance sheet.
   - Reporting Receivables on the Balance Sheet

At a Glance | Menu | Turn to pg 416

South-Western

1 Describe the common classes of receivables.

Classification of Receivables

The receivables that result from sales on account are normally accounts receivable or notes receivable. The term **receivables** includes all money claims against other entities, including people, companies, and other organizations. Receivables are usually a significant portion of the total current assets.

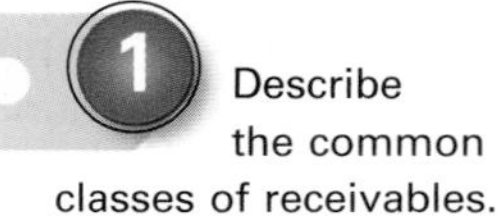

An annual report of La-Z-Boy Incorporated reported that receivables made up over 48% of La-Z-Boy's current assets.

Accounts Receivable

The most common transaction creating a receivable is selling merchandise or services on account (on credit). The receivable is recorded as a debit to Accounts Receivable. Such **accounts receivable** are normally collected within a short period, such as 30 or 60 days. They are classified on the balance sheet as a current asset.

Notes Receivable

Notes receivable are amounts that customers owe for which a formal, written instrument of credit has been issued. If notes receivable are expected to be collected within a year, they are classified on the balance sheet as a current asset.

Notes are often used for credit periods of more than 60 days. For example, an automobile dealer may require a down payment at the time of sale and accept a note or a series of notes for the remainder. Such notes usually provide for monthly payments.

Notes may also be used to settle a customer's account receivable. Notes and accounts receivable that result from sales transactions are sometimes called *trade receivables.* We assume that all notes and accounts receivable in this chapter are from sales transactions.

If you have purchased an automobile on credit, you probably signed a note. From your viewpoint, the note is a note payable. From the creditor's viewpoint, the note is a note receivable.

Other Receivables

Other receivables include interest receivable, taxes receivable, and receivables from officers or employees. Other receivables are normally reported separately on the balance sheet. If they are expected to be collected within one year, they are classified as current assets. If collection is expected beyond one year, they are classified as noncurrent assets and reported under the caption *Investments.*

2 Describe the accounting for uncollectible receivables.

Uncollectible Receivables

In prior chapters, the accounting for sales of merchandise or services on account (on credit) was described and illustrated. A major issue that has not yet been discussed is that some customers will not pay their accounts. That is, some accounts receivable will be uncollectible.

Companies may shift the risk of uncollectible receivables to other companies. For example, some retailers do not accept sales on account, but will only accept cash or credit cards. Such policies shift the risk to the credit card companies.

Companies may also sell their receivables. This is often the case when a company issues its own credit card. For example, Macy's and JCPenney issue their own credit cards. Selling receivables is called *factoring* the receivables. The buyer of the receivables is called a *factor*. An advantage of factoring is that the company selling its receivables immediately receives cash for operating and other needs. Also, depending on the factoring agreement, some of the risk of uncollectible accounts is shifted to the factor.

Regardless of how careful a company is in granting credit, some credit sales will be uncollectible. The operating expense recorded from uncollectible receivables is called **bad debt expense**, *uncollectible accounts expense*, or *doubtful accounts expense.*

There is no general rule for when an account becomes uncollectible. Some indications that an account may be uncollectible include the following:

1. The receivable is past due.
2. The customer does not respond to the company's attempts to collect.
3. The customer files for bankruptcy.
4. The customer closes its business.
5. The company cannot locate the customer.

Adams, Stevens & Bradley, Ltd. is a collection agency that operates on a contingency basis. That is, its fees are based on what it collects.

If a customer doesn't pay, a company may turn the account over to a collection agency. After the collection agency attempts to collect payment, any remaining balance in the account is considered worthless.

The two methods of accounting for uncollectible receivables are as follows:

1. The **direct write-off method** records bad debt expense only when an account is determined to be worthless.
2. The **allowance method** records bad debt expense by estimating uncollectible accounts at the end of the accounting period.

The direct write-off method is often used by small companies and companies with few receivables.[1] Generally accepted accounting principles (GAAP), however, require companies with a large amount of receivables to use the allowance method. As a result, most well-known companies such as General Electric, Pepsi, Intel, and FedEx use the allowance method.

1 The direct write-off method is also required for federal income tax purposes.

Describe the direct write-off method of accounting for uncollectible receivables.

Direct Write-Off Method for Uncollectible Accounts

Under the direct write-off method, Bad Debt Expense is not recorded until the customer's account is determined to be worthless. At that time, the customer's account receivable is written off.

To illustrate, assume that a $4,200 account receivable from D. L. Ross has been determined to be uncollectible. The entry to write off the account is as follows:

May	10	Bad Debt Expense		4,200	
		Accounts Receivable—D. L. Ross			4,200

An account receivable that has been written off may be collected later. In such cases, the account is reinstated by an entry that reverses the write-off entry. The cash received in payment is then recorded as a receipt on account.

To illustrate, assume that the D. L. Ross account of $4,200 written off on May 10 is later collected on November 21. The reinstatement and receipt of cash is recorded as follows:

Nov.	21	Accounts Receivable—D. L. Ross		4,200	
		Bad Debt Expense			4,200
	21	Cash		4,200	
		Accounts Receivable—D. L. Ross			4,200

The direct write-off method is used by businesses that sell most of their goods or services for cash or accept only MasterCard or VISA, which are recorded as cash sales. In such cases, receivables are a small part of the current assets and any bad debt expense is small. Examples of such businesses are a restaurant, a convenience store, and a small retail store.

Example Exercise 9-1 Direct Write-off Method 3

Journalize the following transactions using the direct write-off method of accounting for uncollectible receivables:

July 9. Received $1,200 from Jay Burke and wrote off the remainder owed of $3,900 as uncollectible.
Oct. 11. Reinstated the account of Jay Burke and received $3,900 cash in full payment.

Follow My Example 9-1

July 9	Cash	1,200	
	Bad Debt Expense	3,900	
	Accounts Receivable—Jay Burke		5,100
Oct. 11	Accounts Receivable—Jay Burke	3,900	
	Bad Debt Expense		3,900
11	Cash	3,900	
	Accounts Receivable—Jay Burke		3,900

For Practice: PE 9-1A, PE 9-1B

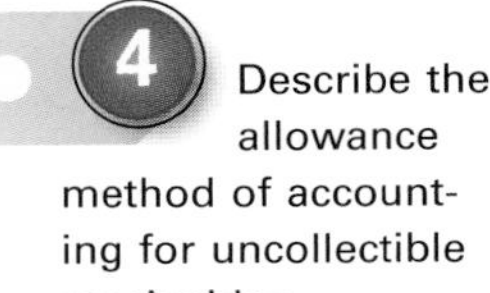

Describe the allowance method of accounting for uncollectible receivables.

Allowance Method for Uncollectible Accounts

The allowance method estimates the uncollectible accounts receivable at the end of the accounting period. Based on this estimate, Bad Debt Expense is recorded by an adjusting entry.

To illustrate, assume that ExTone Company began operations August 1. As of the end of its accounting period on December 31, 2009, ExTone has an accounts receivable balance of $200,000. This balance includes some past due accounts. Based on industry averages, ExTone estimates that $30,000 of the December 31 accounts receivable will be uncollectible. However, on December 31, ExTone doesn't know which customer accounts will be uncollectible. Thus, specific customer accounts cannot be decreased or credited. Instead, a contra asset account, **Allowance for Doubtful Accounts**, is credited for the estimated bad debts.

Using the $30,000 estimate, the following adjusting entry is made on December 31:

2009 Dec.	31	Bad Debt Expense		30,000	
		Allowance for Doubtful Accounts			30,000
		Uncollectible accounts estimate.			

The adjusting entry reduces receivables to their net realizable value and matches the uncollectible expense with revenues.

The preceding adjusting entry affects the income statement and balance sheet. On the income statement, the $30,000 of Bad Debt Expense will be matched against the related revenues of the period. On the balance sheet, the value of the receivables is reduced to the amount that is expected to be collected or realized. This amount, $170,000 ($200,000 − $30,000), is called the **net realizable value** of the receivables.

After the preceding adjusting entry is recorded, Accounts Receivable still has a debit balance of $200,000. This balance is the total amount owed by customers on account on December 31 as supported by the accounts receivable subsidiary ledger. The accounts receivable contra account, Allowance for Doubtful Accounts, has a credit balance of $30,000.

Integrity, Objectivity, and Ethics in Business

SELLER BEWARE

A company in financial distress will still try to purchase goods and services on account. In these cases, rather than "buyer beware," it is more like "seller beware." Sellers must be careful in advancing credit to such companies, because trade creditors have low priority for cash payments in the event of bankruptcy. To help suppliers, third-party services specialize in evaluating financially distressed customers. These services analyze credit risk for these firms by evaluating recent management payment decisions (who is getting paid and when), court actions (if in bankruptcy), and other supplier credit tightening or suspension actions. Such information helps monitor and adjust trade credit amounts and terms with the financially distressed customer.

Write-Offs to the Allowance Account

When a customer's account is identified as uncollectible, it is written off against the allowance account. This requires the company to remove the specific accounts receivable and an equal amount from the allowance account.

To illustrate, on January 21, 2010, John Parker's account of $6,000 with ExTone Company is written off as follows:

2010 Jan.	21	Allowance for Doubtful Accounts		6,000	
		Accounts Receivable—John Parker			6,000

At the end of a period, Allowance for Doubtful Accounts will normally have a balance. This is because Allowance for Doubtful Accounts is based on an estimate. As a result, the total write-offs to the allowance account during the period will rarely equal the balance of the account at the beginning of the period. The allowance account will have a credit balance at the end of the period if the write-offs during the period are less than the beginning balance. It will have a debit balance if the write-offs exceed the beginning balance.

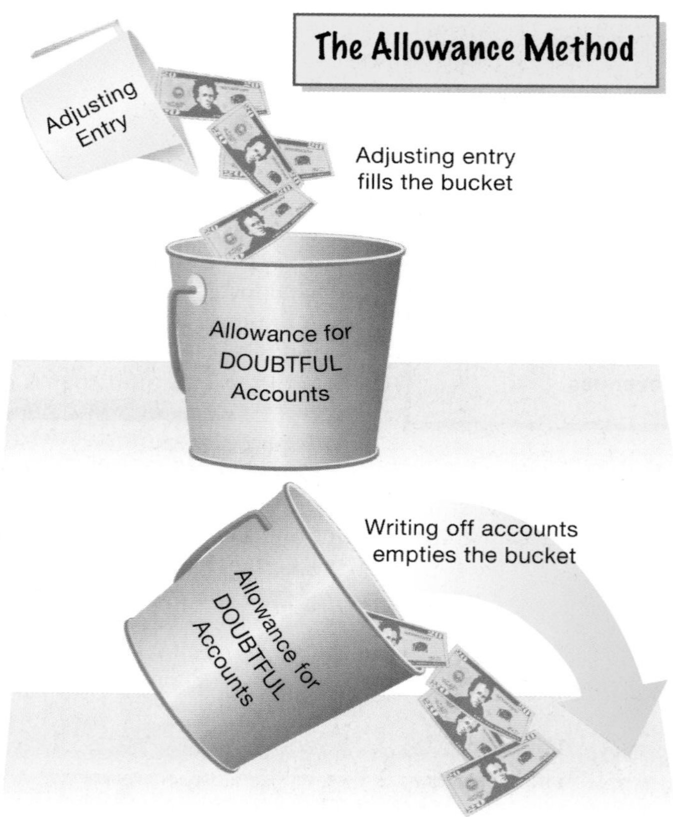

To illustrate, assume that during 2010 ExTone Company writes off $26,750 of uncollectible accounts, including the $6,000 account of John Parker recorded on January 21. Allowance for Doubtful Accounts will have a credit balance of $3,250 ($30,000 – $26,750), as shown below.

ALLOWANCE FOR DOUBTFUL ACCOUNTS

	Debit		Credit	
			Jan. 1, 2010 Balance	30,000
Total accounts written off $26,750	Jan. 21	6,000		
	Feb. 2	3,900		
	⋮	⋮		
			Dec. 31, 2010 Unadjusted balance	3,250

If ExTone Company had written off $32,100 in accounts receivable during 2010, Allowance for Doubtful Accounts would have a debit balance of $2,100, as shown below.

ALLOWANCE FOR DOUBTFUL ACCOUNTS

			Jan. 1, 2010	Balance	30,000
Total accounts written off $32,100	Jan. 21	6,000			
	Feb. 2	3,900			
	⋮	⋮			
Dec. 31, 2010	Unadjusted balance	2,100			

The allowance account balances (credit balance of $3,250 and debit balance of $2,100) in the preceding illustrations are *before* the end-of-period adjusting entry. After the end-of-period adjusting entry is recorded, Allowance for Doubtful Accounts should always have a credit balance.

An account receivable that has been written off against the allowance account may be collected later. Like the direct write-off method, the account is reinstated by an entry that reverses the write-off entry. The cash received in payment is then recorded as a receipt on account.

To illustrate, assume that Nancy Smith's account of $5,000 which was written off on April 2 is collected later on June 10. ExTone Company records the reinstatement and the collection as follows:

June	10	Accounts Receivable—Nancy Smith		5,000	
		Allowance for Doubtful Accounts			5,000
	10	Cash		5,000	
		Accounts Receivable—Nancy Smith			5,000

Example Exercise 9-2 Allowance Method

4

Journalize the following transactions using the allowance method of accounting for uncollectible receivables.

July 9. Received $1,200 from Jay Burke and wrote off the remainder owed of $3,900 as uncollectible.
Oct. 11. Reinstated the account of Jay Burke and received $3,900 cash in full payment.

Follow My Example 9-2

July 9	Cash	1,200	
	Allowance for Doubtful Accounts	3,900	
	Accounts Receivable—Jay Burke		5,100
Oct. 11	Accounts Receivable—Jay Burke	3,900	
	Allowance for Doubtful Accounts		3,900
11	Cash	3,900	
	Accounts Receivable—Jay Burke		3,900

For Practice: PE 9-2A, PE 9-2B

Estimating Uncollectibles

The allowance method requires an estimate of uncollectible accounts at the end of the period. This estimate is normally based on past experience, industry averages, and forecasts of the future.

The two methods used to estimate uncollectible accounts are as follows:

1. Percent of sales method.
2. Analysis of the receivables method.

Percent of Sales Method Since accounts receivable are created by credit sales, uncollectible accounts can be estimated as a percent of credit sales. If the portion of credit sales to sales is relatively constant, the percent may be applied to total sales or net sales.

To illustrate, assume the following data for ExTone Company on December 31, 2010, before any adjustments:

Balance of Accounts Receivable	$240,000
Balance of Allowance for Doubtful Accounts	3,250 (Cr.)
Total credit sales	3,000,000
Bad debt as a percent of credit sales	3/4%

Bad Debt Expense of $22,500 is estimated as follows:

Bad Debt Expense = Credit Sales × Bad Debt as a Percent of Credit Sales
Bad Debt Expense = $3,000,000 × 3/4% = $22,500

The adjusting entry for uncollectible accounts on December 31, 2010, is as follows:

Dec.	31	Bad Debt Expense		22,500	
		Allowance for Doubtful Accounts			22,500
		Uncollectible accounts estimate.			
		($3,000,000 × 0.0075 = $22,500)			

After the adjusting entry is posted to the ledger, Bad Debt Expense will have an adjusted balance of $22,500. Allowance for Doubtful Accounts will have an adjusted balance of $25,750 ($3,250 + $22,500). Both T accounts are shown below.

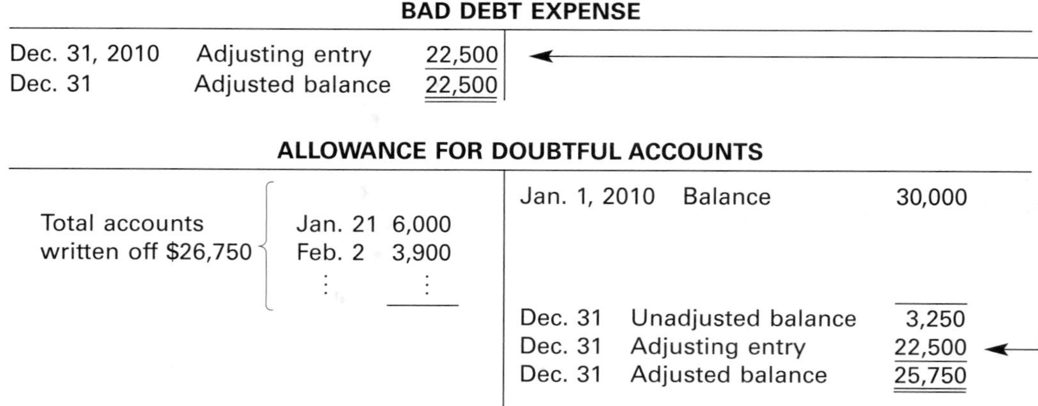

Under the percent of sales method, the amount of the adjusting entry is the amount estimated for Bad Debt Expense. This estimate is credited to whatever the unadjusted balance is for Allowance for Doubtful Accounts.

The estimate based on sales is added to any balance in Allowance for Doubtful Accounts.

To illustrate, assume that in the preceding example the unadjusted balance of Allowance for Doubtful Accounts on December 31, 2010, had been a $2,100 debit balance instead of a $3,250 credit balance. The adjustment would still have been

$22,500. However, the December 31, 2010, ending adjusted balance of Allowance for Doubtful Accounts would have been $20,400 ($22,500 − $2,100).

Example Exercise 9-3 Percent of Sales Method 4

At the end of the current year, Accounts Receivable has a balance of $800,000; Allowance for Doubtful Accounts has a credit balance of $7,500; and net sales for the year total $3,500,000. Bad debt expense is estimated at ½ of 1% of net sales.

Determine (a) the amount of the adjusting entry for uncollectible accounts; (b) the adjusted balances of Accounts Receivable, Allowance for Doubtful Accounts, and Bad Debt Expense; and (c) the net realizable value of accounts receivable.

Follow My Example 9-3

a. $17,500 ($3,500,000 × 0.005)

b.	Adjusted Balance
Accounts Receivable	$800,000
Allowance for Doubtful Accounts ($7,500 + $17,500)	25,000
Bad Debt Expense	17,500

c. $775,000 ($800,000 − $25,000)

For Practice: PE 9-3A, PE 9-3B

The percentage of uncollectible accounts will vary across companies and industries. For example, in their recent annual reports, JCPenney reported 1.7% of its receivables as uncollectible, Deere & Company (manufacturer of John Deere tractors, etc.) reported only 1.0% of its dealer receivables as uncollectible, and HCA Inc., a hospital management company, reported 42% of its receivables as uncollectible.

Analysis of Receivables Method The analysis of receivables method is based on the assumption that the longer an account receivable is outstanding, the less likely that it will be collected. The analysis of receivables method is applied as follows:

Step 1. The due date of each account receivable is determined.

Step 2. The number of days each account is past due is determined. This is the number of days between the due date of the account and the date of the analysis.

Step 3. Each account is placed in an aged class according to its days past due. Typical aged classes include the following:
- Not past due
- 1–30 days past due
- 31–60 days past due
- 61–90 days past due
- 91–180 days past due
- 181–365 days past due
- Over 365 days past due

Step 4. The totals for each aged class are determined.

Step 5. The total for each aged class is multiplied by an estimated percentage of uncollectible accounts for that class.

Step 6. The estimated total of uncollectible accounts is determined as the sum of the uncollectible accounts for each aged class.

The preceding steps are summarized in an aging schedule, and this overall process is called **aging the receivables**.

To illustrate, assume that ExTone Company uses the analysis of receivables method instead of the percent of sales method. ExTone prepared an aging schedule for its accounts receivable of $240,000 as of December 31, 2010, as shown in Exhibit 1.

Exhibit 1

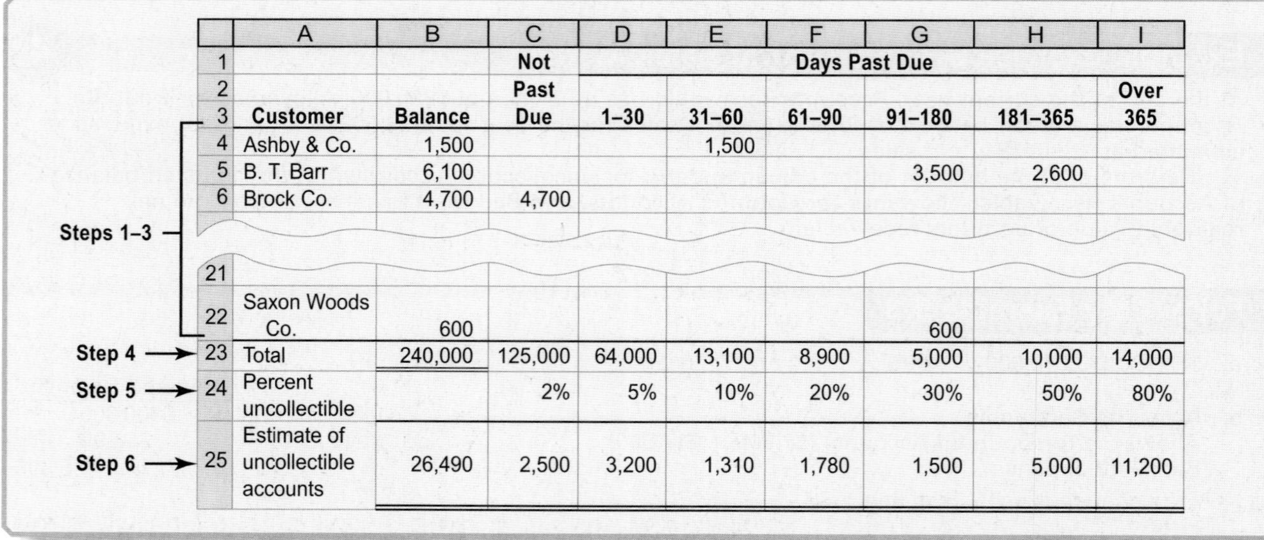

Aging of Receivables Schedule
December 31, 2010

		A	B	C	D	E	F	G	H	I
	1			Not			Days Past Due			
	2			Past						Over
	3	Customer	Balance	Due	1–30	31–60	61–90	91–180	181–365	365
Steps 1–3	4	Ashby & Co.	1,500			1,500				
	5	B. T. Barr	6,100					3,500	2,600	
	6	Brock Co.	4,700	4,700						
	21									
	22	Saxon Woods Co.	600					600		
Step 4 →	23	Total	240,000	125,000	64,000	13,100	8,900	5,000	10,000	14,000
Step 5 →	24	Percent uncollectible		2%	5%	10%	20%	30%	50%	80%
Step 6 →	25	Estimate of uncollectible accounts	26,490	2,500	3,200	1,310	1,780	1,500	5,000	11,200

Assume that ExTone Company sold merchandise to Saxon Woods Co. on August 29 with terms 2/10, n/30. Thus, the due date (Step 1) of Saxon Woods' account is September 28, as shown below.

Credit terms, net	30 days
Less: Aug. 29 to Aug. 30	2 days
Days in September	28 days

As of December 31, Saxon Woods' account is 94 days past due (Step 2), as shown below.

Number of days past due in September	2 days (30 – 28)
Number of days past due in October	31 days
Number of days past due in November	30 days
Number of days past due in December	31 days
Total number of days past due	94 days

The estimate based on receivables is compared to the balance in the allowance account to determine the amount of the adjusting entry.

Exhibit 1 shows that the $600 account receivable for Saxon Woods Co. was placed in the 91–180 days past due class (Step 3).

The total for each of the aged classes is determined (Step 4). Exhibit 1 shows that $125,000 of the accounts receivable are not past due, while $64,000 are 1–30 days past due. ExTone Company applies a different estimated percentage of uncollectible accounts to the totals of each of the aged classes (Step 5). As shown in Exhibit 1, the percent is 2% for accounts not past due, while the percent is 80% for accounts over 365 days past due.

The sum of the estimated uncollectible accounts for each aged class (Step 6) is the estimated uncollectible accounts on December 31, 2010. This is the desired adjusted balance for Allowance for Doubtful Accounts. For ExTone Company, this amount is $26,490, as shown in Exhibit 1.

Comparing the estimate of $26,490 with the unadjusted balance of the allowance account determines the amount of the adjustment for Bad Debt Expense. For ExTone, the unadjusted balance of the allowance account is a credit balance of $3,250. The amount to be added to this balance is therefore $23,240 ($26,490 – $3,250). The adjusting entry is as follows:

Dec.	31	Bad Debt Expense Allowance for Doubtful Accounts Uncollectible accounts estimate. ($26,490 – $3,250)	23,240	23,240

The Commercial Collection Agency Section of the Commercial Law League of America reported the following collection rates by number of months past due:

After the preceding adjusting entry is posted to the ledger, Bad Debt Expense will have an adjusted balance of $23,240. Allowance for Doubtful Accounts will have an adjusted balance of $26,490, and the net realizable value of the receivables is $213,510 ($240,000 – $26,490). Both T accounts are shown below.

BAD DEBT EXPENSE

Dec. 31, 2010	Adjusting entry	23,240	
Dec. 31	Adjusting balance	23,240	

ALLOWANCE FOR DOUBTFUL ACCOUNTS

	Dec. 31, 2010	Unadjusted balance	3,250
	Dec. 31	Adjusting entry	23,240
	Dec. 31	Adjusted balance	26,490

Under the analysis of receivables method, the amount of the adjusting entry is the amount that will yield an adjusted balance for Allowance for Doubtful Accounts equal to that estimated by the aging schedule.

To illustrate, if the unadjusted balance of the allowance account had been a debit balance of $2,100, the amount of the adjustment would have been $28,590 ($26,490 + $2,100). In this case, Bad Debt Expense would have an adjusted balance of $28,590. However, the adjusted balance of Allowance for Doubtful Accounts would still have been $26,490. After the adjusting entry is posted, both T accounts are shown below.

BAD DEBT EXPENSE

Dec. 31, 2010	Adjusting entry	28,590	
Dec. 31	Adjusting balance	28,590	

ALLOWANCE FOR DOUBTFUL ACCOUNTS

Dec. 31, 2010	Unadjusted balance	2,100			
			Aug. 31	Adjusted entry	28,590
			Aug. 31	Adjusted balance	26,490

Example Exercise 9-4 Analysis of Receivables Method

4

At the end of the current year, Accounts Receivable has a balance of $800,000; Allowance for Doubtful Accounts has a credit balance of $7,500; and net sales for the year total $3,500,000. Using the aging method, the balance of Allowance for Doubtful Accounts is estimated as $30,000.

Determine (a) the amount of the adjusting entry for uncollectible accounts; (b) the adjusted balances of Accounts Receivable, Allowance for Doubtful Accounts, and Bad Debt Expense; and (c) the net realizable value of accounts receivable.

Follow My Example 9-4

a. $22,500 ($30,000 – $7,500)

b.

	Adjusted Balance
Accounts Receivable	$800,000
Allowance for Doubtful Accounts	30,000
Bad Debt Expense	22,500

c. $770,000 ($800,000 – $30,000)

For Practice: PE 9-4A, PE 9-4B

Comparing Estimation Methods Both the percent of sales and analysis of receivables methods estimate uncollectible accounts. However, each method has a slightly different focus and financial statement emphasis.

Under the percent of sales method, Bad Debt Expense is the focus of the estimation process. The percent of sales method places more emphasis on matching revenues and expenses and, thus, emphasizes the income statement. That is, the amount of the adjusting entry is based on the estimate of Bad Debt Expense for the period. Allowance for Doubtful Accounts is then credited for this amount.

Under the analysis of receivables method, Allowance for Doubtful Accounts is the focus of the estimation process. The analysis of receivables method places more emphasis on the net realizable value of the receivables and, thus, emphasizes the balance sheet. That is, the amount of the adjusting entry is the amount that will yield an adjusted balance for Allowance for Doubtful Accounts equal to that estimated by the aging schedule. Bad Debt Expense is then debited for this amount.

Exhibit 2 summarizes these differences between the percent of sales and the analysis of receivables methods. Exhibit 2 also shows the results of the ExTone Company illustration for the percent of sales and analysis of receivables methods. The amounts shown in Exhibit 2 assume that an unadjusted credit balance of $3,250 for Allowance for Doubtful Accounts. While the methods normally yield different amounts for any one period, over several periods the amounts should be similar.

Exhibit 2

Differences Between Estimation Methods

			ExTone Company Example	
	Focus of Method	**Financial Statement Emphasis**	**Bad Debt Expense Estimate ****	**Allowance for Doubtful Accounts Estimate**
Percent of Sales Method	Bad Debt Expense Estimate	Income Statement	$22,500	$25,750* ($22,500 + $3,250)
Analysis of Receivables Method	Allowance for Doubtful Accounts Estimate	Balance Sheet	$23,240* ($26,490 − $3,250)	$26,490

*Indicates that the estimate was derived (sometimes called plugged) from the estimate on which this method focuses.
** Amount of adjusting entry.

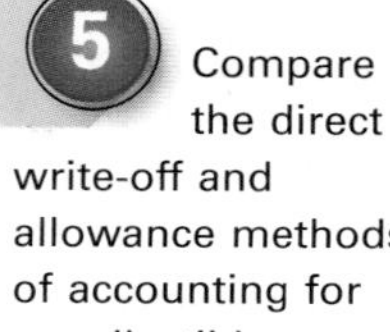

5 Compare the direct write-off and allowance methods of accounting for uncollectible accounts.

Comparing Direct Write-Off and Allowance Methods

The journal entries for the direct write-off and allowance methods are illustrated and compared in this section. As a basis for our illustration, the following selected transactions, taken from the records of Hobbs Company for the year ending December 31, 2009, are used:

Mar. 1. Wrote off account of C. York, $3,650

Apr. 12. Received $2,250 as partial payment on the $5,500 account of Cary Bradshaw. Wrote off the remaining balance as uncollectible.

June 22. Received the $3,650 from C. York, which had been written off on March 1. Reinstated the account and recorded the cash receipt.

Sept. 7. Wrote off the following accounts as uncollectible (record as one journal entry):

Jason Bigg	$1,100	Stanford Noonan	$1,360
Steve Bradey	2,220	Aiden Wyman	990
Samantha Neeley	775		

Dec. 31. Hobbs Company uses the percent of credit sales method of estimating uncollectible expenses. Based on past history and industry averages, 1.25% of credit sales are expected to be uncollectible. Hobbs recorded $3,400,000 of credit sales during 2009.

Exhibit 3 illustrates the journal entries for Hobbs Company using the direct write-off and allowance methods. Using the direct write-off method, there is no adjusting entry on December 31 for uncollectible accounts. In contrast, the allowance method records an adjusting entry for estimated uncollectible accounts of $42,500.

Exhibit 3

Comparing Direct Write-Off and Allowance Methods

		Direct Write-Off Method			Allowance Method		
2009 Mar.	1	Bad Debt Expense	3,650		Allowance for Doubtful Accounts	3,650	
		Accounts Receivable—C. York		3,650	Accounts Receivable—C. York		3,650
Apr.	12	Cash	2,250		Cash	2,250	
		Bad Debt Expense	3,250		Allowance for Doubtful Accounts	3,250	
		Accounts Receivable—Cary Bradshaw		5,500	Accounts Receivable—Cary Bradshaw		5,500
June	22	Accounts Receivable—C. York	3,650		Accounts Receivable—C. York	3,650	
		Bad Debt Expense		3,650	Allowance for Doubtful Accounts		3,650
	22	Cash	3,650		Cash	3,650	
		Accounts Receivable—C. York		3,650	Accounts Receivable—C. York		3,650
Sept.	7	Bad Debt Expense	6,445		Allowance for Doubtful Accounts	6,445	
		Accounts Receivable—Jason Bigg		1,100	Accounts Receivable—Jason Bigg		1,100
		Accounts Receivable—Steve Bradey		2,220	Accounts Receivable—Steve Bradey		2,220
		Accounts Receivable—Samantha Neeley		775	Accounts Receivable—Samantha Neeley		775
		Accounts Receivable—Stanford Noonan		1,360	Accounts Receivable—Stanford Noonan		1,360
		Accounts Receivable—Aiden Wyman		990	Accounts Receivable—Aiden Wyman		990
Dec.	31	No Entry			Bad Debt Expense	42,500	
					Allowance for Doubtful Accounts		42,500
					Uncollectible accounts estimate. ($3,400,000 × 0.0125 = $42,500)		

The primary differences between the direct write-off and allowance methods are summarized below.

COMPARING THE DIRECT WRITE-OFF AND ALLOWANCE METHODS

	Direct Write-Off Method	Allowance Method
Bad debt expense is recorded	When the specific customer accounts are determined to be uncollectible.	Using estimate based on (1) a percent of sales or (2) an analysis of receivables.
Allowance account	No allowance account is used.	The allowance account is used.
Primary users	Small companies and companies with few receivables.	Large companies and those with a large amount of receivables.

Integrity, Objectivity, and Ethics in Business

RECEIVABLES FRAUD

Financial reporting frauds are often tied to accounts receivable, because receivables allow companies to record revenue before cash is received. Take, for example, the case of entrepreneur Michael Weinstein, who acquired Coated Sales, Inc. with the dream of growing the small specialty company into a major corporation. To acquire funding that would facilitate this growth, Weinstein had to artificially boost the company's sales. He accomplished this by adding millions in false accounts receivable to existing customer accounts.

The company's auditors began to sense a problem when they called one of the company's customers to confirm a large order. When the customer denied placing the order, the auditors began to investigate the company's receivables more closely. Their analysis revealed a fraud which overstated profits by $55 million and forced the company into bankruptcy, costing investors and creditors over $160 million.

Source: Joseph T. Wells, "Follow Fraud to the Likely Perpetrator," *The Journal of Accountancy,* March 2001.

Describe the accounting for notes receivable.

Notes Receivable

A note has some advantages over an account receivable. By signing a note, the debtor recognizes the debt and agrees to pay it according to its terms. Thus, a note is a stronger legal claim.

Characteristics of Notes Receivable

A promissory note is a written promise to pay the face amount, usually with interest, on demand or at a date in the future.[2] Characteristics of a promissory note are as follows:

1. The *maker* is the party making the promise to pay.
2. The *payee* is the party to whom the note is payable.
3. The *face amount* is the amount the note is written for on its face.
4. The *issuance date* is the date a note is issued.
5. The *due date* or *maturity date* is the date the note is to be paid.
6. The *term* of a note is the amount of time between the issuance and due dates.
7. The *interest rate* is that rate of interest that must be paid on the face amount for the term of the note.

Exhibit 4 illustrates a promissory note. The maker of the note is Selig Company, and the payee is Pearland Company. The face value of the note is $2,000, and the issuance date is March 16, 2009. The term of the note is 90 days, which results in a due date of June 14, 2009, as shown below and at the top of page 410.

Days in March	31 days
Minus issuance date of note	16
Days remaining in March	15 days
Add days in April	30
Add days in May	31
Add days in June (due date of June 14)	14
Term of note	90 days

2 You may see references to non-interest-bearing notes. Such notes are not widely used and carry an assumed or implicit interest rate.

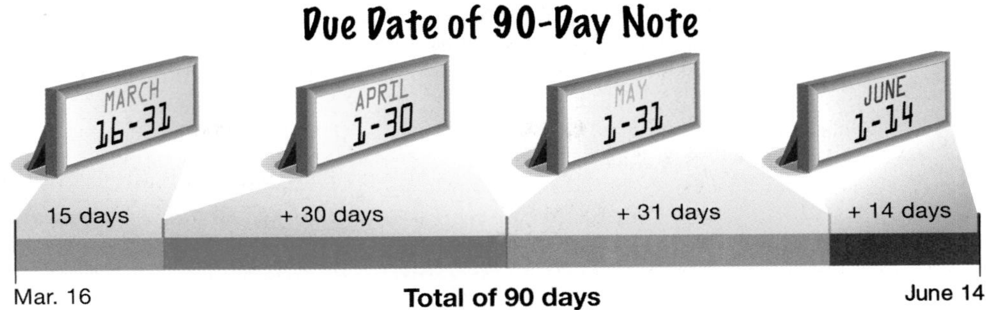

In Exhibit 4, the term of the note is 90 days and has an interest rate of 10%.

Exhibit 4

Promissory Note

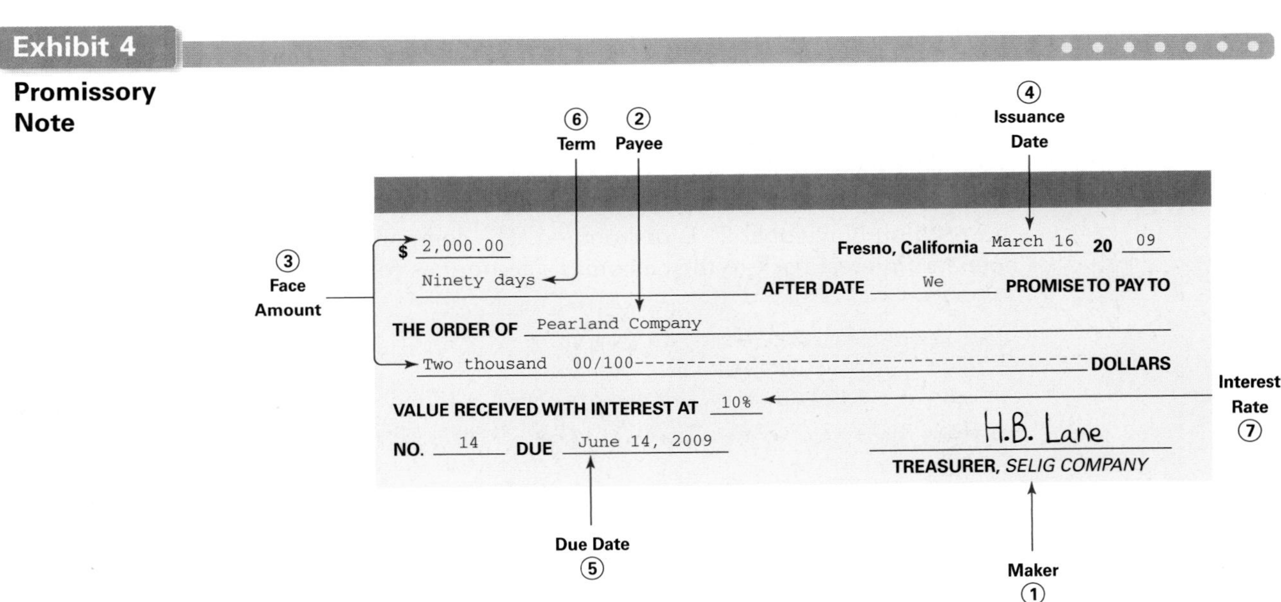

The interest on a note is computed as follows:

$$\text{Interest} = \text{Face Amount} \times \text{Interest Rate} \times (\text{Term}/360 \text{ days})$$

Your credit card balances that are not paid at the end of the month incur an interest charge expressed as a percent per month. Interest charges of 1½% per month are common. Such charges approximate an annual interest rate of 18% per year (1½% × 12). Thus, if you can borrow money at less than 18%, you are better off borrowing the money to pay off the credit card balance.

The interest rate is stated on an annual (yearly) basis, while the term is expressed as days. Thus, the interest on the note in Exhibit 4 is computed as follows:

$$\text{Interest} = \$2{,}000 \times 10\% \times (90/360) = \$50$$

To simplify, we will use 360 days per year. In practice, companies such as banks and mortgage companies use the exact number of days in a year, 365.

The **maturity value** is the amount that must be paid at the due date of the note, which is the sum of the face amount and the interest. The maturity value of the note in Exhibit 4 is $2,050 ($2,000 + $50).

Accounting for Notes Receivable

A promissory note may be received by a company from a customer to replace an account receivable. In such cases, the promissory note is recorded as a note receivable.[3]

3 The accounting for notes payable is described and illustrated in Chapter 14.

To illustrate, assume that a company accepts a 30-day, 12% note dated November 21, 2010, in settlement of the account of W. A. Bunn Co., which is past due and has a balance of $6,000. The company records the receipt of the note as follows:

Nov.	21	Notes Receivable—W. A. Bunn Co.		6,000	
		Accounts Receivable—W. A. Bunn Co.			6,000

At the due date, the company records the receipt of $6,060 ($6,000 face amount plus $60 interest) as follows:

Dec.	21	Cash		6,060	
		Notes Receivable—W. A. Bunn Co.			6,000
		Interest Revenue			60
		$6,060 = [$6,000 + ($6,000 × 12% × 30/360)].			

If the maker of a note fails to pay the note on the due date, the note is a **dishonored note receivable**. A company that holds a dishonored note transfers the face amount of the note plus any interest due back to an accounts receivable account. For example, assume that the $6,000, 30-day, 12% note received from W. A. Bunn Co. and recorded on November 21 is dishonored. The company holding the note transfers the note and interest back to the customer's account as follows:

Dec.	21	Accounts Receivable—W. A. Bunn Co.		6,060	
		Notes Receivable—W. A. Bunn Co.			6,000
		Interest Revenue			60

The company has earned the interest of $60, even though the note is dishonored. If the account receivable is uncollectible, the company will write off $6,060 against Allowance for Doubtful Accounts.

A company receiving a note should record an adjusting entry for any accrued interest at the end of the period. For example, assume that Crawford Company issues a $4,000, 90-day, 12% note dated December 1, 2010, to settle its account receivable. If the accounting period ends on December 31, the company receiving the note would record the following entries:

2010 Dec.	1	Notes Receivable—Crawford Company		4,000	
		Accounts Receivable—Crawford Company			4,000
	31	Interest Receivable		40	
		Interest Revenue			40
		Accrued interest.			
		($4,000 × 12% × 30/360)			
2011 Mar.	1	Cash		4,120	
		Notes Receivable—Crawford Company			4,000
		Interest Receivable			40
		Interest Revenue			80
		Total interest of $120.			
		($4,000 × 12% × 90/360)			

The interest revenue account is closed at the end of each accounting period. The amount of interest revenue is normally reported in the Other income section of the income statement.

Example Exercise 9-5 Note Receivable 

Same Day Surgery Center received a 120-day, 6% note for $40,000, dated March 14 from a patient on account.

a. Determine the due date of the note.
b. Determine the maturity value of the note.
c. Journalize the entry to record the receipt of the payment of the note at maturity.

Follow My Example 9-5

a. The due date of the note is July 12, determined as follows:

March	17 days (31 − 14)
April	30 days
May	31 days
June	30 days
July	12 days
Total	120 days

b. $40,800 [$40,000 + ($40,000 × 6% × 120/360)]

c. July 12			
	Cash	40,800	
	Notes Receivable		40,000
	Interest Revenue		800

For Practice: PE 9-5A, PE 9-5B

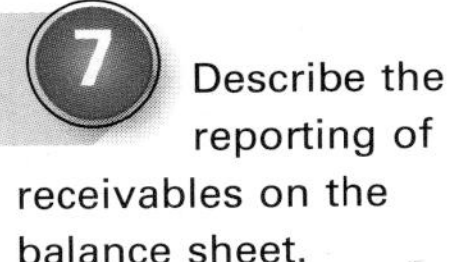

Describe the reporting of receivables on the balance sheet.

Reporting Receivables on the Balance Sheet

All receivables that are expected to be realized in cash within a year are reported in the Current Assets section of the balance sheet. Current assets are normally reported in the order of their liquidity, beginning with cash and cash equivalents.

The balance sheet presentation for receivables for Mornin' Joe is shown below.

Mornin' Joe
Balance Sheet
December 31, 2010

Assets

Current assets:		
Cash and cash equivalents		$235,000
Trading investments (at cost)	$420,000	
Plus valuation allowance for trading investments	45,000	465,000
Accounts receivable	$305,000	
Less allowance for doubtful accounts	12,300	292,700

In Mornin Joe's financial statements, the allowance for doubtful accounts is subtracted from accounts receivable. Some companies report receivables at their net realizable value with a note showing the amount of the allowance.

Other disclosures related to receivables are reported either on the face of the financial statements or in the financial statement notes. Such disclosures include the market (fair) value of the receivables. In addition, if unusual credit risks exist within the receivables, the nature of the risks are disclosed. For example, if the majority of the receivables are due from one customer or are due from customers located in one area of the country or one industry, these facts are disclosed.[4]

Financial Analysis and Interpretation

Two financial measures that are especially useful in evaluating efficiency in collecting receivables are (1) the accounts receivable turnover and (2) the number of days' sales in receivables.

The **accounts receivable turnover** measures how frequently during the year the accounts receivable are being converted to cash. For example, with credit terms of 2/10, n/30, the accounts receivable should turn over more than 12 times per year. The accounts receivable turnover is computed as follows:[5]

$$\text{Accounts Receivable Turnover} = \frac{\text{Net Sales}}{\text{Average Accounts Receivable}}$$

The average accounts receivable can be determined by using monthly data or by simply adding the beginning and ending accounts receivable balances and dividing by two. For example, using the following financial data (in millions) for FedEx, the 2007 and 2006 accounts receivable turnover is computed as 10.5 and 7.7, respectively.

	2007		2006		2005
Net sales	$22,527		$21,296		—
Accounts receivable	1,429		2,860		$2,703
Average accounts receivable	2,145	[($1,429 + $2,860)/2]	2,782	[($2,860 + $2,703)/2]	
Accounts receivable turnover	10.5	($22,527/$2,145)	7.7	($21,296/$2,782)	

Comparing 2007 and 2006 indicates that the accounts receivable turnover has increased from 7.7 to 10.5. Thus, FedEx's management of accounts receivable has improved in 2007.

The **number of days' sales in receivables** is an estimate of the length of time the accounts receivable have been outstanding. With credit terms of 2/10, n/30, the number of days' sales in receivables should be less than 20 days. It is computed as follows:

$$\text{Number of Days' Sales in Receivables} = \frac{\text{Average Accounts Receivable}}{\text{Average Daily Sales}}$$

Average daily sales are determined by dividing net sales by 365 days. For example, using the preceding data for FedEx, the number of days' sales in receivables is 34.8 and 47.7 for 2007 and 2006, respectively, as shown below.

	2007		2006	
Net sales	$22,527		$21,296	
Average accounts receivable	2,145	[($1,429 + $2,860)/2]	2,782	[($2,860 + $2,703)/2]
Average daily sales	61.7	($22,527/365)	58.3	($21,296/365)
Days' sales in receivables	34.8	($2,145/61.7)	47.7	($2,782/58.3)

The number of days' sales in receivables confirms an improvement in managing accounts receivable during 2007. That is, the efficiency in collecting accounts receivable has improved when the number of days' sales in receivables decreases. During 2007, FedEx's days in receivables decreased from 47.7 in 2006 to 34.8. However, these measures should also be compared with similar companies within the industry.

4 *Statement of Financial Accounting Standards No. 105*, "Disclosures of Information about Financial Instruments with Off-Balance Sheet Risk and Financial Instruments with Concentrations of Credit Risk," and *No. 107*, "Disclosures about Fair Value of Financial Instruments" (Norwalk, CT: Financial Accounting Standards Board).

5 If known, credit sales can be used in the numerator. However, because credit sales are not normally disclosed to external users, most analysts use net sales in the numerator.

Business Connection

DELTA AIR LINES

Delta Air Lines is a major air carrier that services cities throughout the United States and the world. In its operations, Delta generates accounts receivable as reported in the following note to its financial statements:

© AP Photo/Ric Field

Our accounts receivable are generated largely from the sale of passenger airline tickets and cargo transportation services. The majority of these sales are processed through major credit card companies, resulting in accounts receivable which are generally short-term in duration. We also have receivables from the sale of mileage credits to partners, such as credit card companies, hotels and car rental agencies, that participate in our SkyMiles program. We believe that the credit risk associated with these receivables is minimal and that the allowance for uncollectible accounts that we have provided is appropriate.

In its December 31, 2007, balance sheet, Delta reported the following accounts receivable (in millions):

	Dec. 31, 2007	Dec. 31, 2006
Current Assets:		
. . .		
Accounts receivable, net of an allowance for uncollectible accounts of $26 at December 31, 2007 and $21 at December 31, 2006	$1,066	$915

APPENDIX

Discounting Notes Receivable

A company may endorse a note receivable and transfer it to a bank in return for cash. This is called *discounting notes receivable*. The bank pays cash (the *proceeds*) to the company after deducting a *discount* (interest). The discount is computed using a *discount rate* on the maturity value of the note for the discount period. The *discount period* is the time that the bank must hold the note before it becomes due.

To illustrate, assume that on May 3 a note receivable from Pryor & Co is discounted by Deacon Company at its bank. The related data are as follows:

Face amount of note	$1,800
Issuance date of note	April 8
Interest rate on note	12%
Term of note	90 days
Due date of note	July 7
Maturity value of note	$1,854 [$1,800 + ($1,800 × 12% × 90/360)]
Discount date	May 3
Discount period	65 days (May 3 to July 7)
Discount rate	14%
Discount	$46.87 ($1,854 × 14% × 65/360)
Discount proceeds	$1,807.13 ($1,854.00 − $46.87)

Deacon Company records the receipt of the proceeds as follows:

May	3	Cash		1,807.13	
		Notes Receivable			1,800.00
		Interest Revenue			7.13
		Discounted $1,800, 90-day, 12% note at 14%.			

If the proceeds had been less than the face amount, Deacon Company would have recorded the excess of the face amount over the proceeds as interest expense. For example, if the proceeds had been $1,785, Deacon Company would have recorded interest expense of $15 ($1,800 − $1,785). The length of the discount period, interest rate, and discount rate determine whether interest expense or interest revenue is recorded.

Without a statement limiting responsibility, Deacon Company must pay the maturity value of the note if the maker defaults. This potential liability is called a *contingent liability*. If the maker pays the maturity value, the contingent liability ceases to exist. If, on the other hand, the maker dishonors the note, the contingent liability becomes a liability that must be paid.

If a discounted note receivable is dishonored, the bank notifies the company and asks for payment. In some cases, the bank may charge a *protest fee* on dishonored notes. The entire amount paid to the bank, including the maturity value and protest fee, is debited to the account receivable of the maker.

To illustrate, assume that Pryor & Co. dishonors the $1,800, 90-day, 12% note that was discounted on May 3. The bank charges a protest fee of $12. Deacon Company's entry to record the payment to the bank is as follows:

July	7	Accounts Receivable—Pryor & Co.		1,866	
		Cash			1,866
		Paid dishonored, discounted note (maturity value of $1,854 plus protest fee of $12).			

At a Glance 9

1 Describe the common classes of receivables.

Key Points	Key Learning Outcomes	Example Exercises	Practice Exercises
The term *receivables* includes all money claims against other entities, including people, business firms, and other organizations. Receivables are normally classified as accounts receivable, notes receivable, or other receivables.	• Define the term *receivables*. • List some common classifications of receivables.		

2 Describe the accounting for uncollectible receivables.

Key Points	Key Learning Outcomes	Example Exercises	Practice Exercises
Regardless of the care used in granting credit and the collection procedures used, a part of the credit sales will not be collectible. The operating expense recorded from uncollectible receivables is called *bad debt expense*. The two methods of accounting for uncollectible receivables are the direct write-off method and the allowance method.	• Describe how a company may shift the risk of uncollectible receivables to other companies.		
	• List factors that indicate an account receivable is uncollectible.		
	• Describe two methods of accounting for uncollectible accounts receivable.		

3 Describe the direct write-off method of accounting for uncollectible receivables.

Key Points	Key Learning Outcomes	Example Exercises	Practice Exercises
Under the direct write-off method, the entry to write off an account debits Bad Debt Expense and credits Accounts Receivable. Neither an allowance account nor an adjusting entry is needed at the end of the period.	• Prepare journal entries to write off an account using the direct method.	**9-1**	9-1A, 9-1B
	• Prepare journal entries for the reinstatement and collection of an account previously written off.	**9-1**	9-1A, 9-1B

4 Describe the allowance method of accounting for uncollectible receivables.

Key Points	Key Learning Outcomes	Example Exercises	Practice Exercises
Under the allowance method, an adjusting entry is made for uncollectible accounts. When an account is determined to be uncollectible, it is written off against the allowance account. The allowance account normally has a credit balance after the adjusting entry has been posted and is a contra asset account.	• Prepare journal entries to write off an account using the allowance method.	**9-2**	9-2A, 9-2B
The estimate of uncollectibles may be based on a percent of sales or an analysis of receivables. Using the percent of sales, the adjusting entry is made without regard to the balance of the allowance account. Using the analysis of receivables, the adjusting entry is made so that the balance of the allowance account will equal the estimated uncollectibles at the end of the period.	• Prepare journal entries for the reinstatement and collection of an account previously written off.	**9-2**	9-2A, 9-2B
	• Determine the adjustment, bad debt expense, and net realizable value of accounts receivable using the percent of sales method.	**9-3**	9-3A, 9-3B
	• Determine the adjustment, bad debt expense, and net realizable value of accounts receivable using the analysis of receivables method.	**9-4**	9-4A, 9-4B

5 Compare the direct write-off and allowance methods of accounting for uncollectible accounts.

Key Points	Key Learning Outcomes	Example Exercises	Practice Exercises
The direct write-off and allowance methods of accounting for uncollectible accounts are recorded differently in the accounts and presented differently in the financial statements. Exhibit 3 illustrates both methods of accounting for uncollectible accounts.	• Describe the differences in accounting for uncollectible accounts under the direct write-off and allowance methods.		
	• Record journal entries using the direct write-off and allowance methods.		

6 Describe the accounting for notes receivable.

Key Points	Key Learning Outcomes	Example Exercises	Practice Exercises
A note received in settlement of an account receivable is recorded as a debit to Notes Receivable and a credit to Accounts Receivable. When a note matures, Cash is debited, Notes Receivable is credited, and Interest Revenue is credited. If the maker of a note fails to pay the debt on the due date, the dishonored note is recorded by debiting an accounts receivable account for the amount of the claim against the maker of the note.	• Describe the characteristics of a note receivable.		
	• Determine the due date and maturity value of a note receivable.	**9-5**	9-5A, 9-5B
	• Prepare journal entries for the receipt of the payment of a note receivable.	**9-5**	9-5A, 9-5B
	• Prepare a journal entry for the dishonored note receivable.		

7 Describe the reporting of receivables on the balance sheet.

Key Points	Key Learning Outcomes	Example Exercises	Practice Exercises
All receivables that are expected to be realized in cash within a year are reported in the Current Assets section of the balance sheet in the order in which they can be converted to cash in normal operations. In addition to the allowance for doubtful accounts, additional receivable disclosures include the market (fair) value and unusual credit risks.	• Describe how receivables are reported in the Current Assets section of the balance sheet.		
	• Describe disclosures related to receivables that should be reported in the financial statements.		

Key Terms

accounts receivable (398)
accounts receivable turnover (414)
aging the receivables (405)
Allowance for Doubtful Accounts (401)
allowance method (399)
bad debt expense (399)
direct write-off method (399)
dishonored note receivable (412)
maturity value (411)
net realizable value (401)
notes receivable (398)
number of days' sales in receivables (414)
receivables (398)

Illustrative Problem

Ditzler Company, a construction supply company, uses the allowance method of accounting for uncollectible accounts receivable. Selected transactions completed by Ditzler Company are as follows:

Feb. 1. Sold merchandise on account to Ames Co., $8,000. The cost of the merchandise sold was $4,500.
Mar. 15. Accepted a 60-day, 12% note for $8,000 from Ames Co. on account.
Apr. 9. Wrote off a $2,500 account from Dorset Co. as uncollectible.
21. Loaned $7,500 cash to Jill Klein, receiving a 90-day, 14% note.
May 14. Received the interest due from Ames Co. and a new 90-day, 14% note as a renewal of the loan. (Record both the debit and the credit to the notes receivable account.)
June 13. Reinstated the account of Dorset Co., written off on April 9, and received $2,500 in full payment.
July 20. Jill Klein dishonored her note.
Aug. 12. Received from Ames Co. the amount due on its note of May 14.
19. Received from Jill Klein the amount owed on the dishonored note, plus interest for 30 days at 15%, computed on the maturity value of the note.
Dec. 16. Accepted a 60-day, 12% note for $12,000 from Global Company on account.
31. It is estimated that 3% of the credit sales of $1,375,000 for the year ended December 31 will be uncollectible.

Instructions

1. Journalize the transactions.
2. Journalize the adjusting entry to record the accrued interest on December 31 on the Global Company note.

Solution

1.

Feb.	1	Accounts Receivable—Ames Co.		8,000.00	
		Sales			8,000.00
	1	Cost of Merchandise Sold		4,500.00	
		Merchandise Inventory			4,500.00
Mar.	15	Notes Receivable—Ames Co.		8,000.00	
		Accounts Receivable—Ames Co.			8,000.00
Apr.	9	Allowance for Doubtful Accounts		2,500.00	
		Accounts Receivable—Dorset Co.			2,500.00
	21	Notes Receivable—Jill Klein		7,500.00	
		Cash			7,500.00
May	14	Notes Receivable—Ames Co.		8,000.00	
		Cash		160.00	
		Notes Receivable—Ames Co.			8,000.00
		Interest Revenue			160.00
June	13	Accounts Receivable—Dorset Co.		2,500.00	
		Allowance for Doubtful Accounts			2,500.00
	13	Cash		2,500.00	
		Accounts Receivable—Dorset Co.			2,500.00
July	20	Accounts Receivable—Jill Klein		7,762.50	
		Notes Receivable—Jill Klein			7,500.00
		Interest Revenue			262.50
Aug.	12	Cash		8,280.00	
		Notes Receivable—Ames Co.			8,000.00
		Interest Revenue			280.00
	19	Cash		7,859.53	
		Accounts Receivable—Jill Klein			7,762.50
		Interest Revenue			97.03
		($7,762.50 × 15% × 30/360).			
Dec.	16	Notes Receivable—Global Company		12,000.00	
		Accounts Receivable—Global Company			12,000.00
	31	Bad Debt Expense		41,250.00	
		Allowance for Doubtful Accounts			41,250.00
		Uncollectible accounts estimate.			
		($1,375,000 × 3%)			

2.

Dec.	31	Interest Receivable		60.00	
		Interest Revenue			60.00
		Accrued interest.			
		($12,000 × 12% × 15/360)			

Self-Examination Questions (Answers at End of Chapter)

1. At the end of the fiscal year, before the accounts are adjusted, Accounts Receivable has a balance of $200,000 and Allowance for Doubtful Accounts has a credit balance of $2,500. If the estimate of uncollectible accounts determined by aging the receivables is $8,500, the amount of bad debt expense is:
   A. $2,500.
   B. $6,000.
   C. $8,500.
   D. $11,000.
2. At the end of the fiscal year, Accounts Receivable has a balance of $100,000 and Allowance for Doubtful Accounts has a balance of $7,000. The expected net realizable value of the accounts receivable is:
   A. $7,000.
   B. $93,000.
   C. $100,000.
   D. $107,000.
3. What is the maturity value of a 90-day, 12% note for $10,000?
   A. $8,800
   B. $10,000
   C. $10,300
   D. $11,200
4. What is the due date of a $12,000, 90-day, 8% note receivable dated August 5?
   A. October 31
   B. November 2
   C. November 3
   D. November 4
5. When a note receivable is dishonored, Accounts Receivable is debited for what amount?
   A. The face value of the note
   B. The maturity value of the note
   C. The maturity value of the note less accrued interest
   D. The maturity value of the note plus accrued interest

Eye Openers

1. What are the three classifications of receivables?
2. What types of transactions give rise to accounts receivable?
3. In what section of the balance sheet should a note receivable be listed if its term is (a) 90 days, (b) six years?
4. Give two examples of other receivables.
5. Gallatin Hardware is a small hardware store in the rural township of Willow Creek that rarely extends credit to its customers in the form of an account receivable. The few customers that are allowed to carry accounts receivable are long-time residents of Willow Creek and have a history of doing business at Gallatin Hardware. What method of accounting for uncollectible receivables should Gallatin Hardware use? Why?
6. Which of the two methods of accounting for uncollectible accounts provides for the recognition of the expense at the earlier date?
7. What kind of an account (asset, liability, etc.) is Allowance for Doubtful Accounts, and is its normal balance a debit or a credit?
8. After the accounts are adjusted and closed at the end of the fiscal year, Accounts Receivable has a balance of $298,150 and Allowance for Doubtful Accounts has a balance of $31,200. Describe how the accounts receivable and the allowance for doubtful accounts are reported on the balance sheet.
9. A firm has consistently adjusted its allowance account at the end of the fiscal year by adding a fixed percent of the period's net sales on account. After seven years, the balance in Allowance for Doubtful Accounts has become very large in relationship to the balance in Accounts Receivable. Give two possible explanations.
10. Which of the two methods of estimating uncollectibles provides for the most accurate estimate of the current net realizable value of the receivables?
11. For a business, what are the advantages of a note receivable in comparison to an account receivable?
12. Blanchard Company issued a note receivable to Tucker Company. (a) Who is the payee? (b) What is the title of the account used by Tucker Company in recording the note?
13. If a note provides for payment of principal of $90,000 and interest at the rate of 7%, will the interest amount to $6,300? Explain.

14. The maker of a $10,000, 8%, 90-day note receivable failed to pay the note on the due date of June 30. What accounts should be debited and credited by the payee to record the dishonored note receivable?
15. The note receivable dishonored in Eye Opener 14 is paid on July 30 by the maker, plus interest for 30 days, 10%. What entry should be made to record the receipt of the payment?
16. Under what section should accounts receivable be reported on the balance sheet?

Practice Exercises

PE 9-1A
Direct write-off method
obj. 3
EE 9-1 p. 400

Journalize the following transactions using the direct write-off method of accounting for uncollectible receivables:

Sept. 19. Received $100 from Pat Roark and wrote off the remainder owed of $500 as uncollectible.

Dec. 20. Reinstated the account of Pat Roark and received $500 cash in full payment.

PE 9-1B
Direct write-off method
obj. 3
EE 9-1 p. 400

Journalize the following transactions using the direct write-off method of accounting for uncollectible receivables:

Feb. 25. Received $500 from Jason Wilcox and wrote off the remainder owed of $4,000 as uncollectible.

May 9. Reinstated the account of Jason Wilcox and received $4,000 cash in full payment.

PE 9-2A
Allowance method
obj. 4
EE 9-2 p. 403

Journalize the following transactions using the allowance method of accounting for uncollectible receivables:

Sept. 19. Received $100 from Pat Roark and wrote off the remainder owed of $500 as uncollectible.

Dec. 20. Reinstated the account of Pat Roark and received $500 cash in full payment.

PE 9-2B
Allowance method
obj. 4
EE 9-2 p. 403

Journalize the following transactions using the allowance method of accounting for uncollectible receivables:

Feb. 25. Received $500 from Jason Wilcox and wrote off the remainder owed of $4,000 as uncollectible.

May 9. Reinstated the account of Jason Wilcox and received $4,000 cash in full payment.

PE 9-3A
Percent of sales method
obj. 4
EE 9-3 p. 405

At the end of the current year, Accounts Receivable has a balance of $1,400,000; Allowance for Doubtful Accounts has a debit balance of $2,250; and net sales for the year total $9,500,000. Bad debt expense is estimated at ¼ of 1% of net sales.

Determine (1) the amount of the adjusting entry for uncollectible accounts; (2) the adjusted balances of Accounts Receivable, Allowance for Doubtful Accounts, and Bad Debt Expense; and (3) the net realizable value of accounts receivable.

PE 9-3B
Percent of sales method
obj. 4

At the end of the current year, Accounts Receivable has a balance of $750,000; Allowance for Doubtful Accounts has a credit balance of $11,250; and net sales for the year total $4,100,000. Bad debt expense is estimated at ½ of 1% of net sales.

EE 9-3 p. 405

Determine (1) the amount of the adjusting entry for uncollectible accounts; (2) the adjusted balances of Accounts Receivable, Allowance for Doubtful Accounts, and Bad Debt Expense; and (3) the net realizable value of accounts receivable.

PE 9-4A
Analysis of receivables method
obj. 4
EE 9-4 p. 407

At the end of the current year, Accounts Receivable has a balance of $1,400,000; Allowance for Doubtful Accounts has a debit balance of $2,250; and net sales for the year total $9,500,000. Using the aging method, the balance of Allowance for Doubtful Accounts is estimated as $24,000.

Determine (1) the amount of the adjusting entry for uncollectible accounts; (2) the adjusted balances of Accounts Receivable, Allowance for Doubtful Accounts, and Bad Debt Expense; and (3) the net realizable value of accounts receivable.

PE 9-4B
Analysis of receivables method
obj. 4
EE 9-4 p. 407

At the end of the current year, Accounts Receivable has a balance of $750,000; Allowance for Doubtful Accounts has a credit balance of $11,250; and net sales for the year total $4,150,000. Using the aging method, the balance of Allowance for Doubtful Accounts is estimated as $30,000.

Determine (1) the amount of the adjusting entry for uncollectible accounts; (2) the adjusted balances of Accounts Receivable, Allowance for Doubtful Accounts, and Bad Debt Expense; and (3) the net realizable value of accounts receivable.

PE 9-5A
Note receivable
obj. 6
EE 9-5 p. 413

Cannondale Supply Company received a 120-day, 9% note for $200,000, dated March 13 from a customer on account.

a. Determine the due date of the note.
b. Determine the maturity value of the note.
c. Journalize the entry to record the receipt of the payment of the note at maturity.

PE 9-5B
Note receivable
obj. 6
EE 9-5 p. 413

Northrop Supply Company received a 30-day, 6% note for $40,000, dated September 23 from a customer on account.

a. Determine the due date of the note.
b. Determine the maturity value of the note.
c. Journalize the entry to record the receipt of the payment of the note at maturity.

Exercises

EX 9-1
Classifications of receivables
obj. 1

Boeing is one of the world's major aerospace firms, with operations involving commercial aircraft, military aircraft, missiles, satellite systems, and information and battle management systems. As of December 31, 2007, Boeing had $2,838 million of receivables involving U.S. government contracts and $1,232 million of receivables involving commercial aircraft customers, such as Delta Air Lines and United Airlines.

Should Boeing report these receivables separately in the financial statements, or combine them into one overall accounts receivable amount? Explain.

EX 9-2
Nature of uncollectible accounts

The MGM Mirage owns and operates casinos including the MGM Grand and the Bellagio in Las Vegas, Nevada. As of December 31, 2007, the MGM Mirage reported accounts and notes receivable of $452,945,000 and allowance for doubtful accounts of $90,024,000.

obj. 2

✔ a. 19.9%

Johnson & Johnson manufactures and sells a wide range of health care products including Band-Aids and Tylenol. As of December 31, 2006, Johnson & Johnson reported accounts receivable of $8,872,000,000 and allowance for doubtful accounts of $160,000,000.

a. Compute the percentage of the allowance for doubtful accounts to the accounts and notes receivable as of December 31, 2006, for The MGM Mirage.
b. Compute the percentage of the allowance for doubtful accounts to the accounts receivable as of December 31, 2006, for Johnson & Johnson.
c. Discuss possible reasons for the difference in the two ratios computed in (a) and (b).

EX 9-3
Entries for uncollectible accounts, using direct write-off method

obj. 3

Journalize the following transactions in the accounts of Laser Tech Co., a medical equipment company that uses the direct write-off method of accounting for uncollectible receivables:

Feb. 23. Sold merchandise on account to Dr. Judith Salazar, $41,500. The cost of the merchandise sold was $22,300.
May 10. Received $10,000 from Dr. Judith Salazar and wrote off the remainder owed on the sale of February 23 as uncollectible.
Dec. 2. Reinstated the account of Dr. Judith Salazar that had been written off on May 10 and received $31,500 cash in full payment.

EX 9-4
Entries for uncollectible receivables, using allowance method

obj. 4

Journalize the following transactions in the accounts of Food Unlimited Company, a restaurant supply company that uses the allowance method of accounting for uncollectible receivables:

Jan. 18. Sold merchandise on account to Wings Co., $13,200. The cost of the merchandise sold was $9,500.
Mar. 31. Received $5,000 from Wings Co. and wrote off the remainder owed on the sale of January 18 as uncollectible.
Sept. 3. Reinstated the account of Wings Co. that had been written off on March 31 and received $8,200 cash in full payment.

EX 9-5
Entries to write off accounts receivable

objs. 3, 4

Tech Savvy, a computer consulting firm, has decided to write off the $8,375 balance of an account owed by a customer, Nick Wadle. Journalize the entry to record the write-off, assuming that (a) the direct write-off method is used and (b) the allowance method is used.

EX 9-6
Providing for doubtful accounts

obj. 4

✔ a. $23,500
✔ b. $24,800

At the end of the current year, the accounts receivable account has a debit balance of $825,000 and net sales for the year total $9,400,000. Determine the amount of the adjusting entry to provide for doubtful accounts under each of the following assumptions:

a. The allowance account before adjustment has a credit balance of $11,200. Bad debt expense is estimated at ¼ of 1% of net sales.
b. The allowance account before adjustment has a credit balance of $11,200. An aging of the accounts in the customer ledger indicates estimated doubtful accounts of $36,000.
c. The allowance account before adjustment has a debit balance of $6,000. Bad debt expense is estimated at ½ of 1% of net sales.
d. The allowance account before adjustment has a debit balance of $6,000. An aging of the accounts in the customer ledger indicates estimated doubtful accounts of $49,500.

EX 9-7
Number of days past due

Bubba's Auto Supply distributes new and used automobile parts to local dealers throughout the Southeast. Bubba's credit terms are n/30. As of the end of business on July 31, the following accounts receivable were past due:

obj. 4

✔ AAA Pickup Shop, 62 days

Account	Due Date	Amount
AAA Pickup Shop	May 30	$6,000
Best Auto	July 14	3,000
Downtown Repair	March 18	2,000
Luke's Auto Repair	June I	5,000
New or Used Auto	June 18	750
Sally's	April 12	2,800
Trident Auto	May 31	1,500
Washburn Repair & Tow	March 13	7,500

Determine the number of days each account is past due.

EX 9-8
Aging of receivables schedule

obj. 4

The accounts receivable clerk for Summit Industries prepared the following partially completed aging of receivables schedule as of the end of business on November 30:

	A	B	C	D	E	F	G
1			Not	Days Past Due			
2			Past				Over
3	Customer	Balance	Due	1–30	31–60	61–90	90
4	Abbott Brothers Inc.	2,000	2,000				
5	Alonso Company	1,500		1,500			
21	Ziel Company	5,000			5,000		
22	Subtotals	807,500	475,000	180,000	78,500	42,300	31,700

The following accounts were unintentionally omitted from the aging schedule and not included in the subtotals above:

Customer	Balance	Due Date
Cottonwood Industries	$14,300	July 6
Fargo Company	17,700	September 17
Garfield Inc.	8,500	October 17
Sadler Company	10,000	November 2
Twitty Company	25,000	December 23

a. Determine the number of days past due for each of the preceding accounts.
b. Complete the aging-of-receivables schedule by including the omitted accounts.

EX 9-9
Estimating allowance for doubtful accounts

obj. 4

✔ $77,800

Summit Industries has a past history of uncollectible accounts, as shown below. Estimate the allowance for doubtful accounts, based on the aging of receivables schedule you completed in Exercise 9-8.

Age Class	Percent Uncollectible
Not past due	1%
1–30 days past due	6
31–60 days past due	20
61–90 days past due	35
Over 90 days past due	50

EX 9-10
Adjustment for uncollectible accounts

obj. 4

Using data in Exercise 9-8, assume that the allowance for doubtful accounts for Summit Industries has a credit balance of $16,175 before adjustment on November 30. Journalize the adjusting entry for uncollectible accounts as of November 30.

EX 9-11
Estimating doubtful accounts
obj. 4

Fonda Bikes Co. is a wholesaler of motorcycle supplies. An aging of the company's accounts receivable on December 31, 2010, and a historical analysis of the percentage of uncollectible accounts in each age category are as follows:

Age Interval	Balance	Percent Uncollectible
Not past due	$567,000	½%
1–30 days past due	58,000	3
31–60 days past due	29,000	7
61–90 days past due	20,500	15
91–180 days past due	15,000	40
Over 180 days past due	10,500	75
	$700,000	

Estimate what the proper balance of the allowance for doubtful accounts should be as of December 31, 2010.

EX 9-12
Entry for uncollectible accounts
obj. 4

Using the data in Exercise 9-11, assume that the allowance for doubtful accounts for Fonda Bikes Co. had a debit balance of $4,145 as of December 31, 2010.

Journalize the adjusting entry for uncollectible accounts as of December 31, 2010.

EX 9-13
Entries for bad debt expense under the direct write-off and allowance methods
obj. 5
✔ c. $6,025 higher

The following selected transactions were taken from the records of Lights of the West Company for the first year of its operations ending December 31, 2010:

Jan. 24. Wrote off account of J. Huntley, $3,000.
Feb. 17. Received $1,500 as partial payment on the $4,000 account of Karlene Solomon. Wrote off the remaining balance as uncollectible.
May 29. Received $3,000 from J. Huntley, which had been written off on January 24. Reinstated the account and recorded the cash receipt.
Nov. 30. Wrote off the following accounts as uncollectible (record as one journal entry):

Don O'Leary	$2,000
Kim Snider	1,500
Jennifer Kerlin	900
Tracy Lane	1,250
Lynn Fuqua	450

Dec. 31. Lights of the West Company uses the percent of credit sales method of estimating uncollectible accounts expense. Based on past history and industry averages, 1½% of credit sales are expected to be uncollectible. Lights of the West Company recorded $975,000 of credit sales during 2010.

a. Journalize the transactions for 2010 under the direct write-off method.
b. Journalize the transactions for 2010 under the allowance method.
c. How much higher (lower) would Lights of the West Company's net income have been under the direct write-off method than under the allowance method?

EX 9-14
Entries for bad debt expense under the direct write-off and allowance methods
obj. 5
✔ c. $17,200 higher

The following selected transactions were taken from the records of Burrito Company for the year ending December 31, 2010:

Mar. 13. Wrote off account of B. Hall, $4,200.
Apr. 19. Received $3,000 as partial payment on the $7,500 account of M. Rainey. Wrote off the remaining balance as uncollectible.
July 9. Received the $4,200 from B. Hall, which had been written off on March 13. Reinstated the account and recorded the cash receipt.
Nov. 23. Wrote off the following accounts as uncollectible (record as one journal entry):

Rai Quinn	$1,200
P. Newman	750
Ned Berry	2,900
Mary Adams	1,675
Nichole Chapin	480

Dec. 31. The company prepared the following aging schedule for its accounts receivable:

Aging Class (Number of Days Past Due)	Receivables Balance on December 31	Estimated Percent of Uncollectible Accounts
0–30 days	$200,000	2%
31–60 days	75,000	8
61–90 days	24,000	25
91–120 days	9,000	40
More than 120 days	12,000	80
Total receivables	$320,000	

a. Journalize the transactions for 2010 under the direct write-off method.
b. Journalize the transactions for 2010 under the allowance method, assuming that the allowance account had a beginning balance of $12,000 on January 1, 2010, and the company uses the analysis of receivables method.
c. How much higher (lower) would Burrito's 2010 net income have been under the direct write-off method than under the allowance method?

EX 9-15
Effect of doubtful accounts on net income
obj. 5

During its first year of operations, Master Plumbing Supply Co. had net sales of $3,500,000, wrote off $50,000 of accounts as uncollectible using the direct write-off method, and reported net income of $390,500. Determine what the net income would have been if the allowance method had been used, and the company estimated that 1¾% of net sales would be uncollectible.

EX 9-16
Effect of doubtful accounts on net income
obj. 5
✔ b. $24,750 credit balance

Using the data in Exercise 9-15, assume that during the second year of operations Master Plumbing Supply Co. had net sales of $4,200,000, wrote off $60,000 of accounts as uncollectible using the direct write-off method, and reported net income of $425,000.

a. Determine what net income would have been in the second year if the allowance method (using 1¾% of net sales) had been used in both the first and second years.
b. Determine what the balance of the allowance for doubtful accounts would have been at the end of the second year if the allowance method had been used in both the first and second years.

EX 9-17
Entries for bad debt expense under the direct write-off and allowance methods
obj. 5
✔ c. $7,000 higher

Isner Company wrote off the following accounts receivable as uncollectible for the first year of its operations ending December 31, 2010:

Customer	Amount
L. Hearn	$10,000
Carrie Murray	9,500
Kelly Salkin	13,100
Shana Wagnon	2,400
Total	$35,000

a. Journalize the write-offs for 2010 under the direct write-off method.
b. Journalize the write-offs for 2010 under the allowance method. Also, journalize the adjusting entry for uncollectible accounts. The company recorded $2,400,000 of credit sales during 2010. Based on past history and industry averages, 1¾% of credit sales are expected to be uncollectible.
c. How much higher (lower) would Isner Company's 2010 net income have been under the direct write-off method than under the allowance method?

EX 9-18
Entries for bad debt expense under the direct write-off and allowance methods
obj. 5

OK International wrote off the following accounts receivable as uncollectible for the year ending December 31, 2010:

Customer	Amount
Eva Fry	$ 6,500
Lance Landau	11,200
Marcie Moffet	3,800
Jose Reis	3,500
Total	$25,000

The company prepared the following aging schedule for its accounts receivable on December 31, 2010:

Aging Class (Number of Days Past Due)	Receivables Balance on December 31	Estimated Percent of Uncollectible Accounts
0–30 days	$480,000	1%
31–60 days	100,000	3
61–90 days	40,000	20
91–120 days	25,000	30
More than 120 days	5,000	40
Total receivables	$650,000	

a. Journalize the write-offs for 2010 under the direct write-off method.
b. Journalize the write-offs and the year-end adjusting entry for 2010 under the allowance method, assuming that the allowance account had a beginning balance of $22,500 on January 1, 2010, and the company uses the analysis of receivables method.

EX 9-19
Determine due date and interest on notes
obj. 6

✔ d. May 5, $225

Determine the due date and the amount of interest due at maturity on the following notes:

	Date of Note	Face Amount	Interest Rate	Term of Note
a.	October 1	$10,500	8%	60 days
b.	August 30	18,000	10	120 days
c.	May 30	12,000	12	90 days
d.	March 6	15,000	9	60 days
e.	May 23	9,000	10	60 days

EX 9-20
Entries for notes receivable
obj. 6
✔ b. $40,600

South Bay Interior Decorators issued a 90-day, 6% note for $40,000, dated April 15, to Miami Furniture Company on account.

a. Determine the due date of the note.
b. Determine the maturity value of the note.
c. Journalize the entries to record the following: (1) receipt of the note by Miami Furniture and (2) receipt of payment of the note at maturity.

EX 9-21
Entries for notes receivable
obj. 6

The series of seven transactions recorded in the following T accounts were related to a sale to a customer on account and the receipt of the amount owed. Briefly describe each transaction.

CASH

	Debit		Credit
(7)	30,955		

NOTES RECEIVABLE

	Debit		Credit
(5)	30,000	(6)	30,000

ACCOUNTS RECEIVABLE

	Debit		Credit
(1)	35,000	(3)	5,000
(6)	30,750	(5)	30,000
		(7)	30,750

SALES RETURNS AND ALLOWANCES

	Debit		Credit
(3)	5,000		

MERCHANDISE INVENTORY

	Debit		Credit
(4)	3,000	(2)	21,000

COST OF MERCHANDISE SOLD

	Debit		Credit
(2)	21,000	(4)	3,000

SALES

	Debit		Credit
		(1)	35,000

INTEREST REVENUE

	Debit		Credit
		(6)	750
		(7)	205

EX 9-22
Entries for notes receivable, including year-end entries
obj. 6

The following selected transactions were completed by Alcor Co., a supplier of Velcro™ for clothing:

2009

Dec. 13. Received from Penick Clothing & Bags Co., on account, an $84,000, 90-day, 9% note dated December 13.

31. Recorded an adjusting entry for accrued interest on the note of December 13.

31. Recorded the closing entry for interest revenue.

2010

Mar. 12. Received payment of note and interest from Penick Clothing & Bags Co.

Journalize the transactions.

EX 9-23
Entries for receipt and dishonor of note receivable
obj. 6

Journalize the following transactions of Funhouse Productions:

July 8. Received a $120,000, 90-day, 8% note dated July 8 from Mystic Mermaid Company on account.

Oct. 6. The note is dishonored by Mystic Mermaid Company.

Nov. 5. Received the amount due on the dishonored note plus interest for 30 days at 10% on the total amount charged to Mystic Mermaid Company on October 6.

EX 9-24
Entries for receipt and dishonor of notes receivable
objs. 4, 6

Journalize the following transactions in the accounts of Lemon Grove Co., which operates a riverboat casino:

Mar. 1. Received a $30,000, 60-day, 6% note dated March 1 from Bradshaw Co. on account.

18. Received a $25,000, 60-day, 9% note dated March 18 from Soto Co. on account.

Apr. 30. The note dated March 1 from Bradshaw Co. is dishonored, and the customer's account is charged for the note, including interest.

May 17. The note dated March 18 from Soto Co. is dishonored, and the customer's account is charged for the note, including interest.

July 29. Cash is received for the amount due on the dishonored note dated March 1 plus interest for 90 days at 8% on the total amount debited to Bradshaw Co. on April 30.

Aug. 23. Wrote off against the allowance account the amount charged to Soto Co. on May 17 for the dishonored note dated March 18.

EX 9-25
Receivables on the balance sheet
obj. 7

List any errors you can find in the following partial balance sheet:

Jennett Company
Balance Sheet
December 31, 2010

Assets		
Current assets:		
Cash		$ 95,000
Notes receivable	$250,000	
Less interest receivable	15,000	235,000
Accounts receivable	$398,000	
Plus allowance for doubtful accounts	36,000	434,000

Appendix
EX 9-26
Discounting notes receivable

✔ a. $61,800

D. Stoner Co., a building construction company, holds a 120-day, 9% note for $60,000, dated August 7, which was received from a customer on account. On October 6, the note is discounted at the bank at the rate of 12%.

a. Determine the maturity value of the note.
b. Determine the number of days in the discount period.
c. Determine the amount of the discount.
d. Determine the amount of the proceeds.
e. Journalize the entry to record the discounting of the note on October 6.

Appendix EX 9-27
Entries for receipt and discounting of note receivable and dishonored notes

Journalize the following transactions in the accounts of Zion Theater Productions:

Mar. 1.	Received a $40,000, 90-day, 8% note dated March 1 from Gymboree Company on account.
31.	Discounted the note at Security Credit Bank at 10%.
May 30.	The note is dishonored by Gymboree Company; paid the bank the amount due on the note, plus a protest fee of $200.
June 29.	Received the amount due on the dishonored note plus interest for 30 days at 12% on the total amount charged to Gymboree Company on May 30.

EX 9-28
Accounts receivable turnover and days' sales in receivables

✔ a. 2007: 8.4

Polo Ralph Lauren Corporation designs, markets, and distributes a variety of apparel, home decor, accessory, and fragrance products. The company's products include such brands as Polo by Ralph Lauren, Ralph Lauren Purple Label, Ralph Lauren, Polo Jeans Co., and Chaps. Polo Ralph Lauren reported the following (in thousands):

	For the Period Ending	
	March 31, 2007	**April 1, 2006**
Net sales	$4,295,400	$3,746,300
Accounts receivable	511,900	516,600

Assume that accounts receivable (in millions) were $530,503 at the beginning of the 2006 fiscal year.

a. Compute the accounts receivable turnover for 2007 and 2006. Round to one decimal place.
b. Compute the days' sales in receivables for 2007 and 2006. Round to one decimal place.
c. What conclusions can be drawn from these analyses regarding Ralph Lauren's efficiency in collecting receivables?

EX 9-29
Accounts receivable turnover and days' sales in receivables

✔ a. 2007: 9.0

H.J. Heinz Company was founded in 1869 at Sharpsburg, Pennsylvania, by Henry J. Heinz. The company manufactures and markets food products throughout the world, including ketchup, condiments and sauces, frozen food, pet food, soups, and tuna. For the fiscal years 2007 and 2006, H.J. Heinz reported the following (in thousands):

	Year Ending	
	May 2, 2007	**May 3, 2006**
Net sales	$9,001,630	$8,643,438
Accounts receivable	996,852	1,002,125

Assume that the accounts receivable (in thousands) were $1,092,394 at the beginning of 2006.

a. Compute the accounts receivable turnover for 2007 and 2006. Round to one decimal place.
b. Compute the days' sales in receivables at the end of 2007 and 2006. Round to one decimal place.
c. What conclusions can be drawn from these analyses regarding Heinz's efficiency in collecting receivables?

EX 9-30
Accounts receivable turnover and days' sales in receivables

The Limited, Inc., sells women's and men's clothing through specialty retail stores. The Limited sells women's intimate apparel and personal care products through Victoria's Secret and Bath & Body Works stores. The Limited reported the following (in millions):

	For the Period Ending	
	Feb. 3, 2007	**Jan. 28, 2006**
Net sales	$10,671	$9,699
Accounts receivable	176	182

Assume that accounts receivable (in millions) were $128 on January 29, 2005.

a. Compute the accounts receivable turnover for 2007 and 2006. Round to one decimal place.
b. Compute the day's sales in receivables for 2007 and 2006. Round to one decimal place.
c. What conclusions can be drawn from these analyses regarding The Limited's efficiency in collecting receivables?

EX 9-31
Accounts receivable turnover

Use the data in Exercises 9-29 and 9-30 to analyze the accounts receivable turnover ratios of H.J. Heinz Company and The Limited, Inc.

a. Compute the average accounts receivable turnover ratio for The Limited, Inc., and H.J. Heinz Company for the years shown in Exercises 9-29 and 9-30.
b. Does The Limited or H.J. Heinz Company have the higher average accounts receivable turnover ratio?
c. Explain the logic underlying your answer in (b).

Problems Series A

PR 9-1A
Entries related to uncollectible accounts
obj. 4

✔ 3. $918,750

The following transactions were completed by The Bronze Gallery during the current fiscal year ended December 31:

June 6. Reinstated the account of Ian Netti, which had been written off in the preceding year as uncollectible. Journalized the receipt of $1,945 cash in full payment of Ian's account.
July 19. Wrote off the $11,150 balance owed by Rancho Rigging Co., which is bankrupt.
Aug. 13. Received 35% of the $20,000 balance owed by Santori Co., a bankrupt business, and wrote off the remainder as uncollectible.
Sept. 2. Reinstated the account of Sheryl Capers, which had been written off two years earlier as uncollectible. Recorded the receipt of $3,170 cash in full payment.
Dec. 31. Wrote off the following accounts as uncollectible (compound entry): Jacoba Co., $8,390; Garcia Co., $2,500; Summit Furniture, $6,400; Jill DePuy, $1,800.
31. Based on an analysis of the $960,750 of accounts receivable, it was estimated that $42,000 will be uncollectible. Journalized the adjusting entry.

Instructions

1. Record the January 1 credit balance of $40,000 in a T account for Allowance for Doubtful Accounts.
2. Journalize the transactions. Post each entry that affects the following T accounts and determine the new balances:

   Allowance for Doubtful Accounts
   Bad Debt Expense

3. Determine the expected net realizable value of the accounts receivable as of December 31.
4. Assuming that instead of basing the provision for uncollectible accounts on an analysis of receivables, the adjusting entry on December 31 had been based on an estimated expense of ¾ of 1% of the net sales of $6,000,000 for the year, determine the following:
   a. Bad debt expense for the year.
   b. Balance in the allowance account after the adjustment of December 31.
   c. Expected net realizable value of the accounts receivable as of December 31.

PR 9-2A
Aging of receivables; estimating allowance for doubtful accounts
obj. 4

✔ 3. $67,210

Wigs Plus Company supplies wigs and hair care products to beauty salons throughout California and the Pacific Northwest. The accounts receivable clerk for Wigs Plus prepared the following partially completed aging of receivables schedule as of the end of business on December 31, 2009:

	A	B	C	D	E	F	G	H
1			Not	Days Past Due				
2			Past					
3	Customer	Balance	Due	1–30	31–60	61–90	91–120	Over 120
4	Alpha Beauty	20,000	20,000					
5	Blonde Wigs	11,000			11,000			
30	Zahn's Beauty	2,900		2,900				
31	Subtotals	900,000	498,600	217,250	98,750	33,300	29,950	22,150

The following accounts were unintentionally omitted from the aging schedule:

Customer	Due Date	Balance
Sun Coast Beauty	May 30, 2009	$2,850
Paradise Beauty Store	Sept. 15, 2009	6,050
Helix Hair Products	Oct. 17, 2009	800
Hairy's Hair Care	Oct. 20, 2009	2,000
Surf Images	Nov. 18, 2009	700
Oh The Hair	Nov. 29, 2009	3,500
Mountain Coatings	Dec. 1, 2009	2,250
Lasting Images	Jan. 9, 2010	7,400

Wigs Plus has a past history of uncollectible accounts by age category, as follows:

Age Class	Percent Uncollectible
Not past due	2%
1–30 days past due	4
31–60 days past due	10
61–90 days past due	15
91–120 days past due	35
Over 120 days past due	80

Instructions

1. Determine the number of days past due for each of the preceding accounts.
2. Complete the aging of receivables schedule.
3. Estimate the allowance for doubtful accounts, based on the aging of receivables schedule.
4. Assume that the allowance for doubtful accounts for Wigs Plus has a credit balance of $1,710 before adjustment on December 31, 2009. Journalize the adjustment for uncollectible accounts.

PR 9-3A
Compare two methods of accounting for uncollectible receivables
objs. 3, 4, 5

✔ 1. Year 4: Balance of allowance account, end of year, $13,350

J. J. Technology Company, which operates a chain of 30 electronics supply stores, has just completed its fourth year of operations. The direct write-off method of recording bad debt expense has been used during the entire period. Because of substantial increases in sales volume and the amount of uncollectible accounts, the firm is considering changing to the allowance method. Information is requested as to the effect that an annual provision of $\frac{1}{2}$% of sales would have had on the amount of bad debt expense reported for each of the past four years. It is also considered desirable to know what the balance of Allowance for Doubtful Accounts would have been at the end of each year. The following data have been obtained from the accounts:

			Year of Origin of Accounts Receivable Written Off as Uncollectible			
Year	Sales	Uncollectible Accounts Written Off	1st	2nd	3rd	4th
1st	$1,300,000	$ 1,200	$1,200			
2nd	$1,750,000	3,000	1,400	$1,600		
3rd	$3,000,000	13,000	3,800	3,000	$6,200	
4th	$3,600,000	17,700		4,000	6,100	$7,600

Instructions

1. Assemble the desired data, using the following column headings:

	Bad Debt Expense			
Year	Expense Actually Reported	Expense Based on Estimate	Increase (Decrease) in Amount of Expense	Balance of Allowance Account, End of Year

2. Experience during the first four years of operations indicated that the receivables were either collected within two years or had to be written off as uncollectible. Does the estimate of $\frac{1}{2}$% of sales appear to be reasonably close to the actual experience with uncollectible accounts originating during the first two years? Explain.

PR 9-4A
Details of notes receivable and related entries
obj. 6

✔1. Note 2: Due date, Sept. 13; Interest due at maturity, $150

Boutique Ads Co. produces advertising videos. During the last six months of the current fiscal year, Boutique Ads Co. received the following notes:

	Date	Face Amount	Term	Interest Rate
1.	May 9	$19,200	45 days	9%
2.	July 15	11,250	60 days	8
3.	Aug. 1	43,200	90 days	7
4.	Sept. 4	20,000	90 days	6
5.	Nov. 26	13,500	60 days	8
6.	Dec. 16	21,600	60 days	13

Instructions

1. Determine for each note (a) the due date and (b) the amount of interest due at maturity, identifying each note by number.
2. Journalize the entry to record the dishonor of Note (3) on its due date.
3. Journalize the adjusting entry to record the accrued interest on Notes (5) and (6) on December 31.
4. Journalize the entries to record the receipt of the amounts due on Notes (5) and (6) in January and February.

PR 9-5A
Notes receivable entries
obj. 6

The following data relate to notes receivable and interest for Vidovich Co., a financial services company. (All notes are dated as of the day they are received.)

Mar. 3. Received a $72,000, 9%, 60-day note on account.
25. Received a $10,000, 8%, 90-day note on account.
May 2. Received $73,080 on note of March 3.
16. Received a $40,000, 7%, 90-day note on account.
31. Received a $25,000, 6%, 30-day note on account.
June 23. Received $10,200 on note of March 25.
30. Received $25,125 on note of May 31.
July 1. Received a $7,500, 12%, 30-day note on account.
31. Received $7,575 on note of July 1.
Aug. 14. Received $40,700 on note of May 16.

Instructions

Journalize the entries to record the transactions.

PR 9-6A
Sales and notes receivable transactions
obj. 6

The following were selected from among the transactions completed during the current year by Bonita Co., an appliance wholesale company:

Jan. 20. Sold merchandise on account to Wilding Co., $30,750. The cost of merchandise sold was $18,600.
Mar. 3. Accepted a 60-day, 8% note for $30,750 from Wilding Co. on account.
May 2. Received from Wilding Co. the amount due on the note of March 3.
June 10. Sold merchandise on account to Foyers for $13,600. The cost of merchandise sold was $8,200.

June 15. Loaned $18,000 cash to Michele Hobson, receiving a 30-day, 6% note.
20. Received from Foyers the amount due on the invoice of June 10, less 2% discount.
July 15. Received the interest due from Michele Hobson and a new 60-day, 9% note as a renewal of the loan of June 15. (Record both the debit and the credit to the notes receivable account.)
Sept. 13. Received from Michele Hobson the amount due on her note of July 15.
13. Sold merchandise on account to Rainbow Co., $20,000. The cost of merchandise sold was $11,500.
Oct. 12. Accepted a 60-day, 6% note for $20,000 from Rainbow Co. on account.
Dec. 11. Rainbow Co. dishonored the note dated October 12.
26. Received from Rainbow Co. the amount owed on the dishonored note, plus interest for 15 days at 12% computed on the maturity value of the note.

Instructions

Journalize the transactions.

Problems Series B

PR 9-1B
Entries related to uncollectible accounts
obj. 4

✔ 3. $750,375

The following transactions were completed by Interia Management Company during the current fiscal year ended December 31:

Feb. 24. Received 40% of the $18,000 balance owed by Broudy Co., a bankrupt business, and wrote off the remainder as uncollectible.
May 3. Reinstated the account of Irma Alonso, which had been written off in the preceding year as uncollectible. Journalized the receipt of $1,725 cash in full payment of Alonso's account.
Aug. 9. Wrote off the $3,600 balance owed by Tux Time Co., which has no assets.
Nov. 20. Reinstated the account of Pexis Co., which had been written off in the preceding year as uncollectible. Journalized the receipt of $6,140 cash in full payment of the account.
Dec. 31. Wrote off the following accounts as uncollectible (compound entry): Siena Co., $2,400; Kommers Co., $1,800; Butte Distributors, $6,000; Ed Ballantyne, $1,750.
31. Based on an analysis of the $768,375 of accounts receivable, it was estimated that $18,000 will be uncollectible. Journalized the adjusting entry.

Instructions

1. Record the January 1 credit balance of $15,500 in a T account for Allowance for Doubtful Accounts.
2. Journalize the transactions. Post each entry that affects the following selected T accounts and determine the new balances:

   Allowance for Doubtful Accounts
   Bad Debt Expense

3. Determine the expected net realizable value of the accounts receivable as of December 31.
4. Assuming that instead of basing the provision for uncollectible accounts on an analysis of receivables, the adjusting entry on December 31 had been based on an estimated expense of ½ of 1% of the net sales of $4,100,000 for the year, determine the following:
   a. Bad debt expense for the year.
   b. Balance in the allowance account after the adjustment of December 31.
   c. Expected net realizable value of the accounts receivable as of December 31.

PR 9-2B
Aging of receivables; estimating allowance for doubtful accounts
obj. 4

✔ 3. $72,270

Cutthroat Company supplies flies and fishing gear to sporting goods stores and outfitters throughout the western United States. The accounts receivable clerk for Cutthroat prepared the following partially completed aging of receivables schedule as of the end of business on December 31, 2009:

	A	B	C	D	E	F	G	H
1			Not	Days Past Due				
2			Past					
3	Customer	Balance	Due	1–30	31–60	61–90	91–120	Over 120
4	Alder Fishery	15,000	15,000					
5	Brown Trout	5,500			5,500			
30	Zug Bug Sports	2,900		2,900				
31	Subtotals	850,000	422,450	247,250	103,850	33,300	25,000	18,150

The following accounts were unintentionally omitted from the aging schedule:

Customer	Due Date	Balance
AAA Sports & Flies	June 14, 2009	$2,850
Blackmon Flies	Aug. 30, 2009	1,200
Charlie's Fish Co.	Sept. 30, 2009	1,800
Firehole Sports	Oct. 17, 2009	600
Green River Sports	Nov. 7, 2009	950
Smith River Co.	Nov. 28, 2009	2,200
Wintson Company	Dec. 1, 2009	2,250
Wolfe Bug Sports	Jan. 6, 2010	6,550

Cutthroat Company has a past history of uncollectible accounts by age category, as follows:

Age Class	Percent Uncollectible
Not past due	2%
1–30 days past due	5
31–60 days past due	10
61–90 days past due	25
91–120 days past due	45
Over 120 days past due	90

Instructions

1. Determine the number of days past due for each of the preceding accounts.
2. Complete the aging of receivables schedule.
3. Estimate the allowance for doubtful accounts, based on the aging of receivables schedule.
4. Assume that the allowance for doubtful accounts for Cutthroat Company has a debit balance of $1,370 before adjustment on December 31, 2009. Journalize the adjusting entry for uncollectible accounts.

PR 9-3B
Compare two methods of accounting for uncollectible receivables
objs. 3, 4, 5

✔ 1. Year 4: Balance of allowance account, end of year, $13,700

Maywood Company, a telephone service and supply company, has just completed its fourth year of operations. The direct write-off method of recording bad debt expense has been used during the entire period. Because of substantial increases in sales volume and the amount of uncollectible accounts, the firm is considering changing to the allowance method. Information is requested as to the effect that an annual provision of $\frac{3}{4}$% of sales would have had on the amount of bad debt expense reported for each of the past four years. It is also considered desirable to know what the balance of Allowance for Doubtful Accounts would have been at the end of each year. The following data have been obtained from the accounts:

Year	Sales	Uncollectible Accounts Written off	Year of Origin of Accounts Receivable Written Off as Uncollectible 1st	2nd	3rd	4th
1st	$ 680,000	$2,600	$2,600			
2nd	800,000	3,100	2,000	$1,100		
3rd	1,000,000	6,000	750	4,200	$1,050	
4th	2,000,000	8,200		1,260	2,700	$4,240

Instructions

1. Assemble the desired data, using the following column headings:

	Bad Debt Expense			
Year	Expense Actually Reported	Expense Based on Estimate	Increase (Decrease) in Amount of Expense	Balance of Allowance Account, End of Year

2. Experience during the first four years of operations indicated that the receivables were either collected within two years or had to be written off as uncollectible. Does the estimate of ¾% of sales appear to be reasonably close to the actual experience with uncollectible accounts originating during the first two years? Explain.

PR 9-4B
Details of notes receivable and related entries
obj. 6

✔ 1. Note 2: Due date, July 26; Interest due at maturity, $185

Hauser Co. wholesales bathroom fixtures. During the current fiscal year, Hauser Co. received the following notes:

	Date	Face Amount	Term	Interest Rate
1.	Apr. 4	$30,000	60 days	8%
2.	June 26	18,500	30 days	12
3.	July 5	16,200	120 days	6
4.	Oct. 31	36,000	60 days	9
5.	Nov. 23	21,000	60 days	6
6.	Dec. 27	40,500	30 days	12

Instructions

1. Determine for each note (a) the due date and (b) the amount of interest due at maturity, identifying each note by number.
2. Journalize the entry to record the dishonor of Note (3) on its due date.
3. Journalize the adjusting entry to record the accrued interest on Notes (5) and (6) on December 31.
4. Journalize the entries to record the receipt of the amounts due on Notes (5) and (6) in January.

PR 9-5B
Notes receivable entries
obj. 6

The following data relate to notes receivable and interest for Optic Co., a cable manufacturer and supplier. (All notes are dated as of the day they are received.)

June 10. Received a $15,000, 9%, 60-day note on account.
July 13. Received a $54,000, 10%, 120-day note on account.
Aug. 9. Received $15,225 on note of June 10.
Sept. 4. Received a $24,000, 9%, 60-day note on account.
Nov. 3. Received $24,360 on note of September 4.
5. Received a $24,000, 7%, 30-day note on account.
10. Received $55,800 on note of July 13.
30. Received a $15,000, 10%, 30-day note on account.
Dec. 5. Received $24,140 on note of November 5.
30. Received $15,125 on note of November 30.

Instructions

Journalize entries to record the transactions.

PR 9-6B
Sales and notes receivable transactions
obj. 6

The following were selected from among the transactions completed by Mair Co. during the current year. Mair Co. sells and installs home and business security systems.

Jan. 10. Loaned $12,000 cash to Jas Caudel, receiving a 90-day, 8% note.
Feb. 4. Sold merchandise on account to Periman & Co., $28,000. The cost of the merchandise sold was $16,500.
13. Sold merchandise on account to Centennial Co., $30,000. The cost of merchandise sold was $17,600.
Mar. 6. Accepted a 60-day, 6% note for $28,000 from Periman & Co. on account.
14. Accepted a 60-day, 12% note for $30,000 from Centennial Co. on account.
Apr. 10. Received the interest due from Jas Caudel and a new 90-day, 10% note as a renewal of the loan of January 10. (Record both the debit and the credit to the notes receivable account.)
May 5. Received from Periman & Co. the amount due on the note of March 6.
13. Centennial Co. dishonored its note dated March 14.
June 12. Received from Centennial Co. the amount owed on the dishonored note, plus interest for 30 days at 12% computed on the maturity value of the note.
July 9. Received from Jas Caudel the amount due on his note of April 10.
Aug. 10. Sold merchandise on account to Lindenfield Co., $13,600. The cost of the merchandise sold was $8,000.
20. Received from Lindenfield Co. the amount of the invoice of August 10, less 1% discount.

Instructions

Journalize the transactions.

Special Activities

SA 9-1
Ethics and professional conduct in business

Mirna Gaymer, vice president of operations for Rocky Mountain County Bank, has instructed the bank's computer programmer to use a 365-day year to compute interest on depository accounts (payables). Mirna also instructed the programmer to use a 360-day year to compute interest on loans (receivables).

Discuss whether Mirna is behaving in a professional manner.

SA 9-2
Estimate uncollectible accounts

For several years, Halsey Co.'s sales have been on a "cash only" basis. On January 1, 2007, however, Halsey Co. began offering credit on terms of n/30. The amount of the adjusting entry to record the estimated uncollectible receivables at the end of each year has been ¼ of 1% of credit sales, which is the rate reported as the average for the industry. Credit sales and the year-end credit balances in Allowance for Doubtful Accounts for the past four years are as follows:

Year	Credit Sales	Allowance for Doubtful Accounts
2007	$6,120,000	$ 6,390
2008	6,300,000	11,880
2009	6,390,000	17,000
2010	6,540,000	24,600

Javier Cernao, president of Halsey Co., is concerned that the method used to account for and write off uncollectible receivables is unsatisfactory. He has asked for your advice in the analysis of past operations in this area and for recommendations for change.

1. Determine the amount of (a) the addition to Allowance for Doubtful Accounts and (b) the accounts written off for each of the four years.
2. a. Advise Javier Cernao as to whether the estimate of ¼ of 1% of credit sales appears reasonable.

(continued)

b. Assume that after discussing (a) with Javier Cernao, he asked you what action might be taken to determine what the balance of Allowance for Doubtful Accounts should be at December 31, 2010, and what possible changes, if any, you might recommend in accounting for uncollectible receivables. How would you respond?

SA 9-3
Accounts receivable turnover and days' sales in receivables

Best Buy is a specialty retailer of consumer electronics, including personal computers, entertainment software, and appliances. Best Buy operates retail stores in addition to the Best Buy, Media Play, On Cue, and Magnolia Hi-Fi Web sites. For two recent years, Best Buy reported the following (in millions):

	Year Ending	
	Mar. 3, 2007	**Feb. 25, 2006**
Net sales	$35,934	$30,848
Accounts receivable at end of year	548	506

Assume that the accounts receivable (in millions) were $375 at the beginning of the year ending February 25, 2006.

1. Compute the accounts receivable turnover for 2007 and 2006. Round to one decimal place.
2. Compute the days' sales in receivables at the end of 2007 and 2006.
3. What conclusions can be drawn from (1) and (2) regarding Best Buy's efficiency in collecting receivables?
4. For its years ending in 2007 and 2006, Circuit City Stores, Inc., has an accounts receivable turnover of 30.7 and 50.6, respectively. Compare Best Buy's efficiency in collecting receivables with that of Circuit City.
5. What assumption did we make about sales for the Circuit City and Best Buy ratio computations that might distort the two company ratios and therefore cause the ratios not to be comparable?

SA 9-4
Accounts receivable turnover and days' sales in receivables

Apple Computer, Inc., designs, manufactures, and markets personal computers and related personal computing and communicating solutions for sale primarily to education, creative, consumer, and business customers. Substantially all of the company's net sales over the last five years are from sales of its Macs, Ipods, and related software and peripherals. For two recent fiscal years, Apple reported the following (in millions):

	Year Ending	
	Sept. 30, 2006	**Sept. 24, 2005**
Net sales	$19,315	$13,931
Accounts receivable at end of year	1,252	895

Assume that the accounts receivable (in millions) were $774 at the beginning of 2005.

1. Compute the accounts receivable turnover for 2006 and 2005. Round to one decimal place.
2. Compute the days' sales in receivables at the end of 2006 and 2005.
3. What conclusions can be drawn from (1) and (2) regarding Apple's efficiency in collecting receivables?

SA 9-5
Accounts receivable turnover and days' sales in receivables

EarthLink, Inc., is a nationwide Internet Service Provider (ISP). EarthLink provides a variety of services to its customers, including narrowband access, broadband or high-speed access, and Web hosting services. For two recent years, EarthLink reported the following (in thousands):

	Year Ending	
	Dec. 31, 2006	Dec. 31, 2005
Net sales	$1,301,267	$1,290,072
Accounts receivable at end of year	51,054	36,033

Assume that the accounts receivable (in thousands) were $30,733 at January 1, 2005.

1. Compute the accounts receivable turnover for 2006 and 2005. Round to one decimal place.
2. Compute the days' sales in receivables at the end of 2006 and 2005.
3. What conclusions can be drawn from (1) and (2) regarding EarthLink's efficiency in collecting receivables?
4. Given the nature of EarthLink's operations, do you believe EarthLink's accounts receivable turnover ratio would be higher or lower than a typical manufacturing company, such as Boeing or Kellogg Company? Explain.

SA 9-6
Accounts receivable turnover

The accounts receivable turnover ratio will vary across companies, depending on the nature of the company's operations. For example, an accounts receivable turnover of 6 for an Internet Service Provider is unacceptable but might be excellent for a manufacturer of specialty milling equipment. A list of well-known companies follows.

Alcoa Inc.	The Coca-Cola Company	Kroger
AutoZone, Inc.	Delta Air Lines	Procter & Gamble
Barnes & Noble, Inc.	The Home Depot	Wal-Mart
Caterpillar	IBM	Whirlpool Corporation

1. Categorize each of the preceding companies as to whether its turnover ratio is likely to be above or below 15.
2. Based on (1), identify a characteristic of companies with accounts receivable turnover ratios above 15.

Answers to Self-Examination Questions

1. **B** The estimate of uncollectible accounts, $8,500 (answer C), is the amount of the desired balance of Allowance for Doubtful Accounts after adjustment. The amount of the current provision to be made for uncollectible accounts expense is thus $6,000 (answer B), which is the amount that must be added to the Allowance for Doubtful Accounts credit balance of $2,500 (answer A) so that the account will have the desired balance of $8,500.
2. **B** The amount expected to be realized from accounts receivable is the balance of Accounts Receivable, $100,000, less the balance of Allowance for Doubtful Accounts, $7,000, or $93,000 (answer B).
3. **C** Maturity value is the amount that is due at the maturity or due date. The maturity value of $10,300 (answer C) is determined as follows:

Face amount of note	$10,000
Plus interest ($10,000 × 0.12 × 90/360)	300
Maturity value of note	$10,300

4. **C** November 3 is the due date of a $12,000, 90-day, 8% note receivable dated August 5 [26 days in August (31 days − 5 days) + 30 days in September + 31 days in October + 3 days in November].
5. **B** If a note is dishonored, Accounts Receivable is debited for the maturity value of the note (answer B). The maturity value of the note is its face value (answer A) plus the accrued interest. The maturity value of the note less accrued interest (answer C) is equal to the face value of the note. The maturity value of the note plus accrued interest (answer D) is incorrect, since the interest would be added twice.

CHAPTER 10

Fixed Assets and Intangible Assets

© AP Photo/W. A. Harewood

FATBURGER INC.

Do you remember purchasing your first car? You probably didn't buy your first car like you would buy a CD. Purchasing a new or used car is expensive. In addition, you would drive (use) the car for the next 3–5 years or longer. As a result, you might spend hours or weeks considering different makes and models, safety ratings, warranties, and operating costs before deciding on the final purchase.

Like buying her first car, Lovie Yancey spent a lot of time before deciding to open her first restaurant. In 1952, she created the biggest, juiciest hamburger that anyone had ever seen. She called it a Fatburger. The restaurant initially started as a 24-hour operation to cater to the schedules of professional musicians. As a fan of popular music and its performers, Yancey played rhythm and blues, jazz, and blues recordings for her customers. Fatburger's popularity with entertainers was illustrated when its name was used in a 1992 rap by Ice Cube. "Two in the mornin' got the Fatburger," Cube said, in "It Was a Good Day," a track on his *Predator* album.

The demand for this incredible burger was such that, in 1980, Ms. Yancey decided to offer Fatburger franchise opportunities. In 1990, with the goal of expanding Fatburger throughout the world, Fatburger Inc. purchased the business from Ms. Yancey. Today, Fatburger has grown to a multi-restaurant chain with owners and investors such as talk show host Montel Williams, Cincinnati Bengals' tackle Willie Anderson, comedian David Spade, and musicians Cher, Janet Jackson, and Pharrell.

So, how much would it cost you to open a Fatburger restaurant? The total investment begins at over $750,000 per restaurant. Thus, in starting a Fatburger restaurant, you would be making a significant investment that would affect your life for years to come. In this chapter, we discuss the accounting for investments in fixed assets such as those used to open a Fatburger restaurant. We also explain how to determine the portion of the fixed asset that becomes an expense over time. Finally, we discuss the accounting for the disposal of fixed assets and accounting for intangible assets such as patents and copyrights. **http://www.fatburger.com**

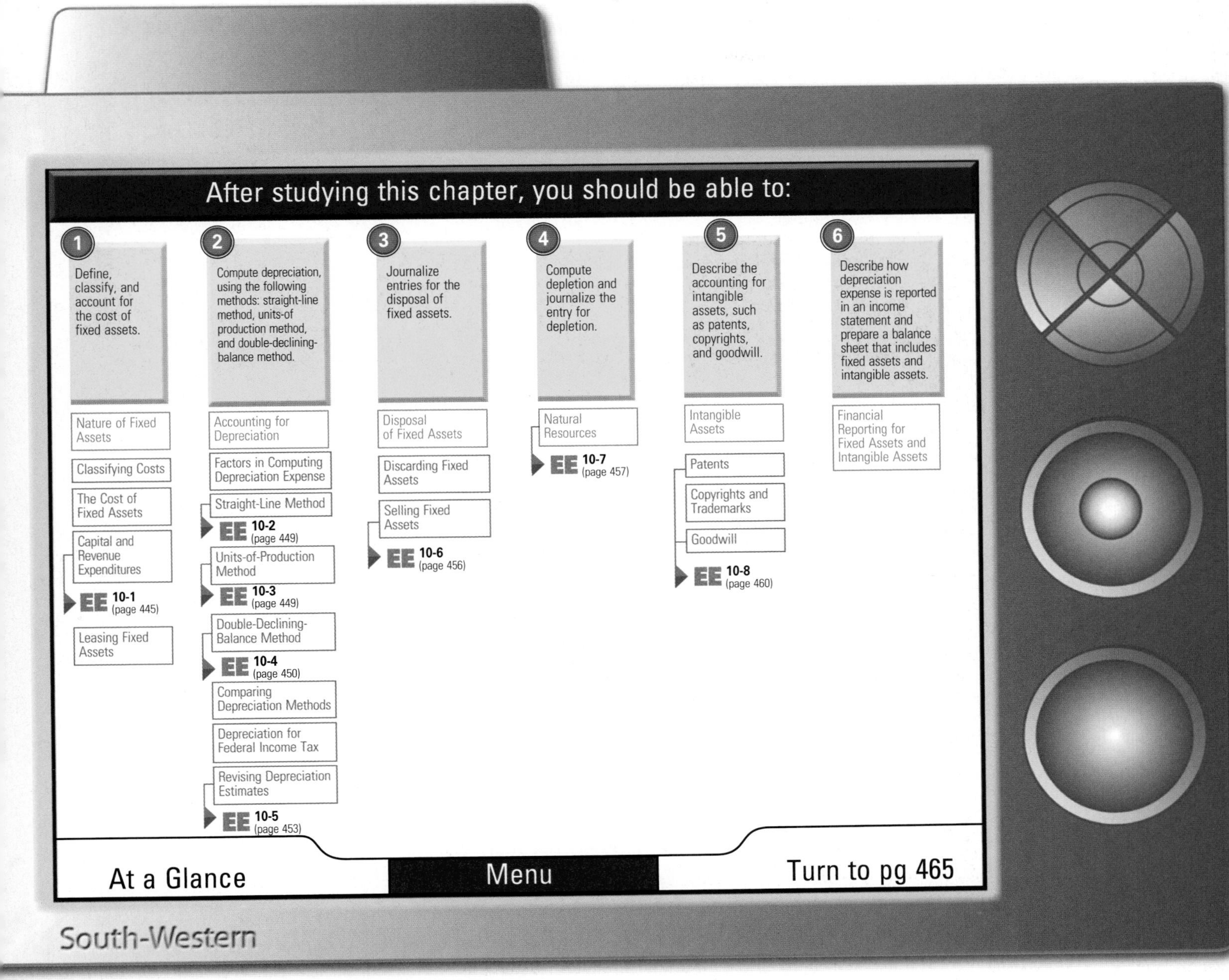

After studying this chapter, you should be able to:

1 Define, classify, and account for the cost of fixed assets.
- Nature of Fixed Assets
- Classifying Costs
- The Cost of Fixed Assets
- Capital and Revenue Expenditures
- EE 10-1 (page 445)
- Leasing Fixed Assets

2 Compute depreciation, using the following methods: straight-line method, units-of-production method, and double-declining-balance method.
- Accounting for Depreciation
- Factors in Computing Depreciation Expense
- Straight-Line Method
- EE 10-2 (page 449)
- Units-of-Production Method
- EE 10-3 (page 449)
- Double-Declining-Balance Method
- EE 10-4 (page 450)
- Comparing Depreciation Methods
- Depreciation for Federal Income Tax
- Revising Depreciation Estimates
- EE 10-5 (page 453)

3 Journalize entries for the disposal of fixed assets.
- Disposal of Fixed Assets
- Discarding Fixed Assets
- Selling Fixed Assets
- EE 10-6 (page 456)

4 Compute depletion and journalize the entry for depletion.
- Natural Resources
- EE 10-7 (page 457)

5 Describe the accounting for intangible assets, such as patents, copyrights, and goodwill.
- Intangible Assets
- Patents
- Copyrights and Trademarks
- Goodwill
- EE 10-8 (page 460)

6 Describe how depreciation expense is reported in an income statement and prepare a balance sheet that includes fixed assets and intangible assets.
- Financial Reporting for Fixed Assets and Intangible Assets

At a Glance | Menu | Turn to pg 465

South-Western

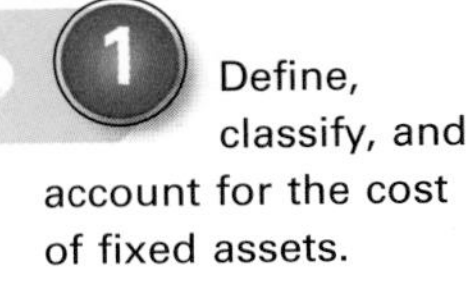
Define, classify, and account for the cost of fixed assets.

Nature of Fixed Assets

Fixed assets are long-term or relatively permanent assets such as equipment, machinery, buildings, and land. Other descriptive titles for fixed assets are *plant assets* or *property, plant, and equipment*. Fixed assets have the following characteristics:

1. They exist physically and, thus, are *tangible* assets.
2. They are owned and used by the company in its normal operations.
3. They are not offered for sale as part of normal operations.

Exhibit 1 shows the percent of fixed assets to total assets for some select companies. As shown in Exhibit 1, fixed assets are often a significant portion of the total assets of a company.

Exhibit 1

Fixed Assets as a Percent of Total Assets—Selected Companies

	Fixed Assets as a Percent of Total Assets
Alcoa Inc.	40%
ExxonMobil Corporation	60
Ford Motor Company	35
Kroger	55
Marriott International, Inc.	31
United Parcel Service, Inc.	53
Verizon Communications	45
Walgreen Co.	46
Wal-Mart	53

Classifying Costs

A cost that has been incurred may be classified as a fixed asset, an investment, or an expense. Exhibit 2 shows how to determine the proper classification of a cost and, thus, how it should be recorded. As shown in Exhibit 2, classifying a cost involves the following steps:

Step 1. Is the purchased item (cost) long-lived?

If *yes*, the item is capitalized as an asset on the balance sheet as either a fixed asset or an investment. Proceed to Step 2.

If *no*, the item is classified and recorded as an *expense*.

Step 2. Is the asset used in normal operations?

If *yes*, the asset is classified and recorded as a *fixed asset*.

If *no*, the asset is classified and recorded as an *investment*.

Costs that are classified and recorded as fixed assets include the purchase of land, buildings, or equipment. Such assets normally last more than a year and are used in

Exhibit 2

Classifying Costs

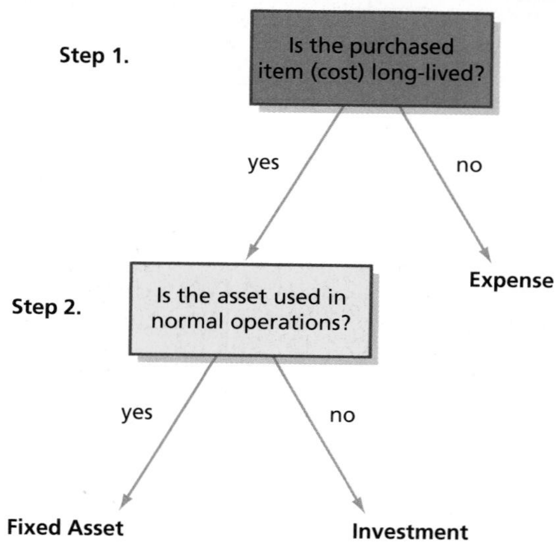

the normal operations. However, standby equipment for use during peak periods or when other equipment breaks down is still classified as a fixed asset even though it is not used very often. In contrast, fixed assets that have been abandoned or are no longer used in operations are not fixed assets.

Although fixed assets may be sold, they should not be offered for sale as part of normal operations. For example, cars and trucks offered for sale by an automotive dealership are not fixed assets of the dealership. On the other hand, a tow truck used in the normal operations of the dealership is a fixed asset of the dealership.

Investments are long-lived assets that are not used in the normal operations and are held for future resale. Such assets are reported on the balance sheet in a section entitled *Investments*. For example, undeveloped land acquired for future resale would be classified and reported as an investment, not land.

The Cost of Fixed Assets

The costs of acquiring fixed assets include all amounts spent to get the asset in place and ready for use. For example, freight costs and the costs of installing equipment are part of the asset's total cost.

Exhibit 3 summarizes some of the common costs of acquiring fixed assets. These costs are recorded by debiting the related fixed asset account, such as Land,[1] Building, Land Improvements, or Machinery and Equipment.

Exhibit 3

Costs of Acquiring Fixed Assets

Building

- Architects' fees
- Engineers' fees
- Insurance costs incurred during construction
- Interest on money borrowed to finance construction
- Walkways to and around the building
- Sales taxes
- Repairs (purchase of existing building)
- Reconditioning (purchase of existing building)
- Modifying for use
- Permits from government agencies

Machinery & Equipment

- Sales taxes
- Freight
- Installation
- Repairs (purchase of used equipment)
- Reconditioning (purchase of used equipment)
- Insurance while in transit
- Assembly
- Modifying for use
- Testing for use
- Permits from government agencies

Land

- Purchase price
- Sales taxes
- Permits from government agencies
- Broker's commissions
- Title fees
- Surveying fees
- Delinquent real estate taxes
- Removing unwanted building less any salvage
- Grading and leveling
- Paving a public street bordering the land

1 As discussed here, land is assumed to be used only as a location or site and not for its mineral deposits or other natural resources.

Only costs necessary for preparing the fixed asset for use are included as a cost of the asset. Unnecessary costs that do not increase the asset's usefulness are recorded as an expense. For example, the following costs are included as an expense:

1. Vandalism
2. Mistakes in installation
3. Uninsured theft
4. Damage during unpacking and installing
5. Fines for not obtaining proper permits from governmental agencies

Intel Corporation recently reported almost $3 billion of construction in progress, which was 7% of its total fixed assets.

A company may incur costs associated with constructing a fixed asset such as a new building. The direct costs incurred in the construction, such as labor and materials, should be capitalized as a debit to an account entitled Construction in Progress. When the construction is complete, the costs are reclassified by crediting Construction in Progress and debiting the proper fixed asset account such as Building. For some companies, construction in progress can be significant.

Capital and Revenue Expenditures

Once a fixed asset has been acquired and placed in service, costs may be incurred for ordinary maintenance and repairs. In addition, costs may be incurred for improving an asset or for extraordinary repairs that extend the asset's useful life. Costs that benefit only the current period are called **revenue expenditures**. Costs that improve the asset or extend its useful life are **capital expenditures**.

Ordinary Maintenance and Repairs Costs related to the ordinary maintenance and repairs of a fixed asset are recorded as an expense of the current period. Such expenditures are *revenue expenditures* and are recorded as increases to Repairs and Maintenance Expense. For example, $300 paid for a tune-up of a delivery truck is recorded as follows:

		Repairs and Maintenance Expense		300	
		Cash			300

Asset Improvements After a fixed asset has been placed in service, costs may be incurred to improve the asset. For example, the service value of a delivery truck might be improved by adding a $5,500 hydraulic lift to allow for easier and quicker loading of cargo. Such costs are *capital expenditures* and are recorded as increases to the fixed asset account. In the case of the hydraulic lift, the expenditure is recorded as follows:

		Delivery Truck		5,500	
		Cash			5,500

Because the cost of the delivery truck has increased, depreciation for the truck would also change over its remaining useful life.

Extraordinary Repairs After a fixed asset has been placed in service, costs may be incurred to extend the asset's useful life. For example, the engine of a forklift that is near the end of its useful life may be overhauled at a cost of $4,500, extending its useful life by eight years. Such costs are *capital expenditures* and are recorded as a decrease in an accumulated depreciation account. In the case of the fork-lift, the expenditure is recorded as follows:

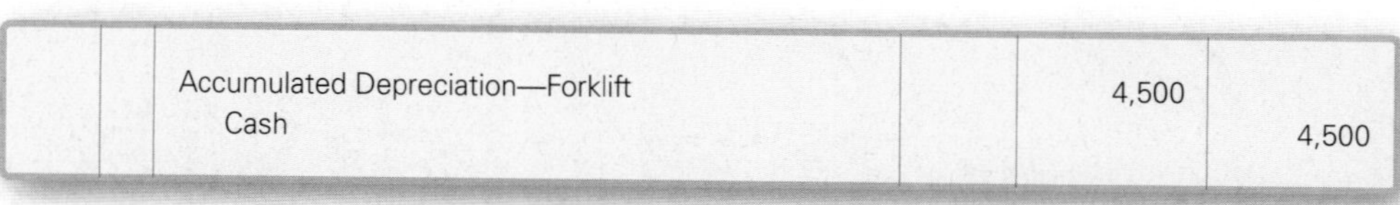

		Accumulated Depreciation—Forklift		4,500	
		Cash			4,500

Integrity, Objectivity, and Ethics in Business

CAPITAL CRIME

One of the largest alleged accounting frauds in history involved the improper accounting for capital expenditures. WorldCom, the second largest telecommunications company in the United States at the time, improperly treated maintenance expenditures on its telecommunications network as capital expenditures. As a result, the company had to restate its prior years' earnings downward by nearly $4 billion to correct this error. The company declared bankruptcy within months of disclosing the error, and the CEO was sentenced to 25 years in prison.

Because the forklift's remaining useful life has changed, depreciation for the forklift would also change based on the new book value of the forklift.

The accounting for revenue and capital expenditures is summarized below.

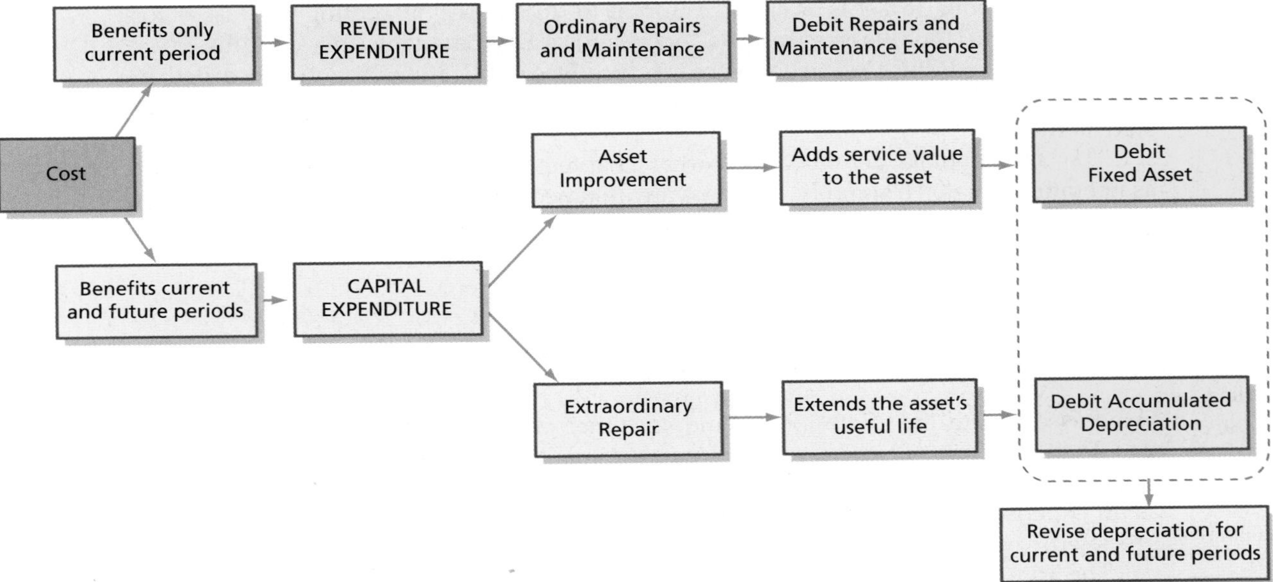

Example Exercise 10-1 Capital and Revenue Expenditures

On June 18, GTS Co. paid $1,200 to upgrade a hydraulic lift and $45 for an oil change for one of its delivery trucks. Journalize the entries for the hydraulic lift upgrade and oil change expenditures.

Follow My Example 10-1

June 18	Delivery Truck	1,200	
	Cash		1,200
18	Repairs and Maintenance Expense	45	
	Cash		45

For Practice: PE 10-1A, PE 10-1B

Leasing Fixed Assets

A *lease* is a contract for the use of an asset for a period of time. Leases are often used in business. For example, automobiles, computers, medical equipment, buildings, and airplanes are often leased.

The two parties to a lease contract are as follows:

1. The *lessor* is the party who owns the asset.
2. The *lessee* is the party to whom the rights to use the asset are granted by the lessor.

On December 31, 2007, Delta Air Lines operated 137 aircraft under operating leases and 48 aircraft under capital leases with future lease commitments of over $8 billion.

Under a lease contract, the lessee pays rent on a periodic basis for the lease term. The lessee accounts for a lease contract in one of two ways depending on how the lease contract is classified. A lease contract can be classified as either a:

1. *Capital lease* or
2. *Operating lease*

A **capital lease** is accounted for as if the lessee has purchased the asset. The lessee debits an asset account for the fair market value of the asset and credits a long-term lease liability account. The asset is then written off as an expense (amortized) over the life of the capital lease. The accounting for capital leases is discussed in more advanced accounting texts.

An **operating lease** is accounted for as if the lessee is renting the asset for the lease term. The lessee records operating lease payments by debiting *Rent Expense* and crediting *Cash*. The lessee's future lease obligations are not recorded in the accounts. However, such obligations are disclosed in notes to the financial statements.

The asset rentals described in earlier chapters of this text were accounted for as operating leases. To simplify, all leases are assumed to be operating leases throughout this text.

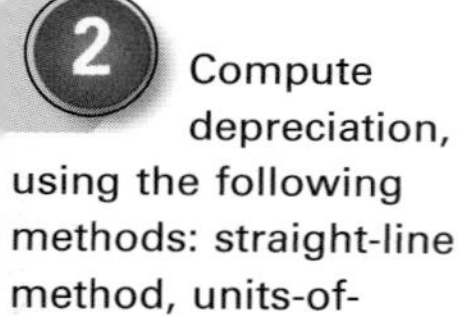

2 Compute depreciation, using the following methods: straight-line method, units-of-production method, and double-declining-balance method.

Accounting for Depreciation

Fixed assets, with the exception of land, lose their ability, over time, to provide services. Thus, the costs of fixed assets such as equipment and buildings should be recorded as an expense over their useful lives. This periodic recording of the cost of fixed assets as an expense is called **depreciation**. Because land has an unlimited life, it is not depreciated.

The adjusting entry to record depreciation debits *Depreciation Expense* and credits a *contra asset* account entitled *Accumulated Depreciation* or *Allowance for Depreciation*. The use of a contra asset account allows the original cost to remain unchanged in the fixed asset account.

Depreciation can be caused by physical or functional factors.

The adjusting entry to record depreciation debits Depreciation Expense and credits Accumulated Depreciation.

1. *Physical depreciation* factors include wear and tear during use or from exposure to weather.
2. *Functional depreciation* factors include obsolescence and changes in customer needs that cause the asset to no longer provide services for which it was intended. For example, equipment may become obsolete due to changing technology.

Two common misunderstandings exist about *depreciation* as used in accounting include:

Would you have more cash if you depreciated your car? The answer is no. Depreciation does not affect your cash flows. Likewise, depreciation does not affect the cash flows of a business. However, depreciation is subtracted in determining net income.

1. Depreciation does not measure a decline in the market value of a fixed asset. Instead, depreciation is an allocation of a fixed asset's cost to expense over the asset's useful life. Thus, the book value of a fixed asset (cost less accumulated depreciation) usually does not agree with the asset's market value. This is justified in accounting because a fixed asset is for use in a company's operations rather than for resale.
2. Depreciation does not provide cash to replace fixed assets as they wear out. This misunderstanding may occur because depreciation, unlike most expenses, does not require an outlay of cash when it is recorded.

Factors in Computing Depreciation Expense

Three factors determine the depreciation expense for a fixed asset. These three factors are as follows:

1. The asset's initial cost
2. The asset's expected useful life
3. The asset's estimated residual value

The initial *cost* of a fixed asset is determined using the concepts discussed and illustrated earlier in this chapter.

The *expected useful life* of a fixed asset is estimated at the time the asset is placed into service. Estimates of expected useful lives are available from industry trade associations. The Internal Revenue Service also publishes guidelines for useful lives, which may be helpful for financial reporting purposes. However, it is not uncommon for different companies to use a different useful life for similar assets.

JCPenney depreciates buildings over 50 years, while Tandy Corporation depreciates buildings over 10–40 years.

The **residual value** of a fixed asset at the end of its useful life is estimated at the time the asset is placed into service. Residual value is sometimes referred to as *scrap value, salvage value*, or *trade-in value*. The difference between a fixed asset's initial cost and its residual value is called the asset's *depreciable cost*. The depreciable cost is the amount of the asset's cost that is allocated over its useful life as depreciation expense. If a fixed asset has no residual value, then its entire cost should be allocated to depreciation.

Exhibit 4 shows the relationship between depreciation expense and a fixed asset's initial cost, expected useful life, and estimated residual value.

Exhibit 4

Depreciation Expense Factors

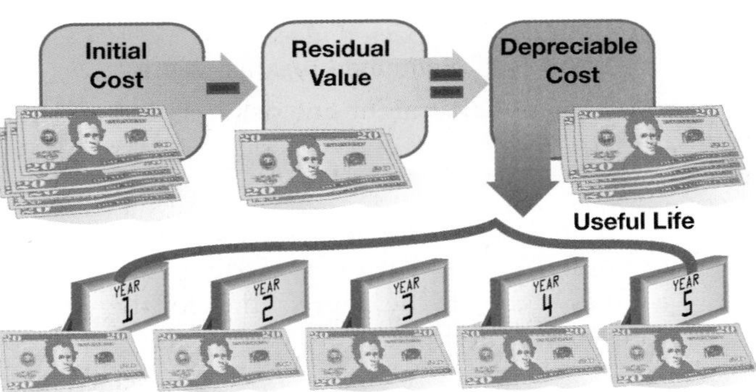

For an asset placed into or taken out of service during the first half of a month, many companies compute depreciation on the asset for the entire month. That is, the asset is treated as having been purchased or sold on the first day of *that* month. Likewise, purchases and sales during the second half of a month are treated as having occurred on the first day of the *next* month. To simplify, this practice is used in this chapter.

The three depreciation methods used most often are as follows:[2]

1. Straight-line depreciation
2. Units-of-production depreciation
3. Double-declining-balance depreciation

Exhibit 5 shows how often these methods are used in financial statements.

It is not necessary that a company use one method of computing depreciation for all of its fixed assets. For example, a company may use one method for depreciating

2 Another method not often used today, called the *sum-of-the-years-digits method*, is described and illustrated in Appendix 1 at the end of this chapter.

Exhibit 5

Use of Depreciation Methods

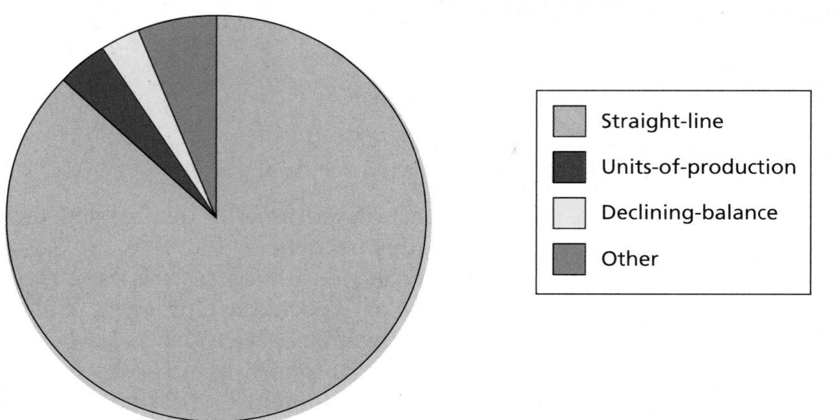

Source: *Accounting Trends & Techniques,* 61st ed., American Institute of Certified Public Accountants, New York, 2007.

equipment and another method for depreciating buildings. A company may also use different methods for determining income and property taxes.

Straight-Line Method

The **straight-line method** provides for the same amount of depreciation expense for each year of the asset's useful life. As shown in Exhibit 5, the straight-line method is the most widely used depreciation method.

To illustrate, assume that equipment was purchased on January 1 as follows:

Initial cost	$24,000
Expected useful life	5 years
Estimated residual value	$2,000

The annual straight-line depreciation of $4,400 is computed below.

$$\text{Annual Depreciation} = \frac{\text{Cost} - \text{Residual Value}}{\text{Useful Life}} = \frac{\$24{,}000 - \$2{,}000}{5 \text{ Years}} = \$4{,}400$$

If an asset is used for only part of a year, the annual depreciation is prorated. For example, assume that the preceding equipment was purchased and placed into service on October 1. The depreciation for the year ending December 31 would be **$1,100**, computed as follows:

$$\textit{First-Year Partial Depreciation} = \$4{,}400 \times 3/12 = \$1{,}100$$

The computation of straight-line depreciation may be simplified by converting the annual depreciation to a percentage of depreciable cost.[3] The straight-line percentage is determined by dividing 100% by the number of years of expected useful life, as shown below.

Expected Years of Useful Life	Straight-Line Percentage
5 years	20% (100%/5)
8 years	12.5% (100%/8)
10 years	10% (100%/10)
20 years	5% (100%/20)
25 years	4% (100%/25)

For the preceding equipment, the annual depreciation of $4,400 can be computed by multiplying the depreciable cost of $22,000 by 20% (100%/5).

As shown above, the straight-line method is simple to use. When an asset's revenues are about the same from period to period, straight-line depreciation provides a good matching of depreciation expense with the asset's revenues.

3 The depreciation rate may also be expressed as a fraction. For example, the annual straight-line rate for an asset with a three-year useful life is 1/3.

Example Exercise 10-2 Straight-Line Depreciation

Equipment acquired at the beginning of the year at a cost of $125,000 has an estimated residual value of $5,000 and an estimated useful life of 10 years. Determine (a) the depreciable cost, (b) the straight-line rate, and (c) the annual straight-line depreciation.

Follow My Example 10-2

a. $120,000 ($125,000 − $5,000)
b. 10% = 1/10
c. $12,000 ($120,000 × 10%), or ($120,000/10 years)

For Practice: PE 10-2A, PE 10-2B

Units-of-Production Method

Norfolk Southern Corporation depreciates its train engines based on hours of operation.

The **units-of-production method** provides the same amount of depreciation expense for each unit of production. Depending on the asset, the units of production can be expressed in terms of hours, miles driven, or quantity produced.

The units-of-production method is applied in two steps.

Step 1. Determine the depreciation per unit as:

$$\text{Depreciation per Unit} = \frac{\text{Cost} - \text{Residual Value}}{\text{Total Units of Production}}$$

Step 2. Compute the depreciation expense as:

$$\text{Depreciation Expense} = \text{Depreciation per Unit} \times \text{Total Units of Production Used}$$

To illustrate, assume that the equipment in the preceding example is expected to have a useful life of 10,000 operating hours. During the year, the equipment was operated 2,100 hours. The units-of-production depreciation for the year is $4,620, as shown below.

Step 1. Determine the depreciation per hour as:

$$\text{Depreciation per Hour} = \frac{\text{Cost} - \text{Residual Value}}{\text{Total Units of Production}} = \frac{\$24{,}000 - \$2{,}000}{10{,}000 \text{ Hours}} = \$2.20 \text{ per Hour}$$

Step 2. Compute the depreciation expense as:

$$\text{Depreciation Expense} = \text{Depreciation per Unit} \times \text{Total Units of Production Used}$$

$$\text{Depreciation Expense} = \$2.20 \text{ per Hour} \times 2{,}100 \text{ Hours} = \$4{,}620$$

The units-of-production method is often used when a fixed asset's in-service time (or use) varies from year to year. In such cases, the units-of-production method matches depreciation expense with the asset's revenues.

Example Exercise 10-3 Units-of-Production Depreciation

Equipment acquired at a cost of $180,000 has an estimated residual value of $10,000, has an estimated useful life of 40,000 hours, and was operated 3,600 hours during the year. Determine (a) the depreciable cost, (b) the depreciation rate, and (c) the units-of-production depreciation for the year.

Follow My Example 10-3

a. $170,000 ($180,000 − $10,000)
b. $4.25 per hour ($170,000/40,000 hours)
c. $15,300 (3,600 hours × $4.25)

For Practice: PE 10-3A, PE 10-3B

Double-Declining-Balance Method

The **double-declining-balance method** provides for a declining periodic expense over the expected useful life of the asset. The double-declining-balance method is applied in three steps.

Step 1. Determine the straight-line percentage using the expected useful life.
Step 2. Determine the double-declining-balance rate by multiplying the straight-line rate from Step 1 by two.
Step 3. Compute the depreciation expense by multiplying the double-declining-balance rate from Step 2 times the book value of the asset.

To illustrate, the equipment purchased in the preceding example is used to compute double-declining-balance depreciation. For the first year, the depreciation is **$9,600**, as shown below.

Step 1. Straight-line percentage = 20% (100%/5)
Step 2. Double-declining-balance rate = 40% (20% × 2)
Step 3. Depreciation expense = $9,600 ($24,000 × 40%)

For the first year, the book value of the equipment is its initial cost of $24,000. After the first year, the **book value** (cost minus accumulated depreciation) declines and, thus, the depreciation also declines. The double-declining-balance depreciation for the full five-year life of the equipment is shown below.

Year	Cost	Acc. Dep. at Beginning of Year	Book Value at Beginning of Year		Double-Declining-Balance Rate	Depreciation for Year	Book Value at End of Year
1	$24,000		$24,000.00	×	40%	$9,600.00	$14,400.00
2	24,000	$ 9,600.00	14,400.00	×	40%	5,760.00	8,640.00
3	24,000	15,360.00	8,640.00	×	40%	3,456.00	5,184.00
4	24,000	18,816.00	5,184.00	×	40%	2,073.60	3,110.40
5	24,000	20,889.60	3,110.40		—	1,110.40	2,000.00

When the double-declining-balance method is used, the estimated residual value is *not* considered. However, the asset should not be depreciated below its estimated residual value. In the above example, the estimated residual value was $2,000. Therefore, the depreciation for the fifth year is $1,110.40 ($3,110.40 − $2,000.00) instead of $1,244.16 (40% × $3,110.40).

Like straight-line depreciation, if an asset is used for only part of a year, the annual depreciation is prorated. For example, assume that the preceding equipment was purchased and placed into service on October 1. The depreciation for the year ending December 31 would be $2,400, computed as follows:

First-Year Partial Depreciation = $9,600 × 3/12 = $2,400

The depreciation for the second year would then be $8,640, computed as follows:

Second-Year Depreciation = $8,640 = [40% × ($24,000 − $2,400)]

The double-declining-balance method provides a higher depreciation in the first year of the asset's use, followed by declining depreciation amounts. For this reason, the double-declining-balance method is called an **accelerated depreciation method**.

An asset's revenues are often greater in the early years of its use than in later years. In such cases, the double-declining-balance method provides a good matching of depreciation expense with the asset's revenues.

Example Exercise 10-4 Double-Declining-Balance Depreciation 2

Equipment acquired at the beginning of the year at a cost of $125,000 has an estimated residual value of $5,000 and an estimated useful life of 10 years. Determine (a) the double-declining-balance rate and (b) the double-declining-balance depreciation for the first year.

Follow My Example 10-4

a. 20% [(1/10) × 2]

b. $25,000 ($125,000 × 20%)

For Practice: PE 10-4A, PE 10-4B

Comparing Depreciation Methods

The three depreciation methods are summarized in Exhibit 6. All three methods allocate a portion of the total cost of an asset to an accounting period, while never depreciating an asset below its residual value.

Exhibit 6

Summary of Depreciation Methods

Method	Useful Life	Depreciable Cost	Depreciation Rate	Depreciation Expense
Straight-line	Years	Cost less residual value	Straight-line rate*	Constant
Units-of-production	Total units of production	Cost less residual value	(Cost − Residual value)/Total units of production	Variable
Double-declining-balance	Years	Declining book value, but not below residual value	Straight-line rate* × 2	Declining

*Straight-line rate = (1/Useful life)

The straight-line method provides for the same periodic amounts of depreciation expense over the life of the asset. The units-of-production method provides for periodic amounts of depreciation expense that vary, depending on the amount the asset is used. The double-declining-balance method provides for a higher depreciation amount in the first year of the asset's use, followed by declining amounts.

The depreciation for the straight-line, units-of-production, and double-declining-balance methods is shown in Exhibit 7. The depreciation in Exhibit 7 is based on the

Exhibit 7

Comparing Depreciation Methods

	Depreciation Expense		
Year	Straight-Line Method	Units-of-Production Method	Double-Declining-Balance Method
1	$ 4,400*	$ 4,620 ($2.20 × 2,100 hrs)	$ 9,600.00 ($24,000 × 40%)
2	4,400	3,300 ($2.20 × 1,500 hrs.)	5,760.00 ($14,400 × 40%)
3	4,400	5,720 ($2.20 × 2,600 hrs.)	3,456.00 ($8,640 × 40%)
4	4,400	3,960 ($2.20 × 1,800 hrs.)	2,073.60 ($5,184 × 40%)
5	4,400	4,400 ($2.20 × 2,000 hrs.)	1,110.40**
Total	$22,000	$22,000	$22,000.00

*$4,400 = ($24,000 − $2,000)/5 years

**$3,110.40 − $2,000.00 because the equipment cannot be depreciated below its residual value of $2,000.

equipment purchased in our prior illustrations. For the units-of-production method, we assume that the equipment was used as follows:

Year 1	2,100 hours
Year 2	1,500
Year 3	2,600
Year 4	1,800
Year 5	2,000
Total	10,000 hours

Depreciation for Federal Income Tax

Tax Code Section 179 allows a business to deduct a portion of the cost of qualified property in the year it is placed into service.

The Internal Revenue Code uses the *Modified Accelerated Cost Recovery System (MACRS)* to compute depreciation for tax purposes. MACRS has eight classes of useful life and depreciation rates for each class. Two of the most common classes are the five-year class and the seven-year class.[4] The five-year class includes automobiles and light-duty trucks. The seven-year class includes most machinery and equipment. Depreciation for these two classes is similar to that computed using the double-declining-balance method.

In using the MACRS rates, residual value is ignored. Also, all fixed assets are assumed to be put in and taken out of service in the middle of the year. For the five-year-class assets, depreciation is spread over six years, as shown below.

Year	MACRS 5-Year-Class Depreciation Rates
1	20.0%
2	32.0
3	19.2
4	11.5
5	11.5
6	5.8
	100.0%

To simplify, a company will sometimes use MACRS for both financial statement and tax purposes. This is acceptable if MACRS does not result in significantly different amounts than would have been reported using one of the three depreciation methods discussed in this chapter.

Revising Depreciation Estimates

St. Paul Companies recently shortened the useful life of its application software at its data center.

Estimates of residual values and useful lives of fixed assets may change due to abnormal wear and tear or obsolescence. When new estimates are determined, they are used to determine the depreciation expense in future periods. The depreciation expense recorded in earlier years is not affected.[5]

To illustrate, assume the following data for a machine that was purchased on January 1, 2009.

Initial machine cost	$140,000
Expected useful life	5 years
Estimated residual value	$10,000
Annual depreciation using the straight-line method [($140,000 − $10,000)/5 years]	$26,000

4 Real estate is in either a 27½-year or a 31½-year class and is depreciated by the straight-line method.

5 *Statement of Financial Accounting Standards No. 154,* "Accounting Changes and Error Corrections" (Financial Accounting Standards Board, Norwalk, CT: 2005).

At the end of 2010, the machine's book value (undepreciated cost) is $88,000, as shown below.

Initial machine cost	$140,000
Less accumulated depreciation ($26,000 per year × 2 years)	52,000
Book value (undepreciated cost), end of second year	$ 88,000

During 2011, the company estimates that the machine's remaining useful life is eight years (instead of three) and that its residual value is $8,000 (instead of $10,000). The depreciation expense for each of the remaining eight years is $10,000, computed as follows:

Book value (undepreciated cost), end of second year	$88,000
Less revised estimated residual value	8,000
Revised remaining depreciable cost	$80,000
Revised annual depreciation expense [($88,000 − $8,000)/8 years]	$10,000

Exhibit 8 shows the book value of the asset over its original and revised lives. After the depreciation is revised at the end of 2010, book value declines at a slower rate. At the end of year 2018, the book value reaches the revised residual value of $8,000.

Exhibit 8

Book Value of Asset with Change in Estimate

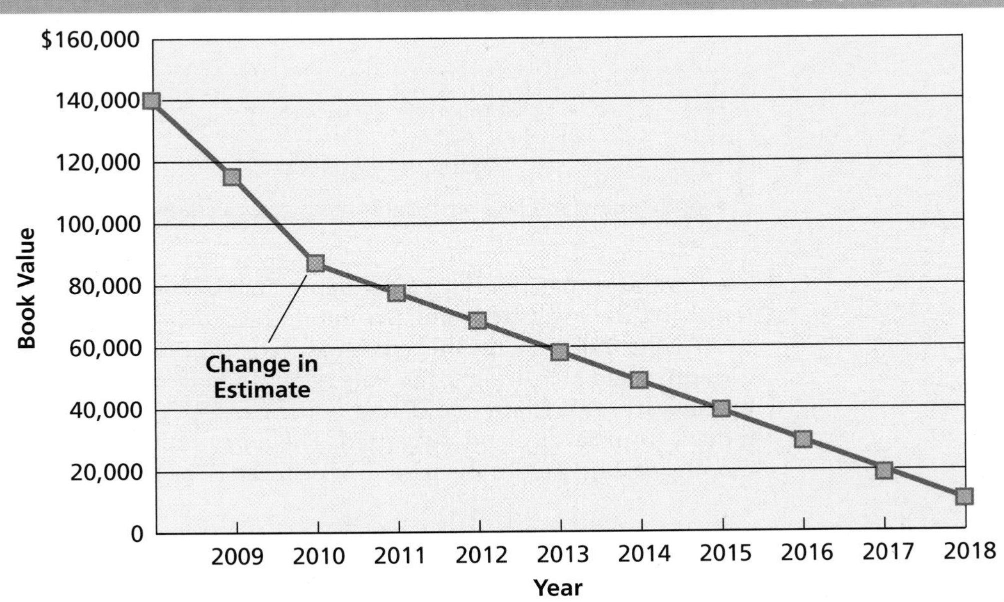

Example Exercise 10-5 Revision of Depreciation

2

A warehouse with a cost of $500,000 has an estimated residual value of $120,000, has an estimated useful life of 40 years, and is depreciated by the straight-line method. (a) Determine the amount of the annual depreciation. (b) Determine the book value at the end of the twentieth year of use. (c) Assuming that at the start of the twenty-first year the remaining life is estimated to be 25 years and the residual value is estimated to be $150,000, determine the depreciation expense for each of the remaining 25 years.

Follow My Example 10-5

a. $9,500 [($500,000 − $120,000)/40]

b. $310,000 [$500,000 − ($9,500 × 20)]

c. $6,400 [($310,000 − $150,000)/25]

For Practice: PE 10-5A, PE 10-5B

3 Journalize entries for the disposal of fixed assets.

Disposal of Fixed Assets

Fixed assets that are no longer useful may be discarded or sold.[6] In such cases, the fixed asset is removed from the accounts. Just because a fixed asset is fully depreciated, however, does not mean that it should be removed from the accounts.

The entry to record the disposal of a fixed asset removes the cost of the asset and its accumulated depreciation from the accounts.

If a fixed asset is still being used, its cost and accumulated depreciation should remain in the ledger even if the asset is fully depreciated. This maintains accountability for the asset in the ledger. If the asset was removed from the ledger, the accounts would contain no evidence of the continued existence of the asset. In addition, cost and accumulated depreciation data on such assets are often needed for property tax and income tax reports.

Discarding Fixed Assets

If a fixed asset is no longer used and has no residual value, it is discarded. For example, assume that a fixed asset that is fully depreciated and has no residual value is discarded. The entry to record the discarding removes the asset and its related accumulated depreciation from the ledger.

To illustrate, assume that equipment acquired at a cost of $25,000 is fully depreciated at December 31, 2009. On February 14, 2010, the equipment is discarded. The entry to record the discard is as follows:

Feb.	14	Accumulated Depreciation—Equipment		25,000	
		Equipment			25,000
		To write off equipment discarded.			

If an asset has not been fully depreciated, depreciation should be recorded before removing the asset from the accounting records.

To illustrate, assume that equipment costing $6,000 with no estimated residual value is depreciated at a straight-line rate of 10%. On December 31, 2009, the accumulated depreciation balance, after adjusting entries, is $4,750. On March 24, 2010, the asset is removed from service and discarded. The entry to record the depreciation for the three months of 2010 before the asset is discarded is as follows:

Mar.	24	Depreciation Expense—Equipment		150	
		Accumulated Depreciation—Equipment			150
		To record current depreciation on equipment discarded ($600 × 3/12).			

The discarding of the equipment is then recorded as follows:

Mar.	24	Accumulated Depreciation—Equipment		4,900	
		Loss on Disposal of Equipment		1,100	
		Equipment			6,000
		To write off equipment discarded.			

6 The accounting for the exchange of fixed assets is described and illustrated in Appendix 2 at the end of this chapter.

The loss of $1,100 is recorded because the balance of the accumulated depreciation account ($4,900) is less than the balance in the equipment account ($6,000). Losses on the discarding of fixed assets are nonoperating items and are normally reported in the Other expense section of the income statement.

Selling Fixed Assets

The entry to record the sale of a fixed asset is similar to the entries for discarding an asset. The only difference is that the receipt of cash is also recorded. If the selling price is more than the book value of the asset, a gain is recorded. If the selling price is less than the book value, a loss is recorded.

To illustrate, assume that equipment is purchased at a cost of $10,000 with no estimated residual value and is depreciated at a straight-line rate of 10%. The equipment is sold for cash on October 12 of the eighth year of its use. The balance of the accumulated depreciation account as of the preceding December 31 is $7,000. The entry to update the depreciation for the nine months of the current year is as follows:

Oct.	12	Depreciation Expense—Equipment		750	
		Accumulated Depreciation—Equipment			750
		To record current depreciation on			
		equipment sold ($10,000 × 9/12 × 10%).			

After the current depreciation is recorded, the book value of the asset is $2,250 ($10,000 − $7,750). The entries to record the sale, assuming three different selling prices, are as follows:

Sold at book value, for $2,250. No gain or loss.

Oct.	12	Cash		2,250	
		Accumulated Depreciation—Equipment		7,750	
		Equipment			10,000

Sold below book value, for $1,000. Loss of $1,250.

Oct.	12	Cash		1,000	
		Accumulated Depreciation—Equipment		7,750	
		Loss on Sale of Equipment		1,250	
		Equipment			10,000

Sold above book value, for $2,800. Gain of $550.

Oct.	12	Cash		2,800	
		Accumulated Depreciation—Equipment		7,750	
		Equipment			10,000
		Gain on Sale of Equipment			550

Example Exercise 10-6 Sale of Equipment 3

Equipment was acquired at the beginning of the year at a cost of $91,000. The equipment was depreciated using the straight-line method based on an estimated useful life of nine years and an estimated residual value of $10,000.

a. What was the depreciation for the first year?

b. Assuming the equipment was sold at the end of the second year for $78,000, determine the gain or loss on sale of the equipment.

c. Journalize the entry to record the sale.

Follow My Example 10-6

a. $9,000 [($91,000 – $10,000)/9]

b. $5,000 gain {$78,000 – [$91,000 – ($9,000 × 2)]}

c.

Cash	78,000	
Accumulated Depreciation—Equipment	18,000	
Equipment		91,000
Gain on Sale of Equipment		5,000

For Practice: PE 10-6A, PE 10-6B

4 Compute depletion and journalize the entry for depletion.

Natural Resources

The fixed assets of some companies include timber, metal ores, minerals, or other natural resources. As these resources are harvested or mined and then sold, a portion of their cost is debited to an expense account. This process of transferring the cost of natural resources to an expense account is called **depletion**.

Depletion is determined as follows:[7]

Step 1. Determine the depletion rate as:

$$\text{Depletion Rate} = \frac{\text{Cost of Resource}}{\text{Estimated Total Units of Resource}}$$

Step 2. Multiply the depletion rate by the quantity extracted from the resource during the period.

$$\text{Depletion Expense} = \text{Depletion Rate} \times \text{Quantity Extracted}$$

To illustrate, assume that Karst Company purchased mining rights as follows:

Cost of mineral deposit	$400,000
Estimated total units of resource	1,000,000 tons
Tons mined during year	90,000 tons

The depletion expense of $36,000 for the year is computed, as shown below.

Step 1.

$$\text{Depletion Rate} = \frac{\text{Cost of Resource}}{\text{Estimated Total Units of Resource}} = \frac{\$400{,}000}{1{,}000{,}000 \text{ Tons}} = \$0.40 \text{ per Ton}$$

Step 2.

$$\text{Depletion Expense} = \$0.40 \text{ per Ton} \times 90{,}000 \text{ Tons} = \$36{,}000$$

7 We assume that there is no significant residual value left after all the natural resource is extracted.

The adjusting entry to record the depletion is shown below.

Dec.	31	Depletion Expense Accumulated Depletion Depletion of mineral deposit.		36,000	36,000

Like the accumulated depreciation account, Accumulated Depletion is a *contra asset* account. It is reported on the balance sheet as a deduction from the cost of the mineral deposit.

Example Exercise 10-7 Depletion

4

Earth's Treasures Mining Co. acquired mineral rights for $45,000,000. The mineral deposit is estimated at 50,000,000 tons. During the current year, 12,600,000 tons were mined and sold.

a. Determine the depletion rate.
b. Determine the amount of depletion expense for the current year.
c. Journalize the adjusting entry on December 31 to recognize the depletion expense.

Follow My Example 10-7

a. $0.90 per ton ($45,000,000/50,000,000 tons)
b. $11,340,000 (12,600,000 tons × $0.90 per ton)
c.

Dec. 31	Depletion Expense	11,340,000	
	Accumulated Depletion.		11,340,000
	Depletion of mineral deposit.		

For Practice: PE 10-7A, PE 10-7B

Describe the accounting for intangible assets, such as patents, copyrights, and goodwill.

Intangible Assets

Patents, copyrights, trademarks, and goodwill are long-lived assets that are used in the operations of a business and are not held for sale. These assets are called **intangible assets** because they do not exist physically.

The accounting for intangible assets is similar to that for fixed assets. The major issues are:

1. Determining the initial cost.
2. Determining the **amortization**, which is the amount of cost to transfer to expense.

Amortization results from the passage of time or a decline in the usefulness of the intangible asset.

Patents

Manufacturers may acquire exclusive rights to produce and sell goods with one or more unique features. Such rights are granted by **patents,** which the federal government issues to inventors. These rights continue in effect for 20 years. A business may purchase patent rights from others, or it may obtain patents developed by its own research and development.

The initial cost of a purchased patent, including any legal fees, is debited to an asset account. This cost is written off, or amortized, over the years of the patent's expected useful life. The expected useful life of a patent may be less than its legal life. For example, a patent may become worthless due to changing technology or consumer tastes.

Apple Computer, Inc., amortizes intangible assets over 3–10 years.

Patent amortization is normally computed using the straight-line method. The amortization is recorded by debiting an amortization expense account and crediting the patents account. A separate contra asset account is usually *not* used for intangible assets.

To illustrate, assume that at the beginning of its fiscal year, a company acquires patent rights for $100,000. Although the patent will not expire for 14 years, its remaining useful life is estimated as five years. The adjusting entry to amortize the patent at the end of the year is as follows:

Dec.	31	Amortization Expense—Patents		20,000	
		Patents			20,000
		Patent amortization ($100,000/5).			

Some companies develop their own patents through research and development. In such cases, any *research and development costs* are usually recorded as current operating expenses in the period in which they are incurred. This accounting for research and development costs is justified on the basis that any future benefits from research and development are highly uncertain.

Sony Corporation of America amortizes its artist contracts and music catalogs over 16 years and 21 years.

Coke® is one of the world's most recognizable trademarks. As stated in *LIFE*, "Two-thirds of the earth is covered by water; the rest is covered by Coke. If the French are known for wine and the Germans for beer, America achieved global beverage dominance with fizzy water and caramel color."

Copyrights and Trademarks

The exclusive right to publish and sell a literary, artistic, or musical composition is granted by a **copyright**. Copyrights are issued by the federal government and extend for 70 years beyond the author's death. The costs of a copyright include all costs of creating the work plus any other costs of obtaining the copyright. A copyright that is purchased is recorded at the price paid for it. Copyrights are amortized over their estimated useful lives.

A **trademark** is a name, term, or symbol used to identify a business and its products. Most businesses identify their trademarks with ® in their advertisements and on their products.

Under federal law, businesses can protect their trademarks by registering them for 10 years and renewing the registration for 10-year periods. Like a copyright, the legal costs of registering a trademark are recorded as an asset.

If a trademark is purchased from another business, its cost is recorded as an asset. In such cases, the cost of the trademark is considered to have an indefinite useful life. Thus, trademarks are not amortized. Instead, trademarks are reviewed periodically for impaired value. When a trademark is impaired, the trademark should be written down and a loss recognized.

Integrity, Objectivity, and Ethics in Business

21ST CENTURY PIRATES

Pirated software is a major concern of software companies. For example, during a recent global sweep, Microsoft Corporation seized nearly 5 million units of counterfeit Microsoft software with an estimated retail value of $1.7 billion. U.S. copyright laws and practices are sometimes ignored or disputed in other parts of the world.

Businesses must honor the copyrights held by software companies by eliminating pirated software from corporate computers. The Business Software Alliance (BSA) represents the largest software companies in campaigns to investigate illegal use of unlicensed software by businesses. The BSA estimates software industry losses of nearly $12 billion annually from software piracy. Employees using pirated software on business assets risk bringing legal penalties to themselves and their employers.

eBay recorded an impairment of $1.39 billion in the goodwill created from its purchase of Skype.

Goodwill

Goodwill refers to an intangible asset of a business that is created from such favorable factors as location, product quality, reputation, and managerial skill. Goodwill allows a business to earn a greater rate of return than normal.

Generally accepted accounting principles (GAAP) allow goodwill to be recorded only if it is objectively determined by a transaction. An example of such a transaction is the purchase of a business at a price in excess of the fair value of its net assets (assets − liabilities). The excess is recorded as goodwill and reported as an intangible asset.

Unlike patents and copyrights, goodwill is not amortized. However, a loss should be recorded if the future prospects of the purchased firm become impaired. This loss would normally be disclosed in the Other expense section of the income statement.

To illustrate, assume that on December 31 FaceCard Company has determined that $250,000 of the goodwill created from the purchase of electronic Systems is impaired. The entry to record the impairment is as follows:

Dec.	31	Loss from Impaired Goodwill		250,000	
		Goodwill			250,000
		Impaired goodwill.			

Exhibit 9 shows intangible asset disclosures for 600 large firms. Goodwill is the most often reported intangible asset. This is because goodwill arises from merger transactions, which are common.

Exhibit 9

Frequency of Intangible Asset Disclosures for 600 Firms

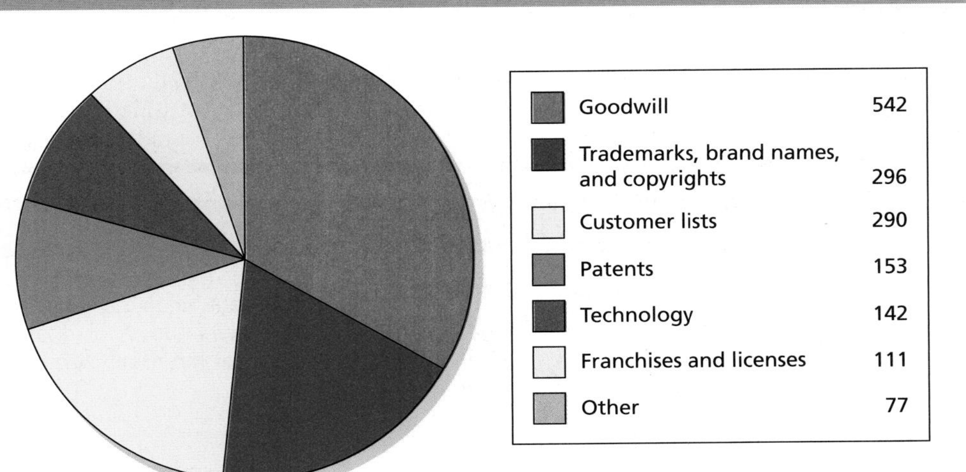

Source: *Accounting Trends & Techniques*, 61st ed., American Institute of Certified Public Accountants, New York, 2007.
Note: Some firms have multiple disclosures.

Exhibit 10 summarizes the characteristics of intangible assets.

Exhibit 10

Comparison of Intangible Assets

Intangible Asset	Description	Amortization Period	Periodic Expense
Patent	Exclusive right to benefit from an innovation.	Estimated useful life not to exceed legal life.	Amortization expense.
Copyright	Exclusive right to benefit from a literary, artistic, or musical composition.	Estimated useful life not to exceed legal life.	Amortization expense.
Trademark	Exclusive use of a name, term, or symbol.	None	Impairment loss if fair value less than carrying value (impaired).
Goodwill	Excess of purchase price of a business over the fair value of its net assets (assets − liabilities).	None	Impairment loss if fair value less than carrying value (impaired).

Example Exercise 10-8 Impaired Goodwill and Amortization of Patent

On December 31, it was estimated that goodwill of $40,000 was impaired. In addition, a patent with an estimated useful economic life of 12 years was acquired for $84,000 on July 1.

a. Journalize the adjusting entry on December 31 for the impaired goodwill.
b. Journalize the adjusting entry on December 31 for the amortization of the patent rights.

Follow My Example 10-8

a. Dec. 31	Loss from Impaired Goodwill	40,000	
	Goodwill		40,000
	Impaired goodwill.		
b. Dec. 31	Amortization Expense—Patents	3,500	
	Patents		3,500
	Amortized patent rights [($84,000/12) × (6/12)].		

For Practice: PE 10-8A, PE 10-8B

Integrity, Objectivity, and Ethics in Business

WHEN DOES GOODWILL BECOME WORTHLESS?

The timing and amount of goodwill write-offs can be very subjective. Managers and their accountants should fairly estimate the value of goodwill and record goodwill impairment when it occurs. It would be unethical to delay a write-down of goodwill when it is determined that the asset is impaired.

6 Describe how depreciation expense is reported in an income statement and prepare a balance sheet that includes fixed assets and intangible assets.

Financial Reporting for Fixed Assets and Intangible Assets

In the income statement, depreciation and amortization expense should be reported separately or disclosed in a note. A description of the methods used in computing depreciation should also be reported.

In the balance sheet, each class of fixed assets should be disclosed on the face of the statement or in the notes. The related accumulated depreciation should also be disclosed, either by class or in total. The fixed assets may be shown at their *book value* (cost less accumulated depreciation), which can also be described as their *net* amount.

If there are many classes of fixed assets, a single amount may be presented in the balance sheet, supported by a note with a separate listing. Fixed assets may be reported under the more descriptive caption of property, plant, and equipment.

Intangible assets are usually reported in the balance sheet in a separate section following fixed assets. The balance of each class of intangible assets should be disclosed net of any amortization.

The balance sheet presentation for Mornin' Joe's fixed and intangible assets is shown below.

Mornin' Joe
Balance Sheet
December 31, 2010

Property, plant, and equipment:			
Land		$1,850,000	
Buildings	$2,650,000		
Less accumulated depreciation	420,000	2,230,000	
Office equipment	$ 350,000		
Less accumulated depreciation	102,000	248,000	
Total property, plant, and equipment			$4,328,000
Intangible assets:			
Patents			140,000

The cost and related accumulated depletion of mineral rights are normally shown as part of the Fixed Assets section of the balance sheet. The mineral rights may be shown net of depletion on the face of the balance sheet. In such cases, a supporting note discloses the accumulated depletion.

Business Connection

HUB-AND-SPOKE OR POINT-TO-POINT?

Southwest Airlines Co. uses a simple fare structure, featuring low, unrestricted, unlimited, everyday coach fares. These fares are made possible by Southwest's use of a point-to-point, rather than a hub-and-spoke, business approach. United Airlines, Inc., Delta Air Lines, and American Airlines employ a hub-and-spoke approach in which an airline establishes major hubs that serve as connecting links to other cities. For example, Delta has established major connecting hubs in Atlanta, Cincinnati, and Salt Lake City. In contrast, Southwest focuses on point-to-point service between selected cities with over 400 one-way, nonstop city pairs with an average length of just over 600 miles and average flying time of 1.8 hours. As a result, Southwest minimizes connections, delays, and total trip time. Southwest also focuses on serving conveniently located satellite or downtown airports, such as Dallas Love Field, Houston Hobby, and Chicago Midway. Because these airports are normally less congested than hub airports, Southwest is better able to maintain high employee productivity and reliable on-time performance. This operating approach permits the company to achieve high utilization of its fixed assets, such as its 737 aircraft. For example, aircraft are scheduled to minimize time spent at the gate, thereby reducing the number of aircraft and gate facilities that would otherwise be required.

© AP Photo/Matt Slocum

Financial Analysis and Interpretation

Fixed assets can be evaluated by their ability to generate revenue. One measure of the revenue-generating ability of fixed assets is the fixed asset turnover ratio. The **fixed asset turnover ratio** measures the number of dollars of revenue earned per dollar of fixed assets and is computed as follows:

$$\text{Fixed Asset Turnover Ratio} = \frac{\text{Revenue}}{\text{Average Book Value of Fixed Assets}}$$

To illustrate, the following fixed asset balance sheet information is used for Marriott International, Inc.:

	December 29, 2006 (in millions)	December 30, 2005 (in millions)
Property and equipment (net)	$1,238	$2,341

Marriott reported revenue of $12,160 million for 2006. Thus, the fixed asset turnover ratio is calculated as follows:

$$\text{Fixed Asset Turnover Ratio} = \frac{\$12{,}160}{(1{,}238 + 2{,}341)/2} = 6.80$$

For every dollar of fixed assets, Marriott earns $6.80 of revenue. The larger this ratio, the more efficiently a business is using its fixed assets. This ratio can be compared across time within a single firm or to other companies in the industry to evaluate overall fixed asset turnover performance.

The fixed asset turnover ratio for a number of different companies is shown below. The smaller ratios are associated with companies that require large fixed asset investments. The larger fixed asset turnover ratios are associated with firms that are more labor-intensive and require smaller fixed asset investments.

Company (industry)	Fixed Asset Turnover Ratio
Comcast Corporation (cable)	1.25
Google (Internet)	6.32
Manpower Inc. (temporary employment)	88.14
Norfolk Southern Corporation (railroad)	0.45
Ruby Tuesday, Inc. (restaurant)	1.40
Southwest Airlines Co. (airline)	0.93

APPENDIX 1

Sum-of-the-Years-Digits Depreciation

A recent edition of *Accounting Trends & Techniques* reported that only 1%–2% of the surveyed companies now use this method for financial reporting purposes.

Under the *sum-of-the-years-digits method,* depreciation expense is determined by multiplying the original cost of the asset less its estimated residual value by a smaller fraction each year. Thus, the sum-of-the-years-digits method is similar to the double-declining-balance method in that the depreciation expense declines each year.

The denominator of the fraction used in determining the depreciation expense is the sum of the digits of the years of the asset's useful life. For example, an asset with a useful life of five years would have a denominator of 15 (5 + 4 + 3 + 2 + 1). The denominator can also be determined using the following formula where N is the useful life of the assest:

$$\text{Sum of Years of Useful Life} = \frac{N(N + 1)}{2} = \frac{5(5 + 1)}{2} = 15$$

The numerator of the fraction is the number of years of useful life remaining at the beginning of each year for which depreciation is being computed. Thus, the numerator decreases each year by 1. For a useful life of five years, the numerator is 5 the first year, 4 the second year, 3 the third year, and so on.

To illustrate, the equipment example from the illustrations for the straight-line, units-of-production, and double-declining-balance methods is used. This equipment was purchased on January 1 as follows:

Initial cost	$24,000
Expected useful life	5 years
Estimated residual value	$2,000

Using the sum-of-the-years-digits method, the depreciation is computed as shown below.

Year	Cost Less Residual Value	Rate	Depreciation for Year	Acc. Dep. at End of Year	Book Value at End of Year
1	$22,000	$^5/_{15}$	$7,333.33	$ 7,333.33	$16,666.67
2	22,000	$^4/_{15}$	5,866.67	13,200.00	10,800.00
3	22,000	$^3/_{15}$	4,400.00	17,600.00	6,400.00
4	22,000	$^2/_{15}$	2,933.33	20,533.33	3,466.67
5	22,000	$^1/_{15}$	1,466.67	22,000.00	2,000.00

If an asset is used for only part of a year, the annual depreciation is prorated. For example, assume that the preceding equipment was purchased and placed into service on October 1. The depreciation for the year ending December 31 would be **$1,833.33**, computed as follows:

First-Year Partial Depreciation = $7,333.33 × 3/12 = $1,833 .33

The depreciation for the second year would then be $6,966.67, computed as follows:

Second-Year Depreciation = ($^9/_{12}$ × $^5/_{15}$ × $22,000) + ($^3/_{12}$ × $^4/_{15}$ × $22,000)

Second-Year Depreciation = $5,500.00 + $1,466.67 = $6,966.67

At one time, the sum-of-the-years-digits method of depreciation was widely used. However, MACRS and current tax law changes have limited its use.

APPENDIX 2

Exchanging Similar Fixed Assets

Old equipment is often traded in for new equipment having a similar use. In such cases, the seller allows the buyer an amount for the old equipment traded in. This amount, called the **trade-in allowance**, may be either greater or less than the book value of the old equipment. The remaining balance—the amount owed—is either paid in cash or recorded as a liability. It is normally called **boot**, which is its tax name.

Accounting for the exchange of similar assets depends on whether the transaction has *commercial substance*.[9] An exchange has commercial substance if future cash flows change as a result of the exchange. If an exchange of similar assets has commercial substance, a gain or loss is recognized based on the difference between the book value of the asset given up (exchanged) and the fair market value of the asset received. In such cases, the exchange is accounted for similar to that of a sale of a fixed asset.

9 *Statement of Financial Accounting Standards No. 153*, "Exchanges of Nonmonetary Assets" (Financial Accounting Standards Board, Norwalk, CT: 2004).

Gain on Exchange

To illustrate a gain on an exchange of similar assets, assume the following:

Similar equipment acquired (new):	
Price (fair market value) of new equipment	$5,000
Trade-in allowance on old equipment	1,100
Cash paid at June 19, date of exchange	$3,900
Equipment traded in (old):	
Cost of old equipment	$4,000
Accumulated depreciation at date of exchange	3,200
Book value at June 19, date of exchange	$ 800

The entry to record this exchange and payment of cash is as follows:

June 19	Accumulated Depreciation—Equipment	3,200	
	Equipment (new equipment)	5,000	
	Equipment (old equipment)		4,000
	Cash		3,900
	Gain on Exchange of Equipment		300

The gain on the exchange, $300, is the difference between the fair market value of the new asset of $5,000 and the book value of the old asset traded in of $800 plus the cash paid of $3,900 as shown below.

Price (fair market value) of new equipment		$5,000
Less assets given up in exchange:		
Book value of old equipment ($4,000 – $3,200)	$ 800	
Cash paid on the exchange	3,900	4,700
Gain on exchange of assets		$ 300

Loss on Exchange

To illustrate a loss on an exchange of similar assets, assume that instead of a trade-in allowance of $1,100, a trade-in allowance of only $675 was allowed in the preceding example. In this case, the cash paid on the exchange is $4,325 as shown below.

Price (fair market value) of new equipment	$5,000
Trade-in allowance of old equipment	675
Cash paid at June 19, date of exchange	$4,325

The entry to record this exchange and payment of cash is as follows:

June 19	Accumulated Depreciation—Equipment	3,200	
	Equipment (new equipment)	5,000	
	Loss on Exchange of Equipment	125	
	Equipment (old equipment)		4,000
	Cash		4,325

The loss on the exchange, $125, is the difference between the fair market value of the new asset of $5,000 and the book value of the old asset traded in of $800 plus the cash paid of $4,325 as shown below.

Price (fair market value) of new equipment		$5,000
Less assets given up in exchange:		
Book value of old equipment ($4,000 – $3,200)	$ 800	
Cash paid on the exchange	4,325	5,125
Loss on exchange of assets		$ (125)

In those cases where an asset exchange *lacks commercial substance*, no gain is recognized on the exchange. Instead, the cost of the new asset is adjusted for any gain. For example, in the first illustration, the gain of $300 would be subtracted from the purchase price of $5,000 and the new asset would be recorded at $4,700. Accounting for the exchange of assets that lack commercial substance is discussed in more advanced accounting texts.[10]

10 The exchange of similar assets also involves complex tax issues that are discussed in advanced accounting courses.

1 Define, classify, and account for the cost of fixed assets.

Key Points	Key Learning Outcomes	Example Exercises	Practice Exercises
Fixed assets are long-term tangible assets that are owned by the business and are used in the normal operations of the business such as equipment, buildings, and land. The initial cost of a fixed asset includes all amounts spent to get the asset in place and ready for use. Once an asset is placed into service, revenue and capital expenditures may be incurred. Revenue expenditures include ordinary repairs and maintenance. Capital expenditures include asset improvements and extraordinary repairs. Fixed assets may also be leased and accounted for as capital or operating leases.	• Define *fixed assets.*		
	• List types of costs that should and should not be included in the cost of a fixed asset.		
	• Provide examples of ordinary repairs, asset improvements, and extraordinary repairs.		
	• Prepare journal entries for ordinary repairs, asset improvements, and extraordinary repairs.	**10-1**	10-1A, 10-1B

2 Compute depreciation, using the following methods: straight-line method, units-of-production method, and double-declining-balance method.

Key Points	Key Learning Outcomes	Example Exercises	Practice Exercises
All fixed assets except land lose their ability to provide services and should be depreciated over time. Three factors are considered in determining depreciation: (1) the fixed asset's initial cost, (2) the useful life of the asset, and (3) the residual value of the asset.	• Define and describe *depreciation.*		
	• List the factors used in determining depreciation.		
The straight-line method spreads the initial cost less the residual value equally over the useful life. The units-of-production method spreads the initial cost less the residual value equally over the units expected to be produced by the asset during its useful life. The double-declining-balance method is applied by multiplying the declining book value of the asset by twice the straight-line rate.	• Compute straight-line depreciation.	**10-2**	10-2A, 10-2B
	• Compute units-of-production depreciation.	**10-3**	10-3A, 10-3B
	• Compute double-declining-balance depreciation.	**10-4**	10-4A, 10-4B
Depreciation may be revised for changes in an asset's useful life or residual value. Such changes affect future depreciation.	• Compute revised depreciation for a change in an asset's useful life and residual value.	**10-5**	10-5A, 10-5B

3 Journalize entries for the disposal of fixed assets.

Key Points	Key Learning Outcomes	Example Exercises	Practice Exercises
To record disposals of fixed assets, any depreciation for the current period should be recorded, and the book value of the asset is then removed from the accounts. For assets discarded from service, a loss may be recorded for any remaining book value of the asset.	• Prepare the journal entry for discarding a fixed asset.		
When a fixed asset is sold, the book value is removed, and the cash or other asset received is recorded. If the selling price is more than the book value of the asset, the transaction results in a gain. If the selling price is less than the book value, there is a loss.	• Prepare journal entries for the sale of a fixed asset.	**10-6**	10-6A, 10-6B

4 Compute depletion and journalize the entry for depletion.

Key Points	Key Learning Outcomes	Example Exercises	Practice Exercises
The amount of periodic depletion is computed by multiplying the quantity of minerals extracted during the period by a depletion rate. The depletion rate is computed by dividing the cost of the mineral deposit by its estimated total units of resource. The entry to record depletion debits a depletion expense account and credits an accumulated depletion account.	• Define and describe *depletion.*		
	• Compute a depletion rate.	**10-7**	10-7A, 10-7B
	• Prepare the journal entry to record depletion.	**10-7**	10-7A, 10-7B

5 Describe the accounting for intangible assets, such as patents, copyrights, and goodwill.

Key Points	Key Learning Outcomes	Example Exercises	Practice Exercises
Long-term assets such as patents, copyrights, trademarks, and goodwill that are without physical attributes but are used in the business are intangible assets. The initial cost of an intangible asset should be debited to an asset account. The cost of patents and copyrights should be amortized over the years of the asset's expected usefulness by debiting an expense account and crediting the intangible asset account. Trademarks and goodwill are not amortized, but are written down only upon impairment.	• Define, describe, and provide examples of intangible assets.		
	• Prepare a journal entry for the purchase of an intangible asset.		
	• Prepare a journal entry to amortize the costs of patents and copyrights.	**10-8**	10-8A, 10-8B
	• Prepare the journal entry to record the impairment of goodwill.	**10-8**	10-8A, 10-8B

6 **Describe how depreciation expense is reported in an income statement and prepare a balance sheet that includes fixed assets and intangible assets.**

Key Points	Key Learning Outcomes	Example Exercises	Practice Exercises
The amount of depreciation expense and the method or methods used in computing depreciation should be disclosed in the financial statements. In addition, each major class of fixed assets should be disclosed, along with the related accumulated depreciation. Intangible assets are usually presented in the balance sheet in a separate section immediately following fixed assets. Each major class of intangible assets should be disclosed at an amount net of the amortization recorded to date.	• Describe and illustrate how fixed assets are reported in the income statement and balance sheet. • Describe and illustrate how intangible assets are reported in the income statement and balance sheet.		

Key Terms

accelerated depreciation method (450)
amortization (457)
book value (450)
boot (463)
capital expenditures (444)
capital lease (446)
copyright (458)
depletion (456)
depreciation (446)
double-declining-balance method (450)
fixed asset turnover ratio (462)
fixed assets (441)
goodwill (459)
intangible assets (457)
operating lease (446)
patents (457)
residual value (447)
revenue expenditures (444)
straight-line method (448)
trade-in allowance (463)
trademark (458)
units-of-production method (449)

Illustrative Problem

McCollum Company, a furniture wholesaler, acquired new equipment at a cost of $150,000 at the beginning of the fiscal year. The equipment has an estimated life of five years and an estimated residual value of $12,000. Ellen McCollum, the president, has requested information regarding alternative depreciation methods.

Instructions

1. Determine the annual depreciation for each of the five years of estimated useful life of the equipment, the accumulated depreciation at the end of each year, and the book value of the equipment at the end of each year by (a) the straight-line method and (b) the double-declining-balance method.
2. Assume that the equipment was depreciated under the double-declining-balance method. In the first week of the fifth year, the equipment was sold for $10,000. Journalize the entry to record the sale.

Solution

1.

	Year	Depreciation Expense	Accumulated Depreciation, End of Year	Book Value, End of Year
a.	1	$27,600*	$ 27,600	$122,400
	2	27,600	55,200	94,800
	3	27,600	82,800	67,200
	4	27,600	110,400	39,600
	5	27,600	138,000	12,000

*$27,600 = ($150,000 − $12,000) ÷ 5

	Year	Depreciation Expense	Accumulated Depreciation, End of Year	Book Value, End of Year
b.	1	$60,000**	$ 60,000	$ 90,000
	2	36,000	96,000	54,000
	3	21,600	117,600	32,400
	4	12,960	130,560	19,440
	5	7,440***	138,000	12,000

**$60,000 = $150,000 × 40%

***The asset is not depreciated below the estimated residual value of $12,000.
$7,440 = $150,000 − $130,560 − $12,000

	Cash		10,000	
	Accumulated Depreciation—Equipment		130,560	
	Loss on Sale of Equipment		9,440	
	Equipment			150,000

Self-Examination Questions (Answers at End of Chapter)

1. Which of the following expenditures incurred in connection with acquiring machinery is a proper charge to the asset account?
   A. Freight
   B. Installation costs
   C. Both A and B
   D. Neither A nor B
2. What is the amount of depreciation, using the double-declining-balance method for the second year of use for equipment costing $9,000, with an estimated residual value of $600 and an estimated life of three years?
   A. $6,000
   B. $3,000
   C. $2,000
   D. $400
3. An example of an accelerated depreciation method is:
   A. straight-line.
   B. double-declining-balance.
   C. units-of-production.
   D. depletion.
4. Equipment purchased on January 3, 2008, for $80,000 was depreciated using the straight-line method based upon a 5-year life and $7,500 residual value. The equipment was sold on December 31, 2010, for $40,000. What is the gain on the sale of the equipment?
   A. $3,500
   B. $14,500
   C. $36,500
   D. $43,500
5. Which of the following is an example of an intangible asset?
   A. Patents
   B. Goodwill
   C. Copyrights
   D. All of the above

Eye Openers

1. Which of the following qualities are characteristic of fixed assets? (a) tangible, (b) capable of repeated use in the operations of the business, (c) held for sale in the normal course of business, (d) used rarely in the operations of the business, (e) long-lived.
2. Mancini Office Supplies has a fleet of automobiles and trucks for use by salespersons and for delivery of office supplies and equipment. East Village Auto Sales Co. has automobiles and trucks for sale. Under what caption would the automobiles and trucks be reported in the balance sheet of (a) Mancini Office Supplies, (b) East Village Auto Sales Co.?
3. Just Animals Co. acquired an adjacent vacant lot with the hope of selling it in the future at a gain. The lot is not intended to be used in Just Animals' business operations. Where should such real estate be listed in the balance sheet?
4. My Mother's Closet Company solicited bids from several contractors to construct an addition to its office building. The lowest bid received was for $375,000. My Mother's Closet Company decided to construct the addition itself at a cost of $298,500. What amount should be recorded in the building account?
5. Distinguish between the accounting for capital expenditures and revenue expenditures.
6. Immediately after a used truck is acquired, a new motor is installed at a total cost of $3,175. Is this a capital expenditure or a revenue expenditure?
7. How does the accounting for a capital lease differ from the accounting for an operating lease?
8. Are the amounts at which fixed assets are reported in the balance sheet their approximate market values as of the balance sheet date? Discuss.
9. a. Does the recognition of depreciation in the accounts provide a special cash fund for the replacement of fixed assets? Explain.
   b. Describe the nature of depreciation as the term is used in accounting.
10. Pac Vac Company purchased a machine that has a manufacturer's suggested life of 15 years. The company plans to use the machine on a special project that will last 12 years. At the completion of the project, the machine will be sold. Over how many years should the machine be depreciated?
11. Is it necessary for a business to use the same method of computing depreciation (a) for all classes of its depreciable assets, (b) for financial statement purposes and in determining income taxes?
12. a. Under what conditions is the use of an accelerated depreciation method most appropriate?
    b. Why is an accelerated depreciation method often used for income tax purposes?
    c. What is the Modified Accelerated Cost Recovery System (MACRS), and under what conditions is it used?
13. A company revised the estimated useful lives of its fixed assets, which resulted in an increase in the remaining lives of several assets. Can the company include, as income of the current period, the cumulative effect of the changes, which reduces the depreciation expense of past periods? Discuss.
14. For some of the fixed assets of a business, the balance in Accumulated Depreciation is exactly equal to the cost of the asset. (a) Is it permissible to record additional depreciation on the assets if they are still useful to the business? Explain. (b) When should an entry be made to remove the cost and the accumulated depreciation from the accounts?
15. a. Over what period of time should the cost of a patent acquired by purchase be amortized?
    b. In general, what is the required accounting treatment for research and development costs?
    c. How should goodwill be amortized?

Practice Exercises

PE 10-1A
Capital and revenue expenditures
obj. 1
EE 10-1 p. 445

On May 27, Linoleum Associates Co. paid $950 to repair the transmission on one of its delivery vans. In addition, Linoleum Associates paid $450 to install a GPS system in its van. Journalize the entries for the transmission and GPS system expenditures.

PE 10-1B
Capital and revenue expenditures
obj. 1
EE 10-1 p. 445

On October 9, Wonder Inflatables Co. paid $1,150 to install a hydraulic lift and $40 for an air filter for one of its delivery trucks. Journalize the entries for the new lift and air filter expenditures.

PE 10-2A
Straight-line depreciation
obj. 2
EE 10-2 p. 449

A building acquired at the beginning of the year at a cost of $485,000 has an estimated residual value of $75,000 and an estimated useful life of 25 years. Determine (a) the depreciable cost, (b) the straight-line rate, and (c) the annual straight-line depreciation.

PE 10-2B
Straight-line depreciation
obj. 2
EE 10-2 p. 449

Equipment acquired at the beginning of the year at a cost of $125,000 has an estimated residual value of $5,000 and an estimated useful life of eight years. Determine (a) the depreciable cost, (b) the straight-line rate, and (c) the annual straight-line depreciation.

PE 10-3A
Units-of-production depreciation
obj. 2
EE 10-3 p. 449

A truck acquired at a cost of $134,000 has an estimated residual value of $35,000, has an estimated useful life of 300,000 miles, and was driven 52,000 miles during the year. Determine (a) the depreciable cost, (b) the depreciation rate, and (c) the units-of-production depreciation for the year.

PE 10-3B
Units-of-production depreciation
obj. 2
EE 10-3 p. 449

A tractor acquired at a cost of $95,000 has an estimated residual value of $15,000, has an estimated useful life of 40,000 hours, and was operated 5,100 hours during the year. Determine (a) the depreciable cost, (b) the depreciation rate, and (c) the units-of-production depreciation for the year.

PE 10-4A
Double-declining-balance depreciation
obj. 2
EE 10-4 p. 450

A building acquired at the beginning of the year at a cost of $650,000 has an estimated residual value of $125,000 and an estimated useful life of 40 years. Determine (a) the double-declining-balance rate and (b) the double-declining-balance depreciation for the first year.

PE 10-4B
Double-declining-balance depreciation
obj. 2
EE 10-4 p. 450

Equipment acquired at the beginning of the year at a cost of $145,000 has an estimated residual value of $18,000 and an estimated useful life of five years. Determine (a) the double-declining-balance rate and (b) the double-declining-balance depreciation for the first year.

PE 10-5A
Revision of depreciation
obj. 2
EE 10-5 p. 453

Equipment with a cost of $250,000 has an estimated residual value of $34,000, has an estimated useful life of 18 years, and is depreciated by the straight-line method. (a) Determine the amount of the annual depreciation. (b) Determine the book value at the end of the tenth year of use. (c) Assuming that at the start of the eleventh year the remaining life is estimated to be eight years and the residual value is estimated to be $6,000, determine the depreciation expense for each of the remaining eight years.

PE 10-5B
Revision of depreciation
obj. 2
EE 10-5 p. 453

A truck with a cost of $80,000 has an estimated residual value of $15,000, has an estimated useful life of eight years, and is depreciated by the straight-line method. (a) Determine the amount of the annual depreciation. (b) Determine the book value at the end of the fourth year of use. (c) Assuming that at the start of the fifth year the remaining life is estimated to be five years and the residual value is estimated to be $10,000, determine the depreciation expense for each of the remaining five years.

PE 10-6A
Sale of equipment
obj. 3
EE 10-6 p. 456

Equipment was acquired at the beginning of the year at a cost of $324,000. The equipment was depreciated using the double-declining-balance method based on an estimated useful life of eight years and an estimated residual value of $43,000.

a. What was the depreciation for the first year?
b. Assuming the equipment was sold at the end of the second year for $200,000, determine the gain or loss on the sale of the equipment.
c. Journalize the entry to record the sale.

PE 10-6B
Sale of equipment
obj. 3
EE 10-6 p. 456

Equipment was acquired at the beginning of the year at a cost of $160,000. The equipment was depreciated using the straight-line method based on an estimated useful life of 15 years and an estimated residual value of $17,500.

a. What was the depreciation for the first year?
b. Assuming the equipment was sold at the end of the sixth year for $90,000, determine the gain or loss on the sale of the equipment.
c. Journalize the entry to record the sale.

PE 10-7A
Depletion
obj. 4
EE 10-7 p. 457

Montana Mining Co. acquired mineral rights for $120,000,000. The mineral deposit is estimated at 200,000,000 tons. During the current year, 31,155,000 tons were mined and sold.

a. Determine the depletion rate.
b. Determine the amount of depletion expense for the current year.
c. Journalize the adjusting entry on December 31 to recognize the depletion expense.

PE 10-7B
Depletion
obj. 4
EE 10-7 p. 457

Cooke City Mining Co. acquired mineral rights for $50,000,000. The mineral deposit is estimated at 125,000,000 tons. During the current year, 42,385,000 tons were mined and sold.

a. Determine the depletion rate.
b. Determine the amount of depletion expense for the current year.
c. Journalize the adjusting entry on December 31 to recognize the depletion expense.

PE 10-8A
Impaired goodwill and amortization of patent
obj. 5
EE 10-8 p. 460

On December 31, it was estimated that goodwill of $500,000 was impaired. In addition, a patent with an estimated useful economic life of eight years was acquired for $388,000 on July 1.

a. Journalize the adjusting entry on December 31 for the impaired goodwill.
b. Journalize the adjusting entry on December 31 for the amortization of the patent rights.

PE 10-8B
Impaired goodwill and amortization of patent
obj. 5
EE 10-8 p. 460

On December 31, it was estimated that goodwill of $875,000 was impaired. In addition, a patent with an estimated useful economic life of 17 years was acquired for $425,000 on April 1.

a. Journalize the adjusting entry on December 31 for the impaired goodwill.
b. Journalize the adjusting entry on December 31 for the amortization of the patent rights.

Exercises

EX 10-1
Costs of acquiring fixed assets
obj. 1

Catherine Simpkins owns and operates Speedy Print Co. During February, Speedy Print Co. incurred the following costs in acquiring two printing presses. One printing press was new, and the other was used by a business that recently filed for bankruptcy.

Costs related to new printing press:

1. Sales tax on purchase price
2. Freight
3. Special foundation
4. Insurance while in transit
5. New parts to replace those damaged in unloading
6. Fee paid to factory representative for installation

Costs related to used printing press:

7. Fees paid to attorney to review purchase agreement
8. Freight
9. Installation
10. Repair of vandalism during installation
11. Replacement of worn-out parts
12. Repair of damage incurred in reconditioning the press

a. Indicate which costs incurred in acquiring the new printing press should be debited to the asset account.
b. Indicate which costs incurred in acquiring the used printing press should be debited to the asset account.

EX 10-2
Determine cost of land
obj. 1

Bridger Ski Co. has developed a tract of land into a ski resort. The company has cut the trees, cleared and graded the land and hills, and constructed ski lifts. (a) Should the tree cutting, land clearing, and grading costs of constructing the ski slopes be debited to the land account? (b) If such costs are debited to Land, should they be depreciated?

EX 10-3
Determine cost of land
obj. 1
✔ $327,425

Fastball Delivery Company acquired an adjacent lot to construct a new warehouse, paying $30,000 and giving a short-term note for $270,000. Legal fees paid were $1,425, delinquent taxes assumed were $12,000, and fees paid to remove an old building from the land were $18,500. Materials salvaged from the demolition of the building were sold for $4,500. A contractor was paid $910,000 to construct a new warehouse. Determine the cost of the land to be reported on the balance sheet.

EX 10-4
Capital and revenue expenditures
obj. 1

Connect Lines Co. incurred the following costs related to trucks and vans used in operating its delivery service:

1. Replaced a truck's suspension system with a new suspension system that allows for the delivery of heavier loads.
2. Installed a hydraulic lift to a van.

3. Repaired a flat tire on one of the vans.
4. Overhauled the engine on one of the trucks purchased three years ago.
5. Removed a two-way radio from one of the trucks and installed a new radio with a greater range of communication.
6. Rebuilt the transmission on one of the vans that had been driven 40,000 miles. The van was no longer under warranty.
7. Changed the radiator fluid on a truck that had been in service for the past four years.
8. Tinted the back and side windows of one of the vans to discourage theft of contents.
9. Changed the oil and greased the joints of all the trucks and vans.
10. Installed security systems on four of the newer trucks.

Classify each of the costs as a capital expenditure or a revenue expenditure.

EX 10-5
Capital and revenue expenditures
obj. 1

Jaime Baldwin owns and operates Love Transport Co. During the past year, Jaime incurred the following costs related to an 18-wheel truck:

1. Changed engine oil.
2. Installed a wind deflector on top of the cab to increase fuel mileage.
3. Replaced fog and cab light bulbs.
4. Modified the factory-installed turbo charger with a special-order kit designed to add 50 more horsepower to the engine performance.
5. Replaced a headlight that had burned out.
6. Removed the old CB radio and replaced it with a newer model with a greater range.
7. Replaced the old radar detector with a newer model that detects the KA frequencies now used by many of the state patrol radar guns. The detector is wired directly into the cab, so that it is partially hidden. In addition, Jaime fastened the detector to the truck with a locking device that prevents its removal.
8. Replaced the hydraulic brake system that had begun to fail during his latest trip through the Rocky Mountains.
9. Installed a television in the sleeping compartment of the truck.
10. Replaced a shock absorber that had worn out.

Classify each of the costs as a capital expenditure or a revenue expenditure.

EX 10-6
Capital and revenue expenditures
obj. 1

Easy Move Company made the following expenditures on one of its delivery trucks:

Feb. 16. Replaced transmission at a cost of $3,150.
July 15. Paid $1,100 for installation of a hydraulic lift.
Oct. 3. Paid $72 to change the oil and air filter.

Prepare journal entries for each expenditure.

EX 10-7
Nature of depreciation
obj. 2

Legacy Ironworks Co. reported $3,175,000 for equipment and $2,683,000 for accumulated depreciation—equipment on its balance sheet.

Does this mean (a) that the replacement cost of the equipment is $3,175,000 and (b) that $2,683,000 is set aside in a special fund for the replacement of the equipment? Explain.

EX 10-8
Straight-line depreciation rates
obj. 2
✓ c. 10%

Convert each of the following estimates of useful life to a straight-line depreciation rate, stated as a percentage, assuming that the residual value of the fixed asset is to be ignored: (a) 2 years, (b) 8 years, (c) 10 years, (d) 20 years, (e) 25 years, (f) 40 years, (g) 50 years.

EX 10-9
Straight-line depreciation
obj. 2
✓ $3,350

A refrigerator used by a meat processor has a cost of $93,750, an estimated residual value of $10,000, and an estimated useful life of 25 years. What is the amount of the annual depreciation computed by the straight-line method?

EX 10-10
Depreciation by units-of-production method
obj. 2
✔ $276

A diesel-powered tractor with a cost of $145,000 and estimated residual value of $7,000 is expected to have a useful operating life of 75,000 hours. During July, the generator was operated 150 hours. Determine the depreciation for the month.

EX 10-11
Depreciation by units-of-production method
obj. 2
✔ a. Truck #1, credit Accumulated Depreciation, $6,670

Prior to adjustment at the end of the year, the balance in Trucks is $250,900 and the balance in Accumulated Depreciation—Trucks is $88,200. Details of the subsidiary ledger are as follows:

Truck No.	Cost	Estimated Residual Value	Estimated Useful Life	Accumulated Depreciation at Beginning of Year	Miles Operated During Year
1	$50,000	$ 6,500	150,000 miles	—	23,000 miles
2	72,900	9,900	300,000	$60,000	25,000
3	38,000	3,000	200,000	8,050	36,000
4	90,000	13,000	200,000	20,150	40,000

a. Determine the depreciation rates per mile and the amount to be credited to the accumulated depreciation section of each of the subsidiary accounts for the miles operated during the current year.
b. Journalize the entry to record depreciation for the year.

EX 10-12
Depreciation by two methods
obj. 2
✔ a. $3,750

A Kubota tractor acquired on January 9 at a cost of $75,000 has an estimated useful life of 20 years. Assuming that it will have no residual value, determine the depreciation for each of the first two years (a) by the straight-line method and (b) by the double-declining-balance method.

EX 10-13
Depreciation by two methods
obj. 2
✔ a. $19,000

A storage tank acquired at the beginning of the fiscal year at a cost of $172,000 has an estimated residual value of $20,000 and an estimated useful life of eight years. Determine the following: (a) the amount of annual depreciation by the straight-line method and (b) the amount of depreciation for the first and second years computed by the double-declining-balance method.

EX 10-14
Partial-year depreciation
obj. 2
✔ a. First year, $2,000

Sandblasting equipment acquired at a cost of $85,000 has an estimated residual value of $5,000 and an estimated useful life of 10 years. It was placed in service on October 1 of the current fiscal year, which ends on December 31. Determine the depreciation for the current fiscal year and for the following fiscal year by (a) the straight-line method and (b) the double-declining-balance method.

EX 10-15
Revision of depreciation
obj. 2
✔ a. $17,500

A building with a cost of $1,050,000 has an estimated residual value of $420,000, has an estimated useful life of 36 years, and is depreciated by the straight-line method. (a) What is the amount of the annual depreciation? (b) What is the book value at the end of the twentieth year of use? (c) If at the start of the twenty-first year it is estimated that the remaining life is 20 years and that the residual value is $300,000, what is the depreciation expense for each of the remaining 20 years?

EX 10-16
Capital expenditure and depreciation
objs. 1, 2
✔ b. Depreciation Expense, $600

Crane Company purchased and installed carpet in its new general offices on March 30 for a total cost of $12,000. The carpet is estimated to have a 15-year useful life and no residual value.

a. Prepare the journal entries necessary for recording the purchase of the new carpet.
b. Record the December 31 adjusting entry for the partial-year depreciation expense for the carpet, assuming that Crane Company uses the straight-line method.

EX 10-17
Entries for sale of fixed asset
obj. 3

Equipment acquired on January 3, 2007, at a cost of $504,000, has an estimated useful life of 12 years, has an estimated residual value of $42,000, and is depreciated by the straight-line method.

a. What was the book value of the equipment at December 31, 2010, the end of the year?
b. Assuming that the equipment was sold on April 1, 2011, for $315,000, journalize the entries to record (1) depreciation for the three months until the sale date, and (2) the sale of the equipment.

EX 10-18
Disposal of fixed asset
obj. 3
✔ b. $177,750

Equipment acquired on January 3, 2007, at a cost of $265,500, has an estimated useful life of eight years and an estimated residual value of $31,500.

a. What was the annual amount of depreciation for the years 2007, 2008, and 2009, using the straight-line method of depreciation?
b. What was the book value of the equipment on January 1, 2010?
c. Assuming that the equipment was sold on January 4, 2010, for $168,500, journalize the entry to record the sale.
d. Assuming that the equipment had been sold on January 4, 2010, for $180,000 instead of $168,500, journalize the entry to record the sale.

EX 10-19
Depletion entries
obj. 4
✔ a. $2,475,000

Cikan Mining Co. acquired mineral rights for $16,200,000. The mineral deposit is estimated at 90,000,000 tons. During the current year, 13,750,000 tons were mined and sold.

a. Determine the amount of depletion expense for the current year.
b. Journalize the adjusting entry to recognize the depletion expense.

EX 10-20
Amortization entries
obj. 5
✔ a. $57,500

Isolution Company acquired patent rights on January 4, 2007, for $750,000. The patent has a useful life equal to its legal life of 15 years. On January 7, 2010, Isolution successfully defended the patent in a lawsuit at a cost of $90,000.

a. Determine the patent amortization expense for the current year ended December 31, 2010.
b. Journalize the adjusting entry to recognize the amortization.

EX 10-21
Book value of fixed assets
obj. 6

Apple Computer, Inc., designs, manufactures, and markets personal computers and related software. Apple also manufactures and distributes music players (Ipod) along with related accessories and services including the online distribution of third-party music. The following information was taken from a recent annual report of Apple:

Property, Plant, and Equipment (in millions):

	Current Year	Preceding Year
Land and buildings	$626	$361
Machinery, equipment, and internal-use software	595	470
Office furniture and equipment	94	81
Other fixed assets related to leases	760	569
Accumulated depreciation and amortization	794	664

a. Compute the book value of the fixed assets for the current year and the preceding year and explain the differences, if any.
b. Would you normally expect the book value of fixed assets to increase or decrease during the year?

EX 10-22
Balance sheet presentation
obj. 6

List the errors you find in the following partial balance sheet:

Hobart Company
Balance Sheet
December 31, 2010

Assets

	Replacement Cost	Accumulated Depreciation	Book Value	
Total current assets				$350,000
Property, plant, and equipment:				
Land	$ 60,000	$ 12,000	$ 48,000	
Buildings	156,000	45,600	110,400	
Factory equipment	330,000	175,200	154,800	
Office equipment	72,000	48,000	24,000	
Patents	48,000	—	48,000	
Goodwill	27,000	3,000	24,000	
Total property, plant, and equipment	$693,000	$283,800		409,200

Appendix 1
EX 10-23
Sum-of-the-years-digits depreciation

✔ First year: $7,143

Based on the data in Exercise 10-12, determine the depreciation for the Kubota tractor for each of the first two years, using the sum-of-the-years-digits depreciation method. Round to the nearest dollar.

Appendix 1
EX 10-24
Sum-of-the-years-digits depreciation

✔ First year: $33,778

Based on the data in Exercise 10-13, determine the depreciation for the storage tank for each of the first two years, using the sum-of-the-years-digits depreciation method. Round to the nearest dollar.

Appendix 1
EX 10-25
Partial-year depreciation

✔ First year: $3,636

Based on the data in Exercise 10-14, determine the depreciation for the sandblasting equipment for each of the first two years, using the sum-of-the-years-digits depreciation method. Round to the nearest dollar.

Appendix 2
EX 10-26
Asset traded for similar asset

✔ a. $180,000

A printing press priced at a fair market value of $300,000 is acquired in a transaction that has commercial substance by trading in a similar press and paying cash for the difference between the trade-in allowance and the price of the new press.

a. Assuming that the trade-in allowance is $120,000, what is the amount of cash given?
b. Assuming that the book value of the press traded in is $115,500, what is the gain or loss on the exchange?

Appendix 2
EX 10-27
Asset traded for similar asset

✔ a. $180,000

Assume the same facts as in Exercise 10-26, except that the book value of the press traded in is $127,750. (a) What is the amount of cash given? (b) What is the gain or loss on the exchange?

Appendix 2
EX 10-28
Entries for trade of fixed asset

On October 1, Hot Springs Co., a water distiller, acquired new bottling equipment with a list price (fair market value) of $462,000. Hot Springs received a trade-in allowance of $96,000 on the old equipment of a similar type and paid cash of $366,000. The following information about the old equipment is obtained from the account in the equipment ledger: cost, $336,000; accumulated depreciation on December 31, the end of the preceding fiscal year, $220,000; annual depreciation, $20,000. Assuming the exchange has commercial substance, journalize the entries to record (a) the current depreciation of the old equipment to the date of trade-in and (b) the exchange transaction on October 1.

Appendix 2
EX 10-29
Entries for trade of fixed asset

On April 1, Gyminny Delivery Services acquired a new truck with a list price (fair market value) of $150,000. Gyminny received a trade-in allowance of $30,000 on an old truck of similar type and paid cash of $120,000. The following information about the old truck is obtained from the account in the equipment ledger: cost, $96,000; accumulated depreciation on December 31, the end of the preceding fiscal year, $64,000; annual depreciation, $16,000. Assuming the exchange has commercial substance, journalize the entries to record (a) the current depreciation of the old truck to the date of trade-in and (b) the transaction on April 1.

EX 10-30
Fixed asset turnover ratio

Verizon Communications is a major telecommunications company in the United States. Verizon's balance sheet disclosed the following information regarding fixed assets:

	Dec. 31, 2007 (in millions)	Dec. 31, 2006 (in millions)
Plant, property, and equipment	$ 213,994	$204,109
Less accumulated depreciation	128,700	121,753
	$ 85,294	$ 82,356

Verizon's revenue for 2007 was $93,469 million. The fixed asset turnover for the telecommunications industry averages 1.10.

a. Determine Verizon's fixed asset turnover ratio. Round to two decimal places.
b. Interpret Verizon's fixed asset turnover ratio.

EX 10-31
Fixed asset turnover ratio

The following table shows the revenue and average net fixed assets (in millions) for a recent fiscal year for Best Buy and Circuit City Stores, Inc.:

	Revenue	Average Net Fixed Assets
Best Buy	35,934	2,825
Circuit City Stores, Inc.	12,430	880

a. Compute the fixed asset turnover for each company. Round to two decimal places.
b. Which company uses its fixed assets more efficiently? Explain.

Problems Series A

PR 10-1A
Allocate payments and receipts to fixed asset accounts
obj. 1

✔ Land, $469,450

The following payments and receipts are related to land, land improvements, and buildings acquired for use in a wholesale apparel business. The receipts are identified by an asterisk.

a. Finder's fee paid to real estate agency	$ 4,000
b. Cost of real estate acquired as a plant site: Land	375,000
Building	25,000
c. Fee paid to attorney for title search	2,500
d. Delinquent real estate taxes on property, assumed by purchaser	31,750
e. Architect's and engineer's fees for plans and supervision	36,000
f. Cost of removing building purchased with land in (b)	10,000
g. Proceeds from sale of salvage materials from old building	3,000*

h. Cost of filling and grading land	15,200
i Premium on one-year insurance policy during construction	5,400
j. Money borrowed to pay building contractor	600,000*
k. Special assessment paid to city for extension of water main to the property	9,000
l. Cost of repairing windstorm damage during construction	3,000
m. Cost of repairing vandalism damage during construction	1,800
n. Cost of trees and shrubbery planted	12,000
o. Cost of paving parking lot to be used by customers	14,500
p. Interest incurred on building loan during construction	33,000
q. Proceeds from insurance company for windstorm and vandalism damage	4,500*
r. Payment to building contractor for new building	700,000
s. Refund of premium on insurance policy (j) canceled after 10 months	450*

Instructions

1. Assign each payment and receipt to Land (unlimited life), Land Improvements (limited life), Building, or Other Accounts. Indicate receipts by an asterisk. Identify each item by letter and list the amounts in columnar form, as follows:

Item	Land	Land Improvements	Building	Other Accounts

2. Determine the amount debited to Land, Land Improvements, and Building.
3. The costs assigned to the land, which is used as a plant site, will not be depreciated, while the costs assigned to land improvements will be depreciated. Explain this seemingly contradictory application of the concept of depreciation.

PR 10-2A
Compare three depreciation methods
obj. 2

✔ a. 2009: straight-line depreciation, $86,000

Newbirth Coatings Company purchased waterproofing equipment on January 2, 2009, for $380,000. The equipment was expected to have a useful life of four years, or 8,000 operating hours, and a residual value of $36,000. The equipment was used for 3,000 hours during 2009, 2,500 hours in 2010, 1,400 hours in 2011, and 1,100 hours in 2012.

Instructions

Determine the amount of depreciation expense for the years ended December 31, 2009, 2010, 2011, and 2012, by (a) the straight-line method, (b) the units-of-production method, and (c) the double-declining-balance method. Also determine the total depreciation expense for the four years by each method. The following columnar headings are suggested for recording the depreciation expense amounts:

	Depreciation Expense		
Year	Straight-Line Method	Units-of-Production Method	Double-Declining-Balance Method

PR 10-3A
Depreciation by three methods; partial years
obj. 2

✔ a. 2008, $7,600

Razar Sharp Company purchased tool sharpening equipment on July 1, 2008, for $48,600. The equipment was expected to have a useful life of three years, or 7,500 operating hours, and a residual value of $3,000. The equipment was used for 1,800 hours during 2008, 2,600 hours in 2009, 2,000 hours in 2010, and 1,100 hours in 2011.

Instructions

Determine the amount of depreciation expense for the years ended December 31, 2008, 2009, 2010, and 2011, by (a) the straight-line method, (b) the units-of-production method, and (c) the double-declining-balance method.

PR 10-4A
Depreciation by two methods; sale of fixed asset
objs. 2, 3

New tire retreading equipment, acquired at a cost of $144,000 at the beginning of a fiscal year, has an estimated useful life of four years and an estimated residual value of $10,800. The manager requested information regarding the effect of alternative methods on the amount of depreciation expense each year. On the basis of the data presented to the manager, the double-declining-balance method was selected.

✔ 1. b. Year 1, $72,000 depreciation expense

In the first week of the fourth year, the equipment was sold for $19,750.

Instructions

1. Determine the annual depreciation expense for each of the estimated four years of use, the accumulated depreciation at the end of each year, and the book value of the equipment at the end of each year by (a) the straight-line method and (b) the double-declining-balance method. The following columnar headings are suggested for each schedule:

Year	Depreciation Expense	Accumulated Depreciation, End of Year	Book Value, End of Year

2. Journalize the entry to record the sale.
3. Journalize the entry to record the sale, assuming that the equipment sold for $14,900 instead of $19,750.

PR 10-5A
Transactions for fixed assets, including sale
objs. 1, 2, 3

The following transactions, adjusting entries, and closing entries were completed by King Furniture Co. during a three-year period. All are related to the use of delivery equipment. The double-declining-balance method of depreciation is used.

2008
- Jan. 7. Purchased a used delivery truck for $45,600, paying cash.
- Feb. 27. Paid garage $130 for changing the oil, replacing the oil filter, and tuning the engine on the delivery truck.
- Dec. 31. Recorded depreciation on the truck for the fiscal year. The estimated useful life of the truck is eight years, with a residual value of $10,000 for the truck.

2009
- Jan. 8. Purchased a new truck for $75,000, paying cash.
- Mar. 13. Paid garage $200 to tune the engine and make other minor repairs on the used truck.
- Apr. 30. Sold the used truck for $30,000. (Record depreciation to date in 2009 for the truck.)
- Dec. 31. Record depreciation for the new truck. It has an estimated trade-in value of $13,500 and an estimated life of 10 years.

2010
- July 1. Purchased a new truck for $82,000, paying cash.
- Oct. 4. Sold the truck purchased January 8, 2009, for $53,000. (Record depreciation for the year.)
- Dec. 31. Recorded depreciation on the remaining truck. It has an estimated residual value of $15,000 and an estimated useful life of 10 years.

Instructions

Journalize the transactions and the adjusting entries.

PR 10-6A
Amortization and depletion entries
objs. 4, 5

✔ b. $33,750

Data related to the acquisition of timber rights and intangible assets during the current year ended December 31 are as follows:

a. On December 31, the company determined that $20,000,000 of goodwill was impaired.
b. Governmental and legal costs of $675,000 were incurred on June 30 in obtaining a patent with an estimated economic life of 10 years. Amortization is to be for one-half year.
c. Timber rights on a tract of land were purchased for $1,665,000 on February 16. The stand of timber is estimated at 9,000,000 board feet. During the current year, 2,400,000 board feet of timber were cut and sold.

Instructions

1. Determine the amount of the amortization, depletion, or impairment for the current year for each of the foregoing items.
2. Journalize the adjusting entries to record the amortization, depletion, or impairment for each item.

Problems Series B

PR 10-1B
Allocate payments and receipts to fixed asset accounts
obj. 1

✔ Land, $356,200

The following payments and receipts are related to land, land improvements, and buildings acquired for use in a wholesale ceramic business. The receipts are identified by an asterisk.

a. Fee paid to attorney for title search	$ 1,500
b. Cost of real estate acquired as a plant site: Land	270,000
Building	30,000
c. Special assessment paid to city for extension of water main to the property	20,000
d. Cost of razing and removing building	5,000
e. Proceeds from sale of salvage materials from old building	3,600*
f. Delinquent real estate taxes on property, assumed by purchaser	15,800
g. Premium on one-year insurance policy during construction	4,200
h. Cost of filling and grading land	17,500
i. Architect's and engineer's fees for plans and supervision	18,000
j. Money borrowed to pay building contractor	750,000*
k. Cost of repairing windstorm damage during construction	4,500
l. Cost of paving parking lot to be used by customers	15,000
m. Cost of trees and shrubbery planted	9,000
n. Cost of floodlights installed on parking lot	1,100
o. Cost of repairing vandalism damage during construction	1,500
p. Proceeds from insurance company for windstorm and vandalism damage	6,000*
q. Payment to building contractor for new building	800,000
r. Interest incurred on building loan during construction	45,000
s. Refund of premium on insurance policy (g) canceled after 11 months	350*

Instructions

1. Assign each payment and receipt to Land (unlimited life), Land Improvements (limited life), Building, or Other Accounts. Indicate receipts by an asterisk. Identify each item by letter and list the amounts in columnar form, as follows:

Item	Land	Land Improvements	Building	Other Accounts

2. Determine the amount debited to Land, Land Improvements, and Building.
3. The costs assigned to the land, which is used as a plant site, will not be depreciated, while the costs assigned to land improvements will be depreciated. Explain this seemingly contradictory application of the concept of depreciation.

PR 10-2B
Compare three depreciation methods
obj. 2

✔ a. 2008: straight-line depreciation, $21,000

Mammoth Company purchased packaging equipment on January 3, 2008, for $67,500. The equipment was expected to have a useful life of three years, or 25,000 operating hours, and a residual value of $4,500. The equipment was used for 12,000 hours during 2008, 9,000 hours in 2009, and 4,000 hours in 2010.

Instructions

Determine the amount of depreciation expense for the years ended December 31, 2008, 2009, and 2010, by (a) the straight-line method, (b) the units-of-production method, and (c) the double-declining-balance method. Also determine the total depreciation expense for the three years by each method. The following columnar headings are suggested for recording the depreciation expense amounts:

	Depreciation Expense		
Year	Straight-Line Method	Units-of-Production Method	Double-Declining-Balance Method

PR 10-3B
Depreciation by three methods; partial years
obj. 2

✔ a. 2008: $2,510

Quality IDs Company purchased plastic laminating equipment on July 1, 2008, for $15,660. The equipment was expected to have a useful life of three years, or 18,825 operating hours, and a residual value of $600. The equipment was used for 3,750 hours during 2008, 7,500 hours in 2009, 5,000 hours in 2010, and 2,575 hours in 2011.

Instructions

Determine the amount of depreciation expense for the years ended December 31, 2008, 2009, 2010, and 2011, by (a) the straight-line method, (b) the units-of-production method, and (c) the double-declining-balance method. Round to the nearest dollar.

PR 10-4B
Depreciation by two methods; sale of fixed asset
objs. 2, 3

✔ b. Year 1: $52,500 depreciation expense

New lithographic equipment, acquired at a cost of $131,250 at the beginning of a fiscal year, has an estimated useful life of five years and an estimated residual value of $11,250. The manager requested information regarding the effect of alternative methods on the amount of depreciation expense each year. On the basis of the data presented to the manager, the double-declining-balance method was selected.

In the first week of the fifth year, the equipment was sold for $21,500.

Instructions

1. Determine the annual depreciation expense for each of the estimated five years of use, the accumulated depreciation at the end of each year, and the book value of the equipment at the end of each year by (a) the straight-line method and (b) the double-declining-balance method. The following columnar headings are suggested for each schedule:

Year	Depreciation Expense	Accumulated Depreciation, End of Year	Book Value, End of Year

2. Journalize the entry to record the sale.
3. Journalize the entry to record the sale, assuming that the equipment was sold for $12,500 instead of $21,500.

PR 10-5B
Transactions for fixed assets, including sale
objs. 1, 2, 3

The following transactions, adjusting entries, and closing entries were completed by Trail Creek Furniture Co. during a three-year period. All are related to the use of delivery equipment. The double-declining-balance method of depreciation is used.

2008

Jan. 6. Purchased a used delivery truck for $24,000, paying cash.
July 19. Paid garage $500 for miscellaneous repairs to the truck.
Dec. 31. Recorded depreciation on the truck for the year. The estimated useful life of the truck is four years, with a residual value of $4,000 for the truck.

2009

Jan. 2. Purchased a new truck for $69,000, paying cash.
Aug. 1. Sold the used truck for $10,250. (Record depreciation to date in 2009 for the truck.)
Oct. 24. Paid garage $415 for miscellaneous repairs to the truck.
Dec. 31. Record depreciation for the new truck. It has an estimated residual value of $15,000 and an estimated life of five years.

2010

July 1. Purchased a new truck for $70,000, paying cash.
Oct. 1. Sold the truck purchased January 2, 2009, for $25,000. (Record depreciation for the year.)
Dec. 31. Recorded depreciation on the remaining truck. It has an estimated residual value of $18,000 and an estimated useful life of eight years.

Instructions

Journalize the transactions and the adjusting entries.

PR 10-6B
Amortization and depletion entries
objs. 4, 5
✔ 1. a. $356,200

Data related to the acquisition of timber rights and intangible assets during the current year ended December 31 are as follows:

a. Timber rights on a tract of land were purchased for $1,170,000 on July 5. The stand of timber is estimated at 4,500,000 board feet. During the current year, 1,370,000 board feet of timber were cut and sold.
b. On December 31, the company determined that $5,000,000 of goodwill was impaired.
c. Governmental and legal costs of $234,000 were incurred on April 4 in obtaining a patent with an estimated economic life of 12 years. Amortization is to be for three-fourths of a year.

Instructions

1. Determine the amount of the amortization, depletion, or impairment for the current year for each of the foregoing items.
2. Journalize the adjusting entries required to record the amortization, depletion, or impairment for each item.

Special Activities

SA 10-1
Ethics and professional conduct in business

Esteban Appleby, CPA, is an assistant to the controller of Summerfield Consulting Co. In his spare time, Esteban also prepares tax returns and performs general accounting services for clients. Frequently, Esteban performs these services after his normal working hours, using Summerfield Consulting Co.'s computers and laser printers. Occasionally, Esteban's clients will call him at the office during regular working hours. Discuss whether Esteban is performing in a professional manner.

SA 10-2
Financial vs. tax depreciation

The following is an excerpt from a conversation between two employees of Quantum Technologies, Pat Gapp and Faye Dalby. Pat is the accounts payable clerk, and Faye is the cashier.

Pat: Faye, could I get your opinion on something?

Faye: Sure, Pat.

Pat: Do you know Julie, the fixed assets clerk?

Faye: I know who she is, but I don't know her real well. Why?

Pat: Well, I was talking to her at lunch last Monday about how she liked her job, etc. You know, the usual . . . and she mentioned something about having to keep two sets of books . . . one for taxes and one for the financial statements. That can't be good accounting, can it? What do you think?

Faye: Two sets of books? It doesn't sound right.

Pat: It doesn't seem right to me either. I was always taught that you had to use generally accepted accounting principles. How can there be two sets of books? What can be the difference between the two?

How would you respond to Faye and Pat if you were Julie?

SA 10-3
Effect of depreciation on net income

Lonesome Dove Construction Co. specializes in building replicas of historic houses. Mike Jahn, president of Lonesome Dove Construction, is considering the purchase of various items of equipment on July 1, 2008, for $200,000. The equipment would have a useful life of five years and no residual value. In the past, all equipment has been leased. For tax purposes, Mike is considering depreciating the equipment by the straight-line method. He discussed the matter with his CPA and learned that, although the straight-line method could be elected, it was to his advantage to use the Modified Accelerated Cost Recovery System (MACRS) for tax purposes. He asked for your advice as to which method to use for tax purposes.

1. Compute depreciation for each of the years (2008, 2009, 2010, 2011, 2012, and 2013) of useful life by (a) the straight-line method and (b) MACRS. In using the straight-line method, one-half year's depreciation should be computed for 2008 and 2013. Use the MACRS rates presented on page 452.
2. Assuming that income before depreciation and income tax is estimated to be $500,000 uniformly per year and that the income tax rate is 40%, compute the net

income for each of the years 2008, 2009, 2010, 2011, 2012, and 2013, if (a) the straight-line method is used and (b) MACRS is used.

3. What factors would you present for Mike's consideration in the selection of a depreciation method?

SA 10-4
Shopping for a delivery truck

Group Project

You are planning to acquire a delivery truck for use in your business for five years. In groups of three or four, explore a local dealer's purchase and leasing options for the truck. Summarize the costs of purchasing versus leasing, and list other factors that might help you decide whether to buy or lease the truck.

SA 10-5
Applying for patents, copyrights, and trademarks

Internet Project

Go to the Internet and review the procedures for applying for a patent, a copyright, and a trademark. One Internet site that is useful for this purpose is **idresearch.com,** which is linked to the text's Web site at **academic.cengage.com/accounting/warren.** Prepare a written summary of these procedures.

SA 10-6
Fixed asset turnover: three industries

The following table shows the revenues and average net fixed assets for a recent fiscal year for three different companies from three different industries: retailing, manufacturing, and communications.

	Revenues (in millions)	Average Net Fixed Assets (in millions)
Wal-Mart	$348,650	$83,865
Alcoa Inc.	30,379	14,495
Comcast Corporation	24,966	20,009

a. For each company, determine the fixed asset turnover ratio. Round to two decimal places.
b. Explain Wal-Mart's ratio relative to the other two companies.

Answers to Self-Examination Questions

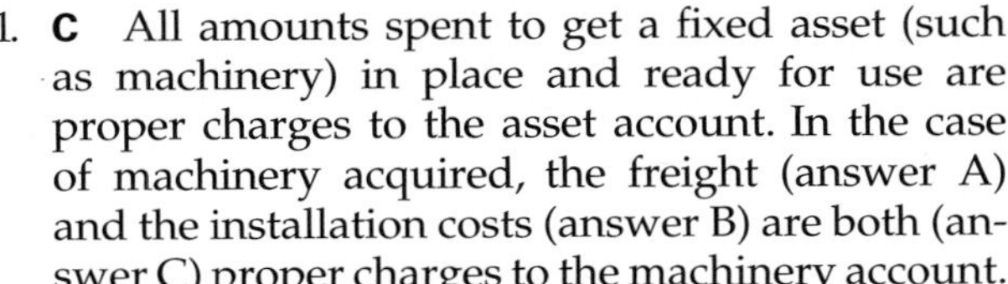

1. **C** All amounts spent to get a fixed asset (such as machinery) in place and ready for use are proper charges to the asset account. In the case of machinery acquired, the freight (answer A) and the installation costs (answer B) are both (answer C) proper charges to the machinery account.
2. **C** The periodic charge for depreciation under the double-declining-balance method for the second year is determined by first computing the depreciation charge for the first year. The depreciation for the first year of $6,000 (answer A) is computed by multiplying the cost of the equipment, $9,000, by 2/3 (the straight-line rate of 1/3 multiplied by 2). The depreciation for the second year of $2,000 (answer C) is then determined by multiplying the book value at the end of the first year, $3,000 (the cost of $9,000 minus the first-year depreciation of $6,000), by 2/3. The third year's depreciation is $400 (answer D). It is determined by multiplying the book value at the end of the second year, $1,000, by 2/3, thus yielding $667. However, the equipment cannot be depreciated below its residual value of $600; thus, the third-year depreciation is $400 ($1,000 − $600).
3. **B** A depreciation method that provides for a higher depreciation amount in the first year of the use of an asset and a gradually declining periodic amount thereafter is called an accelerated depreciation method. The double-declining-balance method (answer B) is an example of such a method.
4. **A** A gain of $3,500 was recognized on the sale of the equipment as shown below.

Annual depreciation [($80,000 − $7,500)/5 years]	$14,500	(Answer B)
Cost of equipment	$80,000	
Accumulated depreciation on December 31, 2010 ($14,500 × 3)	43,500	(Answer D)
Book value of equipment on December 31, 2010	$36,500	(Answer C)
Selling price	$40,000	
Book value of equipment on December 31, 2010	36,500	
Gain on sale of equipment	$ 3,500	

5. **D** Long-lived assets that are useful in operations, not held for sale, and without physical qualities are called intangible assets. Patents, goodwill, and copyrights are examples of intangible assets (answer D).

CHAPTER 11

Current Liabilities and Payroll

© AP Photo/Tom Gannam

PANERA BREAD

Banks and other financial institutions provide loans or credit to buyers for purchases of various items. Using credit to purchase items is probably as old as commerce itself. In fact, the Babylonians were lending money to support trade as early as 1300 B.C. The use of credit provides *individuals* convenience and buying power. Credit cards provide individuals convenience over writing checks and make purchasing over the Internet easier. Credit cards also provide individuals control over cash by providing documentation of their purchases through receipt of monthly credit card statements and by allowing them to avoid carrying large amounts of cash and to purchase items before they are paid.

Short-term credit is also used by *businesses* to provide convenience in purchasing items for manufacture or resale. More importantly, short-term credit gives a business control over the payment for goods and services. For example, Panera Bread, a chain of bakery-cafés located throughout the United States, uses short-term trade credit, or accounts payable, to purchase ingredients for making bread products in its bakeries. Short-term trade credit gives Panera control over cash payments by separating the purchase function from the payment function. Thus, the employee responsible for purchasing the bakery ingredients is separated from the employee responsible for paying for the purchase. This separation of duties can help prevent unauthorized purchases or payments.

In addition to accounts payable, a business like Panera Bread can also have current liabilities related to payroll, payroll taxes, employee benefits, short-term notes, unearned revenue, and contingencies. We will discuss each of these types of current liabilities in this chapter.

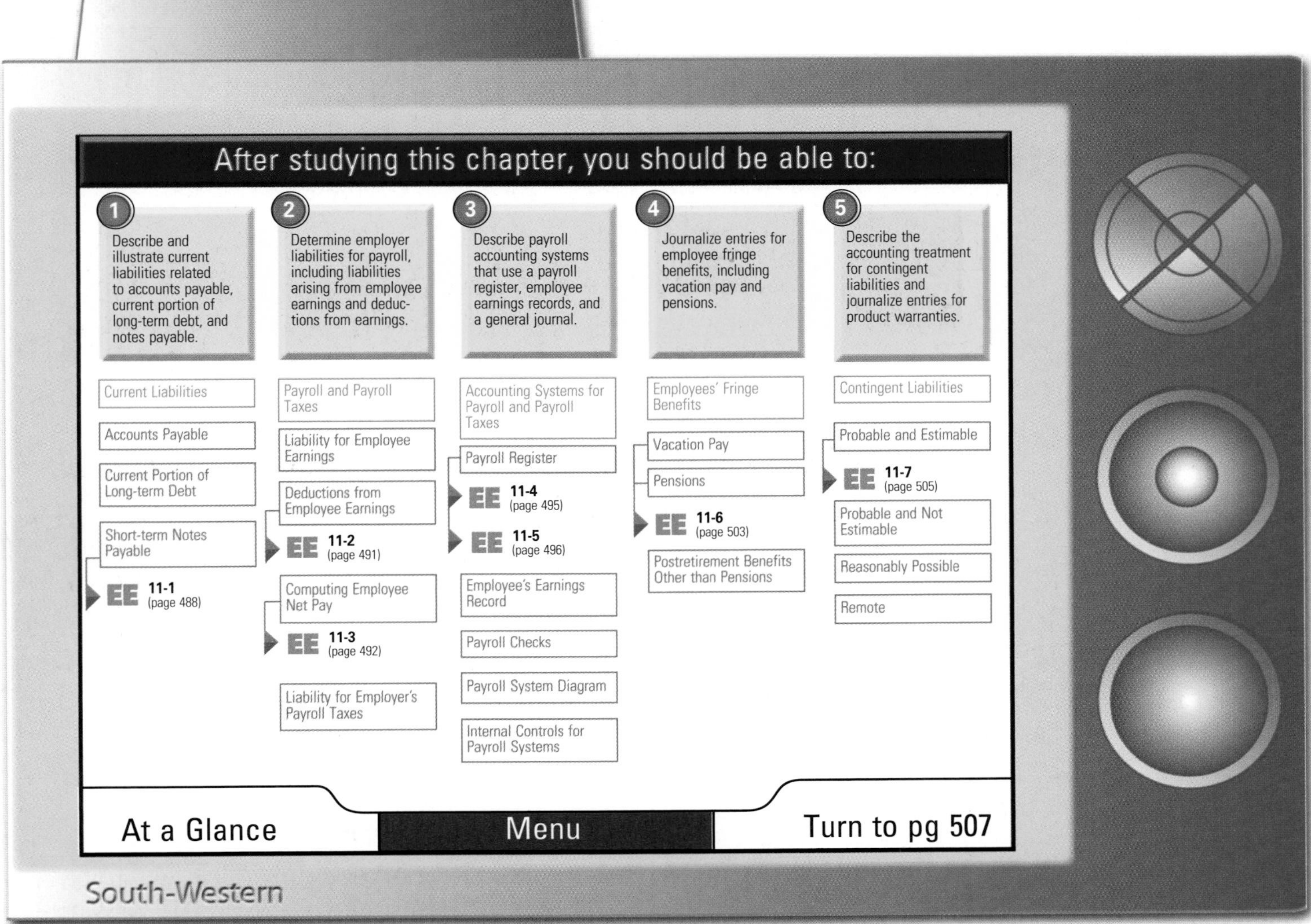

1 Describe and illustrate current liabilities related to accounts payable, current portion of long-term debt, and notes payable.

Current Liabilities

When a company or a bank advances *credit*, it is making a loan. The company or bank is called a *creditor* (or *lender*). The individuals or companies receiving the loan are called *debtors* (or *borrowers*).

Debt is recorded as a liability by the debtor. *Long-term liabilities* are debt due beyond one year. Thus, a 30-year mortgage used to purchase property is a long-term liability. *Current liabilities* are debt that will be paid out of current assets and are due within one year.

Three types of current liabilities are discussed in this section—accounts payable, current portion of long-term debt, and notes payable.

Accounts Payable

Accounts payable transactions have been described and illustrated in earlier chapters. These transactions involved a variety of purchases on account, including the purchase of merchandise and supplies. For most companies, accounts payable is the largest current liability. Exhibit 1 shows the accounts payable balance as a percent of total current liabilities for a number of companies.

Exhibit 1

Accounts Payable as a Percent of Total Current Liabilities

Company	Accounts Payable as a Percent of Total Current Liabilities
Alcoa Inc.	39%
AT&T	16
Gap Inc.	47
IBM	22
Nissan Motor Co. Ltd.	25
Rite Aid Corp.	51
ChevronTexaco	54

Current Portion of Long-Term Debt

Long-term liabilities are often paid back in periodic payments, called *installments.* Such installments that are due *within* the coming year are classified as a current liability. The installments due *after* the coming year are classified as a long-term liability.

To illustrate, Starbucks Corporation reported the following debt payments schedule in its September 30, 2007, annual report to shareholders:

Fiscal year ending	
2008	$ 775,000
2009	789,000
2010	337,000
2011	56,000
2012	0
Thereafter	550,000,000
Total principal payments	$551,957,000

The debt of $775,000 due in 2008 would be reported as a current liability on the September 30, 2007, balance sheet. The remaining debt of $551,182,000 ($551,957,000 – $775,000) would be reported as a long-term liability on the balance sheet.

Short-Term Notes Payable

Notes may be issued to purchase merchandise or other assets. Notes may also be issued to creditors to satisfy an account payable created earlier.[1]

To illustrate, assume that Nature's Sunshine Company issued a 90-day, 12% note for $1,000, dated August 1, 2009, to Murray Co. for a $1,000 overdue account. The entry to record the issuance of the note is as follows:

Aug.	1	Accounts Payable—Murray Co.		1,000	
		Notes Payable			1,000
		Issued a 90-day, 12% note on account.			

1 The accounting for notes received to satisfy an account receivable was described and illustrated in Chapter 9, Receivables.

When the note matures, the entry to record the payment of $1,000 plus $30 interest ($1,000 × 12% × 90/360) is as follows:

Oct.	30	Notes Payable		1,000	
		Interest Expense		30	
		Cash			1,030
		Paid principal and interest due on note.			

The interest expense is reported in the Other expense section of the income statement for the year ended December 31, 2009. The interest expense account is closed at December 31.

Each note transaction affects a debtor (borrower) and creditor (lender). The following illustration shows how the same transactions are recorded by the debtor and creditor. In this illustration, the debtor (borrower) is Bowden Co., and the creditor (lender) is Coker Co.

	Bowden Co. (Borrower)			Coker Co. (Creditor)		
May 1. Bowden Co. purchased merchandise on account from Coker Co., $10,000, 2/10, n/30. The merchandise cost Coker Co. $7,500.	Merchandise Inventory	10,000		Accounts Receivable	10,000	
	Accounts Payable		10,000	Sales		10,000
				Cost of Merchandise Sold	7,500	
				Merchandise Inventory		7,500
May 31. Bowden Co. issued a 60-day, 12% note for $10,000 to Coker Co. on account.	Accounts Payable	10,000		Notes Receivable	10,000	
	Notes Payable		10,000	Accounts Receivable		10,000
July 30. Bowden Co. paid Coker Co. the amount due on the note of May 31. Interest: $10,000 × 12% × 60/360.	Notes Payable	10,000		Cash	10,200	
	Interest Expense	200		Interest Revenue		200
	Cash		10,200	Notes Receivable		10,000

A company may borrow from a bank by issuing a note. To illustrate, assume that on September 19 Iceburg Company issues a $4,000, 90-day, 15% note to First National Bank. The entry to record the issuance of the note is as follows:

Sept.	19	Cash		4,000	
		Notes Payable			4,000
		Issued a 90-day, 15% note to First National Bank.			

On the due date of the note (December 18), Iceburg Company owes $4,000 plus interest of $150 ($4,000 × 15% × 90/360). The entry to record the payment of the note is as follows:

Dec.	18	Notes Payable		4,000	
		Interest Expense		150	
		Cash			4,150
		Paid principal and interest due on note.			

The U.S. Treasury issues short-term treasury bills to investors at a discount.

In some cases, a *discounted note* may be issued rather than an interest-bearing note. A discounted note has the following characteristics:

1. The creditor (lender) requires an interest rate, called the *discount rate.*
2. Interest, called the *discount*, is computed on the face amount of the note.
3. The debtor (borrower) receives the face amount of the note less the discount, called the *proceeds*.
4. The debtor pays the face amount of the note on the due date.

To illustrate, assume that on August 10, Cary Company issues a $20,000, 90-day discounted note to Western National Bank. The discount rate is 15%, and the amount of the discount is $750 ($20,000 × 15% × 90/360). Thus, the proceeds received by Cary Company are $19,250. The entry by Cary Company is as follows:

Aug.	10	Cash		19,250	
		Interest Expense		750	
		Notes Payable			20,000
		Issued a 90-day discounted note to Western National Bank at a 15% discount rate.			

The entry when Cary Company pays the discounted note on November 8 is as follows:[2]

Nov.	8	Notes Payable		20,000	
		Cash			20,000
		Paid note due.			

Other current liabilities that have been discussed in earlier chapters include accrued expenses, unearned revenue, and interest payable. The accounting for wages and salaries, termed *payroll accounting*, is discussed next.

Example Exercise 11-1 Proceeds from Notes Payable

1

On July 1, Bella Salon Company issued a 60-day note with a face amount of $60,000 to Delilah Hair Products Company for merchandise inventory.

a. Determine the proceeds of the note, assuming the note carries an interest rate of 6%.
b. Determine the proceeds of the note, assuming the note is discounted at 6%.

Follow My Example 11-1

a. $60,000.
b. $59,400 [$60,000 − ($60,000 × 6% × 60/360)].

For Practice: PE 11-1A, PE 11-1B

2 If the accounting period ends before a discounted note is paid, an adjusting entry should record the prepaid (deferred) interest that is not yet an expense. This deferred interest would be deducted from Notes Payable in the Current Liabilities section of the balance sheet.

2 Determine employer liabilities for payroll, including liabilities arising from employee earnings and deductions from earnings.

Payroll and Payroll Taxes

In accounting, **payroll** refers to the amount paid employees for services they provided during the period. A company's payroll is important for the following reasons:

1. Employees are sensitive to payroll errors and irregularities.
2. Good employee morale requires payroll to be paid timely and accurately.
3. Payroll is subject to federal and state regulations.
4. Payroll and related payroll taxes significantly affect the net income of most companies.

Liability for Employee Earnings

Salary usually refers to payment for managerial and administrative services. Salary is normally expressed in terms of a month or a year. *Wages* usually refers to payment for employee manual labor. The rate of wages is normally stated on an hourly or a weekly basis. The salary or wage of an employee may be increased by bonuses, commissions, profit sharing, or cost-of-living adjustments.

Employee salaries and wages are expenses to an employer.

Companies engaged in interstate commerce must follow the Fair Labor Standards Act. This act, sometimes called the Federal Wage and Hour Law, requires employers to pay a minimum rate of $1\frac{1}{2}$ times the regular rate for all hours worked in excess of 40 hours per week. Exemptions are provided for executive, administrative, and some supervisory positions. Increased rates for working overtime, nights, or holidays are common, even when not required by law. These rates may be as much as twice the regular rate.

Information on average salaries for a variety of professions can be found on Internet job sites such as **monster.com**.

To illustrate computing an employee's earnings, assume that John T. McGrath is a salesperson employed by McDermott Supply Co. McGrath's regular rate is $34 per hour, and any hours worked in excess of 40 hours per week are paid at $1\frac{1}{2}$ times the regular rate. McGrath worked 42 hours for the week ended December 27. His earnings of **$1,462** for the week are computed as follows:

Earnings at regular rate (40 hrs. × $34)	$1,360
Earnings at overtime rate [2 hrs. × ($34 × 1½)]	102
Total earnings	**$1,462**

Deductions from Employee Earnings

The total earnings of an employee for a payroll period, including any overtime pay, are called **gross pay**. From this amount is subtracted one or more *deductions* to arrive at the **net pay**. Net pay is the amount paid the employee. The deductions normally include federal, state, and local income taxes, medical insurance, and pension contributions.

Income Taxes Employers normally withhold a portion of employee earnings for payment of the employees' federal income tax. Each employee authorizes the amount to be withheld by completing an "Employee's Withholding Allowance Certificate," called a W-4. Exhibit 2 is the W-4 form submitted by John T. McGrath.

On the W-4, an employee indicates marital status and the number of withholding allowances. A single employee may claim one withholding allowance. A married employee may claim an additional allowance for a spouse. An employee may also claim an allowance for each dependent other than a spouse. Each allowance reduces the federal income tax withheld from the employee's check. Exhibit 2 indicates that John T. McGrath is single and, thus, claimed one withholding allowance.

The federal income tax withheld depends on each employee's gross pay and W-4 allowance. Withholding tables issued by the Internal Revenue Service (IRS) are used to determine amounts to withhold. Exhibit 3 is an example of an IRS wage withholding table for a single person who is paid weekly.[3]

3 IRS withholding tables are also available for married employees and for pay periods other than weekly.

Exhibit 2

Employee's Withholding Allowance Certificate (W-4 Form)

Cut here and give Form W-4 to your employer. Keep the top part for your records.

Form **W-4** — Department of the Treasury, Internal Revenue Service

Employee's Withholding Allowance Certificate

▶ Whether you are entitled to claim a certain number of allowances or exemption from withholding is subject to review by the IRS. Your employer may be required to send a copy of this form to the IRS.

OMB No. 1545-0074 — **2008**

1 Type or print your first name and middle initial.	Last name	2 Your social security number
John T.	McGrath	381 : 48 : 9120

Home address (number and street or rural route): 1830 4th Street

3 ☒ Single ☐ Married ☐ Married, but withhold at higher Single rate.
Note. If married, but legally separated, or spouse is a nonresident alien, check the "Single" box.

City or town, state, and ZIP code: Clinton, Iowa 52732-6142

4 If your last name differs from that shown on your social security card, check here. You must call 1-800-772-1213 for a new card. ▶ ☐

5 Total number of allowances you are claiming (from line H above or from the applicable worksheet on page 2) — 5: 1

6 Additional amount, if any, you want withheld from each paycheck . . . . — 6: $

7 I claim exemption from withholding for 2008, and I certify that I meet both of the following conditions for exemption.
- Last year I had a right to a refund of all federal income tax withheld because I had no tax liability and
- This year I expect a refund of all federal income tax withheld because I expect to have no tax liability.

If you meet both conditions, write "Exempt" here . . . . ▶ 7

Under penalties of perjury, I declare that I have examined this certificate and to the best of my knowledge and belief, it is true, correct, and complete.

Employee's signature (Form is not valid unless you sign it.) ▶ *John T. McGrath* Date ▶ June 2, 2008

8 Employer's name and address (Employer: Complete lines 8 and 10 only if sending to the IRS.)	9 Office code (optional)	10 Employer identification number (EIN)

Cat. No. 10220Q Form **W-4** (2008)

In Exhibit 3, each row is the employee's wages after deducting the employee's withholding allowances. Each year, the amount of the standard withholding allowance is determined by the IRS. For a single person paid weekly, we assume the standard withholding allowance to be deducted in Exhibit 3 is $67.[4] Thus, if two withholding allowances are claimed, $134 ($67 × 2) is deducted.

To illustrate, John T. McGrath made $1,462 for the week ended December 27. McGrath's W-4 claims one withholding allowance of $67. Thus, the wages used in determining McGrath's withholding bracket in Exhibit 3 are $1,395 ($1,462 − $67).

After the person's withholding wage bracket has been computed, the federal income tax to be withheld is determined as follows:

Step 1. Locate the proper withholding wage bracket in Exhibit 3.

McGrath's wages after deducting one standard IRS withholding allowance are $1,395 ($1,462 − $67). Therefore, the wage bracket for McGrath is $653–$1,533.

Step 2. Compute the withholding for the proper wage bracket using the directions in the two right-hand columns in Exhibit 3.

For McGrath's wage bracket, the withholding is computed as "$82.95 plus 25% of the excess over $653." Hence, McGrath's withholding is $268.45, as shown below.

Initial withholding from wage bracket	*$ 82.95*
Plus [25% × ($1,395 − $653)]	*185.50*
Total withholding	*$268.45*

Exhibit 3

Wage Bracket Withholding Table

Table for Percentage Method of Withholding WEEKLY Payroll Period

(a) SINGLE person (including head of household) —

If the amount of wages (after subtracting withholding allowances) is: Not over $51 . . . . The amount of income tax to withhold is: $0

Over—	But not over—		of excess over—	
$51	—$198 . .	10%	—$51	
$198	—$653 . .	$14.70 plus 15%	—$198	
$653	—$1,533 . .	$82.95 plus 25%	—$653	← McGrath wage bracket
$1,533	—$3,202 . .	$302.95 plus 28%	—$1,533	
$3,202	—$6,916 . .	$770.27 plus 33%	—$3,202	
$6,916	. . . .	$1,995.89 plus 35%	—$6,916	

Source: Publication 15, *Employer's Tax Guide*, Internal Revenue Service, 2008.

4 The actual IRS standard withholding allowance changes every year and was $67.31 for 2008.

Employers may also be required to withhold state or city income taxes. The amounts to be withheld are determined on state-by-state and city-by-city bases.

Residents of New York City must pay federal, state, and city income taxes.

Example Exercise 11-2 Federal Income Tax Withholding 2

Karen Dunn's weekly gross earnings for the present week were $2,250. Dunn has two exemptions. Using the wage bracket withholding table in Exhibit 3 with a $67 standard withholding allowance for each exemption, what is Dunn's federal income tax withholding?

Follow My Example 11-2

Total wage payment		$ 2,250
One allowance (provided by IRS)	$67	
Multiplied by allowances claimed on Form W-4	× 2	134
Amount subject to withholding		$ 2,116
Initial withholding from wage bracket in Exhibit 3		$302.95
Plus additional withholding: 28% of excess over $1,533		163.24*
Federal income tax withholding		$466.19

*28% × ($2,116 − $1,533)

For Practice: PE 11-2A, PE 11-2B

FICA Tax Employers are required by the Federal Insurance Contributions Act (FICA) to withhold a portion of the earnings of each employee. The **FICA tax** withheld contributes to the following two federal programs:

1. *Social security,* which provides payments for retirees, survivors, and disability insurance (OASDI).
2. *Medicare,* which provides health insurance for senior citizens.

The amount withheld from each employee is based on the employee's earnings *paid* in the *calendar* year. The withholding tax rates and maximum earnings subject to tax are often revised by Congress. To simplify, this chapter assumes the following rates and earnings subject to tax:

1. Social security: 6% on the first $100,000 of annual earnings
2. Medicare: 1.5% on all earnings

To illustrate, assume that John T. McGrath's annual earnings prior to the payroll period ending on December 27 total $99,038. Since McGrath's earnings for the week are $1,462, the total FICA tax to be withheld is **$79.65**, as shown below.

Earnings subject to 6% social security tax ($100,000 − $99,038)	$ 962	
Social security tax rate	× 6%	
Social security tax		$57.72
Earnings subject to 1.5% Medicare tax	$1,462	
Medicare tax rate	× 1.5%	
Medicare tax		21.93
Total FICA tax		$79.65

Other Deductions Employees may choose to have additional amounts deducted from their gross pay. For example, an employee may authorize deductions for retirement savings, for charitable contributions, or life insurance. A union contract may also require the deduction of union dues.

Computing Employee Net Pay

Gross earnings less payroll deductions equals *net pay*, sometimes called *take-home pay*. Assuming that John T. McGrath authorized deductions for retirement savings and for a United Fund contribution, McGrath's net pay for the week ended December 27 is $1,088.90, as shown below.

Gross earnings for the week		$1,462.00
Deductions:		
Social security tax	$ 57.72	
Medicare tax	21.93	
Federal income tax	268.45	
Retirement savings	20.00	
United Fund	5.00	
Total deductions		373.10
Net pay		$1,088.90

Example Exercise 11-3 Employee Net Pay

2

Karen Dunn's weekly gross earnings for the week ending December 3 were $2,250, and her federal income tax withholding was $466.19. Prior to this week, Dunn had earned $98,000 for the year. Assuming the social security rate is 6% on the first $100,000 of annual earnings and Medicare is 1.5% of all earnings, what is Dunn's net pay?

Follow My Example 11-3

Total wage payment			$2,250.00
Less: Federal income tax withholding		$466.19	
Earnings subject to social security tax ($100,000 − $98,000)	$2,000		
Social security tax rate	× 6%		
Social security tax		120.00	
Medicare tax ($2,250 × 1.5%)		33.75	619.94
Net pay			$1,630.06

For Practice: PE 11-3A, PE 11-3B

Liability for Employer's Payroll Taxes

Employers are subject to the following payroll taxes for amounts paid their employees:

1. *FICA Tax*: Employers must match the employee's FICA tax contribution.
2. *Federal Unemployment Compensation Tax (FUTA)*: This employer tax provides for temporary payments to those who become unemployed. The tax collected by the federal government is allocated among the states for use in state programs rather than paid directly to employees. Congress often revises the FUTA tax rate and maximum earnings subject to tax. In this chapter, the FUTA rate and earnings subject to tax are assumed to be 6.2% rate on first $7,000 of annual earnings paid each employee during the calendar year.
3. *State Unemployment Compensation Tax (SUTA)*: This employer tax also provides temporary payments to those who become unemployed. The FUTA and SUTA programs are closely coordinated, with the states distributing the unemployment checks.[5] SUTA tax rates and earnings subject to tax vary by state.[6]

5 This rate may be reduced to 0.8% for credits for state unemployment compensation tax.

6 As of January 1, 2008, the maximum state rate credited against the federal unemployment rate was 5.4% of the first $7,000 of each employee's earnings during a calendar year.

The preceding employer taxes are an operating expense of the company. Exhibit 4 summarizes the responsibility for employee and employer payroll taxes.

Exhibit 4

Responsibility for Tax Payments

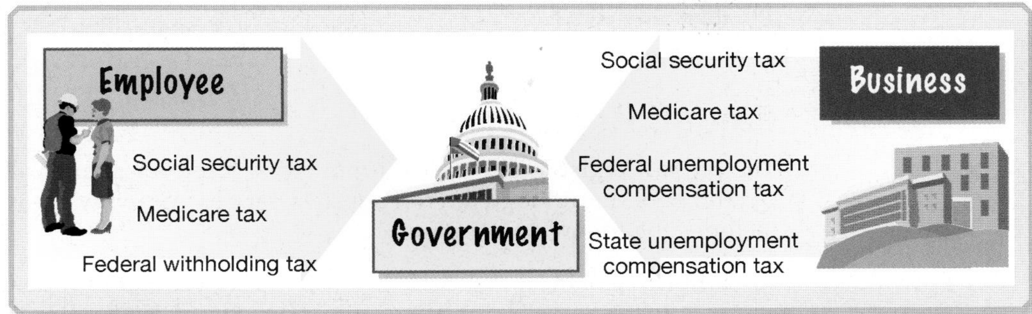

Business Connection

THE MOST YOU WILL EVER PAY

In 1936, the Social Security Board described how the tax was expected to affect a worker's pay, as follows:

The taxes called for in this law will be paid both by your employer and by you. For the next 3 years you will pay maybe 15 cents a week, maybe 25 cents a week, maybe 30 cents or more, according to what you earn. That is to say, during the next 3 years, beginning January 1, 1937, you will pay 1 cent for every dollar you earn, and at the same time your employer will pay 1 cent for every dollar you earn, up to $3,000 a year. . . .

. . . Beginning in 1940 you will pay, and your employer will pay, 1½ cents for each dollar you earn, up to $3,000 a year . . . and then beginning in 1943, you will pay 2 cents, and so will your employer, for every dollar you earn for the next three years. After that, you and your employer will each pay half a cent more for 3 years, and finally, beginning in 1949, . . . you and your employer will each pay 3 cents on each dollar you earn, up to $3,000 a year. That is the most you will ever pay.

The rate on January 1, 2008, was 7.65 cents per dollar earned (7.65%). The social security portion was 6.20% on the first $102,000 of earnings. The Medicare portion was 1.45% on all earnings.

Source: Arthur Lodge, "That Is the Most You Will Ever Pay," *Journal of Accountancy*, October 1985, p. 44.

Integrity, Objectivity, and Ethics in Business

RESUMÉ PADDING

Misrepresenting your accomplishments on your resumé could come back to haunt you. In one case, the chief financial officer (CFO) of Veritas Software was forced to resign his position when it was discovered that he had lied about earning an MBA from Stanford University, when in actuality he had earned only an undergraduate degree from Idaho State University.

Source: Reuters News Service, October 4, 2002.

3 Describe payroll accounting systems that use a payroll register, employee earnings records, and a general journal.

Accounting Systems for Payroll and Payroll Taxes

Payroll systems should be designed to:

1. Pay employees accurately and timely.
2. Meet regulatory requirements of federal, state, and local agencies.
3. Provide useful data for management decision-making needs.

Although payroll systems differ among companies, the major elements of most payroll systems are:

1. Payroll register
2. Employee's earnings record
3. Payroll checks

Payroll Register

The **payroll register** is a multicolumn report used for summarizing the data for each payroll period. Although payroll registers vary by company, a payroll register normally includes the following columns:

1. Employee name
2. Total hours worked
3. Regular earnings
4. Overtime earnings
5. Total gross earnings
6. Social security tax withheld
7. Medicare tax withheld
8. Federal income tax withheld
9. Retirement savings withheld
10. Miscellaneous items withheld
11. Total withholdings
12. Net pay
13. Check number of payroll check issued
14. Accounts debited for payroll expense

Exhibit 5 illustrates a payroll register. The right-hand columns of the payroll register indicate the accounts debited for the payroll expense. These columns are often referred to as the *payroll distribution*.

Recording Employees' Earnings The column totals of the payroll register provide the basis for recording the journal entry for payroll. The entry based on the payroll register in Exhibit 5 is shown on the next page.

Payroll taxes become a liability to the employer when the payroll is paid.

Recording and Paying Payroll Taxes Payroll taxes are recorded as liabilities when the payroll is *paid* to employees. In addition, employers compute and report payroll taxes on a *calendar-year* basis, which may differ from the company's fiscal year.

Exhibit 5

Payroll Register

			Earnings			
	Employee Name	Total Hours	Regular	Overtime	Total	
1	Abrams, Julie S.	40	500.00		500.00	1
2	Elrod, Fred G.	44	392.00	58.80	450.80	2
3	Gomez, Jose C.	40	840.00		840.00	3
4	McGrath, John T.	42	1,360.00	102.00	1,462.00	4
25	Wilkes, Glenn K.	40	480.00		480.00	25
26	Zumpano, Michael W.	40	600.00		600.00	26
27	Total		13,328.00	574.00	13,902.00	27
28						28

Dec.	27	Sales Salaries Expense		11,122.00	
		Office Salaries Expense		2,780.00	
		Social Security Tax Payable			643.07
		Medicare Tax Payable			208.53
		Employees Federal Income Tax Payable			3,332.00
		Retirement Savings Deductions Payable			680.00
		United Fund Deductions Payable			470.00
		Accounts Receivable—Fred G. Elrod (emp.)			50.00
		Salaries Payable			8,518.40
		Payroll for week ended December 27.			

Example Exercise 11-4 Journalize Period Payroll

3

The payroll register of Chen Engineering Services indicates $900 of social security withheld and $225 of Medicare tax withheld on total salaries of $15,000 for the period. Federal withholding for the period totaled $2,925.

Provide the journal entry for the period's payroll.

Follow My Example 11-4

Salaries Expense	15,000	
Social Security Tax Payable		900
Medicare Tax Payable		225
Employees Federal Withholding Tax Payable		2,925
Salaries Payable		10,950

For Practice: PE 11-4A, PE 11-4B

To illustrate, assume that Everson Company's fiscal year ends on April 30. Also, assume the following payroll data on December 31, 2009:

Wages owed employees on December 31	$26,000
Wages subject to payroll taxes:	
Social security tax (6.0%)	$18,000
Medicare tax (1.5%)	26,000
State (5.4%) and federal (0.8%) unemployment compensation tax	1,000

Exhibit 5

(Concluded)

	Deductions						Paid		Accounts Debited		
	Social Security Tax	Medicare Tax	Federal Income Tax	Retirement Savings	Misc.	Total	Net Pay	Check No.	Sales Salaries Expense	Office Salaries Expense	
1	30.00	7.50	74.00	20.00	UF 10.00	141.50	358.50	6857	500.00		1
2	27.05	6.76	62.00		AR 50.00	145.81	304.99	6858		450.80	2
3	50.40	12.60	131.00	25.00	UF 10.00	229.00	611.00	6859	840.00		3
4	57.72	21.93	268.45	20.00	UF 5.00	373.10	1,088.90	6860	1,462.00		4
25	28.80	7.20	69.00	10.00		115.00	365.00	6880	480.00		25
26	36.00	9.00	79.00	5.00	UF 2.00	131.00	469.00	6881		600.00	26
27	643.07	208.53	3,332.00	680.00	UF 470.00	5,383.60	8,518.40		11,122.00	2,780.00	27
28					AR 50.00						28

Miscellaneous Deductions: UF—United Fund; AR—Accounts Receivable

If the payroll is paid on December 31, the payroll taxes are computed as follows:

Social security	$1,080 ($18,000 × 6.0%)
Medicare tax	390 ($26,000 × 1.5%)
State unemployment compensation tax (SUTA)	54 ($1,000 × 5.4%)
Federal unemployment compensation tax (FUTA)	8 ($1,000 × 0.8%)
Total payroll taxes	$1,532

If the payroll is paid on January 2, however, the *entire* $26,000 is subject to *all* payroll taxes. This is because the maximum earnings limit for social security and unemployment taxes starts on January 1 of each year. Thus, if the payroll is paid on January 2, the payroll taxes are computed as follows:

Social security	$1,560 ($26,000 × 6.0%)
Medicare tax	390 ($26,000 × 1.5%)
State unemployment compensation tax (SUTA)	1,404 ($26,000 × 5.4%)
Federal unemployment compensation tax (FUTA)	208 ($26,000 × 0.8%)
Total payroll taxes	$3,562

The payroll register in Exhibit 5 indicates that social security tax of $643.07 and Medicare tax of $208.53 were withheld. Employers must match the employees' FICA contributions. Thus, the employer's social security and Medicare payroll tax will also be $643.07 and $208.53, respectively.

Assume that in Exhibit 5 the earnings subject to state and federal unemployment compensation taxes are $2,710. In addition, assume a SUTA rate of 5.4% and a FUTA rate of 0.8%. The payroll taxes based on Exhibit 5 are $1,019.62, as shown below.

Social security	$ 643.07 (from Social Security Tax column of Exhibit 5)
Medicare tax	208.53 (from Medicare Tax column of Exhibit 5)
SUTA	146.34 ($2,710 × 5.4%)
FUTA	21.68 ($2,710 × 0.8%)
Total payroll taxes	$1,019.62

The entry to journalize the payroll tax expense for Exhibit 5 is shown below.

Dec.	27	Payroll Tax Expense		1,019.62	
		Social Security Tax Payable			643.07
		Medicare Tax Payable			208.53
		State Unemployment Tax Payable			146.34
		Federal Unemployment Tax Payable			21.68
		Payroll taxes for week ended December 27.			

The preceding entry records a liability for each payroll tax. When the payroll taxes are paid, an entry is recorded debiting the payroll tax liability accounts and crediting Cash.

Example Exercise 11-5 Journalize Payroll Tax 3

The payroll register of Chen Engineering Services indicates $900 of social security withheld and $225 of Medicare tax withheld on total salaries of $15,000 for the period. Assume earnings subject to state and federal unemployment compensation taxes are $5,250, at the federal rate of 0.8% and the state rate of 5.4%.

Provide the journal entry to record the payroll tax expense for the period.

Follow My Example 11-5

Payroll Tax Expense	1,450.50	
Social Security Tax Payable		900.00
Medicare Tax Payable		225.00
State Unemployment Tax Payable		283.50*
Federal Unemployment Tax Payable		42.00**

*$5,250 × 5.4%
**$5,250 × 0.8%

For Practice: PE 11-5A, PE 11-5B

Employee's Earnings Record

Each employee's earnings to date must be determined at the end of each payroll period. This total is necessary for computing the employee's social security tax withholding and the employer's payroll taxes. Thus, detailed payroll records must be kept for each employee. This record is called an **employee's earnings record**.

Exhibit 6, on pages 498–499, shows a portion of John T. McGrath's employee's earnings record. An employee's earnings record and the payroll register are interrelated. For example, McGrath's earnings record for December 27 can be traced to the fourth line of the payroll register in Exhibit 5.

As shown in Exhibit 6, an employee's earnings record has quarterly and yearly totals. These totals are used for tax, insurance, and other reports. For example, one such report is the Wage and Tax Statement, commonly called a *W-2*. This form is provided annually to each employee as well as to the Social Security Administration. The W-2 shown below is based on John T. McGrath's employee's earnings record shown in Exhibit 6.

22222 Void ☐ | a Employee's social security number 381-48-9120 | For Office Use Only ► OMB No. 1545–0008

b Employer identification number (EIN) 61-8436524	1 Wages, tips, other compensation 100,500.00	2 Federal income tax withheld 21,387.65
c Employer's name, address, and ZIP code McDermott Supply Co. 415 5th Ave. So. Dubuque, IA 52736-0142	3 Social security wages 100,000.00	4 Social security tax withheld 6,000.00
	5 Medical wages and tips 100,500.00	6 Medicare tax withheld 1,507.50
	7 Social security tips	8 Allocated tips
d Control number	9 Advance EIC payment	10 Dependent care benefits
e Employee's first name and initial: John T. — Last name: McGrath — Suff.	11 Nonqualified plans	12a See instructions for box 12
1830 4th St. Clinton, IA 52732-6142	13 Statutory employee ☐ Retirement plan ☐ Third party sick pay ☐	12b
	14 Other	12c
f Employee's address, and ZIP code		12d

15 State	Employer's state ID number	16 State wages, tips, etc.	17 State income tax	18 Local wages, tips, etc.	19 Local income tax	20 Locality name
IA						Dubuque

Form **W-2** Wage and Tax Statement **2009**

Department of the Treasury—Internal Revenue Service

For Privacy Act and Paperwork Reduction Act Notice, see back of Copy D.

Cat. No. 10134D

Copy A For Social Security Administration — Send this entire page with Form W-3 to the Social Security Administration; photocopies are **not** acceptable.

Do Not Cut, Fold, or Staple Forms on This Page — Do Not Cut, Fold, or Staple Forms on This Page

Payroll Checks

Companies may pay employees, especially part-time employees, by issuing *payroll checks*. Each check includes a detachable statement showing how the net pay was computed. Exhibit 7, on page 500, illustrates a payroll check for John T. McGrath.

Exhibit 6

Employee's Earnings Record

John T. McGrath
1830 4th St.
Clinton, IA 52732-6142 **PHONE: 555-3148**

SINGLE **NUMBER OF WITHHOLDING ALLOWANCES: 1** **PAY RATE: $1,360.00 Per Week**

OCCUPATION: Salesperson **EQUIVALENT HOURLY RATE: $34**

			Earnings				
	Period Ending	Total Hours	Regular Earnings	Overtime Earnings	Total Earnings	Total	
42	SEPT. 27	53	1,360.00	663.00	2,023.00	75,565.00	42
43	THIRD QUARTER		17,680.00	7,605.00	25,285.00		43
44	OCT. 4	51	1,360.00	561.00	1,921.00	77,486.00	44
50	NOV. 15	50	1,360.00	510.00	1,870.00	89,382.00	50
51	NOV. 22	53	1,360.00	663.00	2,023.00	91,405.00	51
52	NOV. 29	47	1,360.00	357.00	1,717.00	93,122.00	52
53	DEC. 6	53	1,360.00	663.00	2,023.00	95,145.00	53
54	DEC.13	52	1,360.00	612.00	1,972.00	97,117.00	54
55	DEC. 20	51	1,360.00	561.00	1,921.00	99,038.00	55
56	DEC. 27	42	1,360.00	102.00	1,462.00	100,500.00	56
57	FOURTH QUARTER		17,680.00	7,255.00	24,935.00		57
58	YEARLY TOTAL		70,720.00	29,780.00	100,500.00		58

Most companies issuing payroll checks use a special payroll bank account. In such cases, payroll is processed as follows:

1. The total net pay for the period is determined from the payroll register.
2. The company authorizes an electronic funds transfer (EFT) from its regular bank account to the special payroll bank account for the total net pay.
3. Individual payroll checks are written from the payroll account.
4. The numbers of the payroll checks are inserted in the payroll register.

An advantage of using a separate payroll bank account is that reconciling the bank statements is simplified. In addition, a payroll bank account establishes control over payroll checks and, thus, prevents their theft or misuse.

Many companies use electronic funds transfer to pay their employees. In such cases, each pay period an employee's net pay is deposited directly into the employee checking account. Later, employees receive a payroll statement summarizing how the net pay was computed.

Payroll System Diagram

Exhibit 8, on page 500, shows the flow of data and the interactions among the elements of a payroll system. As shown in Exhibit 8, the inputs into a payroll system may be classified as:

1. Constants, which are data that remain unchanged from payroll to payroll.

   Examples: Employee names, social security numbers, marital status, number of income tax withholding allowances, rates of pay, tax rates, and withholding tables.

Exhibit 6

(Concluded)

SOC. SEC. NO.: 381-48-9120 **EMPLOYEE NO.: 814**

DATE OF BIRTH: February 15, 1982

DATE EMPLOYMENT TERMINATED:

	Deductions							Paid		
	Social Security Tax	Medicare Tax	Federal Income Tax	Retirement Savings	Other		Total	Net Amount	Check No.	
42	121.38	30.35	429.83	20.00			601.56	1,421.44	6175	42
43	1,517.10	379.28	5,391.71	260.00	UF	40.00	7,588.09	17,696.91		43
44	115.26	28.82	401.27	20.00			565.35	1,355.65	6225	44
50	112.20	28.05	386.99	20.00			547.24	1,322.76	6530	50
51	121.38	30.35	429.83	20.00			601.56	1,421.44	6582	51
52	103.02	25.76	344.15	20.00			492.93	1,224.07	6640	52
53	121.38	30.35	429.83	20.00	UF	5.00	606.56	1,416.44	6688	53
54	118.32	29.58	415.55	20.00			583.45	1,388.55	6743	54
55	115.26	28.82	401.27	20.00			565.35	1,355.65	6801	55
56	57.72	21.93	268.45	20.00	UF	5.00	373.10	1,088.90	6860	56
57	1,466.10	374.03	5,293.71	260.00	UF	15.00	7,408.84	17,526.16		57
58	6,000.00	1,507.50	21,387.65	1,040.00	UF	100.00	30,035.15	70,464.85		58

2. Variables, which are data that change from payroll to payroll.

   Examples: Number of hours or days worked for each employee, accrued days of sick leave, vacation credits, total earnings to date, and total taxes withheld.

Many computerized payroll systems are offered on the Internet for a monthly fee. Internet-based payroll systems have the advantage of maintaining current federal and state tax rates.

In a computerized accounting system, constants are stored within a payroll file. The variables are input each pay period by a payroll clerk. In some systems, employees swipe their identification (ID) cards when they report for and leave work. In such cases, the hours worked by each employee are automatically updated.

A computerized payroll system also maintains electronic versions of the payroll register and employee earnings records. Payroll system outputs, such as payroll checks, EFTs, and tax records, are automatically produced each pay period.

Internal Controls For Payroll Systems

The cash payment controls described in Chapter 8, *Sarbanes-Oxley, Internal Control, and Cash,* also apply to payrolls. Some examples of payroll controls include the following:

Payroll frauds often involve a supervisor who cashes the payroll checks of fictitious employees or fired employees who are kept on the payroll.

1. If a check-signing machine is used, blank payroll checks and access to the machine should be restricted to prevent their theft or misuse.
2. The hiring and firing of employees should be properly authorized and approved in writing.
3. All changes in pay rates should be properly authorized and approved in writing.

Exhibit 7

Payroll Check

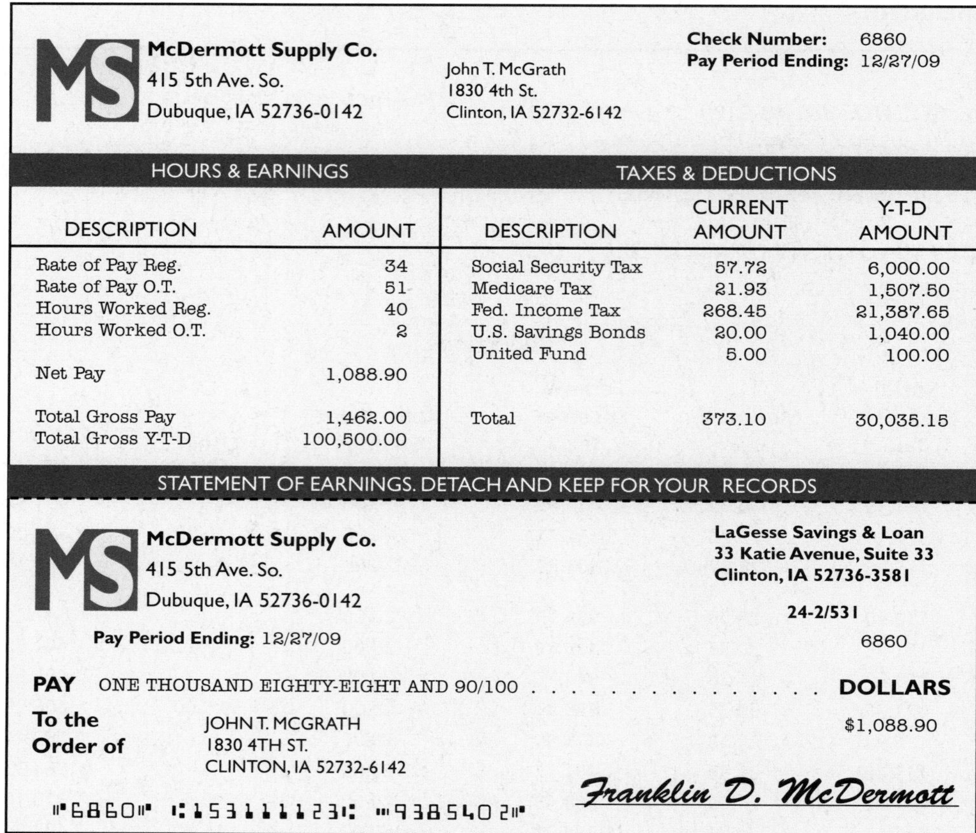

McDermott Supply Co.
415 5th Ave. So.
Dubuque, IA 52736-0142

John T. McGrath
1830 4th St.
Clinton, IA 52732-6142

Check Number: 6860
Pay Period Ending: 12/27/09

HOURS & EARNINGS		TAXES & DEDUCTIONS		
DESCRIPTION	AMOUNT	DESCRIPTION	CURRENT AMOUNT	Y-T-D AMOUNT
Rate of Pay Reg.	34	Social Security Tax	57.72	6,000.00
Rate of Pay O.T.	51	Medicare Tax	21.93	1,507.50
Hours Worked Reg.	40	Fed. Income Tax	268.45	21,387.65
Hours Worked O.T.	2	U.S. Savings Bonds	20.00	1,040.00
		United Fund	5.00	100.00
Net Pay	1,088.90			
Total Gross Pay	1,462.00	Total	373.10	30,035.15
Total Gross Y-T-D	100,500.00			

STATEMENT OF EARNINGS. DETACH AND KEEP FOR YOUR RECORDS

McDermott Supply Co.
415 5th Ave. So.
Dubuque, IA 52736-0142

Pay Period Ending: 12/27/09

LaGesse Savings & Loan
33 Katie Avenue, Suite 33
Clinton, IA 52736-3581

24-2/531

6860

PAY ONE THOUSAND EIGHTY-EIGHT AND 90/100 . . . . **DOLLARS**

To the Order of JOHN T. MCGRATH
1830 4TH ST.
CLINTON, IA 52732-6142

$1,088.90

Franklin D. McDermott

⑈6860⑈ ⑆153111123⑆ ⑈938540 2⑈

4. Employees should be observed when arriving for work to verify that employees are "checking in" for work only once and only for themselves. Employees may "check in" for work by using a time card or by swiping their employee ID card.
5. Payroll checks should be distributed by someone other than employee supervisors.
6. A special payroll bank account should be used.

Exhibit 8

Flow of Data in a Payroll System

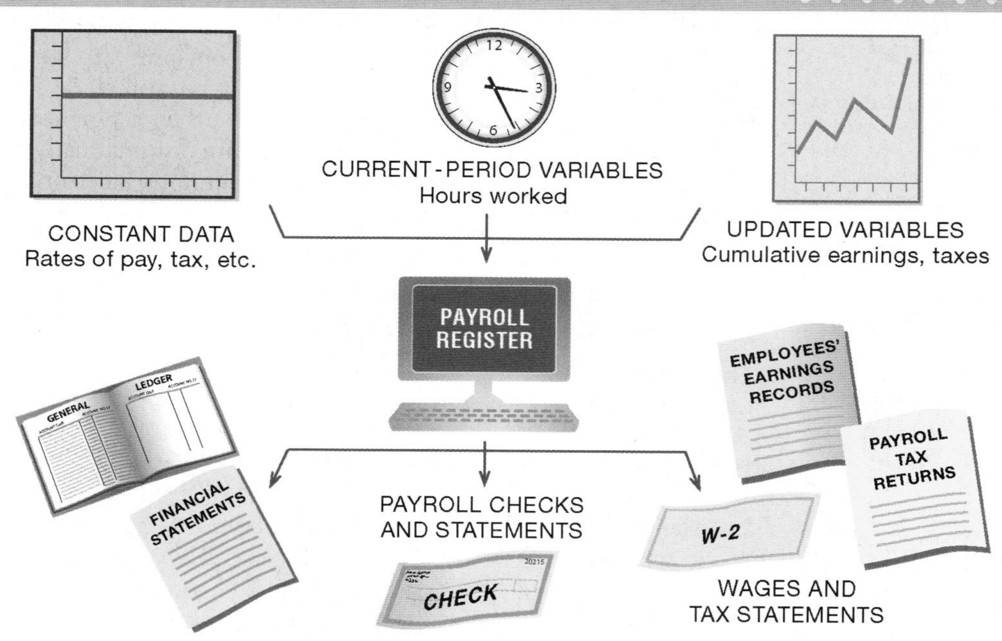

Integrity, Objectivity, and Ethics in Business

$8 MILLION FOR 18 MINUTES OF WORK

Computer system controls can be very important in issuing payroll checks. In one case, a Detroit schoolteacher was paid $4,015,625 after deducting $3,884,375 in payroll deductions for 18 minutes of overtime work. The error was caused by a computer glitch when the teacher's employee identification number was substituted incorrectly in the "hourly wage" field and wasn't caught by the payroll software. After six days, the error was discovered and the money was returned. "One of the things that came with (the software) is a fail-safe that prevents that. It doesn't work," a financial officer said. The district has since installed a program to flag any paycheck exceeding $10,000.

Source: Associated Press, September 27, 2002.

4 Journalize entries for employee fringe benefits, including vacation pay and pensions.

Employees' Fringe Benefits

Many companies provide their employees benefits in addition to salary and wages earned. Such **fringe benefits** may include vacation, medical, and retirement benefits. Exhibit 9 shows these three fringe benefits as a percent of total payroll costs.[7]

Exhibit 9

Benefit Dollars as a Percent of Payroll Costs

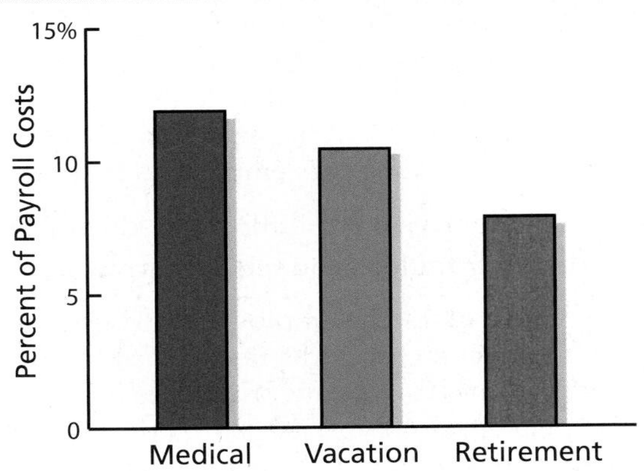

The U.S. Chamber of Commerce estimates that fringe benefits, excluding FICA, average about 33% of gross pay.

The cost of employee fringe benefits is recorded as an expense by the employer. To match revenues and expenses, the estimated cost of fringe benefits is recorded as an expense during the period in which the employees earn the benefits.

Vacation Pay

Most employers provide employees vacations, sometimes called *compensated absences*. The liability to pay for employee vacations could be accrued as a liability at the end of each pay period. However, many companies wait and record an adjusting entry for accrued vacation at the end of the year.

Vacation pay becomes the employer's liability as the employee earns vacation rights.

To illustrate, assume that employees earn one day of vacation for each month worked. The estimated vacation pay for the year ending December 31 is $325,000. The adjusting entry for the accrued vacation is shown below.

Dec.	31	Vacation Pay Expense		325,000	
		Vacation Pay Payable			325,000
		Accrued vacation pay for the year.			

7 *2005 Employee Benefits Study*, U.S. Chamber of Commerce, 2006.

Employees may be required to take all their vacation time within one year. In such cases, any accrued vacation pay will be paid within one year. Thus, the vacation pay payable is reported as a current liability on the balance sheet. If employees are allowed to accumulate their vacation pay, the estimated vacation pay payable that will *not* be taken within a year is reported as a long-term liability.

When employees take vacations, the liability for vacation pay is decreased by debiting Vacation Pay Payable. Salaries or Wages Payable and the other related payroll accounts for taxes and withholdings are credited.

Pensions

A **pension** is a cash payment to retired employees. Pension rights are accrued by employees as they work, based on the employer's pension plan. Two basic types of pension plans are:

1. Defined contribution plan
2. Defined benefit plan

In 90% of 401k plans, the employer matches some portion of the employee's contribution. As a result, nearly 70% of eligible employees elect to enroll in a 401k.

Source: "Employees Sluggish in Interacting with 401k Plans," Hewitt Associates, December 26, 2005.

In a **defined contribution plan**, the company invests contributions on behalf of the employee during the employee's working years. Normally, the employee and employer contribute to the plan. The employee's pension depends on the total contributions and the investment returns earned on those contributions.

One of the more popular defined contribution plans is the 401k plan. Under this plan, employees contribute a portion of their gross pay to investments, such as mutual funds. A 401k plan offers employees two advantages.

1. The employee contribution is deducted before taxes.
2. The contributions and related earnings are not taxed until withdrawn at retirement.

In most cases, the employer matches some portion of the employee's contribution. The employer's cost is debited to *Pension Expense*. To illustrate, assume that Heaven Scent Perfumes Company contributes 10% of employee monthly salaries to an employee 401k plan. Assuming $500,000 of monthly salaries, the journal entry to record the monthly contribution is shown below.

Dec.	31	Pension Expense		50,000	
		Cash			50,000
		Contributed 10% of monthly salaries to pension plan.			

Twenty percent of private industry uses defined benefit plans, while 43% uses defined contribution plans.

Source: Bureau of Labor Statistics, "Employee Benefits in Private Industry," 2007.

In a **defined benefit plan**, the company pays the employee a fixed annual pension based on a formula. The formula is normally based on such factors as the employee's years of service, age, and past salary.

Annual Pension = 1.5% × Years of Service × Highest 3-Year Average Salary

In a defined benefit plan, the employer is obligated to pay for (fund) the employee's future pension benefits. As a result, many companies are replacing their defined benefit plans with defined contribution plans.

The pension cost of a defined benefit plan is debited to *Pension Expense*. Cash is credited for the amount contributed (funded) by the employer. Any unfunded amount is credited to *Unfunded Pension Liability*.

To illustrate, assume that the defined benefit plan of Hinkle Co. requires an annual pension cost of $80,000. This annual contribution is based on estimates of Hinkle's future pension liabilities. On December 31, Hinkle Co. pays $60,000 to the pension fund. The entry to record the payment and unfunded liability is shown below.

Dec.	31	Pension Expense		80,000	
		Cash			60,000
		Unfunded Pension Liability			20,000
		Annual pension cost and contribution.			

If the unfunded pension liability is to be paid within one year, it is reported as a current liability on the balance sheet. Any portion of the unfunded pension liability that will be paid beyond one year is a long-term liability.

The accounting for pensions is complex due to the uncertainties of estimating future pension liabilities. These estimates depend on such factors as employee life expectancies, employee turnover, expected employee compensation levels, and investment income on pension contributions. Additional accounting and disclosures related to pensions are covered in advanced accounting courses.

Example Exercise 11-6 Vacation Pay and Pension Benefits

Manfield Services Company provides its employees vacation benefits and a defined contribution pension plan. Employees earned vacation pay of $44,000 for the period. The pension plan requires a contribution to the plan administrator equal to 8% of employee salaries. Salaries were $450,000 during the period.

Provide the journal entry for the (a) vacation pay and (b) pension benefit.

Follow My Example 11-6

a.	Vacation Pay Expense	44,000	
	Vacation Pay Payable		44,000
	Vacation pay accrued for the period.		
b.	Pension Expense	36,000	
	Cash		36,000
	Pension contribution, 8% of $450,000 salary.		

For Practice: PE 11-6A, PE 11-6B

Postretirement Benefits Other than Pensions

Employees may earn rights to other postretirement benefits from their employer. Such benefits may include dental care, eye care, medical care, life insurance, tuition assistance, tax services, and legal services.

The accounting for other postretirement benefits is similar to that of defined benefit pension plans. The estimate of the annual benefits expense is recorded by debiting *Postretirement Benefits Expense*. If the benefits are fully funded, Cash is credited for the same amount. If the benefits are not fully funded, a postretirement benefits plan liability account is also credited.

The financial statements should disclose the nature of the postretirement benefit liabilities. These disclosures are usually included as notes to the financial statements. Additional accounting and disclosures for postretirement benefits are covered in advanced accounting courses.

Current Liabilities on the Balance Sheet

Accounts payable, the current portion of long-term debt, notes payable, and any other debts that are due within one year are reported as current liabilities on the balance sheet. The balance sheet presentation of current liabilities for Mornin' Joe is as follows:

Mornin' Joe Balance Sheet December 31, 2010		
Liabilities		
Current liabilities:		
Accounts payable	$133,000	
Notes payable (current portion)	200,000	
Salaries and wages payable	42,000	
Payroll taxes payable	16,400	
Interest payable	40,000	
Total current liabilities		$431,400

Describe the accounting treatment for contingent liabilities and journalize entries for product warranties.

Contingent Liabilities

Some liabilities may arise from past transactions if certain events occur in the future. These *potential* liabilities are called **contingent liabilities.**

The accounting for contingent liabilities depends on the following two factors:

1. Likelihood of occurring: Probable, reasonably possible, or remote
2. Measurement: Estimable or not estimable

The likelihood that the event creating the liability occurring is classified as *probable, reasonably possible*, or *remote*. The ability to estimate the potential liability is classified as *estimable* or *not estimable*.

Probable and Estimable

If a contingent liability is *probable* and the amount of the liability can be *reasonably estimated*, it is recorded and disclosed. The liability is recorded by debiting an expense and crediting a liability.

To illustrate, assume that during June a company sold a product for $60,000 that includes a 36-month warranty for repairs. The average cost of repairs over the warranty period is 5% of the sales price. The entry to record the estimated product warranty expense for June is as shown below.

June	30	Product Warranty Expense		3,000	
		Product Warranty Payable			3,000
		Warranty expense for June, 5% × $60,000.			

The estimated costs of warranty work on new car sales are a contingent liability for Ford Motor Company.

The preceding entry records warranty expense in the same period in which the sale is recorded. In this way, warranty expense is matched with the related revenue (sales).

If the product is repaired under warranty, the repair costs are recorded by debiting *Product Warranty Payable* and crediting *Cash, Supplies, Wages Payable,* or other appropriate accounts. Thus, if a $200 part is replaced under warranty on August 16, the entry is as follows:

Aug.	16	Product Warranty Payable		200	
		Supplies			200
		Replaced defective part under warranty.			

Example Exercise 11-7 Estimated Warranty Liability

Cook-Rite Co. sold $140,000 of kitchen appliances during August under a six-month warranty. The cost to repair defects under the warranty is estimated at 6% of the sales price. On September 11, a customer required a $200 part replacement, plus $90 of labor under the warranty.

Provide the journal entry for (a) the estimated warranty expense on August 31 and (b) the September 11 warranty work.

Follow My Example 11-7

a.	Product Warranty Expense	8,400	
	Product Warranty Payable		8,400
	To record warranty expense for August, 6% × $140,000.		
b.	Product Warranty Payable	290	
	Supplies		200
	Wages Payable		90
	Replaced defective part under warranty.		

For Practice: PE 11-7A, PE 11-7B

Probable and Not Estimable

A contingent liability may be probable, but cannot be estimated. In this case, the contingent liability is disclosed in the notes to the financial statements. For example, a company may have accidentally polluted a local river by dumping waste products. At the end of the period, the cost of the cleanup and any fines may not be able to be estimated.

Reasonably Possible

A contingent liability may be only possible. For example, a company may have lost a lawsuit for infringing on another company's patent rights. However, the verdict is under appeal and the company's lawyers feel that the verdict will be reversed or significantly reduced. In this case, the contingent liability is disclosed in the notes to the financial statements.

Remote

A contingent liability may be remote. For example, a ski resort may be sued for injuries incurred by skiers. In most cases, the courts have found that a skier accepts the risk of injury when participating in the activity. Thus, unless the ski resort is grossly negligent, the resort will not incur a liability for ski injuries. In such cases, no disclosure needs to be made in the notes to the financial statements.

The accounting treatment of contingent liabilities is summarized in Exhibit 10.

Exhibit 10

Accounting Treatment of Contingent Liabilities

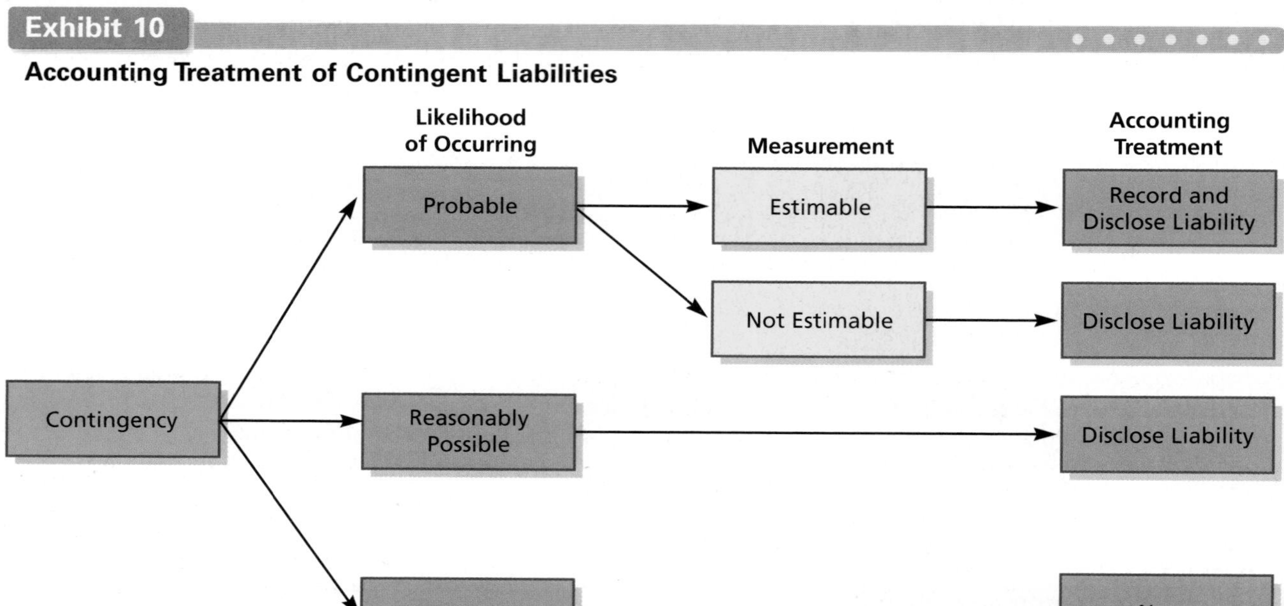

Common examples of contingent liabilities disclosed in notes to the financial statements are litigation, environmental matters, guarantees, and contingencies from the sale of receivables.

An example of a contingent liability disclosure from a recent annual report of Google Inc. is shown below.

> *—Certain entities have also filed copyright claims against us, alleging that certain of our products, including Google Web Search, Google News, Google Image Search, and Google Book Search, infringe their rights. Adverse results in these lawsuits may include awards of damages and may also result in, or even compel, a change in our business practices, which could result in a loss of revenue for us or otherwise harm our business.*
>
> *—Although the results of litigation and claims cannot be predicted with certainty, we believe that the final outcome of the matters discussed above will not have a material adverse effect on our business. . . .*

Professional judgment is necessary in distinguishing between classes of contingent liabilities. This is especially the case when distinguishing between probable and reasonably possible contingent liabilities.

Integrity, Objectivity, and Ethics in Business

TODAY'S MISTAKES CAN BE TOMORROW'S LIABILITY

Environmental and public health claims are quickly growing into some of the largest contingent liabilities facing companies. For example, tobacco, asbestos, and environmental cleanup claims have reached billions of dollars and have led to a number of corporate bankruptcies. Managers must be careful that today's decisions do not become tomorrow's nightmare.

Financial Analysis and Interpretation

The Current Assets and Current Liabilities sections of the balance sheet for Noble Co. and Hart Co. are illustrated as follows:

	Noble Co.	Hart Co.
Current assets:		
Cash	$147,000	$120,000
Accounts receivable (net)	84,000	472,000
Inventory	150,000	200,000
Total current assets	$381,000	$792,000
Current liabilities:		
Accounts payable	$ 75,000	$227,000
Wages payable	30,000	193,000
Notes payable	115,000	320,000
Total current liabilities	$220,000	$740,000

We can use this information to evaluate Noble's and Hart's ability to pay their current liabilities within a short period of time, using the **quick ratio** or *acid-test ratio*. The quick ratio is computed as follows:

$$\text{Quick Ratio} = \frac{\text{Quick Assets}}{\text{Current Liabilities}}$$

The quick ratio measures the "instant" debt-paying ability of a company, using quick assets. **Quick assets** are cash, receivables, and other current assets that can quickly be converted into cash. It is often considered desirable to have a quick ratio exceeding 1.0. A ratio less than 1.0 would indicate that current liabilities cannot be covered by cash and "near cash" assets.

To illustrate, the quick ratios for both companies would be as follows:

$$\text{Noble Co: } \frac{\$147{,}000 + \$84{,}000}{\$220{,}000} = 1.05$$

$$\text{Hart Co: } \frac{\$120{,}000 + \$472{,}000}{\$740{,}000} = 0.80$$

As you can see, Noble Co. has quick assets in excess of current liabilities, or a quick ratio of 1.05. The ratio exceeds 1.0, indicating that the quick assets should be sufficient to meet current liabilities. Hart Co., however, has a quick ratio of 0.8. Its quick assets will not be sufficient to cover the current liabilities. Hart could solve this problem by working with a bank to convert its short-term debt of $320,000 into a long-term obligation. This would remove the notes payable from current liabilities. If Hart did this, then its quick ratio would improve to 1.4 ($592,000/$420,000), which would be sufficient for quick assets to cover current liabilities.

f·a·i

At a Glance 11

1 Describe and illustrate current liabilities related to accounts payable, current portion of long-term debt, and notes payable.

Key Points	Key Learning Outcomes	Example Exercises	Practice Exercises
Current liabilities are obligations that are to be paid out of current assets and are due within a short time, usually within one year. The three primary types of current liabilities are accounts payable, notes payable, and current portion of long-term debt.	• Identify and define the most frequently reported current liabilities on the balance sheet.		
	• Determine the interest from interest-bearing and discounted notes payable.	11-1	11-1A, 11-1B

2 Determine employer liabilities for payroll, including liabilities arising from employee earnings and deductions from earnings.

Key Points	Key Learning Outcomes	Example Exercises	Practice Exercises
An employer's liability for payroll is determined from employee total earnings, including overtime pay. From this amount, employee deductions are subtracted to arrive at the net pay to be paid to each employee. Most employers also incur liabilities for payroll taxes, such as social security tax, Medicare tax, federal unemployment compensation tax, and state unemployment compensation tax.	• Compute the federal withholding tax from a wage bracket withholding table.	**11-2**	11-2A, 11-2B
	• Compute employee net pay, including deductions for social security and Medicare tax.	**11-3**	11-3A, 11-3B

3 Describe payroll accounting systems that use a payroll register, employee earnings records, and a general journal.

Key Points	Key Learning Outcomes	Example Exercises	Practice Exercises
The payroll register is used in assembling and summarizing the data needed for each payroll period. The payroll register is supported by a detailed payroll record for each employee, called an *employee's earnings record.*	• Journalize the employee's earnings, net pay, and payroll liabilities from the payroll register.	**11-4**	11-4A, 11-4B
	• Journalize the payroll tax expense.	**11-5**	11-5A, 11-5B
	• Describe elements of a payroll system, including the employee's earnings record, payroll checks, and internal controls.		

4 Journalize entries for employee fringe benefits, including vacation pay and pensions.

Key Points	Key Learning Outcomes	Example Exercises	Practice Exercises
Fringe benefits are expenses of the period in which the employees earn the benefits. Fringe benefits are recorded by debiting an expense account and crediting a liability account.	• Journalize vacation pay.	**11-6**	11-6A, 11-6B
	• Distinguish and journalize defined contribution and defined benefit pension plans.	**11-6**	11-6A, 11-6B

5 Describe the accounting treatment for contingent liabilities and journalize entries for product warranties.

Key Points	Key Learning Outcomes	Example Exercises	Practice Exercises
A contingent liability is a potential obligation that results from a past transaction but depends on a future event. The accounting for contingent liabilities is summarized in Exhibit 10.	• Describe the accounting for contingent liabilities.		
	• Journalize estimated warranty obligations and services granted under warranty.	**11-7**	11-7A, 11-7B

Key Terms

contingent liabilities (504)
defined benefit plan (502)
defined contribution plan (502)
employee's earnings record (497)
FICA tax (491)
fringe benefits (501)
gross pay (489)
net pay (489)
payroll (489)
payroll register (494)
pension (502)
quick assets (507)
quick ratio (507)

Illustrative Problem

Selected transactions of Taylor Company, completed during the fiscal year ended December 31, are as follows:

Mar. 1. Purchased merchandise on account from Kelvin Co., $20,000.
Apr. 10. Issued a 60-day, 12% note for $20,000 to Kelvin Co. on account.
June 9. Paid Kelvin Co. the amount owed on the note of April 10.
Aug. 1. Issued a $50,000, 90-day note to Harold Co. in exchange for a building. Harold Co. discounted the note at 15%.
Oct. 30. Paid Harold Co. the amount due on the note of August 1.
Dec. 27. Journalized the entry to record the biweekly payroll. A summary of the payroll record follows:

Salary distribution:		
Sales	$63,400	
Officers	36,600	
Office	10,000	$110,000
Deductions:		
Social security tax	$ 5,050	
Medicare tax	1,650	
Federal income tax withheld	17,600	
State income tax withheld	4,950	
Savings bond deductions	850	
Medical insurance deductions	1,120	31,220
Net amount		$ 78,780

27. Journalized the entry to record payroll taxes for social security and Medicare from the biweekly payroll.
30. Issued a check in payment of liabilities for employees' federal income tax of $17,600, social security tax of $10,100, and Medicare tax of $3,300.
31. Issued a check for $9,500 to the pension fund trustee to fully fund the pension cost for December.
31. Journalized an entry to record the employees' accrued vacation pay, $36,100.
31. Journalized an entry to record the estimated accrued product warranty liability, $37,240.

Instructions

Journalize the preceding transactions.

Solution

Date		Description	Post. Ref.	Debit	Credit
Mar.	1	Merchandise Inventory		20,000	
		Accounts Payable—Kelvin Co.			20,000
Apr.	10	Accounts Payable—Kelvin Co.		20,000	
		Notes Payable			20,000
June	9	Notes Payable		20,000	
		Interest Expense		400	
		Cash			20,400
Aug.	1	Building		48,125	
		Interest Expense		1,875	
		Notes Payable			50,000
Oct.	30	Notes Payable		50,000	
		Cash			50,000
Dec.	27	Sales Salaries Expense		63,400	
		Officers Salaries Expense		36,600	
		Office Salaries Expense		10,000	
		Social Security Tax Payable			5,050
		Medicare Tax Payable			1,650
		Employees Federal Income Tax Payable			17,600
		Employees State Income Tax Payable			4,950
		Bond Deductions Payable			850
		Medical Insurance Payable			1,120
		Salaries Payable			78,780
	27	Payroll Tax Expense		6,700	
		Social Security Tax Payable			5,050
		Medicare Tax Payable			1,650
	30	Employees Federal Income Tax Payable		17,600	
		Social Security Tax Payable		10,100	
		Medicare Tax Payable		3,300	
		Cash			31,000
	31	Pension Expense		9,500	
		Cash			9,500
		Fund pension cost.			
	31	Vacation Pay Expense		36,100	
		Vacation Pay Payable			36,100
		Accrue vacation pay.			
	31	Product Warranty Expense		37,240	
		Product Warranty Payable			37,240
		Accrue warranty expense.			

Self-Examination Questions (Answers at End of Chapter)

1. A business issued a $5,000, 60-day, 12% note to the bank. The amount due at maturity is:
   A. $4,900.
   B. $5,000.
   C. $5,100.
   D. $5,600.
2. A business issued a $5,000, 60-day note to a supplier, which discounted the note at 12%. The proceeds are:
   A. $4,400.
   B. $4,900.
   C. $5,000.
   D. $5,100.
3. Which of the following taxes are employers usually not required to withhold from employees?
   A. Federal income tax
   B. Federal unemployment compensation tax
   C. Medicare tax
   D. State and local income tax
4. An employee's rate of pay is $40 per hour, with time and a half for all hours worked in excess of 40 during a week. The social security rate is 6.0% on the first $100,000 of annual earnings, and the Medicare rate is 1.5% on all earnings. The following additional data are available:

Hours worked during current week	45
Year's cumulative earnings prior to current week	$99,400
Federal income tax withheld	$450

   Based on these data, the amount of the employee's net pay for the current week is:
   A. $1,307.50.
   B. $1,405.00.
   C. $1,450.00.
   D. $1,385.50.
5. Within limitations on the maximum earnings subject to the tax, employers do not incur an expense for which of the following payroll taxes?
   A. Social security tax
   B. Federal unemployment compensation tax
   C. State unemployment compensation tax
   D. Employees' federal income tax

Eye Openers

1. Does a discounted note payable provide credit without interest? Discuss.
2. Employees are subject to taxes withheld from their paychecks.
   a. List the federal taxes withheld from most employee paychecks.
   b. Give the title of the accounts credited by amounts withheld.
3. For each of the following payroll-related taxes, indicate whether there is a ceiling on the annual earnings subject to the tax: (a) federal income tax, (b) Medicare tax, (c) social security tax, (d) federal unemployment compensation tax.
4. Why are deductions from employees' earnings classified as liabilities for the employer?
5. Taylor Company, with 20 employees, is expanding operations. It is trying to decide whether to hire one full-time employee for $25,000 or two part-time employees for a total of $25,000. Would any of the employer's payroll taxes discussed in this chapter have a bearing on this decision? Explain.
6. For each of the following payroll-related taxes, indicate whether they generally apply to (a) employees only, (b) employers only, or (c) both employees and employers:
   1. Federal income tax
   2. Medicare tax
   3. Social security tax
   4. Federal unemployment compensation tax
   5. State unemployment compensation tax
7. What are the principal reasons for using a special payroll checking account?
8. In a payroll system, what types of input data are referred to as (a) constants and (b) variables?
9. Explain how a payroll system that is properly designed and operated tends to ensure that (a) wages paid are based on hours actually worked and (b) payroll checks are not issued to fictitious employees.
10. To match revenues and expenses properly, should the expense for employee vacation pay be recorded in the period during which the vacation privilege is earned or during the period in which the vacation is taken? Discuss.

11. Identify several factors that influence the future pension obligation of an employer under a defined benefit pension plan.
12. When should the liability associated with a product warranty be recorded? Discuss.

13. General Motors Corporation reported $10.1 billion of product warranties in the Current Liabilities section of a recent balance sheet. How would costs of repairing a defective product be recorded?
14. The "Questions and Answers Technical Hotline" in the *Journal of Accountancy* included the following question:

    Several years ago, Company B instituted legal action against Company A. Under a memorandum of settlement and agreement, Company A agreed to pay Company B a total of $17,500 in three installments—$5,000 on March 1, $7,500 on July 1, and the remaining $5,000 on December 31. Company A paid the first two installments during its fiscal year ended September 30. Should the unpaid amount of $5,000 be presented as a current liability at September 30?

    How would you answer this question?

Practice Exercises

PE 11-1A
Proceeds from notes payable
obj. 1
EE 11-1 p. 488

On September 1, Klondike Co. issued a 60-day note with a face amount of $100,000 to Arctic Apparel Co. for merchandise inventory.

a. Determine the proceeds of the note, assuming the note carries an interest rate of 6%.
b. Determine the proceeds of the note, assuming the note is discounted at 6%.

PE 11-1B
Proceeds from notes payable
obj. 1
EE 11-1 p. 488

On February 1, Electronic Warehouse Co. issued a 45-day note with a face amount of $80,000 to Yamura Products Co. for cash.

a. Determine the proceeds of the note, assuming the note carries an interest rate of 10%.
b. Determine the proceeds of the note, assuming the note is discounted at 10%.

PE 11-2A
Federal income tax withholding
obj. 2
EE 11-2 p. 491

Todd Hackworth's weekly gross earnings for the present week were $2,000. Hackworth has two exemptions. Using the wage bracket withholding table in Exhibit 3 with a $67 standard withholding allowance for each exemption, what is Hackworth's federal income tax withholding?

PE 11-2B
Federal income tax withholding
obj. 2
EE 11-2 p. 491

Robert Clowney's weekly gross earnings for the present week were $800. Clowney has one exemption. Using the wage bracket withholding table in Exhibit 3 with a $67 standard withholding allowance for each exemption, what is Clowney's federal income tax withholding?

PE 11-3A
Employee net pay
obj. 2
EE 11-3 p. 492

Todd Hackworth's weekly gross earnings for the week ending December 18 were $2,000, and his federal income tax withholding was $396.19. Prior to this week, Hackworth had earned $98,500 for the year. Assuming the social security rate is 6% on the first $100,000 of annual earnings and Medicare is 1.5% of all earnings, what is Hackworth's net pay?

PE 11-3B
Employee net pay
obj. 2
EE 11-3 p. 492

Robert Clowney's weekly gross earnings for the week ending September 5 were $800, and his federal income tax withholding was $102.95. Prior to this week, Clowney had earned $24,000 for the year. Assuming the social security rate is 6% on the first $100,000 of annual earnings and Medicare is 1.5% of all earnings, what is Clowney's net pay?

PE 11-4A
Journalize period payroll
obj. 3
EE 11-4 p. 495

The payroll register of Woodard Construction Co. indicates $2,552 of social security withheld and $660 of Medicare tax withheld on total salaries of $44,000 for the period. Federal withholding for the period totaled $8,712.

Provide the journal entry for the period's payroll.

PE 11-4B
Journalize period payroll
obj. 3
EE 11-4 p. 495

The payroll register of Salem Communications Co. indicates $29,580 of social security withheld and $7,650 of Medicare tax withheld on total salaries of $510,000 for the period. Retirement savings withheld from employee paychecks were $30,600 for the period. Federal withholding for the period totaled $100,980.

Provide the journal entry for the period's payroll.

PE 11-5A
Journalize payroll tax
obj. 3
EE 11-5 p. 496

The payroll register of Woodard Construction Co. indicates $2,552 of social security withheld and $660 of Medicare tax withheld on total salaries of $44,000 for the period. Assume earnings subject to state and federal unemployment compensation taxes are $10,500, at the federal rate of 0.8% and the state rate of 5.4%.

Provide the journal entry to record the payroll tax expense for the period.

PE 11-5B
Journalize payroll tax
obj. 3
EE 11-5 p. 496

The payroll register of Salem Communications Co. indicates $29,580 of social security withheld and $7,650 of Medicare tax withheld on total salaries of $510,000 for the period. Assume earnings subject to state and federal unemployment compensation taxes are $16,000, at the federal rate of 0.8% and the state rate of 5.4%.

Provide the journal entry to record the payroll tax expense for the period.

PE 11-6A
Vacation pay and pension benefits
obj. 4
EE 11-6 p. 503

Blount Company provides its employees with vacation benefits and a defined contribution pension plan. Employees earned vacation pay of $30,000 for the period. The pension plan requires a contribution to the plan administrator equal to 10% of employee salaries. Salaries were $400,000 during the period.

Provide the journal entry for the (a) vacation pay and (b) pension benefit.

PE 11-6B
Vacation pay and pension benefits
obj. 4
EE 11-6 p. 503

Hobson Equipment Company provides its employees vacation benefits and a defined benefit pension plan. Employees earned vacation pay of $20,000 for the period. The pension formula calculated a pension cost of $140,000. Only $106,000 was contributed to the pension plan administrator.

Provide the journal entry for the (a) vacation pay and (b) pension benefit.

PE 11-7A
Estimated warranty liability
obj. 5
EE 11-7 p. 505

Akine Co. sold $600,000 of equipment during April under a one-year warranty. The cost to repair defects under the warranty is estimated at 6% of the sales price. On August 4, a customer required a $140 part replacement, plus $80 of labor under the warranty.

Provide the journal entry for (a) the estimated warranty expense on April 30 and (b) the August 4 warranty work.

PE 11-7B
Estimated warranty liability
obj. 5
EE 11-7 p. 505

Robin Industries sold $350,000 of consumer electronics during May under a nine-month warranty. The cost to repair defects under the warranty is estimated at 3% of the sales price. On July 16, a customer was given $140 cash under terms of the warranty.

Provide the journal entry for (a) the estimated warranty expense on May 31 and (b) the July 16 cash payment.

Exercises

EX 11-1
Current liabilities
obj. 1
✔ Total current liabilities, $790,000

I-Generation Co. sold 14,000 annual subscriptions of *Climber's World* for $60 during December 2010. These new subscribers will receive monthly issues, beginning in January 2011. In addition, the business had taxable income of $400,000 during the first calendar quarter of 2011. The federal tax rate is 40%. A quarterly tax payment will be made on April 7, 2011.

Prepare the Current Liabilities section of the balance sheet for I-Generation Co. on March 31, 2011.

EX 11-2
Entries for discounting notes payable
obj. 1

U-Build It Warehouse issues a 45-day note for $800,000 to Thomson Home Furnishings Co. for merchandise inventory. Thomson Home Furnishings Co. discounts the note at 7%.

a. Journalize U-Build It Warehouse's entries to record:
   1. the issuance of the note.
   2. the payment of the note at maturity.
b. Journalize Thomson Home Furnishings Co.'s entries to record:
   1. the receipt of the note.
   2. the receipt of the payment of the note at maturity.

EX 11-3
Evaluate alternative notes
obj. 1

A borrower has two alternatives for a loan: (1) issue a $240,000, 60-day, 8% note or (2) issue a $240,000, 60-day note that the creditor discounts at 8%.

a. Calculate the amount of the interest expense for each option.
b. Determine the proceeds received by the borrower in each situation.
c. Which alternative is more favorable to the borrower? Explain.

EX 11-4
Entries for notes payable
obj. 1

A business issued a 30-day, 4% note for $60,000 to a creditor on account. Journalize the entries to record (a) the issuance of the note and (b) the payment of the note at maturity, including interest.

EX 11-5
Entries for discounted note payable
obj. 1

A business issued a 60-day note for $45,000 to a creditor on account. The note was discounted at 6%. Journalize the entries to record (a) the issuance of the note and (b) the payment of the note at maturity.

EX 11-6
Fixed asset purchases with note
obj. 1

On June 30, Rioux Management Company purchased land for $400,000 and a building for $600,000, paying $500,000 cash and issuing a 6% note for the balance, secured by a mortgage on the property. The terms of the note provide for 20 semiannual payments of $25,000 on the principal plus the interest accrued from the date of the preceding payment. Journalize the entry to record (a) the transaction on June 30, (b) the payment of the first installment on December 31, and (c) the payment of the second installment the following June 30.

EX 11-7
Current portion of long-term debt
obj. 1

P.F. Chang's China Bistro, Inc., the operator of P.F. Chang restaurants, reported the following information about its long-term debt in the notes to a recent financial statement:

Long-term debt is comprised of the following:

	December 31,	
	2006	2005
Notes payable	$19,210,000	$10,470,000
Less current portion	(5,487,000)	(5,110,000)
Long-term debt	$13,723,000	$ 5,360,000

a. How much of the notes payable was disclosed as a current liability on the December 31, 2006, balance sheet?
b. How much did the total current liabilities change between 2005 and 2006 as a result of the current portion of long-term debt?
c. If P.F. Chang's did not issue additional notes payable during 2007, what would be the total notes payable on December 31, 2007?

EX 11-8
Calculate payroll
obj. 2
✔ b. Net pay, $2,061.00

An employee earns $40 per hour and 1.75 times that rate for all hours in excess of 40 hours per week. Assume that the employee worked 60 hours during the week, and that the gross pay prior to the current week totaled $58,000. Assume further that the social security tax rate was 6.0% (on earnings up to $100,000), the Medicare tax rate was 1.5%, and federal income tax to be withheld was $714.

a. Determine the gross pay for the week.
b. Determine the net pay for the week.

EX 11-9
Calculate payroll
obj. 2
✔ Administrator net pay, $1,423.57

Reaves Professional Services has three employees—a consultant, a computer programmer, and an administrator. The following payroll information is available for each employee:

	Consultant	Computer Programmer	Administrator
Regular earnings rate	$3,000 per week	$24 per hour	$36 per hour
Overtime earnings rate	Not applicable	2 times hourly rate	2 times hourly rate
Gross pay prior to current pay period	$118,000	$45,000	$99,000
Number of withholding allowances	2	1	2

For the current pay period, the computer programmer worked 50 hours and the administrator worked 46 hours. The federal income tax withheld for all three employees, who are single, can be determined from the wage bracket withholding table in Exhibit 3 in the chapter. Assume further that the social security tax rate was 6.0% on the first $100,000 of annual earnings, the Medicare tax rate was 1.5%, and one withholding allowance is $67.

Determine the gross pay and the net pay for each of the three employees for the current pay period.

EX 11-10
Summary payroll data
objs. 2, 3

✔ a. (3) Total earnings, $400,000

In the following summary of data for a payroll period, some amounts have been intentionally omitted:

Earnings:	
1. At regular rate	?
2. At overtime rate	$ 60,000
3. Total earnings	?
Deductions:	
4. Social security tax	23,200
5. Medicare tax	6,000
6. Income tax withheld	99,600
7. Medical insurance	14,000
8. Union dues	?
9. Total deductions	147,800
10. Net amount paid	252,200
Accounts debited:	
11. Factory Wages	210,000
12. Sales Salaries	?
13. Office Salaries	80,000

a. Calculate the amounts omitted in lines (1), (3), (8), and (12).
b. Journalize the entry to record the payroll accrual.
c. Journalize the entry to record the payment of the payroll.
d. From the data given in this exercise and your answer to (a), would you conclude that this payroll was paid sometime during the first few weeks of the calendar year? Explain.

EX 11-11
Payroll tax entries
obj. 3

According to a summary of the payroll of Scofield Industries Co., $600,000 was subject to the 6.0% social security tax and $740,000 was subject to the 1.5% Medicare tax. Also, $20,000 was subject to state and federal unemployment taxes.

a. Calculate the employer's payroll taxes, using the following rates: state unemployment, 4.2%; federal unemployment, 0.8%.
b. Journalize the entry to record the accrual of payroll taxes.

EX 11-12
Payroll entries
obj. 3

The payroll register for Gentry Company for the week ended December 17 indicated the following:

Salaries	$540,000
Social security tax withheld	25,380
Medicare tax withheld	8,100
Federal income tax withheld	108,000

In addition, state and federal unemployment taxes were calculated at the rate of 5.2% and 0.8%, respectively, on $10,000 of salaries.

a. Journalize the entry to record the payroll for the week of December 17.
b. Journalize the entry to record the payroll tax expense incurred for the week of December 17.

EX 11-13
Payroll entries
obj. 3

Thorup Company had gross wages of $200,000 during the week ended December 10. The amount of wages subject to social security tax was $180,000, while the amount of wages subject to federal and state unemployment taxes was $25,000. Tax rates are as follows:

Social security	6.0%
Medicare	1.5%
State unemployment	5.3%
Federal unemployment	0.8%

The total amount withheld from employee wages for federal taxes was $40,000.

a. Journalize the entry to record the payroll for the week of December 10.
b. Journalize the entry to record the payroll tax expense incurred for the week of December 10.

EX 11-14
Payroll internal control procedures
obj. 3

Hillman Pizza is a pizza restaurant specializing in the sale of pizza by the slice. The store employs 7 full-time and 13 part-time workers. The store's weekly payroll averages $3,800 for all 20 workers.

Hillman Pizza uses a personal computer to assist in preparing paychecks. Each week, the store's accountant collects employee time cards and enters the hours worked into the payroll program. The payroll program calculates each employee's pay and prints a paycheck. The accountant uses a check-signing machine to sign the paychecks. Next, the restaurant's owner authorizes the transfer of funds from the restaurant's regular bank account to the payroll account.

For the week of July 11, the accountant accidentally recorded 250 hours worked instead of 40 hours for one of the full-time employees.

Does Hillman Pizza have internal controls in place to catch this error? If so, how will this error be detected?

EX 11-15
Internal control procedures
obj. 3

Kailua Motors is a small manufacturer of specialty electric motors. The company employs 26 production workers and 7 administrative persons. The following procedures are used to process the company's weekly payroll:

a. All employees are required to record their hours worked by clocking in and out on a time clock. Employees must clock out for lunch break. Due to congestion around the time clock area at lunch time, management has not objected to having one employee clock in and out for an entire department.
b. Whenever a salaried employee is terminated, Personnel authorizes Payroll to remove the employee from the payroll system. However, this procedure is not required when an hourly worker is terminated. Hourly employees only receive a paycheck if their time cards show hours worked. The computer automatically drops an employee from the payroll system when that employee has six consecutive weeks with no hours worked.
c. Whenever an employee receives a pay raise, the supervisor must fill out a wage adjustment form, which is signed by the company president. This form is used to change the employee's wage rate in the payroll system.
d. Kailua Motors maintains a separate checking account for payroll checks. Each week, the total net pay for all employees is transferred from the company's regular bank account to the payroll account.
e. Paychecks are signed by using a check-signing machine. This machine is located in the main office so that it can be easily accessed by anyone needing a check signed.

State whether each of the procedures is appropriate or inappropriate after considering the principles of internal control. If a procedure is inappropriate, describe the appropriate procedure.

EX 11-16
Payroll procedures
obj. 3

The fiscal year for Grain-Crop Stores Inc. ends on June 30. In addition, the company computes and reports payroll taxes on a fiscal-year basis. Thus, it applies social security and FUTA maximum earnings limitations to the fiscal-year payroll.

What is wrong with these procedures for accounting for payroll taxes?

EX 11-17
Accrued vacation pay
obj. 4

A business provides its employees with varying amounts of vacation per year, depending on the length of employment. The estimated amount of the current year's vacation pay is $80,400. Journalize the adjusting entry required on January 31, the end of the first month of the current year, to record the accrued vacation pay.

EX 11-18
Pension plan entries
obj. 4

Washington Co. operates a chain of bookstores. The company maintains a defined contribution pension plan for its employees. The plan requires quarterly installments to be paid to the funding agent, Hamilton Funds, by the fifteenth of the month following the end of each quarter. Assuming that the pension cost is $124,600 for the quarter ended December 31, journalize entries to record (a) the accrued pension liability on December 31 and (b) the payment to the funding agent on January 15.

EX 11-19
Defined benefit pension plan terms
obj. 4

In a recent year's financial statements, Procter & Gamble showed an unfunded pension liability of $2,637 million and a periodic pension cost of $183 million.

Explain the meaning of the $2,637 million unfunded pension liability and the $183 million periodic pension cost.

EX 11-20
Accrued product warranty
obj. 5

Lachgar Industries warrants its products for one year. The estimated product warranty is 4% of sales. Assume that sales were $210,000 for June. In July, a customer received warranty repairs requiring $140 of parts and $95 of labor.

a. Journalize the adjusting entry required at June 30, the end of the first month of the current fiscal year, to record the accrued product warranty.
b. Journalize the entry to record the warranty work provided in July.

EX 11-21
Accrued product warranty
obj. 5

Ford Motor Company disclosed estimated product warranty payable for comparative years as follows:

	(in millions)	
	12/31/06	12/31/05
Current estimated product warranty payable	$13,644	$13,074
Noncurrent estimated product warranty payable	8,289	7,359
Total	$21,933	$20,433

Ford's sales were $160,123 million in 2005 and increased to $176,896 million in 2006. Assume that the total paid on warranty claims during 2006 was $14,000 million.

a. Why are short- and long-term estimated warranty liabilities separately disclosed?
b. Provide the journal entry for the 2006 product warranty expense.

EX 11-22
Contingent liabilities
obj. 5

Several months ago, Welker Chemical Company experienced a hazardous materials spill at one of its plants. As a result, the Environmental Protection Agency (EPA) fined the company $410,000. The company is contesting the fine. In addition, an employee is seeking $400,000 damages related to the spill. Lastly, a homeowner has sued the company for $260,000. The homeowner lives 30 miles from the plant, but believes that the incident has reduced the home's resale value by $260,000.

Welker's legal counsel believes that it is probable that the EPA fine will stand. In addition, counsel indicates that an out-of-court settlement of $170,000 has recently been reached with the employee. The final papers will be signed next week. Counsel believes that the homeowner's case is much weaker and will be decided in favor of Welker. Other litigation related to the spill is possible, but the damage amounts are uncertain.

a. Journalize the contingent liabilities associated with the hazardous materials spill. Use the account "Damage Awards and Fines" to recognize the expense for the period.
b. Prepare a note disclosure relating to this incident.

EX 11-23
Quick ratio

✔ a. 2010: 1.10

Austin Technology Co. had the following current assets and liabilities for two comparative years:

	Dec. 31, 2010	Dec. 31, 2009
Current assets:		
Cash	$370,000	$ 448,000
Accounts receivable	400,000	410,000
Inventory	220,000	180,000
Total current assets	$990,000	$1,038,000

	Dec. 31, 2010	Dec. 31, 2009
Current liabilities:		
Current portion of long-term debt	$110,000	$ 100,000
Accounts payable	220,000	200,000
Accrued and other current liabilities	370,000	360,000
Total current liabilities	$700,000	$ 660,000

a. Determine the quick ratio for December 31, 2010 and 2009.
b. Interpret the change in the quick ratio between the two balance sheet dates.

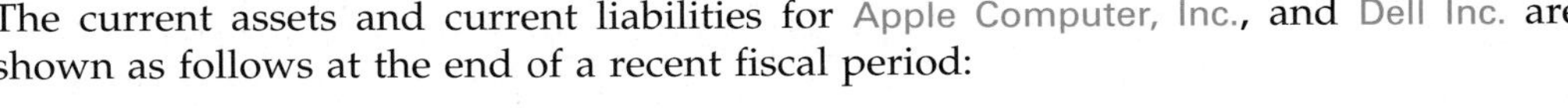

EX 11-24
Quick ratio

The current assets and current liabilities for Apple Computer, Inc., and Dell Inc. are shown as follows at the end of a recent fiscal period:

	Apple Computer, Inc. (In millions) Sept. 29, 2007	Dell Inc. (In millions) Feb. 2, 2007
Current assets:		
Cash and cash equivalents	$ 9,352	$ 9,546
Short-term investments	6,034	752
Accounts receivable	4,029	6,152
Inventories	346	660
Other current assets*	2,195	2,829
Total current assets	$21,956	$19,939
Current liabilities:		
Accounts payable	$ 4,970	$10,430
Accrued and other current liabilities	4,329	7,361
Total current liabilities	$ 9,299	$17,791

*These represent prepaid expense and other nonquick current assets.

a. Determine the quick ratio for both companies.
b. Interpret the quick ratio difference between the two companies.

Problems Series A

PR 11-1A
Liability transactions
objs. 1, 5

The following items were selected from among the transactions completed by Emerald Bay Stores Co. during the current year:

Jan. 15. Purchased merchandise on account from Hood Co., $220,000, terms n/30.
Feb. 14. Issued a 60-day, 6% note for $220,000 to Hood Co., on account.
Apr. 15. Paid Hood Co. the amount owed on the note of February 14.
June 2. Borrowed $187,500 from Acme Bank, issuing a 60-day, 8% note.
July 10. Purchased tools by issuing a $190,000, 90-day note to Columbia Supply Co., which discounted the note at the rate of 6%.
Aug. 1. Paid Acme Bank the interest due on the note of June 2 and renewed the loan by issuing a new 60-day, 10% note for $187,500. (Journalize both the debit and credit to the notes payable account.)
Sept. 30. Paid Acme Bank the amount due on the note of August 1.
Oct. 8. Paid Columbia Supply Co. the amount due on the note of July 10.
Dec. 1. Purchased office equipment from Mountain Equipment Co. for $120,000, paying $20,000 and issuing a series of ten 6% notes for $10,000 each, coming due at 30-day intervals.
5. Settled a product liability lawsuit with a customer for $76,000, payable in January. Emerald Bay accrued the loss in a litigation claims payable account.
31. Paid the amount due Mountain Equipment Co. on the first note in the series issued on December 1.

Instructions

1. Journalize the transactions.
2. Journalize the adjusting entry for each of the following accrued expenses at the end of the current year: (a) product warranty cost, $16,400; (b) interest on the nine remaining notes owed to Mountain Equipment Co.

PR 11-2A
Entries for payroll and payroll taxes
objs. 2, 3

✔ 1. (b) Dr. Payroll Tax Expense, $36,026

The following information about the payroll for the week ended December 30 was obtained from the records of Arnsparger Equipment Co.:

Salaries:		Deductions:	
Sales salaries	$244,000	Income tax withheld	$ 88,704
Warehouse salaries	135,000	Social security tax withheld	27,216
Office salaries	125,000	Medicare tax withheld	7,560
	$504,000	U.S. savings bonds	11,088
		Group insurance	9,072
			$143,640

Tax rates assumed:
Social security, 6% on first $100,000 of employee annual earnings
Medicare, 1.5%
State unemployment (employer only), 4.2%
Federal unemployment (employer only), 0.8%

Instructions

1. Assuming that the payroll for the last week of the year is to be paid on December 31, journalize the following entries:
   a. December 30, to record the payroll.
   b. December 30, to record the employer's payroll taxes on the payroll to be paid on December 31. Of the total payroll for the last week of the year, $25,000 is subject to unemployment compensation taxes.
2. Assuming that the payroll for the last week of the year is to be paid on January 5 of the following fiscal year, journalize the following entries:
   a. December 30, to record the payroll.
   b. January 5, to record the employer's payroll taxes on the payroll to be paid on January 5.

PR 11-3A
Wage and tax statement data on employer FICA tax
objs. 2, 3

✔ 2. (e) $28,503

Gridiron Concepts Co. began business on January 2, 2009. Salaries were paid to employees on the last day of each month, and social security tax, Medicare tax, and federal income tax were withheld in the required amounts. An employee who is hired in the middle of the month receives half the monthly salary for that month. All required payroll tax reports were filed, and the correct amount of payroll taxes was remitted by the company for the calendar year. Early in 2010, before the Wage and Tax Statements (Form W-2) could be prepared for distribution to employees and for filing with the Social Security Administration, the employees' earnings records were inadvertently destroyed.

None of the employees resigned or were discharged during the year, and there were no changes in salary rates. The social security tax was withheld at the rate of 6.0% on the first $100,000 of salary and Medicare tax at the rate of 1.5% on salary. Data on dates of employment, salary rates, and employees' income taxes withheld, which are summarized as follows, were obtained from personnel records and payroll records:

Employee	Date First Employed	Monthly Salary	Monthly Income Tax Withheld
Brooks	Jan. 2	$ 3,400	$ 502
Croom	June 16	5,600	1,052
Fulmer	Apr. 1	2,500	310
Johnson	Oct. 1	2,500	310
Nutt	Jan. 2	10,000	2,253
Richt	Jan. 16	3,600	552
Spurrier	Mar. 1	8,600	1,861

Instructions

1. Calculate the amounts to be reported on each employee's Wage and Tax Statement (Form W-2) for 2009, arranging the data in the following form:

Employee	Gross Earnings	Federal Income Tax Withheld	Social Security Tax Withheld	Medicare Tax Withheld

2. Calculate the following employer payroll taxes for the year: (a) social security; (b) Medicare; (c) state unemployment compensation at 4.8% on the first $8,000 of each employee's earnings; (d) federal unemployment compensation at 0.8% on the first $8,000 of each employee's earnings; (e) total.

PR 11-4A
Payroll register
objs. 2, 3

✔ 3. Dr. Payroll Tax Expense, $773.71

If the working papers correlating with this textbook are not used, omit Problem 11-4A.

The payroll register for Namesake Co. for the week ended September 12, 2010, is presented in the working papers.

Instructions

1. Journalize the entry to record the payroll for the week.
2. Journalize the entry to record the issuance of the checks to employees.
3. Journalize the entry to record the employer's payroll taxes for the week. Assume the following tax rates: state unemployment, 3.2%; federal unemployment, 0.8%. Of the earnings, $1, 500 is subject to unemployment taxes.
4. Journalize the entry to record a check issued on September 15 to Fourth National Bank in payment of employees' income taxes, $1,944.78, social security taxes, $1,084.32, and Medicare taxes, $343.10.

PR 11-5A
Payroll register
objs. 2, 3

✔ 1. Total net amount payable, $9,260.56

The following data for Enrichment Industries, Inc. relate to the payroll for the week ended December 10, 2010:

Employee	Hours Worked	Hourly Rate	Weekly Salary	Federal Income Tax	U.S. Savings Bonds	Accumulated Earnings, Dec. 3
Beilein	32	$16.00		$102.40	10	$ 24,576
Calhoun	50	32.00		369.60	10	84,480
Calipari	40	28.00		240.80	20	53,760
Knight	42	32.00		316.48		66,048
Odom			$3,400	748.00	90	163,200
Olson			1,600	384.00		76,800
Pitino	34	18.00		91.80		29,376
Ryan	44	34.00		297.16	20	75,072
Thompson	40	26.00		218.40	35	49,920

Employees Olson and Odom are office staff, and all of the other employees are sales personnel. All sales personnel are paid $1\frac{1}{2}$ times the regular rate for all hours in excess of 40 hours per week. The social security tax rate is 6.0% on the first $100,000 of each employee's annual earnings, and Medicare tax is 1.5% of each employee's annual earnings. The next payroll check to be used is No. 345.

Instructions

1. Prepare a payroll register for Enrichment Industries, Inc. for the week ended December 10, 2010. Use the following columns for the payroll register: Name, Total Hours, Regular Earnings, Overtime Earnings, Total Earnings, Social Security Tax, Medicare Tax, Federal Income Tax, U.S. Savings Bonds, Total Deductions, Net Pay, Ck. No., Sales Salaries Expense, and Office Salaries Expense.
2. Journalize the entry to record the payroll sales for the week.

PR 11-6A
Payroll accounts and year-end entries
objs. 2, 3, 4

The following accounts, with the balances indicated, appear in the ledger of Wadsley Gifts Co. on December 1 of the current year:

211	Salaries Payable	—	218	Bond Deductions Payable	$ 2,800
212	Social Security Tax Payable	$ 7,234	219	Medical Insurance Payable	22,000
213	Medicare Tax Payable	1,904	611	Operations Salaries Expense	766,000
214	Employees Federal Income Tax Payable	11,739	711	Officers Salaries Expense	504,000
215	Employees State Income Tax Payable	11,422	712	Office Salaries Expense	126,000
216	State Unemployment Tax Payable	1,200	719	Payroll Tax Expense	109,318
217	Federal Unemployment Tax Payable	400			

The following transactions relating to payroll, payroll deductions, and payroll taxes occurred during December:

Dec. 2. Issued Check No. 321 for $2,800 to Johnson Bank to purchase U.S. savings bonds for employees.

3. Issued Check No. 322 to Johnson Bank for $20,877, in payment of $7,234 of social security tax, $1,904 of Medicare tax, and $11,739 of employees' federal income tax due.

14. Journalized the entry to record the biweekly payroll. A summary of the payroll record follows:

Salary distribution:		
Operations	$34,800	
Officers	22,900	
Office	5,700	$63,400
Deductions:		
Social security tax	$ 3,550	
Medicare tax	951	
Federal income tax withheld	11,285	
State income tax withheld	2,853	
Savings bond deductions	1,400	
Medical insurance deductions	3,667	23,706
Net amount		$39,694

14. Issued Check No. 331 in payment of the net amount of the biweekly payroll.

14. Journalized the entry to record payroll taxes on employees' earnings of December 14: social security tax, $3,550; Medicare tax, $951; state unemployment tax, $300; federal unemployment tax, $100.

17. Issued Check No. 335 to Johnson Bank for $20,287, in payment of $7,100 of social security tax, $1,902 of Medicare tax, and $11,285 of employees' federal income tax due.

18. Issued Check No. 340 to Tidy Insurance Company for $22,000, in payment of the semiannual premium on the group medical insurance policy.

28. Journalized the entry to record the biweekly payroll. A summary of the payroll record follows:

Salary distribution:		
Operations	$34,200	
Officers	22,400	
Office	5,400	$62,000
Deductions:		
Social security tax	$ 3,348	
Medicare tax	930	
Federal income tax withheld	11,036	
State income tax withheld	2,790	
Savings bond deductions	1,400	19,504
Net amount		$42,496

28. Issued Check No. 352 in payment of the net amount of the biweekly payroll.

28. Journalized the entry to record payroll taxes on employees' earnings of December 28: social security tax, $3,348; Medicare tax, $930; state unemployment tax, $150; federal unemployment tax, $50.

30. Issued Check No. 354 to Johnson Bank for $2,800 to purchase U.S. savings bonds for employees.

30. Issued Check No. 356 for $17,065 to Johnson Bank in payment of employees' state income tax due on December 31.

Dec. 31. Paid $34,000 to the employee pension plan. The annual pension cost is $40,000. (Record both the payment and unfunded pension liability.)

Instructions

1. Journalize the transactions.
2. Journalize the following adjusting entries on December 31:
   a. Salaries accrued: operations salaries, $3,420; officers salaries, $2,240; office salaries, $540. The payroll taxes are immaterial and are not accrued.
   b. Vacation pay, $11,500.

Problems Series B

PR 11-1B
Liability transactions
objs. 1, 5

The following items were selected from among the transactions completed by Paulson, Inc. during the current year:

Apr. 1. Borrowed $60,000 from McCaw Company, issuing a 45-day, 6% note for that amount.

26. Purchased equipment by issuing a $160,000, 180-day note to Houston Manufacturing Co., which discounted the note at the rate of 8%.

May 16. Paid McCaw Company the interest due on the note of April 1 and renewed the loan by issuing a new 30-day, 10% note for $60,000. (Record both the debit and credit to the notes payable account.)

June 15. Paid McCaw Company the amount due on the note of May 16.

Sept. 3. Purchased merchandise on account from Oatley Co., $42,000, terms, n/30.

Oct. 3. Issued a 30-day, 9% note for $42,000 to Oatley Co., on account.

23. Paid Houston Manufacturing Co. the amount due on the note of April 26.

Nov. 2. Paid Oatley Co. the amount owed on the note of October 3.

10. Purchased store equipment from Biden Technology Co. for $200,000, paying $60,000 and issuing a series of seven 9% notes for $20,000 each, coming due at 30-day intervals.

Dec. 10. Paid the amount due Biden Technology Co. on the first note in the series issued on November 10.

16. Settled a personal injury lawsuit with a customer for $42,500, to be paid in January. Paulson, Inc. accrued the loss in a litigation claims payable account.

Instructions

1. Journalize the transactions.
2. Journalize the adjusting entry for each of the following accrued expenses at the end of the current year:
   a. Product warranty cost, $10,400.
   b. Interest on the six remaining notes owed to Biden Technology Co.

PR 11-2B
Entries for payroll and payroll taxes
objs. 2, 3

✔ 1. (b) Dr. Payroll Tax Expense, $68,304

The following information about the payroll for the week ended December 30 was obtained from the records of Vienna Co.:

Salaries:		Deductions:	
Sales salaries	$ 670,000	Income tax withheld	$198,744
Warehouse salaries	110,000	Social security tax withheld	51,714
Office salaries	234,000	Medicare tax withheld	15,210
	$1,014,000	U.S. savings bonds	30,420
		Group insurance	45,630
			$341,718

Tax rates assumed:
- Social security, 6% on first $100,000 of employee annual earnings
- Medicare, 1.5%
- State unemployment (employer only), 3.8%
- Federal unemployment (employer only), 0.8%

Instructions

1. Assuming that the payroll for the last week of the year is to be paid on December 31, journalize the following entries:
   a. December 30, to record the payroll.
   b. December 30, to record the employer's payroll taxes on the payroll to be paid on December 31. Of the total payroll for the last week of the year, $30,000 is subject to unemployment compensation taxes.
2. Assuming that the payroll for the last week of the year is to be paid on January 4 of the following fiscal year, journalize the following entries:
   a. December 30, to record the payroll.
   b. January 4, to record the employer's payroll taxes on the payroll to be paid on January 4.

PR 11-3B
Wage and tax statement data and employer FICA tax
objs. 2, 3

✔ 2. (e) $26,019.00

CTU Industries, Inc., began business on January 2, 2009. Salaries were paid to employees on the last day of each month, and social security tax, Medicare tax, and federal income tax were withheld in the required amounts. An employee who is hired in the middle of the month receives half the monthly salary for that month. All required payroll tax reports were filed, and the correct amount of payroll taxes was remitted by the company for the calendar year. Early in 2010, before the Wage and Tax Statements (Form W-2) could be prepared for distribution to employees and for filing with the Social Security Administration, the employees' earnings records were inadvertently destroyed.

None of the employees resigned or were discharged during the year, and there were no changes in salary rates. The social security tax was withheld at the rate of 6.0% on the first $100,000 of salary and Medicare tax at the rate of 1.5% on salary. Data on dates of employment, salary rates, and employees' income taxes withheld, which are summarized as follows, were obtained from personnel records and payroll records:

Employee	Date First Employed	Monthly Salary	Monthly Income Tax Withheld
Brown	Aug. 1	$3,600	$ 552
Carroll	Jan. 2	9,500	2,113
Grobe	May 1	6,500	1,277
Meyer	July 1	4,200	702
Saban	Jan. 2	5,100	927
Tressel	Apr. 16	3,200	452
Weis	Oct. 1	3,000	402

Instructions

1. Calculate the amounts to be reported on each employee's Wage and Tax Statement (Form W-2) for 2009, arranging the data in the following form:

Employee	Gross Earnings	Federal Income Tax Withheld	Social Security Tax Withheld	Medicare Tax Withheld

2. Calculate the following employer payroll taxes for the year: (a) social security; (b) Medicare; (c) state unemployment compensation at 4.8% on the first $10,000 of each employee's earnings; (d) federal unemployment compensation at 0.8% on the first $10,000 of each employee's earnings; (e) total.

PR 11-4B
Payroll register
objs. 2, 3

✔ 3. Dr. Payroll Tax Expense, $788.40

If the working papers correlating with this textbook are not used, omit Problem 11-4B.

The payroll register for Gogol Manufacturing Co. for the week ended September 12, 2010, is presented in the working papers.

Instructions

1. Journalize the entry to record the payroll for the week.
2. Journalize the entry to record the issuance of the checks to employees.
3. Journalize the entry to record the employer's payroll taxes for the week. Assume the following tax rates: state unemployment, 3.2%; federal unemployment, 0.8%. Of the earnings, $1,800 is subject to unemployment taxes.
4. Journalize the entry to record a check issued on September 15 to Third National Bank in payment of employees' income taxes, $2,337.88, social security taxes, $1,021.44, and Medicare taxes, $411.36.

PR 11-5B
Payroll register
objs. 2, 3

✔ 1. Total net amount payable, $8,610.31

The following data for Burtard Industries, Inc., relate to the payroll for the week ended December 10, 2010:

Employee	Hours Worked	Hourly Rate	Weekly Salary	Federal Income Tax	U.S. Savings Bonds	Accumulated Earnings, Dec. 3
Barnes			$3,000	$645.00		$144,000
Calhoun	50	$32.00		369.60	20	84,480
Crean			1,800	432.00	50	86,400
Donovan	34	20.00		136.00		32,640
Izzo	45	25.00		178.13		57,000
Matta	46	24.00		223.44	25	56,448
Self	40	23.00		193.20	40	44,160
Smith	40	22.00		202.40	30	42,240
Williams	36	18.00		142.56	30	31,104

Employees Barnes and Crean are office staff, and all of the other employees are sales personnel. All sales personnel are paid $1\frac{1}{2}$ times the regular rate for all hours in excess of 40 hours per week. The social security tax rate is 6.0% on the first $100,000 of each employee's annual earnings, and Medicare tax is 1.5% of each employee's annual earnings. The next payroll check to be used is No. 652.

Instructions

1. Prepare a payroll register for Burtard Industries, Inc. for the week ended December 10, 2010. Use the following columns for the payroll register: Name, Total Hours, Regular Earnings, Overtime Earnings, Total Earnings, Social Security Tax, Medicare Tax, Federal Income Tax, U.S. Savings Bonds, Total Deductions, Net Pay, Ck. No., Sales Salaries Expense, and Office Salaries Expense.
2. Journalize the entry to record the payroll sales for the week.

PR 11-6B
Payroll accounts and year-end entries
objs. 2, 3, 4

The following accounts, with the balances indicated, appear in the ledger of Yukon Kayak Co. on December 1 of the current year:

211	Salaries Payable	—
212	Social Security Tax Payable	$4,880
213	Medicare Tax Payable	1,236
214	Employees Federal Income Tax Payable	7,540
215	Employees State Income Tax Payable	7,038
216	State Unemployment Tax Payable	1,000
217	Federal Unemployment Tax Payable	280
218	Bond Deductions Payable	$ 1,800
219	Medical Insurance Payable	2,000
611	Sales Salaries Expense	556,000
711	Officers Salaries Expense	266,400
712	Office Salaries Expense	99,200
719	Payroll Tax Expense	74,316

The following transactions relating to payroll, payroll deductions, and payroll taxes occurred during December:

Dec. 1. Issued Check No. 510 to Tidy Insurance Company for $2,000, in payment of the semiannual premium on the group medical insurance policy.

2. Issued Check No. 511 to Johnson Bank for $13,656, in payment for $4,880 of social security tax, $1,236 of Medicare tax, and $7,540 of employees' federal income tax due.

3. Issued Check No. 512 for $1,800 to Johnson Bank to purchase U.S. savings bonds for employees.

14. Journalized the entry to record the biweekly payroll. A summary of the payroll record follows:

Salary distribution:		
Sales	$25,000	
Officers	12,100	
Office	4,500	$41,600
Deductions:		
Social security tax	$ 2,288	
Medicare tax	624	
Federal income tax withheld	7,405	
State income tax withheld	1,872	
Savings bond deductions	900	
Medical insurance deductions	333	13,422
Net amount		$28,178

Dec. 14. Issued Check No. 520 in payment of the net amount of the biweekly payroll.

14. Journalized the entry to record payroll taxes on employees' earnings of December 14: social security tax, $2,288; Medicare tax, $624; state unemployment tax, $250; federal unemployment tax, $60.

17. Issued Check No. 528 to Johnson Bank for $13,229, in payment for $4,576 of social security tax, $1,248 of Medicare tax, and $7,405 of employees' federal income tax due.

28. Journalized the entry to record the biweekly payroll. A summary of the payroll record follows:

Salary distribution:		
Sales	$25,400	
Officers	12,400	
Office	4,800	$42,600
Deductions:		
Social security tax	$ 2,300	
Medicare tax	639	
Federal income tax withheld	7,583	
State income tax withheld	1,917	
Savings bond deductions	900	13,339
Net amount		$29,261

28. Issued Check No. 540 for the net amount of the biweekly payroll.

28. Journalized the entry to record payroll taxes on employees' earnings of December 28: social security tax, $2,300; Medicare tax, $639; state unemployment tax, $120; federal unemployment tax, $30.

30. Issued Check No. 551 for $10,827 to Johnson Bank, in payment of employees' state income tax due on December 31.

30. Issued Check No. 552 to Johnson Bank for $1,800 to purchase U.S. savings bonds for employees.

31. Paid $44,000 to the employee pension plan. The annual pension cost is $52,000. (Record both the payment and the unfunded pension liability.)

Instructions

1. Journalize the transactions.
2. Journalize the following adjusting entries on December 31:
   a. Salaries accrued: sales salaries, $2,540; officers salaries, $1,240; office salaries, $480. The payroll taxes are immaterial and are not accrued.
   b. Vacation pay, $10,600.

Comprehensive Problem 3

✔ 5. Total assets, $1,567,300

Selected transactions completed by Blackwell Company during its first fiscal year ending December 31 were as follows:

Jan. 2. Issued a check to establish a petty cash fund of $2,000.

Mar. 4. Replenished the petty cash fund, based on the following summary of petty cash receipts: office supplies, $789; miscellaneous selling expense, $256; miscellaneous administrative expense, $378.

Apr. 5. Purchased $14,000 of merchandise on account, terms 1/10, n/30. The perpetual inventory system is used to account for inventory.

May 7. Paid the invoice of April 5 after the discount period had passed.

10. Received cash from daily cash sales for $9,455. The amount indicated by the cash register was $9,545.

June 2. Received a 60-day, 9% note for $80,000 on the Stevens account.

Aug. 1. Received amount owed on June 2 note, plus interest at the maturity date.

8. Received $3,400 on the Jacobs account and wrote off the remainder owed on a $4,000 accounts receivable balance. (The allowance method is used in accounting for uncollectible receivables.)

Aug. 25. Reinstated the Jacobs account written off on August 8 and received $600 cash in full payment.

Sept. 2. Purchased land by issuing a $300,000, 90-day note to Ace Development Co., which discounted it at 10%.

Oct. 2. Sold office equipment in exchange for $60,000 cash plus receipt of a $40,000, 120-day, 6% note. The equipment had cost $140,000 and had accumulated depreciation of $25,000 as of October 1.

Nov. 30. Journalized the monthly payroll for November, based on the following data:

Salaries		Deductions	
Sales salaries	$60,400	Income tax withheld	$17,082
Office salaries	34,500	Social security tax withheld	5,450
	$94,900	Medicare tax withheld	1,424

Unemployment tax rates:	
State unemployment	4.0%
Federal unemployment	0.8%
Amount subject to unemployment taxes:	
State unemployment	$4,000
Federal unemployment	4,000

30. Journalized the employer's payroll taxes on the payroll.

Dec. 1. Journalized the payment of the September 2 note at maturity.

30. The pension cost for the year was $85,000, of which $62,400 was paid to the pension plan trustee.

Instructions

1. Journalize the selected transactions.
2. Based on the following data, prepare a bank reconciliation for December of the current year:
   a. Balance according to the bank statement at December 31, $126,400.
   b. Balance according to the ledger at December 31, $109,650.
   c. Checks outstanding at December 31, $30,600.
   d. Deposit in transit, not recorded by bank, $13,200.
   e. Bank debit memo for service charges, $350.
   f. A check for $530 in payment of an invoice was incorrectly recorded in the accounts as $230.
3. Based on the bank reconciliation prepared in (2), journalize the entry or entries to be made by Blackwell Company.
4. Based on the following selected data, journalize the adjusting entries as of December 31 of the current year:
   a. Estimated uncollectible accounts at December 31, $7,200, based on an aging of accounts receivable. The balance of Allowance for Doubtful Accounts at December 31 was $750 (debit).
   b. The physical inventory on December 31 indicated an inventory shrinkage of $1,480.
   c. Prepaid insurance expired during the year, $10,200.
   d. Office supplies used during the year, $1,760.
   e. Depreciation is computed as follows:

Asset	Cost	Residual Value	Acquisition Date	Useful Life in Years	Depreciation Method Used
Buildings	$400,000	$ 0	January 2	40	Straight-line
Office Equip.	110,000	10,000	July 1	4	Straight-line
Store Equip.	50,000	5,000	January 3	8	Double-declining-balance (at twice the straight-line rate)

   f. A patent costing $22,500 when acquired on January 2 has a remaining legal life of 10 years and is expected to have value for five years.
   g. The cost of mineral rights was $220,000. Of the estimated deposit of 400,000 tons of ore, 24,000 tons were mined and sold during the year.

h. Vacation pay expense for December, $4,800.
i. A product warranty was granted beginning December 1 and covering a one-year period. The estimated cost is 2.5% of sales, which totaled $840,000 in December.
j. Interest was accrued on the note receivable received on October 2.

5. Based on the following information and the post-closing trial balance shown below, prepare a balance sheet in report form at December 31 of the current year.

The merchandise inventory is stated at cost by the LIFO method.

The product warranty payable is a current liability.

Vacation pay payable:

Current liability	$3,200
Long-term liability	1,600

The unfunded pension liability is a long-term liability.

Notes payable:

Current liability	$25,000
Long-term liability	75,000

Blackwell Company
Post-Closing Trial Balance
December 31, 2010

	Debit Balances	Credit Balances
Petty Cash	2,000	
Cash	109,000	
Notes Receivable	40,000	
Accounts Receivable	210,000	
Allowance for Doubtful Accounts		7,200
Merchandise Inventory	144,200	
Interest Receivable	600	
Prepaid Insurance	20,400	
Office Supplies	6,000	
Land	292,500	
Buildings	400,000	
Accumulated Depreciation—Buildings		10,000
Office Equipment	110,000	
Accumulated Depreciation—Office Equipment		12,500
Store Equipment	50,000	
Accumulated Depreciation—Store Equipment		12,500
Mineral Rights	220,000	
Accumulated Depletion		13,200
Patents	18,000	
Social Security Tax Payable		10,420
Medicare Tax Payable		2,550
Employees Federal Income Tax Payable		17,260
State Unemployment Tax Payable		100
Federal Unemployment Tax Payable		20
Salaries Payable		85,000
Accounts Payable		140,000
Interest Payable		3,200
Product Warranty Payable		21,000
Vacation Pay Payable		4,800
Unfunded Pension Liability		22,600
Notes Payable		100,000
J. Crane, Capital		1,160,350
	1,622,700	1,622,700

6. On February 7 of the following year, the merchandise inventory was destroyed by fire. Based on the following data obtained from the accounting records, estimate the cost of the merchandise destroyed:

Jan. 1 Merchandise inventory	$144,200
Jan. 1–Feb. 7 Purchases (net)	40,000
Jan. 1–Feb. 7 Sales (net)	70,000
Estimated gross profit rate	40%

Special Activities

SA 11-1
Ethics and professional conduct in business

Suzanne Thompson is a certified public accountant (CPA) and staff accountant for Deuel and Soldner, a local CPA firm. It had been the policy of the firm to provide a holiday bonus equal to two weeks' salary to all employees. The firm's new management team announced on November 15 that a bonus equal to only one week's salary would be made available to employees this year. Suzanne thought that this policy was unfair because she and her coworkers planned on the full two-week bonus. The two-week bonus had been given for 10 straight years, so it seemed as though the firm had breached an implied commitment. Thus, Suzanne decided that she would make up the lost bonus week by working an extra six hours of overtime per week over the next five weeks until the end of the year. Deuel and Soldner's policy is to pay overtime at 150% of straight time.

Suzanne's supervisor was surprised to see overtime being reported, since there is generally very little additional or unusual client service demands at the end of the calendar year. However, the overtime was not questioned, since firm employees are on the "honor system" in reporting their overtime.

Discuss whether the firm is acting in an ethical manner by changing the bonus. Is Suzanne behaving in an ethical manner?

SA 11-2
Recognizing pension expense

The annual examination of Tidal Company's financial statements by its external public accounting firm (auditors) is nearing completion. The following conversation took place between the controller of Tidal Company (Jose) and the audit manager from the public accounting firm (Cara).

Cara: You know, Jose, we are about to wrap up our audit for this fiscal year. Yet, there is one item still to be resolved.

Jose: What's that?

Cara: Well, as you know, at the beginning of the year, Tidal began a defined benefit pension plan. This plan promises your employees an annual payment when they retire, using a formula based on their salaries at retirement and their years of service. I believe that a pension expense should be recognized this year, equal to the amount of pension earned by your employees.

Jose: Wait a minute. I think you have it all wrong. The company doesn't have a pension expense until it actually pays the pension in cash when the employee retires. After all, some of these employees may not reach retirement, and if they don't, the company doesn't owe them anything.

Cara: You're not really seeing this the right way. The pension is earned by your employees during their working years. You actually make the payment much later—when they retire. It's like one long accrual—much like incurring wages in one period and paying them in the next. Thus, I think that you should recognize the expense in the period the pension is earned by the employees.

Jose: Let me see if I've got this straight. I should recognize an expense this period for something that may or may not be paid to the employees in 20 or 30 years, when they finally retire. How am I supposed to determine what the expense is for the current year? The amount of the final retirement depends on many uncertainties: salary levels, employee longevity, mortality rates, and interest earned on investments to fund the pension. I don't think that an amount can be determined, even if I accepted your arguments.

Evaluate Cara's position. Is she right or is Jose correct?

SA 11-3
Executive bonuses and accounting methods

Paul Sheile, the owner of Sheile Trucking Company, initiated an executive bonus plan for his chief executive officer (CEO). The new plan provides a bonus to the CEO equal to 3% of the income before taxes. Upon learning of the new bonus arrangement, the CEO issued instructions to change the company's accounting for trucks. The CEO has asked the controller to make the following two changes:

a. Change from the double-declining-balance method to the straight-line method of depreciation.
b. Add 50% to the useful lives of all trucks.

Why did the CEO ask for these changes? How would you respond to the CEO's request?

SA 11-4
Ethics and professional conduct in business

Fio Barellis was discussing summer employment with Sara Rida, president of Xanadu Construction Service:

Sara: I'm glad that you're thinking about joining us for the summer. We could certainly use the help.

Fio: Sounds good. I enjoy outdoor work, and I could use the money to help with next year's school expenses.

Sara: I've got a plan that can help you out on that. As you know, I'll pay you $12 per hour, but in addition, I'd like to pay you with cash. Since you're only working for the summer, it really doesn't make sense for me to go to the trouble of formally putting you on our payroll system. In fact, I do some jobs for my clients on a strictly cash basis, so it would be easy to just pay you that way.

Fio: Well, that's a bit unusual, but I guess money is money.

Sara: Yeah, not only that, it's tax-free!

Fio: What do you mean?

Sara: Didn't you know? Any money that you receive in cash is not reported to the IRS on a W-2 form; therefore, the IRS doesn't know about the income—hence, it's the same as tax-free earnings.

a. Why does Sara Rida want to conduct business transactions using cash (not check or credit card)?
b. How should Fio respond to Sara's suggestion?

SA 11-5
Payroll forms

Group Project

Internet Project

Payroll accounting involves the use of government-supplied forms to account for payroll taxes. Three common forms are the W-2, Form 940, and Form 941. Form a team with three of your classmates and retrieve copies of each of these forms. They may be obtained from a local IRS office, a library, or downloaded from the Internet at **http://www.irs.gov** (go to forms and publications).

Briefly describe the purpose of each of the three forms.

SA 11-6
Contingent liabilities

Internet Project

Altria Group, Inc., has over 24 pages dedicated to describing contingent liabilities in the notes to recent financial statements. These pages include extensive descriptions of multiple contingent liabilities. Use the Internet to research Altria Group, Inc., at **http://www.altria.com**.

a. What are the major business units of Altria Group?
b. Based on your understanding of this company, why would Altria Group require 11 pages of contingency disclosure?

Answers to Self-Examination Questions

1. **C** The maturity value is $5,100, determined as follows:

Face amount of note	$5,000
Plus interest ($5,000 × 12% × 60/360)	100
Maturity value	$5,100

2. **B** The net amount available to a borrower from discounting a note payable is called the proceeds. The proceeds of $4,900 (answer B) is determined as follows:

Face amount of note	$5,000
Less discount ($5,000 × 12% × 60/360)	100
Proceeds	$4,900

3. **B** Employers are usually required to withhold a portion of their employees' earnings for payment of federal income taxes (answer A), Medicare tax (answer C), and state and local income taxes (answer D). Generally, federal unemployment compensation taxes (answer B) are levied against the employer only and thus are not deducted from employee earnings.

4. **D** The amount of net pay of $1,385.50 (answer D) is determined as follows:

Gross pay:			
40 hours at $40		$1,600.00	
5 hours at $60		300.00	$1,900.00
Deductions:			
Federal income tax withheld		$ 450.00	
FICA:			
Social security tax ($600 × 0.06)	$ 36.00		
Medicare tax ($1,900 × 0.015)	28.50	64.50	514.50
			$1,385.50

5. **D** The employer incurs an expense for social security tax (answer A), federal unemployment compensation tax (answer B), and state unemployment compensation tax (answer C). The employees' federal income tax (answer D) is not an expense of the employer. It is withheld from the employees' earnings.

CHAPTER 13

Corporations: Organization, Stock Transactions, and Dividends

© Susan Van Etten

HASBRO

If you purchase a share of stock from Hasbro, you own a small interest in the company. You may request a Hasbro stock certificate as an indication of your ownership.

As you may know, Hasbro is one of the world's largest toy manufacturers and produces popular children's toys such as G.I. Joe, Play-Doh, Tonka toys, Mr. Potato Head, and Nerf balls. In addition, Hasbro manufactures family entertainment products such as Monopoly, Scrabble, and Trivial Pursuit under the Milton Bradley and Parker Brothers labels. In fact, the stock certificate of Hasbro has a picture of Uncle Pennybags, the Monopoly game icon, printed on it.

Purchasing a share of stock from Hasbro may be a great gift idea for the "hard-to-shop-for person." However, a stock certificate represents more than just a picture that you can frame. In fact, the stock certificate is a document that reflects legal ownership of the future financial prospects of Hasbro. In addition, as a shareholder, it represents your claim against the assets and earnings of the corporation.

If you are purchasing Hasbro stock as an investment, you should analyze Hasbro's financial statements and management's plans for the future. For example, Hasbro has a unique relationship with Disney that allows it to produce and sell licensed Disney products. Should this Disney relationship affect how much you are willing to pay for the stock? Also, you might want to know if Hasbro plans to pay cash dividends or whether management is considering issuing additional shares of stock.

In this chapter, we describe and illustrate the nature of corporations including the accounting for stock and dividends. This discussion will aid you in making decisions such as whether or not to buy Hasbro stock.

After studying this chapter, you should be able to:

1. Describe the nature of the corporate form of organization.
   - Nature of a Corporation
   - Characteristics of a Corporation
   - Forming a Corporation
2. Describe the two main sources of stockholders' equity.
   - Stockholders' Equity
3. Describe and illustrate the characteristics of stock, classes of stock, and entries for issuing stock.
   - Paid-In Capital from Issuing Stock
   - Characteristics of Stock
   - Classes of Stock
   - EE 13-1 (page 581)
   - Issuing Stock
   - Premium on Stock
   - No-Par Stock
   - EE 13-2 (page 584)
4. Describe and illustrate the accounting for cash dividends and stock dividends.
   - Accounting for Dividends
   - Cash Dividends
   - EE 13-3 (page 586)
   - Stock Dividends
   - EE 13-4 (page 587)
5. Describe and illustrate the accounting for treasury stock transactions.
   - Treasury Stock Transactions
   - EE 13-5 (page 588)
6. Describe and illustrate the reporting of stockholders' equity.
   - Reporting Stockholders' Equity
   - Stockholders' Equity in the Balance Sheet
   - EE 13-6 (page 590)
   - Reporting Retained Earnings
   - EE 13-7 (page 592)
   - Statement of Stockholders' Equity
   - Reporting Stockholders' Equity for Mornin' Joe
7. Describe the effect of stock splits on corporate financial statements.
   - Stock Splits

At a Glance | Menu | Turn to pg 595

South-Western

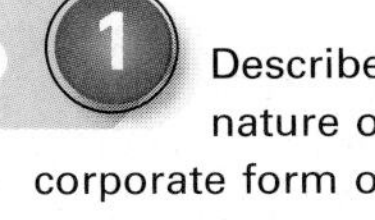

Nature of a Corporation

1 Describe the nature of the corporate form of organization.

Most large businesses are organized as corporations. As a result, corporations generate more than 90% of the total business dollars in the United States. In contrast, most small businesses are organized as proprietorships, partnerships, or limited liability companies.

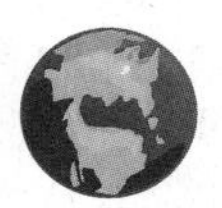

A corporation was defined in the Dartmouth College case of 1819, in which Chief Justice Marshall of the United States Supreme Court stated: "A corporation is an artificial being, invisible, intangible, and existing only in contemplation of the law."

Characteristics of a Corporation

A *corporation* is a legal entity, distinct and separate from the individuals who create and operate it. As a legal entity, a corporation may acquire, own, and dispose of property in its own name. It may also incur liabilities and enter into contracts. Most importantly, it can sell shares of ownership, called **stock**. This characteristic gives corporations the ability to raise large amounts of capital.

The **stockholders** or *shareholders* who own the stock own the corporation. They can buy and sell stock without affecting the corporation's operations or continued

The Coca-Cola Company is a well-known public corporation. Mars, Incorporated, which is owned by family members, is a well-known private corporation.

existence. Corporations whose shares of stock are traded in public markets are called *public corporations*. Corporations whose shares are not traded publicly are usually owned by a small group of investors and are called *nonpublic* or *private corporations*.

The stockholders of a corporation have *limited liability*. This means that creditors usually may not go beyond the assets of the corporation to satisfy their claims. Thus, the financial loss that a stockholder may suffer is limited to the amount invested.

The stockholders control a corporation by electing a *board of directors*. This board meets periodically to establish corporate policies. It also selects the chief executive officer (CEO) and other major officers to manage the corporation's day-to-day affairs. Exhibit 1 shows the organizational structure of a corporation.

Exhibit 1

Organizational Structure of a Corporation

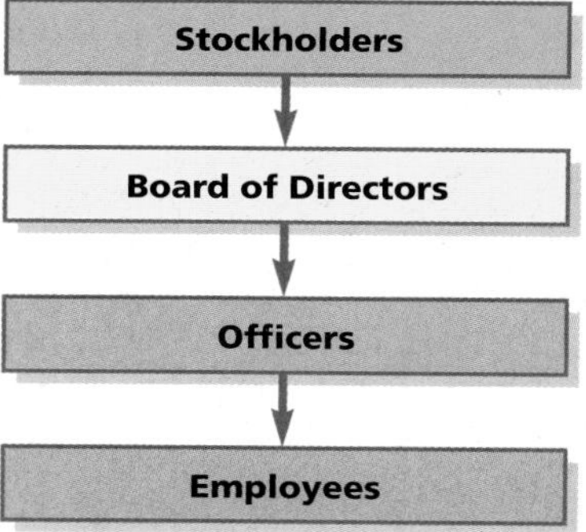

Corporations have a separate legal existence, transferable units of ownership, and limited stockholder liability.

As a separate entity, a corporation is subject to taxes. For example, corporations must pay federal income taxes on their income.[1] Thus, corporate income that is distributed to stockholders in the form of *dividends* has already been taxed. In turn, stockholders must pay income taxes on the dividends they receive. This *double taxation* of corporate earnings is a major disadvantage of the corporate form.[2] The advantages and disadvantages of the corporate form are listed in Exhibit 2.

Integrity, Objectivity, and Ethics in Business

THE RESPONSIBLE BOARD

Recent accounting scandals, such as those involving Enron, WorldCom, and Fannie Mae, have highlighted the roles of boards of directors in executing their responsibilities. For example, eighteen of Enron's former directors and their insurance providers have settled shareholder litigation for $168 million, of which $13 million is to come from the directors' personal assets. Board members are now on notice that their directorship responsibilities are being taken seriously by stockholders.

Forming a Corporation

The first step in forming a corporation is to file an *application of incorporation* with the state. State incorporation laws differ, and corporations often organize in those states with the more favorable laws. For this reason, more than half of the largest companies are incorporated in Delaware. Exhibit 3 lists some corporations, their states of incorporation, and the location of their headquarters.

After the application of incorporation has been approved, the state grants a *charter* or *articles of incorporation*. The articles of incorporation formally create the corporation.[3]

1 A majority of states also require corporations to pay income taxes.

2 Dividends presently receive a preferential individual tax rate of 15% to reduce the impact of double taxation.

3 The articles of incorporation may also restrict a corporation's activities in certain areas, such as owning certain types of real estate, conducting certain types of business activities, or purchasing its own stock.

Exhibit 2

Advantages and Disadvantages of the Corporate Form

Advantages	Explanation
Separate legal existence	A corporation exists separately from its owners.
Continuous life	A corporation's life is separate from its owners; therefore, it exists indefinitely.
Raising large amounts of capital	The corporate form is suited for raising large amounts of money from shareholders.
Ownership rights are easily transferable	A corporation sells shares of ownership, called *stock*. The stockholders of a public company can transfer their shares of stock to other stockholders through stock markets, such as the New York Stock Exchange.
Limited liability	A corporation's creditors usually may not go beyond the assets of the corporation to satisfy their claims. Thus, the financial loss that a stockholder may suffer is limited to the amount invested.
Disadvantages	
Owner is separate from management	Stockholders control management through a board of directors. The board of directors should represent shareholder interests; however, the board is often more closely tied to management than to shareholders. As a result, the board of directors and management may not always behave in the best interests of stockholders.
Double taxation of dividends	As a separate legal entity, a corporation is subject to taxation. Thus, net income distributed as dividends will be taxed once at the corporation level, and then again at the individual level.
Regulatory costs	Corporations must satisfy many requirements such as those required by the Sarbanes-Oxley Act of 2002.

The corporate management and board of directors then prepare a set of *bylaws*, which are the rules and procedures for conducting the corporation's affairs.

Costs may be incurred in organizing a corporation. These costs include legal fees, taxes, state incorporation fees, license fees, and promotional costs. Such costs are debited to an expense account entitled *Organizational Expenses*.

A Financial Executives International survey estimated that Sarbanes-Oxley costs the average public company over $3 million per year.

To illustrate, a corporation's organizing costs of $8,500 on January 5 are recorded as shown below.

Jan.	5	Organizational Expenses		8,500	
		Cash			8,500
		Paid costs of organizing the corporation.			

Exhibit 3

Examples of Corporations and Their States of Incorporation

Corporation	State of Incorporation	Headquarters
Caterpillar	Delaware	Peoria, Ill.
Delta Air Lines	Delaware	Atlanta, Ga.
The Dow Chemical Company	Delaware	Midland, Mich.
General Electric Company	New York	Fairfield, Conn.
The Home Depot	Delaware	Atlanta, Ga.
Kellogg Company	Delaware	Battle Creek, Mich.
3M	Delaware	St. Paul, Minn.
R.J. Reynolds Tobacco Company	Delaware	Winston-Salem, N.C.
Starbucks Corporation	Washington	Seattle, Wash.
Sun Microsystems, Inc.	Delaware	Palo Alto, Calif.
The Washington Post Company	Delaware	Washington, D.C.
Whirlpool Corporation	Delaware	Benton Harbor, Mich.

Integrity, Objectivity, and Ethics in Business

NOT-FOR-PROFIT, OR NOT?

Corporations can be formed for not-for-profit purposes by making a request to the Internal Revenue Service under *Internal Revenue Code* section 501(c)3. Such corporations, such as the Sierra Club and the National Audubon Society, are exempt from federal taxes. Forming businesses inside a 501(c)3 exempt organization that competes with profit-making (and hence, tax-paying) businesses is very controversial. For example, should the local YMCA receive a tax exemption for providing similar services as the local health club business? The IRS is now challenging such businesses and is withholding 501(c)3 status to many organizations due to this issue.

2 Describe the two main sources of stockholders' equity.

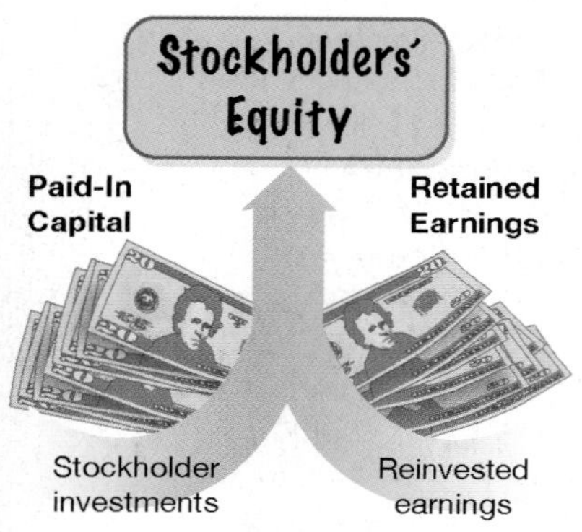

Stockholders' Equity

The owners' equity in a corporation is called **stockholders' equity**, *shareholders' equity, shareholders' investment,* or *capital.* In the balance sheet, stockholders' equity is reported by its two main sources.

1. Capital contributed to the corporation by the stockholders, called **paid-in capital** or *contributed capital.*
2. Net income retained in the business, called **retained earnings**.

A Stockholders' Equity section of a balance sheet is shown below.[4]

Stockholders' Equity

Paid-in capital:		
Common stock	$330,000	
Retained earnings	80,000	
Total stockholders' equity		$410,000

The paid-in capital contributed by the stockholders is recorded in separate accounts for each class of stock. If there is only one class of stock, the account is entitled *Common Stock* or *Capital Stock.*

Retained earnings is a corporation's cumulative net income that has not been distributed as dividends. **Dividends** are distributions of a corporation's earnings to stockholders. Sometimes retained earnings that are not distributed as dividends are referred to in the financial statements as *earnings retained for use in the business* and *earnings reinvested in the business.*

Net income increases retained earnings, while a net loss and dividends decrease retained earnings. The net increase or decrease in retained earnings for a period is recorded by the following closing entries:

1. The balance of Income Summary (the net income or net loss) is transferred to Retained Earnings. For *net income,* Income Summary is debited and Retained Earnings is credited. For a *net loss,* Retained Earnings is debited and Income Summary is credited.
2. The balance of the dividends account, which is similar to the drawing account for a proprietorship, is transferred to Retained Earnings. Retained Earnings is debited and Dividends is credited for the balance of the dividends account.

Most companies generate net income. In addition, most companies do not pay out all of their net income in dividends. As a result, Retained Earnings normally has a credit balance. However, in some cases, a debit balance in Retained Earnings may occur. A debit balance in Retained Earnings is called a **deficit**. Such a balance often results from cumulated net losses. In the Stockholders' Equity section, a deficit is deducted from paid-in capital in determining total stockholders' equity.

The balance of Retained Earnings does not represent surplus cash or cash left over for dividends. This is because cash generated from operations is normally used to improve or expand operations. As cash is used, its balance decreases; however, the balance of

4 The reporting of stockholders' equity is further discussed and illustrated later in this chapter.

the retained earnings account is unaffected. As a result, over time the balance in Retained Earnings becomes less and less related to the balance of Cash.

Describe and illustrate the characteristics of stock, classes of stock, and entries for issuing stock.

Paid-In Capital from Issuing Stock

The two main sources of stockholders' equity are paid-in capital (or contributed capital) and retained earnings. The main source of paid-in capital is from issuing stock.

Characteristics of Stock

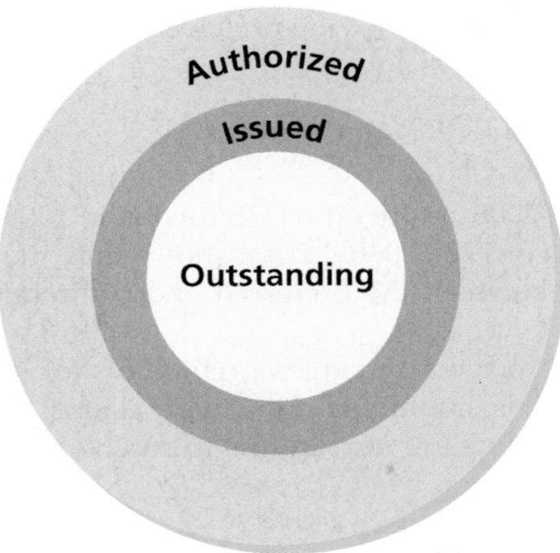

Number of shares authorized, issued, and outstanding

The number of shares of stock that a corporation is *authorized* to issue is stated in its charter. The term *issued* refers to the shares issued to the stockholders. A corporation may reacquire some of the stock that it has issued. The stock remaining in the hands of stockholders is then called **outstanding stock**. The relationship between authorized, issued, and outstanding stock is shown in the graphic at the left.

Upon request, corporations may issue stock certificates to stockholders to document their ownership. Printed on a stock certificate is the name of the company, the name of the stockholder, and the number of shares owned. The stock certificate may also indicate a dollar amount assigned to each share of stock, called **par** value. Stock may be issued without par, in which case it is called *no-par stock*. In some states, the board of directors of a corporation is required to assign a *stated value* to no-par stock.

Corporations have limited liability and, thus, creditors have no claim against stockholders' personal assets. To protect creditors, however, some states require corporations to maintain a minimum amount of paid-in capital. This minimum amount, called *legal capital,* usually includes the par or stated value of the shares issued.

The major rights that accompany ownership of a share of stock are as follows:

1. The right to vote in matters concerning the corporation.
2. The right to share in distributions of earnings.
3. The right to share in assets on liquidation.

These stock rights normally vary with the class of stock.

Some corporations have stopped issuing stock certificates except on special request. In these cases, the corporation maintains records of ownership.

Classes of Stock

When only one class of stock is issued, it is called **common stock**. Each share of common stock has equal rights.

A corporation may also issue one or more classes of stock with various preference rights such as a preference to dividends. Such a stock is called a **preferred stock**. The dividend rights of preferred stock are stated either as dollars per share or as a percent of par. For example, a $50 par value preferred stock with a $4 per share dividend may be described as either:[5]

The two primary classes of paid-in capital are common stock and preferred stock.

$4 preferred stock, $50 par
or
8% preferred stock, $50 par

Because they have first rights (preference) to any dividends, preferred stockholders have a greater chance of receiving dividends than common stockholders. However, since dividends are normally based on earnings, a corporation cannot guarantee dividends even to preferred stockholders.

5 In some cases, preferred stock may receive additional dividends if certain conditions are met. Such stock, called *participating preferred stock,* is not often used.

The payment of dividends is authorized by the corporation's board of directors. When authorized, the directors are said to have *declared* a dividend.

Cumulative preferred stock has a right to receive regular dividends that were not declared (paid) in prior years. Noncumulative preferred stock does not have this right.

Cumulative preferred stock dividends that have not been paid in prior years are said to be **in arrears**. Any preferred dividends in arrears must be paid before any common stock dividends are paid. In addition, any dividends in arrears are normally disclosed in notes to the financial statements.

To illustrate, assume that a corporation has issued the following preferred and common stock:

1,000 shares of $4 cumulative preferred stock, $50 par
4,000 shares of common stock, $15 par

The corporation was organized on January 1, 2008, and paid no dividends in 2008 and 2009. In 2010, the corporation paid dividends of $22,000. Exhibit 4 shows how the $22,000 of dividends paid in 2010 is distributed between the preferred and common stockholders.

In addition to dividend preference, preferred stock may be given preferences to assets if the corporation goes out of business and is liquidated. However, claims of creditors must be satisfied first. Preferred stockholders are next in line to receive any remaining assets, followed by the common stockholders.

Exhibit 4

Dividends to Cumulative Preferred Stock

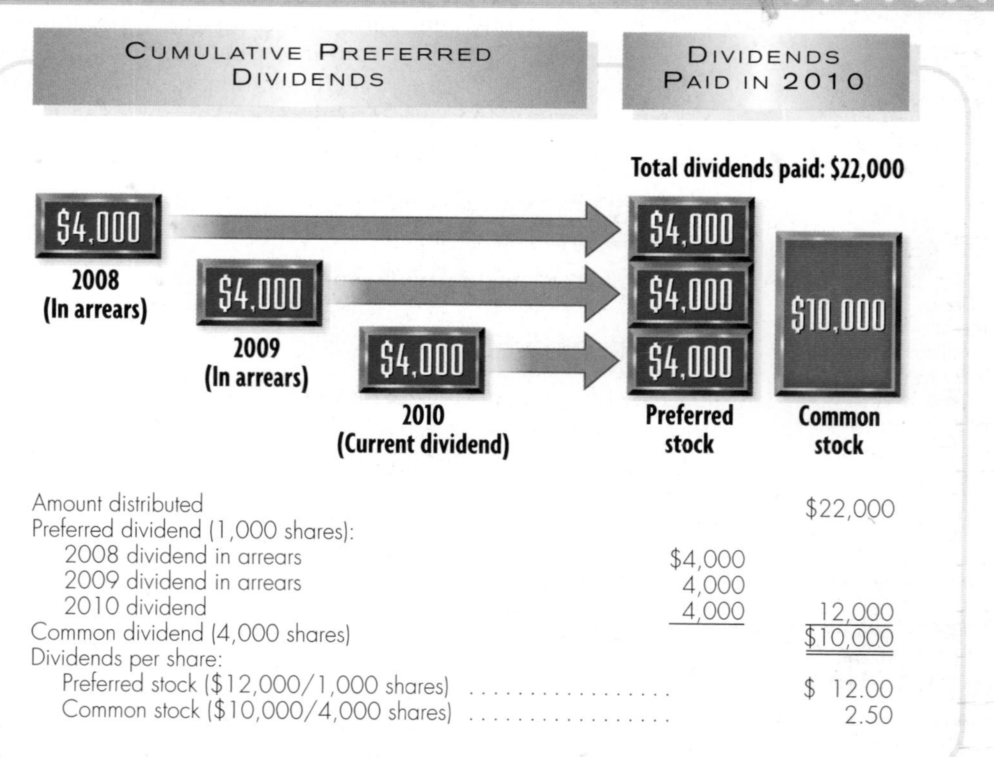

Amount distributed		$22,000
Preferred dividend (1,000 shares):		
2008 dividend in arrears	$4,000	
2009 dividend in arrears	4,000	
2010 dividend	4,000	12,000
Common dividend (4,000 shares)		$10,000
Dividends per share:		
Preferred stock ($12,000/1,000 shares)		$ 12.00
Common stock ($10,000/4,000 shares)		2.50

Example Exercise 13-1 Dividends per Share 3

Sandpiper Company has 20,000 shares of 1% cumulative preferred stock of $100 par and 100,000 shares of $50 par common stock. The following amounts were distributed as dividends:

Year 1	$10,000
Year 2	45,000
Year 3	80,000

Determine the dividends per share for preferred and common stock for each year.

Follow My Example 13-1

	Year 1	Year 2	Year 3
Amount distributed	$10,000	$45,000	$80,000
Preferred dividend (20,000 shares)	10,000	30,000*	20,000
Common dividend (100,000 shares)	$ 0	$15,000	$60,000
*($10,000 + $20,000)			
Dividends per share:			
Preferred stock	$0.50	$1.50	$1.00
Common stock	None	$0.15	$0.60

For Practice: PE 13-1A, PE 13-1B

Issuing Stock

A separate account is used for recording the amount of each class of stock issued to investors in a corporation. For example, assume that a corporation is authorized to issue 10,000 shares of $100 par preferred stock and 100,000 shares of $20 par common stock. The corporation issued 5,000 shares of preferred stock and 50,000 shares of common stock at par for cash. The corporation's entry to record the stock issue is as follows: [6]

			Debit	Credit
	Cash		1,500,000	
	Preferred Stock			500,000
	Common Stock			1,000,000
	Issued preferred stock and common stock at par for cash.			

Stock is often issued by a corporation at a price other than its par. The price at which stock is sold depends on a variety of factors, such as the following:

1. The financial condition, earnings record, and dividend record of the corporation.
2. Investor expectations of the corporation's potential earning power.
3. General business and economic conditions and expectations.

If stock is issued (sold) for a price that is more than its par, the stock has been sold at a **premium**. For example, if common stock with a par of $50 is sold for $60 per share, the stock has sold at a premium of $10.

If stock is issued (sold) for a price that is less than its par, the stock has been sold at a **discount**. For example, if common stock with a par of $50 is sold for $45 per share, the stock has sold at a discount of $5. Many states do not permit stock to be sold at a discount. In other states, stock may be sold at a discount in only unusual cases. Since stock is rarely sold at a discount, it is not illustrated.

6 The accounting for investments in stocks from the point of view of the investor is discussed in Chapter 15.

The following price quotation for Wal-Mart is taken from Yahoo Finance at http://finance.yahoo.com/q?s=WMT on May 6, 2008:

Trade Time:	10:37 AM ET	52wk Range:	42.09–59.09
Change:	↓0.47 (0.82%)	Volume:	4,695,512
Prev Close:	56.97	Avg Vol (3m):	22,486,000
Open:	56.99	Market Cap:	223.43B
Bid:	N/A	P/E (ttm):	18.07
Ask:	N/A	EPS (ttm):	3.13
1y Target Est:	59.00	Div & Yield:	0.95 (1.70%)

In order to distribute dividends, financial statements, and other reports, a corporation must keep track of its stockholders. Large public corporations normally use a financial institution, such as a bank, for this purpose.[7] In such cases, the financial institution is referred to as a *transfer agent* or *registrar*.

Premium on Stock

When stock is issued at a premium, Cash is debited for the amount received. Common Stock or Preferred Stock is credited for the par amount. The excess of the amount paid over par is part of the paid-in capital. An account entitled *Paid-In Capital in Excess of Par* is credited for this amount.

To illustrate, assume that Caldwell Company issues 2,000 shares of $50 par preferred stock for cash at $55. The entry to record this transaction is as follows:

		Cash		110,000	
		Preferred Stock			100,000
		Paid-In Capital in Excess of Par— Preferred Stock			10,000
		Issued $50 par preferred stock at $55.			

When stock is issued in exchange for assets other than cash, such as land, buildings, and equipment, the assets acquired are recorded at their fair market value. If this value cannot be determined, the fair market price of the stock issued is used.

The transfer agent and registrar for The Coca-Cola Company is First Chicago Trust Company of New York.

To illustrate, assume that a corporation acquired land with a fair market value that cannot be determined. In exchange, the corporation issued 10,000 shares of its $10 par common. If the stock has a market price of $12 per share, the transaction is recorded as follows:

		Land		120,000	
		Common Stock			100,000
		Paid-In Capital in Excess of Par			20,000
		Issued $10 par common stock, valued at $12 per share, for land.			

No-Par Stock

In most states, no-par preferred and common stock may be issued. When no-par stock is issued, Cash is debited and Common Stock is credited for the proceeds. As no-par stock is issued over time, this entry is the same even if the issuing price varies.

To illustrate, assume that on January 9 a corporation issues 10,000 shares of no-par common stock at $40 a share. On June 27, the corporation issues an additional 1,000 shares at $36. The entries to record these issuances of the no-par stock are as follows:

7 Small corporations may use a subsidiary ledger, called a *stockholders ledger*. In this case, the stock accounts (Preferred Stock and Common Stock) are controlling accounts for the subsidiary ledger.

Jan.	9	Cash		400,000	
		Common Stock			400,000
		Issued 10,000 shares of no-par common at $40.			
June	27	Cash		36,000	
		Common Stock			36,000
		Issued 1,000 shares of no-par common at $36.			

Business Connection

CISCO SYSTEMS, INC.

Cisco Systems, Inc., manufactures and sells networking and communications products worldwide. Some excerpts of its bylaws are shown below.

ARTICLE 2
SHAREHOLDERS' MEETINGS
Section 2.01 Annual Meetings. The annual meeting of the shareholders of the Corporation . . . shall be held each year on the second Thursday in November at 10:00 A.M. . . .

ARTICLE 3
BOARD OF DIRECTORS
Section 3.02 Number and Qualification of Directors. The number of authorized directors of this Corporation shall be not less than eight (8) nor more than fifteen (15), . . . to be (determined) by . . . the Board of Directors or shareholders.

Section 3.04 Special Meetings. Special meetings of the Board of Directors may be called at any time by the Chairman of the Board, the President of the Corporation or any two (2) directors.

ARTICLE 4
OFFICERS
Section 4.01 Number and Term. The officers of the Corporation shall include a President, a Secretary and a Chief Financial Officer, all of which shall be chosen by the Board of Directors. . . .

Section 4.05 Chairman of the Board. The Chairman of the Board shall preside at all meetings of the Board of Directors.

© AP PHOTO/PAUL SAKUMA

Section 4.06 President. The President shall be the general manager and chief executive officer of the Corporation, . . . shall preside at all meetings of shareholders, shall have general supervision of the affairs of the Corporation. . . .

Section 4.08 Secretary. The Secretary shall keep . . . minutes of all meetings, shall have charge of the seal and the corporate books. . . .

Section 4.10 Treasurer. The Treasurer shall have custody of all moneys and securities of the Corporation and shall keep regular books of account. . . .

Section 5.04 Fiscal Year. The fiscal year of the Corporation shall end on the last Saturday of July.

In some states, no-par stock may be assigned a *stated value per share.* The stated value is recorded like a par value. Any excess of the proceeds over the stated value is credited to *Paid-in Capital in Excess of Stated Value.*

To illustrate, assume that in the preceding example the no-par common stock is assigned a stated value of $25. The issuance of the stock on January 9 and June 27 is recorded as follows:

Jan.	9	Cash		400,000	
		Common Stock			250,000
		Paid-In Capital in Excess of Stated Value			150,000
		Issued 10,000 shares of no-par common at $40; stated value, $25.			
June	27	Cash		36,000	
		Common Stock			25,000
		Paid-In Capital in Excess of Stated Value			11,000
		Issued 1,000 shares of no-par common at $36; stated value, $25.			

Example Exercise 13-2 Entries for Issuing Stock 3

On March 6, Limerick Corporation issued for cash 15,000 shares of no-par common stock at $30. On April 13, Limerick issued at par 1,000 shares of 4%, $40 par preferred stock for cash. On May 19, Limerick issued for cash 15,000 shares of 4%, $40 par preferred stock at $42.

Journalize the entries to record the March 6, April 13, and May 19 transactions.

Follow My Example 13-2

Mar. 6	Cash	450,000	
	Common Stock		450,000
	(15,000 shares × $30).		
Apr. 13	Cash	40,000	
	Preferred Stock		40,000
	(1,000 shares × $40).		
May 19	Cash	630,000	
	Preferred Stock		600,000
	Paid-In Capital in Excess of Par		30,000
	(15,000 shares × $42).		

For Practice: PE 13-2A, PE 13-2B

Describe and illustrate the accounting for cash dividends and stock dividends.

Accounting for Dividends

When a board of directors declares a cash dividend, it authorizes the distribution of cash to stockholders. When a board of directors declares a stock dividend, it authorizes the distribution of its stock. In both cases, declaring a dividend reduces the retained earnings of the corporation.[8]

Cash Dividends

A cash distribution of earnings by a corporation to its shareholders is a **cash dividend.** Although dividends may be paid in other assets, cash dividends are the most common.

Three conditions for a cash dividend are as follows:

1. Sufficient retained earnings
2. Sufficient cash
3. Formal action by the board of directors

There must be a sufficient (large enough) balance in Retained Earnings to declare a cash dividend. That is, the balance of Retained Earnings must be large enough so that the dividend does not create a debit balance in the retained earnings account. However,

8 In rare cases, when a corporation is reducing its operations or going out of business, a dividend may be a distribution of paid-in capital. Such a dividend is called a *liquidating dividend.*

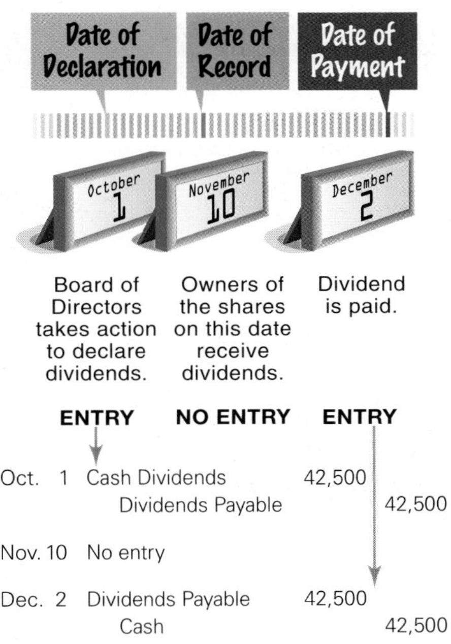

a large Retained Earnings balance does not mean that there is cash available to pay dividends. This is because the balances of Cash and Retained Earnings are often unrelated.

Even if there are sufficient retained earnings and cash, a corporation's board of directors is not required to pay dividends. Nevertheless, many corporations pay quarterly cash dividends to make their stock more attractive to investors. *Special* or *extra* dividends may also be paid when a corporation experiences higher than normal profits.

Three dates included in a dividend announcement are as follows:

1. Date of declaration
2. Date of record
3. Date of payment

The *date of declaration* is the date the board of directors formally authorizes the payment of the dividend. On this date, the corporation incurs the liability to pay the amount of the dividend.

The *date of record* is the date the corporation uses to determine which stockholders will receive the dividend. During the period of time between the date of declaration and the date of record, the stock price is quoted as selling *with-dividends.* This means that any investors purchasing the stock before the date of record will receive the dividend.

The *date of payment* is the date the corporation will pay the dividend to the stockholders who owned the stock on the date of record. During the period of time between the record date and the payment date, the stock price is quoted as selling *ex-dividends.* This means that since the date of record has passed, any new investors will not receive the dividend.

The Campbell Soup Company declared on March 27 a quarterly cash dividend of $0.22 to common stockholders of record as of the close of business on April 17, payable on April 28.

To illustrate, assume that on October 1 Hiber Corporation declares the cash dividends shown below with a date of record of November 10 and a date of payment of December 2.

	Dividend per Share	Total Dividends
Preferred stock, $100 par, 5,000 shares outstanding	$2.50	$12,500
Common stock, $10 par, 100,000 shares outstanding	$0.30	30,000
Total		$42,500

On October 1, the declaration date, Hiber Corporation records the following entry:

Oct.	1	Cash Dividends		42,500	
		Cash Dividends Payable			42,500
		Declared cash dividends.			

On November 10, the date of record, no entry is necessary. This date merely determines which stockholders will receive the dividends.

On December 2, the date of payment, Hiber Corporation records the payment of the dividends as follows:

Dec.	2	Cash Dividends Payable		42,500	
		Cash			42,500
		Paid cash dividends.			

At the end of the accounting period, the balance in Cash Dividends will be transferred to Retained Earnings as part of the closing process. This closing entry debits Retained Earnings and credits Cash Dividends for the balance of the cash dividends account. If the cash dividends have not been paid by the end of the period, Cash Dividends Payable will be reported on the balance sheet as a current liability.

Example Exercise 13-3 Entries for Cash Dividends

The important dates in connection with a cash dividend of $75,000 on a corporation's common stock are February 26, March 30, and April 2. Journalize the entries required on each date.

Follow My Example 13-3

Feb. 26	Cash Dividends	75,000	
	Cash Dividends Payable		75,000
Mar. 30	No entry required.		
Apr. 2	Cash Dividends Payable	75,000	
	Cash		75,000

For Practice: PE 13-3A, PE 13-3B

Integrity, Objectivity, and Ethics in Business

THE PROFESSOR WHO KNEW TOO MUCH

A major Midwestern university released a quarterly "American Customer Satisfaction Index" based on its research of customers of popular U.S. products and services. Before the release of the index to the public, the professor in charge of the research bought and sold stocks of some of the companies in the report. The professor was quoted as saying that he thought it was important to test his theories of customer satisfaction with "real" [his own] money.

Is this proper or ethical? Apparently, the dean of the Business School didn't think so. In a statement to the press, the dean stated: "I have instructed anyone affiliated with the (index) not to make personal use of information gathered in the course of producing the quarterly index, prior to the index's release to the general public, and they [the researchers] have agreed."

Sources: Jon E. Hilsenrath and Dan Morse, "Researcher Uses Index to Buy, Short Stocks," *The Wall Street Journal*, February 18, 2003; and Jon E. Hilsenrath, "Satisfaction Theory: Mixed Results," *The Wall Street Journal*, February 19, 2003.

Stock Dividends

A **stock dividend** is a distribution of shares of stock to stockholders. Stock dividends are normally declared only on common stock and issued to common stockholders.

The recording of a stock dividend affects only stockholders' equity. Specifically, the amount of the stock dividend is transferred from Retained Earnings to Paid-in Capital. The amount transferred is normally the fair value (market price) of the shares issued in the stock dividend.[9]

To illustrate, assume that the stockholders' equity accounts of Hendrix Corporation as of December 15 are as follows:

Common Stock, $20 par (2,000,000 shares issued)	$40,000,000
Paid-In Capital in Excess of Par—Common Stock	9,000,000
Retained Earnings	26,600,000

On December 15, Hendrix Corporation declares a stock dividend of 5% or 100,000 shares (2,000,000 shares × 5%) to be issued on January 10 to stockholders of record on December 31. The market price of the stock on December 15 (the date of declaration) is $31 per share.

The entry to record the stock dividend is as follows:

Dec.	15	Stock Dividends		3,100,000	
		Stock Dividends Distributable			2,000,000
		Paid-In Capital in Excess of Par—Common Stock			1,100,000
		Declared 5% (100,000 share) stock dividend on $20 par common stock with a market price of $31 per share.			

9 The use of fair market value is justified as long as the number of shares issued for the stock dividend is small (less than 25% of the shares outstanding).

After the preceding entry is recorded, Stock Dividends will have a debit balance of $3,100,000. Like cash dividends, the stock dividends account is closed to Retained Earnings at the end of the accounting period. This closing entry debits Retained Earnings and credits Stock Dividends.

At the end of the period, the *stock dividends distributable* and *paid-in capital in excess of par—common stock* accounts are reported in the Paid-in Capital section of the balance sheet. Thus, the effect of the preceding stock dividend is to transfer $3,100,000 of retained earnings to paid-in capital.

On January 10, the stock dividend is distributed to stockholders by issuing 100,000 shares of common stock. The issuance of the stock is recorded by the following entry:

Jan.	10	Stock Dividends Distributable		2,000,000	
		Common Stock			2,000,000
		Issued stock as stock dividend.			

A stock dividend does not change the assets, liabilities, or total stockholders' equity of a corporation. Likewise, a stock dividend does not change an individual stockholder's proportionate interest (equity) in the corporation.

To illustrate, assume a stockholder owns 1,000 of a corporation's 10,000 shares outstanding. If the corporation declares a 6% stock dividend, the stockholder's proportionate interest will not change as shown below.

	***Before* Stock Dividend**	***After* Stock Dividend**
Total shares issued	10,000	10,600 [10,000 + (10,000 × 6%)]
Number of shares owned	1,000	1,060 [1,000 + (1,000 × 6%)]
Proportionate ownership	10% (1,000/10,000)	10% (1,060/10,600)

Example Exercise 13-4 Entries for Stock Dividends (4)

Vienna Highlights Corporation has 150,000 shares of $100 par common stock outstanding. On June 14, Vienna Highlights declared a 4% stock dividend to be issued August 15 to stockholders of record on July 1. The market price of the stock was $110 per share on June 14.

Journalize the entries required on June 14, July 1, and August 15.

Follow My Example 13-4

June 14	Stock Dividends (150,000 × 4% × $110)	660,000	
	Stock Dividends Distributable (6,000 × $100)		600,000
	Paid-In Capital in Excess of Par—Common Stock ($660,000 − $600,000)		60,000
July 1	No entry required.		
Aug. 15	Stock Dividends Distributable	600,000	
	Common Stock		600,000

For Practice: PE 13-4A, PE 13-4B

Describe and illustrate the accounting for treasury stock transactions.

Treasury Stock Transactions

Treasury stock is stock that a corporation has issued and then reacquired. A corporation may reacquire (purchase) its own stock for a variety of reasons including the following:

1. To provide shares for resale to employees
2. To reissue as bonuses to employees, or
3. To support the market price of the stock

The 2007 edition of *Accounting Trends & Techniques* indicated that over 66% of the companies surveyed reported treasury stock.

The *cost method* is normally used for recording the purchase and resale of treasury stock.[10] Using the cost method, *Treasury Stock* is debited for the cost (purchase price) of the stock. When the stock is resold, Treasury Stock is credited for its cost. Any difference between the cost and the selling price is debited or credited to *Paid-In Capital from Sale of Treasury Stock.*

To illustrate, assume that a corporation has the following paid-in capital on January 1:

Common stock, $25 par (20,000 shares authorized and issued)	$500,000
Excess of issue price over par	150,000
	$650,000

On February 13, the corporation purchases 1,000 shares of its common stock at $45 per share. The entry to record the purchase of the treasury stock is as follows:

Feb.	13	Treasury Stock		45,000	
		Cash			45,000
		Purchased 1,000 shares of treasury stock at $45.			

On April 29, the corporation sells 600 shares of the treasury stock for $60. The entry to record the sale is as follows:

Apr.	29	Cash		36,000	
		Treasury Stock			27,000
		Paid-In Capital from Sale of Treasury Stock			9,000
		Sold 600 shares of treasury stock at $60.			

A sale of treasury stock may result in a decrease in paid-in capital. To the extent that Paid-In Capital from Sale of Treasury Stock has a credit balance, it is debited for any such decrease. Any remaining decrease is then debited to the retained earnings account.

To illustrate, assume that on October 4, the corporation sells the remaining 400 shares of treasury stock for $40 per share. The entry to record the sale is as follows:

Oct.	4	Cash		16,000	
		Paid-In Capital from Sale of Treasury Stock		2,000	
		Treasury Stock			18,000
		Sold 400 shares of treasury stock at $40.			

The October 4 entry shown above decreases paid-in capital by $2,000. Since Paid-In Capital from Sale of Treasury Stock has a credit balance of $9,000, the entire $2,000 was debited to Paid-In Capital from Sale of Treasury Stock.

No dividends (cash or stock) are paid on the shares of treasury stock. To do so would result in the corporation earning dividend revenue from itself.

Example Exercise 13-5 Entries for Treasury Stock 5

On May 3, Buzz Off Corporation reacquired 3,200 shares of its common stock at $42 per share. On July 22, Buzz Off sold 2,000 of the reacquired shares at $47 per share. On August 30, Buzz Off sold the remaining shares at $40 per share.

Journalize the transactions of May 3, July 22, and August 30.

(continued)

10 Another method that is infrequently used, called the *par value method,* is discussed in advanced accounting texts.

Follow My Example 13-5

May 3	Treasury Stock (3,200 × $42)	134,400	
	Cash		134,400
July 22	Cash (2,000 × $47)	94,000	
	Treasury Stock (2,000 × $42)		84,000
	Paid-In Capital from Sale of Treasury Stock [2,000 × ($47 − $42)]		10,000
Aug. 30	Cash (1,200 × $40)	48,000	
	Paid-In Capital from Sale of Treasury Stock [1,200 × ($42 − $40)]	2,400	
	Treasury Stock (1,200 × $42)		50,400

For Practice: PE 13-5A, PE 13-5B

Describe and illustrate the reporting of stockholders' equity.

Reporting Stockholders' Equity

As with other sections of the balance sheet, alternative terms and formats may be used in reporting stockholders' equity. Also, changes in retained earnings and paid-in capital may be reported in separate statements or notes to the financial statements.

Stockholders' Equity in the Balance Sheet

Exhibit 5 shows two methods for reporting stockholders' equity for the December 31, 2010, balance sheet for Telex Inc.

Method 1. Each class of stock is reported, followed by its related paid-in capital accounts. Retained earnings is then reported followed by a deduction for treasury stock.

Method 2. The stock accounts are reported, followed by the paid-in capital reported as a single item, Additional paid-in capital. Retained earnings is then reported followed by a deduction for treasury stock.

Exhibit 5

Stockholders' Equity Section of a Balance Sheet

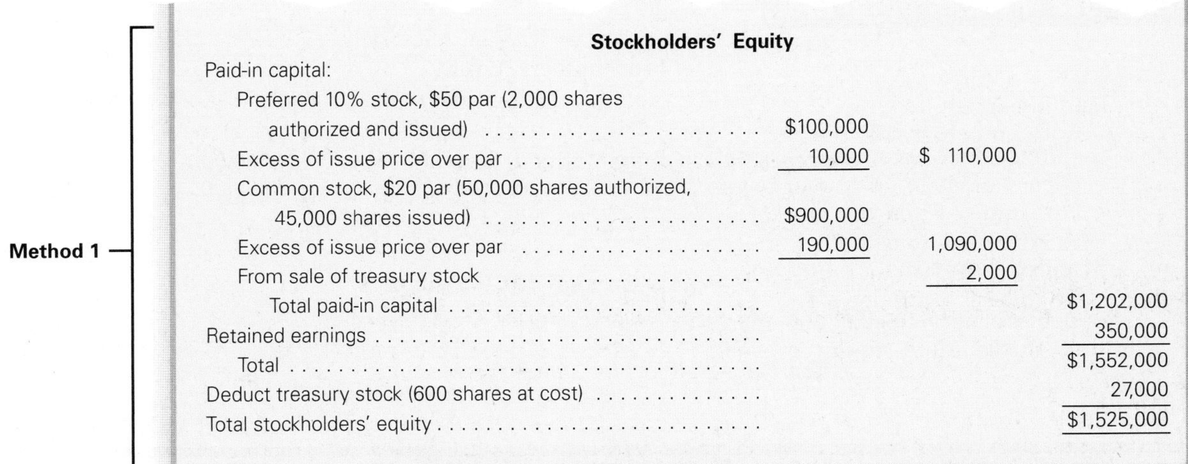

Telex Inc.
Balance Sheet
December 31, 2010

Method 1

Stockholders' Equity

Paid-in capital:			
Preferred 10% stock, $50 par (2,000 shares authorized and issued)	$100,000		
Excess of issue price over par	10,000	$ 110,000	
Common stock, $20 par (50,000 shares authorized, 45,000 shares issued)	$900,000		
Excess of issue price over par	190,000	1,090,000	
From sale of treasury stock		2,000	
Total paid-in capital			$1,202,000
Retained earnings			350,000
Total			$1,552,000
Deduct treasury stock (600 shares at cost)			27,000
Total stockholders' equity			$1,525,000

(continued)

Exhibit 5 (continued)

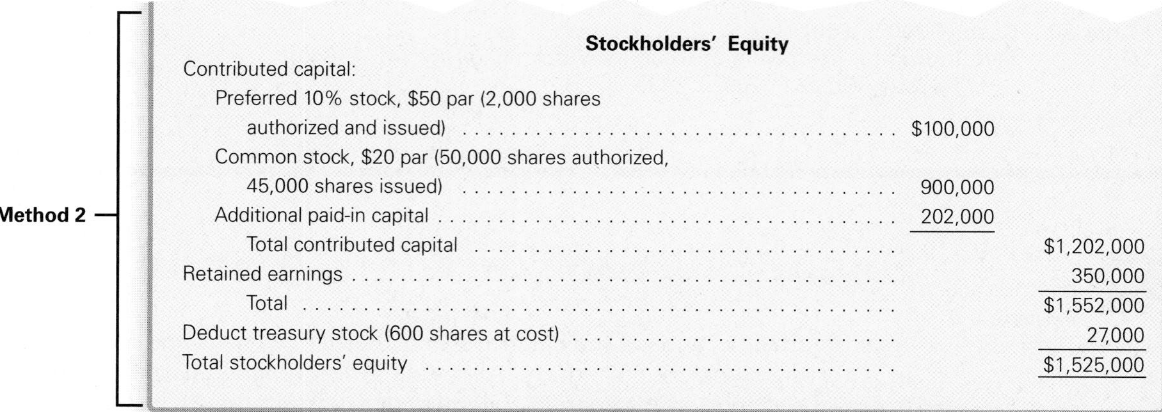

Telex Inc.
Balance Sheet
December 31, 2010

Method 2

Stockholders' Equity		
Contributed capital:		
Preferred 10% stock, $50 par (2,000 shares authorized and issued)	$100,000	
Common stock, $20 par (50,000 shares authorized, 45,000 shares issued)	900,000	
Additional paid-in capital	202,000	
Total contributed capital		$1,202,000
Retained earnings		350,000
Total		$1,552,000
Deduct treasury stock (600 shares at cost)		27,000
Total stockholders' equity		$1,525,000

Significant changes in stockholders' equity during a period may also be presented in a statement of stockholders' equity or in the notes to the financial statements. The statement of stockholders' equity is illustrated later in this section.

Relevant rights and privileges of the various classes of stock outstanding should also be reported.[11] Examples include dividend and liquidation preferences, conversion rights, and redemption rights. Such information may be disclosed on the face of the balance sheet or in the notes to the financial statements.

Example Exercise 13-6 Reporting Stockholders' Equity — 6

Using the following accounts and balances, prepare the Stockholders' Equity section of the balance sheet. Forty thousand shares of common stock are authorized, and 5,000 shares have been reacquired.

Common Stock, $50 par	$1,500,000
Paid-In Capital in Excess of Par	160,000
Paid-In Capital from Sale of Treasury Stock	44,000
Retained Earnings	4,395,000
Treasury Stock	120,000

Follow My Example 13-6

Stockholders' Equity		
Paid-in capital:		
Common stock, $50 par (40,000 shares authorized, 30,000 shares issued)	$1,500,000	
Excess of issue price over par	160,000	$1,660,000
From sale of treasury stock		44,000
Total paid-in capital		$1,704,000
Retained earnings		4,395,000
Total		$6,099,000
Deduct treasury stock (5,000 shares at cost)		120,000
Total stockholders' equity		$5,979,000

For Practice: PE 13-6A, PE 13-6B

11 *Statement of Financial Accounting Standards No. 129*, "Disclosure Information about Capital Structure" (Financial Accounting Standards Board, Norwalk, CT: 1997).

Reporting Retained Earnings

Changes in retained earnings may be reported using one of the following:

1. Separate retained earnings statement
2. Combined income and retained earnings statement
3. Statement of stockholders' equity

Changes in retained earnings may be reported in a separate retained earnings statement. When a separate **retained earnings statement** is prepared, the beginning balance of retained earnings is reported. The net income is then added (or net loss is subtracted) and any dividends are subtracted to arrive at the ending retained earnings for the period.

To illustrate, a retained earnings statement for Telex Inc. is shown in Exhibit 6.

Exhibit 6

Retained Earnings Statement

Telex Inc.
Retained Earnings Statement
For the Year Ended December 31, 2010

Retained earnings, January 1, 2010			$245,000
Net income		$180,000	
Less dividends:			
Preferred stock	$10,000		
Common stock	65,000	75,000	
Increase in retained earnings			105,000
Retained earnings, December 31, 2010			$350,000

Changes in retained earnings may also be reported in combination with the income statement. This format emphasizes net income as the connecting link between the income statement and ending retained earnings. Since this format is not often used, we do not illustrate it.

Changes in retained earnings may also be reported in a statement of stockholders' equity. An example of reporting changes in retained earnings in a statement of stockholders' equity for Telex Inc. is shown in Exhibit 7.

The 2007 edition of *Accounting Trends & Techniques* indicated that 0.5% of the companies surveyed presented a separate statement of retained earnings, 0.5% presented a combined income and retained earnings statement, and 1% presented changes in retained earnings in the notes to the financial statements. The other 98% of the companies presented changes in retained earnings in a statement of stockholders' equity.

Restrictions The use of retained earnings for payment of dividends may be restricted by action of a corporation's board of directors. Such **restrictions,** sometimes called *appropriations*, remain part of the retained earnings.

Restrictions of retained earnings are classified as:

1. *Legal.* State laws may require a restriction of retained earnings.

   Example: States may restrict retained earnings by the amount of treasury stock purchased. In this way, legal capital cannot be used for dividends.

2. *Contractual.* A corporation may enter into contracts that require restrictions of retained earnings.

   Example: A bank loan may restrict retained earnings so that money for repaying the loan cannot be used for dividends.

3. *Discretionary.* A corporation's board of directors may restrict retained earnings voluntarily.

   Example: The board may restrict retained earnings and, thus, limit dividend distributions so that more money is available for expanding the business.

Restrictions of retained earnings must be disclosed in the financial statements. Such disclosures are usually included in the notes to the financial statements.

Example Exercise 13-7 Retained Earnings Statement 6

Dry Creek Cameras Inc. reported the following results for the year ending March 31, 2010:

Retained earnings, April 1, 2009	$3,338,500
Net income	461,500
Cash dividends declared	80,000
Stock dividends declared	120,000

Prepare a retained earnings statement for the fiscal year ended March 31, 2010.

Follow My Example 13-7

DRY CREEK CAMERAS INC.
RETAINED EARNINGS STATEMENT
For the Year Ended March 31, 2010

Retained earnings, April 1, 2009		$3,338,500
Net income	$461,500	
Less dividends declared	200,000	
Increase in retained earnings		261,500
Retained earnings, March 31, 2010		$3,600,000

For Practice: PE 13-7A, PE 13-7B

Prior Period Adjustments An error may arise from a mathematical mistake or from a mistake in applying accounting principles. Such errors may not be discovered within the same period in which they occur. In such cases, the effect of the error should not affect the current period's net income. Instead, the correction of the error, called a **prior period adjustment**, is reported in the retained earnings statement. Such corrections are reported as an adjustment to the beginning balance of retained earnings.[12]

Statement of Stockholders' Equity

When the only change in stockholders' equity is due to net income or net loss and dividends, a retained earnings statement is sufficient. However, when a corporation also has changes in stock and paid-in capital accounts, a **statement of stockholders' equity** is normally prepared.

A statement of stockholders' equity is normally prepared in a columnar format. Each column is a major stockholders' equity classification. Changes in each classification are then described in the left-hand column. Exhibit 7 illustrates a statement of stockholders' equity for Telex Inc.

Exhibit 7

Statement of Stockholders' Equity

Telex Inc.
Statement of Stockholders' Equity
For the Year Ended December 31, 2010

	Preferred Stock	Common Stock	Additional Paid-In Capital	Retained Earnings	Treasury Stock	Total
Balance, January 1, 2010	$100,000	$850,000	$177,000	$245,000	$ (17,000)	$1,355,000
Net income				180,000		180,000
Dividends on preferred stock				(10,000)		(10,000)
Dividends on common stock				(65,000)		(65,000)
Issuance of additional common stock		50,000	25,000			75,000
Purchase of treasury stock					(10,000)	(10,000)
Balance, December 31, 2010	$100,000	$900,000	$202,000	$350,000	$ (27,000)	$1,525,000

12 Prior period adjustments are illustrated ...

Reporting Stockholders' Equity for Mornin' Joe

Mornin' Joe reports stockholders' equity in its balance sheet. Mornin' Joe also includes a retained earnings statement and statement of stockholders' equity in its financial statements.

The Stockholders' Equity section of Mornin' Joe's balance sheet as of December 31, 2010, is shown below.

Mornin' Joe
Balance Sheet
December 31, 2010

Stockholders' Equity

Paid-in capital:		
Preferred 10% stock, $50 par (6,000 shares authorized and issued)	$ 300,000	
Excess of issue price over par	50,000	$ 350,000
Common stock, $20 par (50,000 shares authorized, 45,000 shares issued)	$ 900,000	
Excess of issue price over par	1,450,000	2,350,000
Total paid-in capital		$2,700,000
Retained earnings		1,200,300
Total		$3,900,300
Deduct treasury stock (1,000 shares at cost)		46,000
Total stockholders' equity		$3,854,300
Total liabilities and stockholders' equity		$6,169,700

Mornin' Joe's retained earnings statement for the year ended December 31, 2010, is as follows:

Mornin' Joe
Retained Earnings Statment
For the Year Ended December 31, 2010

Retained earnings, January 1, 2010			$ 852,700
Net income		$421,600	
Less dividends:			
Preferred stock	$30,000		
Common stock	44,000	74,000	
Increase in retained earnings			347,600
Retained earnings, December 31, 2010			$1,200,300

The statement of stockholders' equity for Mornin' Joe is shown below.

Mornin' Joe
Statement of Stockholders' Equity
For the Year Ended December 31, 2010

	Preferred Stock	Common Stock	Additional Paid-In Capital	Retained Earnings	Treasury Stock	Total
Balance, January 1, 2010	$300,000	$800,000	$1,325,000	$852,700	$ (36,000)	$3,241,700
Net income				421,600		421,600
Dividends on preferred stock				(30,000)		(30,000)
Dividends on common stock				(44,000)		(44,000)
Issuance of additional common stock		100,000	175,000			275,000
Purchase of treasury stock					(10,000)	(10,000)
Balance, December 31, 2010	$300,000	$900,000	$1,500,000	$1,200,300	$ (46,000)	$3,854,300

7 Describe the effect of stock splits on corporate financial statements.

Stock Splits

A **stock split** is a process by which a corporation reduces the par or stated value of its common stock and issues a proportionate number of additional shares. A stock split applies to all common shares including the unissued, issued, and treasury shares.

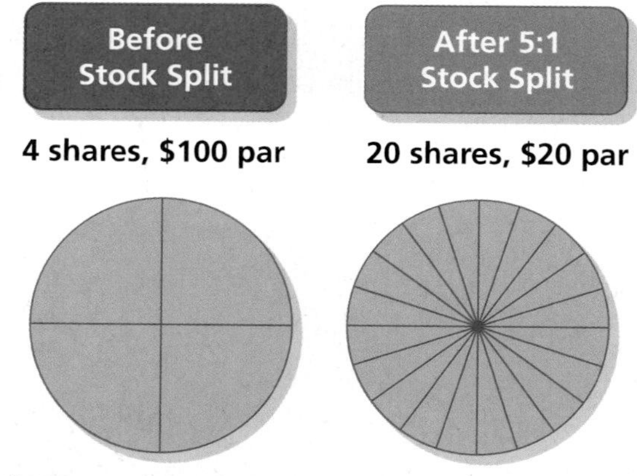

A major objective of a stock split is to reduce the market price per share of the stock. This, in turn, attracts more investors to the stock and broadens the types and numbers of stockholders.

When Nature's Sunshine Products, Inc., declared a 2-for-1 stock split, the company president said:

We believe the split will place our stock price in a range attractive to both individual and institutional investors, broadening the market for the stock.

To illustrate, assume that Rojek Corporation has 10,000 shares of $100 par common stock outstanding with a current market price of $150 per share. The board of directors declares the following stock split:

1. Each common shareholder will receive 5 shares for each share held. This is called a 5-for-l stock split. As a result, 50,000 shares (10,000 shares × 5) will be outstanding.
2. The par of each share of common stock will be reduced to $20 ($100/5).

The par value of the common stock outstanding is $1,000,000 both before and after the stock split as shown below.

	Before Split	After Split
Number of shares	10,000	50,000
Par value per share	× $100	× $20
Total	$1,000,000	$1,000,000

In addition, each Rojek Corporation shareholder owns the same total par amount of stock before and after the stock split. For example, a stockholder who owned 4 shares of $100 par stock before the split (total par of $400) would own 20 shares of $20 par stock after the split (total par of $400). Only the number of shares and the par value per share have changed.

A stock split does not require a journal entry.

Since there are more shares outstanding after the stock split, the market price of the stock should decrease. For example, in the preceding example, there would be 5 times as many shares outstanding after the split. Thus, the market price of the stock would be expected to fall from $150 to about $30 ($150/5).

Stock splits do not require a journal entry since only the par (or stated) value and number of shares outstanding have changed. However, the details of stock splits are normally disclosed in the notes to the financial statements.

Financial Analysis and Interpretation

The amount of net income is often used by investors and creditors in evaluating a company's profitability. However, net income by itself is difficult to use in comparing companies of different sizes. Also, trends in net income may be difficult to evaluate if there have been significant changes in a company's stockholders' equity. Thus, the profitability of companies is often expressed as earnings per share. **Earnings per common share (EPS),** sometimes called *basic earnings per share,* is the net income per share of common stock outstanding during a period. Corporations whose stock is traded in a public market must report earnings per common share on their income statements.

The earnings per share is calculated as follows:

$$\text{Earnings per Share} = \frac{\text{Net Income} - \text{Preferred Dividends}}{\text{Number of Common Shares Outstanding}}$$

If a company has preferred stock outstanding, the net income must be reduced by the amount of any preferred dividends since the numerator represents only those earnings available to the common shareholders. When the number of common shares outstanding has changed during the period, a weighted average number of shares outstanding is used in the denominator.

Earnings per share can be used to compare two companies with different net incomes. For example, the following data are available for a recent year for Blockbuster Inc. and Netflix, Inc., which are two companies in the video rental business:

	Blockbuster Inc. (in millions)	Netflix, Inc. (in millions)
Net income	$54.7	$49.1
Preferred dividends	$11.3	$ 0.0
Number of common shares outstanding	187.1	62.6

The earnings per share for both companies can be calculated as follows:

$$\text{Blockbuster Inc.: } \frac{\$54.7 - \$11.3}{187.1 \text{ common shares outstanding}} = \$0.23 \text{ per common share}$$

$$\text{Netflix, Inc.: } \frac{\$49.1}{62.6 \text{ common shares outstanding}} = \$0.78 \text{ per common share}$$

Thus, while the net income of Blockbuster exceeds that of Netflix, the earnings per share of Netflix is more than three times as great as Blockbuster. This results from Blockbuster's preferred dividends and Netflix's much fewer shares outstanding. Not surprisingly, the stock price of Netflix ($21.60) is greater than Blockbuster's ($3.25), reflecting the superior earnings per share performance.

f·a·i

At a Glance 13

1 Describe the nature of the corporate form of organization.

Key Points	Key Learning Outcomes	Example Exercises	Practice Exercises
Corporations have a separate legal existence, transferable units of stock, unlimited life, and limited stockholders' liability. The advantages and disadvantages of the corporate form are summarized in Exhibit 2. Costs incurred in organizing a corporation are debited to Organizational Expenses.	• Describe the characteristics of corporations. • List the advantages and disadvantages of the corporate form. • Prepare a journal entry for the costs of organizing a corporation.		

2 Describe the two main sources of stockholders' equity.

Key Points	Key Learning Outcomes	Example Exercises	Practice Exercises
The two main sources of stockholders' equity are (1) capital contributed by the stockholders and others, called *paid-in capital*, and (2) net income retained in the business, called *retained earnings*. Stockholders' equity is reported in a corporation balance sheet according to these two sources.	• Describe what is meant by paid-in capital. • Describe what is meant by net income retained in the business. • Prepare a simple Stockholders' Equity section of the balance sheet.		

3 Describe and illustrate the characteristics of stock, classes of stock, and entries for issuing stock.

Key Points	Key Learning Outcomes	Example Exercises	Practice Exercises
The main source of paid-in capital is from issuing common and preferred stock. Stock issued at par is recorded by debiting Cash and crediting the class of stock issued for its par amount. Stock issued for more than par is recorded by debiting Cash, crediting the class of stock for its par, and crediting Paid-In Capital in Excess of Par for the difference. When stock is issued in exchange for assets other than cash, the assets acquired are recorded at their fair market value. When no-par stock is issued, the entire proceeds are credited to the stock account. No-par stock may be assigned a stated value per share, and the excess of the proceeds over the stated value may be credited to Paid-In Capital in Excess of Stated Value.	• Describe the characteristics of common and preferred stock including rights to dividends.	**13-1**	13-1A, 13-1B
	• Journalize the entry for common and preferred stock issued at par.	**13-2**	13-2A, 13-2B
	• Journalize the entry for common and preferred stock issued at more than par.	**13-2**	13-2A, 13-2B
	• Journalize the entry for issuing no-par stock.	**13-2**	13-2A, 13-2B

4 Describe and illustrate the accounting for cash dividends and stock dividends.

Key Points	Key Learning Outcomes	Example Exercises	Practice Exercises
The entry to record a declaration of cash dividends debits Dividends and credits Dividends Payable. When a stock dividend is declared, Stock Dividends is debited for the fair value of the stock to be issued. Stock Dividends Distributable is credited for the par or stated value of the common stock to be issued. The difference between the fair value of the stock and its par or stated value is credited to Paid-In Capital in Excess of Par—Common Stock. When the stock is issued on the date of payment, Stock Dividends Distributable is debited and Common Stock is credited for the par or stated value of the stock issued.	• Journalize the entries for the declaration and payment of cash dividends.	**13-3**	13-3A, 13-3B
	• Journalize the entries for the declaration and payment of stock dividends.	**13-4**	13-4A, 13-4B

5 Describe and illustrate the accounting for treasury stock transactions.

Key Points	Key Learning Outcomes	Example Exercises	Practice Exercises
When a corporation buys its own stock, the cost method of accounting is normally used. Treasury Stock is debited for its cost, and Cash is credited. If the stock is resold, Treasury Stock is credited for its cost and any difference between the cost and the selling price is normally debited or credited to Paid-In Capital from Sale of Treasury Stock.	• Define *treasury stock*.		
	• Describe the accounting for treasury stock.		
	• Journalize entries for the purchase and sale of treasury stock.	**13-5**	13-5A, 13-5B

6 Describe and illustrate the reporting of stockholders' equity.

Key Points	Key Learning Outcomes	Example Exercises	Practice Exercises
Two alternatives for reporting stockholders' equity are shown in Exhibit 5. Changes in retained earnings are reported in a retained earnings statement, as shown in Exhibit 6. Restrictions to retained earnings should be disclosed. Any prior period adjustments are reported in the retained earnings statement. Changes in stockholders' equity may be reported on a statement of stockholders' equity, as shown in Exhibit 7.	• Prepare the Stockholders' Equity section of the balance sheet.	**13-6**	13-6A, 13-6B
	• Prepare a retained earnings statement.	**13-7**	13-7A, 13-7B
	• Describe retained earnings restrictions and prior period adjustments.		
	• Prepare a statement of stockholders' equity.		

7 Describe the effect of stock splits on corporate financial statements.

Key Points	Key Learning Outcomes	Example Exercises	Practice Exercises
When a corporation reduces the par or stated value of its common stock and issues a proportionate number of additional shares, a stock split has occurred. There are no changes in the balances of any accounts, and no entry is required for a stock split.	• Define and give an example of a stock split.		
	• Describe the accounting for and effects of a stock split on the financial statements.		

Key Terms

cash dividend (584)
common stock (579)
cumulative preferred stock (580)
deficit (578)
discount (581)
dividends (578)
earnings per common share (EPS) (595)
in arrears (580)
outstanding stock (579)
paid-in capital (578)
par (579)
preferred stock (579)
premium (581)
prior period adjustments (592)
restrictions (591)
retained earnings (578)
retained earnings statement (591)
statement of stockholders' equity (592)
stock (575)
stock dividend (586)
stock split (594)
stockholders (575)
stockholders' equity (578)
treasury stock (587)

Illustrative Problem

Altenburg Inc. is a lighting fixture wholesaler located in Arizona. During its current fiscal year, ended December 31, 2010, Altenburg Inc. completed the following selected transactions:

Feb. 3. Purchased 2,500 shares of its own common stock at $26, recording the stock at cost. (Prior to the purchase, there were 40,000 shares of $20 par common stock outstanding.)
May 1. Declared a semiannual dividend of $1 on the 10,000 shares of preferred stock and a 30¢ dividend on the common stock to stockholders of record on May 31, payable on June 15.
June 15. Paid the cash dividends.
Sept. 23. Sold 1,000 shares of treasury stock at $28, receiving cash.
Nov. 1. Declared semiannual dividends of $1 on the preferred stock and 30¢ on the common stock. In addition, a 5% common stock dividend was declared on the common stock outstanding, to be capitalized at the fair market value of the common stock, which is estimated at $30.
Dec. 1. Paid the cash dividends and issued the certificates for the common stock dividend.

Instructions

Journalize the entries to record the transactions for Altenburg Inc.

Solution

Date		Account	Post. Ref.	Debit	Credit
2010 Feb.	3	Treasury Stock		65,000	
		Cash			65,000
May	1	Cash Dividends		21,250	
		Cash Dividends Payable			21,250
		(10,000 × $1) + [(40,000 − 2,500) × $0.30].			
June	15	Cash Dividends Payable		21,250	
		Cash			21,250
Sept.	23	Cash		28,000	
		Treasury Stock			26,000
		Paid-In Capital from Sale of Treasury Stock			2,000
Nov.	1	Cash Dividends		21,550	
		Cash Dividends Payable			21,550
		(10,000 × $1) + [(40,000 − 1,500) × $0.30].			
	1	Stock Dividends		57,750*	
		Stock Dividends Distributable			38,500
		Paid-In Capital in Excess of Par—Common Stock			19,250
		*(40,000 − 1,500) × 5% × $30.			
Dec.	1	Cash Dividends Payable		21,550	
		Stock Dividends Distributable		38,500	
		Cash			21,550
		Common Stock			38,500

Self-Examination Questions (Answers at End of Chapter)

1. Which of the following is a disadvantage of the corporate form of organization?
   A. Limited liability
   B. Continuous life
   C. Owner is separate from management
   D. Ability to raise capital
2. Paid-in capital for a corporation may arise from which of the following sources?
   A. Issuing preferred stock
   B. Issuing common stock
   C. Selling the corporation's treasury stock
   D. All of the above
3. The Stockholders' Equity section of the balance sheet may include:
   A. Common Stock.
   B. Stock Dividends Distributable.
   C. Preferred Stock.
   D. All of the above.
4. If a corporation reacquires its own stock, the stock is listed on the balance sheet in the:
   A. Current Assets section.
   B. Long-Term Liabilities section.
   C. Stockholders' Equity section.
   D. Investments section.
5. A corporation has issued 25,000 shares of $100 par common stock and holds 3,000 of these shares as treasury stock. If the corporation declares a $2 per share cash dividend, what amount will be recorded as cash dividends?
   A. $22,000
   B. $25,000
   C. $44,000
   D. $50,000

Eye Openers

1. Describe the stockholders' liability to creditors of a corporation.
2. Why are most large businesses organized as corporations?
3. Of two corporations organized at approximately the same time and engaged in competing businesses, one issued $100 par common stock, and the other issued $0.01 par common stock. Do the par designations provide any indication as to which stock is preferable as an investment? Explain.
4. A stockbroker advises a client to "buy preferred stock. . . . With that type of stock, . . . [you] will never have to worry about losing the dividends." Is the broker right?
5. What are some of the factors that influence the market price of a corporation's stock?
6. When a corporation issues stock at a premium, is the premium income? Explain.
7. (a) What are the three conditions for the declaration and payment of a cash dividend? (b) The dates in connection with the declaration of a cash dividend are February 16, March 18, and April 17. Identify each date.
8. A corporation with both preferred stock and common stock outstanding has a substantial credit balance in its retained earnings account at the beginning of the current fiscal year. Although net income for the current year is sufficient to pay the preferred dividend of $125,000 each quarter and a common dividend of $300,000 each quarter, the board of directors declares dividends only on the preferred stock. Suggest possible reasons for passing the dividends on the common stock.
9. An owner of 500 shares of Microshop Company common stock receives a stock dividend of 5 shares. (a) What is the effect of the stock dividend on the stockholder's proportionate interest (equity) in the corporation? (b) How does the total equity of 505 shares compare with the total equity of 500 shares before the stock dividend?
10. a. Where should a declared but unpaid cash dividend be reported on the balance sheet?
    b. Where should a declared but unissued stock dividend be reported on the balance sheet?
11. a. In what respect does treasury stock differ from unissued stock?
    b. How should treasury stock be presented on the balance sheet?
12. A corporation reacquires 10,000 shares of its own $25 par common stock for $450,000, recording it at cost. (a) What effect does this transaction have on revenue or expense of the period? (b) What effect does it have on stockholders' equity?

13. The treasury stock in Eye Opener 12 is resold for $615,000. (a) What is the effect on the corporation's revenue of the period? (b) What is the effect on stockholders' equity?
14. What is the primary advantage of combining the retained earnings statement with the income statement?
15. What are the three classifications of restrictions of retained earnings, and how are such restrictions normally reported in the financial statements?
16. Indicate how prior period adjustments would be reported on the financial statements presented only for the current period.
17. When is a statement of stockholders' equity normally prepared?
18. What is the primary purpose of a stock split?

Practice Exercises

PE 13-1A
Dividends per share
obj. 3
EE 13-1 p. 581

Taiwanese Company has 5,000 shares of 4% cumulative preferred stock of $40 par and 10,000 shares of $90 par common stock. The following amounts were distributed as dividends:

Year 1	$15,000
Year 2	5,000
Year 3	62,000

Determine the dividends per share for preferred and common stock for each year.

PE 13-1B
Dividends per share
obj. 3
EE 13-1 p. 581

Master Craftmen Company has 10,000 shares of 2% cumulative preferred stock of $50 par and 25,000 shares of $75 par common stock. The following amounts were distributed as dividends:

Year 1	$30,000
Year 2	6,000
Year 3	80,000

Determine the dividends per share for preferred and common stock for each year.

PE 13-2A
Entries for issuing stock
obj. 3
EE 13-2 p. 584

On July 3, Hanoi Artifacts Corporation issued for cash 450,000 shares of no-par common stock at $2.50. On September 1, Hanoi Artifacts issued 10,000 shares of 2%, $25 preferred stock at par for cash. On October 30, Hanoi Artifacts issued for cash 7,500 shares of 2%, $25 par preferred stock at $30.

Journalize the entries to record the July 3, September 1, and October 30 transactions.

PE 13-2B
Entries for issuing stock
obj. 3
EE 13-2 p. 584

On February 13, Elman Corporation issued for cash 75,000 shares of no-par common stock (with a stated value of $125) at $140. On September 9, Elman issued 15,000 shares of 1%, $60 preferred stock at par for cash. On November 23, Elman issued for cash 8,000 shares of 1%, $60 par preferred stock at $70.

Journalize the entries to record the February 13, September 9, and November 23 transactions.

PE 13-3A
Entries for cash dividends
obj. 4
EE 13-3 p. 586

The important dates in connection with a cash dividend of $112,750 on a corporation's common stock are October 6, November 5, and December 5. Journalize the entries required on each date.

PE 13-3B
Entries for cash dividends
obj. 4
EE 13-3 p. 586

The important dates in connection with a cash dividend of $61,500 on a corporation's common stock are July 1, August 1, and September 30. Journalize the entries required on each date.

PE 13-4A
Entries for stock dividends
obj. 4
EE 13-4 p. 587

Self Storage Corporation has 100,000 shares of $40 par common stock outstanding. On May 10, Self Storage Corporation declared a 2% stock dividend to be issued August 1 to stockholders of record on June 9. The market price of the stock was $48 per share on May 10.

Journalize the entries required on May 10, June 9, and August 1.

PE 13-4B
Entries for stock dividends
obj. 4
EE 13-4 p. 587

Spectrum Corporation has 600,000 shares of $75 par common stock outstanding. On February 13, Spectrum Corporation declared a 4% stock dividend to be issued April 30 to stockholders of record on March 14. The market price of the stock was $90 per share on February 13.

Journalize the entries required on February 13, March 14, and April 30.

PE 13-5A
Entries for treasury stock
obj. 5
EE 13-5 p. 588

On October 3, Valley Clothing Inc. reacquired 10,000 shares of its common stock at $9 per share. On November 15, Valley Clothing sold 6,800 of the reacquired shares at $12 per share. On December 22, Valley Clothing sold the remaining shares at $7 per share.

Journalize the transactions of October 3, November 15, and December 22.

PE 13-5B
Entries for treasury stock
obj. 5
EE 13-5 p. 588

On February 1, Motorsports Inc. reacquired 7,500 shares of its common stock at $30 per share. On March 15, Motorsports sold 4,500 of the reacquired shares at $34 per share. On June 2, Motorsports sold the remaining shares at $28 per share.

Journalize the transactions of February 1, March 15, and June 2.

PE 13-6A
Reporting stockholders' equity
obj. 6
EE 13-6 p. 590

Using the following accounts and balances, prepare the Stockholders' Equity section of the balance sheet. Seventy thousand shares of common stock are authorized, and 7,500 shares have been reacquired.

Common Stock, $75 par	$4,725,000
Paid-In Capital in Excess of Par	679,000
Paid-In Capital from Sale of Treasury Stock	25,200
Retained Earnings	2,032,800
Treasury Stock	588,000

PE 13-6B
Reporting stockholders' equity
obj. 6
EE 13-6 p. 590

Using the following accounts and balances, prepare the Stockholders' Equity section of the balance sheet. Sixty thousand shares of common stock are authorized, and 4,000 shares have been reacquired.

Common Stock, $80 par	$4,000,000
Paid-In Capital in Excess of Par	630,000
Paid-In Capital from Sale of Treasury Stock	66,000
Retained Earnings	2,220,000
Treasury Stock	360,000

PE 13-7A
Retained earnings statement
obj. 6
EE 13-7 p. 592

Hornblower Cruises Inc. reported the following results for the year ending October 31, 2010:

Retained earnings, November 1, 2009	$1,500,000
Net income	475,000
Cash dividends declared	50,000
Stock dividends declared	300,000

Prepare a retained earnings statement for the fiscal year ended October 31, 2010.

PE 13-7B
Retained earnings statement
obj. 6
EE 13-7 p. 592

Frontier Leaders Inc. reported the following results for the year ending July 31, 2010:

Retained earnings, August 1, 2009	$875,000
Net income	260,000
Cash dividends declared	20,000
Stock dividends declared	100,000

Prepare a retained earnings statement for the fiscal year ended July 31, 2010.

Exercises

EX 13-1
Dividends per share
obj. 3
✔ Preferred stock, 1st year: $2.00

Fairmount Inc., a developer of radiology equipment, has stock outstanding as follows: 15,000 shares of cumulative 2%, preferred stock of $150 par, and 50,000 shares of $5 par common. During its first four years of operations, the following amounts were distributed as dividends: first year, $30,000; second year, $42,000; third year, $90,000; fourth year, $120,000. Calculate the dividends per share on each class of stock for each of the four years.

EX 13-2
Dividends per share
obj. 3
✔ Preferred stock, 1st year: $0.15

Michelangelo Inc., a software development firm, has stock outstanding as follows: 20,000 shares of cumulative 1%, preferred stock of $25 par, and 25,000 shares of $100 par common. During its first four years of operations, the following amounts were distributed as dividends: first year, $3,000; second year, $4,000; third year, $30,000; fourth year, $80,000. Calculate the dividends per share on each class of stock for each of the four years.

EX 13-3
Entries for issuing par stock
obj. 3

On February 10, Peerless Rocks Inc., a marble contractor, issued for cash 40,000 shares of $10 par common stock at $34, and on May 9, it issued for cash 100,000 shares of $5 par preferred stock at $7.

a. Journalize the entries for February 10 and May 9.
b. What is the total amount invested (total paid-in capital) by all stockholders as of May 9?

EX 13-4
Entries for issuing no-par stock
obj. 3

On June 4, Magic Carpet Inc., a carpet wholesaler, issued for cash 250,000 shares of no-par common stock (with a stated value of $3) at $12, and on October 9, it issued for cash 25,000 shares of $75 par preferred stock at $80.

a. Journalize the entries for June 4 and October 9, assuming that the common stock is to be credited with the stated value.
b. What is the total amount invested (total paid-in capital) by all stockholders as of October 9?

EX 13-5
Issuing stock for assets other than cash
obj. 3

On January 30, Lift Time Corporation, a wholesaler of hydraulic lifts, acquired land in exchange for 18,000 shares of $10 par common stock with a current market price of $15. Journalize the entry to record the transaction.

EX 13-6
Selected stock transactions
obj. 3

Rocky Mountain Sounds Corp., an electric guitar retailer, was organized by Cathy Dewitt, Melody Leimbach, and Mario Torres. The charter authorized 250,000 shares of common stock with a par of $40. The following transactions affecting stockholders' equity were completed during the first year of operations:

a. Issued 10,000 shares of stock at par to Cathy Dewitt for cash.
b. Issued 750 shares of stock at par to Mario Torres for promotional services provided in connection with the organization of the corporation, and issued 20,000 shares of stock at par to Mario Torres for cash.
c. Purchased land and a building from Melody Leimbach. The building is mortgaged for $400,000 for 20 years at 7%, and there is accrued interest of $7,000 on the mortgage note at the time of the purchase. It is agreed that the land is to be priced at $125,000 and the building at $600,000, and that Melody Leimbach's equity will be exchanged for stock at par. The corporation agreed to assume responsibility for paying the mortgage note and the accrued interest.

Journalize the entries to record the transactions.

EX 13-7
Issuing stock
obj. 3

Cashman Nursery, with an authorization of 25,000 shares of preferred stock and 300,000 shares of common stock, completed several transactions involving its stock on July 30, the first day of operations. The trial balance at the close of the day follows:

Cash	475,000	
Land	125,000	
Buildings	200,000	
Preferred 2% Stock, $100 par		250,000
Paid-In Capital in Excess of Par—Preferred Stock		75,000
Common Stock, $40 par		300,000
Paid-In Capital in Excess of Par—Common Stock		175,000
	800,000	800,000

All shares within each class of stock were sold at the same price. The preferred stock was issued in exchange for the land and buildings.

Journalize the two entries to record the transactions summarized in the trial balance.

EX 13-8
Issuing stock
obj. 3

Newgen Products Inc., a wholesaler of office products, was organized on February 20 of the current year, with an authorization of 75,000 shares of 2% preferred stock, $50 par and 400,000 shares of $15 par common stock. The following selected transactions were completed during the first year of operations:

Feb. 20. Issued 150,000 shares of common stock at par for cash.
26. Issued 500 shares of common stock at par to an attorney in payment of legal fees for organizing the corporation.
Mar. 6. Issued 18,000 shares of common stock in exchange for land, buildings, and equipment with fair market prices of $50,000, $275,000, and $60,000, respectively.
Apr. 30. Issued 20,000 shares of preferred stock at $60 for cash.

Journalize the transactions.

EX 13-9
Entries for cash dividends
obj. 4

The important dates in connection with a cash dividend of $69,500 on a corporation's common stock are May 3, June 17, and August 1. Journalize the entries required on each date.

EX 13-10
Entries for stock dividends
obj. 4
✔ b. (1) $12,000,000
(3) $57,000,000

Organic Health Co. is an HMO for businesses in the Chicago area. The following account balances appear on the balance sheet of Organic Health Co.: Common stock (300,000 shares authorized), $100 par, $10,000,000; Paid-in capital in excess of par—common stock, $2,000,000; and Retained earnings, $45,000,000. The board of directors declared a 2% stock dividend when the market price of the stock was $125 a share. Organic Health Co. reported no income or loss for the current year.

a. Journalize the entries to record (1) the declaration of the dividend, capitalizing an amount equal to market value, and (2) the issuance of the stock certificates.
b. Determine the following amounts before the stock dividend was declared: (1) total paid-in capital, (2) total retained earnings, and (3) total stockholders' equity.
c. Determine the following amounts after the stock dividend was declared and closing entries were recorded at the end of the year: (1) total paid-in capital, (2) total retained earnings, and (3) total stockholders' equity.

EX 13-11
Treasury stock transactions
obj. 5
✔ b. $32,000 credit

Beaverhead Creek Inc. bottles and distributes spring water. On March 4 of the current year, Beaverhead Creek reacquired 5,000 shares of its common stock at $90 per share. On August 7, Beaverhead Creek sold 3,500 of the reacquired shares at $100 per share. The remaining 1,500 shares were sold at $88 per share on November 29.

a. Journalize the transactions of March 4, August 7, and November 29.
b. What is the balance in Paid-In Capital from Sale of Treasury Stock on December 31 of the current year?
c. For what reasons might Beaverhead Creek have purchased the treasury stock?

EX 13-12
Treasury stock transactions
objs. 5, 6
✔ b. $54,000 credit

Augusta Gardens Inc. develops and produces spraying equipment for lawn maintenance and industrial uses. On August 30 of the current year, Augusta Gardens Inc. reacquired 17,500 shares of its common stock at $42 per share. On October 31, 14,000 of the reacquired shares were sold at $45 per share, and on November 10, 2,000 of the reacquired shares were sold at $48.

a. Journalize the transactions of August 30, October 31, and November 10.
b. What is the balance in Paid-In Capital from Sale of Treasury Stock on December 31 of the current year?
c. What is the balance in Treasury Stock on December 31 of the current year?
d. How will the balance in Treasury Stock be reported on the balance sheet?

EX 13-13
Treasury stock transactions
objs. 5, 6
✔ b. $37,000 credit

Sweet Water Inc. bottles and distributes spring water. On July 15 of the current year, Sweet Water Inc. reacquired 24,000 shares of its common stock at $60 per share. On August 10, Sweet Water Inc. sold 19,000 of the reacquired shares at $63 per share. The remaining 5,000 shares were sold at $56 per share on December 18.

a. Journalize the transactions of July 15, August 10, and December 18.
b. What is the balance in Paid-In Capital from Sale of Treasury Stock on December 31 of the current year?
c. Where will the balance in Paid-In Capital from Sale of Treasury Stock be reported on the balance sheet?
d. For what reasons might Sweet Water Inc. have purchased the treasury stock?

EX 13-14
Reporting paid-in capital
obj. 6
✔ Total paid-in capital, $2,225,000

The following accounts and their balances were selected from the unadjusted trial balance of REO Inc., a freight forwarder, at October 31, the end of the current fiscal year:

Preferred 2% Stock, $100 par	$ 750,000
Paid-In Capital in Excess of Par—Preferred Stock	90,000
Common Stock, no par, $5 stated value	400,000
Paid-In Capital in Excess of Stated Value—Common Stock	960,000
Paid-In Capital from Sale of Treasury Stock	25,000
Retained Earnings	3,150,000

Prepare the Paid-In Capital portion of the Stockholders' Equity section of the balance sheet. There are 250,000 shares of common stock authorized and 20,000 shares of preferred stock authorized.

EX 13-15
Stockholders' Equity section of balance sheet
obj. 6
✔ Total stockholders' equity, $4,350,000

The following accounts and their balances appear in the ledger of Newberry Properties Inc. on June 30 of the current year:

Common Stock, $75 par	$1,350,000
Paid-In Capital in Excess of Par	108,000
Paid-In Capital from Sale of Treasury Stock	12,000
Retained Earnings	2,950,000
Treasury Stock	70,000

Prepare the Stockholders' Equity section of the balance sheet as of June 30. Forty thousand shares of common stock are authorized, and 875 shares have been reacquired.

EX 13-16
Stockholders' Equity section of balance sheet
obj. 6
✔ Total stockholders' equity, $5,985,000

Race Car Inc. retails racing products for BMWs, Porsches, and Ferraris. The following accounts and their balances appear in the ledger of Race Car Inc. on April 30, the end of the current year:

Common Stock, $10 par	$ 400,000
Paid-In Capital in Excess of Par—Common Stock	120,000
Paid-In Capital in Excess of Par—Preferred Stock	90,000
Paid-In Capital from Sale of Treasury Stock—Common	30,000
Preferred 4% Stock, $50 par	1,500,000
Retained Earnings	3,900,000
Treasury Stock—Common	55,000

Fifty thousand shares of preferred and 200,000 shares of common stock are authorized. There are 5,000 shares of common stock held as treasury stock.

Prepare the Stockholders' Equity section of the balance sheet as of April 30, the end of the current year.

EX 13-17
Retained earnings statement
obj. 6

✔ Retained earnings, January 31, $3,375,000

Bancroft Corporation, a manufacturer of industrial pumps, reports the following results for the year ending January 31, 2010:

Retained earnings, February 1, 2009	$3,175,500
Net income	415,000
Cash dividends declared	75,500
Stock dividends declared	140,000

Prepare a retained earnings statement for the fiscal year ended January 31, 2010.

EX 13-18
Stockholders' Equity section of balance sheet
obj. 6

✔ Corrected total stockholders' equity, $16,758,000

List the errors in the following Stockholders' Equity section of the balance sheet prepared as of the end of the current year.

Stockholders' Equity

Paid-in capital:		
Preferred 2% stock, $150 par		
(10,000 shares authorized and issued)	$1,500,000	
Excess of issue price over par	250,000	$ 1,750,000
Retained earnings		1,450,000
Treasury stock (6,000 shares at cost)		432,000
Dividends payable		135,000
Total paid-in capital		$ 3,767,000
Common stock, $75 par (250,000 shares authorized, 180,000 shares issued)		14,040,000
Organizing costs		50,000
Total stockholders' equity		$17,857,000

EX 13-19
Statement of stockholders' equity
obj. 6

✔ Total stockholders' equity, Dec. 31, $7,182,000

The stockholders' equity T accounts of For All Occasions Greeting Cards Inc. for the current fiscal year ended December 31, 2010, are as follows. Prepare a statement of stockholders' equity for the fiscal year ended December 31, 2010.

COMMON STOCK

			Jan. 1	Balance	2,000,000
			Feb. 20	Issued 18,000 shares	900,000
			Dec. 31	Balance	2,900,000

PAID-IN CAPITAL IN EXCESS OF PAR

			Jan. 1	Balance	320,000
			Feb. 20	Issued 18,000 shares	216,000
			Dec. 31	Balance	536,000

TREASURY STOCK

July 19	Purchased 3,000 shares	144,000			

RETAINED EARNINGS

June 30	Dividend	50,000	Jan. 1	Balance	3,480,000
Dec. 30	Dividend	50,000	Dec. 31	Closing (net income)	510,000
			Dec. 31	Balance	3,890,000

EX 13-20
Effect of stock split
obj. 7

Mia Restaurant Corporation wholesales ovens and ranges to restaurants throughout the Southwest. Mia Restaurant Corporation, which had 40,000 shares of common stock outstanding, declared a 4-for-1 stock split (3 additional shares for each share issued).

a. What will be the number of shares outstanding after the split?
b. If the common stock had a market price of $300 per share before the stock split, what would be an approximate market price per share after the split?

EX 13-21
Effect of cash dividend and stock split
objs. 4, 7

Indicate whether the following actions would (+) increase, (−) decrease, or (0) not affect Indigo Inc.'s total assets, liabilities, and stockholders' equity:

	Assets	Liabilities	Stockholders' Equity
(1) Declaring a cash dividend	______	______	______
(2) Paying the cash dividend declared in (1)	______	______	______
(3) Authorizing and issuing stock certificates in a stock split	______	______	______
(4) Declaring a stock dividend	______	______	______
(5) Issuing stock certificates for the stock dividend declared in (4)	______	______	______

EX 13-22
Selected dividend transactions, stock split
objs. 4, 7

Selected transactions completed by Hartwell Boating Supply Corporation during the current fiscal year are as follows:

Feb. 3. Split the common stock 2 for 1 and reduced the par from $40 to $20 per share. After the split, there were 250,000 common shares outstanding.
Apr. 10. Declared semiannual dividends of $1.50 on 18,000 shares of preferred stock and $0.08 on the common stock to stockholders of record on May 10, payable on June 9.
June 9. Paid the cash dividends.
Oct. 10. Declared semiannual dividends of $1.50 on the preferred stock and $0.04 on the common stock (before the stock dividend). In addition, a 2% common stock dividend was declared on the common stock outstanding. The fair market value of the common stock is estimated at $36.
Dec. 9. Paid the cash dividends and issued the certificates for the common stock dividend.

Journalize the transactions.

EX 13-23
EPS

Crystal Arts, Inc., had earnings of $160,000 for 2010. The company had 20,000 shares of common stock outstanding during the year. In addition, the company issued 2,000 shares of $100 par value preferred stock on January 3, 2010. The preferred stock has a dividend of $7 per share. There were no transactions in either common or preferred stock during 2010.

Determine the basic earnings per share for Crystal Arts.

EX 13-24
EPS

Procter & Gamble (P&G) is one of the largest consumer products companies in the world, famous for such brands as Crest® and Tide®. Financial information for the company for three recent years is as follows:

	Fiscal Years Ended (in millions)		
	2007	2006	2005
Net income	$10,340	$8,684	$6,923
Preferred dividends	$161	$148	$136
Common shares outstanding	3,159	3,055	2,515

a. Determine the earnings per share for fiscal years 2007, 2006, and 2005.
b. Evaluate the growth in earnings per share for the three years in comparison to the growth in net income for the three years.

EX 13-25
EPS

Staples and OfficeMax are two companies competing in the retail office supply business. OfficeMax had a net income of $91,721,000 for a recent year, while Staples had a net income of $973,577,000. OfficeMax had preferred stock of $54,735,000 with a preferred dividend of 7.375% on that amount. Staples had no preferred stock. The outstanding common shares for each company were as follows:

	Common Shares
OfficeMax	73,142,000
Staples	720,528,000

a. Determine the earnings per share for each company.
b. Evaluate the relative profitability of the two companies.

Problem Series A

PR 13-1A
Dividends on preferred and common stock
obj. 3

✔ 1. Common dividends in 2007: $8,000

Bridger Bike Corp. manufactures mountain bikes and distributes them through retail outlets in Montana, Idaho, Oregon, and Washington. Bridger Bike Corp. has declared the following annual dividends over a six-year period ending December 31 of each year: 2005, $5,000; 2006, $18,000; 2007, $45,000; 2008, $45,000; 2009, $60,000; and 2010, $67,000. During the entire period, the outstanding stock of the company was composed of 10,000 shares of 2% cumulative preferred stock, $100 par, and 25,000 shares of common stock, $1 par.

Instructions

1. Determine the total dividends and the per-share dividends declared on each class of stock for each of the six years. There were no dividends in arrears on January 1, 2005. Summarize the data in tabular form, using the following column headings:

		Preferred Dividends		Common Dividends	
Year	**Total Dividends**	**Total**	**Per Share**	**Total**	**Per Share**
2005	$ 5,000				
2006	18,000				
2007	45,000				
2008	45,000				
2009	60,000				
2010	67,000				

2. Determine the average annual dividend per share for each class of stock for the six-year period.
3. Assuming a market price of $125 for the preferred stock and $8 for the common stock, calculate the average annual percentage return on initial shareholders' investment, based on the average annual dividend per share (a) for preferred stock and (b) for common stock.

PR 13-2A
Stock transaction for corporate expansion
obj. 3

Sheldon Optics produces medical lasers for use in hospitals. The accounts and their balances appear in the ledger of Sheldon Optics on October 31 of the current year as follows:

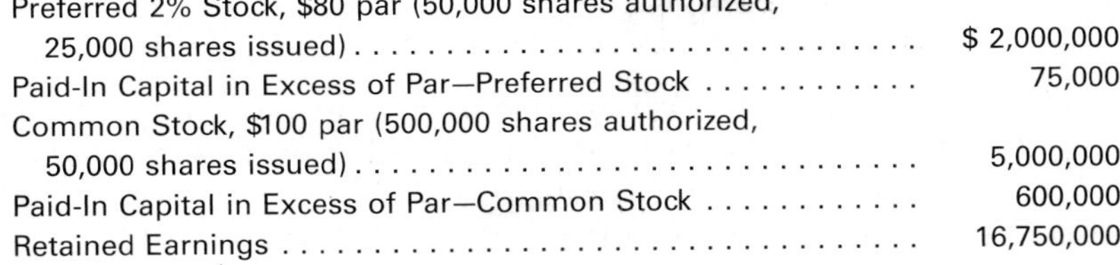

Preferred 2% Stock, $80 par (50,000 shares authorized, 25,000 shares issued)	$ 2,000,000
Paid-In Capital in Excess of Par—Preferred Stock	75,000
Common Stock, $100 par (500,000 shares authorized, 50,000 shares issued)	5,000,000
Paid-In Capital in Excess of Par—Common Stock	600,000
Retained Earnings	16,750,000

At the annual stockholders' meeting on December 7, the board of directors presented a plan for modernizing and expanding plant operations at a cost of approximately $5,300,000. The plan provided (a) that the corporation borrow $2,000,000, (b) that 15,000 shares of the unissued preferred stock be issued through an underwriter, and (c) that a building, valued at $1,850,000, and the land on which it is located, valued at $162,500, be acquired in accordance with preliminary negotiations by the issuance of 17,500 shares of common stock. The plan was approved by the stockholders and accomplished by the following transactions:

Jan. 10. Borrowed $2,000,000 from Whitefish National Bank, giving a 7% mortgage note.
21. Issued 15,000 shares of preferred stock, receiving $84.50 per share in cash.
31. Issued 17,500 shares of common stock in exchange for land and a building, according to the plan.

No other transactions occurred during January.

Instructions

Journalize the entries to record the foregoing transactions.

PR 13-3A
Selected stock transactions
objs. 3, 4, 5

✔ f. Cash dividends, $387,050

Coil Welding Corporation sells and services pipe welding equipment in California. The following selected accounts appear in the ledger of Coil Welding Corporation on February 1, 2010, the beginning of the current fiscal year:

Preferred 2% Stock, $25 par (50,000 shares authorized, 40,000 shares issued)	$ 1,000,000
Paid-In Capital in Excess of Par—Preferred Stock	240,000
Common Stock, $5 par (1,000,000 shares authorized, 750,000 shares issued)	3,750,000
Paid-In Capital in Excess of Par—Common Stock	6,000,000
Retained Earnings	36,785,000

During the year, the corporation completed a number of transactions affecting the stockholders' equity. They are summarized as follows:

a. Purchased 60,000 shares of treasury common for $540,000.
b. Sold 42,000 shares of treasury common for $462,000.
c. Issued 7,500 shares of preferred 2% stock at $38.
d. Issued 120,000 shares of common stock at $15, receiving cash.
e. Sold 13,000 shares of treasury common for $110,500.
f. Declared cash dividends of $0.50 per share on preferred stock and $0.42 per share on common stock.
g. Paid the cash dividends.

Instructions

Journalize the entries to record the transactions. Identify each entry by letter.

PR 13-4A
Entries for selected corporate transactions
objs. 3, 4, 5, 6

✔ 4. Total stockholders' equity, $11,407,975

Krisch Enterprises Inc. produces aeronautical navigation equipment. The stockholders' equity accounts of Krisch Enterprises Inc., with balances on January 1, 2010, are as follows:

Common Stock, $20 stated value (250,000 shares authorized, 175,000 shares issued)	$3,500,000
Paid-In Capital in Excess of Stated Value	1,750,000
Retained Earnings	4,600,000
Treasury Stock (40,000 shares, at cost)	1,000,000

The following selected transactions occurred during the year:

Jan. 6. Paid cash dividends of $0.40 per share on the common stock. The dividend had been properly recorded when declared on November 29 of the preceding fiscal year for $54,000.
Mar. 9. Sold all of the treasury stock for $1,350,000.

Apr. 3. Issued 50,000 shares of common stock for $1,700,000.
July 30. Declared a 2% stock dividend on common stock, to be capitalized at the market price of the stock, which is $36 per share.
Aug. 30. Issued the certificates for the dividend declared on July 30.
Nov. 7. Purchased 25,000 shares of treasury stock for $800,000.
Dec. 30. Declared a $0.45-per-share dividend on common stock.
31. Closed the credit balance of the income summary account, $400,000.
31. Closed the two dividends accounts to Retained Earnings.

Instructions

1. Enter the January 1 balances in T accounts for the stockholders' equity accounts listed. Also prepare T accounts for the following: Paid-In Capital from Sale of Treasury Stock; Stock Dividends Distributable; Stock Dividends; Cash Dividends.
2. Journalize the entries to record the transactions, and post to the eight selected accounts.
3. Prepare a retained earnings statement for the year ended December 31, 2010.
4. Prepare the Stockholders' Equity section of the December 31, 2010, balance sheet.

PR 13-5A
Entries for selected corporate transactions
objs. 3, 4, 5, 7

✔ Sept. 1, Cash dividends, $165,750

Porto Bay Corporation manufactures and distributes leisure clothing. Selected transactions completed by Porto Bay during the current fiscal year are as follows:

Jan. 10. Split the common stock 4 for 1 and reduced the par from $100 to $25 per share. After the split, there were 500,000 common shares outstanding.
Mar. 1. Declared semiannual dividends of $1.20 on 80,000 shares of preferred stock and $0.24 on the 500,000 shares of $25 par common stock to stockholders of record on March 31, payable on April 30.
Apr. 30. Paid the cash dividends.
July 9. Purchased 75,000 shares of the corporation's own common stock at $26, recording the stock at cost.
Aug. 29. Sold 40,000 shares of treasury stock at $32, receiving cash.
Sept. 1. Declared semiannual dividends of $1.20 on the preferred stock and $0.15 on the common stock (before the stock dividend). In addition, a 1% common stock dividend was declared on the common stock outstanding, to be capitalized at the fair market value of the common stock, which is estimated at $30.
Oct. 31. Paid the cash dividends and issued the certificates for the common stock dividend.

Instructions

Journalize the transactions.

Problem Series B

PR 13-1B
Dividends on preferred and common stock
obj. 3

✔ 1. Common dividends in 2007: $16,500

Lone Star Theatre Inc. owns and operates movie theaters throughout Arizona and Texas. Lone Star Theatre has declared the following annual dividends over a six-year period: 2005, $7,500; 2006, $9,000; 2007, $30,000; 2008, $30,000; 2009, $40,000; and 2010, $48,500. During the entire period ending December 31 of each year, the outstanding stock of the company was composed of 10,000 shares of cumulative, 2% preferred stock, $50 par, and 50,000 shares of common stock, $1 par.

Instructions

1. Calculate the total dividends and the per-share dividends declared on each class of stock for each of the six years. There were no dividends in arrears on January 1, 2005. Summarize the data in tabular form, using the following column headings:

Year	Total Dividends	Preferred Dividends		Common Dividends	
		Total	Per Share	Total	Per Share
2005	$ 7,500				
2006	9,000				
2007	30,000				
2008	30,000				
2009	40,000				
2010	48,500				

2. Calculate the average annual dividend per share for each class of stock for the six-year period.
3. Assuming a market price per share of $40 for the preferred stock and $5 for the common stock, calculate the average annual percentage return on initial shareholders' investment, based on the average annual dividend per share (a) for preferred stock and (b) for common stock.

PR 13-2B
Stock transactions for corporate expansion

obj. 3

On February 28 of the current year, the following accounts and their balances appear in the ledger of Wild Things Corp., a meat processor:

Preferred 2% Stock, $25 par (75,000 shares authorized, 30,000 shares issued)	$ 750,000
Paid-In Capital in Excess of Par—Preferred Stock	120,000
Common Stock, $30 par (400,000 shares authorized, 250,000 shares issued)	7,500,000
Paid-In Capital in Excess of Par—Common Stock	500,000
Retained Earnings	12,180,000

At the annual stockholders' meeting on April 2, the board of directors presented a plan for modernizing and expanding plant operations at a cost of approximately $3,650,000. The plan provided (a) that a building, valued at $1,680,000, and the land on which it is located, valued at $420,000, be acquired in accordance with preliminary negotiations by the issuance of 65,000 shares of common stock, (b) that 21,000 shares of the unissued preferred stock be issued through an underwriter, and (c) that the corporation borrow $700,000. The plan was approved by the stockholders and accomplished by the following transactions:

June 9. Issued 65,000 shares of common stock in exchange for land and a building, according to the plan.
13. Issued 21,000 shares of preferred stock, receiving $40 per share in cash.
25. Borrowed $700,000 from Wasburn City Bank, giving an 8% mortgage note.

No other transactions occurred during June.

Instructions

Journalize the entries to record the foregoing transactions.

PR 13-3B
Selected stock transactions

objs. 3, 4, 5

f. Cash dividends, $73,200

The following selected accounts appear in the ledger of Okie Environmental Corporation on August 1, 2010, the beginning of the current fiscal year:

Preferred 2% Stock, $50 par (40,000 shares authorized, 20,000 shares issued)	$1,000,000
Paid-In Capital in Excess of Par—Preferred Stock	100,000
Common Stock, $75 par (100,000 shares authorized, 40,000 shares issued)	3,000,000
Paid-In Capital in Excess of Par—Common Stock	150,000
Retained Earnings	8,170,000

During the year, the corporation completed a number of transactions affecting the stockholders' equity. They are summarized as follows:

a. Issued 17,500 shares of common stock at $81, receiving cash.
b. Issued 8,000 shares of preferred 2% stock at $63.
c. Purchased 5,000 shares of treasury common for $390,000.

d. Sold 3,000 shares of treasury common for $240,000.
e. Sold 1,000 shares of treasury common for $75,000.
f. Declared cash dividends of $1 per share on preferred stock and $0.80 per share on common stock.
g. Paid the cash dividends.

Instructions
Journalize the entries to record the transactions. Identify each entry by letter.

PR 13-4B
Entries for selected corporate transactions
objs. 3, 4, 5, 6

✔ 4. Total stockholders' equity, $11,853,400

Ivy Enterprises Inc. manufactures bathroom fixtures. The stockholders' equity accounts of Ivy Enterprises Inc., with balances on January 1, 2010, are as follows:

Common Stock, $8 stated value (600,000 shares authorized, 400,000 shares issued)	$3,200,000
Paid-In Capital in Excess of Stated Value	600,000
Retained Earnings	7,100,000
Treasury Stock (30,000 shares, at cost)	240,000

The following selected transactions occurred during the year:

Jan. 7. Paid cash dividends of $0.18 per share on the common stock. The dividend had been properly recorded when declared on November 30 of the preceding fiscal year for $66,600.
Feb. 9. Issued 50,000 shares of common stock for $600,000.
May 21. Sold all of the treasury stock for $300,000.
July 1. Declared a 4% stock dividend on common stock, to be capitalized at the market price of the stock, which is $13 per share.
Aug. 15. Issued the certificates for the dividend declared on July 1.
Sept. 30. Purchased 10,000 shares of treasury stock for $100,000.
Dec. 27. Declared a $0.20-per-share dividend on common stock.
31. Closed the credit balance of the income summary account, $485,000.
31. Closed the two dividends accounts to Retained Earnings.

Instructions
1. Enter the January 1 balances in T accounts for the stockholders' equity accounts listed. Also prepare T accounts for the following: Paid-In Capital from Sale of Treasury Stock; Stock Dividends Distributable; Stock Dividends; Cash Dividends.
2. Journalize the entries to record the transactions, and post to the eight selected accounts.
3. Prepare a retained earnings statement for the year ended December 31, 2010.
4. Prepare the Stockholders' Equity section of the December 31, 2010, balance sheet.

PR 13-5B
Entries for selected corporate transactions
objs. 3, 4, 5, 7

✔ Nov. 15, cash dividends, $138,400

Selected transactions completed by Kearny Boating Corporation during the current fiscal year are as follows:

Jan. 8. Split the common stock 3 for 1 and reduced the par from $75 to $25 per share. After the split, there were 600,000 common shares outstanding.
Feb. 13. Purchased 30,000 shares of the corporation's own common stock at $27, recording the stock at cost.
May 1. Declared semiannual dividends of $0.80 on 25,000 shares of preferred stock and $0.18 on the common stock to stockholders of record on May 15, payable on June 1.
June 1. Paid the cash dividends.
Aug. 5. Sold 22,000 shares of treasury stock at $34, receiving cash.
Nov. 15. Declared semiannual dividends of $0.80 on the preferred stock and $0.20 on the common stock (before the stock dividend). In addition, a 2% common stock dividend was declared on the common stock outstanding. The fair market value of the common stock is estimated at $40.
Dec. 31. Paid the cash dividends and issued the certificates for the common stock dividend.

Instructions
Journalize the transactions.

Special Activities

SA 13-1
Board of directors' actions

Bernie Ebbers, the CEO of WorldCom, a major telecommunications company, was having personal financial troubles. Ebbers pledged a large stake of his WorldCom stock as security for some personal loans. As the price of WorldCom stock sank, Ebbers' bankers threatened to sell his stock in order to protect their loans. To avoid having his stock sold, Ebbers asked the board of directors of WorldCom to loan him nearly $400 million of corporate assets at 2.5% interest to pay off his bankers. The board agreed to lend him the money.

Comment on the decision of the board of directors in this situation.

SA 13-2
Ethics and professional conduct in business

Jas Bosley and Nadine Jaffe are organizing Precious Metals Unlimited Inc. to undertake a high-risk gold-mining venture in Canada. Jas and Nadine tentatively plan to request authorization for 90,000,000 shares of common stock to be sold to the general public. Jas and Nadine have decided to establish par of $0.10 per share in order to appeal to a wide variety of potential investors. Jas and Nadine feel that investors would be more willing to invest in the company if they received a large quantity of shares for what might appear to be a "bargain" price.

Discuss whether Jas and Nadine are behaving in a professional manner.

SA 13-3
Issuing stock

Biosciences Unlimited Inc. began operations on January 2, 2010, with the issuance of 100,000 shares of $50 par common stock. The sole stockholders of Biosciences Unlimited Inc. are Rafel Baltis and Dr. Oscar Hansel, who organized Biosciences Unlimited Inc. with the objective of developing a new flu vaccine. Dr. Hansel claims that the flu vaccine, which is nearing the final development stage, will protect individuals against 90% of the flu types that have been medically identified. To complete the project, Biosciences Unlimited Inc. needs $10,000,000 of additional funds. The local banks have been unwilling to loan the funds because of the lack of sufficient collateral and the riskiness of the business.

The following is a conversation between Rafel Baltis, the chief executive officer of Biosciences Unlimited Inc., and Dr. Oscar Hansel, the leading researcher.

Rafel: What are we going to do? The banks won't loan us any more money, and we've got to have $10 million to complete the project. We are so close! It would be a disaster to quit now. The only thing I can think of is to issue additional stock. Do you have any suggestions?

Oscar: I guess you're right. But if the banks won't loan us any more money, how do you think we can find any investors to buy stock?

Rafel: I've been thinking about that. What if we promise the investors that we will pay them 2% of net sales until they have received an amount equal to what they paid for the stock?

Oscar: What happens when we pay back the $10 million? Do the investors get to keep the stock? If they do, it'll dilute our ownership.

Rafel: How about, if after we pay back the $10 million, we make them turn in their stock for $100 per share? That's twice what they paid for it, plus they would have already gotten all their money back. That's a $100 profit per share for the investors.

Oscar: It could work. We get our money, but don't have to pay any interest, dividends, or the $50 until we start generating net sales. At the same time, the investors could get their money back plus $50 per share.

Rafel: We'll need current financial statements for the new investors. I'll get our accountant working on them and contact our attorney to draw up a legally binding contract for the new investors. Yes, this could work.

In late 2010, the attorney and the various regulatory authorities approved the new stock offering, and 200,000 shares of common stock were privately sold to new investors at the stock's par of $50.

In preparing financial statements for 2010, Rafel Baltis and Emma Cavins, the controller for Biosciences Unlimited Inc., have the following conversation:

Emma: Rafel, I've got a problem.

Rafel: What's that, Emma?

Emma: Issuing common stock to raise that additional $10 million was a great idea. But . . .

Rafel: But what?

Emma: I've got to prepare the 2010 annual financial statements, and I am not sure how to classify the common stock.

Rafel: What do you mean? It's common stock.

Emma: I'm not so sure. I called the auditor and explained how we are contractually obligated to pay the new stockholders 2% of net sales until $50 per share is paid. Then, we may be obligated to pay them $100 per share.

Rafel: So . . .

Emma: So the auditor thinks that we should classify the additional issuance of $10 million as debt, not stock! And, if we put the $10 million on the balance sheet as debt, we will violate our other loan agreements with the banks. And, if these agreements are violated, the banks may call in all our debt immediately. If they do that, we are in deep trouble. We'll probably have to file for bankruptcy. We just don't have the cash to pay off the banks.

1. Discuss the arguments for and against classifying the issuance of the $10 million of stock as debt.
2. What do you think might be a practical solution to this classification problem?

SA 13-4
Interpret stock exchange listing

The following stock exchange data for General Electric was taken from the Yahoo! Finance Web site on April 18, 2008:

Gen Electric Co (NYSE: GE)

Last Trade:	32.5815	Prev. Clos:	32.02
Trade Time:	11:03 AM ET	1y Target Est:	36.92
Change:	↑0.5615 (1.75%)	Day's Range:	32.27–32.57
		52wk Range:	31.55–42.15
		Volume:	25,922,495

a. If you owned 500 shares of GE, what amount would you receive as a quarterly dividend?
b. Compute the percentage increase in price from the Previous Close to the Last Trade. Round to two decimal places.
c. What is GE's percentage change in market price from the 52 week low to the Previous Close on April 17, 2008? Round to one decimal place.
d. If you bought 500 shares of GE at the Last Trade price on April 18, 2008, how much would it cost, and who gets the money?

SA 13-5
Dividends

Rainbow Designs Inc. has paid quarterly cash dividends since 1997. These dividends have steadily increased from $0.05 per share to the latest dividend declaration of $0.40 per share. The board of directors would like to continue this trend and is hesitant to suspend or decrease the amount of quarterly dividends. Unfortunately, sales dropped sharply in the fourth quarter of 2010 because of worsening economic conditions and increased competition. As a result, the board is uncertain as to whether it should declare a dividend for the last quarter of 2010.

On November 1, 2010, Rainbow Designs Inc. borrowed $1,200,000 from Washington National Bank to use in modernizing its retail stores and to expand its product line in reaction to its competition. The terms of the 10-year, 6% loan require Rainbow Designs Inc. to:

a. Pay monthly interest on the last day of the month.
b. Pay $120,000 of the principal each November 1, beginning in 2011.

c. Maintain a current ratio (current assets/current liabilities) of 2.
d. Maintain a minimum balance (a compensating balance) of $60,000 in its Washington National Bank account.

On December 31, 2010, $300,000 of the $1,200,000 loan had been disbursed in modernization of the retail stores and in expansion of the product line. Rainbow Designs Inc.'s balance sheet as of December 31, 2010, is shown below.

Rainbow Designs Inc.
Balance Sheet
December 31, 2010

Assets			
Current assets:			
Cash		$ 96,000	
Marketable securities		900,000	
Accounts receivable	$ 219,600		
Less allowance for doubtful accounts	15,600	204,000	
Merchandise inventory		300,000	
Prepaid expenses		10,800	
Total current assets			$1,510,800
Property, plant, and equipment:			
Land		$ 360,000	
Buildings	$2,280,000		
Less accumulated depreciation	516,000	1,764,000	
Equipment	$1,104,000		
Less accumulated depreciation	264,000	840,000	
Total property, plant, and equipment			2,964,000
Total assets			$4,474,800
Liabilities			
Current liabilities:			
Accounts payable	$ 172,320		
Notes payable (Washington National Bank)	120,000		
Salaries payable	7,680		
Total current liabilities		$ 300,000	
Long-term liabilities:			
Notes payable (Washington National Bank)		1,080,000	
Total liabilities			$1,380,000
Stockholders' Equity			
Paid-in capital:			
Common stock, $20 par (100,000 shares authorized, 60,000 shares issued)	$1,200,000		
Excess of issue price over par	96,000		
Total paid-in capital		$1,296,000	
Retained earnings		1,798,800	
Total stockholders' equity			3,094,800
Total liabilities and stockholders' equity			$4,474,800

The board of directors is scheduled to meet January 5, 2011, to discuss the results of operations for 2010 and to consider the declaration of dividends for the fourth quarter of 2010. The chairman of the board has asked for your advice on the declaration of dividends.

1. What factors should the board consider in deciding whether to declare a cash dividend?
2. The board is considering the declaration of a stock dividend instead of a cash dividend. Discuss the issuance of a stock dividend from the point of view of (a) a stockholder and (b) the board of directors.

SA 13-6
Profiling a corporation

Group Project

Internet Project

Select a public corporation you are familiar with or which interests you. Using the Internet, your school library, and other sources, develop a short (1 to 2 pages) profile of the corporation. Include in your profile the following information:

1. Name of the corporation.
2. State of incorporation.
3. Nature of its operations.
4. Total assets for the most recent balance sheet.
5. Total revenues for the most recent income statement.
6. Net income for the most recent income statement.
7. Classes of stock outstanding.
8. Market price of the stock outstanding.
9. High and low price of the stock for the past year.
10. Dividends paid for each share of stock during the past year.

In groups of three or four, discuss each corporate profile. Select one of the corporations, assuming that your group has $100,000 to invest in its stock. Summarize why your group selected the corporation it did and how financial accounting information may have affected your decision. Keep track of the performance of your corporation's stock for the remainder of the term.

Note: Most major corporations maintain "home pages" on the Internet. This home page provides a variety of information on the corporation and often includes the corporation's financial statements. In addition, the New York Stock Exchange Web site (**http://www.nyse.com**) includes links to the home pages of many listed companies. Financial statements can also be accessed using EDGAR, the electronic archives of financial statements filed with the Securities and Exchange Commission (SEC).

SEC documents can also be retrieved using the EdgarScan™ service at **http://www.sec.gov/edgar/searchedgar/webusers.htm**. To obtain annual report information, key in a company name in the appropriate space. Edgar will list the reports available to you for the company you've selected. Select the most recent annual report filing, identified as a 10-K or 10-K405.

Answers to Self-Examination Questions

1. **C** The separation of the owner from management (answer C) is a disadvantage of the corporate form of organization. This is because management may not always behave in the best interests of the owners. Limited liability (answer A), continuous life (answer B), and the ability to raise capital (answer D) are all advantages of the corporate form of organization.
2. **D** Paid-in capital is one of the two major subdivisions of the stockholders' equity of a corporation. It may result from many sources, including the issuance of preferred stock (answer A), issuing common stock (answer B), or the sale of a corporation's treasury stock (answer C).
3. **D** The Stockholders' Equity section of corporate balance sheets is divided into two principal subsections: (1) investments contributed by the stockholders and others and (2) net income retained in the business. Included as part of the investments by stockholders and others is the par of common stock (answer A), stock dividends distributable (answer B), and the par of preferred stock (answer C).
4. **C** Reacquired stock, known as *treasury stock*, should be listed in the Stockholders' Equity section (answer C) of the balance sheet. The price paid for the treasury stock is deducted from the total of all the stockholders' equity accounts.
5. **C** If a corporation that holds treasury stock declares a cash dividend, the dividends are not paid on the treasury shares. To do so would place the corporation in the position of earning income through dealing with itself. Thus, the corporation will record $44,000 (answer C) as cash dividends [(25,000 shares issued less 3,000 shares held as treasury stock) × $2 per share dividend].

CHAPTER 14

Long-Term Liabilities: Bonds and Notes

© UNDER ARMOUR®/PRNEWSFOTO (AP TOPIC GALLERY)

UNDER ARMOUR®

Most of us don't have enough money in our bank accounts to buy a house or a car by simply writing a check. Just imagine if you had to save the complete purchase price of a house before you could buy it! To help us make these types of purchases, banks will typically lend us the money, as long as we agree to repay the loan with interest in smaller future payments. Loans such as this, or long-term debt, allow us to purchase assets such as houses and cars today, which benefit us over the long term.

The use of debt can also help a business reach its objectives. Most businesses have to borrow money in order to acquire assets that they will use to generate income. For example, Under Armour®, a maker of performance athletic clothing, uses debt to acquire assets that it needs to manufacture and sell its products. Since it began in 1995, the company has used long-term debt to transform itself from a small business to a leading athletic wear company. The company now sells products in over 8,000 retail stores across the world. In addition, Under Armour® products are used by a number of teams in the National Football League, Major League Baseball, the National Hockey League, and in Olympic sports.

While debt can help companies like Under Armour® grow to achieve financial success, too much debt can be a financial burden that may even lead to bankruptcy. Just like individuals, businesses must manage debt wisely. In this chapter, we will discuss the nature of, accounting for, analysis of, and investments in long-term debt.

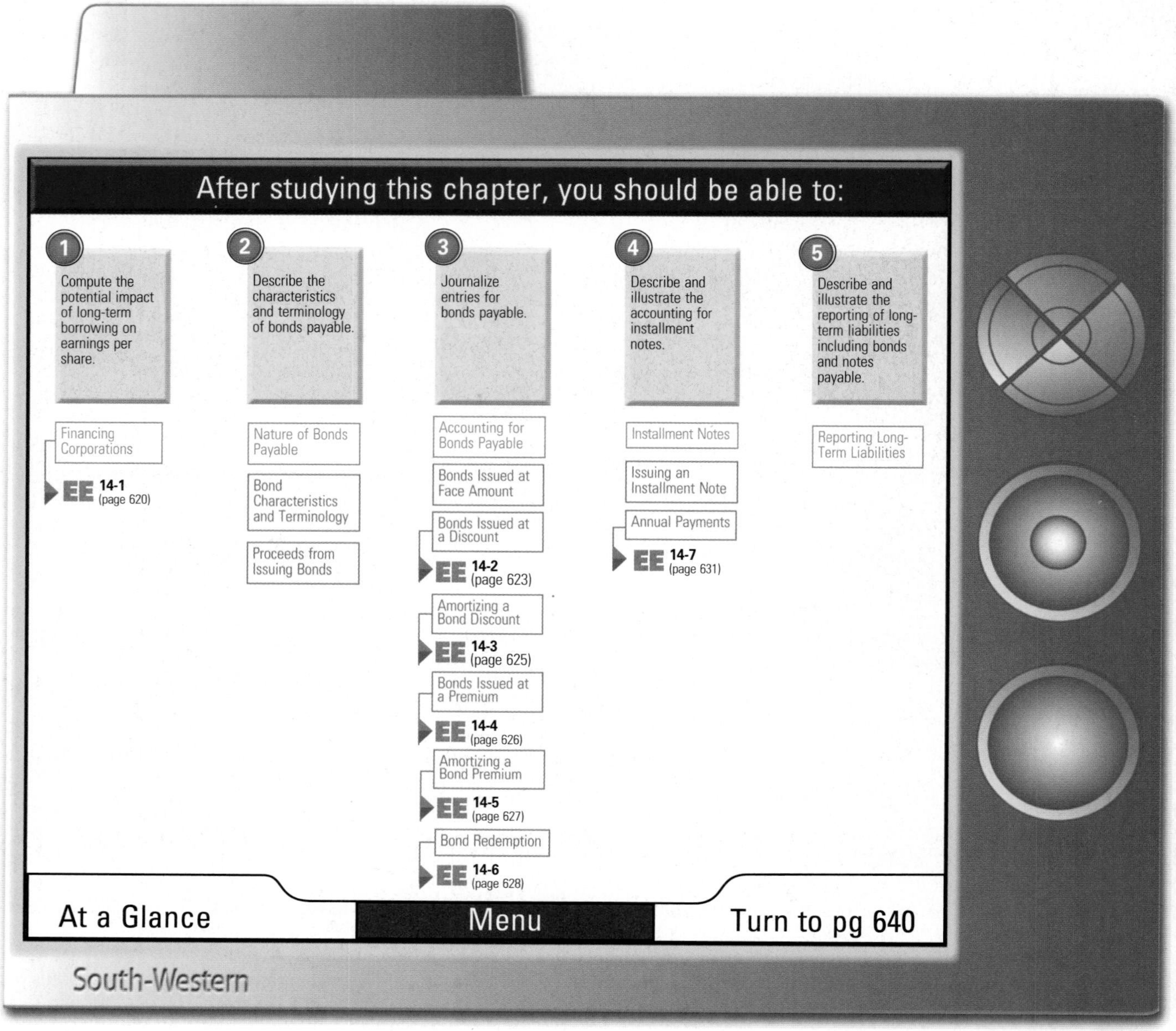

After studying this chapter, you should be able to:

1. Compute the potential impact of long-term borrowing on earnings per share.
   - Financing Corporations
   - EE 14-1 (page 620)
2. Describe the characteristics and terminology of bonds payable.
   - Nature of Bonds Payable
   - Bond Characteristics and Terminology
   - Proceeds from Issuing Bonds
3. Journalize entries for bonds payable.
   - Accounting for Bonds Payable
   - Bonds Issued at Face Amount
   - Bonds Issued at a Discount
   - EE 14-2 (page 623)
   - Amortizing a Bond Discount
   - EE 14-3 (page 625)
   - Bonds Issued at a Premium
   - EE 14-4 (page 626)
   - Amortizing a Bond Premium
   - EE 14-5 (page 627)
   - Bond Redemption
   - EE 14-6 (page 628)
4. Describe and illustrate the accounting for installment notes.
   - Installment Notes
   - Issuing an Installment Note
   - Annual Payments
   - EE 14-7 (page 631)
5. Describe and illustrate the reporting of long-term liabilities including bonds and notes payable.
   - Reporting Long-Term Liabilities

At a Glance | Menu | Turn to pg 640

South-Western

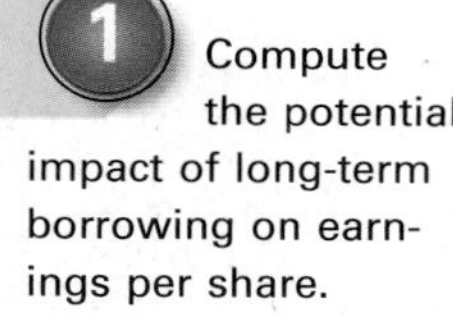

Compute the potential impact of long-term borrowing on earnings per share.

Financing Corporations

Corporations finance their operations using the following:

1. Debt such as purchasing on account or issuing bonds or notes payable
2. Equity such as issuing common stock and, in some cases, preferred stock

Purchasing on account and issuing short-term notes payable as well as issuing common and preferred stock have been discussed in earlier chapters. This chapter focuses on issuing long-term bonds and notes payable to finance a company's operations.

A **bond** is a form of an interest-bearing note. Like a note, a bond requires periodic interest payments with the face amount to be repaid at the maturity date. As creditors of the corporation, bondholder claims on the corporation's assets rank ahead of stockholders.

To illustrate the financing of long-term operations, assume Huckadee Corporation is considering the following plans to issue debt and equity:

	Plan 1		Plan 2		Plan 3	
	Amount	**Percent**	**Amount**	**Percent**	**Amount**	**Percent**
Issue 12% bonds	—	0%	—	0%	$2,000,000	50%
Issue 9% preferred stock, $50 par value	—	0	$2,000,000	50	1,000,000	25
Issue common stock, $10 par value	$4,000,000	100	2,000,000	50	1,000,000	25
Total amount of financing	$4,000,000	100%	$4,000,000	100%	$4,000,000	100%

Each of the preceding plans finances some of the corporation's operations by issuing common stock. However, the percentage financed by common stock varies from 100% (Plan 1) to 25% (Plan 3). In deciding among financing plans, the effect on earnings per share is often considered.

Earnings per share (EPS) measures the income earned by each share of common stock. It is computed as follows:[1]

$$\text{Earnings per Share} = \frac{\text{Net Income} - \text{Preferred Dividends}}{\text{Number of Common Shares Outstanding}}$$

When interest rates are low, corporations usually finance their operations with debt. For example, as interest rates fell in recent years, corporations issued large amounts of new debt.

To illustrate, assume the following data for Huckadee Corporation:

1. Earnings before interest and income taxes are $800,000.
2. The tax rate is 40%.
3. All bonds or stocks are issued at their par or face amount.

The effect of the preceding financing plans on Huckadee's net income and earnings per share is shown in Exhibit 1.

Exhibit 1

Effect of Alternative Financing Plans—$800,000 Earnings

	Plan 1	Plan 2	Plan 3
12% bonds	—	—	$2,000,000
Preferred 9% stock, $50 par	—	$2,000,000	1,000,000
Common stock, $10 par	$4,000,000	2,000,000	1,000,000
Total	$4,000,000	$4,000,000	$4,000,000
Earnings before interest and income tax	$ 800,000	$ 800,000	$ 800,000
Deduct interest on bonds	—	—	240,000
Income before income tax	$ 800,000	$ 800,000	$ 560,000
Deduct income tax	320,000	320,000	224,000
Net income	$ 480,000	$ 480,000	$ 336,000
Dividends on preferred stock	—	180,000	90,000
Available for dividends on common stock	$ 480,000	$ 300,000	$ 246,000
Shares of common stock outstanding	÷ 400,000	÷ 200,000	÷ 100,000
Earnings per share on common stock	$ 1.20	$ 1.50	$ 2.46

Exhibit 1 indicates that Plan 3 yields the highest earnings per share on common stock and, thus, is the most attractive for common stockholders. If the estimated earnings are more than $800,000, the difference between the earnings per share to common stockholders under Plans 1 and 3 is even greater.[2]

1 Earnings per share is also discussed in the *Financial Analysis and Interpretation* section of Chapter 13 and in Chapter 17.

2 The higher earnings per share under Plan 3 is due to a finance concept known as *leverage*. This concept is discussed further in Chapter 17.

If smaller earnings occur, however, Plans 1 and 2 become more attractive to common stockholders. To illustrate, the effect of earnings of $440,000 rather than $800,000 is shown in Exhibit 2.

Exhibit 2

Effect of Alternative Financing Plans—$440,000 Earnings

	Plan 1	Plan 2	Plan 3
12% bonds	—	—	$2,000,000
Preferred 9% stock, $50 par	—	$2,000,000	1,000,000
Common stock, $10 par	$4,000,000	2,000,000	1,000,000
Total	$4,000,000	$4,000,000	$4,000,000
Earnings before interest and income tax	$ 440,000	$ 440,000	$ 440,000
Deduct interest on bonds	—	—	240,000
Income before income tax	$ 440,000	$ 440,000	$ 200,000
Deduct income tax	176,000	176,000	80,000
Net income	$ 264,000	$ 264,000	$ 120,000
Dividends on preferred stock	—	180,000	90,000
Available for dividends on common stock	$ 264,000	$ 84,000	$ 30,000
Shares of common stock outstanding	÷ 400,000	÷ 200,000	÷ 100,000
Earnings per share on common stock	$ 0.66	$ 0.42	$ 0.30

In addition to earnings per share, the corporation should consider other factors in deciding among the financing plans. For example, once bonds are issued, the interest and the face value of the bonds at maturity must be paid. If these payments are not made, the bondholders could seek court action and force the company into bankruptcy. In contrast, a corporation is not legally obligated to pay dividends on preferred or common stock.

Example Exercise 14-1 Alternative Financing Plans

Gonzales Co. is considering the following alternative plans for financing its company:

	Plan 1	Plan 2
Issue 10% bonds (at face value)	—	$2,000,000
Issue common stock, $10 par	$3,000,000	1,000,000

Income tax is estimated at 40% of income.

Determine the earnings per share of common stock under the two alternative financing plans, assuming income before bond interest and income tax is $750,000.

Follow My Example 14-1

	Plan 1	Plan 2
Earnings before bond interest and income tax	$750,000	$750,000
Bond interest	0	200,000[2]
Balance	$750,000	$550,000
Income tax	300,000[1]	220,000[3]
Net income	$450,000	$330,000
Dividends on preferred stock	0	0
Earnings available for common stock	$450,000	$330,000
Number of common shares	÷300,000	÷100,000
Earnings per share on common stock	$ 1.50	$ 3.30

[1]$750,000 × 40% [2]$2,000,000 × 10% [3]$550,000 × 40%

For Practice: PE 14-1A, PE 14-1B

Describe the characteristics and terminology of bonds payable.

Nature of Bonds Payable

Corporate bonds normally differ in face values, interest rates, interest payment dates, and maturity dates. Bonds also differ in other ways such as whether corporate assets are pledged in support of the bonds.

Bond Characteristics and Terminology

The underlying contract between the company issuing bonds and the bondholders is called a **bond indenture** or *trust indenture*. A bond issue is normally divided into a number of individual bonds. Usually, the face value of each bond, called the *principal*, is $1,000 or a multiple of $1,000. The interest on bonds may be payable annually, semiannually, or quarterly. Most bonds pay interest semiannually.

The price of a bond is quoted as a percentage of the bond's face value. For example, a $1,000 bond quoted at 98 could be purchased or sold for $980 ($1,000 × 0.98). Likewise, bonds quoted at 109 could be purchased or sold for $1,090 ($1,000 × 1.09).

When all bonds of an issue mature at the same time, they are called *term bonds*. If the bonds mature over several dates, they are called *serial bonds*. For example, one-tenth of an issue of $1,000,000 bonds, or $100,000, may mature 16 years from the issue date, another $100,000 in the 17th year, and so on.

Time Warner, Inc., 7.625% bonds maturing in 2031 were listed as selling for 106.505 on February 1, 2008.

Bonds that may be exchanged for other securities, such as common stock, are called *convertible bonds*. Bonds that a corporation reserves the right to redeem before their maturity are called *callable bonds*. Bonds issued on the basis of the general credit of the corporation are called *debenture bonds*.

Proceeds from Issuing Bonds

When a corporation issues bonds, the proceeds received for the bonds depend on the following:

1. The face amount of the bonds, which is the amount due at the maturity date.
2. The interest rate on the bonds.
3. The market rate of interest.

Selling price of bond < $1,000

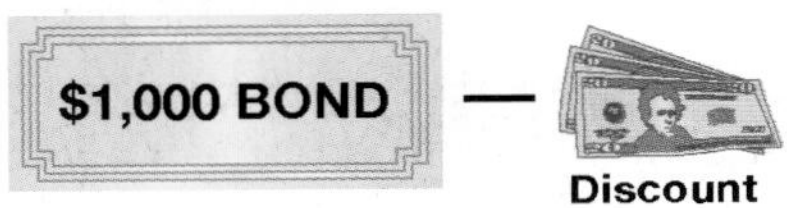

Market Rate < Contract Rate

Selling price of bond > $1,000

The face amount and the interest rate on the bonds are identified in the bond indenture. The interest rate to be paid on the face amount of the bond is called the **contract rate** or *coupon rate*.

The **market rate of interest**, sometimes called the **effective rate of interest**, is the rate determined from sales and purchases of similar bonds. The market rate of interest is affected by a variety of factors, including investors' expectations of current and future economic conditions.

By comparing the market and contract rates of interest, it can be determined whether the selling price of a bond will be equal, less than, or more than the bond's face amount as shown below.

1. Market Rate = Contract Rate
   Selling Price = Face Amount of Bonds
2. Market Rate > Contract Rate
   Selling Price < Face Amount of Bonds
   The face amount of bonds less the selling price is called a **discount**.
3. Market Rate < Contract Rate
   Selling Price > Face Amount of Bonds
   The selling price less the face amount of the bonds is called a **premium**.

A bond sells at a discount because buyers are only willing to pay less than the face amount for bonds whose contract rate is less than the market rate. A bond sells at a premium because buyers are willing to pay more than the face amount for bonds whose contract rate is higher than the market rate.

Integrity, Objectivity, and Ethics in Business

CREDIT QUALITY

The market rate of interest for a corporate bond is influenced by a number of factors, including the credit quality of the issuer. During 2007 and 2008, sub-prime bonds became less secure due to falling house prices and mortgage defaults. As a result, investors in these bonds lost billions of dollars, causing the eventual takeover of Bear Stearns & Co., a Wall Street investment company.

Journalize entries for bonds payable.

Accounting for Bonds Payable

Bonds may be issued at their face amount, a discount, or a premium. When bonds are issued at less or more than their face amount, the discount or premium must be amortized over the life of the bonds. A corporation may redeem bonds before their maturity date.

Bonds Issued at Face Amount

If the market rate of interest is equal to the contract rate of interest, the bonds will sell for their face amount or a price of 100. To illustrate, assume that on January 1, 2009, Eastern Montana Communications Inc. issued the following bonds:

Face amount	$100,000
Contract rate of interest	12%
Interest paid semiannually on June 30 and December 31.	
Term of bonds	5 years
Market rate of interest	12%

Since the contract rate of interest and the market rate of interest are the same, the bonds will sell at their face amount. The entry to record the issuance of the bonds is as follows:

2009 Jan.	1	Cash		100,000	
		Bonds Payable			100,000
		Issued $100,000 bonds payable at face amount.			

Every six months (on June 30 and December 31) after the bonds are issued, interest of $6,000 ($100,000 × 12% × ½) is paid. The first interest payment on June 30, 2009, is recorded as follows:

2009 June	30	Interest Expense		6,000	
		Cash			6,000
		Paid six months' interest on bonds.			

At the maturity date, the payment of the principal of $100,000 is recorded as follows:

2013					
Dec.	31	Bonds Payable		100,000	
		Cash			100,000
		Paid bond principal at maturity date.			

Bonds Issued at a Discount

If the market rate of interest is more than the contract rate of interest, the bonds will sell for less than their face amount. This is because investors are not willing to pay the full face amount for bonds that pay a lower contract rate of interest than the rate they could earn on similar bonds (market rate).[3]

Bonds will sell at a discount when the market rate of interest is higher than the contract rate.

To illustrate, assume that on January 1, 2009, Western Wyoming Distribution Inc. issued the following bonds:

Face amount	$100,000
Contract rate of interest	12%
Interest paid semiannually on June 30 and December 31.	
Term of bonds	5 years
Market rate of interest	13%

Since the contract rate of interest is less than the market rate of interest, the bonds will sell at less than their face amount. Assuming the bonds sell for $96,406, the entry to record the issuance of the bonds is as follows:

2009					
Jan.	1	Cash		96,406	
		Discount on Bonds Payable		3,594	
		Bonds Payable			100,000
		Issued $100,000 bonds at discount.			

The $96,406 may be viewed as the amount investors are willing to pay for bonds that have a lower contract rate of interest (12%) than the market rate (13%). The discount is the market's way of adjusting the contract rate of interest to the higher market rate of interest.

The account, Discount on Bonds Payable, is a contra account to Bonds Payable and has a normal debit balance. It is subtracted from Bonds Payable to determine the carrying amount (or book value) of the bonds payable. Thus, after the preceding entry, the carrying amount of the bonds payable is $96,406 ($100,000 − $3,594).

Example Exercise 14-2 Issuing Bonds at a Discount 3

On the first day of the fiscal year, a company issues a $1,000,000, 6%, five-year bond that pays semiannual interest of $30,000 ($1,000,000 × 6% × ½), receiving cash of $936,420. Journalize the entry to record the issuance of the bonds.

Follow My Example 14-2

Cash	936,420	
Discount on Bonds Payable	63,580	
Bonds Payable		1,000,000

For Practice: PE 14-2A, PE 14-2B

3 The price that investors are willing to pay for the bonds depends on present value concepts. Present value concepts, including the computation of bond prices, are described and illustrated in Appendix 1 at the end of this chapter.

Amortizing a Bond Discount

A bond discount must be amortized to interest expense over the life of the bond. The entry to amortize a bond discount is shown below.

		Interest Expense		XXX	
		Discount on Bonds Payable			XXX

The preceding entry may be made annually as an adjusting entry, or it may be combined with the semiannual interest payment. In the latter case, the entry would be as follows:

		Interest Expense		XXX	
		Discount on Bonds Payable			XXX
		Cash (amount of semiannual interest)			XXX

The two methods of computing the amortization of a bond discount are:

1. *Straight-line method*
2. *Effective interest rate method*, sometimes called the *interest method*

The **effective interest rate method** is required by generally accepted accounting principles. However, the straight-line method may be used if the results do not differ significantly from the interest method. The straight-line method is used in this chapter. The effective interest rate method is described and illustrated in Appendix 2 at the end of this chapter.

The straight-line method provides equal amounts of amortization. To illustrate, amortization of the Western Wyoming Distribution bond discount of $3,594 is computed below.

Discount on bonds payable . .	$3,594.00
Term of bonds	5 years
Semiannual amortization	$359.40 ($3,594/10 periods)

The combined entry to record the first interest payment and the amortization of the discount is as follows:

2009					
June	30	Interest Expense		6,359.40	
		Discount on Bonds Payable			359.40
		Cash			6,000.00
		Paid semiannual interest and			
		amortized 1/10 of bond discount.			

The preceding entry is made on each interest payment date. Thus, the amount of the semiannual interest expense on the bonds ($6,359.40) remains the same over the life of the bonds.

The effect of the discount amortization is to increase the interest expense from $6,000.00 to $6,359.40. In effect, this increases the contract rate of interest from 12% to a rate of interest that approximates the market rate of 13%. In addition, as the discount is amortized, the carrying amount of the bonds increases until it equals the face amount of the bonds on the maturity date.

Example Exercise 14-3 Discount Amortization 3

Using the bond from Example Exercise 14-2, journalize the first interest payment and the amortization of the related bond discount.

Follow My Example 14-3

Interest Expense	36,358	
Discount on Bonds Payable		6,358
Cash		30,000
Paid interest and amortized the bond discount ($63,580/10).		

For Practice: PE 14-3A, PE 14-3B

Bonds will sell at a premium when the market rate of interest is less than the contract rate.

Bonds Issued at a Premium

If the market rate of interest is less than the contract rate of interest (contract rate), the bonds will sell for more than their face amount. This is because investors are willing to pay more for bonds that pay a higher rate of interest (contract rate) than the rate they could earn on similar bonds (market rate).

To illustrate, assume that on January 1, 2009, Northern Idaho Transportation Inc. issued the following bonds:

Face amount	$100,000
Contract rate of interest	12%
Interest paid semiannually on June 30 and December 31.	
Term of bonds	5 years
Market rate of interest	11%

Since the contract rate of interest is more than the market rate of interest, the bonds will sell at more than their face amount. Assuming the bonds sell for $103,769, the entry to record the issuance of the bonds is as follows:

2009 Jan.	1	Cash		103,769	
		Bonds Payable			100,000
		Premium on Bonds Payable			3,769
		Issued $100,000 bonds at a premium.			

The $3,769 premium may be viewed as the extra amount investors are willing to pay for bonds that have a higher rate of interest (12%) than the market rate (11%). The premium is the market's way of adjusting the contract rate of interest to the lower market rate of interest.

The account, Premium on Bonds Payable, has a normal credit balance. It is added to Bonds Payable to determine the carrying amount (or book value) of the bonds payable. Thus, after the preceding entry, the carrying amount of the bonds payable is $103,769 ($100,000 + $3,769).

Example Exercises 14-4 Issuing Bonds at a Premium 3

A company issues a $2,000,000, 12%, five-year bond that pays semiannual interest of $120,000 ($2,000,000 × 12% × ½), receiving cash of $2,154,440. Journalize the bond issuance.

Follow My Example 14-4

Cash	2,154,440	
Premium on Bonds Payable		154,440
Bonds Payable		2,000,000

For Practice: PE 14-4A, PE 14-4B

Amortizing a Bond Premium

Like bond discounts, a bond premium must be amortized over the life of the bond. The amortization can be computed using either the straight-line or the effective interest rate method. The entry to amortize a bond premium is shown below.

		Premium on Bonds Payable		XXX	
		Interest Expense			XXX

The preceding entry may be made annually as an adjusting entry, or it may be combined with the semiannual interest payment. In the latter case, the entry would be as follows:

		Interest Expense		XXX	
		Discount on Bonds Payable			XXX
		Cash (amount of semiannual interest)			XXX

To illustrate, amortization of the preceding premium of $3,769 is computed using the straight-line method as shown below.

Premium on bonds payable	$3,769.00
Term of bonds	5 years
Semiannual amortization	$376.90 ($3,769/10 periods)

The combined entry to record the first interest payment and the amortization of the discount is as follows:

2009 June	30	Interest Expense		5,623.10	
		Premium on Bonds Payable		376.90	
		Cash			6,000.00
		Paid semiannual interest and amortized 1/10 of bond premium.			

The preceding entry is made on each interest payment date. Thus, the amount of the semiannual interest expense ($5,623.10) on the bonds remains the same over the life of the bonds.

The effect of the premium amortization is to decrease the interest expense from $6,000.00 to $5,623.10. In effect, this decreases the contract rate of interest from 12% to a rate of interest that approximates the market rate of 11%. In addition, as the premium is amortized, the carrying amount of the bonds decreases until it equals the face amount of bonds on the maturity date.

Example Exercise 14-5 Premium Amortization 3

Using the bond from Example Exercise 14-4, journalize the first interest payment and the amortization of the related bond premium.

Follow My Example 14-5

Interest Expense	104,556	
Premium on Bonds Payable	15,444	
Cash		120,000
Paid interest and amortized the bond premium ($154,440/10).		

For Practice: PE 14-5A, PE 14-5B

Business Connection

CH-CH-CH-CHANGES IN BOND TRENDS

How would you like to tune into some of the royalties from your favorite rock star or song? In the past decade, several well-known rock stars have offered bonds backed by future royalties from their hit songs and albums. These include rock icons like James Brown, Rod Stewart, and Iron Maiden.

The trend toward linking music royalties to bonds began when rock star David Bowie packaged royalties from his 25-album catalog of over 300 songs as a $55 million bond issue. These "Bowie Bonds" had an average maturity of 10 years and paid 7.9% annual interest. On the issue date, Moody's Investors Service gave the bonds its highest rating, AAA. Potential investors were confident in the bonds, knowing that Bowie never sold fewer than a million albums a year prior to the bond issuance. In addition, Bowie reportedly had a steady cash flow of $1 million per year from his existing music catalog. However, in recent years, investor confidence in these bonds has eroded. In May 2004, Moody's Investors Service downgraded the bonds to Baa3. While Bowie Bonds have fallen on hard times, and are no longer available to the public. However, the recent move to online music retailing has renewed interest in these types of bonds.

© TIM AYLEN/ATLANTIS PARADISE ISLAND/PR NEWSFOTO (AP TOPIC GALLERY)

Bowie Bonds gave rise to a variety of similar bonds that were backed by the future earnings of intellectual property. These include intangibles like copyrights from music and films, patents from prescription drugs and technology, trade secrets, and Internet Web site names.

Bond Redemption

Pacific Bell issued 7.5% bonds, maturing in 2033 but callable in 2023.

A corporation may redeem or call bonds before they mature. This is often done when the market rate of interest declines below the contract rate of interest. In such cases, the corporation may issue new bonds at a lower interest rate and use the proceeds to redeem the original bond issue.

Callable bonds can be redeemed by the issuing corporation within the period of time and at the price stated in the bond indenture. Normally, the call price is above the face value. A corporation may also redeem its bonds by purchasing them on the open market.[4]

A corporation usually redeems its bonds at a price different from the carrying amount (or book value) of the bonds. The **carrying amount** of bonds payable is the face amount of the bonds less any unamortized discount or plus any unamortized premium. A gain or loss may be realized on a bond redemption as follows:

1. A *gain* is recorded if the price paid for redemption is below the bond carrying amount.
2. A *loss* is recorded if the price paid for the redemption is above the carrying amount.

4 Some bond indentures require the corporation issuing the bonds to transfer cash to a special cash fund, called a *sinking fund,* over the life of the bond. Such funds help assure investors that there will be adequate cash to pay the bonds at their maturity date.

Gains and losses on the redemption of bonds are reported in the *Other income (loss)* section of the income statement.

To illustrate, assume that on June 30, 2009, a corporation has the following bond issue:

Face amount of bonds	$100,000
Premium on bonds payable	4,000

On June 30, 2009, the corporation redeemed one-fourth ($25,000) of these bonds in the market for $24,000. The entry to record the redemption is as follows:

2009					
June	30	Bonds Payable		25,000	
		Premium on Bonds Payable		1,000	
		Cash			24,000
		Gain on Redemption of Bonds			2,000
		Redeemed $25,000 bonds for $24,000.			

In the preceding entry, only the portion of the premium related to the redeemed bonds ($1,000) is written off. The difference between the carrying amount of the bonds redeemed, $26,000 ($25,000 + $1,000), and the redemption price, $24,000, is recorded as a gain.

Assume that the corporation calls the remaining $75,000 of outstanding bonds, which are held by a private investor, for $79,500 on July 1, 2009. The entry to record the redemption is as follows:

2009					
July	1	Bonds Payable		75,000	
		Premium on Bonds Payable		3,000	
		Loss on Redemption of Bonds		1,500	
		Cash			79,500
		Redeemed $75,000 bonds for $79,500.			

Example Exercise 14-6 Redemption of Bonds Payable

3

A $500,000 bond issue on which there is an unamortized discount of $40,000 is redeemed for $475,000. Journalize the redemption of the bonds.

Follow My Example 14-6

Bonds Payable	500,000	
Loss on Redemption of Bonds	15,000	
Discount on Bonds Payable		40,000
Cash		475,000

For Practice: PE 14-6A, PE 14-6B

Describe and illustrate the accounting for installment notes.

Installment Notes

Corporations often finance their operations by issuing bonds payable. Corporations may also issue installment notes. An **installment note** is a debt that requires the borrower to make equal periodic payments to the lender for the term of the note. Unlike bonds, each note payment consists of the following:

1. Payment of a portion of the amount initially borrowed, called the *principal*
2. Payment of interest on the outstanding balance

Mortgage notes are used by individuals to buy a car or house.

At the end of the note's term, the principal will have been repaid in full.

Installment notes are often used to purchase assets such as equipment and are usually issued by an individual bank. An installment note may be secured by a pledge of the borrower's assets. Such notes are called **mortgage notes**. If the borrower fails to pay a mortgage note, the lender has the right to take possession of the pledged asset and sell it to pay off the debt.

Issuing an Installment Note

When an installment note is issued, an entry is recorded debiting Cash and crediting Notes Payable. To illustrate, assume that Lewis Company issues the following installment note to City National Bank on January 1, 2008.

Principal amount of note.	\$24,000
Interest rate	6%
Term of note.	5 years
Annual payments	\$5,698[5]

The entry to record the issuance of the note is as follows:

2008 Jan.	1	Cash		24,000	
		Notes Payable			24,000
		Issued installment note for cash.			

Annual Payments

The preceding note payable requires Lewis Company to repay the principal and interest in equal payments of \$5,698 beginning December 31, 2008, for each of the next five years. Unlike bonds, however, each installment note payment includes an interest and principal payment.

The interest portion of an installment note payment is computed by multiplying the interest rate by the carrying amount (book value) of the note at the beginning of the period. The principal portion of the payment is then computed as the difference between the total payment (cash paid) and the interest. These computations are illustrated in Exhibit 3 as follows:

1. The January 1, 2008, carrying value (Column A) equals the amount borrowed from the bank. The January 1 balance in the following years equals the December 31 balance from the prior year.

5 The amount of the annual payment is calculated by using the present value concepts discussed in Appendix 1. The annual payment of \$5,698 is computed by dividing the \$24,000 loan amount by the present value of an annuity of \$1 for 5 periods at 6% (4.21236) from Exhibit 5 (rounded to the nearest dollar).

Exhibit 3

Amortization of Installment Notes

	A	B	C	D	E
For the Year Ending:	January 1 Carrying Amount	Note Payment (cash paid)	Interest Expense (6% of January 1 Note Carrying Amount)	Decrease in Notes Payable (B – C)	December 31 Carrying Amount (A – D)
December 31, 2008	$24,000	$ 5,698	$1,440 (6% of $24,000)	$ 4,258	$19,742
December 31, 2009	19,742	5,698	1,185 (6% of $19,742)	4,513	15,229
December 31, 2010	15,229	5,698	914 (6% of $15,229)	4,784	10,445
December 31, 2011	10,445	5,698	627 (6% of $10,445)	5,071	5,374
December 31, 2012	5,374	5,698	324* (6% of $5,374)	5,374	0
		$28,490	$4,490	$24,000	

*Rounded.

2. The note payment (Column B) remains constant at $5,698, the annual cash payments required by the bank.
3. The interest expense (Column C) is computed at 6% of the installment note carrying amount at the beginning of each year. As a result, the interest expense decreases each year.
4. Notes payable (Column D) decreases each year by the amount of the principal repayment. The principal repayment is computed by subtracting the interest expense (Column C) from the total payment (Column B). The principal repayment increases each year as the interest expense decreases (Column C).
5. The carrying amount on December 31 (Column E) of the note decreases from $24,000, the initial amount borrowed, to $0 at the end of the five years.

The entry to record the first payment on December 31, 2008, is as follows:

2008					
Dec.	31	Interest Expense		1,440	
		Notes Payable		4,258	
		Cash			5,698
		Paid principal and interest on installment note.			

The entry to record the second payment on December 31, 2009, is as follows:

2009					
Dec.	31	Interest Expense		1,185	
		Notes Payable		4,513	
		Cash			5,698
		Paid principal and interest on installment note.			

As the prior entries show, the cash payment is the same in each year. The interest and principal repayment, however, change each year. This is because the carrying amount (book value) of the note decreases each year as principal is repaid, which decreases the interest.

The entry to record the final payment on December 31, 2012, is as follows:

2012					
Dec.	31	Interest Expense		324	
		Notes Payable		5,374	
		Cash			5,698
		Paid principal and interest on installment notes.			

After the final payment, the carrying amount on the note is zero, indicating that the note has been paid in full. Any assets that secure the note would then be released by the bank.

Example Exercise 14-7 Journalizing Installment Notes

On the first day of the fiscal year, a company issues $30,000, 10%, five-year installment note that has annual payments of $7,914. The first note payment consists of $3,000 of interest and $4,914 of principal repayment.

a. Journalize the entry to record the issuance of the installment note.

b. Journalize the first annual note payment.

Follow My Example 14-7

a.

		Cash		30,000	
		Notes Payable			30,000
		Issued $30,000 of installment note for cash.			

b.

		Interest Expense		3,000	
		Notes Payable		4,914	
		Cash			7,914
		Paid principal and interest on installment note.			

For Practice: PE 14-7A, PE 14-7B

5 Describe and illustrate the reporting of long-term liabilities including bonds and notes payable.

Reporting Long-Term Liabilities

Bonds payable and notes payable are reported as liabilities on the balance sheet. Any portion of the bonds or notes that is due within one year is reported as a current liability. Any remaining bonds or notes are reported as a long-term liability.

Any unamortized premium is reported as an addition to the face amount of the bonds. Any unamortized discount is reported as a deduction from the face amount of the bonds. A description of the bonds and notes should also be reported either on the face of the financial statements or in the accompanying notes.

The reporting of bonds and notes payable for Mornin' Joe is shown below.

Mornin' Joe
Balance Sheet
December 31, 2010

Current liabilities:		
Accounts payable	$133,000	
Notes payable (current portion)	200,000	
Salaries and wages payable	42,000	
Payroll taxes payable	16,400	
Interest payable	40,000	
Total current liabilities		$ 431,400
Long-term liabilities:		
Bonds payable, 8%, due December 31, 2030	$500,000	
Less unamortized discount	16,000	$ 484,000
Notes payable		1,400,000
Total long-term liabilities		$1,884,000
Total liabilities		$2,315,400

Financial Analysis and Interpretation

Analysts often assess the relative risk of the bondholders in terms of the **number of times interest charges are earned** during the year. The higher the ratio, the greater the chance that interest payments will continue to be made if earnings decrease.

The amount available to make interest payments is not affected by taxes on income. This is because interest is deductible in determining taxable income. To illustrate, the following data were taken from the 2006 annual report of Briggs & Stratton Corporation:

Interest expense	$ 42,091,000
Income before income tax	$152,366,000

The number of times interest charges are earned, 4.62, is computed at the top of the next column.

Number of Times Interest Charges Are Earned =

$$\frac{\text{Income Before Income Tax} + \text{Interest Expense}}{\text{Interest Expense}}$$

Number of Times Interest Charges Are Earned =

$$\frac{\$152{,}366{,}000 + \$42{,}091{,}000}{\$42{,}091{,}000} = 4.62$$

The number of times interest charges are earned indicates that the debtholders of Briggs & Stratton Corporation have adequate protection against a potential drop in earnings jeopardizing their receipt of interest payments. However, a final assessment should include a review of trends of past years and a comparison with industry averages.

f·a·i

APPENDIX 1

Present Value Concepts and Pricing Bonds Payable

When a corporation issues bonds, the price that investors are willing to pay for the bonds depends on the following:

1. The face amount of the bonds, which is the amount due at the maturity date
2. The periodic interest to be paid on the bonds
3. The market rate of interest

An investor determines how much to pay for the bonds by computing the present value of the bond's future cash receipts, using the market rate of interest. A bond's future cash receipts include its face value at maturity and the periodic interest.

Present Value Concepts

The concept of present value is based on the time value of money. The *time value of money concept* recognizes that cash received today is worth more than the same amount of cash to be received in the future.

To illustrate, what would you rather have: $1,000 today or $1,000 one year from now? You would rather have the $1,000 today because it could be invested to earn interest. For example, if the $1,000 could be invested to earn 10% per year, the $1,000 will accumulate to $1,100 ($1,000 plus $100 interest) in one year. In this sense, you can think of the $1,000 in hand today as the **present value** of $1,100 to be received a year from today. This present value is illustrated below.

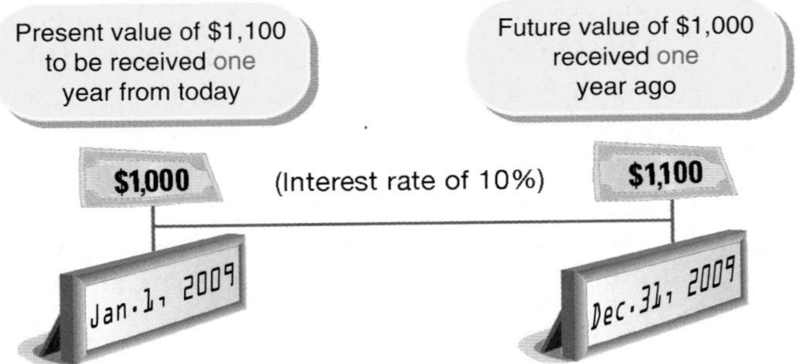

A related concept to present value is **future value**. To illustrate, using the preceding example, the $1,100 to be received on December 31, 2009, is the *future value* of $1,000 on January 1, 2009, assuming an interest rate of 10%.

Present Value of an Amount To illustrate the present value of an amount, assume that $1,000 is to be received in one year. If the market rate of interest is 10%, the present value of the $1,000 is $909.09 ($1,000/1.10). This present value is illustrated below.

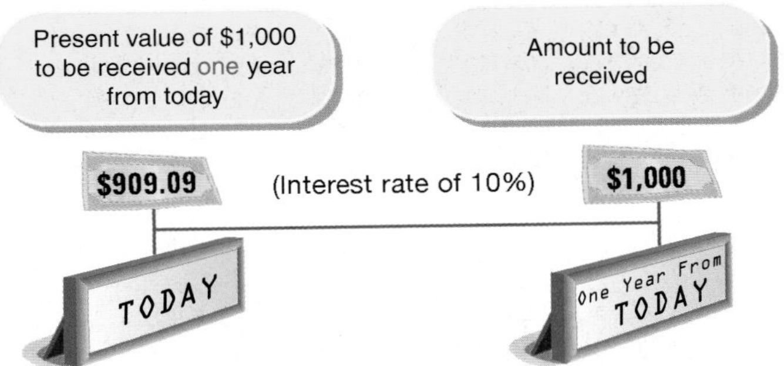

If the $1,000 is to be received in two years, with interest of 10% compounded at the end of the first year, the present value is $826.45 ($909.09/1.10).[6] This present value is illustrated at the top of the next page.

6 Note that the future value of $826.45 in two years, at an interest rate of 10% compounded annually, is $1,000.

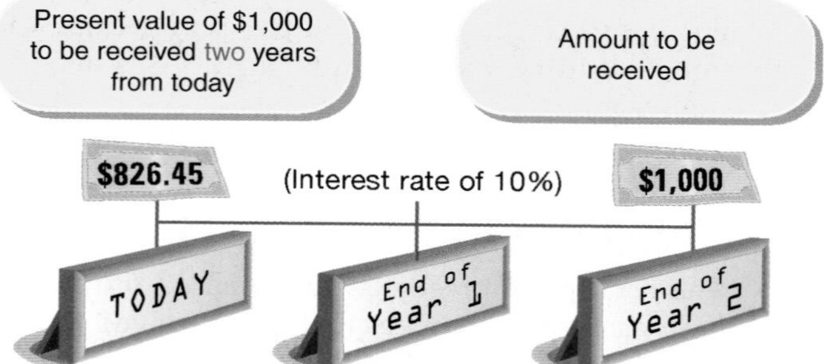

Spreadsheet software with built-in present value functions can be used to calculate present values.

The present value of an amount to be received in the future can be determined by a series of divisions such as illustrated above. In practice, however, it is easier to use a table of present values.

The *present value of $1* table is used to find the present value factor for $1 to be received after a number of periods in the future. The amount to be received is then multiplied by this factor to determine its present value.

To illustrate, Exhibit 4 is a partial table of the present value of $1.[7] Exhibit 4 indicates that the present value of $1 to be received in two years with a market rate of interest of 10% a year is 0.82645. Multiplying $1,000 to be received in two years by 0.82645 yields $826.45 ($1,000 × 0.82645). This amount is the same amount computed above. In Exhibit 4, the Periods column represents the number of compounding periods, and the percentage columns represent the compound interest rate per period. Thus, the present value factor from Exhibit 4 for 12% for five years compounded *semiannually* is 0.55840. Since the interest is compounded semiannually, the interest rate is 6% (12% divided by 2), and the number of periods is 10 (5 years × 2 times per year). Some additional examples using Exhibit 4 are shown below.

Exhibit 4

Present Value of $1 at Compound Interest

Periods	5%	5½%	6%	6½%	7%	10%	11%	12%	13%	14%
1	0.95238	0.94787	0.94340	0.93897	0.93458	0.90909	0.90090	0.89286	0.88496	0.87719
2	0.90703	0.89845	0.89000	0.88166	0.87344	0.82645	0.81162	0.79719	0.78315	0.76947
3	0.86384	0.85161	0.83962	0.82785	0.81630	0.75132	0.73119	0.71178	0.69305	0.67497
4	0.82270	0.80722	0.79209	0.77732	0.76290	0.68301	0.65873	0.63552	0.61332	0.59208
5	0.78353	0.76513	0.74726	0.72988	0.71299	0.62092	0.59345	0.56743	0.54276	0.51937
6	0.74622	0.72525	0.70496	0.68533	0.66634	0.56447	0.53464	0.50663	0.48032	0.45559
7	0.71068	0.68744	0.66506	0.64351	0.62275	0.51316	0.48166	0.45235	0.42506	0.39964
8	0.67684	0.65160	0.62741	0.60423	0.58201	0.46651	0.43393	0.40388	0.37616	0.35056
9	0.64461	0.61763	0.59190	0.56735	0.54393	0.42410	0.39092	0.36061	0.33288	0.30751
10	0.61391	0.58543	0.55840	0.53273	0.50835	0.38554	0.35218	0.32197	0.29459	0.26974

	Number of Periods	Interest Rate	Present Value of $1 Factor from Exhibit 4
10% for *two* years compounded *annually*	2	10%	0.82645
10% for *two* years compounded *semiannually*	4	5%	0.82270
10% for *three* years compounded *semiannually*	6	5%	0.74622
12% for *five* years compounded *semiannually*	10	6%	0.55840

7 To simplify the illustrations and homework assignments, the tables presented in this chapter are limited to 10 periods for a small number of interest rates, and the amounts are carried to only five decimal places. Computer programs are available for determining present value factors for any number of interest rates, decimal places, or periods. More complete interest tables are presented in Appendix A of the text.

Present Value of the Periodic Receipts A series of equal cash receipts at fixed intervals is called an **annuity**. The **present value of an annuity** is the sum of the present values of each cash receipt. To illustrate, assume that $100 is to be received annually for two years and that the market rate of interest is 10%. Using Exhibit 4, the present value of the receipt of the two amounts of $100 is $173.55, as shown below.

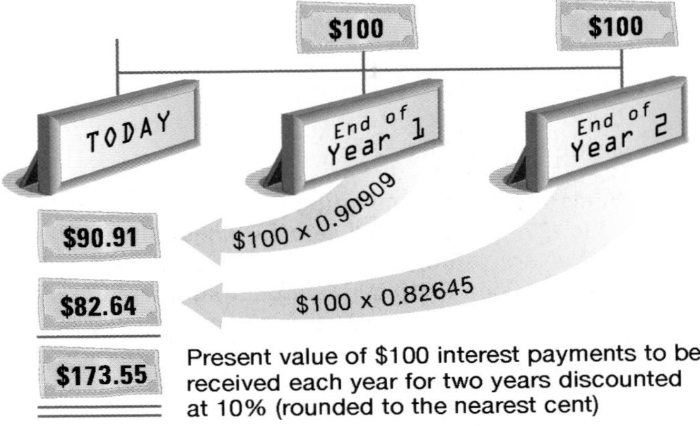

Instead of using present value of $1 tables, such as Exhibit 4, separate present value tables are normally used for annuities. Exhibit 5 is a partial table of the **present value of an annuity of $1** at compound interest. It shows the present value of $1 to be received at the end of each period for various compound rates of interest.

Exhibit 5

Present Value of Annuity of $1 at Compound Interest

Periods	5%	5½%	6%	6½%	7%	10%	11%	12%	13%	14%
1	0.95238	0.94787	0.94340	0.93897	0.93458	0.90909	0.90090	0.89286	0.88496	0.87719
2	1.85941	1.84632	1.83339	1.82063	1.80802	1.73554	1.71252	1.69005	1.66810	1.64666
3	2.72325	2.69793	2.67301	2.64848	2.62432	2.48685	2.44371	2.40183	2.36115	2.32163
4	3.54595	3.50515	3.46511	3.42580	3.38721	3.16987	3.10245	3.03735	2.97447	2.91371
5	4.32948	4.27028	4.21236	4.15568	4.10020	3.79079	3.69590	3.60478	3.51723	3.43308
6	5.07569	4.99553	4.91732	4.84101	4.76654	4.35526	4.23054	4.11141	3.99755	3.88867
7	5.78637	5.68297	5.58238	5.48452	5.38929	4.86842	4.71220	4.56376	4.42261	4.28830
8	6.46321	6.33457	6.20979	6.08875	5.97130	5.33493	5.14612	4.96764	4.79677	4.63886
9	7.10782	6.95220	6.80169	6.65610	6.51523	5.75902	5.53705	5.32825	5.13166	4.94637
10	7.72174	7.53763	7.36009	7.18883	7.02358	6.14457	5.88923	5.65022	5.42624	5.21612

To illustrate, the present value of $100 to be received at the end of each of the next two years at 10% compound interest per period is $173.55 ($100 × 1.73554). This amount is the same amount computed above.

Pricing Bonds

The selling price of a bond is the present value, using the current market rate of interest, of the following:

1. The face amount of the bonds due at the maturity date
2. The periodic interest to be paid on the bonds

To illustrate the pricing of bonds, assume that Southern Utah Communications Inc. issued the following bond on January 1, 2009:

Face amount	$100,000
Contract rate of interest	12%
Interest paid semiannually on June 30 and December 31.	
Term of bonds	5 years

Market Rate of Interest of 12% Assuming a market rate of interest of 12%, the bonds would sell for $100,000, their face amount, as shown by the following present value computations.

Present value of face amount of $100,000 due in 5 years, at 12% compounded semiannually: $100,000 × 0.55840 (present value of $1 for 10 periods at 6% from Exhibit 4)	$ 55,840
Present value of 10 semiannual interest payments of $6,000, at 12% compounded semiannually: $6,000 × 7.36009 (present value of annuity of $1 for 10 periods at 6% from Exhibit 5)	44,160
Total present value of bonds	$100,000

Market Rate of Interest of 13% Assuming a market rate of interest of 13%, the bonds would sell at a discount. As shown by the following present value computations, the bonds would sell for $96,406.[8]

Present value of face amount of $100,000 due in 5 years, at 13% compounded semiannually: $100,000 × 0.53273 (present value of $1 for 10 periods at 6½% from Exhibit 4)	$ 53,273
Present value of 10 semiannual interest payments of $6,000, at 13% compounded semiannually: $6,000 × 7.18883 (present value of an annuity of $1 for 10 periods at 6½% from Exhibit 5)	43,133
Total present value of bonds	$ 96,406

Market Rate of Interest of 11% Assuming a market rate of interest of 11%, the bonds would sell at a premium. As shown by the following present value computations, the bonds would sell for $103,769.

Present value of face amount of $100,000 due in 5 years, at 11% compounded semiannually: $100,000 × 0.58543 (present value of $1 for 10 periods at 5½% from Exhibit 4)	$ 58,543
Present value of 10 semiannual interest payments of $6,000, at 11% compounded semiannually: $6,000 × 7.53763 (present value of an annuity of $1 for 10 periods at 5½% from Exhibit 5)	45,226
Total present value of bonds	$103,769

As shown above, the selling price of the bond varies with the present value of the bond's face amount at maturity, interest payments, and the market rate of interest.

8 Some corporations issue bonds called **zero-coupon bonds** that provide for only the payment of the face amount at maturity. Such bonds sell for large discounts. In this example, such a bond would sell for $53,273, which is the present value of the face amount.

APPENDIX 2

Effective Interest Rate Method of Amortization

The effective interest rate method of amortization provides for a constant *rate* of interest over the life of the bonds. As the discount or premium is amortized, the carrying amount of the bonds changes. As a result, interest expense also changes each period. This is in contrast to the straight-line method, which provides for a constant *amount* of interest expense each period.

The interest rate used in the effective interest rate method of amortization, sometimes called the *interest method*, is the market rate on the date the bonds are issued. The carrying amount of the bonds is multiplied by this interest rate to determine the interest expense for the period. The difference between the interest expense and the interest payment is the amount of discount or premium to be amortized for the period.

Amortization of Discount by the Interest Method

To illustrate, the following data taken from the chapter illustration of issuing bonds at a discount are used:

Face value of 12%, 5-year bonds, interest compounded semiannually	$100,000
Present value of bonds at effective (market) rate of interest of 13%	96,406
Discount on bonds payable	$ 3,594

Exhibit 6 illustrates the interest method for the preceding bonds. Exhibit 6 was prepared as follows:

Step 1. List the interest payments dates in the first column, which for the preceding bond are 10 interest payment dates (semiannual interest over five years). Also, list on the first line the initial amount of discount in Column D and the initial carrying amount (selling price) of the bonds in Column E.

Step 2. List in Column A the semiannual interest payments, which for the preceding bond is $6,000 ($100,000 × 6%).

Step 3. Compute the interest expense in Column B by multiplying the bond carrying amount at the beginning of each period times 6½%, which is the effective interest (market) rate.

Step 4. Compute the discount to be amortized each period in Column C by subtracting the interest payment in Column A ($6,000) from the interest expense for the period shown in Column B.

Step 5. Compute the remaining unamortized discount by subtracting the amortized discount in Column C for the period from the unamortized discount at the beginning of the period in Column D.

Step 6. Compute the bond carrying amount at the end of the period by subtracting the unamortized discount at the end of the period from the face amount of the bonds.

Steps 3–6 are repeated for each interest payment.

As shown in Exhibit 6, the interest expense increases each period as the carrying amount of the bond increases. Also, the unamortized discount decreases each period to zero at the maturity date. Finally, the carrying amount of the bonds increases from $96,406 to $100,000 (the face amount) at maturity.

Exhibit 6

Amortization of Discount on Bonds Payable

Interest Payment Date	A Interest Paid (6% of Face Amount)	B Interest Expense (6½% of Bond Carrying Amount)	C Discount Amortization (B – A)	D Unamortized Discount (D – C)	E Bond Carrying Amount ($100,000 – D)
				$3,594	$ 96,406
June 30, 2009	$6,000	$6,266 (6½% of $96,406)	$266	3,328	96,672
Dec. 31, 2009	6,000	6,284 (6½% of $96,672)	284	3,044	96,956
June 30, 2010	6,000	6,302 (6½% of $96,956)	302	2,742	97,258
Dec. 31, 2010	6,000	6,322 (6½% of $97,258)	322	2,420	97,580
June 30, 2011	6,000	6,343 (6½% of $97,580)	343	2,077	97,923
Dec. 31, 2011	6,000	6,365 (6½% of $97,923)	365	1,712	98,288
June 30, 2012	6,000	6,389 (6½% of $98,288)	389	1,323	98,677
Dec. 31, 2012	6,000	6,414 (6½% of $98,677)	414	909	99,091
June 30, 2013	6,000	6,441 (6½% of $99,091)	441	468	99,532
Dec. 31, 2013	6,000	6,470 (6½% of $99,532)	468*	—	100,000

*Cannot exceed unamortized discount.

The entry to record the first interest payment on June 30, 2009, and the related discount amortization is as follows:

2009					
June	30	Interest Expense		6,266	
		Discount on Bonds Payable			266
		Cash			6,000
		Paid semiannual interest and amortized bond discount for ½ year.			

If the amortization is recorded only at the end of the year, the amount of the discount amortized on December 31, 2009, would be $550. This is the sum of the first two semiannual amortization amounts ($266 and $284) from Exhibit 6.

Amortization of Premium by the Interest Method

To illustrate, the following data taken from the chapter illustration of issuing bonds at a premium are used:

Present value of bonds at effective (market) rate of interest of 11%	$103,769
Face value of 12%, 5-year bonds, interest compounded semiannually . .	100,000
Premium on bonds payable	$ 3,769

Exhibit 7 illustrates the interest method for the preceding bonds. Exhibit 7 was prepared as follows:

Step 1. List the number of interest payments in the first column, which for the preceding bond are 10 interest payments (semiannual interest over 5 years). Also, list on the first line the initial amount of premium in Column D and the initial carrying amount of the bonds in Column E.

Step 2. List in Column A the semiannual interest payments, which for the preceding bond is $6,000 ($100,000 × 6%).

Step 3. Compute the interest expense in Column B by multiplying the bond carrying amount at the beginning of each period times 5½%, which is the effective interest (market) rate.

Step 4. Compute the premium to be amortized each period in Column C by subtracting the interest expense for the period shown in Column B from the interest payment in Column A ($6,000).

Step 5. Compute the remaining unamortized premium by subtracting the amortized premium in Column C for the period from the unamortized premium at the beginning of the period in Column D.

Step 6. Compute the bond carrying amount at the end of the period by adding the unamortized premium at the end of the period to the face amount of the bonds.

Steps 3–6 are repeated for each interest payment.

As shown in Exhibit 7, the interest expense decreases each period as the carrying amount of the bond decreases. Also, the unamortized premium decreases each period to zero at the maturity date. Finally, the carrying amount of the bonds decreases from $103,769 to $100,000 (the face amount) at maturity.

Exhibit 7

Amortization of Premium on Bonds Payable

Interest Payment Date	A Interest Paid (6% of Face Amount)	B Interest Expense (5½% of Bond Carrying Amount)	C Premium Amortization (A − B)	D Unamortized Premium (D − C)	E Bond Carrying Amount ($100,000 + D)
				$3,769	$103,769
June 30, 2009	$6,000	5,707(5½% of $103,769)	$293	3,476	103,476
Dec. 31, 2009	6,000	5,691 (5½% of $103,476)	309	3,167	103,167
June 30, 2010	6,000	5,674 (5½% of $103,167)	326	2,841	102,841
Dec. 31, 2010	6,000	5,656 (5½% of $102,841)	344	2,497	102,497
June 30, 2011	6,000	5,637 (5½% of $102,497)	363	2,134	102,134
Dec. 31, 2011	6,000	5,617 (5½% of $102,134)	383	1,751	101,751
June 30, 2012	6,000	5,596 (5½% of $101,751)	404	1,347	101,347
Dec. 31, 2012	6,000	5,574 (5½% of $101,347)	426	921	100,921
June 30, 2013	6,000	5,551 (5½% of $100,921)	449	472	100,472
Dec. 31, 2013	6,000	5,526 (5½% of $100,472)	472*	—	100,000

*Cannot exceed unamortized premium.

The entry to record the first interest payment on June 30, 2009, and the related premium amortization is as follows:

2009					
June	30	Interest Expense		5,707	
		Premium on Bonds Payable		293	
		Cash			6,000
		Paid semiannual interest and amortized bond premium for ½ year.			

If the amortization is recorded only at the end of the year, the amount of the premium amortized on December 31, 2009, would be $602. This is the sum of the first two semiannual amortization amounts ($293 and $309) from Exhibit 7.

1 Compute the potential impact of long-term borrowing on earnings per share.

Key Points	Key Learning Outcomes	Example Exercises	Practice Exercises
Corporations can finance their operations by issuing bonds or additional equity. A bond is simply a form of an interest-bearing note. One of the many factors that influence a corporation's decision on whether it should issue debt or equity is the effect each alternative has on earnings per share.	• Define the concept of a bond.		
	• Calculate and compare the effect of alternative financing plans on earnings per share.	**14-1**	14-1A, 14-1B

2 Describe the characteristics and terminology of bonds payable.

Key Points	Key Learning Outcomes	Example Exercises	Practice Exercises
A corporation that issues bonds enters into a contract, or bond indenture. The characteristics of a bond depend on the type of bonds issued by a corporation. When a corporation issues bonds, the price that buyers are willing to pay for the bonds depends on (1) the face amount of the bonds, (2) the periodic interest to be paid on the bonds, and (3) the market rate of interest.	• Define the characteristics of a bond. • Describe the various types of bonds. • Describe the factors that determine the price of a bond.		

3 Journalize entries for bonds payable.

Key Points	Key Learning Outcomes	Example Exercises	Practice Exercises
The journal entry for issuing bonds payable debits Cash for the proceeds received and credits Bonds Payable for the face amount of the bonds. Any difference between the face amount of the bonds and the proceeds is debited to Discount on Bonds Payable or credited to Premium on Bonds Payable. A discount or premium on bonds payable is amortized to interest expense over the life of the bonds. At the maturity date, the entry to record the payment at face value of a bond is a debit to Bonds Payable and a credit to Cash. When a corporation redeems bonds, Bonds Payable is debited for the face amount of the bonds, the premium (discount) on bonds payable account is debited (credited) for its balance, Cash is credited, and any gain or loss on the redemption is recorded.	• Journalize the issuance of bonds at face value and the payment of periodic interest.		
	• Journalize the issuance of bonds at a discount.	**14-2**	14-2A, 14-2B
	• Journalize the amortization of a bond discount.	**14-3**	14-3A, 14-3B
	• Journalize the issuance of bonds at a premium.	**14-4**	14-4A, 14-4B
	• Journalize the amortization of a bond premium.	**14-5**	14-5A, 14-5B
	• Describe bond redemptions.		
	• Journalize the redemption of bonds payable.	**14-6**	14-6A, 14-6B

4 Describe and illustrate the accounting for installment notes.

Key Points	Key Learning Outcomes	Example Exercises	Practice Exercises
Companies issue installment notes as an alternative to issuing bonds. An installment note requires the borrower to make equal periodic payments to the lender for the term of the note. Unlike bonds, the annual payment in an installment note consists of both principal and interest. The journal entry for the annual payment debits Interest Expense and Notes Payable and credits Cash for the amount of the payment. After the final payment, the carrying amount on the note is zero.	• Define the characteristics of an installment note.		
	• Journalize the issuance of installment notes.	**14-7**	14-7A, 14-7B
	• Journalize the annual payment for an installment note.		

5 Describe and illustrate the reporting of long-term liabilities including bonds and notes payable.

Key Points	Key Learning Outcomes	Example Exercises	Practice Exercises
Bonds payable and notes payable are usually reported as long-term liabilities. If the balance sheet date is within one year, they are reported as a current liability. A discount on bonds should be reported as a deduction from the related bonds payable. A premium on bonds should be reported as an addition to related bonds payable.	• Illustrate the balance sheet presentation of bonds payable and notes payable.		

Key Terms

bond (618)
bond indenture (621)
carrying amount (627)
contract rate (621)
discount (621)
earnings per share (EPS) (619)
effective interest rate method (624)
effective rate of interest (621)
installment note (629)
market rate of interest (621)
mortgage notes (629)
number of times interest charges are earned (632)
premium (621)

Illustrative Problem

The fiscal year of Russell Inc., a manufacturer of acoustical supplies, ends December 31. Selected transactions for the period 2009 through 2016, involving bonds payable issued by Russell Inc., are as follows:

2009

June 30. Issued $2,000,000 of 25-year, 7% callable bonds dated June 30, 2009, for cash of $1,920,000. Interest is payable semiannually on June 30 and December 31.

Dec. 31. Paid the semiannual interest on the bonds.
31. Recorded straight-line amortization of $1,600 of discount on the bonds.
31. Closed the interest expense account.

2010
June 30. Paid the semiannual interest on the bonds.
Dec. 31. Paid the semiannual interest on the bonds.
31. Recorded straight-line amortization of $3,200 of discount on the bonds.
31. Closed the interest expense account.

2016
June 30. Recorded the redemption of the bonds, which were called at 101.5. The balance in the bond discount account is $57,600 after the payment of interest and amortization of discount have been recorded. (Record the redemption only.)

Instructions

1. Journalize entries to record the preceding transactions.
2. Determine the amount of interest expense for 2009 and 2010.
3. Determine the carrying amount of the bonds as of December 31, 2010.

Solution

1.

Date		Account		Debit	Credit
2009 June	30	Cash		1,920,000	
		Discount on Bonds Payable		80,000	
		Bonds Payable			2,000,000
Dec.	31	Interest Expense		70,000	
		Cash			70,000
	31	Interest Expense		1,600	
		Discount on Bonds Payable			1,600
		Amortization of discount from July 1 to December 31.			
	31	Income Summary		71,600	
		Interest Expense			71,600
2010 June	30	Interest Expense		70,000	
		Cash			70,000
Dec.	31	Interest Expense		70,000	
		Cash			70,000
	31	Interest Expense		3,200	
		Discount on Bonds Payable			3,200
		Amortization of discount from January 1 to December 31.			
	31	Income Summary		143,200	
		Interest Expense			143,200
2016 June	30	Bonds Payable		2,000,000	
		Loss on Redemption of Bonds Payable		87,600	
		Discount on Bonds Payable			57,600
		Cash			2,030,000

2. a. 2009—$71,600
   b. 2010—$143,200
3.

Initial carrying amount of bonds	$1,920,000
Discount amortized on December 31, 2009	1,600
Discount amortized on December 31, 2010	3,200
Carrying amount of bonds, December 31, 2010	$1,924,800

Self-Examination Questions (Answers at End of Chapter)

1. Which of the following measures might a company use to compare alternative financing decisions?
   A. The price of the bond issue
   B. The discount on the bonds payable
   C. Earnings per share
   D. Interest expense
2. If a corporation plans to issue $1,000,000 of 12% bonds at a time when the market rate for similar bonds is 10%, the bonds can be expected to sell at:
   A. their face amount.
   B. a premium.
   C. a discount.
   D. a price below their face amount.
3. If the bonds payable account has a balance of $900,000 and the discount on bonds payable account has a balance of $72,000, what is the carrying amount of the bonds?
   A. $828,000
   B. $900,000
   C. $972,000
   D. $580,000
4. If a company borrows money from a bank as an installment note, the interest portion of each annual payment will:
   A. equal the interest rate on the note times the face amount.
   B. equal the interest rate on the note times the carrying amount of the note at the beginning of the period.
   C. increase over the term of the note.
   D. remain constant over the term of the note.
5. The balance in the discount on bonds payable account would usually be reported on the balance sheet in the:
   A. Current Assets section.
   B. Current Liabilities section.
   C. Long-Term Liabilities section.
   D. Investments section.

Eye Openers

1. Describe the two distinct obligations incurred by a corporation when issuing bonds.
2. Explain the meaning of each of the following terms as they relate to a bond issue: (a) convertible, (b) callable, and (c) debenture.
3. If you asked your broker to purchase for you a 10% bond when the market interest rate for such bonds was 11%, would you expect to pay more or less than the face amount for the bond? Explain.
4. A corporation issues $9,000,000 of 9% bonds to yield interest at the rate of 7%. (a) Was the amount of cash received from the sale of the bonds greater or less than $9,000,000? (b) Identify the following terms related to the bond issue: (1) face amount, (2) market or effective rate of interest, (3) contract rate of interest, and (4) maturity amount.
5. If bonds issued by a corporation are sold at a premium, is the market rate of interest greater or less than the contract rate?
6. The following data relate to a $100,000,000, 12% bond issue for a selected semiannual interest period:

Bond carrying amount at beginning of period	$112,085,373
Interest paid during period	6,000,000
Interest expense allocable to the period	5,623,113

   (a) Were the bonds issued at a discount or at a premium? (b) What is the unamortized amount of the discount or premium account at the beginning of the period? (c) What account was debited to amortize the discount or premium?

7. Assume that Smith Co. amortizes premiums and discounts on bonds payable at the end of the year rather than when interest is paid. What accounts would be debited and credited to record (a) the amortization of a discount on bonds payable and (b) the amortization of a premium on bonds payable?
8. When a corporation issues bonds at a discount, is the discount recorded as income when the bonds are issued? Explain.
9. Assume that two 30-year, 10% bond issues are identical, except that one bond issue is callable at its face amount at the end of five years. Which of the two bond issues do you think will sell for a lower value?
10. Bonds Payable has a balance of $1,000,000, and Discount on Bonds Payable has a balance of $50,000. If the issuing corporation redeems the bonds at 98, is there a gain or loss on the bond redemption?
11. What is a mortgage note?
12. Fleeson Company needs additional funds to purchase equipment for a new production facility and is considering either issuing bonds payable or borrowing the money from a local bank in the form of an installment note. How does an installment note differ from a bond payable?
13. How would a bond payable be reported on the balance sheet if: (a) it is payable within one year and (b) it is payable beyond one year?
14. Sol Company issued $10,000,000 of bonds payable at a price of 102. How would the premium on the bonds payable be presented on the balance sheet?
15. What is meant by the phrase "time value of money"?
16. What has the higher present value: (a) $20,000 to be received at the end of two years, or (b) $10,000 to be received at the end of each of the next two years?

Practice Exercises

PE 14-1A
Alternative financing plans
obj. 1
EE 14-1 p. 620

Folmar Co. is considering the following alternative financing plans:

	Plan 1	Plan 2
Issue 10% bonds (at face value)	$2,000,000	$1,000,000
Issue preferred $1 stock, $5 par	—	1,500,000
Issue common stock, $5 par	2,000,000	1,500,000

Income tax is estimated at 40% of income.

Determine the earnings per share of common stock, assuming income before bond interest and income tax is $800,000.

PE 14-1B
Alternative financing plans
obj. 1
EE 14-1 p. 620

Simonelli Co. is considering the following alternative financing plans:

	Plan 1	Plan 2
Issue 8% bonds (at face value)	$5,000,000	4,000,000
Issue preferred $2.00 stock, $20 par	—	2,000,000
Issue common stock, $25 par	5,000,000	4,000,000

Income tax is estimated at 40% of income.

Determine the earnings per share of common stock, assuming income before bond interest and income tax is $1,000,000.

PE 14-2A
Issuing bonds at a discount
obj. 3
EE 14-2 p. 623

On the first day of the fiscal year, a company issues a $1,000,000, 11%, 10-year bond that pays semiannual interest of $55,000 ($1,000,000 × 11% × ½), receiving cash of $942,646. Journalize the bond issuance.

PE 14-2B
Issuing bonds at a discount
obj. 3
EE 14-2 p. 623

On the first day of the fiscal year, a company issues a $750,000, 7%, five-year bond that pays semiannual interest of $26,250 ($750,000 × 7% × ½), receiving cash of $663,128. Journalize the bond issuance.

PE 14-3A
Discount amortization
obj. 3
EE 14-3 p. 625

Using the bond from Practice Exercise 14-2A, journalize the first interest payment and the amortization of the related bond discount.

PE 14-3B
Discount amortization
obj. 3
EE 14-3 p. 625

Using the bond from Practice Exercise 14-2B, journalize the first interest payment and the amortization of the related bond discount.

PE 14-4A
Issuing bonds at a premium
obj. 3
EE 14-4 p. 626

A company issues a $5,000,000, 11%, five-year bond that pays semiannual interest of $275,000 ($5,000,000 × 11% × ½), receiving cash of $5,193,030. Journalize the bond issuance.

PE 14-4B
Issuing bonds at a premium
obj. 3
EE 14-4 p. 626

A company issues a $3,000,000, 12%, five-year bond that pays semiannual interest of $180,000 ($3,000,000 × 12% × ½), receiving cash of $3,146,200. Journalize the bond issuance.

PE 14-5A
Premium amortization
obj. 3
EE 14-5 p. 627

Using the bond from Practice Exercise 14-4A, journalize the first interest payment and the amortization of the related bond premium.

PE 14-5B
Premium amortization
obj. 3
EE 14-5 p. 627

Using the bond from Practice Exercise 14-4B, journalize the first interest payment and the amortization of the related bond premium.

PE 14-6A
Redemption of bonds payable
obj. 3
EE 14-6 p. 628

A $500,000 bond issue on which there is an unamortized discount of $50,000 is redeemed for $475,000. Journalize the redemption of the bonds.

PE 14-6B
Redemption of bonds payable
obj. 3
EE 14-6 p. 628

A $200,000 bond issue on which there is an unamortized premium of $15,000 is redeemed for $195,000. Journalize the redemption of the bonds.

PE 14-7A
Journalizing installment notes
obj. 4
EE 14-7 p. 631

On the first day of the fiscal year, a company issues $65,000, 10%, six-year installment notes that have annual payments of $14,924. The first note payment consists of $6,500 of interest and $8,424 of principal repayment.

a. Journalize the entry to record the issuance of the installment notes.
b. Journalize the first annual note payment.

PE 14-7B
Journalizing installment notes
obj. 4
EE 14-7 p. 631

On the first day of the fiscal year, a company issues $35,000, 12%, five-year installment notes that have annual payments of $9,709. The first note payment consists of $4,200 of interest and $5,509 of principal repayment.

a. Journalize the entry to record the issuance of the installment notes.
b. Journalize the first annual note payment.

Exercises

EX 14-1
Effect of financing on earnings per share
obj. 1
✔ a. $0.50

Miller Co., which produces and sells skiing equipment, is financed as follows:

Bonds payable, 10% (issued at face amount)	$10,000,000
Preferred $1 stock, $10 par	10,000,000
Common stock, $25 par	10,000,000

Income tax is estimated at 40% of income.

Determine the earnings per share of common stock, assuming that the income before bond interest and income tax is (a) $3,000,000, (b) $4,000,000, and (c) $5,000,000.

EX 14-2
Evaluate alternative financing plans
obj. 1

Based on the data in Exercise 14-1, discuss factors other than earnings per share that should be considered in evaluating such financing plans.

EX 14-3
Corporate financing
obj. 1

The financial statements for Nike, Inc., are presented in Appendix E at the end of the text. What is the major source of financing for Nike?

EX 14-4
Bond price
obj. 3

Procter and Gamble's 8% bonds due in 2024 were reported as selling for 126.987. Were the bonds selling at a premium or at a discount? Explain.

EX 14-5
Entries for issuing bonds
obj. 3

Grodski Co. produces and distributes semiconductors for use by computer manufacturers. Grodski Co. issued $24,000,000 of 20-year, 10% bonds on April 1 of the current year, with interest payable on April 1 and October 1. The fiscal year of the company is the calendar year. Journalize the entries to record the following selected transactions for the current year:

Apr. 1. Issued the bonds for cash at their face amount.
Oct. 1. Paid the interest on the bonds.
Dec. 31. Recorded accrued interest for three months.

EX 14-6
Entries for issuing bonds and amortizing discount by straight-line method
obj. 3
✔ b. $5,130,648

On the first day of its fiscal year, Robbins Company issued $50,000,000 of five-year, 8% bonds to finance its operations of producing and selling home improvement products. Interest is payable semiannually. The bonds were issued at an effective interest rate of 11%, resulting in Robbins Company receiving cash of $44,346,760.

a. Journalize the entries to record the following:
   1. Sale of the bonds.
   2. First semiannual interest payment. (Amortization of discount is to be recorded annually.)
   3. Second semiannual interest payment.
   4. Amortization of discount at the end of the first year, using the straight-line method. (Round to the nearest dollar.)
b. Determine the amount of the bond interest expense for the first year.

EX 14-7
Entries for issuing bonds and amortizing premium by straight-line method
objs. 2, 3

Daan Corporation wholesales repair products to equipment manufacturers. On March 1, 2010, Daan Corporation issued $24,000,000 of five-year, 12% bonds at an effective interest rate of 10%, receiving cash of $25,853,146. Interest is payable semiannually on March 1 and September 1. Journalize the entries to record the following:

a. Sale of bonds on March 1, 2010.
b. First interest payment on September 1, 2010, and amortization of bond premium for six months, using the straight-line method. (Round to the nearest dollar.)

EX 14-8
Entries for issuing and calling bonds; loss
obj. 3

Polders Corp., a wholesaler of office equipment, issued $16,000,000 of 20-year, 11% callable bonds on April 1, 2010, with interest payable on April 1 and October 1. The fiscal year of the company is the calendar year. Journalize the entries to record the following selected transactions:

2010
Apr. 1. Issued the bonds for cash at their face amount.
Oct. 1. Paid the interest on the bonds.

2014
Oct. 1. Called the bond issue at 102, the rate provided in the bond indenture. (Omit entry for payment of interest.)

EX 14-9
Entries for issuing and calling bonds; gain
obj. 3

Vidovich Corp. produces and sells soccer equipment. To finance its operations, Vidovich Corp. issued $15,000,000 of 30-year, 14% callable bonds on January 1, 2010, with interest payable on January 1 and July 1. The fiscal year of the company is the calendar year. Journalize the entries to record the following selected transactions:

2010
Jan. 1. Issued the bonds for cash at their face amount.
July 1. Paid the interest on the bonds.

2016
July 1. Called the bond issue at 98, the rate provided in the bond indenture. (Omit entry for payment of interest.)

EX 14-10
Entries for issuing installment note transactions
obj. 4

On the first day of the fiscal year, Hammond Company obtained a $44,000, seven-year, 5% installment note from Vegas Bank. The note requires annual payments of $7,604, with the first payment occurring on the last day of the fiscal year. The first payment consists of interest of $2,200 and principal repayment of $5,404.

a. Journalize the entries to record the following:
   1. Issued the installment notes for cash on the first day of the fiscal year.
   2. Paid the first annual payment on the note.
b. Determine the amount of bond interest expense for the first year.

EX 14-11
Entries for issuing installment note transactions
obj. 4

On January 1, 2010, Guiado Company obtained a $140,000, 10-year, 11% installment note from Best Bank. The note requires annual payments of $23,772, beginning on December 31, 2010. Journalize the entries to record the following:

2010
Jan. 1 Issued the notes for cash at their face amount.
Dec. 31 Paid the annual payment on the note, which consisted of interest of $15,400 and principal of $8,372.

2019
Dec. 31 Paid the annual payment on the note, which consisted of interest of $2,353 and principal of $21,419.

EX 14-12
Entries for issuing installment note transactions
obj. 4

On January 1, 2010, Zinn Company obtained a $52,000, four-year, 6.5% installment note from Fidelity Bank. The note requires annual payments of $15,179, beginning on December 31, 2011.

a. Prepare an amortization table for this installment note, similar to the one presented in Exhibit 3.
b. Journalize the entries for the issuance of the note and the four annual note payments.

EX 14-13
Reporting bonds
obj. 5

At the beginning of the current year, two bond issues (X and Y) were outstanding. During the year, bond issue X was redeemed and a significant loss on the redemption of bonds was reported as an extraordinary item on the income statement. At the end of the year, bond issue Y was reported as a noncurrent liability. The maturity date on the bonds was early in the following year.

Identify the flaws in the reporting practices related to the two bond issues.

Appendix 1
EX 14-14
Present value of amounts due

Determine the present value of $400,000 to be received in three years, using an interest rate of 10%, compounded annually, as follows:

a. By successive divisions. (Round to the nearest dollar.)
b. By using the present value table in Exhibit 4.

Appendix 1
EX 14-15
Present value of an annuity

Determine the present value of $100,000 to be received at the end of each of four years, using an interest rate of 6%, compounded annually, as follows:

a. By successive computations, using the present value table in Exhibit 4.
b. By using the present value table in Exhibit 5.

Appendix 1
EX 14-16
Present value of an annuity

✔ $21,070,740

On January 1, 2010, you win $30,000,000 in the state lottery. The $30,000,000 prize will be paid in equal installments of $3,000,000 over 10 years. The payments will be made on December 31 of each year, beginning on December 31, 2010. If the current interest rate is 7%, determine the present value of your winnings. Use the present value tables in Appendix A.

Appendix 1
EX 14-17
Present value of an annuity

Assume the same data as in Appendix 1 Exercise 14-16, except that the current interest rate is 14%.

Will the present value of your winnings using an interest rate of 14% be one-half the present value of your winnings using an interest rate of 7%? Why or why not?

Appendix 1
EX 14-18
Present value of bonds payable; discount

Hi-Vis Co. produces and sells high resolution flat panel televisions. To finance its operations, Hi-Vis Co. issued $10,000,000 of five-year, 10% bonds with interest payable semi-annually at an effective interest rate of 12%. Determine the present value of the bonds payable, using the present value tables in Exhibits 4 and 5. Round to the nearest dollar.

Appendix 1
EX 14-19
Present value of bonds payable; premium

✔ $69,265,908

Mason Co. issued $60,000,000 of five-year, 14% bonds with interest payable semiannually, at an effective interest rate of 10%. Determine the present value of the bonds payable, using the present value tables in Exhibits 4 and 5. Round to the nearest dollar.

Appendix 2
EX 14-20
Amortize discount by interest method

✔ b. $2,719,776

On the first day of its fiscal year, Simon Company issued $25,000,000 of 10-year, 10% bonds to finance its operations of producing and selling video equipment. Interest is payable semiannually. The bonds were issued at an effective interest rate of 13%, resulting in Simon Company receiving cash of $20,868,138.

a. Journalize the entries to record the following:
   1. Sale of the bonds.
   2. First semiannual interest payment, including amortization of discount.
   3. Second semiannual interest payment, including amortization of discount.
b. Compute the amount of the bond interest expense for the first year.

Appendix 2
EX 14-21
Amortize premium by interest method

✔ b. $1,027,982

Gary Miller Corporation wholesales bike parts to bicycle manufacturers. On March 1, 2010, Gary Miller Corporation issued $8,000,000 of five-year, 14% bonds at an effective interest rate of 12%, receiving cash of $8,588,850. Interest is payable semiannually. Gary Miller Corporation's fiscal year begins on March 1.

a. Journalize the entries to record the following:
   1. Sale of the bonds.
   2. First semiannual interest payment, including amortization of premium.
   3. Second semiannual interest payment, including amortization of premium.
b. Determine the bond interest expense for the first year.

Appendix 2
EX 14-22
Compute bond proceeds, amortizing premium by interest method, and interest expense

✔ a. $16,078,384
✔ c. $85,099

Motocar Co. produces and sells automobile parts. On the first day of its fiscal year, Motocar Co. issued $15,000,000 of five-year, 15% bonds at an effective interest rate of 13%, with interest payable semiannually. Compute the following, presenting figures used in your computations.

a. The amount of cash proceeds from the sale of the bonds. (Use the tables of present values in Exhibits 4 and 5. Round to the nearest dollar.)
b. The amount of premium to be amortized for the first semiannual interest payment period, using the interest method. (Round to the nearest dollar.)
c. The amount of premium to be amortized for the second semiannual interest payment period, using the interest method. (Round to the nearest dollar.)
d. The amount of the bond interest expense for the first year.

Appendix 2
EX 14-23
Compute bond proceeds, amortizing discount by interest method, and interest expense

✔ a. $35,785,876
✔ b. $305,011

Seward Co. produces and sells restaurant equipment. On the first day of its fiscal year, Seward Co. issued $40,000,000 of five-year, 11% bonds at an effective interest rate of 14%, with interest payable semiannually. Compute the following, presenting figures used in your computations.

a. The amount of cash proceeds from the sale of the bonds. (Use the tables of present values in Exhibits 4 and 5.)
b. The amount of discount to be amortized for the first semiannual interest payment period, using the interest method. (Round to the nearest dollar.)
c. The amount of discount to be amortized for the second semiannual interest payment period, using the interest method. (Round to the nearest dollar.)
d. The amount of the bond interest expense for the first year.

EX 14-24
Number of times interest charges earned

The following data were taken from recent annual reports of Southwest Airlines, which operates a low-fare airline service to over 50 cities in the United States.

	Current Year	Preceding Year
Interest expense	$ 56,000,000	$ 60,000,000
Income before income tax	325,000,000	450,000,000

a. Determine the number of times interest charges were earned for the current and preceding years. Round to one decimal place.
b. What conclusions can you draw?

Problems Series A

PR 14-1A
Effect of financing on earnings per share
obj. 1

✔ 1. Plan 3: $2.60

Three different plans for financing a $10,000,000 corporation are under consideration by its organizers. Under each of the following plans, the securities will be issued at their par or face amount, and the income tax rate is estimated at 40% of income.

	Plan 1	Plan 2	Plan 3
10% bonds	—	—	$ 5,000,000
Preferred 10% stock, $40 par	—	$ 5,000,000	2,500,000
Common stock, $10 par	$10,000,000	5,000,000	2,500,000
Total	$10,000,000	$10,000,000	$10,000,000

Instructions

1. Determine for each plan the earnings per share of common stock, assuming that the income before bond interest and income tax is $2,000,000.
2. Determine for each plan the earnings per share of common stock, assuming that the income before bond interest and income tax is $950,000.
3. Discuss the advantages and disadvantages of each plan.

PR 14-2A
Bond discount, entries for bonds payable transactions
obj. 3

✔ 3. $2,008,143

On July 1, 2010, Brower Industries Inc. issued $32,000,000 of 10-year, 12% bonds at an effective interest rate of 13%, receiving cash of $30,237,139. Interest on the bonds is payable semiannually on December 31 and June 30. The fiscal year of the company is the calendar year.

Instructions

1. Journalize the entry to record the amount of cash proceeds from the sale of the bonds.
2. Journalize the entries to record the following:
   a. The first semiannual interest payment on December 31, 2010, and the amortization of the bond discount, using the straight-line method. (Round to the nearest dollar.)
   b. The interest payment on June 30, 2011, and the amortization of the bond discount, using the straight-line method. (Round to the nearest dollar.)
3. Determine the total interest expense for 2010.
4. Will the bond proceeds always be less than the face amount of the bonds when the contract rate is less than the market rate of interest?

5. (Appendix 1) Compute the price of $30,237,139 received for the bonds by using the tables of present value in Appendix A at end of text. (Round to the nearest dollar.)

PR 14-3A
Bond premium, entries for bonds payable transactions
obj. 3

✔ 3. $164,627

Maui Blends, Inc. produces and sells organically grown coffee. On July 1, 2010, Maui Blends, Inc. issued $3,000,000 of 15-year, 12% bonds at an effective interest rate of 10%, receiving cash of $3,461,181. Interest on the bonds is payable semiannually on December 31 and June 30. The fiscal year of the company is the calendar year.

Instructions

1. Journalize the entry to record the amount of cash proceeds from the sale of the bonds.
2. Journalize the entries to record the following:
   a. The first semiannual interest payment on December 31, 2010, and the amortization of the bond premium, using the straight-line method. (Round to the nearest dollar.)
   b. The interest payment on June 30, 2011, and the amortization of the bond premium, using the straight-line method. (Round to the nearest dollar.)
3. Determine the total interest expense for 2010.
4. Will the bond proceeds always be greater than the face amount of the bonds when the contract rate is greater than the market rate of interest?
5. (Appendix 1) Compute the price of $3,461,181 received for the bonds by using the tables of present value in Appendix A at the end of the text. (Round to the nearest dollar.)

PR 14-4A
Entries for bonds payable and installment note transactions
objs. 3, 4

✔ 3. $17,072,630

The following transactions were completed by Hobson Inc., whose fiscal year is the calendar year:

2010

July 1. Issued $18,000,000 of five-year, 10% callable bonds dated July 1, 2010, at an effective rate of 12%, receiving cash of $16,675,184. Interest is payable semiannually on December 31 and June 30.

Oct. 1. Borrowed $400,000 as a 10-year, 7% installment note from Marble Bank. The note requires annual payments of $56,951, with the first payment occurring on September 30, 2011.

Dec. 31. Accrued $7,000 of interest on the installment note. The interest is payable on the date of the next installment note payment.

31. Paid the semiannual interest on the bonds.

31. Recorded bond discount amortization of $132,482, which was determined using the straight-line method.

31. Closed the interest expense account.

2011

June 30. Paid the semiannual interest on the bonds.

Sept. 30. Paid the annual payment on the note, which consisted of interest of $28,000 and principal of $28,951.

Dec. 31. Accrued $6,493 of interest on the installment note. The interest is payable on the date of the next installment note payment.

31. Paid the semiannual interest on the bonds.

31. Recorded bond discount amortization of $264,964, which was determined using the straight-line method.

31. Closed the interest expense account.

2012

June 30. Recorded the redemption of the bonds, which were called at 97. The balance in the bond discount account is $794,888 after payment of interest and amortization of discount have been recorded. (Record the redemption only.)

Sept. 30. Paid the second annual payment on the note, which consisted of interest of $25,973 and principal of $30,978.

Instructions

1. Journalize the entries to record the foregoing transactions.
2. Indicate the amount of the interest expense in (a) 2010 and (b) 2011.
3. Determine the carrying amount of the bonds as of December 31, 2011.

Appendix 2
PR 14-5A
Bond discount, entries for bonds payable transactions, interest method of amortizing bond discount

✔ 3. $1,965,414

On July 1, 2010, Brower Industries, Inc. issued $32,000,000 of 10-year, 12% bonds at an effective interest rate of 13%, receiving cash of $30,237,139. Interest on the bonds is payable semiannually on December 31 and June 30. The fiscal year of the company is the calendar year.

Instructions

1. Journalize the entry to record the amount of cash proceeds from the sale of the bonds.
2. Journalize the entries to record the following:
   a. The first semiannual interest payment on December 31, 2010, and the amortization of the bond discount, using the interest method. (Round to the nearest dollar.)
   b. The interest payment on June 30, 2011, and the amortization of the bond discount, using the interest method. (Round to the nearest dollar.)
3. Determine the total interest expense for 2010.

Appendix 2
PR 14-6A
Bond premium, entries for bonds payable transactions, interest method of amortizing bond discount

✔ 3. $173,059

Maui Blends, Inc. produces and sells organically grown coffee. On July 1, 2010, Maui Blends, Inc. issued $3,000,000 of 15-year, 12% bonds at an effective interest rate of 10%, receiving cash of $3,461,181. Interest on the bonds is payable semiannually on December 31 and June 30. The fiscal year of the company is the calendar year.

Instructions

1. Journalize the entry to record the amount of cash proceeds from the sale of the bonds.
2. Journalize the entries to record the following:
   a. The first semiannual interest payment on December 31, 2010, and the amortization of the bond discount, using the interest method. (Round to the nearest dollar.)
   b. The interest payment on June 30, 2011, and the amortization of the bond discount, using the interest method. (Round to the nearest dollar.)
3. Determine the total interest expense for 2010.

Problems Series B

PR 14-1B
Effect of financing on earnings per share
obj. 1

✔ 1. Plan 3: $5.12

Three different plans for financing a $60,000,000 corporation are under consideration by its organizers. Under each of the following plans, the securities will be issued at their par or face amount, and the income tax rate is estimated at 40% of income.

	Plan 1	Plan 2	Plan 3
12% bonds	—	—	$40,000,000
Preferred $2 stock, $20 par		$30,000,000	10,000,000
Common stock, $10 par	$60,000,000	30,000,000	10,000,000
Total	$60,000,000	$60,000,000	$60,000,000

Instructions

1. Determine for each plan the earnings per share of common stock, assuming that the income before bond interest and income tax is $15,000,000.
2. Determine for each plan the earnings per share of common stock, assuming that the income before bond interest and income tax is $7,000,000.
3. Discuss the advantages and disadvantages of each plan.

PR 14-2B
Bond discount, entries for bonds payable transactions
obj. 3

✔ 3. $2,726,729

On July 1, 2010, Linux Corporation, a wholesaler of electronics equipment, issued $45,000,000 of 10-year, 10% bonds at an effective interest rate of 14%, receiving cash of $35,465,423. Interest on the bonds is payable semiannually on December 31 and June 30. The fiscal year of the company is the calendar year.

Instructions

1. Journalize the entry to record the amount of cash proceeds from the sale of the bonds.
2. Journalize the entries to record the following:
   a. The first semiannual interest payment on December 31, 2010, and the amortization of the bond discount, using the straight-line method. (Round to the nearest dollar.)
   b. The interest payment on June 30, 2011, and the amortization of the bond discount, using the straight-line method. (Round to the nearest dollar.)
3. Determine the total interest expense for 2010.

4. Will the bond proceeds always be less than the face amount of the bonds when the contract rate is less than the market rate of interest?
5. (Appendix 1) Compute the price of $35,465,423 received for the bonds by using the tables of present value in Appendix A at end of text. (Round to the nearest dollar.)

PR 14-3B
Bond premium, entries for bonds payable transactions
obj. 3

✔ 3. $2,280,494

Prosser Corporation produces and sells baseball cards. On July 1, 2010, Prosser Corporation issued $40,000,000 of 10-year, 12% bonds at an effective interest rate of 11%, receiving cash of $42,390,112. Interest on the bonds is payable semiannually on December 31 and June 30. The fiscal year of the company is the calendar year.

Instructions

1. Journalize the entry to record the amount of cash proceeds from the sale of the bonds.
2. Journalize the entries to record the following:
   a. The first semiannual interest payment on December 31, 2010, and the amortization of the bond premium, using the straight-line method. (Round to the nearest dollar.)
   b. The interest payment on June 30, 2011, and the amortization of the bond premium, using the straight-line method. (Round to the nearest dollar.)
3. Determine the total interest expense for 2010.
4. Will the bond proceeds always be greater than the face amount of the bonds when the contract rate is greater than the market rate of interest?
5. (Appendix 1) Compute the price of $42,390,112 received for the bonds by using the tables of present value in Appendix A at the end of the text. (Round to the nearest dollar.)

PR 14-4B
Entries for bonds payable and installment note transactions
objs. 3, 4

✔ 3. $12,031,573

The following transactions were completed by Hobson Inc., whose fiscal year is the calendar year:

2010
July 1. Issued $10,000,000 of 10-year, 15% callable bonds dated July 1, 2010, at an effective rate of 11%, receiving cash of $12,390,085. Interest is payable semiannually on December 31 and June 30.
Oct. 1. Borrowed $225,000 as a six-year, 8% installment note from Titan Bank. The note requires annual payments of $48,671, with the first payment occurring on September 30, 2011.
Dec. 31. Accrued $4,500 of interest on the installment note. The interest is payable on the date of the next installment note payment.
31. Paid the semiannual interest on the bonds.
31. Recorded bond premium amortization of $119,504, which was determined using the straight-line method.
31. Closed the interest expense account.

2011
June 30. Paid the semiannual interest on the bonds.
Sept. 30. Paid the annual payment on the note, which consisted of interest of $18,000 and principal of $30,671.
Dec. 31. Accrued $3,887 of interest on the installment note. The interest is payable on the date of the next installment note payment.
31. Paid the semiannual interest on the bonds.
31. Recorded bond premium amortization of $239,008, which was determined using the straight-line method.
31. Closed the interest expense account.

2012
June 30. Recorded the redemption of the bonds, which were called at 101.5. The balance in the bond premium account is $1,912,069 after payment of interest and amortization of premium have been recorded. (Record the redemption only.)
Sept. 30. Paid the second annual payment on the note, which consisted of interest of $15,546 and principal of $33,125.

Instructions

1. Journalize the entries to record the foregoing transactions.
2. Indicate the amount of the interest expense in (a) 2010 and (b) 2011.
3. Determine the carrying amount of the bonds as of December 31, 2011.

Appendix 2
PR 14-5B
Bond discount, entries for bonds payable transactions, interest method of amortizing bond discount

✔ 3. $2,482,580

On July 1, 2010, Linux Corporation, a wholesaler of electronics equipment, issued $45,000,000 of 10-year, 10% bonds at an effective interest rate of 14%, receiving cash of $35,465,423. Interest on the bonds is payable semiannually on December 31 and June 30. The fiscal year of the company is the calendar year.

Instructions

1. Journalize the entry to record the amount of cash proceeds from the sale of the bonds.
2. Journalize the entries to record the following:
   a. The first semiannual interest payment on December 31, 2010, and the amortization of the bond discount, using the interest method. (Round to the nearest dollar.)
   b. The interest payment on June 30, 2011, and the amortization of the bond discount, using the interest method. (Round to the nearest dollar.)
3. Determine the total interest expense for 2010.

Appendix 2
PR 14-6B
Bond premium, entries for bonds payable transactions, interest method of amortizing bond premium

✔ 3. $2,331,456

Prosser Corporation produces and sells baseball cards. On July 1, 2010, Prosser Corporation issued $40,000,000 of 10-year, 12% bonds at an effective interest rate of 11%, receiving cash of $42,390,112. Interest on the bonds is payable semiannually on December 31 and June 30. The fiscal year of the company is the calendar year.

Instructions

1. Journalize the entry to record the amount of cash proceeds from the sale of the bonds.
2. Journalize the entries to record the following:
   a. The first semiannual interest payment on December 31, 2010, and the amortization of the bond premium, using the interest method. (Round to the nearest dollar.)
   b. The interest payment on June 30, 2011, and the amortization of the bond premium, using the interest method. (Round to the nearest dollar.)
3. Determine the total interest expense for 2010.

Special Activities

SA 14-1
General Electric bond issuance

General Electric Capital, a division of General Electric, uses long-term debt extensively. In a recent year, GE Capital issued $11 billion in long-term debt to investors, then within days filed legal documents to prepare for another $50 billion long-term debt issue. As a result of the $50 billion filing, the price of the initial $11 billion offering declined (due to higher risk of more debt).

> *Bill Gross, a manager of a bond investment fund, "denounced a 'lack in candor' related to GE's recent debt deal. 'It was the most recent and most egregious example of how bondholders are mistreated.' Gross argued that GE was not forthright when GE Capital recently issued $11 billion in bonds, one of the largest issues ever from a U.S. corporation. What bothered Gross is that three days after the issue the company announced its intention to sell as much as $50 billion in additional debt, warrants, preferred stock, guarantees, letters of credit and promissory notes at some future date."*

In your opinion, did GE Capital act unethically by selling $11 billion of long-term debt without telling those investors that a few days later it would be filing documents to prepare for another $50 billion debt offering?

Source: Jennifer Ablan, "Gross Shakes the Bond Market; GE Calms It, a Bit," *Barron's,* March 25, 2002.

SA 14-2
Ethics and professional conduct in business

Lachgar Industries develops and produces bio diesel, an alternative energy source. The company has an outstanding $200,000,000, 30-year, 12% bond issue dated July 1, 2005. The bond issue is due June 30, 2035. The bond indenture requires a bond sinking fund, which has a balance of $24,000,000 as of July 1, 2010. The company is currently experiencing a shortage of funds due to a recent acquisition. Abdou Hatch, the company's treasurer, is considering using the funds from the bond sinking fund to cover payroll and other bills that are coming due at the end of the month. Abdou's brother-in-law is a trustee in a sinking fund, who has indicated willingness to allow Abdou to use the funds from the sinking fund to temporarily meet the company's cash needs.

Discuss whether Abdou's proposal is appropriate.

SA 14-3
Present values

Finn Kilgallon recently won the jackpot in the Wisconsin lottery while he was visiting his parents. When he arrived at the lottery office to collect his winnings, he was offered the following three payout options:

a. Receive $10,000,000 in cash today.
b. Receive $2,200,000 today and $1,050,000 per year for 15 years, with the first $1,050,000 payment being received one year from today.
c. Receive $1,200,000 per year for 15 years, with the first payment being received one year from today.

Assuming that the effective rate of interest is 12%, which payout option should Finn select? Explain your answer and provide any necessary supporting calculations.

SA 14-4
Preferred stock vs. bonds

Beacon Inc. has decided to expand its operations to owning and operating long-term health care facilities. The following is an excerpt from a conversation between the chief executive officer, Frank Forrest, and the vice president of finance, Rachel Tucker.

Frank: Rachel, have you given any thought to how we're going to finance the acquisition of St. Seniors Health Care?

Rachel: Well, the two basic options, as I see it, are to issue either preferred stock or bonds. The equity market is a little depressed right now. The rumor is that the Federal Reserve Bank's going to increase the interest rates either this month or next.

Frank: Yes, I've heard the rumor. The problem is that we can't wait around to see what's going to happen. We'll have to move on this next week if we want any chance to complete the acquisition of St. Seniors.

Rachel: Well, the bond market is strong right now. Maybe we should issue debt this time around.

Frank: That's what I would have guessed as well. St. Seniors's financial statements look pretty good, except for the volatility of its income and cash flows. But that's characteristic of the industry.

Discuss the advantages and disadvantages of issuing preferred stock versus bonds.

SA 14-5
Financing business expansion

You hold a 25% common stock interest in the family-owned business, a vending machine company. Your sister, who is the manager, has proposed an expansion of plant facilities at an expected cost of $7,500,000. Two alternative plans have been suggested as methods of financing the expansion. Each plan is briefly described as follows:

Plan 1. Issue $7,500,000 of 10-year, 8% notes at face amount.

Plan 2. Issue an additional 100,000 shares of $10 par common stock at $40 per share, and $3,500,000 of 10-year, 8% notes at face amount.

The balance sheet as of the end of the previous fiscal year is as follows:

Thacker, Inc.
Balance Sheet
December 31, 2010

Assets	
Current assets	$ 4,000,000
Property, plant, and equipment	6,000,000
Total assets	$10,000,000
Liabilities and Stockholders' Equity	
Liabilities	$ 3,000,000
Common stock, $5	1,000,000
Paid-in capital in excess of par	100,000
Retained earnings	5,900,000
Total liabilities and stockholders' equity	$10,000,000

Net income has remained relatively constant over the past several years. The expansion program is expected to increase yearly income before bond interest and income tax from $750,000 in the previous year to $1,000,000 for this year. Your sister has asked you, as the company treasurer, to prepare an analysis of each financing plan.

1. Prepare a table indicating the expected earnings per share on the common stock under each plan. Assume an income tax rate of 40%. Round to the nearest cent.
2. a. Discuss the factors that should be considered in evaluating the two plans.
   b. Which plan offers the greater benefit to the present stockholders? Give reasons for your opinion.

SA 14-6
Bond ratings

Internet Project

Moody's Investors Service maintains a Web site at **http://www.Moodys.com**. One of the services offered at this site is a listing of announcements of recent bond rating changes. Visit this site and read over some of these announcements. Write down several of the reasons provided for rating downgrades and upgrades. If you were a bond investor or bond issuer, would you care if Moody's changed the rating on your bonds? Why or why not?

SA 14-7
Number of times interest charges are earned

The following financial data was taken from the financial statements of Williams-Sonoma, Inc.

	Fiscal Year		
	2007	2006	2005
Interest expense	$ 800	$ 774	$ 3,188
Earnings before taxes	36,485	20,108	13,255

1. What is the number of times interest charges are earned for Williams-Sonoma in 2007, 2006, and 2005? (Round your answers to one decimal place.)
2. Evaluate this ratio for Williams-Sonoma.

Answers to Self-Examination Questions

1. **C** Earnings per share is preferred for comparing financing decisions because it captures the effect of alternative decisions on the earnings available to individual shareholders (answer C). The price of the bond issue and the discount on the bond issue relate to the cost of borrowing, but do not reflect the individual shareholder impact (answers A and B). Interest expense reflects the cost of debt financing to the company, but does not capture the effect on individual shareholders (answer D).
2. **B** Since the contract rate on the bonds is higher than the prevailing market rate, a rational investor would be willing to pay more than the face amount, or a premium (answer B), for the bonds. If the contract rate and the market rate were equal, the bonds could be expected to sell at their face amount (answer A). Likewise, if the market rate is higher than the contract rate, the bonds would sell at a price below their face amount (answer D) or at a discount (answer C).
3. **A** The bond carrying amount is the face amount plus unamortized premium or less unamortized discount. For this question, the carrying amount is $900,000 less $72,000, or $828,000 (answer A).
4. **B** The interest portion of an installment note payment is computed by multiplying the interest rate by the carrying amount of the note at the beginning of the period. The periodic interest on bonds payable is computed by multiplying the interest rate times the face amount of the bond (answer A). Because installment note payments include both principal and interest components, the amount of principal is reduced each period which, in turn, reduces the interest portion of each payment (answers C and D).
5. **C** The balance of Discount on Bonds Payable is usually reported as a deduction from Bonds Payable in the Long-Term Liabilities section (answer C) of the balance sheet. Likewise, a balance in a premium on bonds payable account would usually be reported as an addition to Bonds Payable in the Long-Term Liabilities section of the balance sheet.

C H A P T E R 16

Statement of Cash Flows

© AP Photo/Elaine Thompson

JONES SODA CO.

Suppose you were to receive $100 as a result of some event. Would it make a difference what the event was? Yes, it would! If you received $100 for your birthday, then it's a gift. If you received $100 as a result of working part time for a week, then it's the result of your effort. If you received $100 as a loan, then it's money that you will have to pay back in the future. If you received $100 as a result of selling your ipod, then it's the result of giving up something tangible. Thus, the same $100 received can be associated with different types of events, and these events have different meanings to you. You would much rather receive a $100 gift than take out a $100 loan. Likewise, company stakeholders would also view events such as these differently.

Companies are required to report information about the events causing a change in cash over a period time. This information is reported in the statement of cash flows. One such company is Jones Soda Co. Jones began in the late 1980s as an alternative beverage company, known for its customer-provided labels, unique flavors, and support for extreme sports. You have probably seen Jones Soda at Barnes & Noble, Panera Bread, or Starbucks, or maybe sampled some of its unique flavors, such as Fufu Berry®, Blue Bubblegum®, or Lemon Drop®. As with any company, cash is important to Jones Soda. Without cash, Jones would be unable to expand its brands, distribute its product, support extreme sports, or provide a return for its owners. Thus, its managers are concerned about the sources and uses of cash.

In previous chapters, we have used the income statement, balance sheet, retained earnings statement, and other information to analyze the effects of management decisions on a business's financial position and operating performance. In this chapter, we focus on the events causing a change in cash by presenting the preparation and use of the statement of cash flows.

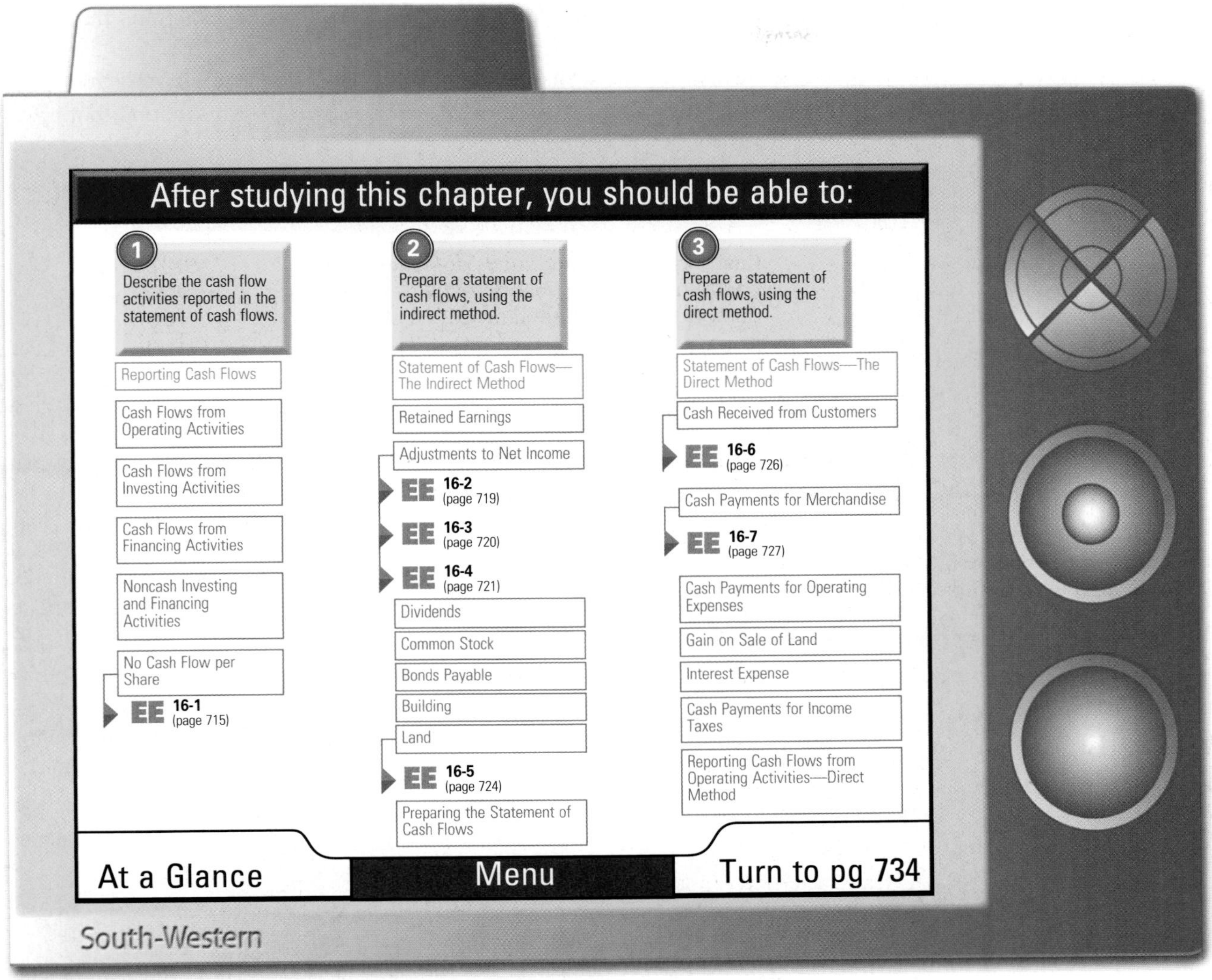

After studying this chapter, you should be able to:

1 Describe the cash flow activities reported in the statement of cash flows.

- Reporting Cash Flows
- Cash Flows from Operating Activities
- Cash Flows from Investing Activities
- Cash Flows from Financing Activities
- Noncash Investing and Financing Activities
- No Cash Flow per Share
- EE 16-1 (page 715)

2 Prepare a statement of cash flows, using the indirect method.

- Statement of Cash Flows—The Indirect Method
- Retained Earnings
- Adjustments to Net Income
- EE 16-2 (page 719)
- EE 16-3 (page 720)
- EE 16-4 (page 721)
- Dividends
- Common Stock
- Bonds Payable
- Building
- Land
- EE 16-5 (page 724)
- Preparing the Statement of Cash Flows

3 Prepare a statement of cash flows, using the direct method.

- Statement of Cash Flows—The Direct Method
- Cash Received from Customers
- EE 16-6 (page 726)
- Cash Payments for Merchandise
- EE 16-7 (page 727)
- Cash Payments for Operating Expenses
- Gain on Sale of Land
- Interest Expense
- Cash Payments for Income Taxes
- Reporting Cash Flows from Operating Activities—Direct Method

At a Glance | Menu | Turn to pg 734

South-Western

1 Describe the cash flow activities reported in the statement of cash flows.

Reporting Cash Flows

The **statement of cash flows** reports a company's cash inflows and outflows for a period.[1] The statement of cash flows provides useful information about a company's ability to do the following:

1. Generate cash from operations
2. Maintain and expand its operating capacity
3. Meet its financial obligations
4. Pay dividends

The statement of cash flows is used by managers in evaluating past operations and in planning future investing and financing activities. It is also used by external users such as investors and creditors to assess a company's profit potential and ability to pay its debt and pay dividends.

The statement of cash flows reports three types of cash flow activities as follows:

1. **Cash flows from operating activities** are cash flows from transactions that affect the net income of the company.

   Example: Purchase and sale of merchandise by a retailer.

1 As used in this chapter, *cash* refers to cash and cash equivalents. Examples of cash equivalents include short-term, highly liquid investments, such as money market accounts, bank certificates of deposit, and U.S. Treasury bills.

2. **Cash flows from investing activities** are cash flows from transactions that affect investments in noncurrent assets of the company.

   Example: Sale and purchase of fixed assets, such as equipment and buildings.

3. **Cash flows from financing activities** are cash flows from transactions that affect the debt and equity of the company.

   Example: Issuing or retiring equity and debt securities.

The cash flows are reported in the statement of cash flows as follows:

Cash flows from operating activities	$XXX
Cash flows from investing activities	XXX
Cash flows from financing activities	XXX
Net increase or decrease in cash for the period	$XXX
Cash at the beginning of the period	XXX
Cash at the end of the period	$XXX

The ending cash on the statement of cash flows equals the cash reported on the company's balance sheet.

The statement of cash flows reports cash flows from operating, investing, and financing activities.

Exhibit 1 illustrates the sources (increases) and uses (decreases) of cash by each of the three cash flow activities. A *source* of cash causes the cash flow to increase and is called a *cash inflow*. A *use* of cash causes cash flow to decrease and is called *cash outflow*.

Exhibit 1

Cash Flows

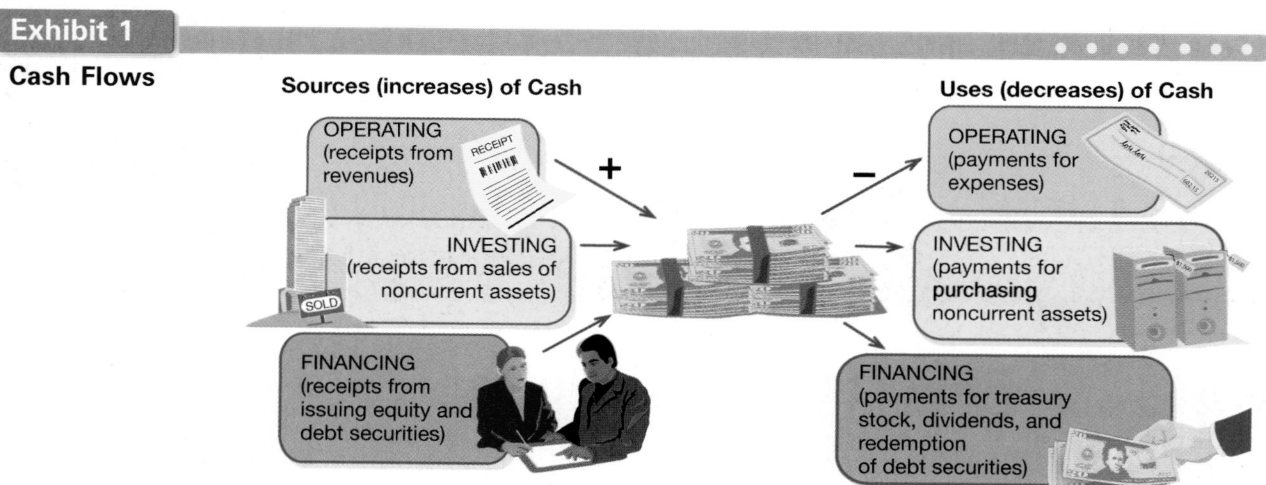

Cash Flows from Operating Activities

There are two methods for reporting cash flows from operating activities in the statement of cash flows. These methods are as follows:

1. Direct method
2. Indirect method

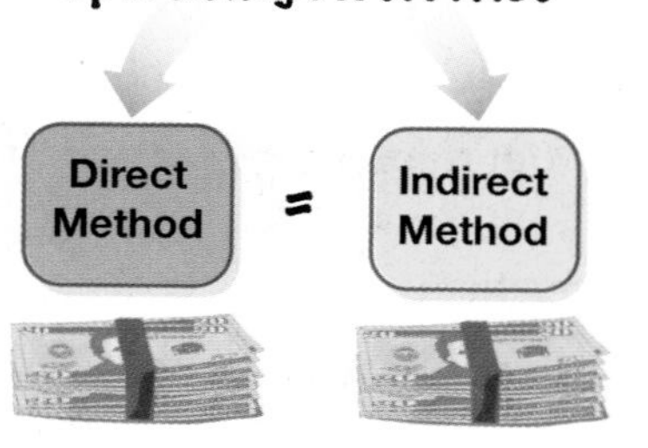

The **direct method** reports operating cash inflows (receipts) and cash outflows (payments) as follows:

Cash flows from operating activities:		
Cash received from customers		$XXX
Less: Cash payments for merchandise	$XXX	
Cash payments for operating expenses	XXX	
Cash payments for interest	XXX	
Cash payments for income taxes	XXX	XXX
Net cash flows from operating activities		$XXX

The primary operating cash inflow is cash received from customers. The primary operating cash outflows are cash payments for merchandise, operating expenses, interest, and income tax payments. The cash received less the cash payments is the net cash flow from operating activities.

The primary advantage of the direct method is that it *directly* reports cash receipts and payments in the statement of cash flows. Its primary disadvantage is that these data may not be readily available in the accounting records. Thus, the direct method is normally more costly to use and, as a result, is used by less than 1% of companies.[2]

The **indirect method** reports operating cash flows by beginning with net income and adjusting it for revenues and expenses that do not involve the receipt or payment of cash as follows:

Cash flows from operating activities:		
Net income	$XXX	
Adjustments to reconcile net income to net cash flow from operating activities	XXX	
Net cash flow from operating activities		$XXX

The adjustments to reconcile net income to net cash flow from operating activities include such items as depreciation and gains (or losses) on fixed assets. Changes in current operating assets and liabilities such as accounts receivable or accounts payable are also added or deducted depending on their effect on cash flows. In effect, these additions and deductions adjust net income, which is reported on an accrual accounting basis, to cash flows from operating activities, which uses a cash basis.

A primary advantage of the indirect method is that it reconciles the differences between net income and net cash flows from operations. In doing so, it shows how net income is related to the ending cash balance that is reported on the balance sheet.

Because the data are readily available, the indirect method is less costly to use than the direct method. As a result, over 99% of companies use the indirect method of reporting cash flows from operations.

netsolutions

Exhibit 2 illustrates the Cash Flows from Operating Activities section of the statement of cash flows for **NetSolutions**. Exhibit 2 shows the direct and indirect methods using the **NetSolutions** data from Chapter 1. As Exhibit 2 illustrates, both methods report the same amount of net cash flow from operating activities, $2,900.

Exhibit 2

Cash Flow from Operations: Direct and Indirect Methods—NetSolutions

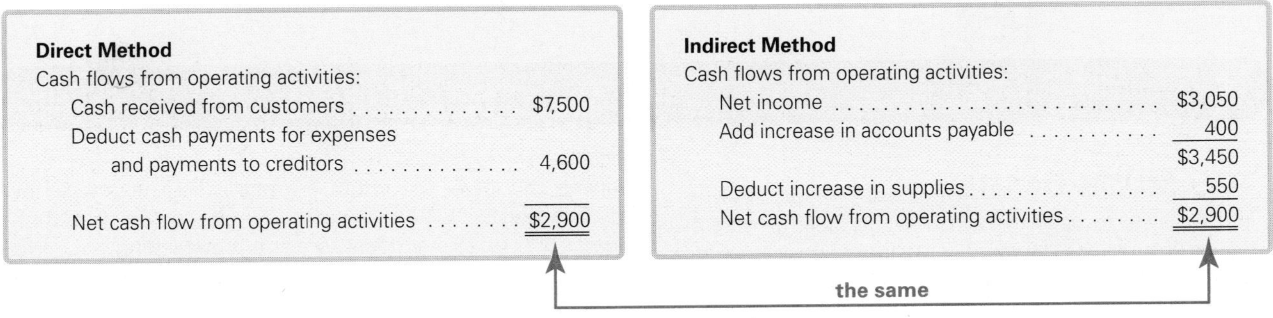

Direct Method	
Cash flows from operating activities:	
Cash received from customers	$7,500
Deduct cash payments for expenses and payments to creditors	4,600
Net cash flow from operating activities	$2,900

Indirect Method	
Cash flows from operating activities:	
Net income	$3,050
Add increase in accounts payable	400
	$3,450
Deduct increase in supplies	550
Net cash flow from operating activities	$2,900

In Chapter 1, the direct method was used to report **NetSolutions'** statement of cash flows. This is because the indirect method requires an understanding of the accrual accounting concepts such as depreciation, which had yet to be covered in Chapter 1.

2 *Accounting Trends & Techniques*, AICPA, 2007 edition.

Cash Flows from Investing Activities

The Walt Disney Company recently invested $1.1 billion in parks, resorts, and other properties, including two new cruise ships and new attractions at Disneyland.

Cash flows from investing activities are reported on the statement of cash flows as follows:

Cash flows from investing activities:		
Cash inflows from investing activities	$XXX	
Less cash used for investing activities	XXX	
Net cash flows from investing activities		$XXX

Cash inflows from investing activities normally arise from selling fixed assets, investments, and intangible assets. Cash outflows normally include payments to purchase fixed assets, investments, and intangible assets.

Cash Flows from Financing Activities

Cash flows from financing activities are reported on the statement of cash flows as follows:

Cash flows from financing activities:		
Cash inflows from financing activities	$XXX	
Less cash used for financing activities	XXX	
Net cash flows from financing activities		$XXX

Cash inflows from financing activities normally arise from issuing debt or equity securities. For example, issuing bonds, notes payable, preferred stock, and common stock creates cash inflows from financing activities. Cash outflows from financing activities include paying cash dividends, repaying debt, and acquiring treasury stock.

Noncash Investing and Financing Activities

Google disclosed the issuance of over $25 million in common stock for business acquisitions in its statement of cash flows as a noncash investing and financing activity.

A company may enter into transactions involving investing and financing activities that do not *directly* affect cash. For example, a company may issue common stock to retire long-term debt. Although this transaction does not directly affect cash, it does eliminate future cash payments for interest and for paying the bonds when they mature. Because such transactions *indirectly* affect cash flows, they are reported in a separate section of the statement of cash flows. This section usually appears at the bottom of the statement of cash flows.

Business Connection

TOO MUCH CASH!

Is it possible to have too much cash? Clearly, most of us would answer no. However, a business views cash differently than an individual. Naturally, a business needs cash to develop and launch new products, expand markets, purchase plant and equipment, and acquire other businesses. However, some businesses have built up huge cash balances beyond even these needs. For example, both Microsoft Corporation and Dell Inc. have accumulated billions of dollars in cash and temporary investments, totaling in excess of 60% of their total assets. Such large cash balances can lower the return on total assets. As stated by one analyst, "When a company sits on cash (which earns 1% or 2%) and leaves equity outstanding . . ., it is tantamount to taking a loan at 15% and investing in a passbook savings account that earns 2%—it destroys value." So while having too much cash is a good problem to have, companies like Microsoft, Cisco Systems, Inc., IBM, Apple Computer Inc., and Dell are under pressure to pay dividends or repurchase common stock. For example, Microsoft declared a $32 billion special dividend to return cash to its shareholders.

No Cash Flow per Share

Cash flow per share is sometimes reported in the financial press. As reported, cash flow per share is normally computed as *cash flow from operations per share.* However, such reporting may be misleading because of the following:

1. Users may misinterpret cash flow per share as the per-share amount available for dividends. This would not be the case if the cash generated by operations is required for repaying loans or for reinvesting in the business.
2. Users may misinterpret cash flow per share as equivalent to (or better than) earnings per share.

For these reasons, the financial statements, including the statement of cash flows, should not report cash flow per share.

Example Exercise 16-1 Classifying Cash Flows

1

Identify whether each of the following would be reported as an operating, investing, or financing activity in the statement of cash flows.

a. Purchase of patent
b. Payment of cash dividend
c. Disposal of equipment
d. Cash sales
e. Purchase of treasury stock
f. Payment of wages expense

Follow My Example 16-1

a. Investing
b. Financing
c. Investing
d. Operating
e. Financing
f. Operating

For Practice: PE 16-1A, PE 16-1B

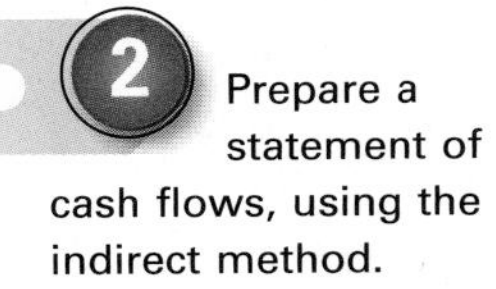

Prepare a statement of cash flows, using the indirect method.

Statement of Cash Flows— The Indirect Method

The indirect method of reporting cash flows from operating activities uses the logic that a change in any balance sheet account (including cash) can be analyzed in terms of changes in the other balance sheet accounts. Thus, by analyzing changes in noncash balance sheet accounts, any change in the cash account can be *indirectly* determined.

To illustrate, the accounting equation can be solved for cash as shown below.

Assets = Liabilities + Stockholders' Equity
Cash + Noncash Assets = Liabilities + Stockholders' Equity
Cash = Liabilities + Stockholders' Equity − Noncash Assets

Therefore, any change in the cash account can be determined by analyzing changes in the liability, stockholders' equity, and noncash asset accounts as shown below.

Change in Cash = *Change* in Liabilities + *Change* in Stockholders' Equity
− *Change* in Noncash Assets

Under the indirect method, there is no order in which the balance sheet accounts must be analyzed. However, net income (or net loss) is the first amount reported on the statement of cash flows. Since net income (or net loss) is a component of any change in Retained Earnings, the first account normally analyzed is Retained Earnings.

To illustrate the indirect method, the income statement and comparative balance sheets for Rundell Inc. shown in Exhibit 3 are used. Ledger accounts and

Exhibit 3

Income Statement and Comparative Balance Sheet

Rundell Inc.
Income Statement
For the Year Ended December 31, 2010

Sales		$1,180,000
Cost of merchandise sold		790,000
Gross profit		$ 390,000
Operating expenses:		
Depreciation expense	$ 7,000	
Other operating expenses	196,000	
Total operating expenses		203,000
Income from operations		$ 187,000
Other income:		
Gain on sale of land	$ 12,000	
Other expense:		
Interest expense	8,000	4,000
Income before income tax		$ 191,000
Income tax expense		83,000
Net income		$ 108,000

Rundell Inc.
Comparative Balance Sheet
December 31, 2010 and 2009

	2010	2009	Increase Decrease*
Assets			
Cash	$ 97,500	$ 26,000	$ 71,500
Accounts receivable (net)	74,000	65,000	9,000
Inventories	172,000	180,000	8,000*
Land	80,000	125,000	45,000*
Building	260,000	200,000	60,000
Accumulated depreciation—building	(65,300)	(58,300)	7,000
Total assets	$618,200	$537,700	$ 80,500
Liabilities			
Accounts payable (merchandise creditors)	$ 43,500	$ 46,700	$ 3,200*
Accrued expenses payable (operating expenses)	26,500	24,300	2,200
Income taxes payable	7,900	8,400	500*
Dividends payable	14,000	10,000	4,000
Bonds payable	100,000	150,000	50,000*
Total liabilities	$191,900	$239,400	$ 47,500*
Stockholders' Equity			
Common stock ($2 par)	$ 24,000	$ 16,000	$ 8,000
Paid-in capital in excess of par	120,000	80,000	40,000
Retained earnings	282,300	202,300	80,000
Total stockholders' equity	$426,300	$298,300	$128,000
Total liabilities and stockholders' equity	$618,200	$537,700	$ 80,500

other data supporting the income statement and balance sheet are presented as needed.[3]

Retained Earnings

The comparative balance sheet for Rundell Inc. shows that retained earnings increased $80,000 during the year. The retained earnings account shown below indicates how this change occurred.

Account *Retained Earnings*					Account No.	
					Balance	
Date		**Item**	**Debit**	**Credit**	**Debit**	**Credit**
2010						
Jan.	1	Balance				202,300
Dec.	31	Net income		108,000		310,300
	31	Cash dividends	28,000			282,300

The retained earnings account indicates that the $80,000 ($108,000 – $28,000) change resulted from net income of $108,000 and cash dividends of $28,000. The net income of $108,000 is the first amount reported in the Cash Flows from Operating Activities section.

Adjustments to Net Income

The net income of $108,000 reported by Rundell Inc. does not equal the cash flows from operating activities for the period. This is because net income is determined using the accrual method of accounting.

Under the accrual method of accounting, revenues and expenses are recorded at different times from when cash is received or paid. For example, merchandise may be sold on account and the cash received at a later date. Likewise, insurance premiums may be paid in the current period, but expensed in a following period.

Thus, under the indirect method, adjustments to net income must be made to determine cash flows from operating activities. The typical adjustments to net income are shown in Exhibit 4.[4]

Net income is normally adjusted to cash flows from operating activities using the following steps:

Step 1. Expenses that do not affect cash are added. Such expenses decrease net income, but did not involve cash payments and, thus, are added to net income.

Examples: *Depreciation* of fixed assets and *amortization* of intangible assets are added to net income.

3 An appendix that discusses using a spreadsheet (work sheet) as an aid in assembling data for the statement of cash flows is presented at the end of this chapter. This appendix illustrates the use of this spreadsheet in reporting cash flows from operating activities using the indirect method.

4 Other items that also require adjustments to net income to obtain cash flows from operating activities include amortization of bonds payable discounts (add), losses on debt retirement (add), amortization of bonds payable premiums (deduct), and gains on retirement of debt (deduct).

Exhibit 4

Adjustments to Net Income (Loss) Using the Indirect Method

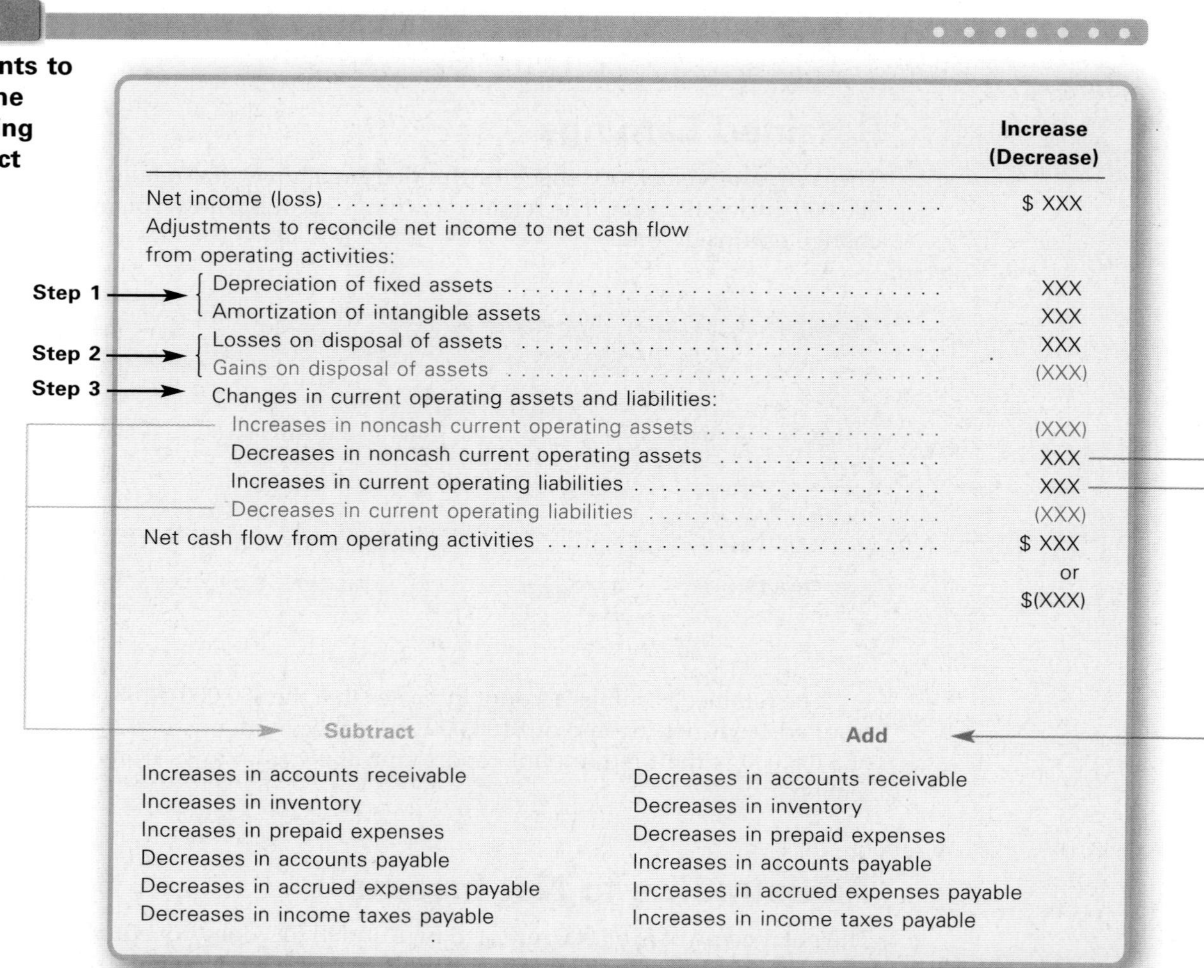

	Increase (Decrease)
Net income (loss)	$ XXX
Adjustments to reconcile net income to net cash flow from operating activities:	
Step 1 → Depreciation of fixed assets	XXX
Amortization of intangible assets	XXX
Step 2 → Losses on disposal of assets	XXX
Gains on disposal of assets	(XXX)
Step 3 → Changes in current operating assets and liabilities:	
Increases in noncash current operating assets	(XXX)
Decreases in noncash current operating assets	XXX
Increases in current operating liabilities	XXX
Decreases in current operating liabilities	(XXX)
Net cash flow from operating activities	$ XXX or $(XXX)

Subtract	Add
Increases in accounts receivable	Decreases in accounts receivable
Increases in inventory	Decreases in inventory
Increases in prepaid expenses	Decreases in prepaid expenses
Decreases in accounts payable	Increases in accounts payable
Decreases in accrued expenses payable	Increases in accrued expenses payable
Decreases in income taxes payable	Increases in income taxes payable

Step 2. Losses and gains on disposal of assets are added or deducted. The disposal (sale) of assets is an investing activity rather than an operating activity. However, such losses and gains are reported as part of net income. As a result, any *losses* on disposal of assets are *added* back to net income. Likewise, any *gains* on disposal of assets are *deducted* from net income.

Example: Land costing $100,000 is sold for $90,000. The loss of $10,000 is added back to net income.

Step 3. Changes in current operating assets and liabilities are added or deducted as follows:

Increases in noncash current operating assets are deducted.
Decreases in noncash current operating assets are added.
Increases in current operating liabilities are added.
Decreases in current operating liabilities are deducted.

Example: A sale of $10,000 on account increases accounts receivable by $10,000. However, cash is not affected. Thus, an increase in accounts receivable of $10,000 is deducted. Similar adjustments are required for the changes in the other current asset and liability accounts such as inventory, prepaid expenses, accounts payable, accrued expenses payable, and income taxes payable as shown in Exhibit 4.

Example Exercise 16-2 Adjustments to Net Income—Indirect Method

Omni Corporation's accumulated depreciation increased by $12,000, while, $3,400 of patents were amortized between balance sheet dates. There were no purchases or sales of depreciable or intangible assets during the year. In addition, the income statement showed a gain of $4,100 from the sale of land. Reconcile a net income of $50,000 to net cash flow from operating activities.

Follow My Example 16-2

Net income	$50,000
Adjustments to reconcile net income to net cash flow from operating activities:	
Depreciation	12,000
Amortization of patents	3,400
Gain from sale of land	(4,100)
Net cash flow from operating activities	$61,300

For Practice: PE 16-2A, PE 16-2B

To illustrate, the cash flows from operating activities section of Rundell's statement of cash flows is shown in Exhibit 5. Rundell's net income of $108,000 is converted to cash flows from operating activities of $100,500 as follows:

Exhibit 5

Cash Flows from Operating Activities—Indirect Method

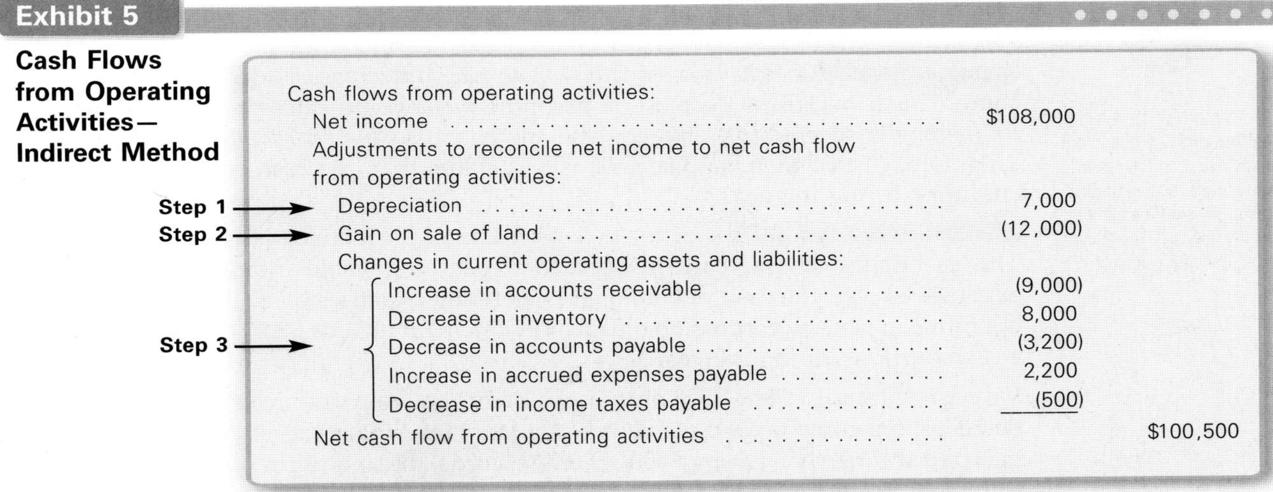

	Cash flows from operating activities:		
	Net income		$108,000
	Adjustments to reconcile net income to net cash flow from operating activities:		
Step 1 →	Depreciation	7,000	
Step 2 →	Gain on sale of land	(12,000)	
	Changes in current operating assets and liabilities:		
Step 3 →	Increase in accounts receivable	(9,000)	
	Decrease in inventory	8,000	
	Decrease in accounts payable	(3,200)	
	Increase in accrued expenses payable	2,200	
	Decrease in income taxes payable	(500)	
	Net cash flow from operating activities		$100,500

Step 1. Add depreciation of $7,000.

Analysis: The comparative balance sheet in Exhibit 3 indicates that Accumulated Depreciation—Building increased by $7,000. The account, shown below, indicates that depreciation for the year was $7,000 for the building.

Account *Accumulated Depreciation—Building* Account No.

Date		Item	Debit	Credit	Balance Debit	Balance Credit
2010						
Jan.	1	Balance				58,300
Dec.	31	Depreciation for year		7,000		65,300

Step 2. Deduct the gain on the sale of land of $12,000.

Analysis: The income statement in Exhibit 3 reports a gain from the sale of land of $12,000. The proceeds, which include the gain, are reported in the Investing section of the statement of cash flows.[5] Thus, the gain of $12,000 is deducted from net income in determining cash flows from operating activities.

Step 3. Add and deduct changes in current operating assets and liabilities.

Analysis: The increases and decreases in the current operating asset and current liability accounts are shown below.

	December 31		Increase
Accounts	**2010**	**2009**	**Decrease***
Accounts Receivable (net)	$ 74,000	$ 65,000	$9,000
Inventories	172,000	180,000	8,000*
Accounts Payable (merchandise creditors)	43,500	46,700	3,200*
Accrued Expenses Payable (operating expenses)	26,500	24,300	2,200
Income Taxes Payable	7,900	8,400	500*

Accounts receivable (net): The $9,000 increase is deducted from net income. This is because the $9,000 increase in accounts receivable indicates that sales on account were $9,000 more than the cash received from customers. Thus, sales (and net income) includes $9,000 that was not received in cash during the year.

Inventories: The $8,000 decrease is added to net income. This is because the $8,000 decrease in inventories indicates that the cost of merchandise *sold* exceeds the cost of the merchandise *purchased* during the year by $8,000. In other words, cost of merchandise sold includes $8,000 that was not purchased (used cash) during the year.

Ford Motor Company had a net loss of $12.6 billion but a positive cash flow from operating activities of $3.3 billion. This difference was mostly due to $16.5 billion of depreciation expenses.

Accounts payable (merchandise creditors): The $3,200 decrease is deducted from net income. This is because a decrease in accounts payable indicates that the cash *payments* to merchandise creditors exceeds the merchandise *purchased on account* by $3,200. Therefore, cost of merchandise sold is $3,200 less than the cash paid to merchandise creditors during the year.

Accrued expenses payable (operating expenses): The $2,200 increase is added to net income. This is because an increase in accrued expenses payable indicates that operating expenses exceed the cash payments for operating expenses by $2,200. In other words, operating expenses reported on the income statement include $2,200 that did not require a cash outflow during the year.

Income taxes payable: The $500 decrease is deducted from net income. This is because a decrease in income taxes payable indicates that taxes paid exceed the amount of taxes incurred during the year by $500. In other words, the amount reported on the income statement for income tax expense is less than the amount paid by $500.

Example Exercise 16-3 Changes in Current Operating Assets and Liabilities—Indirect Method 2

Victor Corporation's comparative balance sheet for current assets and liabilities was as follows:

	Dec. 31, 2011	Dec. 31, 2010
Accounts receivable	$ 6,500	$ 4,900
Inventory	12,300	15,000
Accounts payable	4,800	5,200
Dividends payable	5,000	4,000

Adjust net income of $70,000 for changes in operating assets and liabilities to arrive at cash flows from operating activities.

(continued)

5 The reporting of the proceeds (cash flows) from the sale of land as part of investing activities is discussed later in this chapter.

Follow My Example 16-3

Net income	$70,000
Adjustments to reconcile net income to net cash flow from operating activities:	
Changes in current operating assets and liabilities:	
Increase in accounts receivable	(1,600)
Decrease in inventory	2,700
Decrease in accounts payable	(400)
Net cash flow from operating activities	$70,700

For Practice: PE 16-3A, PE 16-3B

Using the preceding analyses, Rundell's net income of $108,000 is converted to cash flows from operating activities of $100,500 as shown in Exhibit 5, on page 719.

Exercise 16-4 Cash Flows from Operating Activities—Indirect Method

2

Omicron Inc. reported the following data:

Net income	$120,000
Depreciation expense	12,000
Loss on disposal of equipment	15,000
Increase in accounts receivable	5,000
Decrease in accounts payable	2,000

Prepare the Cash Flows from Operating Activities section of the statement of cash flows using the indirect method.

Follow My Example 16-4

Cash flows from operating activities:		
Net income	$120,000	
Adjustments to reconcile net income to net cash flow from operating activities:		
Depreciation expense	12,000	
Loss on disposal of equipment	15,000	
Changes in current operating assets and liabilities:		
Increase in accounts receivable	(5,000)	
Decrease in accounts payable	(2,000)	
Net cash flow from operating activities		$140,000

Note: The change in dividends payable impacts the cash paid for dividends, which is disclosed under financing activities.

For Practice: PE 16-4A, PE 16-4B

Integrity, Objectivity, and Ethics in Business

CREDIT POLICY AND CASH FLOW

One would expect customers to pay for products and services sold on account. Unfortunately, that is not always the case. Collecting accounts receivable efficiently is the key to turning a current asset into positive cash flow. Most entrepreneurs would rather think about the exciting aspects of their business—such as product development, marketing, sales, and advertising—rather than credit collection. This can be a mistake. Hugh McHugh of Overhill Flowers, Inc., decided that he would have no more trade accounts after dealing with Christmas orders that weren't paid for until late February, or sometimes not paid at all. As stated by one collection service, "One thing business owners always tell me is that they never thought about [collections] when they started their own business." To the small business owner, the collection of accounts receivable may mean the difference between succeeding and failing.

Source: Paulette Thomas, "Making Them Pay: The Last Thing Most Entrepreneurs Want to Think About Is Bill Collection; It Should Be One of the First Things," *The Wall Street Journal*, September 19, 2005, p. R6.

Dividends

The retained earnings account of Rundell Inc., shown on page 717, indicates cash dividends of $28,000 during the year. However, the dividends payable account, shown below, indicates that only $24,000 of the dividends was paid during the year.

Account *Dividends Payable* — Account No.

Date		Item	Debit	Credit	Balance Debit	Balance Credit
2010						
Jan.	1	Balance				10,000
	10	Cash paid	10,000		—	—
June	20	Dividends declared		14,000		14,000
July	10	Cash paid	14,000		—	—
Dec.	20	Dividends declared		14,000		14,000

Since dividend payments are a financing activity, the dividend payment of $24,000 is reported in the Financing Activities section of the statement of cash flows, as shown below.

Cash flows from financing activities:	
Cash paid for dividends	$24,000

Common Stock

XM Satellite Radio has had negative cash flows from operations for most of its young corporate life. However, it has been able to grow by obtaining cash from the sale of common stock and issuing debt.

The common stock account increased by $8,000, and the paid-in capital in excess of par—common stock account increased by $40,000, as shown below. These increases were from issuing 4,000 shares of common stock for $12 per share.

Account *Common Stock* — Account No.

Date		Item	Debit	Credit	Balance Debit	Balance Credit
2010						
Jan.	1	Balance				16,000
Nov.	1	4,000 shares issued for cash		8,000		24,000

Account *Paid-In Capital in Excess of Par—Common Stock* — Account No.

Date		Item	Debit	Credit	Balance Debit	Balance Credit
2010						
Jan.	1	Balance				80,000
Nov.	1	4,000 shares issued for cash		40,000		120,000

This cash inflow is reported in the Financing Activities section as follows:

Cash flows from financing activities:	
Cash received from sale of common stock	$48,000

Bonds Payable

The bonds payable account decreased by $50,000, as shown below. This decrease is from retiring the bonds by a cash payment for their face amount.

Account *Bonds Payable* — Account No.

Date		Item	Debit	Credit	Balance Debit	Balance Credit
2010						
Jan.	1	Balance				150,000
June	30	Retired by payment of cash at face amount	50,000			100,000

This cash outflow is reported in the Financing Activities section as follows:

Cash flows from financing activities:
Cash paid to retire bonds payable $50,000

Building

The building account increased by $60,000, and the accumulated depreciation—building account increased by $7,000, as shown below.

Account *Building* — Account No.

Date		Item	Debit	Credit	Balance Debit	Balance Credit
2010						
Jan.	1	Balance			200,000	
Dec.	27	Purchased for cash	60,000		260,000	

Account *Accumulated Depreciation—Building* — Account No.

Date		Item	Debit	Credit	Balance Debit	Balance Credit
2010						
Jan.	1	Balance				58,300
Dec.	31	Depreciation for the year		7,000		65,300

The purchase of a building for cash of $60,000 is reported as an outflow of cash in the Investing Activities section as follows:

Cash flows from investing activities:
Cash paid for purchase of building $60,000

The credit in the accumulated depreciation—building account represents depreciation expense for the year. This depreciation expense of $7,000 on the building was added to net income in determining cash flows from operating activities, as reported in Exhibit 5, on page 719.

Land

The $45,000 decline in the land account was from two transactions, as shown below.

Account *Land*					Account No.	
					Balance	
Date		**Item**	**Debit**	**Credit**	**Debit**	**Credit**
2010						
Jan.	1	Balance			125,000	
June	8	Sold for $72,000 cash		60,000	65,000	
Oct.	12	Purchased for $15,000 cash	15,000		80,000	

The June 8 transaction is the sale of land with a cost of $60,000 for $72,000 in cash. The $72,000 proceeds from the sale are reported in the Investing Activities section, as follows:

Cash flows from investing activities:
Cash received from sale of land $72,000

The proceeds of $72,000 include the $12,000 gain on the sale of land and the $60,000 cost (book value) of the land. As shown in Exhibit 5, on page 719, the $12,000 gain is deducted from net income in the Cash Flows from Operating Activities section. This is so that the $12,000 cash inflow related to the gain is not included twice as a cash inflow.

The October 12 transaction is the purchase of land for cash of $15,000. This transaction is reported as an outflow of cash in the Investing Activities section, as follows:

Cash flows from investing activities:
Cash paid for purchase of land $15,000

Example Exercise 16-5 Land Transactions on the Statement of Cash Flows

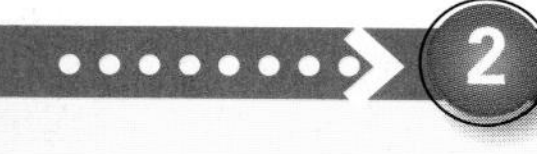

Alpha Corporation purchased land for $125,000. Later in the year, the company sold land with a book value of $165,000 for $200,000. How are the effects of these transactions reported on the statement of cash flows?

Follow My Example 16-5

The gain on sale of land is deducted from net income as shown below.
Gain on sale of land . . . . $ (35,000)

The purchase and sale of land is reported as part of cash flows from investing activities as shown below.
Cash received for sale of land 200,000
Cash paid for purchase of land . . . . (125,000)

For Practice: PE 16-5A, PE 16-5B

Preparing the Statement of Cash Flows

The statement of cash flows for Rundell Inc. using the indirect method is shown in Exhibit 6. The statement of cash flows indicates that cash increased by $71,500 during the year. The most significant increase in net cash flows ($100,500) was from operating activities. The most significant use of cash ($26,000) was for financing activities. The ending balance of cash on December 31, 2010, is $97,500. This ending cash balance is also reported on the December 31, 2010, balance sheet shown in Exhibit 3, on page 716.

Exhibit 6

Statement of Cash Flows—Indirect Method

Rundell Inc. Statement of Cash Flows For the Year Ended December 31, 2010			
Cash flows from operating activities:			
Net income		$108,000	
Adjustments to reconcile net income to net cash flow from operating activities:			
Depreciation		7,000	
Gain on sale of land		(12,000)	
Changes in current operating assets and liabilities:			
Increase in accounts receivable		(9,000)	
Decrease in inventory		8,000	
Decrease in accounts payable		(3,200)	
Increase in accrued expenses payable		2,200	
Decrease in income taxes payable		(500)	
Net cash flow from operating activities			$100,500
Cash flows from investing activities:			
Cash from sale of land		$ 72,000	
Less: Cash paid to purchase land	$15,000		
Cash paid for purchase of building	60,000	75,000	
Net cash flow used for investing activities			(3,000)
Cash flows from financing activities:			
Cash received from sale of common stock		$ 48,000	
Less: Cash paid to retire bonds payable	$50,000		
Cash paid for dividends	24,000	74,000	
Net cash flow used for financing activities			(26,000)
Increase in cash			$ 71,500
Cash at the beginning of the year			26,000
Cash at the end of the year			$ 97,500

Prepare a statement of cash flows, using the direct method.

Statement of Cash Flows—The Direct Method

The direct method reports cash flows from operating activities as follows:

Cash flows from operating activities:		
Cash received from customers		$XXX
Less: Cash payments for merchandise	$XXX	
Cash payments for operating expenses	XXX	
Cash payments for interest	XXX	
Cash payments for income taxes	XXX	XXX
Net cash flows from operating activities		$XXX

The Cash Flows from Investing and Financing Activities sections of the statement of cash flows are the same under the direct and indirect methods. The amount of cash flows from operating activities is also the same.

Under the direct method, the income statement is adjusted to cash flows from operating activities as follows:

Income Statement	Adjusted to	Cash Flows from Operating Activities
Sales	→	Cash received from customers
Cost of merchandise sold	→	Cash payments for merchandise
Operating expenses:		
Depreciation expense	N/A	N/A
Other operating expenses	→	Cash payments for operating expenses
Gain on sale of land	N/A	N/A
Interest expense	→	Cash payments for interest
Income tax expense	→	Cash payments for income taxes
Net income	→	Cash flows from operating activities

N/A—Not applicable

As shown above, depreciation expense is not adjusted or reported as part of cash flows from operating activities. This is because deprecation expense does not involve a cash outflow. The gain on sale of land is also not adjusted or reported as part of cash flows from operating activities. This is because the sale of land is reported as an investing activity rather than an operating activity.

To illustrate the direct method, the income statement and comparative balance sheet for Rundell Inc. shown in Exhibit 3, on page 716, are used.

Cash Received from Customers

The income statement (shown in Exhibit 3) of Rundell Inc. reports sales of $1,180,000. To determine the *cash received from customers*, the $1,180,000 is adjusted for any increase or decrease in accounts receivable. The adjustment is summarized below.

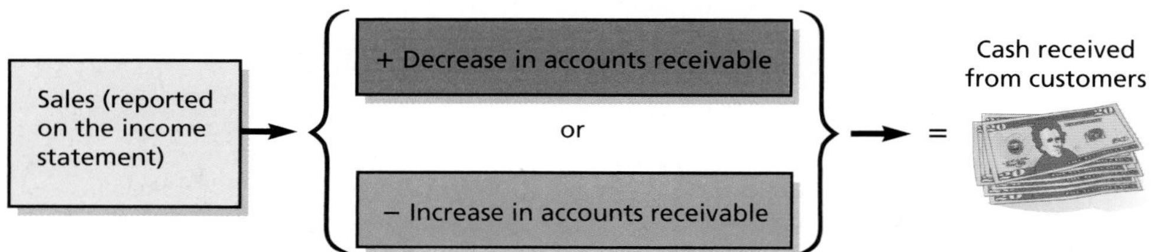

The cash received from customers is $1,171,000, computed as follows:

Sales	$1,180,000
Less increase in accounts receivable	9,000
Cash received from customers	$1,171,000

The increase of $9,000 in accounts receivable (shown in Exhibit 3) during 2010 indicates that sales on account exceeded cash received from customers by $9,000. In other words, sales include $9,000 that did not result in a cash inflow during the year. Thus, $9,000 is deducted from sales to determine the *cash received from customers*.

Example Exercise 16-6 Cash Received from Customers—Direct Method

Sales reported on the income statement were $350,000. The accounts receivable balance declined $8,000 over the year. Determine the amount of cash received from customers.

Follow My Example 16-6

Sales	$350,000
Add decrease in accounts receivable	8,000
Cash received from customers	$358,000

For Practice: PE 16-6A, PE 16-6B

Cash Payments for Merchandise

The income statement (shown in Exhibit 3) for Rundell Inc. reports cost of merchandise sold of $790,000. To determine the *cash payments for merchandise,* the $790,000 is adjusted for any increases or decreases in inventories and accounts payable. Assuming the accounts payable are owed to merchandise suppliers, the adjustment is summarized below.

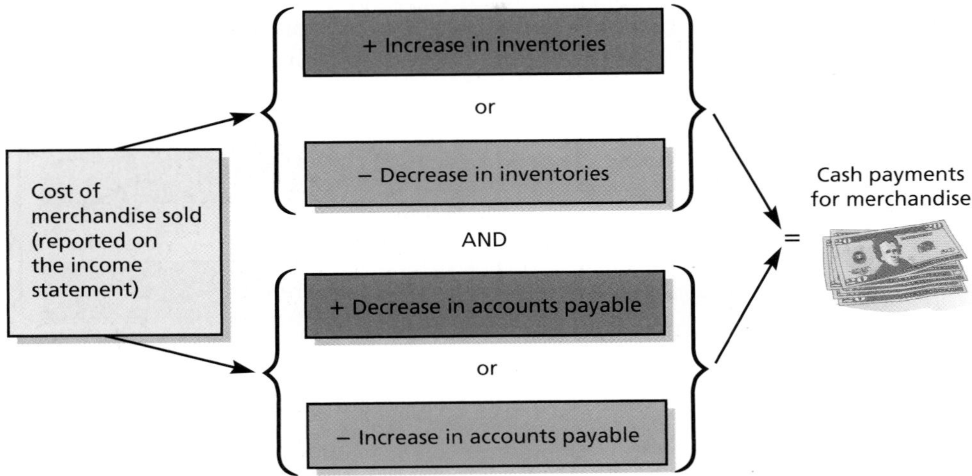

The cash payments for merchandise are $785,200, computed as follows:

Cost of merchandise sold	$790,000
Deduct decrease in inventories	(8,000)
Add decrease in accounts payable	3,200
Cash payments for merchandise	$785,200

The $8,000 decrease in inventories (from Exhibit 3) indicates that the merchandise sold exceeded the cost of the merchandise purchased by $8,000. In other words, cost of merchandise sold includes $8,000 that did not require a cash outflow during the year. Thus, $8,000 is deducted from the cost of merchandise sold in determining the *cash payments for merchandise.*

The $3,200 decrease in accounts payable (from Exhibit 3) indicates that cash payments for merchandise were $3,200 more than the purchases on account during 2010. Therefore, $3,200 is added to the cost of merchandise sold in determining the *cash payments for merchandise.*

Example Exercise 16-7 Cash Payments for Merchandise—Direct Method

Cost of merchandise sold reported on the income statement was $145,000. The accounts payable balance increased $4,000, and the inventory balance increased by $9,000 over the year. Determine the amount of cash paid for merchandise.

Follow My Example 16-7

Cost of merchandise sold	$145,000
Add increase in inventories	9,000
Deduct increase in accounts payable	(4,000)
Cash paid for merchandise	$150,000

For Practice: PE 16-7A, PE 16-7B

Cash Payments for Operating Expenses

The income statement (from Exhibit 3) for Rundell Inc. reports total operating expenses of $203,000, which includes depreciation expense of $7,000. Since depreciation expense does not require a cash outflow, it is omitted from *cash payments for operating expenses*.

To determine the *cash payments for operating expenses*, the other operating expenses (excluding depreciation) of $196,000 ($203,000 − $7,000) are adjusted for any increase or decrease in accrued expenses payable. Assuming that the accrued expenses payable are all operating expenses, this adjustment is summarized below.

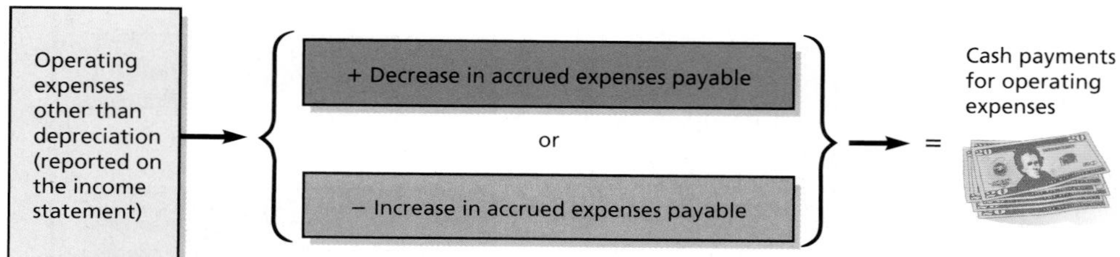

The cash payments for operating expenses is $193,800, computed as follows:

Operating expenses other than depreciation	$196,000
Deduct increase in accrued expenses payable	(2,200)
Cash payments for operating expenses	$193,800

The increase in accrued expenses payable (from Exhibit 3) indicates that the cash payments for operating expenses were $2,200 less than the amount reported for operating expenses during the year. Thus, $2,200 is deducted from the operating expenses in determining the *cash payments for operating expenses*.

Gain on Sale of Land

The income statement for Rundell Inc. (from Exhibit 3) reports a gain of $12,000 on the sale of land. The sale of land is an investing activity. Thus, the proceeds from the sale, which include the gain, are reported as part of the cash flows from investing activities.

Interest Expense

The income statement (from Exhibit 3) for Rundell Inc. reports interest expense of $8,000. To determine the *cash payments for interest*, the $8,000 is adjusted for any increases or decreases in interest payable. The adjustment is summarized below.

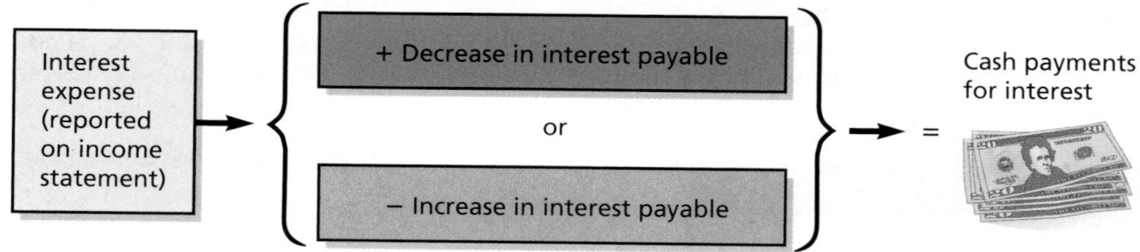

The comparative balance sheet of Rundell Inc. in Exhibit 3 indicates no interest payable. This is because the interest expense on the bonds payable is paid on June 1 and December 31. Since there is no interest payable, no adjustment of the interest expense of $8,000 is necessary.

Cash Payments for Income Taxes

The income statement (from Exhibit 3) for Rundell Inc. reports income tax expense of $83,000. To determine the *Cash payments for income taxes*, the $83,000 is adjusted for any increases or decreases in income taxes payable. The adjustment is summarized below.

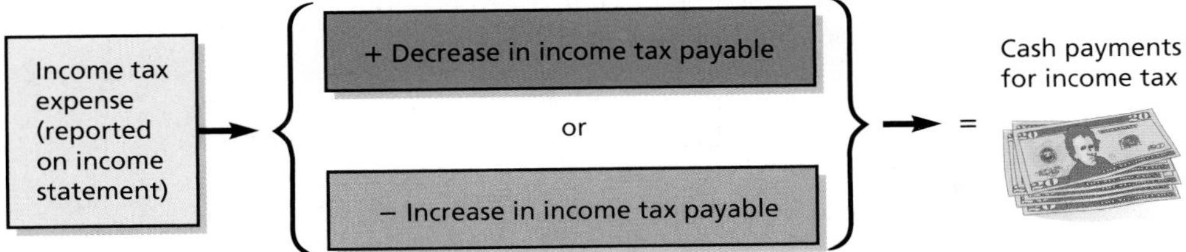

The cash payments for income taxes are $83,500, computed as follows:

Income tax expense	$83,000
Add decrease in income taxes payable	500
Cash payments for income taxes	$83,500

The $500 decrease in income taxes payable (from Exhibit 3) indicates that the cash payments for income taxes were $500 more than the amount reported for income tex expense during 2010. Thus, $500 is added to the income tax expense in determining the *cash payments for income taxes*.

Reporting Cash Flows from Operating Activities—Direct Method

The statement of cash flows for Rundell Inc. using the direct method for reporting cash flows from operating activities is shown in Exhibit 7. The portions of the

Exhibit 7

Statement of Cash Flows—Direct Method

Rundell Inc.
Statement of Cash Flows
For the Year Ended December 31, 2010

Cash flows from operating activities:			
Cash received from customers		$1,171,000	
Deduct: Cash payments for merchandise	$785,200		
Cash payments for operating expenses	193,800		
Cash payments for interest	8,000		
Cash payments for income taxes	83,500	1,070,500	
Net cash flow from operating activities			$100,500
Cash flows from investing activities:			
Cash from sale of land		$ 72,000	
Less: Cash paid to purchase land	$ 15,000		
Cash paid for purchase of building	60,000	75,000	
Net cash flow used for investing activities			(3,000)
Cash flows from financing activities:			
Cash received from sale of common stock		$ 48,000	
Less: Cash paid to retire bonds payable	$ 50,000		
Cash paid for dividends	24,000	74,000	
Net cash flow used for financing activities			(26,000)
Increase in cash			$ 71,500
Cash at the beginning of the year			26,000
Cash at the end of the year			$ 97,500

(continued)

Exhibit 7

(concluded)

Schedule Reconciling Net Income with Cash Flows from Operating Activities:	
Cash flows from operating activities:	
Net income	$108,000
Adjustments to reconcile net income to net cash flow from operating activities:	
Depreciation	7,000
Gain on sale of land	(12,000)
Changes in current operating assets and liabilities:	
Increase in accounts receivable	(9,000)
Decrease in inventory	8,000
Decrease in accounts payable	(3,200)
Increase in accrued expenses payable	2,200
Decrease in income taxes payable	(500)
Net cash flow from operating activities	$100,500

statement that differ from those prepared under the indirect method are highlighted in color.

Exhibit 7 also includes the separate schedule reconciling net income and net cash flow from operating activities. This schedule is included in the statement of cash flows when the direct method is used. This schedule is similar to the Cash Flows from Operating Activities section prepared under the indirect method.

Financial Analysis and Interpretation

A valuable tool for evaluating the cash flows of a business is free cash flow. **Free cash flow** is a measure of operating cash flow available for corporate purposes after providing sufficient fixed asset additions to maintain current productive capacity. Thus, free cash flow can be calculated as follows:

Cash flow from operating activities	$XXX
Less: Investments in fixed assets to maintain current production	XXX
Free cash flow	$XXX

Analysts often use free cash flow, rather than cash flows from operating activities, to measure the financial strength of a business. Many high-technology firms must aggressively reinvest in new technology to remain competitive. This can reduce free cash flow. For example, Verizon Communications Inc.'s free cash flow is less than 30% of the cash flow from operating activities. In contrast, The Coca-Cola Company's free cash flow is approximately 75% of the cash flow from operating activities. Three nonfinancial companies with large free cash flows for a recent year were as follows:

	Free Cash Flow (in millions)
General Electric Company	$13,996
ExxonMobil Corporation	33,824
Microsoft Corporation	15,532

To illustrate, the cash flow from operating activities for Intuit Inc., the developer of TurboTax®, was $727 million in a recent fiscal year. The statement of cash flows indicated that the cash invested in property, plant, and equipment was $105 million. Assuming that the amount invested in property, plant, and equipment maintained existing operations, free cash flow would be calculated as follows (in millions):

Cash flow from operating activities	$727
Less: Investments in fixed assets to maintain current production	105
Free cash flow	$622

During this period, Intuit generated free cash flow in excess of $600 million, which was 86% of cash flows from operations and over 23% of sales.

Positive free cash flow is considered favorable. A company that has free cash flow is able to fund internal growth, retire debt, pay dividends, and enjoy financial flexibility. A company with no free cash flow is unable to maintain current productive capacity. Lack of free cash flow can be an early indicator of liquidity problems. As stated by one analyst, "Free cash flow gives the company firepower to reduce debt and ultimately generate consistent, actual income."[6]

Source: "CFO Free Cash Flow Scorecard," *CFO Magazine*, January 1, 2005.

6 Jill Krutick, *Fortune*, March 30, 1998, p. 106.

APPENDIX

Spreadsheet (Work Sheet) for Statement of Cash Flows— The Indirect Method

A spreadsheet (work sheet) may used in preparing the statement of cash flows. However, whether or not a spreadsheet (work sheet) is used, the concepts presented in this chapter are not affected.

The data for Rundell Inc., presented in Exhibit 3, are used as a basis for illustrating the spreadsheet (work sheet) for the indirect method. The steps in preparing this spreadsheet (work sheet), shown in Exhibit 8, are as follows:

Step 1. List the title of each balance sheet account in the Accounts column.

Step 2. For each balance sheet account, enter its balance as of December 31, 2009, in the first column and its balance as of December 31, 2010, in the last column. Place the credit balances in parentheses.

Step 3. Add the December 31, 2009 and 2010 column totals, which should total to zero.

Step 4. Analyze the change during the year in each noncash account to determine its net increase (decrease) and classify the change as affecting cash flows from operating activities, investing activities, financing activities, or noncash investing and financing activities.

Step 5. Indicate the effect of the change on cash flows by making entries in the Transactions columns.

Step 6. After all noncash accounts have been analyzed, enter the net increase (decrease) in cash during the period.

Step 7. Add the Debit and Credit Transactions columns. The totals should be equal.

Analyzing Accounts

In analyzing the noncash accounts (Step 4), try to determine the type of cash flow activity (operating, investing, or financing) that led to the change in account. As each noncash account is analyzed, an entry (Step 5) is made on the spreadsheet (work sheet) for the type of cash flow activity that caused the change. After all noncash accounts have been analyzed, an entry (Step 6) is made for the increase (decrease) in cash during the period.

The entries made on the spreadsheet are not posted to the ledger. They are only used in preparing and summarizing the data on the spreadsheet.

The order in which the accounts are analyzed is not important. However, it is more efficient to begin with Retained Earnings and proceed upward in the account listing.

Retained Earnings

The spreadsheet (work sheet) shows a Retained Earnings balance of $202,300 at December 31, 2009, and $282,300 at December 31, 2010. Thus, Retained Earnings increased $80,000 during the year. This increase is from the following:

1. Net income of $108,000
2. Declaring cash dividends of $28,000

To identify the cash flows from these activities, two entries are made on the spreadsheet.

The $108,000 is reported on the statement of cash flows as part of "cash flows from operating activities." Thus, an entry is made in the Transactions columns on the spreadsheet as follows:

(a)	Operating Activities—Net Income	108,000	
	Retained Earnings		108,000

The preceding entry accounts for the net income portion of the change to Retained Earnings. It also identifies the cash flow in the bottom portion of the spreadsheet as related to operating activities.

Exhibit 8

End-of-Period Spreadsheet (Work Sheet) for Statement of Cash Flows—Indirect Method

Step 2 (columns C–F)

	A	B	C	D	E	F	G
1	Rundell Inc.						
2	End-of-Period Spreadsheet (Work Sheet) for Statement of Cash Flows						
3	For the Year Ended December 31, 2010						
4	Accounts	Balance,		Transactions			Balance,
5		Dec. 31, 2009		Debit		Credit	Dec. 31, 2010
6	Cash	26,000	(o)	71,500			97,500
7	Accounts receivable (net)	65,000	(n)	9,000			74,000
8	Inventories	180,000			(m)	8,000	172,000
9	Land	125,000	(k)	15,000	(l)	60,000	80,000
10	Building	200,000	(j)	60,000			260,000
11	Accumulated depreciation—building	(58,300)			(i)	7,000	(65,300)
12	Accounts payable (merchandise creditors)	(46,700)	(h)	3,200			(43,500)
13	Accrued expenses payable (operating expenses)	(24,300)			(g)	2,200	(26,500)
14	Income taxes payable	(8,400)	(f)	500			(7,900)
15	Dividends payable	(10,000)			(e)	4,000	(14,000)
16	Bonds payable	(150,000)	(d)	50,000			(100,000)
17	Common stock	(16,000)			(c)	8,000	(24,000)
18	Paid-in capital in excess of par	(80,000)			(c)	40,000	(120,000)
19	Retained earnings	(202,300)	(b)	28,000	(a)	108,000	(282,300)
20	Totals (Step 3 →)	0		237,200		237,200	0 (← Step 3)
21	Operating activities:						
22	Net income		(a)	108,000			
23	Depreciation of building		(i)	7,000			
24	Gain on sale of land				(l)	12,000	
25	Increase in accounts receivable				(n)	9,000	
26	Decrease in inventories		(m)	8,000			
27	Decrease in accounts payable				(h)	3,200	
28	Increase in accrued expenses payable		(g)	2,200			
29	Decrease in income taxes payable				(f)	500	
30	Investing activities:						
31	Sale of land		(l)	72,000			
32	Purchase of land				(k)	15,000	
33	Purchase of building				(j)	60,000	
34	Financing activities:						
35	Issued common stock		(c)	48,000			
36	Retired bonds payable				(d)	50,000	
37	Declared cash dividends				(b)	28,000	
38	Increase in dividends payable		(e)	4,000			
39	Net increase in cash				(o)	71,500	
40	Totals			249,200		249,200	

Step 1 (rows 6–20)

Steps 4–7 (columns C–F, rows 21–40)

The $28,000 of dividends is reported as a financing activity on the statement of cash flows. Thus, an entry is made in the Transactions columns on the spreadsheet as follows:

	Account	Debit	Credit
(b)	Retained Earnings	28,000	
	Financing Activities—Declared Cash Dividends		28,000

The preceding entry accounts for the dividends portion of the change to Retained Earnings. It also identifies the cash flow in the bottom portion of the spreadsheet as related to financing activities. The $28,000 of declared dividends will be adjusted later for the actual amount of cash dividends paid during the year.

Other Accounts

The entries for the other noncash accounts are made in the spreadsheet in a manner similar to entries (a) and (b). A summary of these entries is as follows:

	Account	Debit	Credit
(c)	Financing Activities—Issued Common Stock	48,000	
	Common Stock		8,000
	Paid-In Capital in Excess of Par—Common Stock		40,000
(d)	Bonds Payable	50,000	
	Financing Activities—Retired Bonds Payable		50,000
(e)	Financing Activities—Increase in Dividends Payable	4,000	
	Dividends Payable		4,000
(f)	Income Taxes Payable	500	
	Operating Activities—Decrease in Income Taxes Payable		500
(g)	Operating Activities—Increase in Accrued Expenses Payable	2,200	
	Accrued Expenses Payable		2,200
(h)	Accounts Payable	3,200	
	Operating Activities—Decrease in Accounts Payable		3,200
(i)	Operating Activities—Depreciation of Building	7,000	
	Accumulated Depreciation—Building		7,000
(j)	Building	60,000	
	Investing Activities—Purchase of Building		60,000
(k)	Land	15,000	
	Investing Activities—Purchase of Land		15,000
(l)	Investing Activities—Sale of Land	72,000	
	Operating Activities—Gain on Sale of Land		12,000
	Land		60,000
(m)	Operating Activities—Decrease in Inventories	8,000	
	Inventories		8,000
(n)	Accounts Receivable	9,000	
	Operating Activities—Increase in Accounts Receivable		9,000
(o)	Cash	71,500	
	Net Increase in Cash		71,500

After all the balance sheet accounts are analyzed and the entries made on the spreadsheet (work sheet), all the operating, investing, and financing activities are identified in the bottom portion of the spread sheet. The accuracy of the entries is verified by totaling the Debit and Credit Transactions columns. The totals of the columns should be equal.

Preparing the Statement of Cash Flows

The statement of cash flows prepared from the spreadsheet is identical to the statement in Exhibit 6. The data for the three sections of the statement are obtained from the bottom portion of the spreadsheet.

1 Describe the cash flow activities reported in the statement of cash flows.

Key Points	Key Learning Outcomes	Example Exercises	Practice Exercises
The statement of cash flows reports cash receipts and cash payments by three types of activities: operating activities, investing activities, and financing activities. Investing and financing for a business may be affected by transactions that do not involve cash. The effect of such transactions should be reported in a separate schedule accompanying the statement of cash flows.	• Classify transactions that either provide or use cash into either operating, investing, or financing activities.	**16-1**	16-1A, 16-1B

2 Prepare a statement of cash flows, using the indirect method.

Key Points	Key Learning Outcomes	Example Exercises	Practice Exercises
The changes in the noncash balance sheet accounts are used to develop the statement of cash flows, beginning with the cash flows from operating activities.			
Determine the cash flows from operating activities using the indirect method by adjusting net income for expenses that do not require cash and for gains and losses from disposal of fixed assets.	• Adjust net income for noncash expenses and gains and losses from asset disposals under the indirect method.	**16-2**	16-2A, 16-2B
Determine the cash flows from operating activities using the indirect method by adjusting net income for changes in current operating assets and liabilities.	• Adjust net income for changes in current operating assets and liabilities under the indirect method.	**16-3**	16-3A, 16-3B
Report cash flows from operating activities under the indirect method.	• Prepare the cash flows from operating activities under the indirect method in proper form.	**16-4**	16-4A, 16-4B
Report investing and financing activities on the statement of cash flows.	• Prepare the remainder of the statement of cash flows by reporting investing and financing activities.	**16-5**	16-5A, 16-5B

3 Prepare a statement of cash flows, using the direct method.

Key Points	Key Learning Outcomes	Example Exercises	Practice Exercises
The direct method reports cash flows from operating activities by major classes of operating cash receipts and cash payments. The difference between the major classes of total operating cash receipts and total operating cash payments is the net cash flow from operating activities. The investing and financing activities sections of the statement are the same as under the indirect method.	• Prepare the cash flows from operating activities and the remainder of the statement of cash flows under the direct method.	**16-6** **16-7**	16-6A, 16-6B 16-7A, 16-7B

Key Terms

cash flow per share (715)
cash flows from financing activities (712)
cash flows from investing activities (712)
cash flows from operating activities (711)
direct method (712)
free cash flow (730)
indirect method (713)
statement of cash flows (711)

Illustrative Problem

The comparative balance sheet of Dowling Company for December 31, 2010 and 2009, is as follows:

Dowling Company
Comparative Balance Sheet
December 31, 2010 and 2009

	2010	2009
Assets		
Cash	$ 140,350	$ 95,900
Accounts receivable (net)	95,300	102,300
Inventories	165,200	157,900
Prepaid expenses	6,240	5,860
Investments (long-term)	35,700	84,700
Land	75,000	90,000
Buildings	375,000	260,000
Accumulated depreciation—buildings	(71,300)	(58,300)
Machinery and equipment	428,300	428,300
Accumulated depreciation—machinery and equipment	(148,500)	(138,000)
Patents	58,000	65,000
Total assets	$1,159,290	$1,093,660
Liabilities and Stockholders' Equity		
Accounts payable (merchandise creditors)	$ 43,500	$ 46,700
Accrued expenses payable (operating expenses)	14,000	12,500
Income taxes payable	7,900	8,400
Dividends payable	14,000	10,000
Mortgage note payable, due 2021	40,000	0
Bonds payable	150,000	250,000
Common stock, $30 par	450,000	375,000
Excess of issue price over par—common stock	66,250	41,250
Retained earnings	373,640	349,810
Total liabilities and stockholders' equity	$1,159,290	$1,093,660

The income statement for Dowling Company is shown here.

Dowling Company
Income Statement
For the Year Ended December 31, 2010

Sales		$1,100,000
Cost of merchandise sold		710,000
Gross profit		$ 390,000
Operating expenses:		
Depreciation expense	$ 23,500	
Patent amortization	7,000	
Other operating expenses	196,000	
Total operating expenses		226,500
Income from operations		$ 163,500
Other income:		
Gain on sale of investments	$ 11,000	
Other expense:		
Interest expense	26,000	(15,000)
Income before income tax		$ 148,500
Income tax expense		50,000
Net income		$ 98,500

An examination of the accounting records revealed the following additional information applicable to 2010:

a. Land costing $15,000 was sold for $15,000.
b. A mortgage note was issued for $40,000.
c. A building costing $115,000 was constructed.
d. 2,500 shares of common stock were issued at 40 in exchange for the bonds payable.
e. Cash dividends declared were $74,670.

Instructions

1. Prepare a statement of cash flows, using the indirect method of reporting cash flows from operating activities.
2. Prepare a statement of cash flows, using the direct method of reporting cash flows from operating activities.

Solution

1.

Dowling Company
Statement of Cash Flows—Indirect Method
For the Year Ended December 31, 2010

Cash flows from operating activities:			
Net income		$ 98,500	
Adjustments to reconcile net income to net cash flow from operating activities:			
Depreciation		23,500	
Amortization of patents		7,000	
Gain on sale of investments		(11,000)	
Changes in current operating assets and liabilities:			
Decrease in accounts receivable		7,000	
Increase in inventories		(7,300)	
Increase in prepaid expenses		(380)	
Decrease in accounts payable		(3,200)	
Increase in accrued expenses payable		1,500	
Decrease in income taxes payable		(500)	
Net cash flow from operating activities			$115,120
Cash flows from investing activities:			
Cash received from sale of:			
Investments	$60,000		
Land	15,000	$ 75,000	
Less: Cash paid for construction of building		115,000	
Net cash flow used for investing activities			(40,000)
Cash flows from financing activities:			
Cash received from issuing mortgage note payable		$ 40,000	
Less: Cash paid for dividends		70,670*	
Net cash flow used for financing activities			(30,670)
Increase in cash			$ 44,450
Cash at the beginning of the year			95,900
Cash at the end of the year			$140,350

Schedule of Noncash Investing and Financing Activities:

Issued common stock to retire bonds payable	$100,000

* $70,670 = $74,670 − $4,000 (increase in dividends)

2.

Dowling Company
Statement of Cash Flows—Direct Method
For the Year Ended December 31, 2010

Cash flows from operating activities:			
Cash received from customers[1]		$1,107,000	
Deduct: Cash paid for merchandise[2]	$720,500		
Cash paid for operating expenses[3]	194,880		
Cash paid for interest expense	26,000		
Cash paid for income tax[4]	50,500	991,880	
Net cash flow from operating activities			$115,120
Cash flows from investing activities:			
Cash received from sale of:			
Investments	$ 60,000		
Land	15,000	$ 75,000	
Less: Cash paid for construction of building		115,000	
Net cash flow used for investing activities			(40,000)
Cash flows from financing activities:			
Cash received from issuing mortgage note payable		$ 40,000	
Less: Cash paid for dividends[5]		70,670	
Net cash flow used for financing activities			(30,670)
Increase in cash			$ 44,450
Cash at the beginning of the year			95,900
Cash at the end of the year			$140,350
Schedule of Noncash Investing and Financing Activities:			
Issued common stock to retire bonds payable			$100,000
Schedule Reconciling Net Income with Cash Flows from Operating Activities[6]			

Computations:

[1]$1,100,000 + $7,000 = $1,107,000
[2]$710,000 + $3,200 + $7,300 = $720,500
[3]$196,000 + $380 – $1,500 = $194,880
[4]$50,000 + $500 = $50,500
[5]$74,670 + $10,000 – $14,000 = $70,670
[6]The content of this schedule is the same as the Operating Activities section of part (1) of this solution and is not reproduced here for the sake of brevity.

Self-Examination Questions (Answers at End of Chapter)

1. An example of a cash flow from an operating activity is:
   A. receipt of cash from the sale of stock.
   B. receipt of cash from the sale of bonds.
   C. payment of cash for dividends.
   D. receipt of cash from customers on account.
2. An example of a cash flow from an investing activity is:
   A. receipt of cash from the sale of equipment.
   B. receipt of cash from the sale of stock.
   C. payment of cash for dividends.
   D. payment of cash to acquire treasury stock.
3. An example of a cash flow from a financing activity is:
   A. receipt of cash from customers on account.
   B. receipt of cash from the sale of equipment.
   C. payment of cash for dividends.
   D. payment of cash to acquire land.
4. Which of the following methods of reporting cash flows from operating activities adjusts net income for revenues and expenses not involving the receipt or payment of cash?
   A. Direct method
   B. Purchase method
   C. Reciprocal method
   D. Indirect method

5. The net income reported on the income statement for the year was $55,000, and depreciation of fixed assets for the year was $22,000. The balances of the current asset and current liability accounts at the beginning and end of the year are shown below.

	End	Beginning
Cash	$ 65,000	$ 70,000
Accounts receivable	100,000	90,000
Inventories	145,000	150,000
Prepaid expenses	7,500	8,000
Accounts payable (merchandise creditors)	51,000	58,000

The total amount reported for cash flows from operating activities in the statement of cash flows, using the indirect method, is:

A. $33,000.
B. $55,000.
C. $65,500.
D. $77,000.

Eye Openers

1. What is the principal disadvantage of the direct method of reporting cash flows from operating activities?
2. What are the major advantages of the indirect method of reporting cash flows from operating activities?
3. A corporation issued $500,000 of common stock in exchange for $500,000 of fixed assets. Where would this transaction be reported on the statement of cash flows?
4. A retail business, using the accrual method of accounting, owed merchandise creditors (accounts payable) $300,000 at the beginning of the year and $340,000 at the end of the year. How would the $40,000 increase be used to adjust net income in determining the amount of cash flows from operating activities by the indirect method? Explain.
5. If salaries payable was $90,000 at the beginning of the year and $70,000 at the end of the year, should $20,000 be added to or deducted from income to determine the amount of cash flows from operating activities by the indirect method? Explain.
6. A long-term investment in bonds with a cost of $60,000 was sold for $72,000 cash. (a) What was the gain or loss on the sale? (b) What was the effect of the transaction on cash flows? (c) How should the transaction be reported in the statement of cash flows if cash flows from operating activities are reported by the indirect method?
7. A corporation issued $6,000,000 of 20-year bonds for cash at 104. How would the transaction be reported on the statement of cash flows?
8. Fully depreciated equipment costing $100,000 was discarded. What was the effect of the transaction on cash flows if (a) $24,000 cash is received, (b) no cash is received?
9. For the current year, Bearings Company decided to switch from the indirect method to the direct method for reporting cash flows from operating activities on the statement of cash flows. Will the change cause the amount of net cash flow from operating activities to be (a) larger, (b) smaller, or (c) the same as if the indirect method had been used? Explain.
10. Name five common major classes of operating cash receipts or operating cash payments presented on the statement of cash flows when the cash flows from operating activities are reported by the direct method.
11. In a recent annual report, eBay Inc. reported that during the year it issued stock of $128 million for acquisitions. How would this be reported on the statement of cash flows?

Practice Exercises

PE 16-1A
Classifying cash flows
obj. 1
EE 16-1 p. 715

Identify whether each of the following would be reported as an operating, investing, or financing activity in the statement of cash flows.

a. Issuance of common stock
b. Purchase of land
c. Payment of accounts payable
d. Retirement of bonds payable
e. Payment for administrative expenses
f. Cash received from customers

PE 16-1B
Classifying cash flows
obj. 1
EE 16-1 p. 715

Identify whether each of the following would be reported as an operating, investing, or financing activity in the statement of cash flows.

a. Payment for selling expenses
b. Issuance of bonds payable
c. Disposal of equipment
d. Cash sales
e. Purchase of investments
f. Collection of accounts receivable

PE 16-2A
Adjustments to net income—indirect method
obj. 2
EE 16-2 p. 719

Choi Corporation's accumulated depreciation—furniture increased by $7,000, while $2,600 of patents were amortized between balance sheet dates. There were no purchases or sales of depreciable or intangible assets during the year. In addition, the income statement showed a gain of $15,000 from the sale of land. Reconcile a net income of $140,000 to net cash flow from operating activities.

PE 16-2B
Adjustments to net income—indirect method
obj. 2
EE 16-2 p. 719

Singh Corporation's accumulated depreciation—equipment increased by $6,000, while $2,200 of patents were amortized between balance sheet dates. There were no purchases or sales of depreciable or intangible assets during the year. In addition, the income statement showed a loss of $3,200 from the sale of investments. Reconcile a net income of $86,000 to net cash flow from operating activities.

PE 16-3A
Changes in current operating assets and liabilities—indirect method
obj. 2
EE 16-3 p. 720

Watson Corporation's comparative balance sheet for current assets and liabilities was as follows:

	Dec. 31, 2010	Dec. 31, 2009
Accounts receivable	$30,000	$24,000
Inventory	58,000	49,500
Accounts payable	46,000	34,500
Dividends payable	14,000	18,000

Adjust net income of $320,000 for changes in operating assets and liabilities to arrive at net cash flow from operating activities.

PE 16-3B
Changes in current operating assets and liabilities—indirect method
obj. 2
EE 16-3 p. 720

Chopra Corporation's comparative balance sheet for current assets and liabilities was as follows:

	Dec. 31, 2010	Dec. 31, 2009
Accounts receivable	$15,000	$18,000
Inventory	10,000	8,600
Accounts payable	9,000	7,900
Dividends payable	27,500	29,500

Adjust net income of $115,000 for changes in operating assets and liabilities to arrive at net cash flow from operating activities.

PE 16-4A
Cash flows from operating activities—indirect method
obj. 2
EE 16-4 p. 721

Trahan Inc. reported the following data:

Net income	$175,000
Depreciation expense	30,000
Loss on disposal of equipment	12,200
Increase in accounts receivable	10,800
Increase in accounts payable	5,600

Prepare the Cash Flows from Operating Activities section of the statement of cash flows using the indirect method.

PE 16-4B
Cash flows from operating activities—indirect method
obj. 2
EE 16-4 p. 721

Daly Inc. reported the following data:

Net income	$225,000
Depreciation expense	25,000
Gain on disposal of equipment	20,500
Decrease in accounts receivable	14,000
Decrease in accounts payable	3,600

Prepare the Cash Flows from Operating Activities section of the statement of cash flows using the indirect method.

PE 16-5A
Land transactions on the statement of cash flows
obj. 2
EE 16-5 p. 724

Slocum Corporation purchased land for $600,000. Later in the year, the company sold land with a book value of $360,000 for $410,000. How are the effects of these transactions reported on the statement of cash flows?

PE 16-5B
Land transactions on the statement of cash flows
obj. 2
EE 16-5 p. 724

Verplank Corporation purchased land for $340,000. Later in the year, the company sold land with a book value of $145,000 for $110,000. How are the effects of these transactions reported on the statement of cash flows?

PE 16-6A
Cash received from customers—direct method
obj. 3
EE 16-6 p. 726

Sales reported on the income statement were $46,200. The accounts receivable balance decreased $3,400 over the year. Determine the amount of cash received from customers.

PE 16-6B
Cash received from customers—direct method
obj. 3
EE 16-6 p. 726

Sales reported on the income statement were $521,000. The accounts receivable balance increased $56,000 over the year. Determine the amount of cash received from customers.

PE 16-7A
Cash payments for merchandise—direct method
obj. 3
EE 16-7 p. 727

Cost of merchandise sold reported on the income statement was $130,000. The accounts payable balance increased $6,200, and the inventory balance increased by $11,400 over the year. Determine the amount of cash paid for merchandise.

PE 16-7B
Cash payments for merchandise—direct method
obj. 3
EE 16-7 p. 727

Cost of merchandise sold reported on the income statement was $420,000. The accounts payable balance decreased $22,500, and the inventory balance decreased by $26,000 over the year. Determine the amount of cash paid for merchandise.

Exercises

EX 16-1
Cash flows from operating activities—net loss
obj. 1

On its income statement for a recent year, Continental Airlines, Inc. reported a net *loss* of $68 million from operations. On its statement of cash flows, it reported $457 million of cash flows from operating activities.

Explain this apparent contradiction between the loss and the positive cash flows.

EX 16-2
Effect of transactions on cash flows
obj. 1
✔ c. Cash receipt, $500,000

State the effect (cash receipt or payment and amount) of each of the following transactions, considered individually, on cash flows:

a. Sold a new issue of $200,000 of bonds at 99.
b. Purchased 4,000 shares of $35 par common stock as treasury stock at $70 per share.
c. Sold 10,000 shares of $20 par common stock for $50 per share.
d. Purchased a building by paying $60,000 cash and issuing a $100,000 mortgage note payable.
e. Retired $250,000 of bonds, on which there was $2,500 of unamortized discount, for $260,000.
f. Purchased land for $320,000 cash.
g. Paid dividends of $2.00 per share. There were 25,000 shares issued and 4,000 shares of treasury stock.
h. Sold equipment with a book value of $50,000 for $72,000.

EX 16-3
Classifying cash flows
obj. 1

Identify the type of cash flow activity for each of the following events (operating, investing, or financing):

a. Issued common stock.
b. Redeemed bonds.
c. Issued preferred stock.
d. Purchased patents.
e. Net income.
f. Paid cash dividends.
g. Purchased treasury stock.
h. Sold long-term investments.
i. Sold equipment.
j. Purchased buildings.
k. Issued bonds.

EX 16-4
Cash flows from operating activities—indirect method
obj. 2

Indicate whether each of the following would be added to or deducted from net income in determining net cash flow from operating activities by the indirect method:

a. Decrease in accounts receivable
b. Increase in notes payable due in 90 days to vendors
c. Decrease in salaries payable
d. Decrease in prepaid expenses
e. Gain on retirement of long-term debt
f. Decrease in accounts payable
g. Increase in notes receivable due in 90 days from customers
h. Depreciation of fixed assets
i. Increase in merchandise inventory
j. Amortization of patent
k. Loss on disposal of fixed assets

EX 16-5
Cash flows from operating activities—indirect method

obj. 2

✔ Net cash flow from operating activities, $153,920

The net income reported on the income statement for the current year was $132,000. Depreciation recorded on store equipment for the year amounted to $21,800. Balances of the current asset and current liability accounts at the beginning and end of the year are as follows:

	End of Year	Beginning of Year
Cash	$52,300	$48,200
Accounts receivable (net)	37,500	35,600
Merchandise inventory	51,200	54,220
Prepaid expenses	6,000	4,600
Accounts payable (merchandise creditors)	49,000	45,600
Wages payable	26,800	29,800

Prepare the Cash Flows from Operating Activities section of the statement of cash flows, using the indirect method.

EX 16-6
Cash flows from operating activities—indirect method

objs. 1, 2

✔ Cash flows from operating activities, $258,950

The net income reported on the income statement for the current year was $210,000. Depreciation recorded on equipment and a building amounted to $62,500 for the year. Balances of the current asset and current liability accounts at the beginning and end of the year are as follows:

	End of Year	Beginning of Year
Cash	$ 56,000	$ 59,500
Accounts receivable (net)	71,000	73,400
Inventories	140,000	126,500
Prepaid expenses	7,800	8,400
Accounts payable (merchandise creditors)	62,600	66,400
Salaries payable	9,000	8,250

a. Prepare the Cash Flows from Operating Activities section of the statement of cash flows, using the indirect method.
b. If the direct method had been used, would the net cash flow from operating activities have been the same? Explain.

EX 16-7
Cash flows from operating activities—indirect method

objs. 1, 2

✔ Cash flows from operating activities, $328,700

The income statement disclosed the following items for 2010:

Depreciation expense	$ 36,000
Gain on disposal of equipment	21,000
Net income	317,500

Balances of the current assets and current liability accounts changed between December 31, 2009, and December 31, 2010, as follows:

Accounts receivable	$5,600
Inventory	3,200*
Prepaid insurance	1,200*
Accounts payable	3,800*
Income taxes payable	1,200
Dividends payable	850

*Decrease

Prepare the Cash Flows from Operating Activities section of the statement of cash flows, using the indirect method.

EX 16-8
Determining cash payments to stockholders

obj. 2

The board of directors declared cash dividends totaling $152,000 during the current year. The comparative balance sheet indicates dividends payable of $42,000 at the beginning of the year and $38,000 at the end of the year. What was the amount of cash payments to stockholders during the year?

EX 16-9
Reporting changes in equipment on statement of cash flows
obj. 2

An analysis of the general ledger accounts indicates that office equipment, which cost $67,000 and on which accumulated depreciation totaled $22,500 on the date of sale, was sold for $38,600 during the year. Using this information, indicate the items to be reported on the statement of cash flows.

EX 16-10
Reporting changes in equipment on statement of cash flows
obj. 2

An analysis of the general ledger accounts indicates that delivery equipment, which cost $96,000 and on which accumulated depreciation totaled $42,100 on the date of sale, was sold for $46,500 during the year. Using this information, indicate the items to be reported on the statement of cash flows.

EX 16-11
Reporting land transactions on statement of cash flows
obj. 2

On the basis of the details of the following fixed asset account, indicate the items to be reported on the statement of cash flows:

ACCOUNT *Land* **ACCOUNT NO.**

Date		Item	Debit	Credit	Balance Debit	Balance Credit
2010						
Jan.	1	Balance			1,200,000	
Feb.	5	Purchased for cash	380,000		1,580,000	
Oct.	30	Sold for $210,000		180,000	1,400,000	

EX 16-12
Reporting stockholders' equity items on statement of cash flows
obj. 2

On the basis of the following stockholders' equity accounts, indicate the items, exclusive of net income, to be reported on the statement of cash flows. There were no unpaid dividends at either the beginning or the end of the year.

ACCOUNT *Common Stock, $10 par* **ACCOUNT NO.**

Date		Item	Debit	Credit	Balance Debit	Balance Credit
2010						
Jan.	1	Balance, 60,000 shares				1,200,000
Feb.	11	15,000 shares issued for cash		300,000		1,500,000
June	30	2,200-share stock dividend		44,000		1,544,000

ACCOUNT *Paid-In Capital in Excess of Par—Common Stock* **ACCOUNT NO.**

Date		Item	Debit	Credit	Balance Debit	Balance Credit
2010						
Jan.	1	Balance				200,000
Feb.	11	15,000 shares issued for cash		480,000		680,000
June	30	Stock dividend		79,200		759,200

ACCOUNT *Retained Earnings* ACCOUNT NO.

Date		Item	Debit	Credit	Balance	
					Debit	Credit
2010						
Jan.	1	Balance				1,000,000
June	30	Stock dividend	123,200			876,800
Dec.	30	Cash dividend	115,800			761,000
	31	Net income		720,000		1,481,000

EX 16-13
Reporting land acquisition for cash and mortgage note on statement of cash flows
obj. 2

On the basis of the details of the following fixed asset account, indicate the items to be reported on the statement of cash flows:

ACCOUNT *Land* ACCOUNT NO.

Date		Item	Debit	Credit	Balance	
					Debit	Credit
2010						
Jan.	1	Balance			260,000	
Feb.	10	Purchased for cash	410,000		670,000	
Nov.	20	Purchased with long-term mortgage note	540,000		1,210,000	

EX 16-14
Reporting issuance and retirement of long-term debt
obj. 2

On the basis of the details of the following bonds payable and related discount accounts, indicate the items to be reported in the Financing section of the statement of cash flows, assuming no gain or loss on retiring the bonds:

ACCOUNT *Bonds Payable* ACCOUNT NO.

Date		Item	Debit	Credit	Balance	
					Debit	Credit
2010						
Jan.	1	Balance				500,000
	3	Retire bonds	100,000			400,000
July	30	Issue bonds		300,000		700,000

ACCOUNT *Discount on Bond Payable* ACCOUNT NO.

Date		Item	Debit	Credit	Balance	
					Debit	Credit
2010						
Jan.	1	Balance			22,500	
	3	Retire bonds		8,000	14,500	
July	30	Issue bonds	20,000		34,500	
Dec.	31	Amortize discount		1,750	32,750	

EX 16-15
Determining net income from net cash flow from operating activities

obj. 2

✔ Net income, $155,350

Sanhueza, Inc., reported a net cash flow from operating activities of $162,500 on its statement of cash flows for the year ended December 31, 2010. The following information was reported in the Cash Flows from Operating Activities section of the statement of cash flows, using the indirect method:

Decrease in income taxes payable	$ 3,500
Decrease in inventories	8,700
Depreciation	13,400
Gain on sale of investments	6,000
Increase in accounts payable	2,400
Increase in prepaid expenses	1,350
Increase in accounts receivable	6,500

Determine the net income reported by Sanhueza, Inc., for the year ended December 31, 2010.

EX 16-16
Cash flows from operating activities—indirect method

obj. 2

✔ Net cash flow from operating activities, $3,048

Selected data derived from the income statement and balance sheet of Jones Soda Co. for a recent year are as follows:

Income statement data (in thousands):	
Net earnings	$4,574
Depreciation expense	256
Stock-based compensation expense (noncash)	1,196
Balance sheet data (in thousands):	
Increase in accounts receivable	$3,214
Increase in inventory	1,089
Increase in prepaid expenses	566
Increase in accounts payable	1,891

a. Prepare the Cash Flows from Operating Activities section of the statement of cash flows using the indirect method for Jones Soda Co. for the year.
b. Interpret your results in part (a).

EX 16-17
Statement of cash flows—indirect method

obj. 2

✔ Net cash flow from operating activities, $30

The comparative balance sheet of Tru-Built Construction Inc. for December 31, 2010 and 2009, is as follows:

	Dec. 31, 2010	Dec. 31, 2009
Assets		
Cash	$ 98	$ 32
Accounts receivable (net)	56	40
Inventories	35	22
Land	80	90
Equipment	45	35
Accumulated depreciation—equipment	(12)	(6)
Total	$302	$213
Liabilities and Stockholders' Equity		
Accounts payable (merchandise creditors)	$ 35	$ 32
Dividends payable	6	—
Common stock, $1 par	20	10
Paid-in capital in excess of par—common stock	50	25
Retained earnings	191	146
Total	$302	$213

The following additional information is taken from the records:

a. Land was sold for $25.
b. Equipment was acquired for cash.
c. There were no disposals of equipment during the year.
d. The common stock was issued for cash.
e. There was a $65 credit to Retained Earnings for net income.
f. There was a $20 debit to Retained Earnings for cash dividends declared.

Prepare a statement of cash flows, using the indirect method of presenting cash flows from operating activities.

EX 16-18
Statement of cash flows—indirect method
obj. 2

List the errors you find in the following statement of cash flows. The cash balance at the beginning of the year was $100,320. All other amounts are correct, except the cash balance at the end of the year.

Devon Inc.
Statement of Cash Flows
For the Year Ended December 31, 2010

Cash flows from operating activities:			
Net income		$148,080	
Adjustments to reconcile net income to net cash flow from operating activities:			
Depreciation		42,000	
Gain on sale of investements		7,200	
Changes in current operating assets and liabilities:			
Increase in accounts receivable		11,400	
Increase in inventories		(14,760)	
Increase in accounts payable		(4,440)	
Decrease in accrued expenses payable		(1,080)	
Net cash flow from operating activities			$188,400
Cash flows from investing activities:			
Cash received from sale of investments		$ 102,000	
Less: Cash paid for purchase of land	$ 108,000		
Cash paid for purchase of equipment	180,200	288,200	
Net cash flow used for investing activities			(186,200)
Cash flows from financing activities:			
Cash received from sale of common stock		$128,400	
Cash paid for dividends		54,000	
Net cash flow provided by financing activities			182,400
Increase in cash			$184,600
Cash at the end of the year			126,300
Cash at the beginning of the year			$310,900

EX 16-19
Cash flows from operating activities—direct method
obj. 3
✔ a. $728,500

The cash flows from operating activities are reported by the direct method on the statement of cash flows. Determine the following:

a. If sales for the current year were $685,000 and accounts receivable decreased by $43,500 during the year, what was the amount of cash received from customers?
b. If income tax expense for the current year was $46,000 and income tax payable decreased by $5,200 during the year, what was the amount of cash payments for income tax?

EX 16-20
Cash paid for merchandise purchases
obj. 3

The cost of merchandise sold for Kohl's Corporation for a recent year was $9,891 million. The balance sheet showed the following current account balances (in millions):

	Balance, End of Year	Balance, Beginning of Year
Merchandise inventories	$2,588	$2,238
Accounts payable	934	830

Determine the amount of cash payments for merchandise.

EX 16-21
Determining selected amounts for cash flows from operating activities—direct method
obj. 3
✔ b. $77,870

Selected data taken from the accounting records of Lachgar Inc. for the current year ended December 31 are as follows:

	Balance, December 31	Balance, January 1
Accrued expenses payable (operating expenses)	$ 5,590	$ 6,110
Accounts payable (merchandise creditors)	41,730	46,020
Inventories	77,350	84,110
Prepaid expenses	3,250	3,900

During the current year, the cost of merchandise sold was $448,500, and the operating expenses other than depreciation were $78,000. The direct method is used for presenting the cash flows from operating activities on the statement of cash flows.

Determine the amount reported on the statement of cash flows for (a) cash payments for merchandise and (b) cash payments for operating expenses.

EX 16-22
Cash flows from operating activities—direct method

obj. 3

✔ Net cash flow from operating activities, $69,760

The income statement of Kodiak Industries Inc. for the current year ended June 30 is as follows:

Sales		$364,800
Cost of merchandise sold		207,200
Gross profit		$157,600
Operating expenses:		
Depreciation expense	$28,000	
Other operating expenses	73,920	
Total operating expenses		101,920
Income before income tax		$ 55,680
Income tax expense		15,440
Net income		$ 40,240

Changes in the balances of selected accounts from the beginning to the end of the current year are as follows:

	Increase Decrease*
Accounts receivable (net)	$8,400*
Inventories	2,800
Prepaid expenses	2,720*
Accounts payable (merchandise creditors)	5,760*
Accrued expenses payable (operating expenses)	880
Income tax payable	1,920*

Prepare the Cash Flows from Operating Activities section of the statement of cash flows, using the direct method.

EX 16-23
Cash flows from operating activities—direct method

obj. 3

✔ Net cash flow from operating activities, $56,490

The income statement for M2 Pizza Pie Company for the current year ended June 30 and balances of selected accounts at the beginning and the end of the year are as follows:

Sales		$202,400
Cost of merchandise sold		70,000
Gross profit		$132,400
Operating expenses:		
Depreciation expense	$17,500	
Other operating expenses	52,400	
Total operating expenses		69,900
Income before income tax		$ 62,500
Income tax expense		18,000
Net income		$ 44,500

	End of Year	Beginning of Year
Accounts receivable (net)	$16,300	$14,190
Inventories	41,900	36,410
Prepaid expenses	6,600	7,260
Accounts payable (merchandise creditors)	30,690	28,490
Accrued expenses payable (operating expenses)	8,690	9,460
Income tax payable	1,650	1,650

Prepare the Cash Flows from Operating Activities section of the statement of cash flows, using the direct method.

EX 16-24
Free cash flow

Morrocan Marble Company has cash flows from operating activities of $300,000. Cash flows used for investments in property, plant, and equipment totaled $65,000, of which 75% of this investment was used to replace existing capacity.

Determine the free cash flow for Morrocan Marble Company.

EX 16-25
Free cash flow

The financial statements for Nike, Inc., are provided in Appendix E at the end of the text.

Determine the free cash flow for the year ended May 31, 2007. Assume that 90% of additions to property, plant and equipment were used to maintain productive capacity.

Problems Series A

PR 16-1A
Statement of cash flows—indirect method
obj. 2

✔ Net cash flow from operating activities, $49,520

The comparative balance sheet of Mavenir Technologies Inc. for December 31, 2010 and 2009, is shown as follows:

	Dec. 31, 2010	Dec. 31, 2009
Assets		
Cash	$ 312,880	$ 292,960
Accounts receivable (net)	113,920	104,480
Inventories	320,880	308,560
Investments	0	120,000
Land	164,000	0
Equipment	352,560	276,560
Accumulated depreciation—equipment	(83,200)	(74,000)
	$1,181,040	$1,028,560
Liabilities and Stockholders' Equity		
Accounts payable (merchandise creditors)	$ 214,240	$ 202,480
Accrued expenses payable (operating expenses)	21,120	26,320
Dividends payable	12,000	9,600
Common stock, $10 par	64,000	48,000
Paid-in capital in excess of par—common stock	240,000	140,000
Retained earnings	629,680	602,160
	$1,181,040	$1,028,560

The following additional information was taken from the records:

a. The investments were sold for $140,000 cash.
b. Equipment and land were acquired for cash.
c. There were no disposals of equipment during the year.
d. The common stock was issued for cash.
e. There was a $75,520 credit to Retained Earnings for net income.
f. There was a $48,000 debit to Retained Earnings for cash dividends declared.

Instructions

Prepare a statement of cash flows, using the indirect method of presenting cash flows from operating activities.

PR 16-2A
Statement of cash flows—indirect method
obj. 2

✔ Net cash flow from operating activities, $169,600

The comparative balance sheet of Amelia Enterprises, Inc. at December 31, 2010 and 2009, is as follows:

	Dec. 31, 2010	Dec. 31, 2009
Assets		
Cash	$ 73,300	$ 89,900
Accounts receivable (net)	112,300	121,000
Merchandise inventory	160,800	149,600
Prepaid expenses	6,700	4,800
Equipment	327,500	268,500
Accumulated depreciation—equipment	(85,400)	(66,100)
	$595,200	$567,700
Liabilities and Stockholders' Equity		
Accounts payable (merchandise creditors)	$125,100	$118,800
Mortgage note payable	0	168,000
Common stock, $1 par	24,000	12,000
Paid-in capital in excess of par—common stock	288,000	160,000
Retained earnings	158,100	108,900
	$595,200	$567,700

Additional data obtained from the income statement and from an examination of the accounts in the ledger for 2010 are as follows:

a. Net income, $126,000.
b. Depreciation reported on the income statement, $41,700.
c. Equipment was purchased at a cost of $81,400, and fully depreciated equipment costing $22,400 was discarded, with no salvage realized.
d. The mortgage note payable was not due until 2013, but the terms permitted earlier payment without penalty.
e. 7,000 shares of common stock were issued at $20 for cash.
f. Cash dividends declared and paid, $76,800.

Instructions

Prepare a statement of cash flows, using the indirect method of presenting cash flows from operating activities.

PR 16-3A
Statement of cash flows—indirect method
obj. 2

✔ Net cash flow from operating activities, ($92,000)

The comparative balance sheet of Putnam Cycle Co. at December 31, 2010 and 2009, is as follows:

	Dec. 31, 2010	Dec. 31, 2009
Assets		
Cash	$ 510,000	$ 536,000
Accounts receivable (net)	460,500	423,300
Inventories	704,700	646,100
Prepaid expenses	16,300	19,500
Land	175,500	266,500
Buildings	812,500	500,500
Accumulated depreciation—buildings	(227,000)	(212,400)
Equipment	284,600	252,600
Accumulated depreciation—equipment	(78,500)	(88,200)
	$2,658,600	$2,343,900
Liabilities and Stockholders' Equity		
Accounts payable (merchandise creditors)	$ 512,500	$ 532,400
Bonds payable	150,000	0
Common stock, $1 par	75,000	65,000
Paid-in capital in excess of par—common stock	520,000	310,000
Retained earnings	1,401,100	1,436,500
	$2,658,600	$2,343,900

The noncurrent asset, noncurrent liability, and stockholders' equity accounts for 2010 are as follows:

ACCOUNT ***Land*** **ACCOUNT NO.**

Date		Item	Debit	Credit	Balance Debit	Balance Credit
2010						
Jan.	1	Balance			266,500	
Apr.	20	Realized $84,000 cash from sale		91,000	175,500	

ACCOUNT ***Buildings*** **ACCOUNT NO.**

Date		Item	Debit	Credit	Balance Debit	Balance Credit
2010						
Jan.	1	Balance			500,500	
Apr.	20	Acquired for cash	312,000		812,500	

ACCOUNT ***Accumulated Depreciation—Buildings*** **ACCOUNT NO.**

Date		Item	Debit	Credit	Balance Debit	Balance Credit
2010						
Jan.	1	Balance				212,400
Dec.	31	Depreciation for year		14,600		227,000

ACCOUNT ***Equipment*** **ACCOUNT NO.**

Date		Item	Debit	Credit	Balance Debit	Balance Credit
2010						
Jan.	1	Balance			252,600	
	26	Discarded, no salvage		26,000	226,600	
Aug.	11	Purchased for cash	58,000		284,600	

ACCOUNT ***Accumulated Depreciation—Equipment*** **ACCOUNT NO.**

Date		Item	Debit	Credit	Balance Debit	Balance Credit
2010						
Jan.	1	Balance				88,200
	26	Equipment discarded	26,000			62,200
Dec.	31	Depreciation for year		16,300		78,500

ACCOUNT *Bonds Payable* ACCOUNT NO.

Date		Item	Debit	Credit	Balance Debit	Balance Credit
2010						
May	1	Issued 20-year bonds		150,000		150,000

ACCOUNT *Common Stock, $1 Par* ACCOUNT NO.

Date		Item	Debit	Credit	Balance Debit	Balance Credit
2010						
Jan.	1	Balance				65,000
Dec.	7	Issued 10,000 shares of common stock for $22 per share		10,000		75,000

ACCOUNT *Paid-In Capital in Excess of Par—Common Stock* ACCOUNT NO.

Date		Item	Debit	Credit	Balance Debit	Balance Credit
2010						
Jan.	1	Balance				310,000
Dec.	7	Issued 10,000 shares of common stock for $22 per share		210,000		520,000

ACCOUNT *Retained Earnings* ACCOUNT NO.

Date		Item	Debit	Credit	Balance Debit	Balance Credit
2010						
Jan.	1	Balance				1,436,500
Dec.	31	Net loss	17,400			1,419,100
	31	Cash dividends	18,000			1,401,100

Instructions

Prepare a statement of cash flows, using the indirect method of presenting cash flows from operating activities.

PR 16-4A
Statement of cash flows—direct method
obj. 3

✔ Net cash flow from operating activities, $146,800

The comparative balance sheet of Rucker Photography Products Inc. for December 31, 2011 and 2010, is as follows:

	Dec. 31, 2011	Dec. 31, 2010
Assets		
Cash	$ 321,700	$ 339,700
Accounts receivable (net)	283,400	273,700
Inventories	505,500	491,400
Investments	0	120,000
Land	260,000	0
Equipment	440,000	340,000
Accumulated depreciation	(122,200)	(100,200)
	$1,688,400	$1,464,600

Liabilities and Stockholders' Equity		
Accounts payable (merchandise creditors)	$ 385,900	$ 374,200
Accrued expenses payable (operating expenses)	31,700	35,400
Dividends payable	4,400	3,200
Common stock, $1 par	20,000	16,000
Paid-in capital in excess of par—common stock	208,000	96,000
Retained earnings	1,038,400	939,800
	$1,688,400	$1,464,600

The income statement for the year ended December 31, 2011, is as follows:

Sales		$2,990,000
Cost of merchandise sold		1,226,000
Gross profit		$1,764,000
Operating expenses:		
Depreciation expense	$ 22,000	
Other operating expenses	1,550,000	
Total operating expenses		1,572,000
Operating income		$ 192,000
Other expense:		
Loss on sale of investments		(32,000)
Income before income tax		$ 160,000
Income tax expense		51,400
Net income		$ 108,600

The following additional information was taken from the records:

a. Equipment and land were acquired for cash.
b. There were no disposals of equipment during the year.
c. The investments were sold for $88,000 cash.
d. The common stock was issued for cash.
e. There was a $10,000 debit to Retained Earnings for cash dividends declared.

Instructions

Prepare a statement of cash flows, using the direct method of presenting cash flows from operating activities.

PR 16-5A
Statement of cash flows—direct method applied to PR 16-1A

obj. 3

✔ Net cash flow from operating activities, $49,520

The comparative balance sheet of Mavenir Technologies Inc. for December 31, 2010 and 2009, is as follows:

	Dec. 31, 2010	Dec. 31, 2009
Assets		
Cash	$ 312,880	$ 292,960
Accounts receivable (net)	113,920	104,480
Inventories	320,880	308,560
Investments	0	120,000
Land	164,000	0
Equipment	352,560	276,560
Accumulated depreciation—equipment	(83,200)	(74,000)
	$1,181,040	$1,028,560
Liabilities and Stockholders' Equity		
Accounts payable (merchandise creditors)	$ 214,240	$ 202,480
Accrued expenses payable (operating expenses)	21,120	26,320
Dividends payable	12,000	9,600
Common stock, $10 par	64,000	48,000
Paid-in capital in excess of par—common stock	240,000	140,000
Retained earnings	629,680	602,160
	$1,181,040	$1,028,560

The income statement for the year ended December 31, 2010, is as follows:

Sales		$1,950,699
Cost of merchandise sold		1,200,430
Gross profit		$ 750,269
Operating expenses:		
Depreciation expense	$ 9,200	
Other operating expenses	635,202	
Total operating expenses		644,402
Operating income		$ 105,867
Other income:		
Gain on sale of investments		20,000
Income before income tax		$ 125,867
Income tax expense		50,347
Net income		$ 75,520

The following additional information was taken from the records:

a. The investments were sold for $140,000 cash.
b. Equipment and land were acquired for cash.
c. There were no disposals of equipment during the year.
d. The common stock was issued for cash.
e. There was a $48,000 debit to Retained Earnings for cash dividends declared.

Instructions

Prepare a statement of cash flows, using the direct method of presenting cash flows from operating activities.

Problems Series B

PR 16-1B
Statement of cash flows—indirect method
obj. 2

✔ Net cash flow from operating activities, $86,600

The comparative balance sheet of House Construction Co. for June 30, 2010 and 2009, is as follows:

	June 30, 2010	June 30, 2009
Assets		
Cash	$ 41,600	$ 28,200
Accounts receivable (net)	121,900	110,700
Inventories	175,600	170,500
Investments	0	60,000
Land	174,000	0
Equipment	258,000	210,600
Accumulated depreciation	(58,300)	(49,600)
	$712,800	$530,400
Liabilities and Stockholders' Equity		
Accounts payable (merchandise creditors)	$121,000	$114,200
Accrued expenses payable (operating expenses)	18,000	15,800
Dividends payable	15,000	12,000
Common stock, $1 par	67,200	60,000
Paid-in capital in excess of par—common stock	264,000	120,000
Retained earnings	227,600	208,400
	$712,800	$530,400

The following additional information was taken from the records of House Construction Co.:

a. Equipment and land were acquired for cash.
b. There were no disposals of equipment during the year.
c. The investments were sold for $54,000 cash.
d. The common stock was issued for cash.
e. There was a $79,200 credit to Retained Earnings for net income.
f. There was a $60,000 debit to Retained Earnings for cash dividends declared.

Instructions

Prepare a statement of cash flows, using the indirect method of presenting cash flows from operating activities.

PR 16-2B
Statement of cash flows—indirect method
obj. 2

✔ Net cash flow from operating activities, $200,500

The comparative balance sheet of TorMax Technology, Inc. at December 31, 2010 and 2009, is as follows:

	Dec. 31, 2010	Dec. 31, 2009
Assets		
Cash	$ 158,300	$ 128,900
Accounts receivable (net)	237,600	211,500
Inventories	317,100	365,200
Prepaid expenses	11,300	9,000
Land	108,000	108,000
Buildings	612,000	405,000
Accumulated depreciation—buildings	(166,500)	(148,050)
Machinery and equipment	279,000	279,000
Accumulated depreciation—machinery & equipment	(76,500)	(68,400)
Patents	38,200	43,200
	$1,518,500	$1,333,350
Liabilities and Stockholders' Equity		
Accounts payable (merchandise creditors)	$ 299,100	$ 331,100
Dividends payable	11,700	9,000
Salaries payable	28,200	31,100
Mortgage note payable, due 2017	80,000	—
Bonds payable	—	140,000
Common stock, $1 par	23,000	18,000
Paid-in capital in excess of par—common stock	180,000	45,000
Retained earnings	896,500	759,150
	$1,518,500	$1,333,350

An examination of the income statement and the accounting records revealed the following additional information applicable to 2010:

a. Net income, $184,150.
b. Depreciation expense reported on the income statement: buildings, $18,450; machinery and equipment, $8,100.
c. Patent amortization reported on the income statement, $5,000.
d. A building was constructed for $207,000.
e. A mortgage note for $80,000 was issued for cash.
f. 5,000 shares of common stock were issued at $28 in exchange for the bonds payable.
g. Cash dividends declared, $46,800.

Instructions Prepare a statement of cash flows, using the indirect method of presenting cash flows from operating activities.

PR 16-3B
Statement of cash flows—indirect method
obj. 2

✔ Net cash flow from operating activities, $7,800

The comparative balance sheet of Cantor Industries, Inc. at December 31, 2010 and 2009, is as follows:

	Dec. 31, 2010	Dec. 31, 2009
Assets		
Cash	$ 50,100	$ 56,300
Accounts receivable (net)	117,400	101,600
Inventories	153,100	144,300
Prepaid expenses	3,100	4,400
Land	165,000	231,000
Buildings	330,000	165,000
Accumulated depreciation—buildings	(66,200)	(61,000)
Equipment	110,100	88,300
Accumulated depreciation—equipment	(22,200)	(27,000)
	$840,400	$702,900
Liabilities and Stockholders' Equity		
Accounts payable (merchandise creditors)	$ 99,000	$105,200
Income tax payable	4,400	3,600
Bonds payable	55,000	0
Common stock, $1 par	36,000	30,000
Paid-in capital in excess of par—common stock	195,000	135,000
Retained earnings	451,000	429,100
	$840,400	$702,900

The noncurrent asset, noncurrent liability, and stockholders' equity accounts for 2010 are as follows:

ACCOUNT ***Land*** **ACCOUNT NO.**

Date		Item	Debit	Credit	Balance Debit	Balance Credit
2010						
Jan.	1	Balance			231,000	
Apr.	20	Realized $76,000 cash from sale		66,000	165,000	

ACCOUNT ***Buildings*** **ACCOUNT NO.**

Date		Item	Debit	Credit	Balance Debit	Balance Credit
2010						
Jan.	1	Balance			165,000	
Apr.	20	Acquired for cash	165,000		330,000	

ACCOUNT ***Accumulated Depreciation—Buildings*** **ACCOUNT NO.**

Date		Item	Debit	Credit	Balance Debit	Balance Credit
2010						
Jan.	1	Balance				61,000
Dec.	31	Depreciation for year		5,200		66,200

ACCOUNT ***Equipment*** **ACCOUNT NO.**

Date		Item	Debit	Credit	Balance Debit	Balance Credit
2010						
Jan.	1	Balance			88,300	
	26	Discarded, no salvage		11,000	77,300	
Aug.	11	Purchased for cash	32,800		110,100	

ACCOUNT ***Accumulated Depreciation—Equipment*** **ACCOUNT NO.**

Date		Item	Debit	Credit	Balance Debit	Balance Credit
2010						
Jan.	1	Balance				27,000
	26	Equipment discarded	11,000			16,000
Dec.	31	Depreciation for year		6,200		22,200

ACCOUNT ***Bonds Payable*** **ACCOUNT NO.**

Date		Item	Debit	Credit	Balance Debit	Balance Credit
2010						
May	1	Issued 20-year bonds		55,000		55,000

ACCOUNT *Common Stock, $1 par* ACCOUNT NO.

Date		Item	Debit	Credit	Balance Debit	Balance Credit
2010						
Jan.	1	Balance				30,000
Dec.	7	Issued 6,000 shares of common stock for $11 per share		6,000		36,000

ACCOUNT *Paid-In Capital in Excess of Par—Common Stock* ACCOUNT NO.

Date		Item	Debit	Credit	Balance Debit	Balance Credit
2010						
Jan.	1	Balance				135,000
Dec.	7	Issued 6,000 shares of common stock for $11 per share		60,000		195,000

ACCOUNT *Retained Earnings* ACCOUNT NO.

Date		Item	Debit	Credit	Balance Debit	Balance Credit
2010						
Jan.	1	Balance				429,100
Dec.	31	Net income		35,100		464,200
	31	Cash dividends	13,200			451,000

Instructions

Prepare a statement of cash flows, using the indirect method of presenting cash flows from operating activities.

PR 16-4B
Statement of cash flows—direct method
obj. 3

✔ Net cash flow from operating activities, $169,740

The comparative balance sheet of Lim Garden Supplies Inc. for December 31, 2010 and 2011, is as follows:

	Dec. 31, 2011	Dec. 31, 2010
Assets		
Cash	$ 220,640	$ 227,700
Accounts receivable (net)	330,880	304,800
Inventories	464,800	454,600
Investments	0	144,000
Land	320,000	0
Equipment	408,000	328,000
Accumulated depreciation	(160,500)	(122,800)
	$1,583,820	$1,336,300
Liabilities and Stockholders' Equity		
Accounts payable (merchandise creditors)	$ 360,000	$ 322,200
Accrued expenses payable (operating expenses)	22,600	26,400
Dividends payable	33,600	30,400
Common stock,	16,000	8,000
Paid-in capital in excess of par—common stock	320,000	160,000
Retained earnings	831,620	789,300
	$1,583,820	$1,336,300

The income statement for the year ended December 31, 2011, is as follows:

Sales		$1,504,000
Cost of merchandise sold		784,000
Gross profit		$ 720,000
Operating expenses:		
Depreciation expense	$ 37,700	
Other operating expenses	448,280	
Total operating expenses		485,980
Operating income		$ 234,020
Other income:		
Gain on sale of investments		52,000
Income before income tax		$ 286,020
Income tax expense		99,700
Net income		$ 186,320

The following additional information was taken from the records:

a. Equipment and land were acquired for cash.
b. There were no disposals of equipment during the year.
c. The investments were sold for $196,000 cash.
d. The common stock was issued for cash.
e. There was a $144,000 debit to Retained Earnings for cash dividends declared.

Instructions Prepare a statement of cash flows, using the direct method of presenting cash flows from operating activities.

PR 16-5B
Statement of cash flows—direct method applied to PR 16-1B
obj. 3

✔ Net cash flow from operating activities, $86,600

The comparative balance sheet of House Construction Co. for June 30, 2010 and 2009, is as follows:

	June 30, 2010	June 30, 2009
Assets		
Cash	$ 41,600	$ 28,200
Accounts receivable (net)	121,900	110,700
Inventories	175,600	170,500
Investments	0	60,000
Land	174,000	0
Equipment	258,000	210,600
Accumulated depreciation	(58,300)	(49,600)
	$712,800	$530,400
Liabilities and Stockholders' Equity		
Accounts payable (merchandise creditors)	$121,000	$114,200
Accrued expenses payable (operating expenses)	18,000	15,800
Dividends payable	15,000	12,000
Common stock, $1 par	67,200	60,000
Paid-in capital in excess of par—common stock	264,000	120,000
Retained earnings	227,600	208,400
	$712,800	$530,400

The income statement for the year ended June 30, 2010, is as follows:

Sales		$1,134,900
Cost of merchandise sold		698,400
Gross profit		$ 436,500
Operating expenses:		
Depreciation expense	$ 8,700	
Other operating expenses	289,800	
Total operating expenses		298,500
Operating income		$ 138,000
Other expenses:		
Loss on sale of investments		(6,000)
Income before income tax		$ 132,000
Income tax expense		52,800
Net income		$ 79,200

The following additional information was taken from the records:

a. Equipment and land were acquired for cash.
b. There were no disposals of equipment during the year.
c. The investments were sold for $54,000 cash.
d. The common stock was issued for cash.
e. There was a $60,000 debit to Retained Earnings for cash dividends declared.

Instructions Prepare a statement of cash flows, using the direct method of presenting cash flows from operating activities.

Special Activities

SA 16-1
Ethics and professional conduct in business

Kelly Tough, president of Tu-Rock Industries Inc., believes that reporting operating cash flow per share on the income statement would be a useful addition to the company's just completed financial statements. The following discussion took place between Kelly Tough and Tu-Rock controller, Tripp Kelso, in January, after the close of the fiscal year.

Kelly: I have been reviewing our financial statements for the last year. I am disappointed that our net income per share has dropped by 10% from last year. This is not going to look good to our shareholders. Isn't there anything we can do about this?

Tripp: What do you mean? The past is the past, and the numbers are in. There isn't much that can be done about it. Our financial statements were prepared according to generally accepted accounting principles, and I don't see much leeway for significant change at this point.

Kelly: No, no. I'm not suggesting that we "cook the books." But look at the cash flow from operating activities on the statement of cash flows. The cash flow from operating activities has increased by 20%. This is very good news—and, I might add, useful information. The higher cash flow from operating activities will give our creditors comfort.

Tripp: Well, the cash flow from operating activities is on the statement of cash flows, so I guess users will be able to see the improved cash flow figures there.

Kelly: This is true, but somehow I feel that this information should be given a much higher profile. I don't like this information being "buried" in the statement of cash flows. You know as well as I do that many users will focus on the income statement. Therefore, I think we ought to include an operating cash flow per share number on the face of the income statement—someplace under the earnings per share number. In this way, users will get the complete picture of our operating performance. Yes, our earnings per share dropped this year, but our cash flow from operating activities improved! And all the information is in one place where users can see and compare the figures. What do you think?

Tripp: I've never really thought about it like that before. I guess we could put the operating cash flow per share on the income statement, under the earnings per share. Users would really benefit from this disclosure. Thanks for the idea—I'll start working on it.

Kelly: Glad to be of service.

How would you interpret this situation? Is Tripp behaving in an ethical and professional manner?

SA 16-2
Using the statement of cash flows

You are considering an investment in a new start-up company, Steamboat IQ Inc., an Internet service provider. A review of the company's financial statements reveals a negative retained earnings. In addition, it appears as though the company has been running a negative cash flow from operating activities since the company's inception.

How is the company staying in business under these circumstances? Could this be a good investment?

SA 16-3
Analysis of statement of cash flows

Jim Walker is the president and majority shareholder of Tech Trends Inc., a small retail store chain. Recently, Walker submitted a loan application for Tech Trends Inc. to Yadkin National Bank. It called for a $200,000, 9%, 10-year loan to help finance the construction of a building and the purchase of store equipment, costing a total of $250,000, to enable Tech Trends Inc. to open a store in Yadkin. Land for this purpose was acquired last year. The bank's loan officer requested a statement of cash flows in addition to the most recent income statement, balance sheet, and retained earnings statement that Walker had submitted with the loan application.

As a close family friend, Walker asked you to prepare a statement of cash flows. From the records provided, you prepared the following statement:

Tech Trends Inc.
Statement of Cash Flows
For the Year Ended December 31, 2010

Cash flows from operating activities:		
Net income	$100,000	
Adjustments to reconcile net income to net cash flow from operating activities:		
Depreciation	28,000	
Gain on sale of investments	(10,000)	
Changes in current operating assets and liabilities:		
Decrease in accounts receivable	7,000	
Increase in inventories	(14,000)	
Increase in accounts payable	10,000	
Decrease in accrued expenses payable	(2,000)	
Net cash flow from operating activities		$119,000
Cash flows from investing activities:		
Cash received from investments sold	$60,000	
Less cash paid for purchase of store equipment	(40,000)	
Net cash flow provided by investing activities		20,000
Cash flows from financing activities:		
Cash paid for dividends	$42,000	
Net cash flow used for financing activities		(42,000)
Increase in cash		$ 97,000
Cash at the beginning of the year		36,000
Cash at the end of the year		$133,000
Schedule of Noncash Financing and Investing Activities:		
Issued common stock for land		$ 80,000

After reviewing the statement, Walker telephoned you and commented, "Are you sure this statement is right?" Walker then raised the following questions:

1. "How can depreciation be a cash flow?"
2. "Issuing common stock for the land is listed in a separate schedule. This transaction has nothing to do with cash! Shouldn't this transaction be eliminated from the statement?"
3. "How can the gain on sale of investments be a deduction from net income in determining the cash flow from operating activities?"
4. "Why does the bank need this statement anyway? They can compute the increase in cash from the balance sheets for the last two years."

After jotting down Walkers' questions, you assured him that this statement was "right." But to alleviate Walkers' concern, you arranged a meeting for the following day.

a. How would you respond to each of Walkers' questions?
b. Do you think that the statement of cash flows enhances the chances of Tech Trends Inc. receiving the loan? Discuss.

SA 16-4
Analysis of cash flow from operations

The Retailing Division of Most Excellent Purchase Inc. provided the following information on its cash flow from operations:

Net income	$ 540,000
Increase in accounts receivable	(648,000)
Increase in inventory	(720,000)
Decrease in accounts payable	(108,000)
Depreciation	120,000
Cash flow from operating activities	$(816,000)

The manager of the Retailing Division provided the accompanying memo with this report:

From: Senior Vice President, Retailing Division

I am pleased to report that we had earnings of $540,000 over the last period. This resulted in a return on invested capital of 10%, which is near our targets for this division. I have been *aggressive in building the revenue volume in the division. As a result, I am happy to report that we have increased the number of new credit card customers as a result of an aggressive marketing campaign. In addition, we have found some excellent merchandise opportunities. Some of our suppliers have made some of their apparel merchandise available at a deep discount. We have purchased as much of these goods as possible in order to improve profitability. I'm also happy to report that our vendor payment problems have improved. We are nearly caught up on our overdue payables balances.*

Comment on the senior vice president's memo in light of the cash flow information.

SA 16-5
Statement of cash flows

Group Project

Internet Project

This activity will require two teams to retrieve cash flow statement information from the Internet. One team is to obtain the most recent year's statement of cash flows for Johnson & Johnson, and the other team the most recent year's statement of cash flows for AMR Corp.

The statement of cash flows is included as part of the annual report information that is a required disclosure to the Securities and Exchange Commission (SEC). SEC documents can be retrieved using the EdgarScan™ service at **http://www.sec.gov/edgar/searchedgar/webusers.htm**.

To obtain annual report information, type in a company name in the appropriate space. EdgarScan will list the reports available to you for the company you've selected. Select the most recent annual report filing, identified as a 10-K or 10-K405. EdgarScan provides an outline of the report, including the separate financial statements. You can double-click the income statement and balance sheet for the selected company into an Excel™ spreadsheet for further analysis.

As a group, compare the two statements of cash flows.

a. How are Johnson & Johnson and AMR Corp. similar or different regarding cash flows?
b. Compute and compare the free cash flow for each company, assuming additions to property, plant, and equipment replace current capacity.

Answers to Self-Examination Questions

1. **D** Cash flows from operating activities affect transactions that enter into the determination of net income, such as the receipt of cash from customers on account (answer D). Receipts of cash from the sale of stock (answer A) and the sale of bonds (answer B) and payments of cash for dividends (answer C) are cash flows from financing activities.
2. **A** Cash flows from investing activities include receipts from the sale of noncurrent assets, such as equipment (answer A), and payments to acquire noncurrent assets. Receipts of cash from the sale of stock (answer B) and payments of cash for dividends (answer C) and to acquire treasury stock (answer D) are cash flows from financing activities.
3. **C** Payment of cash for dividends (answer C) is an example of a financing activity. The receipt of cash from customers on account (answer A) is an operating activity. The receipt of cash from the sale of equipment (answer B) is an investing activity. The payment of cash to acquire land (answer D) is an example of an investing activity.
4. **D** The indirect method (answer D) reports cash flows from operating activities by beginning with net income and adjusting it for revenues and expenses not involving the receipt or payment of cash.
5. **C** The Cash Flows from Operating Activities section of the statement of cash flows would report net cash flow from operating activities of $65,500, determined as follows:

Cash flows from operating activities:		
Net income	$55,000	
Adjustments to reconcile net income to net cash flow from operating activities:		
Depreciation	22,000	
Changes in current operating assets and liabilities:		
Increase in accounts receivable	(10,000)	
Decrease in inventories	5,000	
Decrease in prepaid expenses	500	
Decrease in accounts payable	(7,000)	
Net cash flow from operating activities		$65,500

APPENDICES

Appendix A

Interest Tables

Present Value of $1 at Compound Interest Due in *n* Periods

Periods	5%	5.5%	6%	6.5%	7%	8%
1	0.95238	0.94787	0.94334	0.93897	0.93458	0.92593
2	0.90703	0.89845	0.89000	0.88166	0.87344	0.85734
3	0.86384	0.85161	0.83962	0.82785	0.81630	0.79383
4	0.82270	0.80722	0.79209	0.77732	0.76290	0.73503
5	0.78353	0.76513	0.74726	0.72988	0.71290	0.68058
6	0.74622	0.72525	0.70496	0.68533	0.66634	0.63017
7	0.71068	0.68744	0.66506	0.64351	0.62275	0.58349
8	0.67684	0.65160	0.62741	0.60423	0.58201	0.54027
9	0.64461	0.61763	0.59190	0.56735	0.54393	0.50025
10	0.61391	0.58543	0.55840	0.53273	0.50835	0.46319
11	0.58468	0.55491	0.52679	0.50021	0.47509	0.42888
12	0.55684	0.52598	0.49697	0.46968	0.44401	0.39711
13	0.53032	0.49856	0.46884	0.44102	0.41496	0.36770
14	0.50507	0.47257	0.44230	0.41410	0.38782	0.34046
15	0.48102	0.44793	0.41726	0.38883	0.36245	0.31524
16	0.45811	0.42458	0.39365	0.36510	0.33874	0.29189
17	0.43630	0.40245	0.37136	0.34281	0.31657	0.27027
18	0.41552	0.38147	0.35034	0.32189	0.29586	0.25025
19	0.39573	0.36158	0.33051	0.30224	0.27651	0.23171
20	0.37689	0.34273	0.31180	0.28380	0.25842	0.21455
21	0.35894	0.32486	0.29416	0.26648	0.24151	0.19866
22	0.34185	0.30793	0.27750	0.25021	0.22571	0.18394
23	0.32557	0.29187	0.26180	0.23494	0.21095	0.17032
24	0.31007	0.27666	0.24698	0.22060	0.19715	0.15770
25	0.29530	0.26223	0.23300	0.20714	0.18425	0.14602
26	0.28124	0.24856	0.21981	0.19450	0.17211	0.13520
27	0.26785	0.23560	0.20737	0.18263	0.16093	0.12519
28	0.25509	0.22332	0.19563	0.17148	0.15040	0.11591
29	0.24295	0.21168	0.18456	0.16101	0.14056	0.10733
30	0.23138	0.20064	0.17411	0.15119	0.13137	0.09938
31	0.22036	0.19018	0.16426	0.14196	0.12277	0.09202
32	0.20987	0.18027	0.15496	0.13329	0.11474	0.08520
33	0.19987	0.17087	0.14619	0.12516	0.10724	0.07889
34	0.19036	0.16196	0.13791	0.11752	0.10022	0.07304
35	0.18129	0.15352	0.13010	0.11035	0.09366	0.06764
40	0.14205	0.11746	0.09722	0.08054	0.06678	0.04603
45	0.11130	0.08988	0.07265	0.05879	0.04761	0.03133
50	0.08720	0.06877	0.05429	0.04291	0.03395	0.02132

Present Value of $1 at Compound Interest Due in *n* Periods

Periods	9%	10%	11%	12%	13%	14%
1	0.91743	0.90909	0.90090	0.89286	0.88496	0.87719
2	0.84168	0.82645	0.81162	0.79719	0.78315	0.76947
3	0.77218	0.75132	0.73119	0.71178	0.69305	0.67497
4	0.70842	0.68301	0.65873	0.63552	0.61332	0.59208
5	0.64993	0.62092	0.59345	0.56743	0.54276	0.51937
6	0.59627	0.56447	0.53464	0.50663	0.48032	0.45559
7	0.54703	0.51316	0.48166	0.45235	0.42506	0.39964
8	0.50187	0.46651	0.43393	0.40388	0.37616	0.35056
9	0.46043	0.42410	0.39092	0.36061	0.33288	0.30751
10	0.42241	0.38554	0.35218	0.32197	0.29459	0.26974
11	0.38753	0.35049	0.31728	0.28748	0.26070	0.23662
12	0.35554	0.31863	0.28584	0.25668	0.23071	0.20756
13	0.32618	0.28966	0.25751	0.22917	0.20416	0.18207
14	0.29925	0.26333	0.23199	0.20462	0.18068	0.15971
15	0.27454	0.23939	0.20900	0.18270	0.15989	0.14010
16	0.25187	0.21763	0.18829	0.16312	0.14150	0.12289
17	0.23107	0.19784	0.16963	0.14564	0.12522	0.10780
18	0.21199	0.17986	0.15282	0.13004	0.11081	0.09456
19	0.19449	0.16351	0.13768	0.11611	0.09806	0.08295
20	0.17843	0.14864	0.12403	0.10367	0.08678	0.07276
21	0.16370	0.13513	0.11174	0.09256	0.07680	0.06383
22	0.15018	0.12285	0.10067	0.08264	0.06796	0.05599
23	0.13778	0.11168	0.09069	0.07379	0.06014	0.04911
24	0.12640	0.10153	0.08170	0.06588	0.05323	0.04308
25	0.11597	0.09230	0.07361	0.05882	0.04710	0.03779
26	0.10639	0.08390	0.06631	0.05252	0.04168	0.03315
27	0.09761	0.07628	0.05974	0.04689	0.03689	0.02908
28	0.08955	0.06934	0.05382	0.04187	0.03264	0.02551
29	0.08216	0.06304	0.04849	0.03738	0.02889	0.02237
30	0.07537	0.05731	0.04368	0.03338	0.02557	0.01963
31	0.06915	0.05210	0.03935	0.02980	0.02262	0.01722
32	0.06344	0.04736	0.03545	0.02661	0.02002	0.01510
33	0.05820	0.04306	0.03194	0.02376	0.01772	0.01325
34	0.05331	0.03914	0.02878	0.02121	0.01568	0.01162
35	0.04899	0.03558	0.02592	0.01894	0.01388	0.01019
40	0.03184	0.02210	0.01538	0.01075	0.00753	0.00529
45	0.02069	0.01372	0.00913	0.00610	0.00409	0.00275
50	0.01345	0.00852	0.00542	0.00346	0.00222	0.00143

Present Value of Ordinary Annuity of $1 per Period

Periods	5%	5.5%	6%	6.5%	7%	8%
1	0.95238	0.94787	0.94340	0.93897	0.93458	0.92593
2	1.85941	1.84632	1.83339	1.82063	1.80802	1.78326
3	2.72325	2.69793	2.67301	2.64848	2.62432	2.57710
4	3.54595	3.50515	3.46511	3.42580	3.38721	3.31213
5	4.32948	4.27028	4.21236	4.15568	4.10020	3.99271
6	5.07569	4.99553	4.91732	4.84101	4.76654	4.62288
7	5.78637	5.68297	5.58238	5.48452	5.38923	5.20637
8	6.46321	6.33457	6.20979	6.08875	5.97130	5.74664
9	7.10782	6.95220	6.80169	6.65610	6.51523	6.24689
10	7.72174	7.53763	7.36009	7.18883	7.02358	6.71008
11	8.30641	8.09254	7.88688	7.68904	7.49867	7.13896
12	8.86325	8.61852	8.38384	8.15873	7.94269	7.53608
13	9.39357	9.11708	8.85268	8.59974	8.35765	7.90378
14	9.89864	9.58965	9.29498	9.01384	8.74547	8.22424
15	10.37966	10.03758	9.71225	9.40267	9.10791	8.55948
16	10.83777	10.46216	10.10590	9.76776	9.44665	8.85137
17	11.27407	10.86461	10.47726	10.11058	9.76322	9.12164
18	11.68959	11.24607	10.82760	10.43247	10.05909	9.37189
19	12.08532	11.60765	11.15812	10.73471	10.33560	9.60360
20	12.46221	11.95038	11.46992	11.01851	10.59401	9.81815
21	12.82115	12.27524	11.76408	11.28498	10.83553	10.01680
22	13.16300	12.58317	12.04158	11.53520	11.06124	10.20074
23	13.48857	12.87504	12.30338	11.77014	11.27219	10.37106
24	13.79864	13.15170	12.55036	11.99074	11.46933	10.52876
25	14.09394	13.41393	12.78336	12.19788	11.65358	10.67478
26	14.37518	13.66250	13.00317	12.39237	11.82578	10.80998
27	14.64303	13.89810	13.21053	12.57500	11.98671	10.93516
28	14.89813	14.12142	13.40616	12.74648	12.13711	11.05108
29	15.14107	14.33310	13.59072	12.90749	12.27767	11.15841
30	15.37245	14.53375	13.76483	13.05868	12.40904	11.25778
31	15.59281	14.72393	13.92909	13.20063	12.53181	11.34980
32	15.80268	14.90420	14.08404	13.33393	12.64656	11.43500
33	16.00255	15.07507	14.23023	13.45909	12.75379	11.51389
34	16.19290	15.23703	14.36814	13.57661	12.85401	11.58693
35	16.37420	15.39055	14.49825	13.68696	12.94767	11.65457
40	17.15909	16.04612	15.04630	14.14553	13.33171	11.92461
45	17.77407	16.54773	15.45583	14.48023	13.60552	12.10840
50	18.25592	16.93152	15.76186	14.72452	13.80075	12.23348

Present Value of Ordinary Annuity of $1 per Period

Periods	9%	10%	11%	12%	13%	14%
1	0.91743	0.90909	0.90090	0.89286	0.88496	0.87719
2	1.75911	1.73554	1.71252	1.69005	1.66810	1.64666
3	2.53130	2.48685	2.44371	2.40183	2.36115	2.32163
4	3.23972	3.16986	3.10245	3.03735	2.97447	2.91371
5	3.88965	3.79079	3.69590	3.60478	3.51723	3.43308
6	4.48592	4.35526	4.23054	4.11141	3.99755	3.88867
7	5.03295	4.86842	4.71220	4.56376	4.42261	4.28830
8	5.53482	5.33493	5.14612	4.96764	4.79677	4.63886
9	5.99525	5.75902	5.53705	5.32825	5.13166	4.94637
10	6.41766	6.14457	5.88923	5.65022	5.42624	5.21612
11	6.80519	6.49506	6.20652	5.93770	5.68694	5.45273
12	7.16072	6.81369	6.49236	6.19437	5.91765	5.66029
13	7.48690	7.10336	6.74987	6.42355	6.12181	5.84236
14	7.78615	7.36669	6.96187	6.62817	6.30249	6.00207
15	8.06069	7.60608	7.19087	6.81086	6.46238	6.14217
16	8.31256	7.82371	7.37916	6.97399	6.60388	6.26506
17	8.54363	8.02155	7.54879	7.11963	6.72909	6.37286
18	8.75562	8.20141	7.70162	7.24967	6.83991	6.46742
19	8.95012	8.36492	7.83929	7.36578	6.93797	6.55037
20	9.12855	8.51356	7.96333	7.46944	7.02475	6.62313
21	9.29224	8.64869	8.07507	7.56200	7.10155	6.68696
22	9.44242	8.77154	8.17574	7.64465	7.16951	6.74294
23	9.58021	8.88322	8.26643	7.71843	7.22966	6.79206
24	9.70661	8.98474	8.34814	7.78432	7.28288	6.83514
25	9.82258	9.07704	8.42174	7.84314	7.32998	6.87293
26	9.92897	9.16094	8.48806	7.89566	7.37167	6.90608
27	10.02658	9.23722	8.54780	7.94255	7.40856	6.93515
28	10.11613	9.30657	8.60162	7.98442	7.44120	6.96066
29	10.19828	9.36961	8.65011	8.02181	7.47009	6.98304
30	10.27365	9.42691	8.69379	8.05518	7.49565	7.00266
31	10.34280	9.47901	8.73315	8.08499	7.51828	7.01988
32	10.40624	9.52638	8.76860	8.11159	7.53830	7.03498
33	10.46444	9.56943	8.80054	8.13535	7.55602	7.04823
34	10.51784	9.60858	8.82932	8.15656	7.57170	7.05985
35	10.56682	9.64416	8.85524	8.17550	7.58557	7.07005
40	10.75736	9.77905	8.95105	8.24378	7.63438	7.10504
45	10.88118	9.86281	9.00791	8.28252	7.66086	7.12322
50	10.96168	9.91481	9.04165	8.30450	7.67524	7.13266

Appendix B

Reversing Entries

Some of the adjusting entries recorded at the end of the accounting period affect transactions that occur in the next period. In such cases, a reversing entry may be used to simplify the recording of the next period's transactions.

To illustrate, an adjusting entry for accrued wages expense affects the first payment of wages in the next period. Without using a reversing entry, Wages Payable must be debited for the accrued wages at the end of the preceding period. In addition, Wages Expense must also be debited for only that portion of the payroll that is an expense of the current period.

Using a reversing entry, however, simplifies the analysis and recording of the first wages payment in the next period. As the term implies, a *reversing entry* is the exact opposite of the related adjusting entry. The amounts and accounts are the same as the adjusting entry, but the debits and credits are reversed.

netsolutions

Reversing entries are illustrated by using the accrued wages for NetSolutions presented in Chapter 3. These data are summarized in Exhibit 1.

Exhibit 1

Accrued Wages

1. Wages are paid on the second and fourth Fridays for the two-week periods ending on those Fridays. The payments were $950 on December 13 and $1,200 on December 27.
2. The wages accrued for Monday and Tuesday, December 30 and 31, are $250.
3. Wages paid on Friday, January 10, total $1,275.
4. Wages expense, January 1–10, $10,025.

December

S	M	T	W	T	F	S
1	2	3	4	5	6	7
8	9	10	11	12	13	14
15	16	17	18	19	20	21
22	23	24	25	26	27	28
29	30	31				

Wages expense (paid), $950

Wages expense (paid), $1,200

Wages expense (accrued), $250

January

S	M	T	W	T	F	S
			1	2	3	4
5	6	7	8	9	10	11

Wages expense (Jan. 1–10), $1,025

Wages expense (paid), $1,275

The adjusting entry for the accrued wages of December 30 and 31 is as follows:

2009 Dec.	31	Wages Expense	51	250	
		Wages Payable	22		250
		Accrued wages.			

After the adjusting entry is recorded, Wages Expense will have a debit balance of $4,525 ($4,275 + $250), as shown on the top of page B-3. Wages Payable will have a credit balance of $250, as shown on page B-3.

After the closing entries are recorded, Wages Expense will have a zero balance. However, since Wages Payable is a liability account, it is not closed. Thus, Wages Payable will have a credit balance of $250 as of January 1, 2010.

Without recording a reversing entry, the payment of the $1,275 payroll on January 10 would be recorded as follows:

2010 Jan.	10	Wages Payable	22	250	
		Wages Expense	51	1,025	
		Cash	11		1,275

As shown above, to record the January 10 payroll correctly Wages Payable must be debited for $250. This means that the employee who records the January 10 payroll must refer to the December 31, 2009, adjusting entry or to the ledger to determine the amount to debit Wages Payable.

Because the January 10 payroll is not recorded in the normal manner, there is a greater chance that an error may occur. This chance of error is reduced by recording a reversing entry as of the first day of the next period. For example, the reversing entry for the accrued wages expense would be recorded on January 1, 2010, as follows:

2010 Jan.	1	Wages Payable	22	250	
		Wages Expense	51		250
		Reversing entry.			

The preceding reversing entry transfers the $250 liability from Wages Payable to the credit side of Wages Expense. The nature of the $250 is unchanged—it is still a liability. However, because of its unusual nature, an explanation is written under the reversing entry.

When the payroll is paid on January 10, the following entry is recorded:

Jan.	10	Wages Expense	51	1,275	
		Cash	11		1,275

After the January 10 payroll is recorded, Wages Expense has a debit balance of $1,025. This is the wages expense for the period January 1–10, 2010.

Wages Payable and Wages Expense after posting the adjusting, closing, and reversing entries are shown on the next page.

Account *Wages Payable* — Account No. 22

Date		Item	Post. Ref.	Debit	Credit	Balance Debit	Balance Credit
2009 Dec.	31	Adjusting	5		250		250
2010 Jan.	1	Reversing	7	250		—	—

Account *Wages Expense* — Account No. 51

Date		Item	Post. Ref.	Debit	Credit	Balance Debit	Balance Credit
2009 Nov.	30		1	2,125		2,125	
Dec.	13		3	950		3,075	
	27		3	1,200		4,275	
	31	Adjusting	5	250		4,525	
	31	Closing	6		4,525	—	—
2010 Jan.	1	Reversing	7		250		250
	10		7	1,275		1,025	

In addition to accrued expenses (accrued liabilities), reversing entries are also used for accrued revenues (accrued assets). To illustrate, the reversing entry for NetSolutions' accrued fees earned as of December 31, 2009, is as follows:

Jan.	1	Fees Earned	41	500	
		Accounts Receivable	12		500
		Reversing entry.			

The use of reversing entries is optional. However, in computerized accounting systems, data entry employees often input routine accounting entries. In such cases, reversing entries may be useful in avoiding errors.

EX B-1
Adjusting and reversing entries

On the basis of the following data, (a) journalize the adjusting entries at December 31, the end of the current fiscal year, and (b) journalize the reversing entries on January 1, the first day of the following year.

1. Sales salaries are uniformly $17,375 for a five-day workweek, ending on Friday. The last payday of the year was Friday, December 26.
2. Accrued fees earned but not recorded at December 31, $19,850.

EX B-2
Adjusting and reversing entries

On the basis of the following data, (a) journalize the adjusting entries at June 30, the end of the current fiscal year, and (b) journalize the reversing entries on July 1, the first day of the following year.

1. Wages are uniformly $25,900 for a five-day workweek, ending on Friday. The last payday of the year was Friday, June 27.
2. Accrued fees earned but not recorded at June 30, $36,100.

EX B-3
Entries posted to the wages expense account

Portions of the wages expense account of a business are shown below.

a. Indicate the nature of the entry (payment, adjusting, closing, reversing) from which each numbered posting was made.
b. Journalize the complete entry from which each numbered posting was made.

Account ***Wages Expense*** **Account No.** ***53***

Date	Item	Post. Ref.	Dr.	Cr.	Balance Dr.	Balance Cr.
2009						
Dec. 26	(1)	49	27,000		1,400,000	
31	(2)	50	16,200		1,416,200	
31	(3)	51		1,416,200	—	—
2010						
Jan. 1	(4)	52		16,200		16,200
2	(5)	53	27,000		10,800	

EX B-4
Entries posted to the salaries expense account

Portions of the salaries expense account of a business are shown below.

Account ***Salaries Expense*** **Account No.** ***53***

Date	Item	Post. Ref.	Dr.	Cr.	Balance Dr.	Balance Cr.
2009						
Dec. 27	(1)	29	17,500		910,000	
31	(2)	30	7,000		917,000	
31	(3)	31		917,000	—	—
2010						
Jan. 1	(4)	32		7,000		7,000
2	(5)	33	17,500		10,500	

a. Indicate the nature of the entry (payment, adjusting, closing, reversing) from which each numbered posting was made.
b. Journalize the complete entry from which each numbered posting was made.

Appendix C

End-of-Period Spreadsheet (Work Sheet) for a Merchandising Business

A merchandising business may use an end-of-period spreadsheet (work sheet) for preparing financial statements and adjusting and closing entries. This appendix illustrates such a spreadsheet for the perpetual inventory system.

netsolutions

The end-of-period spreadsheet in Exhibit 1 is for NetSolutions on December 31, 2011. Exhibit 1 was prepared using the following steps that are described and illustrated in the appendix to Chapter 4.

Step 1. Enter the Title.
Step 2. Enter the Unadjusted Trial Balance.
Step 3. Enter the Adjustments.
Step 4. Enter the Adjusted Trial Balance.
Step 5. Extend the Accounts to the Income Statement and Balance Sheet columns.
Step 6. Total the Income Statement and Balance Sheet columns, compute the Net Income or Net Loss, and complete the spreadsheet.

The data needed for adjusting the accounts of NetSolutions are as follows:

Physical merchandise inventory on December 31, 2011		$62,150
Office supplies on hand on December 31, 2011		480
Insurance expired during 2011		1,910
Depreciation during 2011 on: Store equipment		3,100
Office equipment		2,490
Salaries accrued on December 31, 2011: Sales salaries	$780	
Office salaries	360	1,140
Rent earned during 2011		600

There is no required order for analyzing the adjustment data and the accounts in the spreadsheet. However, the accounts are normally analyzed in the order in which they appear in the spreadsheet. Using this approach, the adjustment for merchandise inventory shrinkage is listed first as entry (a), followed by the adjustment for office supplies used as entry (b), and so on.

After all the adjustments have been entered, the Adjustments columns are totaled to prove the equality of debits and credits. The adjusted trial balance is entered by combining the adjustments with the unadjusted balances for each account.[1] The Adjusted Trial Balance columns are then totaled to prove the equality of debits and credits. The adjusted balances are then extended to the statement columns. The four statement columns are totaled, and the net income or net loss is determined.

For NetSolutions, the difference between the Credit and Debit columns of the Income Statement section is $75,400, the amount of the net income. The difference between the Debit and Credit columns of the Balance Sheet section is also $75,400, which is the increase in owner's equity as a result of the net income.

1 Some accountants prefer to eliminate the Adjusted Trial Balance columns and to extend the adjusted balances directly to the statement columns. Such a spreadsheet (work sheet) is often used if there are only a few adjustment items.

Exhibit 1

End-of-Period Spreadsheet (Work Sheet) for a Merchandising Business Using Perpetual Inventory System

	A	B	C	D	E	F	G	H	I	J	K
1	NetSolutions										
2	End-of-Period Spreadsheet (Work Sheet)										
3	For the Year Ended December 31, 2011										
4		Unadjusted				Adjusted		Income			
5	Account Title	Trial Balance		Adjustments		Trial Balance		Statement		Balance Sheet	
6		Dr.	Cr.	Dr.	Cr.	Dr.	Cr.	Dr.	Cr.	Dr.	Cr.
7	Cash	52,950				52,950				52,950	
8	Accounts Receivable	91,080				91,080				91,080	
9	Merchandise Inventory	63,950			(a)1,800	62,150				62,150	
10	Office Supplies	1,090			(b) 610	480				480	
11	Prepaid Insurance	4,560			(c)1,910	2,650				2,650	
12	Land	20,000				20,000				20,000	
13	Store Equipment	27,100				27,100				27,100	
14	Accum. Depr.—Store Equipment		2,600		(d)3,100		5,700				5,700
15	Office Equipment	15,570				15,570				15,570	
16	Accum. Depr.—Office Equipment		2,230		(e)2,490		4,720				4,720
17	Accounts Payable		22,420				22,420				22,420
18	Salaries Payable				(f)1,140		1,140				1,140
19	Unearned Rent		2,400	(g) 600			1,800				1,800
20	Notes Payable										
21	(final payment due 2019)		25,000				25,000				25,000
22	Chris Clark, Capital		153,800				153,800				153,800
23	Chris Clark, Drawing	18,000				18,000				18,000	
24	Sales		720,185				720,185		720,185		
25	Sales Returns and Allowances	6,140				6,140		6,140			
26	Sales Discounts	5,790				5,790		5,790			
27	Cost of Merchandise Sold	523,505		(a)1,800		525,305		525,305			
28	Sales Salaries Expense	52,650		(f) 780		53,430		53,430			
29	Advertising Expense	10,860				10,860		10,860			
30	Depr. Exp.—Store Equipment			(d)3,100		3,100		3,100			
31	Delivery Expense	2,800				2,800		2,800			
32	Miscellaneous Selling Expense	630				630		630			
33	Office Salaries Expense	20,660		(f) 360		21,020		21,020			
34	Rent Expense	8,100				8,100		8,100			
35	Depr. Exp.—Office Equipment			(e)2,490		2,490		2,490			
36	Insurance Expense			(c)1,910		1,910		1,910			
37	Office Supplies Expense			(b) 610		610		610			
38	Misc. Administrative Expense	760				760		760			
39	Rent Revenue				(g) 600		600		600		
40	Interest Expense	2,440				2,440		2,440			
41		928,635	928,635	11,650	11,650	935,365	935,365	645,385	720,785	289,980	214,580
42	Net income							75,400			75,400
43								720,785	720,785	289,980	289,980
44											

(a) Merchandise inventory shrinkage for period, $1,800 ($63,950 – $62,150).
(b) Office supplies used, $610 ($1,090 – $480).
(c) Insurance expired, $1,910.
(d) Depreciation of store equipment, $3,100.
(e) Depreciation of office equipment, $2,490.
(f) Salaries accrued but not paid (sales salaries, $780; office salaries, $360), $1,140.
(g) Rent earned from amount received in advance, $600.

The income statement, statement of owner's equity, and balance sheet can be prepared from the spreadsheet (work sheet). These financial statements are shown in Exhibits 1, 4, and 5 in Chapter 6. The Adjustments columns in the spreadsheet (work sheet) may be used as the basis for journalizing the adjusting entries. NetSolutions' adjusting entries at the end of 2011 are shown at the top of the following page.

Journal Page 28

Date		Description	Post. Ref.	Debit	Credit
		Adjusting Entries			
2011 Dec.	31	Cost of Merchandise Sold	510	1,800	
		Merchandise Inventory	115		1,800
		Inventory shrinkage.			
	31	Office Supplies Expense	534	610	
		Office Supplies	116		610
		Supplies used.			
	31	Insurance Expense	533	1,910	
		Prepaid Insurance	117		1,910
		Insurance expired.			
	31	Depr. Expense—Store Equipment	522	3,100	
		Accumulated Depr.—Store Equipment	124		3,100
		Store equipment depreciation.			
	31	Depr. Expense—Office Equipment	532	2,490	
		Accumulated Depr.—Office Equipment	126		2,490
		Office equipment depreciation.			
	31	Sales Salaries Expense	520	780	
		Office Salaries Expense	530	360	
		Salaries Payable	211		1,140
		Accrued salaries.			
	31	Unearned Rent	212	600	
		Rent Revenue	610		600
		Rent earned.			

The Income Statement columns of the work sheet may be used as the basis for preparing the closing entries. The closing entries for NetSolutions at the end of 2011 are shown on page 274 of Chapter 6.

After the closing entries have been prepared and posted to the accounts, a post-closing trial balance may be prepared to verify the debit-credit equality. The only accounts that should appear on the post-closing trial balance are the asset, contra asset, liability, and owner's capital accounts with balances. These are the same accounts that appear on the end-of-period balance sheet.

PR C-1
End-of-period spreadsheet (work sheet), financial statements, and adjusting and closing entries for perpetual inventory system

✔ 2. Net income: $38,800

The accounts and their balances in the ledger of Rack Saver Co. on December 31, 2010, are as follows:

Account	Balance	Account	Balance
Cash	$ 12,000	Sales	$800,000
Accounts Receivable	72,500	Sales Returns and Allowances	11,900
Merchandise Inventory	170,000	Sales Discounts	7,100
Prepaid Insurance	9,700	Cost of Merchandise Sold	500,000
Store Supplies	4,200	Sales Salaries Expense	96,400
Office Supplies	2,100	Advertising Expense	25,000
Store Equipment	360,000	Depreciation Expense—Store Equipment	—
Accumulated Depreciation—Store Equipment	60,300	Store Supplies Expense	—
Office Equipment	70,000	Miscellaneous Selling Expense	1,600
Accumulated Depreciation—Office Equipment	17,200	Office Salaries Expense	64,000
Accounts Payable	46,700	Rent Expense	16,000
Salaries Payable	—	Insurance Expense	—
Unearned Rent	3,000	Depreciation Expense—Office Equipment	—
Note Payable (final payment due 2018)	180,000	Office Supplies Expense	—
Evan Hoffman, Capital	352,750	Miscellaneous Administrative Expense	1,650
Evan Hoffman, Drawing	25,000	Rent Revenue	—
Income Summary	—	Interest Expense	10,800

The data needed for year-end adjustments on December 31 are as follows:

Physical merchandise inventory on December 31		$162,500
Insurance expired during the year		3,600
Supplies on hand on December 31:		
Store supplies		1,050
Office supplies		600
Depreciation for the year:		
Store equipment		6,000
Office equipment		3,000
Salaries payable on December 31:		
Sales salaries	$1,800	
Office salaries	1,200	3,000
Unearned rent on December 31		2,000

Instructions

1. Prepare an end-of-period spreadsheet (work sheet) for the fiscal year ended December 31, 2010. List all accounts in the order given.
2. Prepare a multiple-step income statement.
3. Prepare a statement of owner's equity.
4. Prepare a report form of balance sheet, assuming that the current portion of the note payable is $36,000.
5. Journalize the adjusting entries.
6. Journalize the closing entries.

PR C-2
End-of-period spreadsheet (work sheet), financial statements, and adjusting and closing entries for perpetual inventory system

✔ 1. Net income: $38,450

The accounts and their balances in the ledger of Quality Sports Co. on December 31, 2010, are as follows:

Cash	$ 18,000	Sales Discounts	$ 7,100
Accounts Receivable	42,500	Cost of Merchandise Sold	557,000
Merchandise Inventory	218,000	Sales Salaries Expense	101,400
Prepaid Insurance	8,000	Advertising Expense	45,000
Store Supplies	4,200	Depreciation Expense— Store Equipment	—
Office Supplies	2,100	Delivery Expense	6,000
Store Equipment	282,000	Store Supplies Expense	—
Accumulated Depreciation— Store Equipment	70,300	Miscellaneous Selling Expense	1,600
Office Equipment	60,000	Office Salaries Expense	64,000
Accumulated Depreciation— Office Equipment	17,200	Rent Expense	25,200
Accounts Payable	26,700	Insurance Expense	—
Salaries Payable	—	Depreciation Expense— Office Equipment	—
Unearned Rent	2,500	Office Supplies Expense	—
Note Payable (final payment, 2018)	175,000	Miscellaneous Administrative Expense	1,650
Rosario Noe, Capital	286,450	Rent Revenue	—
Rosario Noe, Drawing	10,000	Interest Expense	10,500
Sales	900,000		
Sales Returns and Allowances	13,900		

The data needed for year-end adjustments on December 31 are as follows:

Merchandise inventory on December 31		$211,000
Insurance expired during the year		5,000
Supplies on hand on December 31:		
Store supplies		1,150
Office supplies		750
Depreciation for the year:		
Store equipment		7,500
Office equipment		3,800
Salaries payable on December 31:		
Sales salaries	$1,500	
Office salaries	1,000	2,500
Unearned rent on December 31		500

Instructions

1. Prepare an end-of-period spreadsheet (work sheet) for the fiscal year ended December 31, listing all accounts in the order given.
2. Prepare a multiple-step income statement.
3. Prepare a statement of owner's equity.
4. Prepare a report form of balance sheet, assuming that the current portion of the note payable is $25,000.
5. Journalize the adjusting entries.
6. Journalize the closing entries.

Appendix D

Accounting for Deferred Income Taxes[1]

A corporation determines its taxable income according to the tax laws and files a corporate tax return. In contrast, a corporation prepares its financial statements using generally accepted accounting principles (GAAP). As a result, *taxable income* normally differs from *income before taxes* reported on the income statement.

Temporary Differences

Some differences between *taxable income* and *income before income taxes* are created because items are recognized in one period for tax purposes and in another period for income statement purposes. Such differences, called *temporary differences*, reverse or turn around in later years. Examples of items that create temporary differences include:

1. Revenues or gains that are taxed *after* they are reported in the income statement.

   Example: In some cases, companies make sales under an installment plan in which customers make periodic payments over future time periods. In such cases, the company recognizes revenue for financial reporting purposes when a sale is made but recognizes revenue for tax purposes when the cash is collected.
2. Expenses or losses that are deducted in determining taxable income *after* they are reported in the income statement.

   Example: Product warranty liability expense is estimated and reported in the year of the sale for financial statement reporting but is deducted for tax reporting when paid.
3. Revenues or gains that are taxed *before* they are reported in the income statement.

   Example: Cash received in advance for magazine subscriptions is included in taxable income when received but included in the income statement only when earned in a future period.
4. Expenses or losses that are deducted in determining taxable income *before* they are reported in the income statement.

   Example: MACRS depreciation is used for tax purposes, and the straight-line method is used for financial reporting purposes.

Since temporary differences reverse in later years, they do not change or reduce the total amount of taxable income over the life of a business. Exhibit 1 illustrates the reversing nature of temporary differences.

In Exhibit 1, a corporation uses MACRS depreciation for tax purposes and straight-line depreciation for financial statement purposes. MACRS recognizes more depreciation in the early years and less depreciation in the later years. However, the total depreciation expense is the same for both methods over the life of the asset.

As Exhibit 1 illustrates, temporary differences affect only the timing of when revenues and expenses are reported for tax purposes. The total amount of taxes paid does not change. In other words, only the timing of the payment of taxes is affected.

1 Accounting for deferred income taxes is a complex topic that is treated in greater detail in advanced accounting texts. The treatment here provides a general overview and conceptual understanding of the topic.

Exhibit 1

Temporary Differences

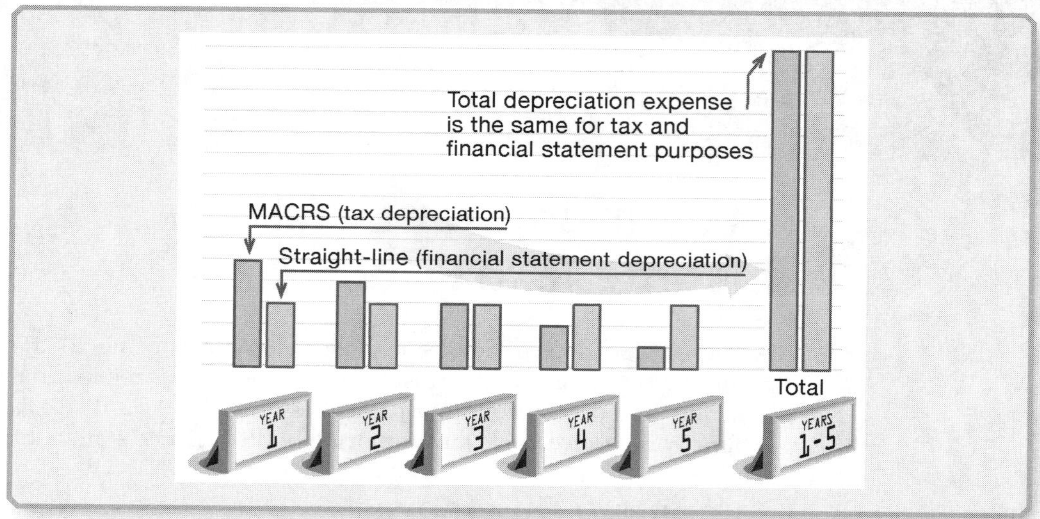

Most corporations use tax-planning methods that delay or defer the payment of taxes to later years. As a result, at the end of each year, most corporations will have two tax liabilities as follows:

1. Current income tax liability, which is due on the current year's taxable income.
2. Postponed or deferred tax liability, which is due in the future when the temporary differences reverse.

To illustrate, assume the following data for the first year of a corporation's operations:

Income before income taxes (income statement)	$ 300,000
Temporary differences	(200,000)
Taxable income (tax return)	$ 100,000
Income tax rate	40%

Based on the preceding data, the income tax expense reported on the income statement is $120,000 ($300,000 × 40%).[2] However, the current income tax liability (income tax due for the year) and reported on the corporate tax return is only $40,000 ($100,000 × 40%). The $80,000 ($120,000 − $40,000) difference is the deferred tax liability that will be paid in future years as shown below.

Income tax expense based on $300,000 reported income at 40%	$120,000
Income tax payable based on $100,000 taxable income at 40%	40,000
Income tax deferred to future years	$ 80,000

On the income statement, income tax expense of $120,000 ($300,000 × 40%) must be reported. This is done so that the current year's expenses (including income tax) are properly matched against the current year's revenue. The entry to record the income tax expense of $120,000 is as shown below.

		Income Tax Expense		120,000	
		Income Tax Payable			40,000
		Deferred Income Tax Payable			80,000
		Record income tax expense for the year.			

2 For purposes of illustration, the 40% rate is assumed to include all federal, state, and local income taxes.

The income tax expense reported on the income statement is the total tax, $120,000. Of this amount, $40,000 is currently due and $80,000 will be due in (deferred to) future years.

As the temporary differences reverse and the taxes become due in future years, the $80,000 in *Deferred Income Tax Payable* will be transferred to *Income Tax Payable*. To illustrate, assume that $48,000 of the deferred tax reverses and becomes due in the second year. The journal entry in the second year would be as follows:

		Deferred Income Tax Payable		48,000	
		Income Tax Payable			48,000
		Record income tax payable.			

Reporting Deferred Taxes

The balance of *Deferred Income Tax Payable* at the end of a year is reported as a liability.[3] The amount due within one year is classified as a current liability. The remainder is classified as a long-term liability or reported in a Deferred Credits section following the Long-Term Liabilities section.[4]

Permanent Differences

Differences between taxable income and income (before taxes) reported on the income statement may also arise because of the following:

1. Some revenues are exempt from tax.
2. Some expenses are not deductible in determining taxable income.

Interest from investments in municipal bonds is also tax exempt for individual taxpayers.

The preceding differences, which will not reverse with the passage of time, are called *permanent differences*. For example, interest income on municipal bonds is exempt from federal taxation.

Permanent differences create no special financial reporting problems. This is because the amount of income tax determined according to the tax laws is the *same* amount reported on the income statement.

3 In some cases, a deferred tax asset may arise for tax benefits to be received in the future. Such deferred tax assets are reported as either current or long-term assets, depending on when the benefits are expected to be realized.

4 Additional note disclosures for deferred income taxes are also required. These are discussed in advanced accounting texts.

EX D-1
Deferred tax entries

Ramsey Inc. has $600,000 of income before income taxes, a 35% tax rate, and $320,000 of taxable income. Provide the journal entry for the current year's taxes.

EX D-2
Deferred tax entries

Downstairs Corp. has $180,000 of income before income taxes, a 40% tax rate, and $90,000 of taxable income. Provide the journal entry for the current year's taxes.

EX D-3
Deferred income taxes

Mattress Systems Inc. recognized service revenue of $500,000 on its financial statements in 2009. Assume, however, that the Tax Code requires this amount to be recognized for tax purposes in 2010. The taxable income for 2009 and 2010 is $1,800,000 and $2,400,000, respectively. Assume a tax rate of 40%.

Prepare the journal entries to record the tax expense, deferred taxes, and taxes payable for 2009 and 2010, respectively.

PR D-1
Deferred taxes

✔ 1. Year-end balance, 3rd year, $30,000

Differences between the accounting methods applied to accounts and financial reports and those used in determining taxable income yielded the following amounts for the first four years of a corporation's operations:

	First Year	Second Year	Third Year	Fourth Year
Income before income taxes	$625,000	$750,000	$1,250,000	$1,000,000
Taxable income	500,000	700,000	1,350,000	1,075,000

The income tax rate for each of the four years was 40% of taxable income, and each year's taxes were promptly paid.

Instructions

1. Determine for each year the amounts described by the following captions, presenting the information in the form indicated:

Year	Income Tax Deducted on Income Statement	Income Tax Payments for the Year	Deferred Income Tax Payable	
			Year's Addition (Deduction)	Year-End Balance

2. Total the first three amount columns.

PR D-2
Deferred taxes

✔ 1. Year-end balance, 3rd year, $12,600

Differences between the accounting methods applied to accounts and financial reports and those used in determining taxable income yielded the following amounts for the first four years of a corporation's operations:

	First Year	Second Year	Third Year	Fourth Year
Income before income taxes	$150,000	$195,000	$270,000	$300,000
Taxable income	105,000	180,000	294,000	336,000

The income tax rate for each of the four years was 35% of taxable income, and each year's taxes were promptly paid.

Instructions

1. Determine for each year the amounts described by the following captions, presenting the information in the form indicated:

Year	Income Tax Deducted on Income Statement	Income Tax Payments for the Year	Deferred Income Tax Payable	
			Year's Addition (Deduction)	Year-End Balance

2. Total the first three amount columns.

Appendix E

FORM 10-K

NIKE INC - NKE

Filed: July 27, 2007 (period: May 31, 2007)

Annual report which provides a comprehensive overview of the company for the past year

Nike Inc. Form 10-K – Annual report [Section 13 or 15(d)] of The Securities Exchange Act of 1934 for the fiscal year ended May 31, 2007.

REPORT OF INDEPENDENT REGISTERED PUBLIC ACCOUNTING FIRM

To the Board of Directors and
Shareholders of NIKE, Inc.:

We have completed integrated audits of NIKE, Inc.'s consolidated financial statements and of its internal control over financial reporting as of May 31, 2007, in accordance with the standards of the Public Company Accounting Oversight Board (United States). Our opinions, based on our audits, are presented below.

Consolidated financial statements and financial statement schedule

In our opinion, the consolidated financial statements listed in the index appearing under Item 15(a)(1) present fairly, in all material respects, the financial position of NIKE, Inc. and its subsidiaries at May 31, 2007 and 2006, and the results of their operations and their cash flows for each of the three years in the period ended May 31, 2007 in conformity with accounting principles generally accepted in the United States of America. In addition, in our opinion, the financial statement schedule listed in the index appearing under Item 15(a)(2) presents fairly, in all material respects, the information set forth therein when read in conjunction with the related consolidated financial statements. These financial statements and financial statement schedule are the responsibility of the Company's management. Our responsibility is to express an opinion on these financial statements and financial statement schedule based on our audits. We conducted our audits of these statements in accordance with the standards of the Public Company Accounting Oversight Board (United States). Those standards require that we plan and perform the audit to obtain reasonable assurance about whether the financial statements are free of material misstatement. An audit of financial statements includes examining, on a test basis, evidence supporting the amounts and disclosures in the financial statements, assessing the accounting principles used and significant estimates made by management, and evaluating the overall financial statement presentation. We believe that our audits provide a reasonable basis for our opinion.

As discussed in Note 1 to the consolidated financial statements, effective June 1, 2006, the Company changed the manner in which it accounts for stock-based compensation in accordance with the Statement of Financial Accounting Standards No. 123R "Share-Based Payment."

Internal control over financial reporting

Also, in our opinion, management's assessment, included in "Management's Annual Report on Internal Control Over Financial Reporting" appearing under Item 8, that the Company maintained effective internal control over financial reporting as of May 31, 2007 based on criteria established in *Internal Control — Integrated Framework* issued by the Committee of Sponsoring Organizations of the Treadway Commission ("COSO"), is fairly stated, in all material respects, based on those criteria. Furthermore, in our opinion, the Company maintained, in all material respects, effective internal control over financial reporting as of May 31, 2007, based on criteria established in *Internal Control — Integrated Framework* issued by the COSO. The Company's management is responsible for maintaining effective internal control over financial reporting and for its assessment of the effectiveness of internal control over financial reporting. Our responsibility is to express opinions on management's assessment and on the effectiveness of the Company's internal control over financial reporting based on our audit. We conducted our audit of internal control over financial reporting in accordance with the standards of the Public Company Accounting Oversight Board (United States). Those standards require that we plan and perform the audit to obtain reasonable assurance about whether effective internal control over financial reporting was maintained in all material respects. An audit of internal control over financial reporting includes obtaining an understanding of internal control over financial reporting, evaluating management's assessment, testing and evaluating the design and operating effectiveness of internal control, and performing such other procedures as we consider necessary in the circumstances. We believe that our audit provides a reasonable basis for our opinions.

A company's internal control over financial reporting is a process designed to provide reasonable assurance regarding the reliability of financial reporting and the preparation of financial statements for external purposes in

Source: NIKE INC, 10-K, July 27, 2007

accordance with generally accepted accounting principles. A company's internal control over financial reporting includes those policies and procedures that (i) pertain to the maintenance of records that, in reasonable detail, accurately and fairly reflect the transactions and dispositions of the assets of the company; (ii) provide reasonable assurance that transactions are recorded as necessary to permit preparation of financial statements in accordance with generally accepted accounting principles, and that receipts and expenditures of the company are being made only in accordance with authorizations of management and directors of the company; and (iii) provide reasonable assurance regarding prevention or timely detection of unauthorized acquisition, use, or disposition of the company's assets that could have a material effect on the financial statements.

Because of its inherent limitations, internal control over financial reporting may not prevent or detect misstatements. Also, projections of any evaluation of effectiveness to future periods are subject to the risk that controls may become inadequate because of changes in conditions, or that the degree of compliance with the policies or procedures may deteriorate.

/s/ PricewaterhouseCoopers LLP

Portland, Oregon
July 26, 2007

Source: NIKE INC, 10-K, July 27, 2007

NIKE, INC.

CONSOLIDATED STATEMENTS OF INCOME

	Year Ended May 31,		
	2007	2006	2005
	(In millions, except per share data)		
Revenues	$ 16,325.9	$ 14,954.9	$ 13,739.7
Cost of sales	9,165.4	8,367.9	7,624.3
Gross margin	7,160.5	6,587.0	6,115.4
Selling and administrative expense	5,028.7	4,477.8	4,221.7
Interest (income) expense, net (Notes 1, 6 and 7)	(67.2)	(36.8)	4.8
Other (income) expense, net (Notes 5 and 16)	(0.9)	4.4	29.1
Income before income taxes	2,199.9	2,141.6	1,859.8
Income taxes (Note 8)	708.4	749.6	648.2
Net income	$ 1,491.5	$ 1,392.0	$ 1,211.6
Basic earnings per common share (Notes 1 and 11)	$ 2.96	$ 2.69	$ 2.31
Diluted earnings per common share (Notes 1 and 11)	$ 2.93	$ 2.64	$ 2.24
Dividends declared per common share	$ 0.71	$ 0.59	$ 0.475

The accompanying notes to consolidated financial statements are an integral part of this statement.

Source: NIKE INC, 10-K, July 27, 2007

NIKE, INC.

CONSOLIDATED BALANCE SHEETS

	May 31, 2007	May 31, 2006
	(In millions)	
ASSETS		
Current assets:		
Cash and equivalents	$ 1,856.7	$ 954.2
Short-term investments	990.3	1,348.8
Accounts receivable, net	2,494.7	2,382.9
Inventories (Note 2)	2,121.9	2,076.7
Deferred income taxes (Note 8)	219.7	203.3
Prepaid expenses and other current assets	393.2	380.1
Total current assets	8,076.5	7,346.0
Property, plant and equipment, net (Note 3)	1,678.3	1,657.7
Identifiable intangible assets, net (Note 4)	409.9	405.5
Goodwill (Note 4)	130.8	130.8
Deferred income taxes and other assets (Note 8)	392.8	329.6
Total assets	$ 10,688.3	$ 9,869.6
LIABILITIES AND SHAREHOLDERS' EQUITY		
Current liabilities:		
Current portion of long-term debt (Note 7)	$ 30.5	$ 255.3
Notes payable (Note 6)	100.8	43.4
Accounts payable (Note 6)	1,040.3	952.2
Accrued liabilities (Notes 5 and 16)	1,303.4	1,276.0
Income taxes payable	109.0	85.5
Total current liabilities	2,584.0	2,612.4
Long-term debt (Note 7)	409.9	410.7
Deferred income taxes and other liabilities (Note 8)	668.7	561.0
Commitments and contingencies (Notes 14 and 16)	—	—
Redeemable Preferred Stock (Note 9)	0.3	0.3
Shareholders' equity:		
Common stock at stated value (Note 10):		
Class A convertible — 117.6 and 127.8 shares outstanding	0.1	0.1
Class B — 384.1 and 384.2 shares outstanding	2.7	2.7
Capital in excess of stated value	1,960.0	1,447.3
Accumulated other comprehensive income (Note 13)	177.4	121.7
Retained earnings	4,885.2	4,713.4
Total shareholders' equity	7,025.4	6,285.2
Total liabilities and shareholders' equity	$ 10,688.3	$ 9,869.6

The accompanying notes to consolidated financial statements are an integral part of this statement.

Source: NIKE INC, 10-K, July 27, 2007

NIKE, INC.

CONSOLIDATED STATEMENTS OF CASH FLOWS

	Year Ended May 31,		
	2007	2006	2005
		(In millions)	
Cash provided (used) by operations:			
Net income	$ 1,491.5	$ 1,392.0	$ 1,211.6
Income charges not affecting cash:			
Depreciation	269.7	282.0	257.2
Deferred income taxes	34.1	(26.0)	21.3
Stock-based compensation (Notes 1 and 10)	147.7	11.8	4.9
Amortization and other	0.5	(2.9)	25.6
Income tax benefit from exercise of stock options	—	54.2	63.1
Changes in certain working capital components and other assets and liabilities:			
Increase in accounts receivable	(39.6)	(85.1)	(93.5)
Increase in inventories	(49.5)	(200.3)	(103.3)
(Increase) decrease in prepaid expenses and other current assets	(60.8)	(37.2)	71.4
Increase in accounts payable, accrued liabilities and income taxes payable	85.1	279.4	112.4
Cash provided by operations	1,878.7	1,667.9	1,570.7
Cash provided (used) by investing activities:			
Purchases of short-term investments	(2,133.8)	(2,619.7)	(1,527.2)
Maturities of short-term investments	2,516.2	1,709.8	1,491.9
Additions to property, plant and equipment	(313.5)	(333.7)	(257.1)
Disposals of property, plant and equipment	28.3	1.6	7.2
Increase in other assets, net of other liabilities	(4.3)	(34.6)	(28.0)
Acquisition of subsidiary, net of cash acquired	—	—	(47.2)
Cash provided (used) by investing activities	92.9	(1,276.6)	(360.4)
Cash provided (used) by financing activities:			
Proceeds from issuance of long-term debt	41.8	—	—
Reductions in long-term debt, including current portion	(255.7)	(6.0)	(9.2)
Increase (decrease) in notes payable	52.6	(18.2)	(81.7)
Proceeds from exercise of stock options and other stock issuances	322.9	225.3	226.8
Excess tax benefits from share-based payment arrangements	55.8	—	—
Repurchase of common stock	(985.2)	(761.1)	(556.2)
Dividends — common and preferred	(343.7)	(290.9)	(236.7)
Cash used by financing activities	(1,111.5)	(850.9)	(657.0)
Effect of exchange rate changes	42.4	25.7	6.8
Net increase (decrease) in cash and equivalents	902.5	(433.9)	560.1
Cash and equivalents, beginning of year	954.2	1,388.1	828.0
Cash and equivalents, end of year	$ 1,856.7	$ 954.2	$ 1,388.1
Supplemental disclosure of cash flow information:			
Cash paid during the year for:			
Interest, net of capitalized interest	$ 60.0	$ 54.2	$ 33.9
Income taxes	601.1	752.6	585.3
Dividends declared and not paid	92.9	79.4	65.3

The accompanying notes to consolidated financial statements are an integral part of this statement.

52

Source: NIKE INC, 10-K, July 27, 2007

NIKE, INC.

CONSOLIDATED STATEMENTS OF SHAREHOLDERS' EQUITY

	Common Stock				Capital in Excess of Stated Value	Accumulated Other Comprehensive Income (Loss)	Retained Earnings	Total
	Class A		Class B					
	Shares	Amount	Shares	Amount				
	(In millions, except per share data)							
Balance at May 31, 2004	155.2	$ 0.1	371.0	$ 2.7	$ 882.3	$ (86.3)	$ 3,982.9	$ 4,781.7
Stock options exercised			8.8		272.2			272.2
Conversion to Class B Common Stock	(11.4)		11.4					—
Repurchase of Class B Common Stock			(13.8)		(8.3)		(547.9)	(556.2)
Dividends on Common stock ($0.475 per share)							(249.4)	(249.4)
Issuance of shares to employees			1.0		21.9			21.9
Stock-based compensation (Note 10):					4.9			4.9
Forfeiture of shares from employees					(1.5)		(0.7)	(2.2)
Comprehensive income (Note 13):								
Net income							1,211.6	1,211.6
Other comprehensive income (net of tax expense of $40.2):								
Foreign currency translation						70.1		70.1
Adjustment for fair value of hedge derivatives						89.6		89.6
Comprehensive income						159.7	1,211.6	1,371.3
Balance at May 31, 2005	143.8	$ 0.1	378.4	$ 2.7	$ 1,171.5	$ 73.4	$ 4,396.5	$ 5,644.2
Stock options exercised			8.0		253.7			253.7
Conversion to Class B Common Stock	(16.0)		16.0					—
Repurchase of Class B Common Stock			(19.0)		(11.3)		(769.9)	(781.2)
Dividends on Common stock ($0.59 per share)							(304.9)	(304.9)
Issuance of shares to employees			1.0		26.9			26.9
Stock-based compensation (Note 10):					11.8			11.8
Forfeiture of shares from employees			(0.2)		(5.3)		(0.3)	(5.6)
Comprehensive income (Note 13):								
Net income							1,392.0	1,392.0
Other comprehensive income (net of tax benefit of $37.8):								
Foreign currency translation						87.1		87.1
Adjustment for fair value of hedge derivatives						(38.8)		(38.8)
Comprehensive income						48.3	1,392.0	1,440.3
Balance at May 31, 2006	127.8	$ 0.1	384.2	$ 2.7	$ 1,447.3	$ 121.7	$ 4,713.4	$ 6,285.2
Stock options exercised			10.7		349.7			349.7
Conversion to Class B Common Stock	(10.2)		10.2					—
Repurchase of Class B Common Stock			(22.1)		(13.2)		(962.0)	(975.2)
Dividends on Common stock ($0.71 per share)							(357.2)	(357.2)
Issuance of shares to employees			1.2		30.1			30.1
Stock-based compensation (Note 10):					147.7			147.7
Forfeiture of shares from employees			(0.1)		(1.6)		(0.5)	(2.1)
Comprehensive income (Note 13):								
Net income							1,491.5	1,491.5
Other comprehensive income (net of tax benefit of $0.5):								
Foreign currency translation						84.6		84.6
Adjustment for fair value of hedge derivatives						(16.7)		(16.7)
Comprehensive income						67.9	1,491.5	1,559.4
Adoption of FAS 158 (net of tax benefit of $5.4) (Note 12):						(12.2)		(12.2)
Balance at May 31, 2007	117.6	$ 0.1	384.1	$ 2.7	$ 1,960.0	$ 177.4	$ 4,885.2	$ 7,025.4

The accompanying notes to consolidated financial statements are an integral part of this statement.

Source: NIKE INC, 10-K, July 27, 2007

NIKE, INC.

NOTES TO CONSOLIDATED FINANCIAL STATEMENTS

Note 1 — Summary of Significant Accounting Policies

Basis of Consolidation

The consolidated financial statements include the accounts of NIKE, Inc. and its subsidiaries (the "Company"). All significant intercompany transactions and balances have been eliminated.

Stock Split

On February 15, 2007 the Board of Directors declared a two-for-one stock split of the Company's Class A and Class B common shares, which was effected in the form of a 100% common stock dividend distributed on April 2, 2007. All references to share and per share amounts in the consolidated financial statements and accompanying notes to the consolidated financial statements have been retroactively restated to reflect the two-for-one stock split.

Recognition of Revenues

Wholesale revenues are recognized when the risks and rewards of ownership have passed to the customer, based on the terms of sale. This occurs upon shipment or upon receipt by the customer depending on the country of the sale and the agreement with the customer. Retail store revenues are recorded at the time of sale. Provisions for sales discounts, returns and miscellaneous claims from customers are made at the time of sale.

Shipping and Handling Costs

Shipping and handling costs are expensed as incurred and included in cost of sales.

Advertising and Promotion

Advertising production costs are expensed the first time the advertisement is run. Media (TV and print) placement costs are expensed in the month the advertising appears.

A significant amount of the Company's promotional expenses result from payments under endorsement contracts. Accounting for endorsement payments is based upon specific contract provisions. Generally, endorsement payments are expensed on a straight-line basis over the term of the contract after giving recognition to periodic performance compliance provisions of the contracts. Prepayments made under contracts are included in prepaid expenses or other assets depending on the period to which the prepayment applies.

Through cooperative advertising programs, the Company reimburses its retail customers for certain of their costs of advertising the Company's products. The Company records these costs in selling and administrative expense at the point in time when it is obligated to its customers for the costs, which is when the related revenues are recognized. This obligation may arise prior to the related advertisement being run.

Total advertising and promotion expenses were $1,912.4 million, $1,740.2 million, and $1,600.7 million for the years ended May 31, 2007, 2006 and 2005, respectively. Prepaid advertising and promotion expenses recorded in prepaid expenses and other assets totaled $253.0 million and $177.1 million at May 31, 2007 and 2006, respectively.

Cash and Equivalents

Cash and equivalents represent cash and short-term, highly liquid investments with maturities of three months or less at date of purchase. The carrying amounts reflected in the consolidated balance sheet for cash and equivalents approximate fair value.

Source: NIKE INC, 10-K, July 27, 2007

NIKE, INC.

NOTES TO CONSOLIDATED FINANCIAL STATEMENTS — (Continued)

Short-term Investments

Short-term investments consist of highly liquid investments, primarily U.S. Treasury debt securities, with maturities over three months from the date of purchase. Debt securities which the Company has the ability and positive intent to hold to maturity are carried at amortized cost. Available-for-sale debt securities are recorded at fair value with any net unrealized gains and losses reported, net of tax, in other comprehensive income. Realized gains or losses are determined based on the specific identification method. The Company holds no investments considered to be trading securities. Amortized cost of both available-for-sale and held-to-maturity debt securities approximates fair market value due to their short maturities. Substantially all short-term investments held at May 31, 2007 have remaining maturities of 180 days or less. Included in interest (income) expense, net for the years ended May 31, 2007, 2006, and 2005, was interest income of $116.9 million, $87.3 million and $34.9 million, respectively, related to short-term investments and cash and equivalents.

Allowance for Uncollectible Accounts Receivable

Accounts receivable consists principally of amounts receivable from customers. We make ongoing estimates relating to the collectibility of our accounts receivable and maintain an allowance for estimated losses resulting from the inability of our customers to make required payments. In determining the amount of the allowance, we consider our historical level of credit losses and make judgments about the creditworthiness of significant customers based on ongoing credit evaluations. Accounts receivable with anticipated collection dates greater than twelve months from the balance sheet date and related allowances are considered non-current and recorded in other assets. The allowance for uncollectible accounts receivable was $71.5 million and $67.6 million at May 31, 2007 and 2006, respectively, of which $33.3 million and $29.2 million was recorded in other assets.

Inventory Valuation

Inventories related to our wholesale operations are stated at lower of cost or market and valued on a first-in, first-out ("FIFO") or moving average cost basis. Inventories related to our retail operations are stated at the lower of average cost or market using the retail inventory method. Under the retail inventory method, the valuation of inventories at cost is calculated by applying a cost-to-retail ratio to the retail value inventories. Permanent and point of sale markdowns, when recorded, reduce both the retail and cost components of inventory on hand so as to maintain the already established cost-to-retail relationship.

Property, Plant and Equipment and Depreciation

Property, plant and equipment are recorded at cost. Depreciation for financial reporting purposes is determined on a straight-line basis for buildings and leasehold improvements over 2 to 40 years and for machinery and equipment over 2 to 15 years. Computer software (including, in some cases, the cost of internal labor) is depreciated on a straight-line basis over 3 to 10 years.

Impairment of Long-Lived Assets

The Company estimates the future undiscounted cash flows to be derived from an asset to assess whether or not a potential impairment exists when events or circumstances indicate the carrying value of a long-lived asset may be impaired. If the carrying value exceeds the Company's estimate of future undiscounted cash flows, the Company then calculates the impairment as the excess of the carrying value of the asset over the Company's estimate of its fair market value.

Source: NIKE INC, 10-K, July 27, 2007

NIKE, INC.

NOTES TO CONSOLIDATED FINANCIAL STATEMENTS — (Continued)

Identifiable Intangible Assets and Goodwill

Goodwill and intangible assets with indefinite lives are not amortized but instead are measured for impairment at least annually in the fourth quarter, or when events indicate that an impairment exists. As required by Statement of Financial Accounting Standards ("SFAS") No. 142, "Goodwill and other Intangible Assets" ("FAS 142"), in the Company's impairment test of goodwill, the Company compares the fair value of the applicable reporting unit to its carrying value. The Company estimates the fair value of its reporting units by using a combination of discounted cash flow analysis and comparisons with the market values of similar publicly traded companies. If the carrying value of the reporting unit exceeds the estimate of fair value, the Company calculates the impairment as the excess of the carrying value of goodwill over its implied fair value. In the impairment tests for indefinite-lived intangible assets, the Company compares the estimated fair value of the indefinite-lived intangible assets to the carrying value. The Company estimates the fair value of indefinite-lived intangible assets and trademarks using the relief from royalty approach, which is a standard form of discounted cash flow analysis used for the valuation of trademarks. If the carrying value exceeds the estimate of fair value, the Company calculates impairment as the excess of the carrying value over the estimate of fair value.

Intangible assets that are determined to have definite lives are amortized over their useful lives and are measured for impairment only when events or circumstances indicate the carrying value may be impaired.

Foreign Currency Translation and Foreign Currency Transactions

Adjustments resulting from translating foreign functional currency financial statements into U.S. dollars are included in the foreign currency translation adjustment, a component of accumulated other comprehensive income in shareholders' equity.

Transaction gains and losses generated by the effect of foreign exchange rates on recorded assets and liabilities denominated in a currency different from the functional currency of the applicable Company entity are recorded in other (income) expense, net, in the period in which they occur.

Accounting for Derivatives and Hedging Activities

The Company uses derivative financial instruments to limit exposure to changes in foreign currency exchange rates and interest rates. The Company accounts for derivatives pursuant to SFAS No. 133, "Accounting for Derivative Instruments and Hedging Activities," as amended and interpreted ("FAS 133"). FAS 133 establishes accounting and reporting standards for derivative instruments and requires that all derivatives be recorded at fair value on the balance sheet. Changes in the fair value of derivative financial instruments are either recognized in other comprehensive income (a component of shareholders' equity) or net income depending on whether the derivative is being used to hedge changes in cash flows or fair value.

See Note 16 for more information on the Company's Risk Management program and derivatives.

Stock-Based Compensation

On June 1, 2006, the Company adopted SFAS No. 123R "Share-Based Payment" ("FAS 123R") which requires the Company to record expense for stock-based compensation to employees using a fair value method. Under FAS 123R, the Company estimates the fair value of options granted under the NIKE, Inc. 1990 Stock Incentive Plan (the "1990 Plan") (see Note 10) and employees' purchase rights under the Employee Stock Purchase Plans ("ESPPs") using the Black-Scholes option pricing model. The Company recognizes this fair value, net of estimated forfeitures, as selling and administrative expense in the Consolidated Statements of Income over the vesting period using the straight-line method.

Source: NIKE INC, 10-K, July 27, 2007

NIKE, INC.

NOTES TO CONSOLIDATED FINANCIAL STATEMENTS — (Continued)

The Company has adopted the modified prospective transition method prescribed by FAS 123R, which does not require the restatement of financial results for previous periods. In accordance with this transition method, the Company's Consolidated Statement of Income for the year ended May 31, 2007 includes (1) amortization of outstanding stock-based compensation granted prior to, but not vested, as of June 1, 2006, based on the fair value estimated in accordance with the original provisions of SFAS No. 123, "Accounting for Stock-Based Compensation" ("FAS 123") and (2) amortization of all stock-based awards granted subsequent to June 1, 2006, based on the fair value estimated in accordance with the provisions of FAS 123R.

The following table summarizes the effects of applying FAS 123R during the year ended May 31, 2007. The resulting stock-based compensation expense primarily relates to stock options.

(in millions, except per share data)	
Addition to selling and administrative expense	$141.9
Reduction to income tax expense	(45.2)
Reduction to net income[(1)]	$ 96.7
Reduction to earnings per share:	
Basic	$ 0.19
Diluted	$ 0.18

(1) In accordance with FAS 123R, stock-based compensation expense reported during the year ended May 31, 2007, includes $24.2 million, net of tax, or $0.04 per diluted share, of accelerated stock-based compensation expense recorded for employees eligible for accelerated stock option vesting upon retirement.

Prior to the adoption of FAS 123R, the Company used the intrinsic value method to account for stock options and ESPP shares in accordance with Accounting Principles Board Opinion No. 25, "Accounting for Stock Issued to Employees" as permitted by FAS 123. If the Company had instead accounted for stock options and ESPP shares issued to employees using the fair value method prescribed by FAS 123 during the years ended May 31, 2006 and 2005 the Company's pro forma net income and pro forma earnings per share would have been reported as follows:

	Year Ended May 31, 2006	2005
	(In millions, except per share data)	
Net income as reported	$ 1,392.0	$ 1,211.6
Add: Stock option expense included in reported net income, net of tax	0.2	0.6
Deduct: Total stock option and ESPP expense under fair value based method for all awards, net of tax[(1)]	(76.8)	(64.1)
Pro forma net income	$ 1,315.4	$ 1,148.1
Earnings per share:		
Basic — as reported	$ 2.69	$ 2.31
Basic — pro forma	2.54	2.19
Diluted — as reported	2.64	2.24
Diluted — pro forma	2.50	2.14

(1) Accelerated stock-based compensation expense for options subject to accelerated vesting due to employee retirement is not included in the pro forma figures shown above for the years ended May 31, 2006 and 2005. This disclosure reflects the expense of such options ratably over the stated vesting period or upon actual employee retirement. Had the Company recognized the fair value for such stock options on an accelerated

Source: NIKE INC, 10-K, July 27, 2007

NIKE, INC.

NOTES TO CONSOLIDATED FINANCIAL STATEMENTS — (Continued)

basis in this pro forma disclosure, the Company would have recognized additional stock-based compensation expense of $17.5 million, net of tax, or $0.03 per diluted share for the year ended May 31, 2006 and $21.8 million, net of tax, or $0.04 per diluted share for the year ended May 31, 2005.

To calculate the excess tax benefits available for use in offsetting future tax shortfalls as of the date of implementation, the Company is following the alternative transition method discussed in FASB Staff Position No. 123R-3, "Transition Election Relating to Accounting for the Tax Effects of Share-Based Payment Awards."

See Note 10 for more information on the Company's stock programs.

Income Taxes

The Company accounts for income taxes using the asset and liability method. This approach requires the recognition of deferred tax assets and liabilities for the expected future tax consequences of temporary differences between the carrying amounts and the tax basis of assets and liabilities. United States income taxes are provided currently on financial statement earnings of non-U.S. subsidiaries that are expected to be repatriated. The Company determines annually the amount of undistributed non-U.S. earnings to invest indefinitely in its non-U.S. operations. See Note 8 for further discussion.

Earnings Per Share

Basic earnings per common share is calculated by dividing net income by the weighted average number of common shares outstanding during the year. Diluted earnings per common share is calculated by adjusting weighted average outstanding shares, assuming conversion of all potentially dilutive stock options and awards. See Note 11 for further discussion.

Management Estimates

The preparation of financial statements in conformity with generally accepted accounting principles requires management to make estimates, including estimates relating to assumptions that affect the reported amounts of assets and liabilities and disclosure of contingent assets and liabilities at the date of financial statements and the reported amounts of revenues and expenses during the reporting period. Actual results could differ from these estimates.

Reclassifications

Certain prior year amounts have been reclassified to conform to fiscal year 2007 presentation. These changes had no impact on previously reported results of operations or shareholders' equity.

Recently Issued Accounting Standards

In June 2006, the Financial Accounting Standards Board ("FASB") ratified the consensus reached on Emerging Issues Task Force ("EITF") Issue No. 06-3, "How Taxes Collected from Customers and Remitted to Governmental Authorities Should Be Presented in the Income Statement (That Is, Gross versus Net Presentation)" ("EITF 06-3"). EITF 06-3 requires disclosure of the method of accounting for the applicable assessed taxes and the amount of assessed taxes that are included in revenues if they are accounted for under the gross method. EITF 06-3 was adopted in the fourth quarter ended May 31, 2007; however, since the Company presents revenues net of any taxes collected from customers, no additional disclosures were required.

Source: NIKE INC, 10-K, July 27, 2007

NIKE, INC.

NOTES TO CONSOLIDATED FINANCIAL STATEMENTS — (Continued)

In September 2006, the FASB issued SFAS No. 158, "Employers' Accounting for Defined Benefit Pension and Other Postretirement Plans" ("FAS 158"). FAS 158 requires employers to fully recognize the obligations associated with single-employer defined benefit pension, retiree healthcare and other postretirement plans in their financial statements. The Company adopted the provisions of FAS 158 in the fourth quarter ended May 31, 2007. See Note 12 for additional details.

In September 2006, the SEC staff issued Staff Accounting Bulletin No. 108, "Considering the Effects of Prior Year Misstatements when Quantifying Misstatements in Current Year Financial Statements" ("SAB 108"). SAB 108 requires public companies to quantify errors using both a balance sheet and income statement approach and evaluate whether either approach results in quantifying a misstatement as material, when all relevant quantitative and qualitative factors are considered. The adoption of SAB 108 at May 31, 2007 did not have a material impact on the Company's consolidated financial position or results of operations.

In June 2006, the FASB issued FASB Interpretation No. 48, "Accounting for Uncertainty in Income Taxes" ("FIN 48"). FIN 48 clarifies the accounting for uncertainty in income taxes recognized in the Company's financial statements in accordance with FASB Statement No. 109, "Accounting for Income Taxes". The provisions of FIN 48 are effective for the fiscal year beginning June 1, 2007. The Company has evaluated the impact of the provisions of FIN 48 and does not expect that the adoption will have a material impact on the Company's consolidated financial position or results of operations.

In June 2006, the FASB ratified the consensus reached on EITF Issue No. 06-2, "Accounting for Sabbatical Leave and Other Similar Benefits Pursuant to FASB Statement No. 43" ("EITF 06-2"). EITF 06-2 clarifies recognition guidance on the accrual of employees' rights to compensated absences under a sabbatical or other similar benefit arrangement. The provisions of EITF 06-2 are effective for the fiscal year beginning June 1, 2007 and will be applied through a cumulative effect adjustment to retained earnings. The Company has evaluated the provisions of EITF 06-2 and does not expect that the adoption will have a material impact on the Company's consolidated financial position or results of operations.

In September 2006, the FASB issued SFAS No. 157, "Fair Value Measurements" ("FAS 157"). FAS 157 defines fair value, establishes a framework for measuring fair value in accordance with generally accepted accounting principles, and expands disclosures about fair value measurements. The provisions of FAS 157 are effective for the fiscal year beginning June 1, 2008. The Company is currently evaluating the impact of the provisions of FAS 157.

In February 2007, the FASB issued SFAS No. 159, "The Fair Value Option for Financial Assets and Financial Liabilities — Including an Amendment of FASB Statement No. 115" ("FAS 159"). FAS 159 permits entities to choose to measure many financial instruments and certain other items at fair value. Unrealized gains and losses on items for which the fair value option has been elected will be recognized in earnings at each subsequent reporting date. The provisions of FAS 159 are effective for the fiscal year beginning June 1, 2008. The Company is currently evaluating the impact of the provisions of FAS 159.

Note 2 — Inventories

Inventory balances of $2,121.9 million and $2,076.7 million at May 31, 2007 and 2006, respectively, were substantially all finished goods.

Source: NIKE INC, 10-K, July 27, 2007

NIKE, INC.

NOTES TO CONSOLIDATED FINANCIAL STATEMENTS — (Continued)

Note 3 — Property, Plant and Equipment

Property, plant and equipment includes the following:

	May 31, 2007	May 31, 2006
	(In millions)	
Land	$ 193.8	$ 195.9
Buildings	840.9	842.6
Machinery and equipment	1,817.2	1,661.7
Leasehold improvements	672.8	626.7
Construction in process	94.4	81.4
	3,619.1	3,408.3
Less accumulated depreciation	1,940.8	1,750.6
	$ 1,678.3	$ 1,657.7

Capitalized interest was not material for the years ended May 31, 2007, 2006 and 2005.

Note 4 — Identifiable Intangible Assets and Goodwill:

The following table summarizes the Company's identifiable intangible assets and goodwill balances as of May 31, 2007 and May 31, 2006:

	May 31, 2007			May 31, 2006		
	Gross Carrying Amount	Accumulated Amortization	Net Carrying Amount	Gross Carrying Amount	Accumulated Amortization	Net Carrying Amount
			(In millions)			
Amortized intangible assets:						
Patents	$ 44.1	$ (12.3)	$ 31.8	$ 34.1	$ (10.5)	$ 23.6
Trademarks	49.8	(17.5)	32.3	46.4	(11.8)	34.6
Other	21.6	(17.3)	4.3	21.5	(15.7)	5.8
Total	$115.5	$ (47.1)	$ 68.4	$102.0	$ (38.0)	$ 64.0
Unamortized intangible assets — Trademarks			$ 341.5			$ 341.5
Total			$ 409.9			$ 405.5
Goodwill			$ 130.8			$ 130.8

Amortization expense of identifiable assets with definite lives, which is included in selling and administrative expense, was $9.9 million, $9.8 million and $9.3 million for the years ended May 31, 2007, 2006, and 2005, respectively. The estimated amortization expense for intangible assets subject to amortization for each of the years ending May 31, 2008 through May 31, 2012 is as follows: 2008: $9.7 million; 2009: $8.7 million; 2010: $8.2 million; 2011: $7.7 million; 2012: $6.9 million.

Source: NIKE INC, 10-K, July 27, 2007

NIKE, INC.

NOTES TO CONSOLIDATED FINANCIAL STATEMENTS — (Continued)

Note 5 — Accrued Liabilities

Accrued liabilities include the following:

	May 31, 2007	May 31, 2006
	(In millions)	
Compensation and benefits, excluding taxes	$ 451.6	$ 427.2
Endorser compensation	139.9	124.7
Taxes other than income taxes	133.4	115.1
Dividends payable	92.9	79.5
Fair value of derivatives	90.5	111.2
Import and logistics costs	81.4	63.3
Advertising and marketing	70.6	75.4
Converse arbitration[(1)]	—	51.9
Other[(2)]	243.1	227.7
	$ 1,303.4	$ 1,276.0

(1) The Converse arbitration relates to a charge taken during the fourth quarter ended May 31, 2006 as a result of a contract dispute between Converse and a former South American licensee. The dispute was settled during the first quarter ended August 31, 2006.

(2) Other consists of various accrued expenses and no individual item accounted for more than $50 million of the balance at May 31, 2007 or 2006.

Note 6 — Short-Term Borrowings and Credit Lines

Notes payable to banks and interest-bearing accounts payable to Sojitz Corporation of America ("Sojitz America") as of May 31, 2007 and 2006, are summarized below:

	2007 Borrowings	2007 Interest Rate	2006 Borrowings	2006 Interest Rate
	(In millions)			
Notes payable:				
U.S. operations	$ 14.6	0.00%[(1)]	$ 21.0	0.00%[(1)]
Non-U.S. operations	86.2	9.85%	22.4	7.72%
	$ 100.8		$ 43.4	
Sojitz America	$ 44.6	6.09%	$ 69.7	5.83%

(1) Weighted average interest rate includes non-interest bearing overdrafts.

The carrying amounts reflected in the consolidated balance sheet for notes payable approximate fair value.

The Company purchases through Sojitz America certain athletic footwear, apparel and equipment it acquires from non-U.S. suppliers. These purchases are for the Company's operations outside of the United States, the Europe, Middle East, and Africa Region and Japan. Accounts payable to Sojitz America are generally due up to 60 days after shipment of goods from the foreign port. The interest rate on such accounts payable is the 60-day London Interbank Offered Rate ("LIBOR") as of the beginning of the month of the invoice date, plus 0.75%.

Source: NIKE INC, 10-K, July 27, 2007

NIKE, INC.

NOTES TO CONSOLIDATED FINANCIAL STATEMENTS — (Continued)

The Company had no borrowings outstanding under its commercial paper program at May 31, 2007 and 2006.

In December 2006, the Company entered into a $1 billion multi-year credit facility that replaced the Company's previous $750 million facility. The facility matures in December 2011, and can be extended for one additional year on both the first and second anniversary date for a total extension of two years. Based on the Company's current long-term senior unsecured debt ratings, the interest rate charged on any outstanding borrowings would be the prevailing LIBOR plus 0.15%. The facility fee is 0.05% of the total commitment. Under this agreement, the Company must maintain, among other things, certain minimum specified financial ratios with which the Company was in compliance at May 31, 2007. No amounts were outstanding under these facilities as of May 31, 2007 or 2006.

In January 2007, one of the Company's Japanese subsidiaries entered into a 3.0 billion yen (approximately $24.7 million as of May 31, 2007) loan facility that replaced certain intercompany borrowings. The interest rate on the facility is based on the six-month Japanese Yen LIBOR plus a spread, resulting in an all-in rate of 0.805% at May 31, 2007. The facility expires December 31, 2007 unless both parties agree to an extension.

Note 7 — Long-Term Debt

Long-term debt includes the following:

	May 31,	
	2007	2006
	(In millions)	
5.5% Corporate Bond, payable August 15, 2006	$ —	$249.3
4.8% Corporate Bond, payable July 9, 2007	25.0	24.7
5.375% Corporate Bond, payable July 8, 2009	24.8	24.6
5.66% Corporate Bond, payable July 23, 2012	24.8	24.6
5.4% Corporate Bond, payable August 7, 2012	14.6	14.4
4.7% Corporate Bond, payable October 1, 2013	50.0	50.0
5.15% Corporate Bonds, payable October 15, 2015	99.6	98.2
4.3% Japanese yen note, payable June 26, 2011	86.4	93.8
1.5% Japanese yen note, payable February 14, 2012	41.1	—
2.6% Japanese yen note, maturing August 20, 2001 through November 20, 2020	51.2	59.7
2.0% Japanese yen note, maturing August 20, 2001 through November 20, 2020	22.9	26.6
Other	—	0.1
Total	440.4	666.0
Less current maturities	30.5	255.3
	$409.9	$410.7

The fair value of long-term debt is estimated using discounted cash flow analyses, based on the Company's incremental borrowing rates for similar types of borrowing arrangements. The fair value of the Company's long-term debt, including current portion, is approximately $443.2 million at May 31, 2007 and $674.0 million at May 31, 2006.

The Company had interest rate swap agreements with the same notional amount and maturity dates as the $250.0 million corporate bond that matured on August 15, 2006, whereby the Company received fixed interest payments at the same rate as the bond and paid variable interest payments based on the three-month LIBOR plus a spread. The interest rate payable on these swap agreements was approximately 6.6% at May 31, 2006.

Source: NIKE INC, 10-K, July 27, 2007

NIKE, INC.

NOTES TO CONSOLIDATED FINANCIAL STATEMENTS — (Continued)

The Company has an effective shelf registration statement with the Securities and Exchange Commission for $1 billion of debt securities. The Company has a medium-term note program under the shelf registration ("medium-term note program") that allows the Company to issue up to $500 million in medium-term notes. The Company has issued $240 million in medium-term notes under this program. During the years ended May 31, 2007 and 2006, no notes were issued under the medium-term note program. The issued notes have coupon rates that range from 4.70% to 5.66%. The maturities range from July 9, 2007 to October 15, 2015. For each of these notes, except for the swap for the $50 million note maturing October 1, 2013, the Company has entered into interest rate swap agreements whereby the Company receives fixed interest payments at the same rate as the notes and pays variable interest payments based on the three-month or six-month LIBOR plus a spread. Each swap has the same notional amount and maturity date as the corresponding note. The swap for the $50 million note maturing October 1, 2013, expired October 2, 2006. At May 31, 2007, the interest rates payable on these swap agreements range from approximately 5.2% to 5.9%.

In June 1996, one of the Company's Japanese subsidiaries, NIKE Logistics YK, borrowed 10.5 billion Japanese yen in a private placement with a maturity of June 26, 2011. Interest is paid semi-annually. The agreement provides for early retirement after year ten.

In July 1999, NIKE Logistics YK assumed 13.0 billion in Japanese yen loans as part of its agreement to purchase a distribution center in Japan, which serves as collateral for the loans. These loans mature in equal quarterly installments during the period August 20, 2001 through November 20, 2020. Interest is also paid quarterly.

In February 2007, NIKE Logistics YK entered into a 5.0 billion yen (approximately $41.1 million at May 31, 2007) term loan maturing February 14, 2012 that replaces certain intercompany borrowings. The interest rate on the loan is approximately 1.5% and interest is paid semi-annually.

Amounts of long-term debt maturities in each of the years ending May 31, 2008 through 2012 are $30.5 million, $5.5 million, $30.5 million, $5.5 million and $133.0 million, respectively.

Note 8 — Income Taxes

Income before income taxes is as follows:

	Year Ended May 31,		
	2007	2006	2005
		(In millions)	
Income before income taxes:			
United States	$ 805.1	$ 838.6	$ 755.5
Foreign	1,394.8	1,303.0	1,104.3
	$ 2,199.9	$ 2,141.6	$ 1,859.8

Source: NIKE INC, 10-K, July 27, 2007

NIKE, INC.

NOTES TO CONSOLIDATED FINANCIAL STATEMENTS — (Continued)

The provision for income taxes is as follows:

	Year Ended May 31, 2007	2006 (In millions)	2005
Current:			
United States			
Federal	$352.6	$359.0	$279.6
State	59.6	60.6	50.7
Foreign	261.9	356.0	292.5
	674.1	775.6	622.8
Deferred:			
United States			
Federal	38.7	(4.2)	21.9
State	(4.8)	(6.8)	(5.3)
Foreign	0.4	(15.0)	8.8
	34.3	(26.0)	25.4
	$708.4	$749.6	$648.2

Deferred tax (assets) and liabilities are comprised of the following:

	May 31, 2007	2006
	(In millions)	
Deferred tax assets:		
Allowance for doubtful accounts	$ (12.4)	$ (10.9)
Inventories	(45.8)	(43.9)
Sales return reserves	(42.1)	(39.4)
Deferred compensation	(132.5)	(110.6)
Stock-based compensation	(30.3)	—
Reserves and accrued liabilities	(46.2)	(50.6)
Property, plant, and equipment	(16.3)	(28.6)
Foreign loss carryforwards	(37.5)	(29.2)
Foreign tax credit carryforwards	(3.4)	(9.5)
Hedges	(26.2)	(25.5)
Other	(33.0)	(29.1)
Total deferred tax assets	(425.7)	(377.3)
Valuation allowance	42.3	36.6
Total deferred tax assets after valuation allowance	(383.4)	(340.7)
Deferred tax liabilities:		
Undistributed earnings of foreign subsidiaries	232.6	135.3
Property, plant and equipment	66.1	91.4
Intangibles	97.2	96.8
Hedges	2.5	7.8
Other	17.8	12.5
Total deferred tax liabilities	416.2	343.8
Net deferred tax liability	$ 32.8	$ 3.1

Source: NIKE INC, 10-K, July 27, 2007

NIKE, INC.

NOTES TO CONSOLIDATED FINANCIAL STATEMENTS — (Continued)

A reconciliation from the U.S. statutory federal income tax rate to the effective income tax rate follows:

	Year Ended May 31,		
	2007	2006	2005
Federal income tax rate	35.0%	35.0%	35.0%
State taxes, net of federal benefit	1.6	1.5	1.8
Foreign earnings	(4.1)	(1.5)	(2.8)
Other, net	(0.3)	—	0.9
Effective income tax rate	32.2%	35.0%	34.9%

The effective tax rate for the year ended May 31, 2007 of 32.2% has decreased from the fiscal 2006 effective tax rate of 35%. The decrease is primarily due to a European tax agreement entered into during the three months ended November 30, 2006. The Company recorded a retroactive benefit for the European tax agreement during the year ended May 31, 2007.

During the quarter ended November 30, 2005, the Company's CEO and Board of Directors approved a domestic reinvestment plan as required by the American Jobs Creation Act of 2004 (the "Act") to repatriate $500 million of foreign earnings in fiscal 2006. The Act created a temporary incentive for U.S. multinational corporations to repatriate accumulated income earned outside the U.S. by providing an 85% dividend received deduction for certain dividends from controlled foreign corporations. A $500 million repatriation was made during the quarter ended May 31, 2006 comprised of both foreign earnings for which U.S. taxes have previously been provided and foreign earnings that had been designated as permanently reinvested. Accordingly, the provisions made did not have a material impact on the Company's income tax expense or effective tax rate for the years ended May 31, 2007, 2006 and 2005.

The Company has indefinitely reinvested approximately $1,185.0 million of the cumulative undistributed earnings of certain foreign subsidiaries. Such earnings would be subject to U.S. taxation if repatriated to the U.S. The amount of unrecognized deferred tax liability associated with the permanently reinvested cumulative undistributed earnings was approximately $248.3 million as of May 31, 2007.

Deferred tax assets at May 31, 2007 and 2006 were reduced by a valuation allowance relating to tax benefits of certain foreign subsidiaries with operating losses where it is more likely than not that the deferred tax assets will not be realized.

During the years ended May 31, 2007, 2006, and 2005, income tax benefits attributable to employee stock-based compensation transactions of $56.6 million, $54.2 million, and $63.1 million, respectively, were allocated to shareholders' equity.

Note 9 — Redeemable Preferred Stock

Sojitz America is the sole owner of the Company's authorized Redeemable Preferred Stock, $1 par value, which is redeemable at the option of Sojitz America or the Company at par value aggregating $0.3 million. A cumulative dividend of $0.10 per share is payable annually on May 31 and no dividends may be declared or paid on the common stock of the Company unless dividends on the Redeemable Preferred Stock have been declared and paid in full. There have been no changes in the Redeemable Preferred Stock in the three years ended May 31, 2007, 2006 and 2005. As the holder of the Redeemable Preferred Stock, Sojitz America does not have general voting rights but does have the right to vote as a separate class on the sale of all or substantially all of the assets of the Company and its subsidiaries, on merger, consolidation, liquidation or dissolution of the Company or on the sale or assignment of the NIKE trademark for athletic footwear sold in the United States.

Source: NIKE INC, 10-K, July 27, 2007

NIKE, INC.

NOTES TO CONSOLIDATED FINANCIAL STATEMENTS — (Continued)

Note 10 — Common Stock

The authorized number of shares of Class A Common Stock, no par value, and Class B Common Stock, no par value, are 350 million and 1.5 billion, respectively. Each share of Class A Common Stock is convertible into one share of Class B Common Stock. Voting rights of Class B Common Stock are limited in certain circumstances with respect to the election of directors.

In 1990, the Board of Directors adopted, and the shareholders approved, the NIKE, Inc. 1990 Stock Incentive Plan (the "1990 Plan"). The 1990 Plan provides for the issuance of up to 132 million previously unissued shares of Class B Common Stock in connection with stock options and other awards granted under the plan. The 1990 Plan authorizes the grant of non-statutory stock options, incentive stock options, stock appreciation rights, stock bonuses and the issuance and sale of restricted stock. The exercise price for non-statutory stock options, stock appreciation rights and the grant price of restricted stock may not be less than 75% of the fair market value of the underlying shares on the date of grant. The exercise price for incentive stock options may not be less than the fair market value of the underlying shares on the date of grant. A committee of the Board of Directors administers the 1990 Plan. The committee has the authority to determine the employees to whom awards will be made, the amount of the awards, and the other terms and conditions of the awards. The committee has granted substantially all stock options and restricted stock at 100% of the market price on the date of grant. Substantially all stock option grants outstanding under the 1990 plan were granted in the first quarter of each fiscal year, vest ratably over four years, and expire 10 years from the date of grant.

The weighted average fair value per share of the options granted during the years ended May 31, 2007, 2006 and 2005, as computed using the Black-Scholes pricing model, was \$8.80, \$9.68 and \$13.95, respectively. The weighted average assumptions used to estimate these fair values are as follows:

	Year Ended May 31,		
	2007	2006	2005
Dividend yield	1.6%	1%	1%
Expected volatility	19%	21%	42%
Weighted average expected life (in years)	5.0	4.5	5.0
Risk-free interest rate	5.0%	4.0%	3.7%

For the years ended May 31, 2007 and 2006, the Company estimated the expected volatility based on the implied volatility in market traded options on the Company's common stock with a term greater than one year, along with other factors. For the year ended May 31, 2005, the Company estimated the expected volatility based on the historical volatility of the Company's common stock. The weighted average expected life of options is based on an analysis of historical and expected future exercise patterns. The interest rate is based on the U.S. Treasury (constant maturity) risk-free rate in effect at the date of grant for periods corresponding with the expected term of the options.

Source: NIKE INC, 10-K, July 27, 2007

NIKE, INC.

NOTES TO CONSOLIDATED FINANCIAL STATEMENTS — (Continued)

The following summarizes the stock option transactions under the plan discussed above:

	Shares (In millions)	Weighted Average Option Price
Options outstanding May 31, 2004	37.6	$ 23.71
Exercised	(8.8)	23.17
Forfeited	(0.9)	26.33
Granted	10.8	36.96
Options outstanding May 31, 2005	38.7	27.49
Exercised	(8.0)	24.68
Forfeited	(1.8)	35.75
Granted	11.5	43.68
Options outstanding May 31, 2006	40.4	32.31
Exercised	(10.7)	27.55
Forfeited	(1.6)	37.17
Granted	11.6	39.54
Options outstanding May 31, 2007	39.7	$ 35.50
Options exercisable at May 31,		
2005	14.7	$ 23.01
2006	16.6	25.68
2007	15.3	29.52

The weighted average contractual life remaining for options outstanding and options exercisable at May 31, 2007 was 7.2 years and 5.4 years, respectively. The aggregate intrinsic value for options outstanding and exercisable at May 31, 2007 was $843.7 million and $417.0 million, respectively. The aggregate intrinsic value was the amount by which the market value of the underlying stock exceeded the exercise price of the options. The total intrinsic value of the options exercised during the years ended May 31, 2007, 2006 and 2005 was $204.9 million, $144.0 million and $145.7 million, respectively.

As of May 31, 2007, the Company had $132.4 million of unrecognized compensation costs from stock options, net of estimated forfeitures, to be recognized as selling and administrative expense over a weighted average period of 2.1 years.

In addition to the 1990 Plan, the Company gives employees the right to purchase shares at a discount to the market price under employee stock purchase plans ("ESPPs"). Employees are eligible to participate through payroll deductions up to 10% of their compensation. At the end of each six-month offering period, shares are purchased by the participants at 85% of the lower of the fair market value at the beginning or the ending of the offering period. During the years ended May 31, 2007, 2006 and 2005, employees purchased 0.8 million, 0.8 million and 0.6 million shares, respectively.

From time to time, the Company grants restricted stock and unrestricted stock to key employees under the 1990 Plan. The number of shares granted to employees during the years ended May 31, 2007, 2006 and 2005 were 345,000, 141,000 and 229,000 with weighted average prices of $39.38, $43.38 and $44.65, respectively. Recipients of restricted shares are entitled to cash dividends and to vote their respective shares throughout the period of restriction. The value of all of the granted shares was established by the market price on the date of grant.

Source: NIKE INC, 10-K, July 27, 2007

NIKE, INC.

NOTES TO CONSOLIDATED FINANCIAL STATEMENTS — (Continued)

The following table summarizes the Company's total stock-based compensation expense recognized in selling and administrative expense:

	Year Ended May 31,		
	2007	2006	2005
	(in millions)		
Stock options	$134.9	$ 0.3	$1.0
ESPPs	7.0	—	—
Restricted stock[1]	5.8	11.5	3.9
Total stock-based compensation expense	$147.7	$11.8	$4.9

(1) The expense related to restricted stock awards was included in selling and administrative expense in prior years and was not affected by the adoption of FAS 123R.

During the years ended May 31, 2007, 2006 and 2005, the Company also granted shares of stock under the Long-Term Incentive Plan ("LTIP"), adopted by the Board of Directors and approved by shareholders in September 1997. The LTIP provides for the issuance of up to 2.0 million shares of Class B Common Stock. Under the LTIP, awards are made to certain executives in their choice of either cash or stock, based on performance targets established over three-year time periods. Once performance targets are achieved, cash or shares of stock are issued. The shares are immediately vested upon grant. The value of the shares is established by the market price on the date of issuance. Under the LTIP, 3,000, 6,000 and 8,000 shares with a price of $38.84, $40.79 and $34.85, respectively, were issued during the years ended May 31, 2007, 2006 and 2005 for the plan years ended May 31, 2006, 2005 and 2004, respectively. The Company recognized nominal expense related to the shares issued during the years ended May 31, 2007 and 2006, and $0.1 million during the year ended May 31, 2005. The Company recognized $30.0 million, $21.7 million and $22.1 million of selling and administrative expense related to the cash awards during the years ended May 31, 2007, 2006 and 2005, respectively. During the year ended May 31, 2007, LTIP participants agreed to amend their grant agreements to eliminate the ability to receive payments in shares of stock, so shares of stock are no longer awarded. Beginning with the plan year ended May 31, 2007, cash will be awarded if performance targets are achieved.

Note 11 — Earnings Per Share

The following represents a reconciliation from basic earnings per share to diluted earnings per share. Options to purchase an additional 9.5 million, 11.3 million and 0.5 million shares of common stock were outstanding at May 31, 2007, 2006 and 2005, respectively, but were not included in the computation of diluted earnings per share because the options were antidilutive.

	Year Ended May 31,		
	2007	2006	2005
	(In millions, except per share data)		
Determination of shares:			
Weighted average common shares outstanding	503.8	518.0	525.2
Assumed conversion of dilutive stock options and awards	6.1	9.6	15.4
Diluted weighted average common shares outstanding	509.9	527.6	540.6
Basic earnings per common share	$ 2.96	$ 2.69	$ 2.31
Diluted earnings per common share	$ 2.93	$ 2.64	$ 2.24

Source: NIKE INC, 10-K, July 27, 2007

NIKE, INC.

NOTES TO CONSOLIDATED FINANCIAL STATEMENTS — (Continued)

Note 12 — Benefit Plans

The Company has a profit sharing plan available to most U.S.-based employees. The terms of the plan call for annual contributions by the Company as determined by the Board of Directors. A subsidiary of the Company also has a profit sharing plan available to its U.S.-based employees. The terms of the plan call for annual contributions as determined by the subsidiary's executive management. Contributions of $31.8 million, $33.2 million, and $29.1 million were made to the plans and are included in selling and administrative expenses in the consolidated financial statements for the years ended May 31, 2007, 2006 and 2005, respectively. The Company has various 401(k) employee savings plans available to U.S.-based employees. The Company matches a portion of employee contributions with common stock or cash. Company contributions to the savings plans were $24.9 million, $22.5 million, and $20.3 million for the years ended May 31, 2007, 2006 and 2005, respectively, and are included in selling and administrative expenses.

The Company has pension plans in various countries worldwide. The pension plans are only available to local employees and are generally government mandated. Upon adoption of FAS 158, "Employers' Accounting for Defined Benefit Pension and Other Postretirement Plans" on May 31, 2007, the Company recorded a liability of $17.6 million related to the unfunded pension liabilities of the plans.

Note 13 — Comprehensive Income

Comprehensive income is as follows:

	Year Ended May 31,		
	2007	2006	2005
	(In millions)		
Net income	$1,491.5	$1,392.0	$1,211.6
Other comprehensive income:			
Change in cumulative translation adjustment and other (net of tax (expense) benefit of ($5.4) in 2007, $19.7 in 2006, and $3.9 in 2005)	84.6	87.1	70.1
Changes due to cash flow hedging instruments (Note 16):			
Net loss on hedge derivatives (net of tax benefit of $9.5 in 2007, $2.8 in 2006 and $28.7 in 2005)	(38.1)	(5.6)	(54.0)
Reclassification to net income of previously deferred losses and (gains) related to hedge derivatives (net of tax expense (benefit) of ($3.6) in 2007, $15.3 in 2006 and ($72.8) in 2005)	21.4	(33.2)	143.6
Other comprehensive income	67.9	48.3	159.7
Total comprehensive income	$1,559.4	$1,440.3	$1,371.3

The components of accumulated other comprehensive income are as follows:

	May 31,	
	2007	2006
	(In millions)	
Cumulative translation adjustment and other[(1)]	$234.3	$161.9
Net deferred loss on hedge derivatives	(56.9)	(40.2)
	$177.4	$121.7

(1) Cumulative translation adjustment and other for the year ended May 31, 2007 includes a $12.2 million net-of-tax adjustment relating to the adoption of FAS 158. See Note 12 for additional details.

Source: NIKE INC, 10-K, July 27, 2007

NIKE, INC.

NOTES TO CONSOLIDATED FINANCIAL STATEMENTS — (Continued)

Note 14 — Commitments and Contingencies

The Company leases space for certain of its offices, warehouses and retail stores under leases expiring from one to twenty-seven years after May 31, 2007. Rent expense was $285.2 million, $252.0 million and $232.6 million for the years ended May 31, 2007, 2006 and 2005, respectively. Amounts of minimum future annual rental commitments under non-cancelable operating leases in each of the five years ending May 31, 2008 through 2012 are $260.9 million, $219.9 million, $183.3 million, $156.7 million, $128.4 million, respectively, and $587.0 million in later years.

As of May 31, 2007 and 2006, the Company had letters of credit outstanding totaling $165.9 million and $347.6 million, respectively. These letters of credit were generally issued for the purchase of inventory.

In connection with various contracts and agreements, the Company provides routine indemnifications relating to the enforceability of intellectual property rights, coverage for legal issues that arise and other items that fall under the scope of FASB Interpretation No. 45, "Guarantor's Accounting and Disclosure Requirements for Guarantees, Including Indirect Guarantees of Indebtedness of Others." Currently, the Company has several such agreements in place. However, based on the Company's historical experience and the estimated probability of future loss, the Company has determined that the fair value of such indemnifications is not material to the Company's financial position or results of operations.

In the ordinary course of its business, the Company is involved in various legal proceedings involving contractual and employment relationships, product liability claims, trademark rights, and a variety of other matters. The Company does not believe there are any pending legal proceedings that will have a material impact on the Company's financial position or results of operations.

Note 15 — Acquisitions

In August 2004, the Company acquired 100% of the equity interests in Official Starter LLC and Official Starter Properties LLC (collectively "Official Starter"). The Exeter Brands Group LLC, a wholly-owned subsidiary of the Company, was formed soon thereafter to develop the Company's business in retail channels serving value-conscious consumers and to operate the Official Starter business. The acquisition was accounted for under the purchase method of accounting. The cash purchase price, including acquisition costs net of cash acquired, was $47.2 million. All assets and liabilities of Exeter Brands Group were initially recorded in the Company's Consolidated Balance Sheet based on their estimated fair values at the date of acquisition. The results of Exeter Brands Group's operations have been included in the consolidated financial statements since the date of acquisition as part of the Company's Other operating segment. The pro forma effect of the acquisition on the combined results of operations was not significant.

Note 16 — Risk Management and Derivatives

The Company is exposed to global market risks, including the effect of changes in foreign currency exchange rates and interest rates. The Company uses derivatives to manage financial exposures that occur in the normal course of business. The Company does not hold or issue derivatives for trading purposes.

The Company formally documents all relationships between hedging instruments and hedged items, as well as its risk-management objective and strategy for undertaking hedge transactions. This process includes linking all derivatives to either specific assets and liabilities on the balance sheet or specific firm commitments or forecasted transactions.

Source: NIKE INC, 10-K, July 27, 2007

NIKE, INC.

NOTES TO CONSOLIDATED FINANCIAL STATEMENTS — (Continued)

Substantially all derivatives outstanding as of May 31, 2007 and 2006 are designated as either cash flow or fair value hedges. All derivatives are recognized on the balance sheet at their fair value. Unrealized gain positions are recorded as other current assets or other non-current assets, depending on the instrument's maturity date. Unrealized loss positions are recorded as accrued liabilities or other non-current liabilities. All changes in fair values of outstanding cash flow hedge derivatives, except the ineffective portion, are recorded in other comprehensive income, until net income is affected by the variability of cash flows of the hedged transaction. Fair value hedges are recorded in net income and are offset by the change in fair value of the underlying asset or liability being hedged.

Cash Flow Hedges

The purpose of the Company's foreign currency hedging activities is to protect the Company from the risk that the eventual cash flows resulting from transactions in foreign currencies, including revenues, product costs, selling and administrative expenses, investments in U.S. dollar-denominated available-for-sale debt securities and intercompany transactions, including intercompany borrowings, will be adversely affected by changes in exchange rates. It is the Company's policy to utilize derivatives to reduce foreign exchange risks where internal netting strategies cannot be effectively employed.

Derivatives used by the Company to hedge foreign currency exchange risks are forward exchange contracts and options. Hedged transactions are denominated primarily in euros, British pounds, Japanese yen, Korean won, Canadian dollars and Mexican pesos. The Company hedges up to 100% of anticipated exposures typically twelve months in advance, but has hedged as much as 32 months in advance. When intercompany loans are hedged, it is typically for their expected duration.

Substantially all foreign currency derivatives outstanding as of May 31, 2007 and 2006 qualify for and are designated as foreign-currency cash flow hedges, including those hedging foreign currency denominated firm commitments.

Changes in fair values of outstanding cash flow hedge derivatives, except the ineffective portion, are recorded in other comprehensive income, until net income is affected by the variability of cash flows of the hedged transaction. In most cases amounts recorded in other comprehensive income will be released to net income some time after the maturity of the related derivative. The consolidated statement of income classification of effective hedge results is the same as that of the underlying exposure. Results of hedges of revenue and product costs are recorded in revenue and cost of sales, respectively, when the underlying hedged transaction affects net income. Results of hedges of selling and administrative expense are recorded together with those costs when the related expense is recorded. Results of hedges of anticipated purchases and sales of U.S. dollar-denominated available-for-sale securities are recorded in other (income) expense, net when the securities are sold.

Results of hedges of anticipated intercompany transactions are recorded in other (income) expense, net when the transaction occurs. Hedges of recorded balance sheet positions are recorded in other (income) expense, net currently together with the transaction gain or loss from the hedged balance sheet position. Net foreign currency transaction gains and losses, which includes hedge results captured in revenues, cost of sales, selling and administrative expense and other (income) expense, net, were a $27.9 million loss, a $49.9 million gain, and a $217.8 million loss for the years ended May 31, 2007, 2006, and 2005, respectively.

Premiums paid on options are initially recorded as deferred charges. The Company assesses effectiveness on options based on the total cash flows method and records total changes in the options' fair value to other comprehensive income to the degree they are effective.

Source: NIKE INC, 10-K, July 27, 2007

NIKE, INC.

NOTES TO CONSOLIDATED FINANCIAL STATEMENTS — (Continued)

As of May 31, 2007, $52.8 million of deferred net losses (net of tax) on both outstanding and matured derivatives accumulated in other comprehensive income are expected to be reclassified to net income during the next twelve months as a result of underlying hedged transactions also being recorded in net income. Actual amounts ultimately reclassified to net income are dependent on the exchange rates in effect when derivative contracts that are currently outstanding mature. As of May 31, 2007, the maximum term over which the Company is hedging exposures to the variability of cash flows for all forecasted and recorded transactions is 18 months.

The Company formally assesses, both at a hedge's inception and on an ongoing basis, whether the derivatives that are used in the hedging transaction have been highly effective in offsetting changes in the cash flows of hedged items and whether those derivatives may be expected to remain highly effective in future periods. When it is determined that a derivative is not, or has ceased to be, highly effective as a hedge, the Company discontinues hedge accounting prospectively.

The Company discontinues hedge accounting prospectively when (1) it determines that the derivative is no longer highly effective in offsetting changes in the cash flows of a hedged item (including hedged items such as firm commitments or forecasted transactions); (2) the derivative expires or is sold, terminated, or exercised; (3) it is no longer probable that the forecasted transaction will occur; or (4) management determines that designating the derivative as a hedging instrument is no longer appropriate.

When the Company discontinues hedge accounting because it is no longer probable that the forecasted transaction will occur in the originally expected period, the gain or loss on the derivative remains in accumulated other comprehensive income and is reclassified to net income when the forecasted transaction affects net income. However, if it is probable that a forecasted transaction will not occur by the end of the originally specified time period or within an additional two-month period of time thereafter, the gains and losses that were accumulated in other comprehensive income will be recognized immediately in net income. In all situations in which hedge accounting is discontinued and the derivative remains outstanding, the Company will carry the derivative at its fair value on the balance sheet, recognizing future changes in the fair value in other (income) expense, net. Any hedge ineffectiveness is recorded in other (income) expense, net. Effectiveness for cash flow hedges is assessed based on forward rates.

For each of the years ended May 31, 2007, 2006 and 2005, the Company recorded in other (income) expense, net an insignificant loss representing the total ineffectiveness of all derivatives. Net income for each of the years ended May 31, 2007, 2006 and 2005 was not materially affected due to discontinued hedge accounting.

Fair Value Hedges

The Company is also exposed to the risk of changes in the fair value of certain fixed-rate debt attributable to changes in interest rates. Derivatives currently used by the Company to hedge this risk are receive-fixed, pay-variable interest rate swaps.

Substantially all interest rate swap agreements are designated as fair value hedges of the related long-term debt and meet the shortcut method requirements under FAS 133. Accordingly, changes in the fair values of the interest rate swap agreements are exactly offset by changes in the fair value of the underlying long-term debt. No ineffectiveness has been recorded to net income related to interest rate swaps designated as fair value hedges for the years ended May 31, 2007, 2006 and 2005.

As discussed in Note 7, during the year ended May 31, 2004, the Company issued a $50 million medium-term note maturing October 1, 2013 and simultaneously entered into a receive-fixed, pay-variable interest rate swap with the same notional amount and fixed interest rate as the note. However, the swap expired

Source: NIKE INC, 10-K, July 27, 2007

NIKE, INC.

NOTES TO CONSOLIDATED FINANCIAL STATEMENTS — (Continued)

October 2, 2006. This interest rate swap was not accounted for as a fair value hedge. Accordingly, changes in the fair value of the swap were recorded to net income each period as a component of other (income) expense, net. The change in the fair value of the swap was not material for the years ended May 31, 2007, 2006 and 2005.

In fiscal 2003, the Company entered into an interest rate swap agreement related to a Japanese yen denominated intercompany loan with one of the Company's Japanese subsidiaries. The Japanese subsidiary pays variable interest on the intercompany loan based on 3-month LIBOR plus a spread. Under the interest rate swap agreement, the subsidiary pays fixed interest payments at 0.8% and receives variable interest payments based on 3-month LIBOR plus a spread based on a notional amount of 8 billion Japanese yen. This interest rate swap is not accounted for as a fair value hedge. Accordingly, changes in the fair value of the swap are recorded to net income each period as a component of other (income) expense, net. The change in the fair value of the swap was not material for the years ended May 31, 2007, 2006 and 2005.

The fair values of all derivatives recorded on the consolidated balance sheet are as follows:

	May 31, 2007	May 31, 2006
	(In millions)	
Unrealized Gains:		
Foreign currency exchange contracts and options	$ 43.5	$ 75.7
Interest rate swaps	0.5	0.9
Unrealized (Losses):		
Foreign currency exchange contracts and options	(90.6)	(122.2)
Interest rate swaps	(2.6)	(6.0)

Concentration of Credit Risk

The Company is exposed to credit-related losses in the event of non-performance by counterparties to hedging instruments. The counterparties to all derivative transactions are major financial institutions with investment grade credit ratings. However, this does not eliminate the Company's exposure to credit risk with these institutions. This credit risk is generally limited to the unrealized gains in such contracts should any of these counterparties fail to perform as contracted. To manage this risk, the Company has established strict counterparty credit guidelines that are continually monitored and reported to senior management according to prescribed guidelines. The Company utilizes a portfolio of financial institutions either headquartered or operating in the same countries the Company conducts its business. As a result of the above considerations, the Company considers the risk of counterparty default to be minimal.

In addition to hedging instruments, the Company is subject to concentrations of credit risk associated with cash and equivalents and accounts receivable. The Company places cash and equivalents with financial institutions with investment grade credit ratings and, by policy, limits the amount of credit exposure to any one financial institution. The Company considers its concentration risk related to accounts receivable to be mitigated by the Company's credit policy, the significance of outstanding balances owed by each individual customer at any point in time and the geographic dispersion of these customers.

Note 17 — Operating Segments and Related Information

Operating Segments. The Company's operating segments are evidence of the structure of the Company's internal organization. The major segments are defined by geographic regions for operations participating in NIKE brand sales activity excluding NIKE Golf and NIKE Bauer Hockey. Each NIKE brand geographic segment operates predominantly in one industry: the design, production, marketing and selling of sports and fitness

NIKE, INC.

NOTES TO CONSOLIDATED FINANCIAL STATEMENTS — (Continued)

footwear, apparel, and equipment. The "Other" category shown below represents activities of Cole Haan, Converse, Exeter Brands Group (beginning August 11, 2004), Hurley, NIKE Bauer Hockey, and NIKE Golf, which are considered immaterial for individual disclosure based on the aggregation criteria in SFAS No. 131 "Disclosures about Segments of an Enterprise and Related Information".

Where applicable, "Corporate" represents items necessary to reconcile to the consolidated financial statements, which generally include corporate activity and corporate eliminations.

Net revenues as shown below represent sales to external customers for each segment. Intercompany revenues have been eliminated and are immaterial for separate disclosure. The Company evaluates performance of individual operating segments based on pre-tax income. On a consolidated basis, this amount represents income before income taxes as shown in the Consolidated Statements of Income. Reconciling items for pre-tax income represent corporate costs that are not allocated to the operating segments for management reporting including corporate activity, certain currency exchange rate gains and losses on transactions and intercompany eliminations for specific income statement items in the Consolidated Statements of Income.

Additions to long-lived assets as presented in the following table represent capital expenditures.

Source: NIKE INC, 10-K, July 27, 2007

NIKE, INC.

NOTES TO CONSOLIDATED FINANCIAL STATEMENTS — (Continued)

Accounts receivable, inventories and property, plant and equipment for operating segments are regularly reviewed by management and are therefore provided below.

Certain prior year amounts have been reclassed to conform to fiscal 2007 presentation.

	Year Ended May 31,		
	2007	2006	2005
		(In millions)	
Net Revenue			
United States	$ 6,107.1	$ 5,722.5	$ 5,129.3
Europe, Middle East and Africa	4,723.3	4,326.6	4,281.6
Asia Pacific	2,283.4	2,053.8	1,897.3
Americas	952.5	904.9	695.8
Other	2,259.6	1,947.1	1,735.7
	$16,325.9	$14,954.9	$13,739.7
Pre-tax Income			
United States	$ 1,300.3	$ 1,244.5	$ 1,127.9
Europe, Middle East and Africa	1,000.7	960.7	917.5
Asia Pacific	483.7	412.5	399.8
Americas	187.4	172.6	116.5
Other	303.7	153.6	154.8
Corporate	(1,075.9)	(802.3)	(856.7)
	$ 2,199.9	$ 2,141.6	$ 1,859.8
Additions to Long-lived Assets			
United States	$ 67.3	$ 59.8	$ 54.8
Europe, Middle East and Africa	94.9	73.6	38.8
Asia Pacific	20.7	16.8	22.0
Americas	5.3	6.9	6.8
Other	36.0	33.2	31.3
Corporate	89.3	143.4	103.4
	$ 313.5	$ 333.7	$ 257.1
Depreciation			
United States	$ 45.4	$ 54.2	$ 49.0
Europe, Middle East and Africa	47.4	46.9	45.2
Asia Pacific	25.2	28.4	28.3
Americas	6.1	6.4	4.0
Other	28.2	29.0	28.5
Corporate	117.4	117.1	102.2
	$ 269.7	$ 282.0	$ 257.2

Source: NIKE INC, 10-K, July 27, 2007

NIKE, INC.

NOTES TO CONSOLIDATED FINANCIAL STATEMENTS — (Continued)

	Year Ended May 31, 2007	2006 (In millions)	2005
Accounts Receivable, net			
United States	$ 806.8	$ 717.2	$ 627.0
Europe, Middle East and Africa	739.1	703.3	711.4
Asia Pacific	296.6	319.7	309.8
Americas	184.1	174.5	168.7
Other	404.9	410.0	394.0
Corporate	63.2	58.2	39.0
	$ 2,494.7	$ 2,382.9	$ 2,249.9
Inventories			
United States	$ 796.0	$ 725.9	$ 639.9
Europe, Middle East and Africa	554.5	590.1	496.5
Asia Pacific	214.1	238.3	228.9
Americas	132.0	147.6	96.8
Other	378.7	330.5	316.2
Corporate	46.6	44.3	32.8
	$ 2,121.9	$ 2,076.7	$ 1,811.1
Property, Plant and Equipment, net			
United States	$ 232.7	$ 219.3	$ 216.0
Europe, Middle East and Africa	325.4	266.6	230.0
Asia Pacific	326.1	354.8	380.4
Americas	16.9	17.0	15.7
Other	103.6	98.2	93.4
Corporate	673.6	701.8	670.3
	$ 1,678.3	$ 1,657.7	$ 1,605.8

Revenues by Major Product Lines. Revenues to external customers for NIKE brand products are attributable to sales of footwear, apparel and equipment. Other revenues to external customers primarily include external sales by Cole Haan Holdings Incorporated, Converse Inc., Exeter Brands Group LLC (beginning August 11, 2004), Hurley International LLC, NIKE Bauer Hockey Corp., and NIKE Golf.

	Year Ended May 31, 2007	2006 (In millions)	2005
Footwear	$ 8,514.0	$ 7,965.9	$ 7,299.7
Apparel	4,576.5	4,168.0	3,879.4
Equipment	975.8	873.9	824.9
Other	2,259.6	1,947.1	1,735.7
	$ 16,325.9	$ 14,954.9	$ 13,739.7

Revenues and Long-Lived Assets by Geographic Area. Geographical area information is similar to that shown previously under operating segments with the exception of the Other activity, which has been allocated to the geographical areas based on the location where the sales originated. Revenues derived in the United States were $7,593.7 million, $7,019.0 million, and $6,284.5 million, for the years ended May 31, 2007, 2006, and

Source: NIKE INC, 10-K, July 27, 2007

NIKE, INC.

NOTES TO CONSOLIDATED FINANCIAL STATEMENTS — (Continued)

2005, respectively. The Company's largest concentrations of long-lived assets are in the United States and Japan. Long-lived assets attributable to operations in the United States, which are comprised of net property, plant & equipment were $991.3 million, $998.2 million, and $956.6 million at May 31, 2007, 2006, and 2005, respectively. Long-lived assets attributable to operations in Japan were $260.6 million, $296.3 million, and $321.0 million at May 31, 2007, 2006, and 2005, respectively.

Major Customers. During the years ended May 31, 2007, 2006 and 2005, revenues derived from Foot Locker, Inc. represented 10 percent, 10 percent and 11 percent of the Company's consolidated revenues, respectively. Sales to this customer are included in all segments of the Company.

Item 9. *Changes In and Disagreements with Accountants on Accounting and Financial Disclosure*

There has been no change of accountants nor any disagreements with accountants on any matter of accounting principles or practices or financial statement disclosure required to be reported under this Item.

Item 9A. *Controls and Procedures*

We maintain disclosure controls and procedures that are designed to ensure that information required to be disclosed in our Exchange Act reports is recorded, processed, summarized and reported within the time periods specified in the Securities and Exchange Commission's rules and forms and that such information is accumulated and communicated to our management, including our Chief Executive Officer and Chief Financial Officer, as appropriate, to allow for timely decisions regarding required disclosure. In designing and evaluating the disclosure controls and procedures, management recognizes that any controls and procedures, no matter how well designed and operated, can provide only reasonable assurance of achieving the desired control objectives, and management is required to apply its judgment in evaluating the cost-benefit relationship of possible controls and procedures.

We carry out a variety of on-going procedures, under the supervision and with the participation of our management, including our Chief Executive Officer and Chief Financial Officer, to evaluate the effectiveness of the design and operation of our disclosure controls and procedures. Based on the foregoing, our Chief Executive Officer and Chief Financial Officer concluded that our disclosure controls and procedures were effective at the reasonable assurance level as of May 31, 2007.

"Management's Annual Report on Internal Control Over Financial Reporting" and the related attestation report of PricewaterhouseCoopers LLP are included in Item 8 on pages 46-49 of this Report.

There has been no change in our internal control over financial reporting during our most recent fiscal quarter that has materially affected, or is reasonable likely to materially affect, our internal control over financial reporting.

Item 9B. *Other Information*

No disclosure is required under this Item.

Source: NIKE INC, 10-K, July 27, 2007

Glossary

A

accelerated depreciation method A depreciation method that provides for a higher depreciation amount in the first year of the asset's use, followed by a gradually declining amount of depreciation. (450)

account An accounting form that is used to record the increases and decreases in each financial statement item. (50)

account form The form of balance sheet that resembles the basic format of the accounting equation, with assets on the left side and Liabilities and Owner's Equity sections on the right side. (17, 258)

account payable The liability created by a purchase on account. (12)

account receivable A claim against the customer created by selling merchandise or services on credit. (12, 62, 398)

accounting An information system that provides reports to stakeholders about the economic activities and condition of a business. (3)

accounting cycle The process that begins with analyzing and journalizing transactions and ends with the post-closing trial balance. (156)

accounting equation Assets = Liabilities + Owner's Equity. (10)

accounting period concept The accounting concept that assumes that the economic life of the business can be divided into time periods. (100)

accounting system The methods and procedures used by a business to collect, classify, summarize, and report financial data for use by management and external users. (202)

accounts payable subsidiary ledger The subsidiary ledger containing the individual accounts with suppliers (creditors). (203)

accounts receivable analysis A company's ability to collect its accounts receivable. (772)

accounts receivable subsidiary ledger The subsidiary ledger containing the individual accounts with customers. (203)

accounts receivable turnover The relationship between net sales and accounts receivable, computed by dividing the net sales by the average net accounts receivable; measures how frequently during the year the accounts receivable are being converted to cash. (414, 772)

accrual basis of accounting Under this basis of accounting, revenues and expenses are reported in the income statement in the period in which they are earned or incurred. (100)

accrued expenses Expenses that have been incurred but not recorded in the accounts. (102)

accrued revenues Revenues that have been earned but not recorded in the accounts. (102)

accumulated depreciation The contra asset account credited when recording the depreciation of a fixed asset. (111)

accumulated other comprehensive income The cumulative effects of other comprehensive income items reported separately in the Stockholders' Equity section of the balance sheet. (681)

adjusted trial balance The trial balance prepared after all the adjusting entries have been posted. (118)

adjusting entries The journal entries that bring the accounts up to date at the end of the accounting period. (101)

adjusting process An analysis and updating of the accounts when financial statements are prepared. (101)

administrative expenses (general expenses) Expenses incurred in the administration or general operations of the business. (257)

aging the receivables The process of analyzing the accounts receivable and classifying them according to various age groupings, with the due date being the base point for determining age. (405)

Allowance for Doubtful Accounts The contra asset account for accounts receivable. (401)

allowance method The method of accounting for uncollectible accounts that provides an expense for uncollectible receivables in advance of their write-off. (399)

amortization The periodic transfer of the cost of an intangible asset to expense. (457)

annuity A series of equal cash flows at fixed intervals. (635)

assets The resources owned by a business. (9, 52)

available-for-sale securities Securities that management expects to sell in the future but which are not actively traded for profit. (671)

average inventory cost flow method The method of inventory costing that is based on the assumption that costs should be charged against revenue by using the weighted average unit cost of the items sold. (314)

B

Bad Debt Expense The operating expense incurred because of the failure to collect receivables. (399)

balance of the account The amount of the difference between the debits and the credits that have been entered into an account. (51)

balance sheet A list of the assets, liabilities, and owner's equity as of a specific date, usually at the close of the last day of a month or a year. (16)

bank reconciliation The analysis that details the items responsible for the difference between the cash balance reported in the bank statement and the balance of the cash account in the ledger. (367)

bank statement A summary of all transactions mailed to the depositor or made available online by the bank each month. (364)

bond A form of an interest-bearing note used by corporations to borrow on a long-term basis. (618)

bond indenture The contract between a corporation issuing bonds and the bondholders. (621)

book value The cost of a fixed asset minus accumulated depreciation on the asset. (450)

book value of the asset (or net book value) The difference between the cost of a fixed asset and its accumulated depreciation. (112)

boot The amount a buyer owes a seller when a fixed asset is traded in on a similar asset. (463)

business An organization in which basic resources (inputs), such as materials and labor, are assembled and processed to provide goods or services (outputs) to customers. (2)

business combination A business making an investment in another business by acquiring a controlling share, often greater than 50%, of the outstanding voting stock of another corporation by paying cash or exchanging stock. (666)

business entity concept A concept of accounting that limits the economic data in the accounting system to data related directly to the activities of the business. (8)

business transaction An economic event or condition that directly changes an entity's financial condition or directly affects its results of operations. (10)

C

capital account An account used for a proprietorship that represents the owner's equity. (52)

capital expenditures The costs of acquiring fixed assets, adding to a fixed asset, improving a fixed asset, or extending a fixed asset's useful life. (444)

capital leases Leases that include one or more provisions that result in treating the leased assets as purchased assets in the accounts. (446)

carrying amount The balance of the bonds payable account (face amount of the bonds) less any unamortized discount or plus any unamortized premium. (627)

cash Coins, currency (paper money), checks, money orders, and money on deposit that is available for unrestricted withdrawal from banks and other financial institutions. (360)

cash basis of accounting Under this basis of accounting, revenues and expenses are reported in the income statement in the period in which cash is received or paid. (100)

cash dividend A cash distribution of earnings by a corporation to its shareholders. (584)

cash equivalents Highly liquid investments that are usually reported with cash on the balance sheet. (373)

cash flow per share Normally computed as cash flow from operations per share. (715)

cash flows from financing activities The section of the statement of cash flows that reports cash flows from transactions affecting the equity and debt of the business. (712)

cash flows from investing activities The section of the statement of cash flows that reports cash flows from transactions affecting investments in noncurrent assets. (712)

cash flows from operating activities The section of the statement of cash flows that reports the cash transactions affecting the determination of net income. (711)

cash payments journal The special journal in which all cash payments are recorded. (214)

cash receipts journal The special journal in which all cash receipts are recorded. (208)

cash short and over account An account which has recorded errors in cash sales or errors in making change causing the amount of actual cash on hand to differ from the beginning amount of cash plus the cash sales for the day. (362)

Certified Public Accountant (CPA) Public accountants who have met a state's education, experience, and examination requirements. (7)

chart of accounts A list of the accounts in the ledger. (52)

clearing account Another name for the income summary account because it has the effect of clearing the revenue and expense accounts of their balances. (151)

closing entries The entries that transfer the balances of the revenue, expense, and drawing accounts to the owner's capital account. (150)

closing process The transfer process of converting temporary account balances to zero by transferring the revenue and expense account balances to Income Summary, transferring the income summary account balance to the owner's capital account, and transferring the owner's drawing account to the owner's capital account. (150)

closing the books The process of transferring temporary accounts balances to permanent accounts at the end of the accounting period. (150)

common stock The stock outstanding when a corporation has issued only one class of stock. (579)

common-sized statement A financial statement in which all items are expressed only in relative terms. (767)

compensating balance A requirement by some banks requiring depositors to maintain minimum cash balances in their bank accounts. (373)

comprehensive income All changes in stockholders' equity during a period, except those resulting from dividends and stockholders' investments. (681)

consigned inventory Merchandise that is shipped by manufacturers to retailers who act as the manufacturer's selling agent. (327)

consignee The name for the retailer in a consigned inventory arrangement. (327)

consignor The name for the manufacturer in a consigned inventory arrangement. (327)

consolidated financial statements Financial statements resulting from combining parent and subsidiary statements. (666)

contingent liabilities Liabilities that may arise from past transactions if certain events occur in the future. (504)

contra account (or contra asset account) An account offset against another account. (111)

contract rate The periodic interest to be paid on the bonds that is identified in the bond indenture; expressed as a percentage of the face amount of the bond. (621)

control environment The overall attitude of management and employees about the importance of controls. (356)

controlling account The account in the general ledger that summarizes the balances of the accounts in a subsidiary ledger. (203)

copyright An exclusive right to publish and sell a literary, artistic, or musical composition. (458)

corporation A business organized under state or federal statutes as a separate legal entity. (8)

correcting journal entry An entry that is prepared when an error has already been journalized and posted. (70)

cost concept A concept of accounting that determines the amount initially entered into the accounting records for purchases. (8)

cost method A method of accounting for equity investments representing less than 20% of the outstanding shares of the investee. The purchase is at original cost, and any gains or losses upon sale are recognized by the difference between the sale proceeds and the original cost. (662)

cost of merchandise purchased The cost of net purchases plus transportation costs. (255)

cost of merchandise sold The cost that is reported as an expense when merchandise is sold. (253)

credit memorandum (credit memo) A form used by a seller to inform the buyer of the amount the seller proposes to credit to the account receivable due from the buyer. (264)

credit period The amount of time the buyer is allowed in which to pay the seller. (263)

credit terms Terms for payment on account by the buyer to the seller. (263)

credits Amounts entered on the right side of an account. (51)

cumulative preferred stock Stock that has a right to receive regular dividends that were not declared (paid) in prior years. (580)

current assets Cash and other assets that are expected to be converted to cash or sold or used up, usually within one year or less, through the normal operations of the business. (149)

current liabilities Liabilities that will be due within a short time (usually one year or less) and that are to be paid out of current assets. (149)

current position analysis A company's ability to pay its current liabilities. (770)

current ratio A financial ratio that is computed by dividing current assets by current liabilities. (770)

D

debit memorandum (debit memo) A form used by a buyer to inform the seller of the amount the buyer proposes to debit to the account payable due the seller. (267)

debits Amounts entered on the left side of an account. (51)

debt securities Notes and bond investments that provide interest revenue over a fixed maturity. (659)

deficiency The debit balance in the owner's equity account of a partner. (550)

deficit A debit balance in the retained earnings account. (578)

defined benefit plan A pension plan that promises employees a fixed annual pension benefit at retirement, based on years of service and compensation levels. (502)

defined contribution plan A pension plan that requires a fixed amount of money to be invested for the employee's behalf during the employee's working years. (502)

depletion The process of transferring the cost of natural resources to an expense account. (456)

depreciate To lose usefulness as all fixed assets except land do. (111)

depreciation The systematic periodic transfer of the cost of a fixed asset to an expense account during its expected useful life. (111, 446)

depreciation expense The portion of the cost of a fixed asset that is recorded as an expense each year of its useful life. (111)

direct method A method of reporting the cash flows from operating activities as the difference between the operating cash receipts and the operating cash payments. (712)

direct write-off method The method of accounting for uncollectible accounts that recognizes the expense only when accounts are judged to be worthless. (399)

discount The interest deducted from the maturity value of a note or the excess of the face amount of bonds over their issue price. (581, 621)

dishonored note receivable A note that the maker fails to pay on the due date. (412)

dividends Distributions of a corporation's earning to stockholders. (578)

dividend yield A ratio, computed by dividing the annual dividends paid per share of common stock by the market price per share at a specific date, that indicates the rate of return to stockholders in terms of cash dividend distributions. (783)

dividends per share Measures the extent to which earnings are being distributed to common shareholders. (783)

double-declining-balance method A method of depreciation that provides periodic depreciation expense based on the declining book value of a fixed asset over its estimated life. (450)

double-entry accounting system A system of accounting for recording transactions, based on recording increases and decreases in accounts so that debits equal credits. (53)

drawing The account used to record amounts withdrawn by an owner of a proprietorship. (52)

E

earnings per common share (EPS) Net income per share of common stock outstanding during a period. (595, 619)

earnings per share (EPS) on common stock The profitability ratio of net income available to common shareholders to the number of common shares outstanding. (619, 781)

e-commerce The use of the Internet for performing business transactions. (222)

effective interest rate method The method of amortizing discounts and premiums that provides for a constant rate of interest on the carrying amount of the bonds at the beginning of each period; often called simply the "interest method." (624)

effective rate of interest The market rate of interest at the time bonds are issued. (621)

electronic funds transfer (EFT) A system in which computers rather than paper (money, checks, etc.) are used to effect cash transactions. (363)

elements of internal control The control environment, risk assessment, control activities, information and communication, and monitoring. (355)

employee fraud The intentional act of deceiving an employer for personal gain. (355)

employee's earnings record A detailed record of each employee's earnings. (498)

equity method A method of accounting for an investment in common stock by which the investment account is adjusted for the investor's share of periodic net income and cash dividends of the investee. (664)

equity securities The common and preferred stock of a firm. (659)

ethics Moral principles that guide the conduct of individuals. (4)

expenses Assets used up or services consumed in the process of generating revenues. (12, 53)

extraordinary item Event or transaction that (1) is significantly different (unusual) from the typical or the normal operating activities of a business and (2) occurs infrequently. (787)

F

fair value The price that would be received for selling an asset or paying off a liability, often the market price for an equity or debt security. (667)

fees earned Revenue from providing services. (12)

FICA tax Federal Insurance Contributions Act tax used to finance federal programs for old-age and disability benefits (social security) and health insurance for the aged (Medicare). (491)

financial accounting The branch of accounting that is concerned with recording transactions using generally accepted accounting principles (GAAP) for a business or other economic unit and with a periodic preparation of various statements from such records. (4)

Financial Accounting Standards Board (FASB) The authoritative body that has the primary responsibility for developing accounting principles. (7)

financial statements Financial reports that summarize the effects of events on a business. (15)

first-in, first-out (FIFO) inventory cost flow method The method of inventory costing based on the assumption that the costs of merchandise sold should be charged against revenue in the order in which the costs were incurred. (314)

fiscal year The annual accounting period adopted by a business. (168)

fixed asset turnover ratio The number of dollars of sales that are generated from each dollar of average fixed assets during the year, computed by dividing the net sales by the average net fixed assets. (462)

fixed assets (or plant assets) Long-term or relatively permanent tangible assets such as equipment, machinery, and buildings that are used in the normal business operations and that depreciate over time. (111, 149, 441)

FOB (free on board) destination Freight terms in which the seller pays the transportation costs from the shipping point to the final destination. (269)

FOB (free on board) shipping point Freight terms in which the buyer pays the transportation costs from the shipping point to the final destination. (269)

free cash flow The amount of operating cash flow remaining after replacing current productive capacity and maintaining current dividends. (730)

freight in Costs of transportation. (255)

fringe benefits Benefits provided to employees in addition to wages and salaries. (501)

future value The estimated worth in the future of an amount of cash on hand today invested at a fixed rate of interest. (633)

G

general journal The two-column form used for entries that do not "fit" in any of the special journals. (205)

general ledger The primary ledger, when used in conjunction with subsidiary ledgers, that contains all of the balance sheet and income statement accounts. (203)

general-purpose financial statements A type of financial accounting report that is distributed to external users. The term "general purpose" refers to the wide range of decision-making needs that the reports are designed to serve. (4)

generally accepted accounting principles (GAAP) Generally accepted guidelines for the preparation of financial statements. (7)

goodwill An intangible asset that is created from such favorable factors as location, product quality, reputation, and managerial skill. (459)

gross pay The total earnings of an employee for an employee for a payroll period. (489)

gross profit Sales minus the cost of merchandise sold. (253)

gross profit method A method of estimating inventory cost that is based on the relationship of gross profit to sales. (332)

H

held-to-maturity securities Investments in bonds or other debt securities that management intends to hold to their maturity. (670)

horizontal analysis Financial analysis that compares an item in a current statement with the same item in prior statements. (71, 764)

I

in arrears Cumulative preferred stock dividends that have not been paid in prior years are said to be in arrears. (580)

income from operations (operating income) Revenues less operating expenses and service department charges for a profit or an investment center. (257)

income statement A summary of the revenue and expenses for a specific period of time, such as a month or a year. (16)

Income Summary An account to which the revenue and expense account balances are transferred at the end of a period. (151)

indirect method A method of reporting the cash flows from operating activities as the net income from operations adjusted for all deferrals of past cash receipts and payments and all accruals of expected future cash receipts and payments. (713)

installment note A debt that requires the borrower to make equal periodic payments to the lender for the term of the note. (629)

intangible assets Long-term assets that are useful in the operations of a business, are not held for sale, and are without physical qualities. (457)

interest revenue Money received for interest. (12)

internal controls The policies and procedures used to safeguard assets, ensure accurate business information, and ensure compliance with laws and regulations. (203, 353)

International Accounting Standards Board (IASB) An organization that issues International Financial Reporting Standards for many countries outside the United States. (7)

inventory analysis A company's ability to manage its inventory effectively. (773)

inventory shrinkage (inventory shortage) The amount by which the merchandise for sale, as indicated by the balance of the merchandise inventory account, is larger than the total amount of merchandise counted during the physical inventory. (273)

inventory turnover The relationship between the volume of goods sold and inventory, computed by dividing the cost of goods sold by the average inventory. (330, 774)

investee The company whose stock is purchased by the investor. (662)

investments The balance sheet caption used to report temporary or long-term investments in stocks or bonds held as either trading, available-for-sale, held-to-maturity, or equity method securities. (659)

investor The company investing in another company's stock. (662)

invoice The bill that the seller sends to the buyer. (206, 262)

J

journal The initial record in which the effects of a transaction are recorded. (55)

journal entry The form of recording a transaction in a journal. (56)

journalizing The process of recording a transaction in the journal. (56)

L

last-in, first-out (LIFO) inventory cost flow method A method of inventory costing based on the assumption that the most recent merchandise inventory costs should be charged against revenue. (314)

ledger A group of accounts for a business. (52)

liabilities The rights of creditors that represent debts of the business. (9, 52)

limited liability company (LLC) A business form consisting of one or more persons or entities filing an operating agreement with a state to conduct business with limited liability to the owners, yet treated as a partnership for tax purposes. (8, 535)

liquidation The winding-up process when a partnership goes out of business. (546)

long-term liabilities Liabilities that usually will not be due for more than one year. (149)

lower-of-cost-or-market (LCM) method A method of valuing inventory that reports the inventory at the lower of its cost or current market value (replacement cost). (325)

M

management (or managerial) accounting The branch of accounting that uses both historical and estimated data in providing information that management uses in conducting daily operations, in planning future operations, and in developing overall business strategies. (4)

Management's Discussion and Analysis (MD&A) An annual report disclosure that provides management's analysis of the results of operations and financial condition. (785)

manufacturing business A type of business that changes basic inputs into products that are sold to individual customers. (3)

market rate of interest The rate determined from sales and purchases of similar bonds. (621)

matching concept (or matching principle) A concept of accounting in which expenses are matched with the revenue generated during a period by those expenses. (16, 100)

maturity value The amount that is due at the maturity or due date of a note. (411)

merchandise available for sale The cost of merchandise available for sale to customers calculated by adding the beginning merchandise inventory to net purchases. (255)

merchandise inventory Merchandise on hand (not sold) at the end of an accounting period. (253)

merchandising business A type of business that purchases products from other businesses and sells them to customers. (3)

mortgage notes An installment note that may be secured by a pledge of the borrower's assets. (629)

multiple-step income statement A form of income statement that contains several sections, subsections, and subtotals. (254)

N

natural business year A fiscal year that ends when business activities have reached the lowest point in an annual operating cycle. (168)

net income or net profit The amount by which revenues exceed expenses. (16)

net loss The amount by which expenses exceed revenues. (16)

net pay Gross pay less payroll deductions; the amount the employer is obligated to pay the employee. (489)

net purchases Determined when purchases returns and allowances and the purchases discounts are deducted from the total purchases. (255)

net realizable value The estimated selling price of an item of inventory less any direct costs of disposal, such as sales commissions. (326, 401)

net sales Revenue received for merchandise sold to customers less any sales returns and allowances and sales discounts. (255)

normal balance of an accout The normal balance of an account can be either a debit or a credit depending on whether increases in the account are recorded as debits or credits. (54)

notes receivable A customer's written promise to pay an amount and possibly interest at an agreed-upon rate. (149, 398)

number of days' sales in inventory The relationship between the volume of sales and inventory, computed by dividing the inventory at the end of the year by the average daily cost of goods sold. (330, 774)

number of days' sales in receivables The relationship between sales and accounts receivable, computed by dividing the net accounts receivable at the end of the year by the average daily sales. (414, 772)

number of times interest charges are earned A ratio that measures creditor margin of safety for interest payments, calculated as income before interest and taxes divided by interest expense. (632, 776)

O

objectivity concept A concept of accounting that requires accounting records and the data reported in financial statements to be based on objective evidence. (9)

operating leases Leases that do not meet the criteria for capital leases and thus are accounted for as operating expenses. (446)

other comprehensive income Specified items that are reported separately from net income, including foreign currency items, pension liability adjustments, and unrealized gains and losses on investments. (681)

other expense Expenses that cannot be traced directly to operations. (257)

other income Revenue from sources other than the primary operating activity of a business. (257)

outstanding stock The stock in the hands of stockholders. (579)

owner's equity The owner's right to the assets of the business. (9, 52)

P

paid-in capital Capital contributed to a corporation by the stockholders and others. (578)

par The monetary amount printed on a stock certificate. (579)

parent company The corporation owning all or a majority of the voting stock of the other corporation. (666)

partnership An unincorporated business form consisting of two or more persons conducting business as co-owners for profit. (8, 534)

partnership agreement The formal written contract creating a partnership. (534)

patents Exclusive rights to produce and sell goods with one or more unique features. (457)

payroll The total amount paid to employees for a certain period. (489)

payroll register A multicolumn report used to assemble and summarize payroll data at the end of each payroll period. (494)

pension A cash payment to retired employees. (502)

periodic inventory system The inventory system in which the inventory records do not show the amount available for sale or sold during the period. (256)

perpetual inventory system The inventory system in which each purchase and sale of merchandise is recorded in an inventory account. (256)

petty cash fund A special cash fund to pay relatively small amounts. (371)

physical inventory A detailed listing of merchandise on hand. (313)

posting The process of transferring the debits and credits from the journal entries to the accounts. (59)

preferred stock A class of stock with preferential rights over common stock. (579)

premium The excess of the issue price of a stock over its par value or the excess of the issue price of bonds over their face amount. (581, 621)

prepaid expenses Items such as supplies that will be used in the business in the future. (12, 102)

present value The estimated worth today of an amount of cash to be received (or paid) in the future. (633)

present value of an annuity The sum of the present values of a series of equal cash flows to be received at fixed intervals. (635)

price-earnings (P/E) ratio The ratio of the market price per share of common stock, at a specific date, to the annual earnings per share. (782)

prior period adjustments Corrections of material errors related to a prior period or periods, excluded from the determination of net income. (591)

private accounting The field of accounting whereby accountants are employed by a business firm or a not-for-profit organization. (4)

profit The difference between the amounts received from customers for goods or services provided and the amounts paid for the inputs used to provide the goods or services. (2)

profitability The ability of a firm to earn income. (769)

proprietorship A business owned by one individual. (8)

public accounting The field of accounting where accountants and their staff provide services on a fee basis. (7)

purchase order The purchase order authorizes the purchase of the inventory from an approved vendor. (313)

purchase return or allowance From the buyer's perspective, returned merchandise or an adjustment for defective merchandise. (255)

purchases discounts Discounts taken by the buyer for early payment of an invoice. (255)

purchases journal The journal in which all items purchased on account are recorded. (211)

Q

quick assets Cash and other current assets that can be quickly converted to cash, such as marketable securities and receivables. (507, 771)

quick ratio A financial ratio that measures the ability to pay current liabilities with quick assets (cash, marketable securities, accounts receivable). (507, 771)

R

rate earned on common stockholders' equity A measure of profitability computed by dividing net income, reduced by preferred dividend requirements, by common stockholders' equity. (779)

rate earned on stockholders' equity A measure of profitability computed by dividing net income by total stockholders' equity. (779)

rate earned on total assets A measure of the profitability of assets, without regard to the equity of creditors and stockholders in the assets. (778)

ratio of fixed assets to long-term liabilities A leverage ratio that measures the margin of safety of long-term creditors, calculated as the net fixed assets divided by the long-term liabilities. (775)

ratio of liabilities to stockholders' equity A comprehensive leverage ratio that measures the relationship of the claims of creditors to stockholders' equity. (775)

ratio of net sales to assets Ratio that measures how effectively a company uses its assets, computed as net sales divided by average total assets. (777)

real (permanent) accounts Term for balance sheet accounts because they are relatively permanent and carried forward from year to year. (150)

realization The sale of assets when a partnership is being liquidated. (546)

receivables All money claims against other entities, including people, business firms, and other organizations. (398)

receiving report The form or electronic transmission used by the receiving personnel to indicate that materials have been received and inspected. (313)

rent revenue Money received for rent. (12)

report form The form of balance sheet with the Liabilities and Owner's Equity sections presented below the Assets section. (258)

residual value The estimated value of a fixed asset at the end of its useful life. (447)

restrictions Amounts of retained earnings that have been limited for use as dividends. (591)

retail inventory method A method of estimating inventory cost that is based on the relationship of gross profit to sales. (330)

retained earnings Net income retained in a corporation. (578)

retained earnings statement A summary of the changes in the retained earnings in a corporation for a specific period of time, such as a month or a year. (591)

revenue expenditures Costs that benefit only the current period or costs incurred for normal maintenance and repairs of fixed assets. (444)

revenue journal The journal in which all sales and services on account are recorded. (205)

revenue recognition concept The accounting concept that supports reporting revenues when the services are provided to customers. (100)

revenues Increases in owner's equity as a result of selling services or products to customers. (12, 53)

rules of debit and credit In the double-entry accounting system, specific rules for recording debits and credits based on the type of account. (53)

S

sales The total amount charged customers for merchandise sold, including cash sales and sales on account. (12, 255)

sales discounts From the seller's perspective, discounts that a seller may offer the buyer for early payment. (255)

sales returns and allowances From the seller's perspective, returned merchandise or an adjustment for defective merchandise. (255)

Sarbanes-Oxley Act of 2002 An act passed by Congress to restore public confidence and trust in the financial statements of companies. (353)

Securities and Exchange Commission (SEC) An agency of the U.S. government that has authority over the accounting and financial disclosures for companies whose shares of ownership (stock) are traded and sold to the public. (7)

selling expenses Expenses that are incurred directly in the selling of merchandise. (257)

service business A business providing services rather than products to customers. (3)

single-step income statement A form of income statement in which the total of all expenses is deducted from the total of all revenues. (258)

slide An error in which the entire number is moved one or more spaces to the right or the left, such as writing $542.00 as $54.20 or $5,420.00. (69)

solvency The ability of a firm to pay its debts as they come due. (769)

special journals Journals designed to be used for recording a single type of transaction. (204)

special-purpose fund A cash fund used for a special business need. (372)

specific identification inventory cost flow method Inventory method in which the unit sold is identified with a specific purchase. (314)

statement of cash flows A summary of the cash receipts and cash payments for a specific period of time, such as a month or a year. (16, 711)

statement of members' equity A summary of the changes in each member's equity in a limited liability corporation that have occurred during a specific period of time. (553)

statement of owner's equity A summary of the changes in owner's equity that have occurred during a specific period of time, such as a month or a year. (16)

statement of partnership equity A summary of the changes in each partner's capital in a partnership that have occurred during a specific period of time. (553)

statement of partnership liquidation A summary of the liquidation process whereby cash is distributed to the partners based on the balances in their capital accounts. (547)

statement of stockholders' equity A summary of the changes in the stockholders' equity in a corporation that have occurred during a specific period of time. (592)

stock Shares of ownership of a corporation. (575)

stock dividend A distribution of shares of stock to its stockholders. (586)

stock split A reduction in the par or stated value of a common stock and the issuance of a proportionate number of additional shares. (594)

stockholders The owners of a corporation. (575)

stockholders' equity The owners' equity in a corporation. (578)

straight-line method A method of depreciation that provides for equal periodic depreciation expense over the estimated life of a fixed asset. (448)

subsidiary company The corporation that is controlled by a parent company. (666)

subsidiary inventory ledger The subsidiary ledger containing individual accounts for items of inventory. (313)

subsidiary ledger A ledger containing individual accounts with a common characteristic. (203)

T

T account The simplest form of an account. (50)

temporary (nominal) accounts Accounts that report amounts for only one period. (150)

trade discounts Discounts from the list prices in published catalogs or special discounts offered to certain classes of buyers. (271)

trade-in allowance The amount a seller allows a buyer for a fixed asset that is traded in for a similar asset. (463)

trademark A name, term, or symbol used to identify a business and its products. (458)

trading securities Securities that management intends to actively trade for profit. (667)

transposition An error in which the order of the digits is changed, such as writing $542 as $452 or $524. (69)

treasury stock Stock that a corporation has once issued and then reacquires. (587)

trial balance A summary listing of the titles and balances of accounts in the ledger. (68)

U

unadjusted trial balance A summary listing of the titles and balances of accounts in the ledger prior to the posting of adjusting entries. (68)

unearned revenue The liability created by receiving revenue in advance. (60, 102)

unit of measure concept A concept of accounting requiring that economic data be recorded in dollars. (9)

units-of-production method A method of depreciation that provides for depreciation expense based on the expected productive capacity of a fixed asset. (449)

unrealized gain or loss Changes in the fair value of equity or debt securities for a period. (667)

V

vertical analysis An analysis that compares each item in a current statement with a total amount within the same statement. (766)

voucher A special form for recording relevant data about a liability and the details of its payment. (363)

voucher system A set of procedures for authorizing and recording liabilities and cash payments. (363)

W

working capital The excess of the current assets of a business over its current liabilities. (770)

Z

zero coupon bonds Bonds that provide for only the payment of the face amount at maturity. (636)

Subject Index

A

B

C

D

E

F

G

H

I

N

O

P

Q

R

S

T

U

V

W

Y

Z